Guide to the Points-Based System

Edited by Duran Seddon

D0552664

Joint Council for the Welfare of Immigrants

JCWI is an independent national organisation that has been campaigning for justice in immigration, nationality and refugee law and policy for over 43 years. It takes on challenging cases and provides expert training in this increasingly complex area of law.

ISBN 978-1-874010-07-4

Cover design: Boldface
Typesetting: Boldface, 35 Eyre Street Hill, London EC1R 5ET
Printing: CPI William Clowes, Copland Way, Ellough,
Beccles, Suffolk, NR34 7TL

JCWI, 115 Old Street, London EC1V 9RT
Tel: 020 7251 8708, Fax: 020 7251 8707
Publications: 020 7553 7458
Email: info@jcwi.org.uk
www.jcwi.org.uk

Preface

Welcome to JCWI's *Guide to the Points-Based System*.

The purpose of this Guide is to help applicants, sponsors and advisers navigate the ever more complex arrangements for applying to come to and remain in the UK for work, study and business purposes. Most of the routes are now contained in the Points-Based System (PBS), but we have included the relevant categories that remain outside the system as well. We have also traced the policy developments on the road that led to the PBS and, in addition, the Guide contains chapters dealing with connected parts of the relevant law and practice, including sponsorship, general grounds of refusal, human rights and challenges to decisions.

I would like to thank the contributors for giving their valuable time to the book. I would like also to express my gratitude to all the staff and management at JCWI but most particularly, Habib Rahman and Hina Majid for their constant support, patience and assistance. I would also like to thank, for their assistance in various ways, although they are not responsible for mistakes, Roger Gherson of Gherson and Barry O'Leary of Wesley Gryk Solicitors. Thanks are also due to Boldface Typesetters and to Cat Wiener for her careful proof reading. I give my personal thanks to Vicky Seddon, Nahid Khaliq, Rafi Seddon and Naila Seddon.

Such is the pace of change that, by the time this Guide is published, work will have commenced on preparing a supplement to capture the changes due to be made by new Immigration Rules and Guidance effective for applications made on or after 6 April 2011. The main changes will be to Chapters 4-6 and will include: the closure of the Tier 1 (General) category (with transitional protection for those already in the UK in that category); the introduction of a new Tier 1 category for the 'exceptionally talented'; amendments to the Tier 1 (Entrepreneur), Tier 1 (Investor), Tier 2 (General) and Tier 2 (Intra-Company Transfer) categories; changes to the sponsorship regime and the introduction of the permanent annual 'cap'. Depending on the timing of changes to Tier 4, they may also be included in the first supplement.

The Guide is up-to-date to 1 January 2011, although we have included details of the proposals made for the above changes as they became known in January and February 2011, as well as some later practice developments and case-law.

Duran Seddon
23 February 2011

Editor

Duran Seddon
Garden Court Chambers

Contributors

Philip Barth
Partner at Penningtons Solicitors

Ramby De Mello
No 5 Chambers

Jonathan Kingham
Solicitor, LexisNexis

Jennifer Lambe
Solicitor, Gherson

Irene McMillan
Immigration Executive, Kingsley Napley

Jo Swaney
Solicitor, Brighton Housing Trust

Shahram Taghavi
Bates Wells & Braithwaite

Colin Yeo
Renaissance Chambers

Hina Majid
Legal Policy Director, JCWI

Summary contents

Full contents

1 The road to the Points-Based System

This chapter covers:

- a brief history of the system for the migration of labour to the UK to 1997 (▶3–4);
- the factors influencing policy changes from 1997 to 2010 (▶4–5);
- six phases of the development of labour migration policy from 1997–2011 (▶5–24); and
- JCWI's critique of the PBS (▶25–33).

OVERVIEW

The aim of this chapter is to examine the roots of the system for controlling the migration of labour to the UK and to provide a basic analysis of the structure as it stands in February 2011. The chapter begins with an overview of the history of the system in place until 1997 when Labour came to power. It moves on to sketch out the social, economic and political factors that propelled change in UK labour migration policy in the late 1990s. Chief amongst these were globalisation and the activities of a group of pro-migration actors.

Chapter 1 then looks at the development of labour migration law and policy from 1997 to date, including the period after the Conservative/Liberal Democrat Coalition Government assumed power. We identify six phases of development as follows:

Phase 1: 1997–2000 This period saw a change in political thinking about immigration. In particular it was now felt that immigration could have potentially positive economic benefits for the UK.

Phase 2: 2000–2004/5 Having taken the decision to expand immigration to the UK, this was a period of innovation and experimentation with the scheme for labour migration. It was underpinned by five themes. These were: meeting labour/skills shortages; encouraging innovation and entrepreneurialism; expanding the UK's share of the Higher and Further Education international student market; developing a self-financing system; and establishing a more rigorous system of control. With the exception of expanding the UK's share of the education market, these policy themes continue to underlie the system.

Phase 3: 2005–2008 During this period hostile public opinion and negative media coverage of immigration, together with the volume of entrants from Eastern Europe, became key factors driving labour migration policy. These factors continue to exert influence on policy making. Although the basic policy themes remained constant, the Government's response was to introduce a blue-print for a 'points-based' system, together with new control mechanisms. However, it also decided to inject social objectives into the labour migration and general immigration systems. Another policy theme, therefore, emerged; that of integration.

Phase 4: 2008–2009 This period saw the launch and implementation of the PBS. This development was inspired by the earlier phases and drew heavily from the preceding innovations. In describing this phase, a comparative table is provided so that the changes and their direct fore-runners can be seen more easily. Reference should also be made to Chapter 2 for an overview of each of the tiers and what they replace.

Phase 5: 2009–2010 This was a period of fine-tuning, tightening and extending the PBS. Modifications were made to the system in order to correct unforeseen consequences and drafting oversights, but also to better reflect the above policy themes. However, the impact of the worst recession since the 1930s, together with growing concerns about 'abuse' of economic routes, also led to greater restriction on routes for migration within the PBS. Additionally, in Phase 5 the Government sought to extend its points-based approach to the scheme for securing both settlement in the UK and British citizenship. The Borders, Citizenship and Immigration Act 2009 laid the foundations for this.

Phase 6: May 2010 to date Following the election of the Coalition Government and the introduction of its 'cap'-based proposals, a new phase is in progress. It is work in progress and, therefore, we simply *touch on* the Coalition Government's response to the wider factors that have been influential in shaping policy so far.

We conclude this chapter by offering JCWI's critique of the PBS. Our concerns are addressed under the following headings:

1) international development and global inequality;

2) international human rights standards;

3) discrimination; and

4) rule of law/accountability and transparency.

For those wishing to know more about the policy and background that has informed the history of labour migration to the UK and the PBS, a list of materials, which we have also drawn on in preparing this commentary, is provided at the end of this chapter (▶33–36).

A BRIEF HISTORY OF THE UK'S IMMIGRATION SYSTEM FOR MIGRANT WORKERS

The period until 1945

Before the First World War, anyone could come and work in the UK from anywhere in the world. In 1919-1920, a system of work permits was introduced. It was an 'employer-driven' scheme. It operated by granting employers permission to employ migrants in the UK provided that it could be shown that:

- such employment was reasonable and necessary;
- adequate efforts to find domestic labour had been made; and
- wages and conditions for the migrant workers were no less favourable than those granted to British employees for similar work. The system was not applicable to citizens of the British colonies, Irish nationals and Commonwealth citizens who entered the UK as British subjects.

In 1945 the Government introduced the European Voluntary Workers' Scheme. It lasted six years, during which the Ministry of Labour allocated jobs in the UK to Europeans from refugee camps.

1962–1971

In 1962, restrictions were imposed on Commonwealth citizens who were, from this time, subjected to a voucher scheme. The scheme consisted of three categories: category A was for those with a job offer; category B was for people with training, skills or education useful to the British economy, and category C was for unskilled workers without a job. In 1965 the voucher scheme was restricted through the use of quotas and category C was abolished.

1971 onwards

In 1971, the voucher scheme was abolished and non-patrial Commonwealth citizens (ie those without the automatic right to enter the UK) were brought into the work permit scheme. The work permit scheme was tightened up by the introduction of the new requirement that the person had a specific job *and* sufficient skills/education. The UK's accession to the European Community in 1973 would later mean that nationals from the (then) European Economic Community would cease to be subject to the Immigration Rules. The UK finally took comprehensive steps to ensure that its system of control complied with European rights of free movement in 1994. These nationals were henceforth treated as part of the 'resident labour force' for work permit purposes. Nationals from countries within the EEA, for example Switzerland, were treated in the same way from 2002. The work permit system co-existed with other routes of entry, such as those for self-employed people, and the permit-free categories for employment, such as ministers of religion, sole representatives of an overseas firm and journalists for foreign media. However, the work permit scheme was the principal route for entering the UK for migrant workers from outside the EEA. It was subject to two reviews prior to 1997. These led to various changes that were designed to streamline and simplify the process. Most significant among these was the introduction, in 1991, of a two-tiered system with a view to simplifying and streamlining the process for highly skilled migrants.

THE LATE 1990S: A SHIFTING LANDSCAPE FOR LABOUR MIGRATION POLICYMAKING IN THE UK

When the Labour Government came to power in 1997 it had no labour migration policy of its own. It simply inherited the pre-existing system that had developed incrementally in a 'haphazard', unco-ordinated, and ad-hoc fashion. It was best described as demand/employer-led in nature and was characterised by multiple routes of entry. It had evolved in a way that kept migration from outside the EEA down to an irreducible minimum. Things were to change. Whereas in 1997 there were 34,000 migrant workers in the UK from outside the EEA, by 2008 that figure had risen to 66,000.

By 1997, the domestic and global economic landscape was undergoing transformation. The economy was experiencing the beginnings of a sustained period of economic growth that would last for a decade. It was also shifting in nature from an economy with a manufacturing base to one heavily structured around the service sector. Economic development and change were becoming even more influenced by global factors relating to supply and demand and there was increasing international competition for skills. The changes that occurred during the Thatcher years meant that the British economy was one of the most open in the world with a deregulated labour market. On top of all of this global mobility had also significantly increased.

The above developments led to calls from what has been referred to as a 'policy community' for a more 'flexible and responsive' labour migration system that could more effectively reflect the transformations that the economy was undergoing. That policy community consisted of individual businesses, employer associations, legal firms representing business interests, research institutes and think tanks such as the IPPR. Importantly, it also included a number of Government departments outside the Home Office, in particular the Treasury (see Somerville, *The Politics and Policy of Skilled Economic Immigration under New Labour 1997–2010*, Migration Policy Institute, forthcoming 2011).

The 'New Labour' Government was a different creature to Labour of the past. The Party had moved to the centre of the political spectrum, was keen to shed its public image as hostile to business and was committed to an open economy and working with the challenges of globalisation. Its vision was of a high-tech, knowledge-intense, innovative and scientific British economy. At least one commentator has suggested that the Party's sense of indebtedness to ethnic minority voters – many of whom played a critical role in bringing Labour to power – together with its own culture of the importance of social justice in the areas of immigration and race, were also influential. Indeed it should not be forgotten that one of the earliest acts of the new Government was to abolish the 'primary purpose' rule, a long-running sore in the politics of race relations.

All of these factors played an important role in ensuring that the Government was particularly receptive to demands for more flexibility in migration. The result was that Labour embarked on an on-going review of immigration policy, a review that would culminate in the establishment of the PBS.

PHASE 1: THE BIRTH OF A NEW APPROACH TO LABOUR MIGRATION (1997–2000)

The process of reforming labour-based immigration policy can be traced back to 1998 with the publication of the Department of Trade and Industry's 1998 White Paper *Our Competitive Future: Building the Knowledge Driven Economy*. The paper concluded that there was a need to attract "bright people with scarce skills" to work in the UK and to set up businesses of their own with a view to creating jobs. It considered what scope there was for lowering the barriers for movement by skilled professionals and entrepreneurs.

The 1998 White Paper was endorsed by the 1999 pre-budget report. This confirmed that the Government would be making it easier for skilled foreign workers in certain areas to come and work in the UK in circumstances "where they have the skills and attitudes to help generate an enterprise economy".

In 2000, Immigration Minister Barbara Roche made a ground-breaking speech. She criticised previous immigration policy and its fixation with stemming the tide of migration and she argued that immigration could bring real benefits to the UK. Subsequently she called for an expansion of primary migration for wealth creators and other migrants who could plug skills shortages.

Roche's speech appears to have been based on research that was subsequently published by the Home Office as part of its major immigration review in 2000. It reflects in particular the thinking in two reports, *International migration and the United Kingdom: Recent Patterns and Trends, Final Report to the Home Office* (Dobson, Koser, McLaughlan and Salt 2001) and *Migration: an Economic and Social Analysis* (Glover *et al* 2001). In summary, the first report observed that there were push and pull factors at work that were resulting in higher levels of migration. Most notable amongst these was the growing demand for labour in the domestic labour market. Globalisation and demographic changes meant that this trend was unlikely to change. The evidence suggested that these immigrant flows were resulting in the creation of new businesses and jobs, the filling of labour market gaps, an improvement in productivity and international competitiveness and the reduction of inflationary pressure, with minimal negative effect on the existing domestic workforce.

The second report, *Migration: an economic and social analysis*, developed the above thinking and went on to map out areas around which Government policy could be developed. Noting that different types of migration impact differently on the labour market, it argued that pre- and post-entry migration policy should be designed in a more co-ordinated way with a view to better reflecting economic objectives. These objectives were meeting labour shortages and encouraging both innovation and entrepreneurialism. The report also suggested that policy should facilitate social objectives such as reducing social exclusion and facilitating migrant integration. Finally, it noted that, while undocumented migration was undesirable on economic and social grounds, its cause, at least in part, was thought to reflect unmet needs in the economy. It recommended enhanced control and a review of the available routes of entry.

Around the same time there was a growing recognition by the Government of the importance of the education industry to the British economy. This led to the launch of the Prime Minister's Initiative in 1999. This was designed to boost significantly the UK's share of the FE and HE student market. The initiative was driven by the Department for Innovation, Universities and Skills, though input was secured from other parts of government including the Home Office and UK Visas. Research commissioned as part of this process showed that immigration procedures and work restrictions were impairing an expansion of the UK's share of the FE/HE student market. The conclusion was that immigration arrangements, in so far as students were concerned, needed to be liberalised.

PHASE 2: A PERIOD OF INNOVATION (2000–2004/5)

Five themes around which policy was developed

Having committed itself to expanding immigration to the UK, the period 2000–2005 can broadly be seen as a period of innovation and experimentation within the confines of this wider objective. Many of the innovations of this period ultimately came to exert considerable influence on the final shape of the PBS.

The innovations during this phase were based around five themes:

- meeting labour/skills shortages;
- encouraging entrepreneurialism and innovation;
- expanding the UK's share of the HE and FE international student market;

- developing a self-financing labour migration system; and
- introducing greater control.

Meeting labour shortages

The White Paper *Secure Borders, Safe Haven Integration with Diversity in Modern Britain* (Cm 5387, 2002) confirmed that there were labour shortages in the UK for both skilled and unskilled positions. To address this in respect of non-EEA migration, the Home Office liberalised the employer-led work permit scheme and expanded 'low-skilled' migration opportunities. In 2000/2001, following the review by the Department for Education and Employment, the work permit scheme was streamlined with a view to making it more responsive to labour shortages. Measures adopted included the following:

- relaxation of the skills threshold for work permit purposes;
- expansion of the occupations that were included in the swifter former Tier 1 procedure;
- abolition of the resident labour market test for work permit extensions;
- transferring the administration of Work Permits UK from the Department of Education and Skills to the Home Office – signifying better co-ordination between migration and economic policy;
- expansion of opportunities for students to switch into work permit employment;
- more flexible application of the work permit scheme; and
- the restructuring of the bureaucracy with a greater 'customer' (ie, employer) focus.

As to the expansion of 'low-skilled' migration opportunities, in 2003 the Government introduced the Sectors-Based Scheme (SBS) for the catering and hospitality industries. Following the *Review of the Seasonal Agricultural Workers Scheme* (Home Office/Work Permits UK, 2002), that scheme was further liberalised through expansion of its coverage and the abolition of the applicable upper age limits. These were, however, subsequently tightened in 2004.

There was also a move towards plugging low-skilled labour market shortages through the use of 'incidental measures'. Students, for example, were given an automatic entitlement to work for 20 hours during term time, and the Working Holidaymaker Scheme was liberalised in 2003 through the removal of limitations on work, although this was subject to revision again in 2005.

In addition, in 2004 the Government, unlike most of its EU partners, allowed immediate access to the domestic labour market for nationals of the ten Accession States upon registration under the Worker Registration Scheme.

Encouraging entrepreneurialism and innovation

The *Secure Borders* White Paper also observed that a number of countries were making attempts to attract highly skilled migrants to their shores. It argued that in order to remain competitive, the UK would need to encourage the movement of business and financial experts and other skilled personnel to the UK with a view to boosting innovation and entrepreneurialism. To this end, the Home Office experimented with the introduction of two new 'supply side' schemes, the Innovator Scheme (2000), and the Highly Skilled Migrants Programme (HSMP) (2002).

The HSMP and the Innovator Scheme were novel in that they provided primary routes of entry leading to settlement for skilled migrants *without* a job offer. While the existence of economic routes of entry for those without existing employment was not new, for the first time these routes enabled the entry of migrants with high levels of human, rather than financial, capital. Human capital was to be evaluated by reference to an entirely new scheme which awarded points for those attributes considered to be associated with labour market success. Applicants were awarded points for education, earnings, attainment in their field, work experience and, in the case of innovators, business experience and the economic benefits potentially arising from their plans. Both schemes underwent further experimentation and modification.

Expanding the UK's share of the FE/HE market

Like many other countries at the time, the UK continued to make various changes to the immigration system with a view to developing a more attractive package for students so as to increase its share of the international HE and FE market and to promote the above objectives. This led to the introduction of various schemes. The Science and Engineering Graduate Scheme (SEGS) was introduced in 2004 and enabled science and engineering graduates to enter or remain in the UK for up to 12 months in order to seek work. The Fresh Talent in Scotland Scheme (2005) allowed those who had studied in Scotland to remain in order to take on work there. This was accompanied by an expansion of categories permitting 'switching' into student routes, and liberalisation of the switching provisions for those who had been students but wished to move to employer-led/supply side schemes. The previous position was that students were required to show that they intended to leave the UK at the end of their studies and had to apply from overseas in order to return under the work permit scheme.

Making the labour migration system self-financing

As *Controlling our borders: Making migration work for Britain, Five year strategy for asylum and immigration* (Cm 6472, 2005) makes clear, another novel development during this period was the move towards making the labour migration system self-financing. The financing of the system had previously been considered largely as a public expense which was to be funded through the general taxation system. The shift to a charging regime was introduced through the 2002 Act and extended under the 2004 Act. This resulted in a pricing scheme that sought 'costs recovery' of the administration and processing costs associated with immigration employment documents.

Greater control

Many of the above measures were designed to shape migratory flows to the UK in line with economic objectives. The flip side of this was that ways were sought to better control the activities of migrants in the UK with a view to ensuring that only those migrants the UK wanted and needed for work purposes were able to engage in work.

In 2001, the Government commissioned research into irregular migration and unlawful working in the UK. The following research studies: *Sizing the unauthorised (illegal) migrant population in the United Kingdom* (2001), *A survey of the illegally resident population in detention in the UK* (2001) and *Employers and Illegal Migrant Workers in the Clothing and Restaurant Industry* (2002) all suggested that illegal working was common in certain sectors and was a growing problem.

In 2002 *Secure Borders* (▶above) argued that illegal working was undermining the economic benefits of immigration. Public revenue from taxation was being lost to the black economy. At the same time this black economy was acting as a pull factor for irregular migrants. It was also argued that, in addition to expanding opportunities for lawful migration, efforts should now be directed to better controlling work by migrants in the UK.

The primary means through which greater control of work was to be exerted was through the expansion of internal controls. In practice these included:

- extending police powers to immigration officers in relation to offences committed by those working unlawfully (the 1999 Act, the 2004 Act and the UK Borders Act 2007);
- introducing streamlined immigration mechanisms for dealing with those who work unlawfully or overstay through the introduction of 'administrative removal' (the 1999 Act);
- making documentary checking requirements more onerous and introducing new offences (the 2004 Act);
- introducing administrative fines and imprisonment for those who knowingly employ unauthorised workers (the 2006 Act, introduced as a Bill in 2005);
- introducing a system of licensing intermediaries in agriculture, food processing and shellfish collection (the Gangmasters (Licensing) Act 2004).

While there was, at this point, no reference to the possibility of a sponsorship system as such, the idea that dealing with irregular migration was no longer the sole responsibility of the state, but one shared by 'all', including business and the general public, received its first airing in *Secure Borders* (2002). There were also changes made to the system of applying from abroad that were linked to the tighter regulation of working in the UK. These included:

- changes to the visa scheme through, for example, the extension of compulsory entry clearance for all work-permit employment exceeding six months;
- the imposition of visa requirements on both visa and non-visa nationals in cases where applicants wish to come to the UK for more than six months; and
- the expansion of carriers' liability and provisions for juxtaposed controls.

PHASE 3: PAVING THE WAY – A BLUEPRINT FOR THE POINTS-BASED SYSTEM (2004/5–2008)

While the changes that took place between 1997–2004/5 were heavily shaped by globalisation and the tight group of highly skilled migrants actors, it has been argued that the period from 2005 to date has been much more political in tone and content. The following factors are said by some to have exerted a far more significant role on policy (see Somerville, *The Politics and Policy of Skilled Economic Immigration under New Labour 1997–2010*, Migration Policy Institute, forthcoming 2011).

- A more hostile public opinion in which immigration was increasingly seen as a key policy issue.
- Negative media coverage linking immigration to crime, security, welfare abuse and problems with public services – there was also, in our view, an increasing fixation with over-population.
- The volume of new arrivals associated with Eastern European migration arising from the Government's decision in 2004 to permit A8 nationals access to work without restrictions, together with liberalised entry to the UK for A2 nationals. Numbers were substantially more than originally predicted. Eastern Europeans therefore became far more visible and negative media coverage began to undermine public confidence in the ability of the Government to regulate immigration.
- The development of a staunch political opposition to the Labour Government's approach to immigration. The Conservative Party adopted a more restrictive approach to migration and there were concerns over the gains being made by the British National Party. The latter were of particular concern given that the skilled working class, traditionally more likely to vote Labour, represented 21% of the UK population and nearly a third (32%) of those who voted for the BNP in 2006.

The Government's initial response to a changing environment

The Labour Government's initial response to the above concerns was three-fold. It:

- published a blueprint for a new Points-Based System, said to be inspired by a similar system implemented in Australia;
- introduced new mechanisms for the control of migrants; and
- focused on migrant integration.

A blueprint for the Points-Based System

Controlling our borders: Making migration work for Britain, Five year strategy for asylum and immigration was the Government's primary response to the above concerns. While there had been a number of changes to the system, it was felt that these were insufficient. Five problems were identified. These were as follows:

- The system was politically ineffectual. Multiple, unco-ordinated routes of entry did not easily lend themselves to comprehensible explanation to the public as to who was coming to the UK and why. This was leading to a perception that migration was 'out of control'.
- The ad-hoc system that existed was still not crafted in a way that was easily amenable to control and regulation by the Government.
- The system was felt to be administratively sluggish, inefficient and unresponsive to the needs of employers and labour markets. In particular, the dual application process for work permits by employers and applicants was time-consuming, unreliable and could not efficiently respond to labour market needs.
- The use of 'subjective tests' for labour and study purposes were considered inefficient. They were generating error, uncertainty, delay and a significant number of successful appeals. Entry clearance applicants were often refused, after lengthy consideration of their applications, on grounds that they did not possess the skills and experience required for the job. This was despite the fact that their employers had been granted work permits. Further, the delay in administering applications arising from these subjective tests was thought to be generating unfounded applications as a means of staying in the UK. This was said, in turn, to creating yet more appeals, pushing up costs and leading to the inefficient deployment of public resources.
- Internal and external immigration control mechanisms to regulate migrant work were considered inadequate. It was felt that a more integrated and intensive approach was required to ensure that migrants complied with the terms of their leave. This could be achieved through devolving control functions to employers, educational establishments, governments of sending states and other sponsors, and also through more rigorous enforcement and the application of civil penalties.

- It was felt that the appeals process was 'hampering' enforcement both preventing swift removal of migrants and encouraging undocumented migrants to enter or remain in the UK. This was thought to be encouraging further irregular migration/residence and unlawful work.

The 'five-year' strategy sought to address these concerns by introducing a blueprint for a Points-Based System. This was followed, in July 2005, by a consultation paper, *Selective Admission: Making Migration Work for Britain*. A yet more developed version of the Points-Based System, together with an explanation of its objectives, was published in the Government's Command Paper of March 2006 *A Points-Based System: Making Migration Work for Britain* (Cm 6471). This was accompanied later in the same year by two further consultation papers. *A Consultation on a New Charging Regime for Immigration and Nationality Fees* in October 2006 examined the basis on which fees should be set. It was followed by *A Consultation on Establishing a Migration Advisory Committee*. The latter developed the idea, advanced in the March 2006 paper, for the establishment of a specific skills advisory board that could offer guidance on shortage occupations.

New control mechanisms

There were five new innovations during this period.

The civil penalties scheme This scheme introduced through the 2006 Act, sought to tighten the structure for unlawful working through the introduction of a system of civil penalties (for further details about civil penalties ▶000). The key features were: on-the-spot fines; an on-going duty to inspect workers' immigration status for certain categories of migrant and the introduction of a new offence of knowingly employing migrant workers without authorisation.

The biometric documents scheme The UK Borders Act 2007 introduced a requirement to apply for a biometric document at the time of making an immigration application.

Tighter control measures for students A mandatory requirement for entry clearance was introduced, non-visa nationals were prevented from switching into the student category and reporting obligations for educational establishments were extended in 2007.

The tightening of the general grounds for refusal The general grounds that can be given for refusing applications (under part IX HC 395) were tightened. In addition, from 2008, a system of 're-entry' bans was introduced into the general refusal grounds. The effect of this was to bar re-entry to the UK for very significant periods of time in cases where a migrant had previously overstayed, breached their conditions of leave (for example conditions relating to work) or used deception in an application to enter or remain in the UK (for further details on this ▶000).

Local immigration teams Local immigration teams were introduced in line with the enforcement strategy set out in *Enforcing the Deal* (2008). Their role is to enforce laws on illegal working, address community concerns, enforce immigration law generally, and find and arrest those who do not comply. Expenditure on enforcement was doubled.

Focus on integration as an objective of the immigration scheme

'Integration' is about securing participation in society by migrants in a range of different spheres, partly as a means of securing their acceptance by society at large. The focus of the Government was on participation in the labour market, and therefore independence of migrants from the welfare state. A commitment to this policy objective began with the HSMP, but was also evident in the extension of English language requirements through English language and life tests which were introduced as a requirement for settlement (indefinite leave to remain) in 2007. There is some empirical research that has linked fluency in the English language to labour market success.

On-going experimentation and innovation

At the same time attempts were being made to mould routes according to economic needs. Cerna, for example, has drawn attention to the addition of a route for those with very well-regarded Masters' degrees in Business Administration under the HSMP. The effect of this is that those who obtained MBAs from a list of 50 schools world-wide were eligible for admission (see L Cerna and A Wietholtz, 'Immigration and immigrant policy-making in the United Kingdom', in G Zincone, R Penninx and M Borkert (eds), *Migratory Policy-Making in Europe*. Amsterdam: Amsterdam University Press, forthcoming 2011).

Additionally, in 2006 the second Prime Minister's Initiative was launched with a view to further increasing international student numbers in the UK. This coincided with various amendments to the Immigration Rules which sought to make studying in the UK more attractive. In March 2006, for example, SEGS was expanded so that all Masters and PhD students, rather than simply those from selected courses, became eligible to apply to remain in the UK for 12 months after completion of their studies. This was followed in 2007 by changes that widened the scope of the scheme so as to include all Bachelor's degrees and all classes of degree as well as postgraduate certificates and diplomas from the UK. These modifications also promoted the aim of meeting labour market shortages and encouraging innovation.

PHASE 4: IMPLEMENTING THE POINTS-BASED SYSTEM (2008–2009)

The PBS was launched in a staggered fashion starting with Tier 1 in March 2008 and ending with Tier 4 in March 2009. An overview of the scheme covering the general contents of each tier and what it replaces, is contained in Chapter 2.

The table below sets out the nature of the changes made by the PBS, by comparing the position before and after the PBS was introduced. For each change, the table identifies the relevant policy objectives by reference to:

1) those contained in *A Points-Based System Making Migration Work for Britain* (Cm 6472, 2006); and

2) the broader aims underpinning the system.

Pre-PBS position	Transition to the PBS	'Points-Based System' Government paper objective	Broader policy objective
Uncoordinated, large number of migration routes with *ad hoc* evolution over time.	Rationalisation of migration routes and establishment of a co-ordinated *system* with a points scheme spanning 5 tiers. Points operate as levers that can be manipulated on a large scale. Points are linked to factors research suggests are indicative of optimum performance in the labour market, ie income, possession of English language, education, youth, and are also tied to immigration control through the requirement of sponsorship certificates.	2, 3, 5, 7	1, 2, 3, 5
Extensive presence in Immigration Rules of 'subjective criteria' including assessment of capability to undertake work/ studies and ability to maintain and accommodate.	Replacement of subjective criteria with 'objective' criteria, eg fixed maintenance requirements, possession of certificate of sponsorship from employer/certificate of acceptance for studies.	1–4, 7	1, 2

Relatively little use of guidance outside the Immigration Rules	Extensive use of detailed and lengthy guidance. Frequently, the guidance itself is referred to in the Immigration Rules.	1, 3, 5	1
Rough and ready system for establishing shortage occupations. Lists were drawn up by civil servants with assistance from panels through the Skills Advisory Board and the Sectors Development Agency. The analysis did not cover all sectors of the economy, there was no formal mechanism for updating the shortage list. Nor was there any methodology for assessing the economic, fiscal and wider impact of migration.	Establishment of the Migration Advisory Committee. This is a far more sophisticated, expert, non-departmental, independent public body supported by a secretariat. Its purpose is to advise on shortage occupations though its terms of reference permit advice on other immigration issues at the request of the Government. Shortage occupation lists are produced every six months following a comprehensive economic analysis of the labour market. The analysis is both 'top down' and 'bottom up' and draws upon information from stakeholders, experts and social contributors. The Committee considers whether occupations are: 'skilled' 'shortage occupations' and whether any gaps can 'be sensibly filled' by migration. The latter assessment takes into account the wider economic and fiscal aspects of the system.	5, 2	1
No institutional mechanism charged with examining the social impact of migration on services and communities.	Establishment of the Migration Impacts Forum. This is an institutional forum at which members consider information and evidence about the social impact of migration on services and communities with a view to developing practices/policies that can accommodate it. The forum is chaired jointly by a Home Office and Communities & Local Government Minister. The forum's findings are shared with all relevant Government Departments.	2	6

Limited immigration responsibilities exercised by employers, educational establishments and overseas countries.	Introduction of a more pervasive, devolved system of immigration control through the requirement that all employers and educational establishments seeking to employ/educate migrants from outside the EU possess a 'sponsor' licence (awards that are based on immigration control risk assessments). As a precondition for securing and maintaining these licences, employers and educational establishments are required to comply with extensive immigration reporting requirements in relation to their employees and students. There is a threat of downgrading of status or withdrawal of licence in the event of non-compliance.	5, 6, 7	5
No requirement that the country of nationality of low-skilled workers must enter into a 'returns' agreement with the UK.	Introduction of effective 'returns' agreements from countries of nationality as a precondition for eligibility for Tier 5 (youth mobility scheme).	6	5, 1
The existence of a 'judicial' right of appeal, on fact and law, to the statutory tribunal against entry clearance decisions relating to work or study.	Abolition of the right of appeal against a work/study based entry clearance decision and its replacement with an administrative process (administrative review) on a point of fact only (save for in limited human rights/ race relations cases).	6, 7	5
No filtering/ advertising mechanism to attract migrant labour and students to the UK.	Introduction of advertising and filtering mechanisms accessible throughout the world through online assessments. PBS calculator permits applicants to self-assess their circumstances against the criteria before deciding whether to make an application.	1–4	1–2

A two-stage process involving officials where immigration issues are assessed by visa-issuing posts abroad and qualifications are assessed by the Home Office in the UK.	A one-stage process involving officials in which immigration issues are assessed by visa posts and qualification is assessed by the sponsoring employer or educational establishment.	3, 4, 5, 7	1
Setting of fees which reflect the administrative costs of processing applications.	Variable fee structure in which fees are levied on the basis of the perceived value of the application to the applicant. The result is that some applications are priced above the administrative processing cost and some below it.	7	1, 2, 5, 6
Existence of 'general' grounds upon which entry clearance and leave to enter/remain should/would be refused.	Introduction of an *additional* immigration penalty in the form of automatic re-entry bans for those who have previously overstayed, breached conditions of stay and/or who have previously used deception. The bans on re-entry operate for different periods of time depending on the terms on which the applicant departed the UK. Addition of the use of false documents and making false representations as a mandatory ground for refusal.	6	5
Existence of a criminal offence for the employment of those who work in the UK unlawfully with statutory defences in cases where the infringement was unintentional and documents were checked and copied	Fortified scheme for preventing unlawful working (ss15 and 21 of the 2006 Act) through the creation of new, more onerous checking requirements and a new civil offence with corresponding defences, and the introduction of a criminal offence of knowingly employing a migrant unlawfully with the new possibility of imprisonment and a fine.	6	5

before starting work (see section 1996 Act).			
No requirement of positive candour in relation to issues that might affect on-going entitlement to leave.	Introduction of biometric documents scheme which requires holders to volunteer relevant information to questions concerning compliance with Immigration Rules. There are corresponding penalties for failure to comply including the cancellation or variation of leave.	6	5

Explanation of definitions for narrow objectives:

1. **Objectivity** – minimising the scope for discretion and subjective evaluation
2. **Transparency** – enabling migrants, the Government and stakeholders to understand how each part of the process works
3. **Operability** – minimising human error
4. **Usability** – enabling different customers to use the scheme
5. **Flexibility** – responding to changes in the labour market
6. **Robust** – minimising non-compliance in the system
7. **Cost effectiveness** – enabling the system to be self-sustaining and keeping costs to a minimum

Broader objectives

1. Meeting labour/skills shortages
2. Encouraging entrepreneurialism and innovation
3. Expanding the UK's share of the FE and the HE international student market
4. Development of a self-financing labour migration system
5. Greater control
6. Integration

The six themes (referred to above) that developed from 2000 onwards went on to underlie the PBS itself: meeting labour/skills shortages, encouraging innovation and entrepreneurialism, expanding the UK's share of the student market, the development of a self-financing system, facilitating 'integration' and establishing greater control.

It is also not difficult to see how influential the preceding period of innovation was on the ultimate design of the PBS. Tier 1 of the PBS draws direct inspiration from the supply side schemes that had previously been introduced, ie HSMP and the route for 'innovators'. The post-study work aspect of Tier 1 developed from the previous Science and Engineering Graduate Scheme (SEGS).

So far as Tier 2 goes, while it remained employer-led in character, it too was heavily influenced by the earlier supply side measures that were grafted on to the Tier through a demanding pointing scheme. The administrative streamlining by replacing the two-step application process with a single-step process continued the administrative liberalisation process that started in 2000/2001. The PBS also continued earlier liberalising reforms such as the abolition of the resident labour market test for extension applications and more generous provision for switching into the category for students.

Tier 3 is suspended as a result of the level of migration from the EEA but its characteristics of being quota-based, operator-led and providing short-term residence entitlements only were all part of the previous Sector-Based and Seasonal Agricultural Workers Schemes. Similarly, Tier 3 reflects its predecessors by excluding settlement and the entry of dependants.

Tier 4 (Study) continued the policy intent of a system designed to encourage international students to come to the UK. Entitlements to switch into work-based tiers were maintained as were incidental rights to work while studying (although they were modified). Tier 4 also continued the control features that had been introduced during the preceding period, ie mandatory entry clearance and limited mandatory reporting requirements.

Tier 5 was less heavily influenced by the preceding developments but still reflected the preoccupation with intensive mechanisms for control. They included civil penalties, mandatory entry clearance requirements and extensive powers for immigration officers to deal with working-related offences.

PHASE 5: FINE-TUNING, TIGHTENING AND EXTENDING THE POINTS-BASED SYSTEM (2009–MAY 2010)

The period 2009–2010 can be seen as the period in which the Government sought to fine-tune, tighten and extend the Points-Based System, in part in response to some of the factors discussed above – in particular growing hostility to migration in the press and public opinion.

Fine-tuning the Points-Based System

A number of changes were made to the system in order to 'fine-tune' it. Their principal aim was to address certain difficulties or gaps that had arisen but in a way that continued to meet the above objectives. Changes included:

- the introduction of a route of entry for Tier 1 migrants with a Bachelor's degree or no degree where their previous earnings were sufficiently high, together with more generous age thresholds;

- broadening the eligibility for Tier 1 post-study work to include migrants studying for an eligible qualification while in the UK in any capacity that does not preclude work;
- no longer requiring those under Tiers 1 and 2 to satisfy further English language tests when applying to extend leave where these requirements had previously been satisfied;
- the introduction of rules allowing for paternity and maternity leave in assessing Tier 2 intra company transfers and applications from those switching from Tier 2 (General) into post-study work;
- removal of the restriction preventing Tier 2 intra company transfers where migrants own more than 10% of the shares;
- the introduction of a new intra company route for graduate trainees;
- changes to the sponsorship scheme so that 'A' rated sponsors could issue undertakings in relation to maintenance payments and also enabling sponsors to make minor changes to the employment details of Tier 2 migrants without having to make an application to the UK Border Agency;
- changes on the rules for switching, eg Representatives of Overseas Business Category into Tier 2
- the reflection of the Sponsor Management System through the introduction of the Confirmation of Acceptance of Studies as a prerequisite for entry and leave extensions under the Points-Based System.

Tightening the Points-Based System

Migrant workers

There were a number of changes during this period which made the requirements for entry and stay more demanding for would-be migrants. In 2010, following the publication of the Migration Advisory Committee reports, *Analysis of the Points-Based System: Tier 2 and Dependants* (October 2009) and *Analysis of the Points-Based System, Tier 1* (December 2009), Tiers 1 and 2 were amended. These changes were:

- the earnings threshold was raised;
- the structure for obtaining successive grants of leave under Tier 1 was changed so applicants would be tested for economic activity at the two, instead of three, year stage;
- the employment conditions attached to leave for Tier 1 applicants became more restrictive (this was also extended to Tier 5); and
- Tier 2 employers were required to conduct a more onerous (and lengthy) search within the domestic labour market before opting to employ foreign nationals.

Growing concerns about the manipulation of the labour migration scheme through fraud led to the following:

- reshaping the intra-company transfer route so that it no longer led to settlement and increasing the qualifying period for previous employment from six to 12 months;

- introducing English language requirements for categories outside the PBS such as sole representatives of overseas businesses;
- changing the post study work requirements so that applicants do not obtain point unless they have UK postgraduate certificates of education; and
- extending visa requirements for entry for short-term purposes.

Students

A key development was the emergence of concerns about the use of Tier 4 for work rather than study purposes. This arose following a report published in *The Times* (15 April 2009 'Bogus foreign students free to flout new laws') that nine Pakistani nationals had been found in the UK with student visas fraudulently facilitated by an organisation calling itself a college. Following the publication of *Bogus Colleges* by the Home Affairs Committee (HC 595, July 2010) and a subsequent review by the UK Border Agency and the Department for Business, Innovation and Skills, the UKBA concluded that Tier 4 needed to be better shaped to ensure that only students, rather than economic migrants, were able to enter the UK under that Tier. This was achieved through Rule changes which:

- prevent Tier 4 students who are studying courses below degree level (except those on a foundation course) from working more than 10 hours per week during term time;
- prevent family members of students who are pursuing courses of six months or less from accompanying the Tier 4 student applicant to the UK;
- prevent family members of students studying at below degree level (except those on foundation courses) from taking up employment unless they qualify under the PBS in their own right;
- increase the standard of English required for Tier 4 (General) courses below degree level; and
- introduce a 'Highly Trusted Sponsor' Scheme so that only accredited organisations are able to provide courses below level 3 of the National Qualifications Framework and offer courses below degree level which provide work placements.

Extending the Points-Based System to the scheme for settlement and citizenship

A consultation paper, *The Path to Citizenship: Next Steps in Reforming the Immigration System* (2008), first aired the idea of 'earned citizenship', although it did not expressly refer to extending the PBS to settlement and citizenship. That paper was followed by the enactment of the Borders, Citizenship and Immigration Act 2009 and a further Government consultation entitled *Earning the Right to Stay: A New Points Test for Citizenship*

(August 2009). The citizenship/naturalisation provisions of the 2009 Act are not in force. It laid the framework for a Points-Based System to apply to naturalisation applications.

The 2009 consultation paper sought views on the criteria that should apply both for settlement and citizenship purposes. The paper makes reference to the growing preoccupation of the media with the size of the population and the level of immigration as justification for the intro-duction of the new measures. It is interesting that the proposals mirror those advanced in September 2008 by the Cross-Party Group on Balanced Migration, chaired by Frank Field MP (see www.frankfield.com) and Nicholas Soames MP (www.nicholassoames.org.uk) in their document *Balanced Migration: A new approach to Controlling Immigration*. The document draws upon research by Migration Watch, which campaigns for a reduction in immigration to the UK.

PHASE 6: THE FUTURE OF THE POINTS-BASED SYSTEM UNDER THE NEW COALITION GOVERNMENT

The new Coalition Government and the cap

In its *Coalition Programme for Government*, published on 20 May 2010, the present Government set out its intention to introduce an annual limit on the number of non-EU economic migrants admitted to the UK to live and work, and to consult on the mechanism for implementing its proposed 'cap' on the numbers coming in. The motive was succinctly described by the Business Secretary, Vince Cable MP, as reflecting the desire simply to "reassure the public that immigration is under control". In other words, it is the Government's response to the concerns identified above. During the election, the Liberal Democrats did not support the cap. They instead argued for the modification of the PBS in a way that could reflect regional considerations. Indeed the Conservative proposal for a cap was heavily criticised by the Liberal Democrats during the election, with the then Liberal Democrat Home Affairs spokesperson, Chris Huhne MP, arguing in JCWI's *Bulletin* that the cap was "at best ludicrous and at worst disastrous for the UK economy".

On 28 June 2010, the Government laid before Parliament a statement of changes to the Immigration Rules for the purpose of implementing an 'interim' cap. This came into force on 19 July 2010. It was a temporary measure intended to apply until April 2011. It was designed to stem sudden surges in visa applications pending reforms to the PBS.

In July 2010, the House of Lords Merits of Statutory Instruments Com-mittee issued a report on the interim cap and, among other matters, suggested that Parliament may wish to take up concerns that JCWI has raised about the changes, including the inadequacy of the equality impact assessment, together with the proposed mode of implementation of the interim cap (HL Paper 17, 16 July 2010). This matter has subsequently been the subject of litigation brought by JCWI (▶58–59).

In June 2010 the Government also issued a consultation paper entitled *Limits on non-EU economic migration* intended to pave the way for a permanent annual limit on migration. It also procured a report in 2010 from the Migration Advisory Committee on the subject.

The Migration Advisory Committee's recommendations and findings can be found in its report *Limits on Migration Limits on Tier 1 and 2 for 2011/2012 and supporting policies*. The Committee was tasked with recommending limits for the cap on the basis of the Government's instruction to find ways to reduce immigration, and as such the report proceeds on this basis. So far as its findings on the previous impact of Tier 1 and 2 migration go, it found that:

- All things being equal, Tier 1 and Tier 2 migration clearly have a positive impact on Gross Domestic Product (GDP).
- Tier 1 and Tier 2 migration make a small but positive contribution to GDP per head.
- The above effects will accumulate over time and become more significant.
- The impact on GDP per head will also be influenced by dynamic factors such as the impact of migration on productivity, trade, investment and skill development of resident workers.
- There is no evidence, at the aggregate level, of adverse labour market impacts.
- Tier 1 and 2 migrants, in the short term at least and on average, almost certainly make a positive net fiscal contribution.
- Tier 1 and 2 migrants and their dependants do consume public services, such as health and education services. They also contribute to the provision of key services as members of the workforce.
- The impact of Tier 1 and 2 migrants on broader outcomes affecting the whole of society, such as crime, congestion and housing, is difficult to estimate. Through their effect in adding to the UK population they will inevitably have an effect on such outcomes. The impact per head is likely to be smaller than that of the migrant population as a whole in relation to some impacts, such as crime. In relation to others, such as congestion, it may be larger.

Following the report by the Migration Advisory Committee, and research entitled *The Migrant Journey, Research Report 43* (Achato, Eaton & Jones 2010), on 6 September the Immigration Minister delivered his speech 'The Real Immigration Question'. He used this to outline the broad thrust of the Government's future approach to labour-based migration. The Minister took the view that there had been a loss of public confidence in the immigration system. Accordingly he reaffirmed that the annual rate of net migration would be reduced to tens of thousands rather than hundreds of thousands in order to address this. He also confirmed that the system would in future, be designed in a way that would make it far more selective, and that strong controls would continue to remain an on-going feature of the system. This was reaffirmed in his subsequent speech of 1 February 2011.

On 3 November 2010, the Home Affairs Committee published its report, *Immigration Cap* (HC 361, November 2010). It expressed concern that the cap would make very little difference to immigration levels overall, that its application might harm certain sectors of the British economy, and that the speed at which policy was being made was cause for concern. It also recommended that visa allocations should be made on a monthly rather than annual basis with provision for emergency cases.

Following the report by the Migration Advisory Committee on 23 November 2010 , the Home Secretary set out in a statement to Parliament her proposals to reform Tiers 1 and 2 of the Points-Based System. A further consultation paper, *The Student Immigration System A Consultation* was issued on 7 December. This consulted on measures to reduce, through changes in the system, the level of migration by students. In February 2011 the UK Border Agency issued its *Statement of Intent for Tier 2 of the Points-Based System*. For further details of the interim and permanent cap, ▶see 55–59, 208–210 and for details of the particular proposals for change to Tier 1, ▶see 140–142; 164–165; 173–174, 203–204; Tier 2 ▶see 207–208 and Tier 4 ▶see 292–294

ANALYSING THE POINTS-BASED SYSTEM

Criticisms of the PBS

JCWI's fundamental objection to the PBS is that it does not adequately reflect the interests of the other parties involved in the 'labour migration equation'. We consider that, in devising labour migration policies, adequate weight must be given, not just to the host economy, but to the rights and interests of migrants and their national states.

In practice, as a minimum, this means that any PBS and its architecture should:

- respect commitments assumed by the international community to promote international development and alleviate global inequality;
- embody international human rights/labour standards and the principles that underlie them;
- reflect the principle of non-discrimination; and
- reflect the principles of the rule of law, accountability and transparency.

While we do not provide an exhaustive critique of the PBS system in this section, we elaborate upon these points below, and identify some of failings that the PBS exhibits by reference to the above principles. More detailed critiques in relation to these points can be found in JCWI's policy papers, its quarterly *Bulletin*, and its policy publications available at www.jcwi.org.uk. Additionally, reference can be made to the materials listed at the end of this chapter.

International development and global inequality

The United Nations Millennium Development Goals are eight international development objectives that the international community has committed itself to achieving by 2015. They include the eradication of extreme poverty, reduction in child mortality and the establishment of a global partnership for development by 2015. They flow from the United Nations Millennium Declaration that has been signed by 189 states, including the UK. These commitments are reflected in the UK's Public Sector Agreement. The principles also appear in the International Labour Organisation's Multilateral Framework on Labour Migration: Non-Binding Principles and Guidelines for a Rights-Based Approach to Labour Migration (MFLM). Undoubtedly labour migration opportunities under the PBS have assisted and indeed continue to assist developing countries through remittances, trade and investment links and in particular through the new skills returning migrants take back. However, the design of the PBS is far more heavily skewed towards the interests of the UK than those of sending developing states. Indeed the UK has received a 'poor' rating for its immigration system from the Centre for Global Development's index rating scheme (2009). A key problem with the PBS has been the courting of very highly skilled migrants in tandem with the closure of routes for those classified as unskilled workers from outside the EU. The latter has been the effect of the suspension of Tier 3, the lack of inclusion of 'unskilled work' on the Tier 2 shortage list and the closure of the Tier 5 Youth Mobility Scheme to developing countries. This will be exacerbated by the changes that are due to be made to the system in April 2011 (▶140–142; 164–165; 173–174; 203–204; 207–212; 292–294).

This closure/suspension of low-skilled routes of entry structurally works against the interests of developing countries for three reasons. Firstly, developing countries have a surplus of 'unskilled labour'. The closure of the UK's doors to one of their most valuable exports therefore represents a significant problem. Secondly, while developing countries have a surplus of unskilled labour, they frequently encounter shortages of skilled labour. Loss of what skilled labour they have has an acute impact on developing countries. For example, the loss of health care professionals in Kenya and Malawi, both of which struggle with the HIV/AIDS epidemic, has been a significant problem for those countries. Thirdly, the terms of exchange for skilled labour are slanted towards the interests of developed countries as the developing country bears the costs of training the labour that then migrates. The effect of this is that the UK receives what amounts to subsidised labour.

Another difficulty with the PBS arises from the increase in the costs of migration through the imposition of fixed maintenance payments that are applicable in Tiers 1, 2, 4 and 5, increasing immigration application fees (to finance the PBS) and language testing. These are all likely to have deterred migration from developing countries. For example, in the context of its submissions to the Home Affairs Committee in 2008, JCWI calculated that it would cost an average sized family from Bangladesh, consisting of a principal applicant, spouse and three children 1,310,150 takas to secure entry to the UK under Tier 1. On the basis of average salaries in Bangladesh, this would take a professor or an accountant, who devoted his/her entire income to achieving this, some 18.7 years to earn. Regrettably the Home Affairs Committee felt that these requirements were reasonable and gave no further consideration to the issue of development in its report.

The use of salary as a criterion for admission and stay within the PBS also has development implications. For example, research carried out by the Equality and Human Rights Commission shows that the scheme appears to be having discriminatory effects for those from developing countries (Kofman, D'Angelo and Montagna 2009). Approval rates for Tier 1 entry were found to be far higher for applicants from developed countries compared to those from developing countries. Kofman, one of the authors of the report, took the view in an article for the JCWI *Bulletin*, that those effects were likely to be amplified due to inequalities in the domestic labour market (JCWI *Bulletin*, Autumn 2009).

The previous Labour Government gave some consideration to the issue of development and immigration in *Earning the Right to Stay: A New Points Test for Citizenship* (3 August 2009). This consultation paper suggested: ethical recruitment lists such as those already used by the NHS 'push button' facilities, permitting migrants to return home during their pathway to settlement and citizenship for development purposes, and the introduction of a two-year period that certain migrants would be able to spend in the UK enhancing their skills. These suggestions showed the beginning of a system that might indeed have made a far more significant contribution to fostering development and minimising global inequality.

Of equal importance at the level of policy-making is the need to integrate the development and migration policy-making process. Although institutional structures for joint policy-making exist in principle, the former Immigration Minister, Phil Woolas, explained to JCWI that, in practice, the policy-making processes are kept separate. The importance of integrating migration and development policy is recognised in recommendation 15.1 of the above MFLM. Other policy proposals that could facilitate international development can be found in JCWI's response to *Earning the Right to Stay: A New Points Test for Citizenship and the MFLM* (JCWI, October 2009).

International human rights standards – 1990 International Convention on the Protection of All Migrant Workers and their Families (MFLM and ILO Conventions)

The international human rights framework for labour-based migration issues can be found in the International Labour Organisation (ILO) Declaration on Fundamental Principles and Rights at Work, the various ILO Conventions, the 1977 European Convention on Migrant Workers, MFLM, and the various UN Conventions including in particular the 1990 International Convention on the Protection of the Rights of All Migrant Workers and Members of their Families.

Despite the recommendation by the United Nations Committee on Economic, Social and Cultural Rights (42nd session, 12 June 2009 E/C.12/ GBR/CO/5), the Government refuses to ratify the 1990 International Convention on the Protection of the Rights of All Migrant Workers and Members of their Families (ICMW). Further, it has not ratified the ILO Migrant Workers (Supplementary Provisions) Convention 143, the European Convention on Migrant Workers, nor indeed the more recent Long-Term Residence Directive.

In spite of the above, all of these instruments still provide a useful measure against which the PBS and its surrounding framework can be assessed, given that they represent statements by the international community on minimum standards below which states should not fall. The ways that the PBS and the structure associated with it fall below these standards are as follows:

Failure to give effect to article 14 (a) of ILO Convention 143 – the right to a free choice of employment for migrant workers Under the Convention, this may only be restricted for a maximum period of two years. States may restrict access to limited 'categories or functions only where this is shown to be necessary in the interests of the state.'

Failure to reflect article 49 (2)–(3) of ICMW Read in accordance with the above ILO Convention, this arguably requires states not to curtail leave before its expiration on the basis of loss of employment and to provide migrant workers with sufficient time to find alternative work for a period corresponding to the period that they would be entitled to employment benefits.

Failure to provide access to migrant workers equal to that enjoyed by nationals in relation to social housing and unemployment benefits These rights also extend to those who are irregular migrant workers (with the exception of unemployment benefits) in accordance with article 27 ICMW.

Failure to reflect article 25.3 of ICMW This requires equal treatment to be given to all migrant workers (including those with irregular status) in all aspects of their employment conditions. It expressly requires that states ensure that employers are not relieved of any legal or contractual obligations. This would ensure that migrant workers under the PBS or otherwise who, for example, fall into irregularity and knowingly enter an employment contract without permission from the immigration authorities to do so, may still enforce their employment rights and the statutory duties upon their employers that flow from them.

Lack of reflection of article 69(1) of ICMW This requires states, in circumstances where migrant workers and their family members are in a territory in an irregular position, to take appropriate measures to ensure that the situation does not continue. Ryan (2009) argues that the effect of this is arguably to require a state to regularise their position.

Lack of reflection of article 44(2) of ICMW This requires states to take measures they deem appropriate to facilitate reunification of migrant workers with their spouses. While Tier 3 (presently suspended) does not allow for the admission of family members, nor do the other temporary work schemes such as those for seasonal agricultural workers.

Lack of reflection of article 33 of ICMW This requires the provision of free information concerning administrative formalities that migrant workers are required to comply with, IMWC rights (some of which are reflected in English law and concern labour law rights) social security rights and information on expulsion and family reunion.

Use of double taxation (in the absence of double taxation agreements) This arises through the levying of immigration application fees set above cost price in a way that is inconsistent with article 48 of ICMW.

During the Home Affairs Committee Inquiry into the PBS, JCWI raised the issue of the rights of migrant workers and, in particular, the need for signature and ratification of the Migrant Workers Convention. Regrettably the Committee did not consider the rights of migrant workers sufficiently important to warrant any further comment.

The principle of non-discrimination

The principle of non-discrimination is embodied in various international instruments including the ECHR, ICCPR, International Convention on the Elimination of All Forms of Discrimination 1963 and the Convention on the Elimination of All Forms of Discrimination Against Women 1967. As the history of labour migration shows, there has been a gradual erosion of immigration opportunities for those from the Commonwealth. This in itself, in our view, is contrary to the principle of non-discrimination. The specific concerns relating to non-discrimination that the PBS raises are as follows:

PBS criteria

The criteria for awarding points within the PBS, in particular salary, age and English language ability, give cause for concern. For example, on salary, it is uncontroversial to acknowledge that women in the UK and throughout the world on average command lower salaries than their male counterparts for identical work, and that other areas of work dominated by women such as care work are undervalued in terms of salary. Equally it is well known that certain ethnic groups earn lower salaries than their white counterparts in the domestic labour market (Black Africans and Bangladeshis earn 25% less than their white counterparts). For this reason the use of salary as criteria in Tiers 1 and 2, its indirect use throughout the system through maintenance payments and its use by the Migration Advisory Committee as one of three factors determining shortage occupation classification, represents a problem.

There has been to date no systematic analysis of the impact of the use of salary and indeed other criteria on the different groups listed above. However, Kofman, Lukes, D'Angelo and Montagna, in a report for the Equality and Human Rights Commission (2009), were critical of Migration Advisory Committee's use of salary in determining shortage occupations in the light of the gender pay gap. Its findings in relation to developing countries and Tier 1 are referred to above. The report went on to recommend that the equality impact assessment process relating to the PBS be improved with a view to offering a systematic and sufficiently rigorous assessment of both the impact and outcomes of the scheme.

Civil penalties scheme

Prior to the implementation of the civil penalties scheme, there was already abundant evidence that wide-scale discrimination against ethnic minorities and migrant workers was taking place. The Commission for Racial Equality (now incorporated into the Equality and Human Rights Commission) argued at the time of the introduction of the civil penalties scheme that it risked further stigmatising ethnic minorities in the work place and would ultimately negatively impact upon the employment of migrants and ethnic minorities generally.

The previous Government took some steps to protect migrant workers under the PBS against discrimination through issuing a Code of Practice, but a report by the Migrants' Rights Network, *Papers Please – The Impact of the Civil Penalty Regime on the Employment Rights of Migrants* (November 2008), drew attention to discrimination and harassment against both regular and undocumented migrants, cases of unfair dismissal as well as a disproportionate enforcement approach to small ethnic catering businesses.

Rule of law, accountability and transparency

The principle of the rule of law requires that laws should be clear and predictable, that adequate protection should be given to fundamental rights (work and education are such rights under the ICCPR) and that adjudicative procedures should be fair. Accountability and transparency require that immigration rules made in a democracy are the subject of a process that embodies these principles. Additionally, given that the PBS rules are not strictly the product of Parliament, but rather the executive, the principle requires that there should be adequate checks on the exercise of that power. Viewed from this perspective the PBS displays several shortcomings as follows:

The use of guidance A feature of the PBS that has recently attracted much attention is its reliance upon guidance. While the use of guidance itself is not new as such, what is innovative is:

- the use of guidance as an integral part of the design of the 'flexible PBS';
- unlike previous guidance which was generally provided as an aid to construction of the Rules (guidance used under the Immigration Rules relating to domestic violence was an exception), it is directly referred to in the Immigration Rules in mandatory and binding terms which seek to prescribe the circumstances in which applicants may qualify; and
- that it is extremely detailed and prescriptive.

Guidance issued in these circumstances hardly satisfies the above requirements. Firstly the guidance receives no Parliamentary scrutiny whatsoever. Secondly, it is capable of being changed at short notice and with regularity and is not predictable. Thirdly, its very specific and often exacting nature in relation to procedure, eg rigid documentary requirements, is at odds with the principle of the rule of law because it enables 'legal' rules to be undermined by bureaucratic barriers. Fourthly it evades accountability and scrutiny by Tribunals. As Clayton points out, given that guidance is treated as part of the requirements for qualifying, and given that grounds of appeal to a Tribunal are limited, there is apparently less scope for the Tribunal to act as a guard on the power of the Executive (Clayton 2010). The Courts have recently expressed a willingness to impose limits on the extent to which guidance can be used in the above way; see the *Pankina* case and *English UK v Secretary of State* (for further details about these cases ▶41–45 and 47–53).

The parliamentary procedure for making the PBS rules While the cases of *Pankina* and *English UK* are no doubt important in the limitations they lay down, their practical effect is in reality more modest given the unaccountable parliamentary process through which the Immigration Rules are themselves made. Currently PBS rules are made through the negative resolution procedure. In contrast to primary legislation which is debated several times, often scrutinised by various parliamentary committees, is capable of being amended and does not come into effect until receiving Royal Assent or through subsequent commencement orders, the Immigration Rules take effect immediately, cannot be amended, but may only be annulled through a resolution of either the House of Commons or the House of Lords. Annulment has happened infrequently. In practice the Rules may not even be debated even in circumstances where this is called for by peers or MPs. Nor are the Rules subject to advance parliamentary scrutiny by the relevant departmental committee, the Home Affairs Committee or the Joint Committee on Human Rights.

In its response to *Simplifying Immigration Law: a New Framework for Immigration Rules* (November 2009), JCWI argued that the Rules should, as per the recommendations of the Joint Committee on Human Rights, be accompanied by a statement of compatibility with the rights incorporated by the Human Rights Act 1998 in the same way that primary legislation is. Additionally, they should, as a minimum, be subject to an affirmative resolution procedure that requires a draft of the Rules to be laid before Parliament and that they receive Parliament's positive assent. While the affirmative resolution procedure itself would represent an improvement on the current position, it would still have shortcomings given that (as with the negative resolution procedure) there is no power to *amend* the Rules in circumstances where there are parliamentary objections. The overall position cannot therefore be satisfactorily resolved without reconsidering the existing parliamentary procedures for law-making. Proposals for reform can be found in *Issues in Law Making*, available on the Hansard Society website (Brazier 2003).

Administrative review Entry clearance decisions have historically been subject to challenge through a judicial process ie a right of appeal to an independent Tribunal. However, in all but a few cases, this has now been replaced with an administrative process of review (indeed termed 'administrative review'). The obvious limitation to this process is that it is conducted by the same body that is responsible for the decision in the first instance and it is far more limited in scope. It is confined to points of fact only and the reviewer may only consider material that was submitted with the application (save for in cases involving deception). *Macdonald's Immigration Law & Practice* (2008) observes that all of these factors seriously limit its fairness given that experience shows that, in most cases, the right decision is achieved through the production of further evidence, the need for which is often not appreciated until notification of the adverse decision made clear quite where the application was thought to be lacking. While judicial review continues to be available, it has severe limitation in the context of the kinds of challenge that arise (it cannot subject the merits to a review) and in its ability to provide an appropriate remedy. Judicial review is also very expensive. JCWI raised the above issues before the Home Affairs Committee during its inquiry into the PBS. The Committee expressed its concerns about this and recommended that the Chief Inspector of the UK Border Agency should be given the power to investigate individual cases and provide remedies. It also concluded that it is unfair to require applicants to make a new application, attracting an additional fee, simply for failing to furnish the UKBA with the precise, rigidly-defined paperwork it requires. The Committee felt that applicants should be allowed to furnish further paperwork, if requested, within the context of the existing application (*Fifth Report of Session 2007–8*, HC 425).

READING

For those wishing to know more about the policy and background relating to labour migration to the UK and the PBS, set out below is a list of materials upon which we have drawn in preparing this chapter and which we can recommend by way of further reading.

Achato, Eaton and Jones (2010)
The Migrant Journey, Research Report 43,
http://rds.homeoffice.gov.uk/rds/pdfs10/horr43c.pdf

Balanced Migration: A New Approach to Controlling Immigration.
www.migrationwatchuk.com/balancedmigration.pdf

Birrell, B, Hawthorne, L and Richardson, S (2006)
Evaluation of the General Skilled Migration Categories
Canberra: Commonwealth of Australia

Brown, Gordon (2010)
Speech on immigration
www.number10.gov.uk/Page21298

Clarke, J and Salt, J (2003)
'Work Permits and Foreign Labour in the UK: a Statistical Review'
Labour Market Trends, vol. 111, No. 11,
London: Office for National Statistics, 563–574

Cerna, L and Wietholtz, A (forthcoming),
'Immigration and immigrant policy-making in the United Kingdom'
in G Zincone, R Penninx and M Borkert (eds)
Migratory Policy-Making in Europe
Amsterdam: Amsterdam University Press

Clayton, G (2010)
Textbook on Immigration and Asylum Law
4th edn, London: Oxford University Press

Dobson, J, Koser, K, McLaughlan, G and Salt, J, (2001)
International Migration and the United Kingdom: Recent Patterns and Trends, Final report to the Home Office
RDS (The Research, Development and Statistics Directorate) Occasional Paper No 75
http://rds.homeoffice.gov.uk/rds/pdfs/occ75.pdf

Glover, S, Gott, C, Loizillon, A, Portes, J, Price, R, Spencer, S, Srinivasan, V and Willis, C (2001)
Migration: an economic and social analysis
RDS Occasional Paper No 67.
http://rds.homeoffice.gov.uk/rds/pdfs/occ67-migration.pdf

Government reply to the first report from the House of Lords Committee on Economic Affairs Session 2007–08 HL Paper 82,
The Economic Impact of Immigration
Cm 7414.

Government reply to the thirteenth report from Home Office Affairs Committee Session 2008–09 HC217
Managed Migration: The Points-Based System

Green, D (6 September, 2011)
The Real Immigration Question
Speech given at the Royal Commonwealth Society, London

Green, D (1 February 2011)
Reforming the immigration system
Speech given to the Reform Think Tank, London

Home Office (2002)
Secure Borders, Safe Haven: Integration with Diversity in Modern Britain
Cm 5387.

Home Office (2002)
Review of the Seasonal Agricultural Workers Scheme

Home Office (2001)
A Survey of the Illegally Resident Population in Detention in the UK
Online Report 20/05, RDS.
http://rds.homeoffice.gov.uk/rds/pdfs05/r224.pdf

Home Office (2005)
Controlling Our Borders: Making migration work for Britain. Five year strategy for asylum and immigration
Cm 6472

Home Office (2006)
A Points-Based System: Making Migration Work for Britain
Cm 6741

Home Office (2006)
A consultation on establishing a Migration Advisory Committee

Home Office (2007), *Results of the public consultation on proposals for a Migration Advisory Committee.*

Home Office (2009)
Earning the Right to Stay: A New Points Test for Citizenship
UK Border Agency consultation

Home Office (2010)
Tier 4: Student visas

Home Office (2010)
Limits on Non-EU Economic Migration
UK Border Agency

Home Office (2011)
Tier 2 of the Points Bases System, Statement of Intent, Transitional Measures and Indefinite Leave to Remain
UK Border Agency

House of Commons Home Affairs Committee (2009)
Bogus Colleges: Eleventh Report of Session 2008–09
HC 595

The Government reply to the eleventh report from the Home Office Affairs Committee Session 2008–09 HC 595
Bogus Colleges

House of Commons Home Affairs Committee (2009)
Managing Migration: Points-Based System
Thirteenth Report of Session 2008–09, Volume II, HC217-ii

House of Commons Home Affairs Committee (2010)
Immigration Cap. First Report of Session 2010–11
HC 361

House of Lords (2008)
The Economic Impact of Immigration, Volume 1
Report, HL Paper 82–I

ILPA briefings
www.ilpa.org.uk

JCWI briefings
www.jcwi.org.uk

JCWI *Bulletin*
Winter 2009.

Kofman, E, D'Angelo, A and Montagna, N (2009)
The equality implications of being a migrant in Britain
Research report 19, Equality and Human Rights Commission

Macdonald, I and Toal R (2008)
Macdonald's Immigration Law and Practice
7th edn. London: Lexis Nexis

Migrants Rights Network (2008)
'Papers Please' – The Impact of the Civil Penalty Regime on the Employment Rights in the UK

Migration Advisory Committee (2009)
Analysis of the Points-Based System, Tier 1

Migration Advisory Committee (2009)
Forthcoming analysis of Tier 1, Tier 2 and dependants under the Points Based System for immigration
Discussion and call for evidence

Migration Advisory Committee (2009)
Review of the UK's transitional measures for nationals of member states that acceded to the European Union in 2004

Migration Advisory Committee (2009)
Skilled Shortage Sensible. First review of the recommended shortage occupation lists for the UK and Scotland

Migration Advisory Committee (2009)
Skilled Shortage Sensible. Second review of the recommended shortage occupation lists for the UK and Scotland
Autumn 2009

Migration Advisory Committee (2009)
Tier 2 and dependants

Migration Advisory Committee (2010)
Skilled Shortage Sensible: Review of Methodology.

Migration Advisory Committee (2010)
Limits on Migration – Limits on Tier 1 and 2 for 2011/2012 and supporting policies

Papademetriou, D and Somerville, W (2008)
Hybrid Immigrant Selection Systems: the Next Generation of Economic Migration Schemes, Migration Policy Institute.
www.migrationpolicy.org/transatlantic/HybridSystems.pdf

Migration Advisory Committee (2010)
Consultation on the level of the first annual limit on economic migration to the UK

Ryan, B (2005)
Labour Migration and Employment Rights
London: The Institute of Employment Rights

Ryan, B (2006)
The Evolving Legal Regime on Unauthorized Work by Migrants in Britain, *Comparative Labor Law and Policy Journal*, 27 (1), pp27–58

Ryan, B (2009)
'Recent policy on the Migrant Workers Convention in the United Kingdom'
in: Cholewinski, Ryszard, de Guchteneire, P and Pecoud, A (eds) (2009)
Migration and Human Rights: The United Nations Convention on Migrant Workers' Rights
Cambridge: Cambridge University Press
http://kar.kent.ac.uk/25061/

Roodman, D, Prieto, C and Lazzarus, E (2009)
Commitment to Development Index 2009, United Kingdom
Centre for Global Development
www.cgdev.org/doc/CDI/2009/country_reports/UK_2009.pdf

Salt, J and Kitching, R (1990)
Labour Migration and the Work Permit System in the United Kingdom
International Migration, 28(3), pp.267–294

Somerville, W (2007)
Immigration under New Labour
Bristol: The Policy Press

Somerville, W (2011)
The Politics and Policy of Skilled Economic Immigration under New Labour 1997–2010
Migration Policy Institute, forthcoming

Woodbridge J (2001)
Sizing the Unauthorised (Illegal) Migrant Population in the United Kingdom in 2001
Home Office Report 29/05.
http://rds.homeoffice.gov.uk/rds/pdfs05/rdsolr2905.pdf

2 Overview: the five tiers, Immigration Rules and Policy Guidance, *Pankina* and related cases

This chapter contains an overview of the Points-Based System and covers the following:

- a summary listing of the five tiers 'at a glance' (▶below);
- a table showing how the previous categories of admission under the Rules have been taken into the PBS (▶38–40);
- the framework of the PBS as contained in Immigration Rules and Policy Guidance, together with a detailed review of the recent case law, including *Pankina* and the following cases considering the role of Policy Guidance (▶40–53);
- a basic review of the allocation of points in the five tiers and the conditions that need to be satisfied in order to score points by meeting common requirements (▶53–55);
- the cap and the 'interim' cap (▶55–59).

THE FIVE TIERS: AT A GLANCE

2008 saw the biggest overhaul of the UK's immigration system for over 45 years with the launch of the Points-Based System. Under the new PBS, 80 or so established routes of entry into the UK were replaced with a system that allowed entry under one of five distinct 'tiers'.

The tiers contain the following categories:

- **Tier 1 (General)** for highly skilled migrants;
- **Tier 1 (Investor)** for high net worth individuals making a substantial financial investment in the UK;
- **Tier 1 (Entrepreneur)** for those investing in the UK by setting up (or taking over) and actively running businesses in the UK;
- **Tier 1 (Post-Study Work)** for international graduates who have studied in the UK;
- **Tier 2 (General)** for sponsored skilled workers from outside the EEA;
- **Tier 2 (Ministers of Religion)** for those coming to the UK as religious workers supporting recognised religions and intending to preach to their community and/or perform a pastoral role;

- **Tier 2 (Sportspeople)** for elite sports persons or coaches who intend to base themselves in the UK, are internationally established at the highest level and whose employment will make a significant contribution to the development of their sport at the highest level in the UK;

- **Tier 3**, for unskilled workers. The government has no plans at present to launch Tier 3 and it remains suspended indefinitely;

- **Tier 4**, for international students;

- **Tier 5** (Youth Mobility Scheme), for young people seeking to come to the UK on a temporary basis and to experience life here;

- **Tier 5** (Temporary Workers – Religious Workers), for ministers of religion coming to the UK on a temporary basis as religious workers, in a non-pastoral role, whose duties include performing religious rites, but not preaching to a congregation.

THE OLD AND THE NEW: WHAT HAS BECOME OF THE OLD CATEGORIES UNDER THE PBS

The table below lists the routes of admission under the Immigration Rules that have been effectively taken over by the PBS and shows where they now slot in under the new system.

CATEGORIES TAKEN OVER BY THE PBS

Previous category	Current PBS category
Highly Skilled Migrant Programme (HSMP)	Tier 1 (General)
Self-employed lawyers	Tier 1 (General)
Writers, composers and artists	Tier 1 (General)
Investors	Tier 1 (Investor)
Business persons	Tier 1 (Entrepreneur)
Innovators	Tier 1 (Entrepreneur)
Fresh Talent: Working in Scotland Scheme	Tier 1 (Post-study work)
International Graduates' Scheme	Tier 1 (Post-study work)
Most long-term work permits , including for entertainers, but *not* for: • sportspeople (▶see below) • workers on training and work experience schemes (▶see 'Temporary workers' below) • workers under the General Agreement on Trade In Services (GATS) (▶see 'Temporary workers' below)	Tier 2 (General)
Long-term work permits for elite sportspeople or coaches at the highest level	Tier 2 (Sportsperson)
Overseas qualified nurses and midwives	Tier 2 (General)

Airline ground crew	Tier 2 (General)
Some seafarers, including those working on vessels on one-port voyages	Tier 2 (General)
Ministers of religion, missionaries, members of religious orders – those in non-pastoral roles coming to the UK for more than two years, or those in pastoral roles that include preaching to a congregation	Tier 2 (Minister of religion)
Work permits for sportspeople or entertainers to do some jobs of less than 12 months, but not to come to the Olympics or other specific event	Tier 5 (Temporary worker – creative and sporting)
Work permits for sportspeople coming to the Olympics or other specific event	Sports visitor
Work permits for entertainers coming to perform at a specific event	Entertainer visitor
Training and work experience scheme	Tier 5 (Temporary worker – government authorised exchange), sponsored by a UK government department
China graduate work experience scheme	Tier 5 (Temporary worker – government authorised exchange), sponsored by the Department for Innovation, Universities and Skills
Overseas government employees	Tier 5 (Temporary worker – international agreement)
General Agreement on Trade in Services (GATS)	Tier 5 (Temporary worker – international agreement)
Private servants in diplomatic households, but not domestic workers in private households (see other categories below)	Tier 5 (Temporary worker – international agreement)
Ministers of religion, missionaries, members of religious orders – those in non-pastoral roles coming to the UK for two years or less	Tier 5 (Temporary worker – religious worker)
Voluntary workers	Tier 5 (Temporary worker – charity worker)
Film crew on location	Business visitor
Overseas qualified doctors taking the professional and linguistic assessments board (PLAB) test	Business visitor
Clinical attachments and dental observer posts	Business visitor
Working holidaymaker scheme	Tier 5 (Youth mobility scheme) – if the applicant is from a participating country

Au pairs	Tier 5 (Youth mobility scheme) – if the applicant is from a participating country
Gap year	Tier 5 (Youth mobility scheme) – if the applicant is from a participating country
Japan: youth exchange scheme	Tier 5 (Youth mobility scheme)

THE FRAMEWORK OF THE PBS: IMMIGRATION RULES, POLICY GUIDANCE AND THE *PANKINA* CASE

Although Tiers 1–5 are routes of admission under the Immigration Rules, the system is heavily supplemented by 'Policy Guidance' to which the Rules themselves refer. Under the heading of 'documentary evidence', the PBS Rules open with the statement (para 245AA(a), HC 395):

"Where Part 6A or Appendices A to C, or E of these Rules state that specified documents must be provided, that means documents specified by the Secretary of State in the Points-Based System Policy Guidance as being specified documents for the route under which the applicant is applying. If the specified documents are not provided, the applicant will not meet the requirement for which the specified documents are required as evidence."

So, the idea is that the Rules contain the 'requirements' for admission but applicants will not be able to show that they meet those requirements and will be refused unless they produce the particular evidence ("specified documents") that are set out in the 'Policy Guidance'.

Policy Guidance also has an important role to play in: (a) setting the criteria for who may be issued with a sponsor licence, thus enabling an organisation to 'sponsor' migrants to work or study in the UK; and (b) in the regulation of those sponsors. In relation to those two questions, legislation and the Rules play only a peripheral role as those matters are almost entirely governed by Guidance issued to sponsors (▶see Chapter 4).

There have been many successive editions of Policy Guidance issued in relation to the different tiers since the introduction of the PBS in March 2008. An important difference between the Immigration Rules and Policy Guidance is that Guidance may be changed by ministers/officials overnight and it is not placed before Parliament. The major concern about this arrangement is the extent to which what applicants have to do in order to quality may be pushed over into largely unaccountable (and changeable) Guidance.

The *BAPIO* case

In April 2008, the House of Lords decided the case of *R (BAPIO Action Ltd & Another) v SSHD*. In that case, external guidance issued by the Secretary of State for Health had the 'side-wind' (although intended) effect of restricting rights under the Immigration Rules. The Lords held that it was unlawful for rights granted under the Rules to be undermined in this way. *BAPIO* did not concern the PBS, although the case was decided at the same time as the PBS began. However, the general legal concern about rights in the Rules being cut down by external Government action provided an omen for the developments (►below) about the interaction between the Rules and external Guidance.

Guidance specifying evidence: a new departure?

The PBS arrangement under which the particular evidence necessary to satisfy the requirements of the Rules is set out in Guidance was new in that it was introduced as a fundamental feature of the entire PBS system. But the mechanism itself was not novel. For example, the Rules on obtaining indefinite leave for the victims of domestic violence require that the applicant "is able to produce such evidence as may be required by the Secretary of State to establish that the relationship was caused to permanently break down…as the result of domestic violence" (para 289A(iv) HC 395).

In *Ahmed Iram Ishtiaq v SSHD*, the Court of Appeal had to decide whether that domestic violence Rule meant that, even if the applicant could prove their case with evidence that was different to that required in the guidance, their application still had to be refused. The Court dealt with the problem by interpreting the Rule in the light of its object and more gently than it first appeared (see the Judgment, paras 31–4). It held that the aim of the Rule was to allow foreign spouses, whose relationships had broken down as the result of domestic violence before the end of the 'probationary' period, to obtain indefinite leave all the same. The Court decided that, because the Rule did not state in terms that an application could only succeed if the particular evidence required by the instructions was produced, the Rule did not have that effect. Applicants could, therefore, use other evidence to prove that the relationship ended due to domestic violence.

But the PBS Rules go further. As set out above, they do exactly what the Court in *Ishtiaq* said would be necessary in order to defeat an application if specified evidence is not produced. They state, in terms, that if the "specified documents" are not provided, the applicant "will not meet" the relevant requirement in the Rules (para 245AA(a), HC 395).

Pankina

In Summer 2010, the Court of Appeal considered the operation of the above PBS Rule in *SSHD v Pankina* (►see box p42). In a nutshell, the Court recognised that it may be lawful for the Rules to refer to outside guidance as to what evidence might be used in order to show that the requirements of the Rules are met. But the Court imposed a strict limitation on how far such guidance can go. It found that it will be unlawful for such guidance, in effect, to impose new substantive requirements on applicants as to the conditions they need to satisfy in order to qualify, even if those requirements are described as guidance about evidence (see box for full findings).

After the case, the particular guidance that was considered in *Pankina*, was put into the Rules. However, the principle that was decided by the Court will be of great continuing importance to the operation of the PBS given the system's heavy reliance on Policy Guidance issued outside the Rules.

THE *PANKINA* CASE

Secretary of State for the Home Department v Pankina was decided by the Court of Appeal on 23 June 2010. It is the first major decision of the higher courts concerning the operation of the PBS. The main judgment was given by Sedley LJ with whom the two other Lord Justices (Rimer LJ and Sullivan LJ) expressed their agreement. The case decided a question of general importance about the constitutional status of the Immigration Rules. In so doing, the Court decided that the Home Office cannot, by guidance/policy issued *outside* the Rules, add to the requirements that must be satisfied in order to obtain leave under the Rules themselves.

Facts

Pankina involved six applicants all of whom were graduates of approved UK educational institutions who had been refused leave to remain in the UK under Tier 1 (Post-Study Work) (see ▶173–180). As regards their maintenance, in five of the cases (*Pankina, Ahmed, Junaideen, Ali, Sankar*), the applicants all had suitable evidence that showed that they had the required £800 in their bank accounts at the time of their applications to the Home Office. But they could not show that they had £800 for three unbroken months before the date of their applications. In the case of one applicant (Malekia), there was no evidence that she had £800 in her bank account at any relevant time (Judgment, paras 6, 37, 38, 50).

Applicable Rules/Policy Guidance

Among the requirements that the applicants had to meet was para 245Z(e) HC 395 which stated that they must have a minimum of 10 points under paras 1–2 of Appendix C of the Rules dealing with maintenance. The relevant wording of Appendix C had been placed into the Rules from 30 June 2008 by HC 607. It stated that the applicants were required to have a level of funds of £800 and to provide "specified documents". It made no reference to an applicant having to show that they had those funds over any particular period of time. It simply stated that applicants were required to have that level of funds. As to "specified documents", they are generally referred to in para 245AA(a) HC 395 ('documentary evidence') as follows:

"…documents specified by the Secretary of State in the [PBS] Policy Guidance as being specified documents for the route under which the applicant is applying."

That Rule also states that failure to produce the documents will mean that the applicant has failed to meet the requirement that relates to them. The relevant Policy Guidance (issued in June 2008) stated that the specified documents were "personal bank or building society statements covering the three-month period immediately before the application" showing "that there are sufficient funds present in the account (the balance must always be at least £800)." In November 2008, the relevant Policy Guidance was modified so that it stated even more clearly (Judgment, para 5):

"Applicants...must have at least £800 of personal savings which must have been held for *at least three months prior to the date of application.*" (emphasis added)

So, the 'three month' funds requirement was part of the Policy Guidance but it was not part of the Rules themselves. The Rules only went as far as referring to the need to produce documents that would be "specified" in Policy Guidance.

Decision of the Court of Appeal

Essential reasoning

The reasoning that was vital to the decision of the Court on the main issue (below) was as follows.

1) In contrast to the system by which the Home Secretary gave instructions to immigration officers under the legislation from the 1900s to the 1960s, the provisions of the Immigration Appeals Act 1969 began to make it clear that what had, by then, become 'Immigration Rules' were more than just 'policy'. By this time, the Rules had lost the most important characteristic of 'policy' which is the ability to be applied flexibly (Judgment, paras 8–10).

2) By the time of the 1971 Act (see ss1(4), 3(2)), the Rules had become an "established category" and had a "life of their own" (Judgment, paras 10–11). The Rules do not "derive from" any "empowering" primary legislation, nor are they made "under" any such legislation – they are not 'subordinate' legislation (Judgment, paras 17 and 44).

3) As a result, the legal status of the Rules was not just "unusual" as being detailed statements by the Minister as to how "the Crown proposed to exercise its executive power to control immigration" and which create "legal rights" (see Lord Hope in *Odelola*, para 6; otherwise referred to as its 'prerogative' power), the Rules are in fact "unique" (Judgment, paras 12–13, 17).

4) The Rules are now "different from and more than policy": they constitute the first ground of appeal under a 2002 Act appeal; they are also described in the 2002 Act as part of "the law" (s86(3)(a)); and they lack the "flexibility" of policy (Judgment, para 16).

5) So, by a combination of "legislative recognition" and "executive practice", the time had come (Judgment, para 17):

"...to recognise...the rules made by Home Secretaries for regulating immigration have ceased to be policy and have acquired *a status akin to that of law.*" (emphasis added)

6) But the British Constitution does not allow 'law' to be created by Ministers (exercising the Crown's prerogative powers). Law can only be made "with the authority of Parliament". That is the explanation for why the 1969 and 1971 Acts

required that the Rules be placed before Parliament so that MPs could, if they wished, vote them down by passing a negative resolution. When the Rules became 'law', it was a constitutional requirement that they had some Parliamentary authority (Judgment, paras 19–21).

Decision on the main issue: could the applicants' cases be rejected because they did not satisfy the 'three month' funds requirement?

Having regard to the above reasoning, the Court found as follows.

1) The 'three month' fund requirement, although contained in 'Policy Guidance', was in fact a legal rule. That is because it was a firm requirement that was not subject to discretion, judgment or flexibility as would be the case with 'policy'. Indeed the Home Office itself claimed that the requirement had become part of the Rules by incorporation – that was the Home Office's intention. If it were policy, then the law might require that it be applied with flexibility so that cases which met its object, ie the exclusion of applicants who could not properly support themselves – but could not meet its very strict terms, would not fail. But that was not the case (Judgment, paras 28, 40).

2) The 'three month' requirement also went beyond what the Rules sometimes legitimately do, that is referring to an outside source in order to *evidence* that the rule itself has been complied with. Instead, the three-month requirement was a rule supplementing the Rules. It was an additional criterion "affecting individuals' status and entitlements" (Judgment, paras 27, 33).

3) Because it was a 'rule' and required to be applied with rigidity, in order for the requirement to be legally effective, it had to have the authority of Parliament (Judgment, paras 29, 33).

4) Did it have the authority of Parliament? The Court found that, in principle, it is possible for external documents, such as guidance, to have legal effect by being treated as part of the rule itself where the rule is placed before Parliament and cross-refers to the outside source (there is "no absolute rule" preventing this, see *ex parte Camden*). But this is only possible if the following three conditions, relating to the external source, are all satisfied. The cross-reference must be to a document or source that is: (a) already in existence; (b) accessible; and (c) permanent, so that it is not open to change without the scrutiny of Parliament (the *Camden* case also required that there be "no question of sub-delegation"). The 'three month' fund requirement did not meet these requirements. In particular, the "critical" failure to meet condition (c) meant that:

"...a discrete element of the rules is placed beyond Parliament's scrutiny and left to the unfettered judgment of the rule-maker." (Judgment, paras 24, 26, 29, 33 and 37).

5) In the light of the above, the fact that the first edition of the Policy Guidance containing the 'three month' requirement was issued *before* the end of the 40-day period that Parliament had to express its disapproval of the Rules was not important. But, if the case had turned on that point, the Court stated that it would still not have found for the Home Office. That was because the 40-day period does not exist in order to give the Home Office more time to lay acceptable rules; rather it is the period allowed to Parliament to consider the new Rules (Judgment, para 36).

In coming to these conclusions, the Court of Appeal implicitly overturned the earlier decision of the AIT in *NA (Tier 1 Post-Study work funds)*. That case had held that the the Rules, read together with the Guidance governing Tier 1 (Post-Study work), required that an applicant show that s/he held at least £800 for each and every day of the period of three months immediately preceding the date of application.

Date of assessment

In case it was not correct in its main finding (above), the Court considered the correct date for assessing whether the applicants had held £800 for three consecutive months. Did this mean that the £800 had to be in the account for the three months before the application itself, or was it enough if the money had been there for three months by the time of the appeal? The Court decided that the answer to this depended on the words of the particular Rules themselves rather than being an issue of general principle. It found that the particular wording clearly required the funds to have been held in the applicant's bank account for three continuous months by the date of the application (Judgment, paras 38–9). In this respect, the Court implicitly upheld the decision of the AIT in *NA (Tier 1 Post-Study work funds)* (▶see further 439–444).

Human rights: art 8 ECHR

Also in the alternative to its main finding and because one of the applicants could not succeed even if the 'three month' requirement had no effect, the Court went on to make important findings as to the need to apply the Rules consistently with the UK's obligations under Art 8 ECHR. What the Court had to say about this has become more important since the Government amended the Rules to include the three month requirement (see below). We deal with the Court's approach to Art 8 in *Pankina* in Chapter 12 on human rights (see ▶412–421).

Outcome of the individual cases

The five applicants who had £800 in their bank accounts at the time of the application all succeeded because they had done as much as was lawfully required of them under the Rules *excluding* the additional requirements of the Guidance. The sixth applicant, who did not at any stage have £800, lost on the facts of her case, both under the Rules and under Art 8 ECHR (Judgment, paras 48–53).

The Government's response to the *Pankina* case

The Court of Appeal rejected the Home Office's application for permission to appeal to the Supreme Court and its application for a stay on the coming into effect of the judgment of the Court of Appeal.

The Home Office general view seems to be that the analysis of the status of the Immigration Rules in *Pankina* as 'akin to law' and distinct from policy (see box above) is inconsistent with existing case law in *Odelola v SSHD* (*Odelola* at paras 6, 33–4), *MB (Somalia)* and *MO (Nigeria)* (▶see the Home Office submissions in the *English UK* case, below, at paras 61 and 63 of that judgment). Despite this, the Home Office has not pursued its attempt to take the matter to the Supreme Court. Instead, the

Home Office introduced new Immigration Rules which include the 'three month' funds requirement for Tiers 1, 2 and 5 (and a '28 day' funds requirement under Tier 4). The new Rules were inserted into HC 395 by HC 382, para 21. They were laid before Parliament on 22 July 2010 and came into force on 23 July 2010. The new wording at para 1A of Appendix C ('Maintenance') (for Tiers 1, 2 and 5) is as follows:

"(b) If the applicant is applying for entry clearance, leave to enter or leave to remain as a Tier 1 Migrant (other than a Tier 1 (Investor) Migrant), a Tier 2 Migrant or a Tier 5 (Temporary Worker) Migrant, the applicant must have had the funds referred to [in the relevant part of Appendix C] for a consecutive 90-day period of time, ending no earlier than one calendar month before the date of the application."

Home Office post-*Pankina* transitional policy

The new Rules (above) only apply to those applicants who apply for entry clearance or leave to remain on or after 23 July 2010. At the same time as amending the Rules, on 23 July 2010, the Home Office issued a transitional policy. That policy was later replaced by a further statement of the transitional policy, issued on 22 November 2010 and entitled *Points-Based System Maintenance (Funds): Policy Document* (version 2.0). It is available on the UKBA website. The 22 November 2010 document applies to applications under Tiers 1, 2, 4 and 5 is to the following effect.

For those who submitted applications for *leave to remain* in the UK before 23 July 2010, UKBA adopts the following policy.

- In respect of outstanding applications, applicants are required to prove that they hold the required level of funds on any one day during the period of one month prior to the date of application. These applications will automatically be considered in line with this policy (Policy, paras 11, 14).

- Those whose applications have been refused may write to request a review (address: PBS (AP & Others), Employment Routes Workflow Team, UK Border Agency, PO Box 3468, Sheffield, S3 8WA) and their application will be reconsidered to determine whether they held the required level of funds on any one day during the period of one month prior to the date of the original application. UKBA states that it will not consider new evidence, but only the evidence provided in support of the original application (Policy, paras 15, 17-18).

- Where there is an appeal outstanding in respect of an applicant refused solely on the basis of maintenance (funds), UKBA will withdraw the decision if the applicant held the required level of funds on any one day during the period of one month prior to the date of the original application. The review will be based solely on the evidence included with the original application (Policy, para 20).

- Where there is a claim for judicial review outstanding in respect of an applicant who was refused solely on the basis of maintenance (funds) and who is presently in the UK, UKBA will withdraw the decision that gave rise to the judicial review if the applicant held the required level of funds on any one day during the period of one month prior to the date of the original application. Again, the review will be based solely on the evidence included with the original application (Policy, paras 23–24).

- Where an applicant left the UK following the refusal of their application, UKBA will consider representations sent to the above address. A certified copy of the applicant's present valid passport, or travel document and biometrics card should be submitted. Again, applicants should show that they held the required level of funds on any one day during the period of one month prior to the date of the original application, but the review will be based only on evidence included with the original application (Policy, paras 26–28). Where the applicant meets these requirements, they will be contacted and asked to forward their passport (Policy, para 29).

For those who submitted applications for *entry clearance* between 23 June–22 July 2010 (inclusive), UKBA adopts the following policy.

- In respect of outstanding applications, applicants should show that they held the required level of funds on any one day during the period of one month prior to the date of the original application. The application should automatically be considered in line with this approach (Policy, paras 33, 35).

- In respect of applications that have been refused and where an administrative review has been dismissed, applicants may contact the entry clearance post which issued the original decision in order to request a review. The application will be reassessed in order to determine whether the applicant held the required level of funds on any one day during the period of one month prior to the date of the original application. Again, only the evidence originally submitted will be considered (Policy, paras 36–39).

Applicants have until 22 June 2011 to take advantage of the above policy (Policy, para 47).

Developments in the case-law following *Pankina*

Since the decision in *Pankina*, there have been several further significant judicial review and Upper Tribunal cases.

The *English UK* case

Following hot on the heels of *Pankina* was *R (English UK) v Secretary of State for the Home Department*, decided on 9 July 2010. A consortium of English language schools challenged an increase in the minimum academic requirements for Tier 4 students intending to study English language courses. The change had been made not through new Rules but by amendments made to the Policy Guidance issued to the sponsors (educational establishments) of the intending students.

The relevant underlying Immigration Rules (HC 314) were laid on 9 March 2009 and stated that the Tier 4 course "must meet the [UKBA's] minimum academic requirements, as set out in sponsor guidance published by the [UKBA]" (para 120(a), Appendix A, HC 395 as amended). Throughout the 40-day period that MPs could consider the newly-laid Rules, Guidance specifying the minimum level of course was in existence. At that time, the Guidance stated that the courses must be at a minimum level of 'A2' (effectively beginner level) on the Council of Europe's Common European Framework of Reference for Languages. However, a year later, in February 2010, the Home Office took the decision to change the Guidance so as to specify a much more severe academic level ('B2') for the majority of courses. The change to the Guidance was made on 3 March 2010 (see, for the facts, Judgment, paras 30–36).

Foskett J held that the binding principle decided in *Pankina* was as follows.

"59...a provision that reflects a *substantive criterion for eligibility for admission for leave to remain* must be the subject of a process that involves true Parliamentary scrutiny... [emphasis in original]

...

"60 It would follow from this that, if a change to current practice (even if reflecting the requirement of a rule) did not involve any alteration of a substantive criterion for admission or for leave to remain, there would be no objection to the change being effected in some form of extrinsic guidance.

...

"106...extrinsic guidance cannot be used in the manner in which it was sought to be used in this case to make a material or substantive change in existing immigration policy without the negative resolution procedure set out in section 3(2) of the Immigration Act being implemented."

Foskett J held that the new guidance clearly did operate to "change materially the substantive criteria" for entry for foreign students who wished to study English in the UK "and that cannot be achieved by a change in guidance – it must be achieved through the medium of a rule change". He therefore declared that the changed minimum educational requirements were unlawful (Judgment, paras 64, 77, 79). The Home Office had tried to distinguish the circumstances in the case from those in *Pankina* on the basis that, in the instant case, the Rules themselves stated an intention to impose minimum educational requirements in the Guidance and Parliament had approved those Rules. The Home Office argued that in *Pankina*, no Rules had authorised the imposition of further and more restrictive requirements under Guidance. However, the judge rejected those submissions (paras 53, 65–6, 78). The Court also rejected the further grounds argued by *English UK* that tried to challenge the rationality of the Guidance and the alleged unlawful delegation of the assessment of a student's abilities to the sponsoring educational institutions.

As with *Pankina*, rather than pursue an appeal against the judgment in the *English UK* case, the Home Office responded by placing the relevant parts of the Guidance into the Rules themselves (see the amendments made by HC 382). As the Explanatory Memo to HC 382 makes clear, the amendment to the Tier 4 Rules "restores the position taken before… judgment was handed down" (see paras 7.11–7.13).

The *Alvi* case

In *R (Hussain Zulfiqar Alvi) v SSHD*, decided on 25 October 2010, the applicant argued that he was entitled to 50 points for attributes under the Tier 2 (General) category under the heading of 'sponsorship' (see App A, Table 11) even though his job as a physiotherapy assistant was not contained in the list of skilled occupations referred to in the notes to that Table (at that time App A, para 82(a)(i) referred to 'UKBA's list of skilled occupations'). The applicant argued before the Court, relying on *Pankina* and *English UK*, that the list of skilled occupations was not part of the Rules and had not been laid before Parliament and that any restriction on the award of points to specified occupations could only lawfully be achieved by setting out the occupations in the Rules themselves (Judgment, paras 19–21).

On the facts of the case, the relevant list of skilled occupations, the 'Tier 2 Codes of Practice', had been placed on the Home Office website on 28 November 2008 which was within the 40-day period for parliamentary scrutiny of the relevant Rules which had been laid on 4 November 2008 (Judgment, paras 23–24). In addition, the Tier 2 Policy Guidance advised persons in the applicant's position that their certificate of sponsorship must confirm that the skill level of the job was at N/SVQ level 3 (Judgment, para 25). The judge concluded that it was not a legal requirement that jobs/skill levels be listed in the Rules themselves (Judgment, para 31):

"It was not the intention of Parliament that the skills list should be an intrinsic part of the Rules or subject to specific Parliamentary legislative approval. The existence of the Tier 2 Codes of Practice and Policy Guidance does not involve changing in a material and substantive way the effect of the Rules or material extrinsic guidance. There is no breach of the principles set out in *Pankina* and in *R (English UK Ltd)*."

The *JCWI/English Community Care Association* case

R (JCWI) v SSHD, R (English Community Care Association) v SSHD was a successful challenge to the Home Office's introduction of an 'interim' cap under Tier 1 (General) and Tier 2 PBS. A long and detailed judgment was delivered orally on 17 December 2010. At the time of writing, there is no approved transcript. For the purposes of this Guide, it is therefore only possible to give brief details of it, rather than fully reflect what was said as part of our ongoing analysis of the post-*Pankina* cases.

For specific details about the background to and operation of the interim cap and the permanent cap and the amending Immigration Rules relating to them, ▶see 55–59. In the legal challenge, JCWI and the English Community Care Association sought judicial review of the Home Office's decision to implement the 'interim' cap, intended to operate until April 2011, arguing that, following *Pankina*, its implementation was unlawful since the actual limits were not stated in the amending Rules that had been laid before Parliament. The amending Rules, which came into force on 19 July 2010 (HC 59 and HC 96), did not state what the interim limits were, but simply that the Tier 1 limit would be published on the UKBA website and that the number of certificates of sponsorship that could be assigned under Tier 2 would be set out in Policy Guidance.

The Court held that:

- Following *Pankina*, it was unlawful to implement new limits on admission under Tiers 1 and 2 when those limits had not been subject to parliamentary scrutiny by being contained in the Rules or in clearly identified extrinsic documents to which the Rules refer and which are available to Parliament.

- Placing the new limits on a website or in guidance on a later date which the Secretary of State may change from time to time, frustrated and evaded the purpose of parliamentary scrutiny of the Immigration Rules that is provided for in section 3(2) 1971 Act and that procedure should not be side-stepped.

The Home Office has been granted a certificate to appeal against the judgment enabling it to appeal directly to the Supreme Court, provided that that Court grants permission to do so. If not, the Home Office may appeal to the Court of Appeal.

Upper Tribunal cases

In subsequent cases before the Upper Tribunal, the Home Office has attempted to argue that the effect of the decision in *Pankina* is confined to the 'three month' funds requirement that was in issue in that case, see: *FA and AA (PBS: effect of Pankina) Nigeria* and *CDS (PBS: 'available': Article 8) Brazil* (both heard on 23 July 2010 before the same constitution of the UT which included the President). In both cases, the UT rejected the idea that *Pankina* was restricted in that way. It held that the Court of Appeal had decided constitutional questions of principle which it then applied to the instant facts of the case and it noted that the *English UK* case also concluded that *Pankina* was of wider application (*FA*, paras 17–18; *CDS*, para 9). As to what *Pankina* had decided, in *CDS* the UT concluded that the decision meant (para 8):

"...that Policy Guidance that had not been laid before Parliament before the inception of the Points-Based System cannot be relied on by the Respondent as a source of additional mandatory requirements not otherwise spelt out in the Immigration Rules themselves."

In *FA*, the question was whether the applicant could meet the Rule contained in Appendix C (maintenance) which required her to show that she had the necessary amount of funds "available" to her, by producing evidence of access to funds held in her *husband's* bank account rather than her own. Again, the Rule required the applicant to produce "the specified documents" to show that the funds were "available". The Policy Guidance stated that, apart from 'official financial sponsors', the bank statement submitted ought to be in the applicant's own name, or that of their parents who were eligible as sponsors. The applicant's husband did not fall into any of these categories specified by the Policy Guidance. Applying *Pankina*, the UT noted that the above requirements contained in the Guidance were not those contained in the Rules (para 13) and that (para 21):

"...once it is established that the Policy Guidance does not have the status of the Immigration Rules for the purpose of immigration appeals, there is no reason why in a particular case an appellant cannot establish that she has funds available to her from a bank account in her husband's name".

On the facts of the case, the UT noted that there was no question that the necessary funds existed, that the husband made them available to the applicant and that the bank account had remained in the husband's name for purely cultural reasons. It followed that the applicant had shown that she had funds "available" to her from a UK bank account and that was enough, "[s]he did not need to go on to comply with additional require- ments of the Policy Guidance" (paras 22, 24–5).

CDS concerned a similar question. The applicant relied on evidence of funds available from two persons, neither of whom fell within the defini- tion of 'sponsor' contained in the Guidance. The UT held that it was an error of law to apply the Guidance "as a source of mandatory additional obligation as to the identity of permissible sponsors" (para 10); that "...in the absence of specific additional requirements of the Immigration Rules, it seems to us that funds are 'available' to a claimant at the material time if they belong to a third party but that party is shown to be willing to deploy them to support the claimant for the purpose contemplated" (para 13); and that the word 'available' in the Rules did not mean "available to her with no assistance from any other person save a parent or guardian" by reference to the Guidance and neither could such requirement "be imported by reference in the Immigration Rules to proving maintenance by relevant documents" (para 14). On the facts, the two sponsors had the necessary resources at the relevant time and were willing to transfer them as needed to ensure that the applicant met the maintenance requirements – accordingly, the applicant had proved her case (paras 12, 14).

Remaining points of uncertainty

We think that the case-law still leaves a number of points for debate, including the following four questions.

1) **Distinction between 'requirement' or 'evidence of compliance with requirements'** As set out above, in *Pankina* the Court appeared to have distinguished between Immigration Rules being supplemented by additional 'rules' (which is objectionable) and Rules that refer to outside Guidance that detail what evidence may be necessary to show that the requirements of the Rules have been complied with (not objectionable) (judgment, para 27). In practice, it may be hard to decide which side of the line any particular criterion falls. The test is variously described in the above case-law as whether the Guidance: imposes an additional condition that "affects" an individual's "status and entitlements" (*Pankina*); imposes a new "substantive criteria for eligibility" or makes a "material or substantive change in existing immigration policy" (*English UK*, above); or acts as a "source of additional mandatory requirements not otherwise spelt out in the Immigration Rules themselves" (*CDS*, above). In the *JCWI* case, the court held that there is a 'spectrum' and that not every alteration in policy needs to be placed before Parliament. It may be that there is no very clear dividing line between what is a separate substantive requirement and guidance about the evidence needed to satisfy what is already a requirement of the Rules. It is possible that, in reality , the distinction may depend on the degree and extent to which the Guidance makes demands about what evidence should be produced.

2) **What is the effect of Guidance that only imposes conditions about evidence of compliance?** The question is: if the Court or Tribunal finds that, in fact, the particular part of the Policy Guidance at issue does not impose a new substantive requirement that is not already contained in the Rules, but only a requirement about the evidence that should be provided to meet it, can the applicant satisfy the requirement by producing evidence other than that which is specified? It appears that the answer may be 'yes' (see, for example, the way in which the UT expressed itself in paragraph 21 of *FA*), but the position is not completely clear. By the same token, if in relation to the same Guidance, the applicant does produce the specified documents, is the Home Office (and the Tribunal) bound to find that the requirement in the Rules is met? The answer may be 'yes' since, even though such Guidance only constitutes policy, the Home Office is generally bound by law to follow its own policy and the Tribunal is also required to allow an appeal where the decision is 'not in accordance with the law' (ss 84(1)(e), 86(3)(a) 2002 Act) and ▶see *HM & Others* (UT) 187–188.

3) **Is a substantive requirement that is contained in Policy Guidance but not in the Rules but which is in existence at the time that the Rules are made and cross-referred to by the Rules, legally effective even if that Guidance may be changed?** In *Pankina*, the first version of the relevant Policy Guidance was brought into existence *within* the 40 days allowed for parliamentary scrutiny of the relevant new Rules. As set out in dealing with *Pankina* (▶above 44), the Court noted that the 40-day period does

not exist in order to give the Home Office more time to lay acceptable rules (see also the *JCWI* case on this point). But, even aside from this, the Court in *Pankina* considered that what was critical to the legal effect of the Guidance was the fact that it was "open to change" rather than "the fact that it has in the event been changed". The Court went on to say that there would be a legal problem if the "reference in the rules were to a categorical criterion in some external but *impermanent or* undetermined source" (*Pankina*, paras 29 and 33, emphasis added). The following case law has not focused on this aspect of *Pankina* (see for example in *R (Pengiliang Fu) v SSHD*, 1 November 2010, which interprets *Pankina* as turning on the question of there being no relevant guidance imposing the new requirement "at the time the rules were laid before Parliament", para 26). In addition, it might be thought that one difficulty with this aspect of *Pankina* is that all guidance is, at least potentially, subject to change.

By contrast with *Pankina* on this point, in the *English UK* case, Foskett J commented that the Guidance relating to the minimum educational requirements that were in existence at the time that the Rules were laid (specifying the lower 'A2' level) did have legal effect (*English UK*, paras 67-9). This seems to be despite the fact that that Guidance was clearly open to change and indeed it did subsequently change in a way that was found to be unlawful. Of course, no one was actually trying to challenge the validity of the original Guidance in *English UK* as there was no need to complain about the original educational standard laid down. In *Alvi* (►49) also, the skills list, contained in materials outside the Rules (Codes of Practice and Policy Guidance) was relied on to show that there had been no "material and substantive" change in the criteria that needed to be satisfied in order to qualify.

4) **What if the Rules expressly state that Guidance may be changed without further Rule changes?** Although he expressly did not decide the question, in the *English UK* case, Foskett J thought that, if the Immigration Rule itself had expressly stated that Guidance relating to minimum educational requirements was to be issued "from time to time", then this might have made changes issued in the form of Guidance legally effective (*English UK*, paras 70, 78). Again, this seems to cut across the requirement in *Pankina* for permanence and also the clear objection stressed in *Pankina*, to the delegation of the making of 'law' beyond the scrutiny and authority of Parliament. It also seems inconsistent with what was said in the *JCWI* case.

THE ALLOCATION OF POINTS UNDER THE PBS

Applicants are only granted leave under the PBS if they score the minimum number of points required. The minimum points required varies depending on the tier under which the applicant is applying and also the category within that tier. With a few exceptions, points are generally awarded for:

- 'attributes';
- 'English language'; and
- 'maintenance'.

The way in which points are allocated for attributes, English language and maintenance, varies according to the particular tier under which the application is made and often according to the particular category within each tier. The way in which points are scored under each tier/category is explained in the relevant part of the Guide. In all cases points are allocated by the Immigration Rules (in the Appendices) which are supplemented by Policy Guidance.

Attributes

Points for attributes are covered in Appendix A of the Rules. All PBS categories require applicants to score a minimum number of points for 'attributes' under Appendix A of the Rules. Depending on the tier/category, points for 'attributes' may be scored on the basis of: educational qualifications; previous earnings; UK experience (in practice previous earnings in the UK); the applicant's age; investment; business activity; job offer; intra-company transfer; certificate of sponsorship; confirmation of acceptance for study and nationality.

English language

The English language requirements under the PBS are contained in Appendix B of the Rules. They only apply in relation to Tier 1 and 2 applicants (although Tier 4 has some separate requirements ▶256–259). The purpose of the English language requirement is that the Home Office considers that "the ability to speak English to a competent level improves an applicant's potential to succeed in the [UK] labour market and assists in integration into the [UK]" (PG T1 (Gen), 9/10, para 173).

Maintenance

Points for maintenance are covered in Appendix C of the Rules. Under the PBS certain Tier 1, 2, 4 and 5 migrants are required to establish that they have adequate funds to support themselves and their dependents whilst in the UK or during their initial period of stay in the UK. Under the old Rules relating to work, study and business (and the still existing Rules for other categories), the level of funding required to qualify was sensitive according to the particular circumstances of the individual and their family. Under the PBS Rules, fixed amounts are specified. It was noted in *Pankina*, that this was a "rough and ready" way of deciding whether a particular applicant had enough to support themselves.

Appendix C sets out the tiers for which applicants have to score the mandatory 10 points for maintenance. All maintenance funds must exist at the date of application and, in some cases they, must be shown to be in existence in the bank account for a set period of time by the date of application. Following *Pankina* (▶42), those requirements have now been made part of the Rules rather than simply being in Policy Guidance. The funds do not have to be in a single account, however, and they can include funds in accounts outside the UK. For more details about scoring points for maintenance generally, ▶see 152–155 Tier 1 and 181–188 (case-law).

THE CAP AND THE INTERIM CAP

The Government's 'cap' on non-EU migration to the UK has travelled a rocky road so far. Below we set out the developments in chronological sequence.

Election pledge and essential thinking

A key pledge made by the Conservative Party during the April–May 2010 general election campaign was that it would introduce a 'cap' on non-EU migration designed to cut back annual net migration from the "hundreds of thousands to the tens of thousands". After the election, the coalition's *Programme for Government*, announced on 20 May 2010, asserted "We will introduce an annual limit on the number of non-EU economic migrants admitted into the UK to live and work". On 28 June 2010, the Home Secretary announced in the House of Commons that the Government would place an 'interim' limit on economic migration. She also stated that the 'permanent' cap would be introduced from April 2011. The Government began a consultation on how the long-term limits would be applied.

In order to give effect to the Home Secretary's plans, on 19 July 2010 two amending statements to the Immigration Rules came into effect, HC 59 and HC 96 (▶see below). The Explanatory Memoranda accompanying them further explained the thinking behind the cap and the interim cap (para 7.4 of both documents):

"...while the United Kingdom can benefit from migration, uncontrolled and unlimited migration places an unacceptable pressure on public services, school places, and the provision of housing, all of which causes problems for certain local communities. The Government is not only concerned to act to limit migration at an early opportunity but is also concerned that the expectation that full limits on migration will be introduced in due course could prompt a surge in applications. The consequences of such a surge would be an immediate increase in net migration. That would be contrary to the Government's policy of reducing net migration and may lead to a more severe correction being required in terms of a future limit than would otherwise be the case. Furthermore, it is in accordance with Government policy in the interests of the economic well-being of the UK to act to prevent a spike in the number of foreign nationals entering the labour market...having regard to the current financial situation and just as the Government introduces a policy aimed at reducing dependence on overseas labour."

These caps have plainly been the cause of friction within the Coalition Government. The Liberal Democrats argued against a cap during the election campaign. The BBC has reported that "tense talks" between the Conservatives and Liberal Democrats subsequently resulted in a compromise. In September 2010, the Business Secretary, Vince Cable MP, was reported as commenting that the interim cap had caused "a lot of damage to British industry".

Interim cap: the amending Immigration Rules from July 2010

The two amending Rules that came into force on 19 July 2010 and their operation are explained below.

HC 59

This statement placed an interim limit on the number of applications for entry clearance and leave to enter within the Tier 1 (General) category that could be granted during a particular period of time. It did not apply to applications for leave to remain, nor to the other categories within Tier 1, and it applied only to applications made on or after 19 July 2010. Applications by dependants were also unaffected. Under the amendments, an application for entry could only be granted if (new para 245C(aa), HC 395):

"The grant allocation relating to the Tier 1 (General) Migrant route would not be exceeded by granting the application for entry clearance or leave to enter in the relevant grant allocation period".

The "relevant grant allocation period" and "grant allocation" were not quantified in the amending Rules. Instead, those Rules defined them, in turn, as a "specified period of time, which will be published by the Secretary of State on the [UKBA] website..." and as a "limit, details of which will be published by the Secretary of State on the [UKBA] website, on the number of grants of entry clearance or leave to enter which may be granted..." (para 6 HC 395 as amended). The stated purpose of publishing the limit on the website, rather than stating it in the Rules, was to provide "flexibility to ensure that the grant allocation remains at the right level" (HC 59 Explanatory Memorandum, para 7.8).

If an application were submitted under Tier 1 (General) and the limit had already been reached for that particular (grant allocation) period and the application did not fall to be refused for any other reason under the Rules, the application would not be refused but rather "reallocated to the next relevant grant allocation period for consideration" (para 245C, HC 395 as amended; HC 59 Explanatory Memorandum, para 7.12). The Tier 1 (General) Sponsor Guidance also stated that an application may "be carried over from one relevant grant period to the next on more than one occasion if a high volume of applications is received".

UKBA later began to administer this limit by calendar month, restricting the number of grants per month to 600. These details were published on the UKBA website. The intention was to limit the number of out-of-country main applicants to the same number as those entering during the equivalent period between 2009–2010. So any application that fell to be refused only because the monthly limit had been reached would be put over to the next month's allocation. There was no attempt to prevent the actual making of an application, even if the monthly limit had been reached.

HC 96

This statement amended Appendix A, HC 395, in very broad terms, inserting (at para 63A) that the:

"...Secretary of State shall be entitled to limit the number of Certificates of Sponsorship available to be assigned to sponsors in any one period, and to limit the number of Certificates of Sponsorship assigned to any specific Sponsor in any one period. These limits will be specified in the Points-Based System guidance."

Of course, an applicant cannot be successful in their application under the PBS if they require, but do not have, a sponsor. Again, no actual limit was specified in the Rules, it was instead left over to the PBS Guidance. The Explanatory Memorandum stated that "For the period of the interim limit announced by the Secretary of State on 28 June", the limit "will only be applied to the Tier 2 (General) category" (para 7.5). An 'addendum' was published to the Guidance issued to sponsors under Tiers 2 and 5 which stated that the "aim" of the interim limit was to achieve an overall reduction of 5% in the Tier 1 (General) and Tier 2 (General) categories. The addendum further stated that:

- the total number of certificates of sponsorship that would available during the period of the interim limit was 18,700;
- in order to achieve this, a limit would be placed on the number of such certificates that each sponsor could assign to migrant workers;
- all Tier 2 sponsors with a licence on 19 July had been notified in writing of their individual certificate allocation – those allocations were arrived at by assessing the certificate usage of each sponsor between 19 July 2009 and 31 March 2010;
- it was for sponsors to decide how to split their allocation between 'new' migrant workers and extension applicants;
- some sponsors had been given a zero allocation;
- a small number of certificates had been set aside for 'exceptional circumstances' – sponsors could apply for such exceptional consideration on the criteria set out in the addendum (paras 26–28).

November 2010: further detail announced regarding the permanent cap

In order to assist in the implementation of the cap, the Government commissioned the Migration Advisory Committee ('MAC') to address the question of what levels the limits on Tiers 1 and 2 should be set at for their first full year of operation (2011–2012) in order to contribute towards the Government's objectives of: (a) reducing net migration to an annual level of tens of thousands by the end of the present Parliament; and (b) taking into account social and public service impacts. In November 2010, MAC published *Limits on Migration, Limits on Tier 1 and Tier 2 for 2011/ 12 and Supporting Policies*. It recommended that the total combined limit for Tier 1 (General) and Tier 2 should be set at between 37,400 and 43,700.

In a statement made the following week, on 23 November 2010, the Home Secretary made the following announcements:

- the permanent cap from April 2011 would incorporate an annual limit of 21,700 for those entering under the 'highly skilled' and 'skilled' routes (ie, Tiers 1 and 2);
- the 'highly skilled' tier will itself be re-modelled and limited to all but entrepreneurs, investors and a new category of 'exceptionally talented' people;
- the annual limit on 'exceptionally talented' entrants will be set at 1,000 (and that will form part of the overall cap of 21,700);
- the 'intra-company transfer' category under Tier 2 will be tightened (the minimum salary for those coming for more than 12 months will be raised to £40,000) but this category *will not* be subject to the cap;
- occupations in Tier 2 will be required to be at graduate level.

For the latest on the permanent cap ▶see 208–210

Decision of the Divisional Court and further amending Rules: December 2010

On 17 December 2010, the Divisional Court ruled that, following *Pankina*, the failure of the Rules to quantify the limits imposed by the interim cap so as to enable Parliament to consider them, was unlawful (*R (JCWI) v SSHD; R (English Community Care Association) v SSHD*, ▶see 49). The judgment applied only to the process by which the interim cap was implemented and does not effect the proposed permanent cap that will be introduced from April 2011. On the day that Judgment was given, the Minister of State, Damian Green MP, announced:

"The court's ruling rests on a technicality. We will set this right within the next few days to ensure we can continue to operate an interim limit."

On 21 December 2010, Mr Green laid before Parliament a further amending statement of Rules, HC 698, the effect of which was to close the Tier 1 (General) category for those applying for entry clearance on or after 23

December 2010 and also to specify, in the Rules, the Tier 2 interim limit with effect from 21 December 2010. The Explanatory Memorandum to the Rules expressed the Government's regret that it had not been possible to comply with the normal convention that changes should be laid before Parliament no less than 21 days before they come into force (para 3.1). In a statement made on the same day, Mr Green indicated that he would "welcome the opportunity to debate [the new Rules] should Members choose to pray against the Statement of Changes".

Closure of Tier 1 (General)

In his 21 December 2010 statement the Minister stated that the reason for the closure of the Tier 1 (General) category to new applicants from over-seas was the high number of applications received since the commence-ment of the interim cap on 19 July 2010, together with the fact that the Government had announced, on 23 November 2010 (►see 58), that Tier 1 (General) would not continue in its existing form beyond March 2011. He explained that because the original interim cap limit or Tier 1 (General) would be reached imminently, with the effect that there may be nowhere for further applications to be 'rolled over' to, the decision had been taken to close the route.

The amendments closing the Tier 1 (General) category delete from the Rules the rule relating to entry clearance/leave to enter as a Tier 1 (General) migrant (para 245B HC 395). The amendments do not apply to applica-tions for entry clearance made before 23 December 2010, nor to those seeking to extend their leave in the UK under this category and nor do they apply to those who seek to switch into this category from their existing status.

Specifying the limit for the Tier 2 (General) category

With effect from 21 December 2010, the amending Rules (HC 698) provide for a 'Tier 2 Interim Limit' on the number of certificates of spon-sorship that can be assigned by the Home Office to sponsors in the Tier 2 (General) Migrant category between 21 December 2010 and 5 April 2011 (para 6 and App A paras 63B–K, HC 395 as amended). The Tier 2 interim limit is 10,832. That figure includes both the number of certificates of sponsorship that UKBA assigns to a particular sponsor and the number of certificates available to be assigned under an 'exceptional consideration process'. The Explanatory Memorandum to HC 698 sets out that, in the *JCWI* case, "...the Divisional Court had determined that in order for the Government's interim limit policy to have legal effect the level of the limit should be specified in the Immigration Rules, as opposed to UK Border Agency Guidance. The Statement of Changes remedies the matter" (para 3.13).

The number of certificates that UKBA will assign to each sponsor is also dealt with in the new rule and the formula is complex – ►see the chapters dealing with sponsorship and Tier 2 at 106–108.

3   Making applications

This chapter covers:

- entry clearance / visas (▶below);
- applying for entry clearance (▶62–67);
- applying for leave to remain (▶67–76);
- applying to 'switch' categories (▶77–78).

This chapter provides details about the *process* of applying to come to live in the UK under the Points-Based System; and the process of extending stay in the UK under PBS for people already here. The requirements for qualifying under the different tiers/categories and the evidence needed to satisfy those requirements is dealt with in the later chapters of the Guide.

All PBS applications are decided at one single stage. In applications from overseas, the decision-maker is the entry clearance officer at the post responsible for deciding the application. In the case of an application made in the UK for 'leave to remain', the decision is made by a UK Border Agency caseworker. This is different from the previous procedures for work permits and the Highly Skilled Migrant Programme (HSMP), where prior approval of the work permit/HSMP application needed to be obtained from Work Permits (UK) before entry clearance or leave to remain could be applied for.

ENTRY CLEARANCE

All those seeking to enter the UK under any of the points-based categories must seek prior entry clearance, regardless of the nationality of the applicant or the proposed length of their stay. The only exception to this is for non-visa nationals applying under the Creative and Sporting subcategory of the Tier 5 (Temporary) Worker category for three months or less.

What is 'entry clearance'?

An 'entry clearance' is a document which is issued by a British post overseas (British embassy, high commission or consulate), which is evidence that the holder is eligible for entry to the UK even though they are not a British citizen (s33(1) 1971 Act). People applying for entry clearance have to satisfy officials at a British post that they qualify under the require-ments in the Immigration Rules for entry in the category in which they are applying, or that entry clearance ought to be granted exceptionally. If entry clearance is granted, it is normally placed in the applicant's passport. As stated above, nearly all PBS applicants from abroad need an entry clearance.

'Visas', 'entry certificates', 'entry clearances' If the applicant is a 'visa national' (ie they are a national of one of the list of countries contained in Appendix 1 to the Rules who require prior entry clearance for any purpose of travel to the UK), the legal term for the entry clearance they get is a 'visa'. If the applicant is a non-visa national, the legal term for the entry clearance they get is an 'entry certificate' (see para. 25, HC 395). Many people simply use the term 'visa' to refer to both of them although this is not technically correct. The proper way to refer to them both is 'entry clearance' and this is the term used throughout this book.

Conditions Entry clearances state the conditions that will apply to the leave that the person obtains when they arrive in the UK. These conditions are sometimes referred to by immigration officers as 'codes' for short-hand. The codes reflect the various different combinations of conditions which a person can be given.

Entry clearances operating as leave to enter

The Immigration Act 1971 (as amended) remains the cornerstone of immigration controls. However, key changes were made to the way the system of entry clearance and 'leave' (permission to be in the UK) operates by the Immigration and Asylum Act 1999 and the Immigration (Leave to Enter and Remain) Order 2000 which was made under it. Important parts of the system brought in by these provisions were:

- entry clearances operate as leave to enter;
- 'leave' to be in the UK can remain in place even when a person embarks from the UK – the technical change that permits this prevents the person's leave from 'lapsing' when they depart;
- leave to enter the UK can be granted to a person before they arrive;
- leave that a person has when they arrive can be 'cancelled' on their arrival;
- leave to be in the UK can remain in place when a person is appealing against a refusal to extend their leave, provided that the application was made 'in time'.

In general, in order for an entry clearance to operate as leave to enter it must state on it the purpose for which it is given (for example, Tier 1 (General) Migrant) and be either (Art 3, Leave to Enter Order 2000, para. 25A, HC 395):

- endorsed with any conditions on which it has been granted (for example, a condition that there is 'no recourse to public funds'); or

- intended to take effect as indefinite leave to enter, in which case it must contain a statement to that effect.

The immigration authorities intend that all entry clearances that are granted will operate as leave to enter. However, an entry clearance which does not in fact satisfy the above conditions will not operate as leave to enter. Such an entry clearance would probably still be valid but leave would not be given unless the immigration officer granted it on entry.

How do these entry clearances work?

Entry clearances have an 'effective date' (which may be later than the date on which they are issued, depending on when the applicant wishes to travel) and an 'expiry date'. On the entry clearance itself, the effective date is shown as 'valid from' and the expiry date is shown as 'valid until'. The 'period of validity' of the entry clearance is the period between these two dates. The conditions of the leave that is given are the conditions that are written on the entry clearance. Applicants must arrive in the UK between these dates. Because the entry clearance itself operates as the grant of leave to enter, when the applicant arrives and is examined by the immigration officer, the officer does not 'grant' leave to enter. After examination, provided everything is in order, the officer will simply allow entry and endorse the passport with a date stamp to show the date on which the person entered.

When a passenger with entry clearance which operates as leave to enter arrives in the UK, they are treated as though they have been granted leave to enter 'before' their arrival but the period of their leave begins on the date of their arrival (see Art 4(2)(2B)(3)(b) Leave to Enter Order 2000; para 25A, HC 395). The intention seems to be to ensure that, although people are treated as already having been given leave, the period over which leave is counted for the purpose of, for example, counting time towards settlement, does not begin until arrival.

It is very important that the 'effective date' is given in accordance with the applicant's plans for their arrival and an opportunity to specify an entry date to the UK is now provided on the application forms.

APPLYING FOR ENTRY CLEARANCE

Which post?

A person must be outside the UK in order to make an application for entry clearance. Applications should be made to the designated British post (British embassy, high commission or consulate) in the country in which the person is 'living'. The Foreign and Commonwealth Office produces a list of designated posts. Most will deal with all types of entry clearance applications but some are restricted to dealing with particular types of applications. Where there is no designated post in their country, applicants can apply to a designated post in another country, which accepts applications in the category in which they wish to enter (para 28, HC 395).

The current Entry Clearance Guidance confirms that applications for entry clearance in all PBS categories (though see below for Tier 5) should be made in an applicant's 'country of residence'. This can be either their country of nationality, or another country where they have permission to reside (other than for short visits). Provision is also made for those applying under the creative and sporting and Youth Mobility Scheme categories of Tier 5 to apply from posts in countries where they are temporarily resident – but applicants should note the particular requirements of each (para 28A(a) and (b), HC 395). Since 2007, UKBA has rolled out a 'hub and spoke' system under which applicatons taken at posts are sent to regional centres for a decision.

Outsourcing from posts

In many countries, all aspects of the entry clearance application process, except the decision itself, have been outsourced to two commercial organisations, VFS and Worldbridge. In these countries, those organisations operate 'Visa Application Centres'. They also maintain websites, email and telephone advice lines which provide applicants with information about the application procedure and give general advice about applications and supporting documents.

Where this system operates, applicants must attend the relevant Visa Application Centre in person, in order to submit their biometrics (►see 64), application forms and supporting documents. The Visa Application Centre will then forward the application to the relevant post for a decision. Often there is provision made for booking appointments to attend the Visa Application Centre. Due to this outsourcing, it is now very difficult to obtain contact details for the posts that operate by use of them.

In other countries applications can be made in person, by post, by courier or online to the post directly (though there will always be a mechanism for the submission of applicants' biometrics).

Using the 'points-based calculator'

In order to qualify for leave to enter the UK as a PBS migrant, applicants are required to show that they can achieve the requisite number of points awarded in a range of areas, which vary between application categories. UKBA has an online tool, called the 'points-based calculator', which allows applicants to determine whether they are eligible to apply under each of the categories by calculating the number of points they can achieve for each area. Together with the main application form, an appendix self-assessment form must also be completed and submitted with the supporting documentation. The appendices can be found on the UK Visa Services website: www.ukvisas.gov.uk. They confirm how many points are scored by the applicant in each area, and what evidence is being provided.

The points-based calculator can be found at www.ukba.homeoffice.gov. uk/pointscalculator.

The application forms

To apply for entry clearance, it is necessary to complete the relevant forms which can be downloaded from the UK Visa Services website (www. ukvisas.gov.uk). Many posts now operate a system where an application can be completed and submitted online. Otherwise, the forms can be obtained free of charge from posts overseas.

While a sponsor, relative or representative may obtain the forms, help fill them in and present them, the applicant must sign and date the 'declaration' at the end to confirm that its contents are correct. The documents that are required depend on the PBS category being applied for. The UK Visa Services website carries notes for guidance for applications in the different categories. Applicants should also consult the PDF guidance booklets that accompany the in-country form on the UKBA website for all PBS applications as they contain details of which documents should be included as supporting evidence. These are the 'specified documents' referred to in the Immigration Rules (▶see 67 dealing with in-country applications). It is very important that the documentary evidence provided complies in full with the relevant guidance.

Fees and date the application is treated as made

Entry clearance applications are not treated as having been made unless the required fee has been paid (para 30, HC 395). The method of payment depends on the country of application.

If the application is submitted and paid for online, then the date of application is the date the fee is paid online. If the application is submitted online, but the fee is paid in person, then the date of application is the date the applicant attends the post or Visa Application Centre and pays the fee.

The date of the application is particularly important for applications made under PBS as it is the relevant date in relation to the mandatory maintenance requirement that applies to most categories. It can also be important when making applications for dependent children, who must be under 18 on the date of application.

Biometrics

All applicants applying for entry clearance to the UK for any purpose must submit their biometric information as part of the application process. In some countries, once an applicant has completed their form online, they will be given an opportunity to book an appointment to submit their biometrics. During the appointment, the applicant will have fingerscans and a digital photograph taken. Depending on the country of application, biometrics are taken at the post or the Visa Application Centre when the application is submitted. If the application is being made in the USA, bio-metrics are at the local 'USCIS' office. Where an applicant is required to submit the application by post, or is submitting their application in the USA through an authorised courier, they must include their biometric evidence with their applications. Applications must be submitted within two weeks of the biometric information being taken.

Those exempt from the biometric process are: minors under six, holders of diplomatic and other official passports, UN officials and holders of a certificate of entitlement to the right of abode.

Dependants

Applications may also be made for a partner and/or children to enter the UK as dependants of the main applicant at the same time (see paras 319AA–D, 319F–I, HC 395). This applies to the dependants of applicants under all PBS categories with the exception of dependants of those in the Tier 5 (Youth Mobility Scheme) category and the dependent children of Tier 4 (Child) Students.

Applications may be made by a spouse or civil partner. Applications may also be made by the main applicant's unmarried or same sex partner, provided that they have been living together in a relationship similar to marriage or civil partnership for at least two years. Children of a PBS main applicant can apply to be their dependant if:

- they are under the age of 18 at the time the application is submitted;
- they are not married or in a civil partnership and have not yet formed an independent life of their own;
- they do not intend to stay in the UK beyond the period of the leave granted to their parent;
- both of their parents are being granted entry clearance at the same time, or are already lawfully present in the UK, unless:
- the main applicant is the sole surviving parent;
- the main applicant has sole responsibility for the dependent child; or
- there are other serious or compelling reasons not to refuse the application and suitable arrangements have been made for the child's care.

Dependants of main applicants in the PBS categories are also subject to maintenance requirements; and the main applicant's and/or the dependant's funds can be used in this regard.

A separate application must be made for each dependant, and each will attract a fee, although they can be submitted at the same time as the main applicant's application. Dependants may also apply after the main applicant has been granted entry clearance.

Dependants will need to provide original evidence of their relationship to the main applicant; which will be the marriage or civil partnership certificate for a spouse or civil partner, evidence of two years' cohabitation for an unmarried partner, or a birth certificate for a child. As with all documents submitted with PBS applications, such documents which are not in English or Welsh are required to be translated by a professional translator and certified in accordance with the guidance.

Further details about the requirements that need to be satisfied by dependants of PBS applicants are contained in Chapter 5 ▶194–203.

Interviews and further investigations

In some cases, the entry clearance officer will interview the applicant and may conduct further investigations such as making enquiries of other agencies before making a decision. Cases involving additional investigations are rare and are likely to involve matters that are not related to the specific PBS criteria but arise instead under the 'general' grounds of refusal contained in part 10 of the Immigration Rules (for example, immigration history or the applicant's general conduct).

Referrals to the UK

Entry clearance officers can refer certain cases to UKBA in the UK for advice and instructions. However, this will be rare for PBS cases. Referrals sometimes take place where UKBA holds information on the person in relation to previous immigration applications. If the application is referred, this will lead to a delay in determining it. When the case has been referred, representations may be made to UKBA instead of to the overseas post.

Time taken to process applications

Processing times vary according to post and type of application. Up-to-date information can be found on the websites of the post concerned, VFS or Worldbridge (the two commercial organisations to which entry clearance services are outsourced in some countries) and UK Visa Services. Note also that the UK Visas website contains a 'Guide to Processing Times' at all posts which is updated every few months.

Entry clearance decisions

If the Entry Clearance Officer (ECO) is satisfied that the requirements of the Rules are met, ie that sufficient points have been scored in the relevant areas, the applicant will be granted entry clearance. If the ECO is not satisfied that the requirements of the Rules are met, then unless it has been shown that it is appropriate to authorise entry outside the Rules, the application will be refused. Given the rigid nature of the PBS, applicants are very unlikely to be granted entry clearance outside the Rules. ECOs must, however, give consideration to rights under the ECHR which have been incorporated into UK law by the Human Rights Act 1998 (para 2, HC 395) (▶see Chapter 12).

It should also be noted that the Rules relating to each PBS category only state that entry clearance or leave *may* be granted if the requirements of the Rules relating to the particular category in question are satisfied. Therefore, even if a person satisfies the Rules for the individual category, they may still be refused an entry clearance under the 'general grounds' on which they can be refused (►see Chapter 11).

Appeals and reviews

Full rights of appeal are not available to PBS applicants applying from outside the UK. The appeal rights available where a PBS application has been refused are generally limited to unlawful discrimination and s6 of the Human Rights Act 1998 (breaches of the ECHR). Instead, applicants have the right to request an 'administrative review'. Such reviews are undertaken by an Entry Clearance Manager, who will look at whether or not an error has been made in the decision-making process. Administrative reviews are restricted to looking at whether points have been correctly awarded and documentation properly assessed. Applicants are not permitted to submit any further evidence not available at the date of decision for the purposes of the review. Appeals, administrative review and other remedies are dealt with in Chapter 13.

APPLYING FOR LEAVE TO REMAIN

Those who have been allowed to enter or remain in the UK, can apply to UKBA to extend their leave. Applications submitted in the UK to extend leave are known as applications for leave to *remain* rather than to enter. Where applicants are applying for leave to remain in a different category to that which they are in at present, the application is commonly referred to as one for 'switching' (►see 76 below). The ability to 'switch' is very tightly controlled.

In most cases, those who entered the UK under one of the PBS categories may apply to extend their leave in that same category. But for some, the possible extensions are very limited. For example, the Skills Transfer and Graduate Trainee sub-categories of the Tier 2 (Intra Company Transfer) category (►see 227, 240–241) are strictly time limited so applicants can extend up to a total maximum of six months and 12 months respectively. Also, those who entered under the Tier 5 (Temporary Workers) category are restricted in terms of the extensions that they may request (►see 310–318). There is no provision in the Rules for applying to extend leave under the Tier 5 (Youth Mobility Scheme).

Application forms

All applications to UKBA for leave to remain must be made on the appropriate prescribed application form. The application forms can be downloaded from the UK Border Agency website (www.ukba.home office.gov.uk). If the applicant is in any doubt about which form to use, it is possible to ask the Immigration Enquiry Bureau (tel 0870 606 7766). However, this Bureau is part of the UK Border Agency and cannot offer independent advice.

Applications *must* be made using the up-to-date form specified for the purpose of the application (para 34, 34(i), HC 395) (▶see further below under 'ensuring the application is valid and in time' 70–72). Application forms are updated regularly, so applicants should check the UKBA website to ensure they are using the most recent version of the form. Applicants are also strongly advised to keep copies of the application form *and* the documents sent.

Common PBS forms are:

PBS Dependant for applications for leave to remain as the dependant of a PBS migrant

Tier 1 Entrepreneur for applications for leave to remain as a Tier 1 (Entrepreneur)

Tier 1 General for applications for leave to remain as a Tier 1 (General) migrant

Tier 1 Investors for applications for leave to remain as a Tier 1 (Investor)

Tier 1 Post-Study Work for applications for leave to remain as a Tier 1 (Post-Study Work) migrant

Tier 2 Sponsored Skilled Worker for applications for leave to remain as a Tier 2 sponsored skilled worker

Tier 4 Student – Adult for applications for leave to remain as a Tier 4 (General) Student

Tier 4 Student – Child for applications for leave to remain as a Tier 4 (Child) Student

Tier 5 Temporary Worker for applications for leave to remain as a Tier 5 (Temporary) Worker

Methods of application

Applications for leave to remain under the PBS can be made in one of the following ways.

Applying by post

The correct postal address for all applications is given in the Guidance Notes of the relevant form and must be checked when sending the application. Payment can be made by providing credit card details or attaching a cheque or postal order. For postal applications, the date of the application is the date it was posted (para 34G(i), HC 395).

UKBA recommends that applicants use recorded or special delivery post as this provides the applicant with proof of posting and also helps UKBA to record receipt of the application. Applicants who do send in their applications by recorded delivery or special delivery should keep the number. UKBA states that it aims to acknowledge applications within one week of receipt. It is worth noting that recorded delivery mail is only 'recorded' at the point of delivery. It is not possible to track items sent this way while they are *en route*.

Generally, when applying for further limited leave to remain under all PBS categories or as a PBS, applicants must now submit their biometrics as part of the application process (and see paras 34A(iv)(v), HC 395). Instead of receiving an endorsement in their passport, such applicants are now issued with Biometric Residence Permits, otherwise referred to as a bio-metric immigration document (BID). These changes have been brought in by the UK Borders Act 2007 and the Biometric Registration Regulations 2008.

If applying by post, the applicant will receive notification from UKBA that their application and supporting documentation has been received and they will be invited to book a biometric appointment. Applicants can arrange to submit their biometrics at one of UKBA's Biometric Enrolment Centres. This can be done by either telephoning the Customer Contact Centre on 0300 123 8895 or by using the UKBA Online Booking Service. Applicants will be given a unique case reference number with which to register their appointment. If an applicant fails to make an appointment, then their application will be rejected.

Alternatively, applicants may choose to submit their biometrics at one of a number of participating regional Post Office Ltd branches which work with UKBA to provide biometric enrolment. Only those residing within certain postcode areas are able to use this service. When submitting biometric information at a Post Office branch, a fee of £8 is payable and can be paid either by cash or debit card. Further information about the biometric process can be seen on the UKBA website at www.ukba.home office.gov.uk/contact/contactspage/biometricenrolment/. Once the bio-metric information has been given, the application will be processed and the applicant will be notified of the decision by post.

Applying by courier

UKBA also accepts PBS applications delivered to them by courier if it is an application for (para 34B (ii), HC 395):

- limited or indefinite leave to remain as a sole representative, retired person of independent means or as a Tier 1 Migrant or Tier 2 Migrant;
- indefinite leave to remain as a businessperson, investor or innovator; or
- limited leave to remain as a Tier 5 (Temporary Worker) Migrant.

There is a separate delivery address on the front of the forms for couriers. The process is the same as outlined above for postal applications, but applicants may want the peace of mind of knowing that the application has been hand-delivered. If the application is submitted in this way, the date of application is the date that UKBA receives it (para. 34G(iii), HC 395).

Applying in person

For most PBS categories, a same-day service is offered to people who apply in person at one of UKBA's Public Enquiry Offices (PEOs). This is referred to as the 'Premium Service' and is only offered for straightforward applications which do not require further enquiries. As far as work and business categories are concerned, in person applications at PEOs are *not* accepted for the following applications (para 34B, HC 395):

- limited or indefinite leave to remain as a sole representative or a retired person of independent means;
- limited or indefinite leave to remain as a Tier 1 (Investor) Migrant or as a Tier 1 (Entrepreneur) Migrant; or
- indefinite leave to remain as a businessperson, investor or innovator.

Applicants who wish to apply in person should make an appointment in advance with one of the PEOs. There are PEOs in Belfast, Birmingham, Brighton, Cardiff, Croydon, Derby, Glasgow, Liverpool, London and Sheffield. The addresses are given on the forms, which also provide the relevant telephone numbers for booking an appointment and state whether the category is one for which the Premium Service can be used. Further up-to-date information on PEOs and contact numbers can be found on the relevant page of the UKBA website. Premium Service appointments for PBS applications are usually booked up months in advance.

All applications submitted via the Premium Service are usually decided on a same-day basis. Applicants will be notified if there are any complications with the application which may result in a delay in the decision-making process. At the Croydon PEO, applications for limited leave may be submitted via the third-party representatives scheme, which is only open to certain registered immigration advisers and solicitors' firms in the following PBS categories: Tier 1 (General); Tier 1 (Post-Study Work); Tier 2 (General); Tier 4; and Tier 5. Similar provisions are in place at other PEOs but representatives should check the website for them and for updates.

Online applications

An applicant may apply online where this option is available on the UKBA website (para 34B(iv), HC 395).

Ensuring that the application is valid and in time

It is essential to ensure that the application is both valid and that it is submitted in time.

Validity of the application

The application form must be (para 34A, HC 395):

- signed and dated by the applicant and, where applicable, the applicant's partner (except that if the applicant is under 18, the form may be signed and dated by the parent or legal guardian of the applicant on the applicant's behalf);
- accompanied by the documents and photographs required by the form and guidance notes; and
- completed in full in accordance with the instructions given on the form.

The application must be made on the correct form and be accompanied by all the documents specified in the forms and in the relevant PBS Policy Guidance (paras 34A, HC 395). The rigidity of the evidential requirements contained in PBS Guidance and the lack of discretion allowed to decision-makers as regards accepting evidence produced in other forms is one of the most controversial aspects of the new system in practice. If supporting documents are not provided in full and they do not meet the requirements in the Guidance as to format it is likely that an application will be rejected. Even at the most mundane level, the specific requirements on format of documents can and do affect the outcome of an application eg how an electronic bank statement must be authenticated and what details it should contain. Immigration advisers repeatedly see refusals where individuals are clearly eligible to meet the relevant points from a common-sense perspective but whose applications have been refused, and no communication is made to the applicant from UKBA to give them a chance to send in evidence in the correct form.

These issues have now been considered by the courts in *Pankina* and the *English (UK)* case (for details, ►see 41–47). Those cases decide that the Guidance alone cannot effectively impose new substantive requirements on applicants that are not contained in the Immigration Rules. However, how that test will apply in each individual case relating to the requirements as to evidence specified in the Guidance, and how officials will deal with applications which do not completely meet the specifications in the Guidance, is not yet certain. We would advise applicants to err on the side of caution and to do what they can to comply with the Guidance. If for any reason they cannot, then they should do as much as they can to show, with whatever evidence they have, that they meet the requirements of the Rules. They should also explain why they cannot produce evidence in the particular form required and whether they will be able to produce it and by what date. Those who are in any doubt about what evidence they should be providing should seek advice. Those who have been refused on the basis of technical points relating to evidence should consider appealing or challenging the decision (►see further Chapters 12 and 13 on human rights and challenging decisions).

Where the application form and accompanying documents do not fulfil the above requirements, the application will be treated as invalid and will not be considered (para 34C, HC 395). Even if the application is then submitted again in a valid form, the applicant may become an overstayer in the meantime (for which, see below). An application that is submitted on a form that has fallen out of date by no more than 21 days by the date that the application is made, will still be treated as having been made on the specified form (para 34I, HC 395). Applications will also not be valid unless the specified fee is paid in accordance with the requirements of the form and Guidance notes (para 34A(ii), HC 395).

Applications should be made in time

Applications for extensions should always be made to UKBA in good time before the current leave expires. If leave has already expired, then legal advice should be obtained about making a further application without delay.

UKBA determines the date the application was submitted (para 34G, HC 395) as:

- the date of the postmark on the envelope, if submitted by post;
- the date it is received, if submitted in person or by courier;
- the date on which it is submitted, if made online.

The consequences of not applying for further leave in time are serious. People who do not make an in-time application for further leave:

- will lose any right of appeal (other than on asylum or human rights grounds);
- will not be able to work lawfully in the UK after the date their leave expires;
- become liable for administrative removal from the UK as overstayers;
- may have subsequent applications for entry clearance or leave to enter refused (▶see Chapter 11 at 379–380, 385–390 for further details); and
- become liable to criminal proceedings, although prosecutions are not frequent.

One present anomaly – given the ongoing restrictive trend on all aspects of immigration control – is that UKBA will accept applications for leave to *remain* in PBS categories from people who have overstayed their leave to enter or remain. The Rules for PBS categories do not prevent this. If such applications meet the requirements of the PBS Rules, then generally they are granted as are in time applications. But, for the reasons given above, we strongly advise that all applications should be submitted well within time.

Dependants

As with applications for entry clearance, applications may also be made for a partner and/or children to enter the UK as dependants of the main applicant at the same time (▶see above 65–66; paras 319AA–D, 319F–I, HC 395). This applies to the dependants of applicants under all PBS categories with the exception of dependants of those in the Tier 5 (Youth Mobility Scheme) category and the dependent children of Tier 4 (Child) Students.

Dependants applying for leave to remain in line with the main applicant under PBS categories must apply on the PBS (Dependant) form. If applying at the same time as the main applicant, they will pay a reduced fee. They are liable to pay the full fee if they apply at a different time.

Where a child of the main applicant originally obtained leave to enter or remain as their dependant but has since turned 18, they will be able to extend their stay on the same basis if they can show that they are still dependent on the main applicant and have not yet formed an independent life of their own. Indeed the PBS Dependant Guidance specifies that all dependants aged over 16 are required to provide specific documentation confirming they are resident at their parent's address (for boarding school pupils and university students they are required to provide specified evidence that they are resident at school/university during term time and at the family home in holidays).

In all categories where the main applicant is required to submit their biometric information, any dependants must also submit their biometrics. Where the dependant is a child under six years, they must submit a digital photograph. Where a child is aged six years or over, they must submit a digital photograph and their fingerscans. As with entry clearance applications, dependants should also submit evidence confirming their relationship to the main applicant.

Further details about the requirements that need to be satisfied by dependants of PBS applicants are contained in Chapter 5 ▶194–203.

Waiting for the decision and requesting the return of passports

Processing times differ according to the type of PBS category and other factors. The UKBA website gives current estimated waiting times on the relevant pages for each category.

UKBA will retain an applicant's passport while the application is under consideration. However, it is sometimes necessary for applicants to request the return of their passport for *non-travel* purposes. In these circumstances, passports can be returned by UKBA without the application being considered as having been withdrawn. However, where an applicant requests the return of their passport for the purposes of travel outside the common travel area (effectively the British Isles), their application for leave will be treated as having been withdrawn as soon as the passport is returned in response to the request (para 34J, HC 395). The applicant will not receive a refund of the fee in these circumstances.

Where an applicant does require the return of their passport for urgent travel purposes, it is also possible to request that UKBA consider the application on an urgent basis. UKBA will usually consider this only where the need for travel is as a result of an emergency, such as a family illness.

Applicants requiring either the return of their passport or other document urgently, or urgent consideration of their applications as the result of an immediate need to travel, should contact UKBA on 0870 606 7766 and select option (2).

Status while waiting for a decision and varying existing applications

In many cases where an in-time application to extend leave is made, it is not possible for UKBA to make a decision on the application before the leave expires. As a result, the legislation requires that a system of automatic grants of leave operates while the applicant is waiting for a decision on an in-time application. This also applies to the period while an applicant is appealing against a refusal to extend leave where the application was made in time.

Section 3C of the Immigration Act 1971 (as amended) provides for these automatic extensions of leave. Under section 3C(1), an applicant has an automatic extension of leave where:

- the applicant has existing limited leave and applies, in time, to extend their leave; and

- the original grant of leave expires before the application to extend leave is determined.

As to the *period* of the automatic extension of leave, leave is extended during all of the following periods (s3C(2) 1971 Act):

- the time during which the application is outstanding and has not been either determined or withdrawn;

- the time after UKBA has refused the application but the applicant is still within time to appeal against the decision (there is no automatic extension after the time for appealing has run out or while the applicant is waiting for a decision on an application to appeal out-of-time); and

- the time during which the appeal is outstanding.

What happens when an application is made during a period of automatic leave?

It is only possible to trigger the automatic extension of leave provisions by making an application once. It is not possible to make a further 'application' for leave during the period when leave is extended under section 3C (s3C(4)). However, it is possible during this period to apply to vary the existing application for leave (s3C(5)). To be valid, the Immigration Rules state that applications to 'vary the application' by relying on a new purpose for being granted leave, should be made on the application form specified for the new purpose and comply with all the normal requirements (para 34E, HC 395). The application as varied will then be decided in accordance with the Rules in force at the time that the variation is made (para 34F, HC 395). The idea behind treating the further representations as a 'variation' of the application is that UKBA will then make a decision on all of the bases put forward for staying in the UK at one time. The operation of section 3C and the ability to vary applications for leave was explained in the decision of the Court of Appeal in *JH (Zimbabwe)* (paras 35–42).

So, UKBA will issue only one decision on the application as varied, which will result in one right of appeal. Although it is a single decision, it will cover both grounds on which the application was based unless, in the 'varied' application, the applicant indicates that they are withdrawing the grounds for the original application in favour of the second one.

Variation applications should be considered by PBS applicants in certain circumstances. For example, where a Tier 1 applicant will not have met the mandatory maintenance requirement for the required full three months (for this requirement, ▶see 152–155) until a short time after their leave would otherwise have expired. In these circumstances an initial application should be submitted to maintain their 3C leave and appeal rights. The covering letter should confirm that a second application is to follow shortly once the relevant funds have been in the individual's account for the 90-day period. The risk with this approach clearly increases the longer the time lag between the date of the original expiry of leave and the point at which the 'three month' requirement can be satisfied. That is because UKBA is not required to delay making a decision on the initial application until they have received the further 'varied' application.

Evidence of automatic extensions

Passports are not endorsed and returned showing that an automatic extension of leave under section 3C has come into operation. It is therefore important that evidence of an in-time application to extend leave is kept in the form of copies of the previous leave, the application form, evidence of recorded/special delivery of an in-time application and the acknowledgment received from UKBA. Although there is no endorsement, this evidence itself can demonstrate that the applicant is not an overstayer.

The decision

UKBA makes decisions by applying the requirements contained in the relevant Immigration Rules. In addition, decisions of UKBA must always comply with an applicant's human rights under the ECHR. The Rules require the immigration authorities to "carry out their duties…in compliance with the provisions of the Human Rights Act 1998" (para. 2, HC 395 and ▶see Chapter 12).

The rules for the different categories in which leave can be granted are set out in the relevant parts of this Guide. However there are also general grounds upon which leave to remain can be refused and these are dealt with in Chapter 11.

If the PBS application to extend leave is successful, UKBA will, in most categories, issue a Biometric Residence Permit showing the immigration status of the holder and the date that their leave is valid until.

If however the application is unsuccessful, then this will also be notified in writing together with information about any right of appeal which exists against the decision. If the applicant will continue to have subsisting and valid leave despite the refusal, they will not have a right of appeal. That is because there is a right of appeal against refusal to vary leave only if the applicant has no leave after the decision. Rights of appeal are generally also denied if, for example, the application was not made in-time or the application was to 'switch' into a category which the Immigration Rules would not allow because the applicant had not been admitted with the relevant entry clearance. In most other cases, provided the application was made in-time, there will be a right of appeal against the decision. Before anyone can be removed from the UK, there is always an in-country right of appeal on asylum or human rights grounds unless that appeal can be certified as clearly unfounded.

For more details about appeals, reviews and challenging decisions, ▶see Chapter 13.

APPLYING TO SWITCH CATEGORIES

'Switching' is the term that is commonly used to describe a situation where an applicant, who has leave to be in the UK in one category, wishes to apply for leave to remain in a different category without leaving the UK in order to apply from abroad.

Traditionally, the question of whether an applicant could 'switch' largely depended on whether they were seeking to remain in the UK in a 'permanent' category (ie one leading to settlement) or a 'temporary' category (ie a category in which the applicant is expected to depart the UK after their period of leave). A general, traditional rule of thumb was that a person could not switch to remain in a permanent category, although switching into a temporary category was permitted. There always were, of course, significant exceptions. For example, a person could switch from any category into the category of spouse or dependent relative of a person settled in the UK.

However, the modern position, following amendments to the Rules, is that the broad traditional rule (▶above) no longer provides a useful or reliable base from which to work. For example, specific temporary categories have been set up under the Immigration Rules which have as their purpose the eventual switch of applicants into other long-term, permanent categories (see for example, the Tier 1 (Post-Study Work) category, ▶173). The Rules on switching have been made very much more detailed throughout. The question of whether an individual can switch under the Rules can no longer be reduced to a simple formula. It depends, instead, on the particular Rules that apply to each situation (and see the relevant chapter in this Guide). Anyone in doubt should take advice.

In *all* cases, applicants must satisfy the full requirements of the category of the Rules into which they wish to switch. In addition, in order to obtain fresh leave, none of the general grounds of refusal must apply. So, although switching may be permitted in principle, in some cases it may also be very unrealistic. For example, nothing technically prevents a visitor switching to stay as a person with long residence. However, a person admitted for a visit for up to six months is very unlikely to have ten years' recent lawful residence in the UK.

In addition, in some cases, the applicant's circumstances and history may be inconsistent with the category into which they could technically switch. For example, in certain categories, in order to be admitted in the first place, applicants have to show that they intend to leave the UK at the end of their period of leave (for example visitors). So, in some circumstances, applications to switch may cast doubt on the genuine nature of the basis of the applicant's original entry. A classic example is the applicant who, shortly after their entry in an unrelated capacity, applies to remain permanently on the basis of marriage or partnership. At worst, such applicants are vulnerable to a decision by UKBA that they are an illegal entrant by deception, having misled the immigration authorities about the true reasons for their original entry to the UK. In most cases, of course, it will be clear that there has been a genuine change in the applicant's circumstances and intentions after their original entry.

In all cases, applications to switch should be carefully considered in the light of the applicant's circumstances, immigration history and the Rules under which they were granted their existing leave. If in doubt, advice should always be taken on these issues.

Switching outside the immigration rules

Even if an applicant cannot switch under the Immigration Rules, in all cases UKBA has a discretion to allow switches outside the Rules where it is satisfied that the circumstances merit it. One purpose of the PBS is to reduce the area for the exercise of discretion and decision-making based on non-objective criteria as far as possible. As a result, UKBA has become less and less inclined to exercise discretion to permit switching outside the Rules. In some situations UKBA has operated concessions to permit a switch. However, the policies operated have been changeable and there have been problems with getting UKBA to apply a consistent practice.

4 Sponsorship under the Points-Based System

This chapter covers:

- sponsorship: fundamentals of the system (▶below);
- requirements for qualifying for a licence to be a sponsor (▶83–95);
- allocating roles in order to become a sponsor (▶95–98);
- procedure for applying to be a sponsor (▶98–100);
- sponsorship decisions and 'rating' sponsors (▶100–104);
- operating as a sponsor and complying with sponsor duties (▶104–120);
- UKBA enforcement of the sponsorship system: monitoring, suspension and withdrawal of sponsor licences (▶119–138).

This chapter refers extensively, by paragraph, to the UKBA guidance that is issued to sponsors. We have abbreviated that guidance as follows:

SG Tiers 2 and 5 of the Points-Based System – Sponsor Guidance, 21 December 2010 (version 12/10);

Student SG Tier 4 of the Points-Based System – Sponsor Guidance, October 2010 (version 10/10).

Note: Although the cut off date for this Guide is pre-April 2011, we have published, in Appendix 2, the summary table of changes to the above SG from 6 April 2011 (▶458).

The purpose of this chapter is to deal with who may become a sponsor and how the system of sponsorship operates. Under the system, 'sponsors' have the first responsibility for deciding whether they are prepared to 'sponsor' any particular applicant so as to enable them to come to the UK.

The question of who may come to the UK as a sponsored migrant, including who the sponsor is entitled to issue a 'Certificate of Sponsorship' or a 'Confirmation of Acceptance of Studies' to (both are referred to in this chapter as 'certificates' or 'certificates of sponsorship') is the focus of Chapters 6 (Tier 2); 8 (Tier 4) and 9 (Tier 5). That is because, firstly, the question of 'who may be a sponsored migrant?' is much more naturally part of the question 'who may come to the UK?' under the various tiers. Also, secondly, although the registered sponsor makes the primary decision about whom it may bring, ultimate control remains with the immigration authorities. As the Sponsor Guidance notes state (SG, para 174):

"A certificate of sponsorship acts as confirmation from a licensed sponsor that it wishes to bring a migrant to the [UK] and that to the best of its knowledge that person meets the rules for the assignment of the certificate of sponsorship. We make the final decision on who is allowed to travel or remain here. This decision will be based on the requirements of the Immigration Rules, including whether the migrant has enough points."

Therefore, in addition to this chapter, the above chapters covering whom a sponsor may bring to come the UK are also relevant to sponsor organisations.

SPONSORSHIP: FUNDAMENTALS OF THE SYSTEM

Although the Immigration Rules refer to the sponsorship system, it is largely governed by Guidance outside those Rules and without any clear grounding in any statutory provisions. This has been of deep concern to many since so much control that is otherwise the responsibility of the Secretary of State and the immigration authorities under the Immigration Act 1971, under the sponsorship system is delegated to private bodies. Individual applicants may well feel aggrieved that their immigration rights are, in part, determined by unaccountable private bodies. Those bodies themselves may feel aggrieved that their recruitment and operations are subject to monitoring, regulation and intervention by UKBA in a way that has not been provided for in any statutory system.

UKBA's decisions about sponsor licences and their withdrawal are, however, subject to the supervision of the Administrative Court according to ordinary principles of UK public law. Suspension and withdrawal of a licence may also raise human rights questions, since it has been acknowledged that a licence is capable of amounting to a 'possession' within the meaning of Article 1 of the First Protocol to the ECHR (*R (The London Reading College Limited) v SSHD*, paras 63–68) (▶see 136–137 and 430–435).

At the outset of the Sponsor Guidance, UKBA states that sponsorship is based on two fundamental principles (SG, para 1):

"(i) those who benefit most directly from migration (that is, employers, education providers or other bodies who are bringing in migrants) should play their part in ensuring that the system is not abused; and
(ii) we need to be sure that those applying to come in to the United Kingdom to do a job or to study are eligible to do so and that a reputable employer or education provider genuinely wishes to take them on."

Who must be sponsored?

Sponsorship is necessary to the following categories of entrant:

- Tier 2 (General) Migrant;

- Tier 2 (Intra Company Transfer) Migrant;
- Tier 2 (Ministers of Religion) Migrant;
- Tier 2 (Sportsperson) Migrant;
- Tier 5 (Creative and Sporting);
- Tier 5 (Religious Worker);
- Tier 5 (Charity Worker);
- Tier 5 (Government-authorised Exchange);
- Tier 5 (International Agreement);
- Tier 4 (General) Student;
- Tier 4 (Child) Student.

Tier 2 Migrants must have a 'Certificate of Sponsorship' in order to score points under the PBS for 'attributes' (Immigration Rules, HC 395, Appendix A, paras 63, Tables 11–13). The same applies to the above five categories of Tier 5 (Temporary Worker) Migrants (Rules, Appendix A, Table 13). Tier 4 (General) Students and Tier 4 (Child) Students must, in order to score points for attributes, have a 'Confirmation of Acceptance of Studies' (CAS). Such confirmations will only be "valid" if they have been issued by an "institution with a Tier 4…Student Sponsor Licence" (Rules, Appendix A, Tables 16–17 and paras 116(d), 124(e)). So, without the necessary 'sponsorship', applicants in the above categories cannot score the required points for 'attributes' under Appendix A and their applications fall to be refused under the Rules. There is no right of appeal against a decision of a proposed sponsor to refuse to sponsor an applicant.

The number of migrants that may be issued with a certificate of sponsorship under the Tier 2 (General) Migrant category is subject to an interim 'cap' until 5 April 2011 and it is likely that the cap for this category will also continue after that date. For more details about the Government's policy on the 'cap' generally, ▶see Chapter 2 at 55–59 and for the interim cap applying to the Tier 2 (General) Migrant category, ▶see 106–108 and for the latest details on the permanent cap ▶see 208–210.

Tier 3 is not operative at the present time. Given that it is intended to be "operator led", it is likely that Tier 3 would also involve sponsorship, even if it were not based on exactly the same model as Tiers 2, 4 and 5.

Those seeking entry under Tier 1 or to study/work in one of the routes that remains outside the PBS (▶see Chapter 10), do not need to comply with the sponsorship requirements.

How does a body 'sponsor' an applicant?

Only those who have a sponsor 'licence' are eligible to be sponsors under the scheme. In order to obtain a licence, the body has to apply to UKBA. Once a licence has been obtained, the body may then assign a 'Certificates of Sponsorship' (COS) (to an employee) and/or a 'Confirmation of

Acceptance of Studies' (CAS) (to a student). Before February 2010, in some cases, the sponsor was able to issue a 'visa letter' instead of a CAS. In this chapter, we shall refer to all three, ie COSs, CASs and visa letters as 'certificates' or 'certificates of sponsorship'.

Each certificate has its own unique reference number which comes into being when the sponsor issues it. When the sponsor assigns a certificate to an applicant, it enters the details on an electronic database known as the 'sponsor management system' (SMS) (for more details about the sponsor SMS, see http://www.ukba.homeoffice.gov.uk/employers/points/sponsoring migrants/sms/whatissms/). Applicants need to be told that reference number because they then provide it in their application to UKBA for entry clearance or leave to remain.

Does sponsorship confer 'leave'?

No. Ultimate responsibility for immigration control remains in the hands of the immigration authorities. Sponsors cannot grant leave. After a sponsor has assigned a certificate to an applicant, it is then used in the application for leave and enables the applicant to score points for 'attributes' under the PBS.

Where are the requirements for becoming a sponsor set out?

In order to qualify to become a sponsor, the body or institution must satisfy the requirements that are set out in the detailed 'Sponsor Guidance' which is available at: www.ukba.homeoffice.gov.uk/sitecontent/documents/employersandsponsors/pbsguidance/. At the point we go to press, there is Sponsor Guidance for Tier 2 and Tier 5 sponsors issued on 21 December 2010 (version 12/10) and separate Guidance for Tier 4 sponsors issued on 1 October 2010 (version 1010). The Guidance is also supported by appendices (listed Appendix A, B etc). There is additional guidance issued for 'Highly Trusted' Sponsors under Tier 4 (▶see 287–291). The UKBA website also contains much of the information contained in the Sponsor Guidance, under a section headed 'How do I sponsor a migrant?'. In this chapter we cover much of the information provided in the Guidance issued to sponsors, although users will note that the Guidance is subject to frequent change.

Although we have, in this chapter, provided paragraph references to the Sponsor Guidance (abbreviated to 'SG' for the Tiers 2 and 5 Guidance and 'Student SG' for the Tier 4 Guidance), users should take note that the paragraph references are likely to change as the scheme continues to be modified. Another form of guidance that is of importance to sponsors is that which relates to illegal working (see www.ukba.homeoffice.gov.uk/employers/.

How does a sponsor apply for a licence?

The sponsor licence application procedure is on-line only and relevant form can be accessed on UKBA's website. The decision is made and sponsor licences are issued by UKBA's 'sponsor licensing team'. The process is more fully described below at ▶98. Processing times can vary but decisions have often taken between two to three months. However, sponsors should expect the process to take longer if UKBA decides to carry out a visit to the sponsor's premises. It is possible to apply for UKBA to expedite the consideration process. If this is necessary, the sponsor should explain fully the reasons why it is imperative that they have an early decision and they should explain also the reasons for the timing of their application for a licence.

Register of sponsors

UKBA maintains a public 'register' of sponsors on its website (www.ukba. homeoffice.gov.uk/employers/points/sponsoringmigrants/registerofspons ors/). Applicants can therefore check the list of licensed sponsors before they set about their plans to come to the UK for sponsored work or study.

REQUIREMENTS FOR QUALIFYING FOR A LICENCE TO BE A SPONSOR

In order to obtain a licence, the relevant employer or educational institution must first make an application to UKBA. The requirements that must be met in order to qualify are outlined in the Sponsor Guidance and they are also contained on other pages of the UKBA website.

Overview of the requirements

The three general questions for UKBA in deciding an application for a body to become a sponsor are as follows (SG, paras 7, 43; Student SG paras 7–8, 64).

- Is the proposed sponsor a genuine organisation, operating lawfully in the UK? The proposed sponsor has to provide certain documents in order to prove that it is.

- Is the proposed sponsor dependable and reliable? Or does it represent a threat to immigration control? To judge this UKBA states that it will look at the history and background of the organisation, at its 'key personnel' (see below) and the people who control it. If there is any evidence of a history of dishonest conduct or immigration crime, this will be viewed seriously and may lead to UKBA refusing the application.

- Is the proposed sponsor capable of carrying out its duties as a sponsor? (for sponsor duties, ▶see 114). UKBA states that it will judge this by looking at the organisation's processes and human resource practices to ensure that it will be able to fulfil its sponsor duties. It may do this by visiting the sponsor, either before the licence is granted, or afterwards. If, after a visit, UKBA has significant doubts, it may award a 'B' rated licence (▶see below 101–102) to the new sponsor. In more serious cases, UKBA may refuse the application.

The particular requirements that must be satisfied in order to obtain a sponsor licence are as follows. The proposed sponsor must (SG, paras 6–7, 54–55, 62–63, 105):

1) meet the 'eligibility' criteria (▶below) ie:
- provide proof that they are based in the UK;
- provide original or certified copies of certain documents to show that they are genuine and operating or trading lawfully in the UK;

2) meet the 'suitability' criteria (▶85) ie that they have effective human resources systems and have personnel who are reliable so that there are no reasons to think that they are a threat to immigration control;

3) meet the specific requirements that apply to the appropriate tier or category under which they are applying to register (▶88);

4) not fall to be refused on the bases of other, general reasons for refusal given in the Sponsor Guidance (▶94); and

5) agree to comply with the duties of sponsorship (▶114).

We look at each of the above in turn immediately below, except that the 'duties' of a sponsor are dealt with at ▶114–120. Sponsorship duties is a topic in itself: they are ongoing and are also relevant to the whether the body will be able to continue to be a sponsor. At the stage of applying for a licence, the requirement is that the proposed sponsor 'agrees' to comply with the duties of sponsorship.

In addition, before a proposed sponsor will be granted a licence, they must complete and submit the appropriate online application and pay the correct fee (SG, para 7). We look more at the procedure for applying to be a sponsor separately (▶98–100).

'Eligibility' criteria

The applicant must (SG, paras 54–55; Student SG, paras 75–76 and SG Appendix A):

- provide proof that they are based in the UK; and
- provide original or certified copies of certain documents to show that they are genuine and operating or trading lawfully in the UK.

The documents that are required are set out in Appendix A to the Guidance which contains three lists, namely documents that are: 'Mandatory' (List A), 'Primary' (List B) and 'Secondary' (List C). The specific documents that are required from those lists depend upon the type of organisation that is applying for a sponsor licence. There are thirteen 'types' of applicant organisation:

- start-up companies,
- public limited companies;
- public bodies;
- overseas governments, international organisations or diplomatic missions;

- private limited companies (there are a number of different entities that fall under this umbrella);
- self-employed (including partnerships, sole traders and franchises);
- universities/education providers;
- nursing homes/care homes;
- hotel/catering establishments;
- charities;
- religious/faith bodies;
- sport;
- companies seeking intra company transfers (ICTs).

For each of the above types of applicant organisation, Appendix A of the Guidance states the documents that are required. The general approach is that the documents in List A are always required; those in List B are mandatory for certain types of organisation only and applicants have a choice of which documents from List C to provide in order to supplement the mandatory documents (see also, SG para 30).

'Suitability' criteria

In order to assess whether the organisation is 'suitable', UKBA will look at the human resources systems that it has in place, at the history of persons within the organisation to see whether they might constitute a threat to the system and at whether there is any evidence of previous non-compliance (SG, paras 62–63; Student SG, para 84).

Human resources systems

UKBA must be satisfied that the sponsor has effective human resource systems in place (SG, para 63). The way in which this is assessed is set out on separate pages of the UKBA website headed 'How do I sponsor a migrant? How we rate human resource systems'. It is dealt with under four main 'areas' as follows:

Area 1: monitoring immigration status and preventing illegal employment Sponsors must have procedures in place to keep a photocopy or electronic copy of each migrant's passport or UK immigration status document (or ID card) showing that they are allowed to work or study. They must also not employ a migrant where they have no leave to enter/remain, or the conditions of their leave prevent them from doing the job. UKBA strongly recommends that sponsors follow the procedures set out in the 'Comprehensive guidance for employers on preventing illegal working' which may be found on the UKBA website.

Area 2: maintaining migrant contact details Sponsors must maintain a procedure for keeping an updated record of each migrant's contact details.

Area 3: Recordkeeping Sponsors must keep easily accessible records concerning each migrant that it is able to make available to UKBA at short notice. The kinds of records concerned are: details of the migrant's recruitment (so that UKBA can judge whether the sponsor is meeting the requirements of the resident labour market test where required) and the migrant's personnel file with copies of any relevant qualifications or professional accreditations and a record of their attendance.

Area 4: Migrant tracking and monitoring Sponsors must have systems in place to track and monitor their sponsored migrants. This area is closely linked to the duties on sponsors to report absences, failures to attend or enrol or other changes in the migrant's circumstances (▶see below at 115–116).

Area 5: Professional accreditations and registrations Sponsors must ensure that they have recruitment systems in place to check professional registrations or accreditations where such are required by law. Copies of the appropriate registration documents should be kept by the sponsor.

History of persons within the organisation

In addition, the applicant organisation will not meet the 'suitability' criteria if any of the following people have a history that shows that the organisation is not suitable to be given a licence, namely any (SG, para 63 read with para 79):

- of the organisation's owners;
- of the organisation's directors;
- person involved in the day-to-day running of the organisation; or
- person who the organisation has named on the sponsor application form as 'authorising officer', 'key contact' or 'level 1 user' (those applying for sponsorship are required to nominate persons within the organisation to fulfil these roles, ▶see further below 95–98 for an explanation of them).

The above people may be treated as having a history that shows that the organisation is not suitable to be given a licence if any of them (SG, para 63 read with SG Appendix B):

- have any criminal convictions in their name for an offence that is listed in Appendix B to the Sponsor Guidance (▶see below) and which is not 'spent' under the Rehabilitation of Offenders Act 1974;
- have any criminal convictions in their name for an offence other than one that is listed in Appendix B, which is not 'spent' under the Rehabilitation of Offenders Act 1974 and which UKBA, at its discretion, decides to take into account; or
- has been given a civil penalty for immigration matters.

Criminal convictions Appendix B of the Sponsor Guidance contains a very long list of immigration-related criminal offences under the following immigration legislation: the Immigration Act 1971; the Asylum and Immigration Act 1996; the Immigration and Asylum Act 1999; the Nationality, Immigration and Asylum Act 2002; the Asylum and Immigration (Treatment of Claimants etc) Act 2004; the Immigration, Asylum and Nationality Act 2006; the UK Border Act 2007; and the Accession (Immigration and Worker Registration) Regulations 2004. The offences include (but are by no means limited to) those related to: entering/remaining in the UK in breach of the immigration law; facilitating breaches of immigration law; making false statements or representations, illegal employment; offences related to the provision and advertisement of immigration advice/services; failure by an employer or financial institution to disclose information to the Secretary of State; trafficking people for exploitation; assaulting/ obstructing officers. Appendix B also specifies certain offences under non-immigration legislation relating to forgery (under the Forgery and Counterfeiting Act 1981), the possession of false identity documents (under the Identity Cards Act 2006) and trafficking for sexual exploitation (under the Sexual Offences Act 2003).

Further details given in the Sponsor Guidance relating to decisions made on applications state that UKBA "will" refuse an application for a licence where the sponsor or any of the above-listed relevant persons have an 'unspent' conviction for (SG, para 105 and footnote 3):

- any offence under the above Acts of 1971, 1999, 2002, 2006 and 2007 (but note that this part of the SG omits reference to the 1996 and 2004 Acts and the 2004 Regulations despite the fact that they are listed in Appendix B – ▶see above);
- any offence under the Immigration Act 1988 or the Asylum and Immigration Appeals Act 1993 (although neither of these Acts are referred to in Appendix B);
- trafficking for sexual exploitation; or
- "any other offence" which, in UKBA's view, suggests that the person is a risk to immigration control, "for example offences involving dishonesty or deception including the offences listed in Appendix B)...".

Both criminal offending and civil penalties (▶below) may also be taken into account in determining how a sponsor will be 'rated', ie if it is granted a licence (▶see 100–102).

Civil penalties The relevant civil penalties (as listed in Appendix C to the SG) are those for:

- carrying clandestine entrants (s32–37 1999 Act);
- carrying passengers without proper documentation (ss40–41 1999 Act);
- bringing passengers to the UK without authority to carry (s124 2002 Act);
- employing an illegal migrant worker (s15 2006 Act).

The Guidance is not entirely clear as to how suitability will be assessed on the basis of such civil penalties. In the main body of the Guidance, it is stated that UKBA will look at the question of whether any of the above named persons have ever been given a civil penalty (SG, para 63). However, Appendix C to the Guidance ('List of Civil Penalties') states that the imposition of a civil penalty within the previous five years may lead to an application being refused. Further details given within the main part of the Guidance state that UKBA will refuse the application if the sponsor or any of the above-listed relevant persons have (SG, para 105 and footnote 3):

- within the past 12 months been issued with a civil penalty under s15 2006 Act for employing one or more migrant workers and certain other criteria (set out in the Guidance) are met; or

- been issued with a civil penalty under any of the provisions listed in Appendix C to the Guidance (▶see above) and have not paid it (unless the penalty was withdrawn or cancelled on appeal).

Summing up on civil penalties, it seems that UKBA will almost certainly refuse the application on the basis of a civil penalty in the circumstances immediately above, that it will consider refusing on the basis of any other civil penalty issued in the previous five years and that it may possibly (but it is unlikely) consider refusing if the penalty was issued before that time.

Other evidence of non-compliance An organisation may also not meet the 'suitability' criteria if UKBA has any other evidence of non-compliance, by the organisation, with the sponsor or immigration system (SG, para 63).

Meeting the requirements that apply to the appropriate tier or category under which they are applying to register

Sponsors are required, on the online application form, to indicate the tiers, categories or sub-categories for which they wish to be issued with a licence. If the application is granted, the sponsor will be able to sponsor migrants but only under the particular tiers/categories that it has applied for and which have been agreed by UKBA (SG, para 37). If the prospective sponsor does not meet any criteria that it is necessary to satisfy in order to sponsor migrants in a particular tier or category, the sponsor will not be granted a licence in that tier/category (SG, para 105, second bullet point).

For details about the separate question of which migrants a sponsor who has obtained a licence may issue a certificate to, ▶see 80–81 in summary and the relevant chapter of this Guide dealing with Tiers 2, 4 and 5.

Identifying the tier or category-specific requirements that need to be satisfied in order to be a sponsor in that particular tier or category is a process that overlaps with the requirement to produce specific documents from Appendix A to the Sponsor Guidance, depending on the particular nature of the proposed sponsor (▶see under 'eligibility' criteria above, 84). However, it is possible to give the following additional 'tier specific' guidance relevant to obtaining a sponsor licence.

Tier 2 (Intra Company Transfer)

A sponsor hoping to bring migrants in under the Tier 2 (Intra Company Transfer) category, must show that it has a direct link, by "common ownership or control" with the overseas entity which employs the proposed sponsored migrant. The sponsor must provide the supporting evidence listed in Appendix A to the SG to show this direct link (SG, paras 228–229, 231). The circumstances in which the corporate relationship between the sponsor and the entity where the migrant is presently employed will amount to "common ownership or control" are set out in some detail in the SG (see at para 229). Note that it will not be sufficient to establish a link for Tier 2 (ICT) purposes simply that one individual owns shares in both companies (SG, para 230).

Tier 2 (Ministers of Religion) and Tier 5 (Temporary Workers) – Religious Workers

A sponsor wishing to apply for a licence under either of these two categories must be a *bona fide* religious organisation which is either a registered, excepted or exempted UK charity according to the relevant charity legislation in force, or an ecclesiastical corporation established for charitable purposes. In Northern Ireland, the organisation must have obtained charitable status for tax purposes from HM Revenue and Customs. Charities which are not registered according to the relevant charity legislation must explain this in the licence application (SG, paras 255, 326).

In addition, the proposed sponsor should be "the structure for a faith-based community with a common system of belief and spiritual goals, codes of behaviour and religious practice, which exists to support and/or propagate those common beliefs and practices" and where such beliefs (SG, paras 255, 326):

- "include any religious belief or similar philosophical belief in something transcendental, metaphysical or ultimate"; and
- "exclude any philosophical or political belief concerned with man, unless that belief is similar to religious belief."

Further, the proposed sponsor must not "exclude from its community on the basis of gender, nationality or ethnicity" and it must receive "financial and material support for its core religious ministry from its congregation or community on a voluntary basis only without promise or coercion". The proposed community must not breach or encourage the breach of UK legislation, nor operate against the public interest or personal or family life (SG, paras 255, 326).

Tier 2 (Sportspersons)

Applications for a licence must be accompanied by the documents listed in Appendix A to the SG. This includes an endorsement from the UKBA-recognised governing body for the sport. If the sport does not have a sports council recognised governing body, contact can be made with UKBA on at EmploymentPolicy@ukba.gsi.gov.uk who will then consult with, among others, the Department for Culture, Media and Sport (SG, paras 263–264)

A sponsor can only tick one sport on the sponsor licence application form. If the body wants to sponsor applicants in more than one sport, then it should list the other sports in the part of the application where it gives its reasons for the number of certificates that it requires. The appropriate governing body for each sport must be provided (SG, para 266).

Tier 4 Students

In order to be a sponsor under Tier 4, the body must be the education provider that offers courses of study to students. The exceptions to this are (Student SG, para 19):

- the Foundation Programme Office can be the sponsor for all migrants on the two-year Foundation Programme for post graduate doctors;
- where the student's programme of study forms part of an overseas degree course and the prospective sponsor in the UK is linked by common ownership or control to the overseas university – in these cases UKBA will ask for proof of those links before it will consider granting a sponsor licence.

State schools, including those with sixth forms, cannot sponsor students under Tier 4. Applications for a Tier 4 licence from a state school will be rejected and the fee will be refunded (Student SG, paras 4, 28). Tier 4 (Child) Student is the route for children aged between 4 and 17 to be educated in the UK. For those over the age of 16, Tier 4 (General) Student is the appropriate route.

Education providers applying for a licence must also show that they (Student SG, para 25):

- have been inspected or audited (▶below); or
- are subject to review by an appropriate body (▶below); or
- hold valid accreditation, or provisional accreditation where permitted (▶below); or
- for overseas providers, directly offer short-term "study abroad" programmes in their own premises in the UK.

An education provider that is subject to the system of public reviews, as the result of being funded publicly or because it has been granted UK degree awarding status, must, show that it has been inspected or audited by one of the following bodies (Student SG, para 26):

- the Quality Assurance Agency for Higher Education (UK wide);
- the Office for Standards in Education ie 'Ofsted' (Ofsted reports for private further education providers that have been inspected by Ofsted because

the provider delivers some courses that are publically funded, are also accepted);

- the Bridge Schools Inspectorate (England);
- the Schools Inspection Service (England);
- Her Majesty's Inspectorate of Education (Scotland);
- Estyn (Wales);
- the Education and Training Inspectorate (Northern Ireland); or
- the Independent Schools Inspectorate (ISI) (UK wide).

An educational provider that is outside the system of public reviews referred to above must hold valid accreditation from one of the following UKBA-approved bodies (Student SG, para 29):

- the Office for Standards in Education (Ofsted);
- Accreditation UK – a British Council scheme offering an accreditation service for English language schools;
- the British Accreditation Council (BAC), which offers a more general accreditation service covering a wide range of educational providers and their courses;
- the Accreditation Service for International Colleges (ASIC), which offers a general accreditation service covering a wide range of educational establishments and their courses;
- the Accreditation Body for Language Services, which offers accreditation for English language schools; or
- the Church of England – Ministry Division, which offers a quality assurance and accreditation service for institutions offering training for Christian ministry in the participating churches.

Where the education provider is a new, private further education institution that has been trading for less than 18 months and is in the process of applying for accreditation from one of the UKBA-approved bodies listed immediately above, UKBA states that it will accept a provisional accreditation (known as 'Stage 2') from one of these accreditation bodies. However, this will be on the condition that the provider obtains full academic accreditation ('Stage 3') within 12 months. New sponsors with Stage 2 accreditation will be 'B' rated until they reach Stage 3 accreditation (Student SG, para 30).

Independent schools that are newly independent and that do not yet have an inspection report from the Independent Schools Inspectorate must show that they are formally registered (in England, that is, through the Department for Children, Schools and Families) (Student SG, para 31).

Where the course is being provided by an overseas higher education institution which offers only part of the course in the UK and part of the course abroad, UK accreditation is not required. However, there are other requirements that apply that are detailed in the Guidance (Student SG, paras 32–35). UK accreditation is required, however, if the overseas provider teaches full programmes to students in the UK or where the study abroad programme is being delivered using a third-party, for example a UK university (Student SG, para 36)

The documents required to be provided in support of an application by a prospective student sponsor are listed in Appendix A to the Sponsor Guidance (in some cases those in Appendix B and C should be provided). Generally prospective student sponsors will need documentary evidence that they are subject to a system of reviews or hold valid accreditation. The last inspection report from the accreditation body should also be provided (Student SG, paras 47–48).

Note that there are procedures in place for education accrediting bodies to inform UKBA promptly when a provider's accreditation is removed (Student SG, para 38).

Tier 5 (Youth Mobility Scheme)

Under the Youth Mobility Scheme, national governments, rather than individual employers or organisations, become sponsors. It is only open to nationals of those countries that the UK does not, in general, consider to be a threat to immigration control and with whom the UK has agreed reciprocal arrangements, enabling young British citizens to travel abroad and be admitted on similar terms.

Tier 5 (Temporary Workers) – Creative and Sporting

A Tier 5 sponsor may not necessarily have a direct employer/employee relationship with the sponsored migrant – UKBA acknowledges that a number of different arrangements exist particularly in the arts and entertainments industry (SG, para 289).

To be issued with a licence under this subcategory ie to sponsor sports people and their entourages, the proposed sponsor must be a (SG, para 305):

- sporting body;
- sports club;
- events organiser; or
- other organiser operating, or intending to operate, in the sporting sector.

As part of the application, the sponsor must submit an endorsement from the UKBA-recognised governing body for the sport (a list is available on the UKBA website) (SG, para 305). An agent cannot be a sponsor under the Tier 5 sporting subcategory (SG, para 306). If the relevant sport is one that does not have a governing body that is recognised for the sport, the proposed sponsor should contact the sport's governing body and ask them to contact UKBA via employmentpolicy@ukba.gsi.gov.uk so that they can apply to be recognised (SG, para 307).

In order to be issued with a licence to sponsor creative workers and their entourage, the proposed sponsor must be operating or intend to operate in the creative sector. Examples include (SG, para 296): a national body; an event organiser; a producer; a venue; an agent; or another similar organisation.

The proposed sponsor must commit to following any applicable Codes of Practice in relation to taking into account the needs of the resident labour market in that particular field. Under this subcategory, the Codes of Practice operate in the following three areas and are available on the UKBA website (SG, para 296):

- dance;
- theatre; and
- film and television.

Tier 5 (Temporary Workers) – Government Authorised Exchange

Individual employers and educational institutions are not permitted to be sponsors under this subcategory. The exceptions to this are where an educational institution is recruiting a sponsored researcher, or where the actual employer is a government department or executive agency of such a department (SG, paras 333, 338). Aside from these exceptions, there will be a separate 'overarching body' which is responsible for administering the exchange scheme. That overarching body will act as the sponsor of the migrant and must apply for a licence.

Both the scheme itself and the overarching body must be supported by a UK government department or one of its executive agencies (SG, para 334). Schemes are only likely to get support if: they will not harm the resident labour market; provide skilled work for the migrant (ie at S/NVQ3 or above); comply with UK and European legislation; and are sufficiently protected from abuse (SG, para 335).

To show that the scheme is supported by a government department (or one of its executive agencies), the relevant accounting officer must write to the Chief Executive of UKBA with details of the overarching body and confirming that (SG, para 336):

- the scheme satisfies all the requirements which government departments must apply when deciding on which exchange schemes to support;
- the scheme will help the relevant department to deliver one or more of its public service agreement (PSA) obligations, or that it will contribute to the department's wider objectives;
- the government department is satisfied to the best of its knowledge that the overarching body is capable of meeting its sponsor duties; and
- if significant numbers of migrants under the exchange scheme breach the Immigration Rules, the supporting government department understands that UKBA may end the scheme.

After the above process has been gone through, the overarching body is to submit an application for a sponsor licence enclosing all the relevant documentation (SG, para 338).

Tier 5 (Temporary workers) – International Agreement

Under this subcategory, a sponsor can bring a migrant to the UK under contract to provide a service that is covered under international law; including: the General Agreement on Trade in Services (GATS); similar agreements between the UK and another country; employees of overseas governments and international organisations; and private servants in diplomatic households (SG, para 341).

To be issued with a licence as a sponsor of private servants in diplomatic households or households of officials working for international organisations, or as the sponsor of employees of overseas governments and international organisations, the proposed sponsor must be a diplomatic mission or an international organisation recognised by the UK (SG, paras 342, 344).

To be licensed to sponsor migrants under GATS or other international agreements, the proposed sponsor must show that the job or employment is covered by the terms of the agreement (SG, para 347).

Other reasons for refusal given in the Sponsor Guidance

There are a number of miscellaneous reasons that are given in the Sponsor Guidance that could lead to a refusal of an application for a licence. The Guidance states that applications "will" be refused if the sponsor (or any of its owners, directors, persons involved in its day-to-day running; or person whom the organisation has named on the sponsor application form either as 'authorising officer', 'key contact' or 'level 1 user' – all referred to below as "relevant persons")) (SG, para 105 and footnote 3):

- submits false documents in support of the application to become a sponsor; or
- is legally prohibited from becoming a company director unless that is because s/he is an undischarged bankrupt (but note that an 'authorising officer' (▶see 95–96) may not be an undischarged bankrupt).

The Guidance further states that UKBA "will normally" refuse an application if the sponsor or any other relevant person has previously been dishonest in its dealings with the immigration authorities (SG, para 106).

Finally, the Guidance states that UKBA "may" refuse an application if the sponsor or any other relevant person (SG, para 108):

- has a previous record of non-compliance or poor compliance with the duties of sponsorship or the work permit scheme;
- has been asked to provide evidence to allow UKBA to determine whether it has been complying with the duties of sponsorship or work permit

arrangements and has refused or failed to do so;

- does not have the ability to comply with the sponsor duties (▶see 114–118);
- has previously had a sponsor licence withdrawn unless they can demonstrate that they have put matters right;
- have, or have been involved with, any organisation that has been removed from the register of education and training providers maintained by the Department for Innovation, Universities and Skills; or
- have or have been involved with any organisation that has had its authorisation removed by the Office of the Immigration Services Commissioner (responsible for supervising those who give immigration advice).

In making its decision in any of the above circumstances in which UKBA "may" refuse the application, it will take into account the seriousness of the past behaviour, the length of time that has since passed and what has been done since then to improve the circumstances (SG, para 109). If a licence is still given although any of these circumstances apply in which UKBA "may" refuse, it is likely that the sponsor will be given a 'B' rating (SG, para 110).

ALLOCATING ROLES IN ORDER TO BECOME A SPONSOR

Sponsors must allocate responsibilities to staff members so that the responsibilities within the organisation for operating the sponsor system are clear. The 'key personnel' are (SG, para 72):

- authorising officer;
- key contact;
- level 1 user;
- level 2 user.

There can only be one authorising officer and one key contact but a sponsor may designate more than one person to fulfil the functions of level 1 and level 2 user (SG, para 74). The authorising officer and the key contact may also be set up as level 1 and 2 users and it is only level 1 or level 2 users who will have access to the 'sponsor management system' (▶104) (SG, para 76). The prospective sponsor must name the authorising officer, key contact and level 1 user on the application form. Level 2 users may only be appointed after a licence has been granted. All of the key personnel must be permanently based in the UK (SG, paras 74–75).

UKBA will take into account failures by the above personnel to properly manage or use the system if it is considering taking any form of enforcement action (▶see below 119–138) in relation to the licence (SG, para 77). In addition, a failure to have an authorising officer in place at all times can result in a sponsor's licence being withdrawn, suspended or downgraded (SG, para 86). Also prior to granting a licence, UKBA will run checks on this history on all the above personnel (other than the level 2 users who are not named at the time of the application), and on the owner/s, director/s and any other person/s involved in the day to day running of the potential sponsor (SG, para 86 and ▶see above at 95).

Authorising officer

Responsibility for the actions of the authorising officer lies with the sponsor themselves and so UKBA suggests that the sponsor ensures that the authorising officer is a responsible and competent person within the organisation (SG, para 81). The authorising officer will be responsible for deciding how many people among the sponsor's staff will have access to the sponsor management system and is also responsible for how they use that system (SG, para 78, 84). The authorising officer must be a paid staff member or office holder in the organisation (SG, para 82). The authorising officer must not be (SG, para 82):

- a representative;
- a contractor or consultant who is contracted for a specific project;
- an employee of a third party organisation engaged to deliver all, or part of, the sponsor's human resource function;
- a temporary member of staff supplied by an agency; or
- an undischarged bankrupt.

Where the sponsor has overseas branches, it can only appoint an authorising officer who is based in the UK branch (SG, para 83).

The authorising officer does not have access to the sponsor management system automatically. To get access to the system, the authorising officer must also be a level 1 or level 2 user (SG, para 85).

Key contact

The key contact acts as the main point of contact between UKBA and the sponsor. The key contact must not be (SG, para 87):

- a contractor;
- a consultant who is contracted for a specific purpose;
- an employee of a third party organisation engaged to deliver all, or part of, the sponsor's human resources functions; or
- a temporary staff member supplied by an agency.

The key contact must be a paid staff member or office holder in the organisation, or a UK based representative (SG, para 87). The key contact also does not have automatic access to the sponsor management system although they can obtain access by being made a level 1 or level 2 user (SG, para 90). Where the sponsor has overseas branches, it can only appoint a key contact who is based in the UK branch (SG, para 88).

Level 1 users

The level 1 user will carry out the sponsor's day to day activities by using the sponsor management system (▶see 104–105). They can (SG, para 91):

- request additional level 1 users and add level 2 users to the sponsor management system or remove them;
- assign certificates of sponsorship to migrants;
- request an increase in the number of certificates that a sponsor can assign (its limit);
- notify UKBA of minor changes to the sponsor's details;
- complete the change of circumstances section on the sponsor management system;
- report migrant activity eg if the migrant goes missing or does not enrol for their course;
- withdraw certificates of sponsorship; and
- amend user details.

When the sponsor applies for a licence, it is only possible to nominate one level 1 user. After the licence has been issued, the sponsor can add further users (SG, para 92). The level 1 user must be a paid staff member or office holder within the sponsor organisation, or an employee of a third party organisation whom the sponsor engages in order to deliver some of their human resources function. The level 1 user must not be (SG, para 94):

- a contractor;
- a consultant who is contracted for a specific project; or
- a temporary staff member supplied by an agency.

A UK-based representative is able to act as the level 1 user (SG, para 95).

Level 2 users

The sponsor may appoint however many level 2 users it requires, although the authorised functions of level 2 users are more restricted than those of level 1 users (SG, para 97).

Level 2 users may (SG, para 97):

- assign certificates to migrants; and
- report migrant activity to UKBA.

The level 2 user must be (SG, para 99):

- a paid staff member or office holder within the sponsor organisation; or
- an employee of a third party organisation engaged by the sponsor to deliver some of their human resource function, or
- a staff member supplied by an employment agency.

A UK-based representative can also act as a level 2 user (SG, para 101).

Level 2 users must not be a contractor or a consultant who is contracted for a specific project (SG, para 100). In the Tier 5 (Government Authorised Exchange) subcategory, the 'overarching' sponsor is able to appoint level 2 users in the organisation that is part of the exchange programme (SG, para 102).

The role of representatives and third party organisations

It will be seen from the above that UK-based representatives can be allocated to the roles of key contact and level 1 and/or level 2 users, but the authorising officer must not be a representative. In addition, level 1 and 2 user roles may be taken up by employees of a third party organisation to which the sponsor has farmed out human resource functions. However, neither the role of authorising officer nor key contact can be allocated to an employee of a third party organisation.

Checks on the authorising officer, key contact and level 1 user

The authorising officer, key contact and level 1 user must be named in the on-line sponsor licence application form and they will therefore be checked by UKBA. As set out above (▶86–88), UKBA will look at whether they have unspent convictions (the police national computer will be used for this) and UKBA will also check its own records including to see whether any of them have been issued with a civil penalty (SG, para 79).

APPLYING TO BE A SPONSOR

Potential sponsors are asked to state, in their application for which tiers, categories or sub-categories they seek a licence. They may only sponsor migrants under the tiers and (sub) categories for which they are licensed. It is also possible to apply for further tiers to be added to the licence once the initial licence has been obtained. If a sponsor wishes to do this, they will need to complete a new online application form, using their unique sponsor licence number, and paying the appropriate additional fee (SG, paras 37–38).

The sponsor licence application

Sponsor applications must be filed on line using the form provided on the UKBA website (SG, paras 6, 18). The application must be made by the proposed sponsor. It may not be submitted by a representative although a representative can of course advise and assist the sponsor through the process. If the application is submitted by a representative, UKBA will refuse it (SG, para 19). UKBA considers that completing the application should take approximately 30 minutes if all of the required information has been gathered in advance (SG, para 21). Sponsors should keep a copy of the form that they have submitted. Sponsors have to pay a fee in order to apply for a licence. For details of fees see http://ukba.homeoffice.gov.uk/employers/points/sponsoringmigrants/costs (SG, paras 7, 20, 39).

The supporting documents

Within 14 days of the online application having been made, the proposed sponsor must send to UKBA the submission sheet for the application, signed by the authorising officer, together with the documents in support of the application and the fee (unless that was paid online) (SG, para 20). The documents sent must either be originals, or certified copies ie copies of the original which have a signed statement, either from the person who issued the document or a solicitor/notary that confirms that it is an accurate copy of the original. UKBA may, however, still ask to see the original document. Documents that need to be translated must be accompanied by a certified translation. The Guidance requires that the translator's credentials should be provided as well as their confirmation that the translation is accurate (SG, paras 33–34).

Single entity and multiple branch registration

UKBA's Guidance appreciates that sponsors may have a number of different offices, UK-based subsidiaries or entities, locations or campuses and refers to all of these different entities as 'branches'. The licensing arrangements for these sponsors can be handled in any of the following ways: (SG, para 44; Student SG, para 65):

- by applying for a single licence that includes the head office and all branches in the UK;
- by grouping a number of branches into a single licence (the example given in the Guidance is where a chain enterprise decides to register all of its branches in a single licence); or
- by each branch applying for its own separate licence.

Where a sponsor applies for a single licence, UKBA states that it reserves the right to request evidence showing that any head office and/or group of branches that have been listed in the application are linked by common ownership or control (SG, para 45).

One advantage of individual licences is that, if one branch has its licence downgraded or withdrawn, UKBA will not automatically take the same action against the other branches. However, in those circumstances, UKBA is likely to investigate the other branches as it is entitled to do if they are all listed under the licence (SG, para 46). However where a single sponsor is licensed as 'head office and all UK branches' (UKBA gives the example of an English language school with branches across the UK – Student SG, para 68), the removal or downgrading of its licences will apply to all branches (SG, para 47).

Tier 4 sponsors Tier 4 sponsors may include a 'partner' institution on their licence. This applies where the partner institution is giving pre-sessional courses to students who will later undertake their main course of study with the sponsor themselves. In these circumstances, UKBA does not require that the sponsor and partner are linked by common ownership or control. UKBA will, however, require evidence that the partner institution has valid accreditation (Student SG, para 66). Note that where a partner institution is named on a standard Tier 4 licence and the partner institution's own licence is withdrawn, UKBA will consider taking action against the sponsor as well (Student SG, para 69). If a Tier 4 sponsor becomes a Highly Trusted Sponsor (HTS), any branches or partner institutions named on the standard licence, will also benefit from the HTS status (Student SG, para 71).

Franchises If an organisation, sole trader or partnership controls a number of franchises, it can either obtain a licence as a 'head office and all UK branches', or it can apply for all of the individual franchises to be licensed separately. But that choice is not available if the franchises are not controlled by one organisation but are separate businesses. If that is the case then each franchise must obtain an individual licence (SG, paras 51–52; Student SG, paras 72–73).

Employment agencies These agencies can only apply for a licence in order to employ migrants within their own organisation. Where an agency is supplying migrants to other businesses then it is those businesses that are responsible for sponsoring them. In addition, they may only do so if they have full responsibility for determining the duties and functions of the migrant and for paying the migrant's wages (SG, para 49).

DECISIONS AND RATINGS

Decisions on applications are made by officers at UKBA's 'Sponsor Licensing Unit'.

UKBA's checks to ensure that sponsors are compliant

UKBA states that it refers all applications for a licence for extensive checks which may include an on-site visit by its 'visiting officers'. As well as investigating issues concerning the licence application, visiting officers can refer cases for civil penalties or for the consideration of criminal prosecution if they find evidence of wrongdoing. Checks may also be made by telephone or letter. UKBA makes risk assessments about compliance so that its visits and checks are targeted on the organisations that it considers the highest risk. For example, if UKBA knows little about an organisation, or is concerned about the evidence it has provided, then it is likely to carry out more intensive checking. The result of the check is reported to the sponsor licensing unit (SG, paras 41–42, 56).

UKBA's checks may include verifying either the correctness of a document (ie that what the document contains is the truth) and the genuineness of a document. In order to do this, UKBA may contact other government departments in the UK and overseas, banks, universities and professional bodies (SG, para 59).

Granting/refusing applications and ratings

UKBA determines whether it will grant or refuse the application. If the application is granted, it may give the sponsor an 'A' or a 'B' rating (►see also below for 'Highly Trusted' Sponsor status for some student sponsors). The rating that the sponsor obtains, if the licence is granted, depends on the assessment of the 'suitability' criteria (►see above 85) and their ability to fulfil their duties as a sponsor. If a licence is granted with only a 'B' rating is given, then UKBA will draw up an action plan for the sponsor to follow (►see below). Sponsors' ratings of 'A' and 'B' are published on the UKBA website (SG, paras 117–119, 126–127).

Consequences of 'A' or 'B' rating There are advantages to being 'A' rather than 'B' rated. Sponsors that are 'A' rated under Tiers 2 and 5 (Temporary Workers) are able to certify that the migrant's maintenance needs will be met (SG, paras 407, 351–355). 'B' rated sponsors are likely to be inspected more often and more rigorously and may be authorised to assign fewer certificates to migrants than would have been the case had they obtained an 'A' rating (SG, para 124, 136).

Highly Trusted Sponsorship

'HTS' status is presently only available for Tier 4 sponsors although UKBA had indicated that it intends to extend this status to Tiers 2 and 5. From 6 April 2010, sponsors with this status have been able to offer a greater range of course levels than others. A non-highly trusted student licence is known as a 'standard' licence and will be rated either 'A' or 'B' (►see above). In order to apply for a HTS licence, the sponsor must have held an 'A' rated licence for a minimum of six months and applicants must demonstrate, among other things, that they have completely complied with their sponsor duties. Separate guidance is available for those who wish to apply for a HTS licence (see http://www.ukba.homeoffice.gov.uk/employers/points/sponsoringmigrants/highly-trusted) (Student SG, paras 5–6).

A Tier 4 sponsor who is issued with a 'standard' licence will be reviewed by UKBA after holding that licence for six months or after it has had an intake of students (whichever occurs soonest). At that stage, it is assessed against another series of ratings criteria, the purpose of which is to make sure that the sponsor has met UKBA's expectations. UKBA will decide again after the review whether the sponsor should be 'A' rated or 'B' rated. A similar review will take place if a standard Tier 4 sponsor applies (but fails) to be upgraded to HTS status (see the Student SG, paras 159–164 which includes a table setting out the ratings criteria).

For further details about HTS status, ►see Chapter 8 at 287–291.

Scoring to determine rating

In order to rate a proposed sponsor, UKBA uses a scoring system which it applies to the requirement of the 'suitability' (►see above 85–88) of the organisation to be a sponsor. Information about scoring can be found on the UKBA website pages marked 'How do I sponsor a migrant – scoring system' and also in the Sponsor Guidance. The categories that UKBA scores are: the proposed sponsor's human resources systems; the civil penalties/criminal convictions of its staff; and any non-compliance by the organisation. The scores available are as follows:

1 = meets all the criteria;

2 = meets only some of the criteria; or

3 = does not meet any of the criteria.

If the proposed sponsor scores '1' in all the categories, then it will be 'A' rated as long as there are no other reasons, considering the other requirements for becoming a sponsor, to either refuse the application or give a 'B' rating. If the application falls below these standards, so that a '2' is scored in any of the three categories, a 'B' rating is likely to be given. If the proposed sponsor scores a '3' in any of the categories, the licence application is likely to be refused. The exception to this seems to be that the sponsor may still be granted a licence if the only '3' score is for human resources. The proposed sponsor will be given a '3' for criminal convictions/civil penalties if any staff member who will have access to the sponsorship management system has an unspent conviction for an offence listed in Appendix B to the SG, or possibly for any other unspent conviction (UKBA website pages on 'scoring' and see also SG, paras 65–70).

The Sponsor Guidance provides some additional information on how UKBA will rate a sponsor depending on criminal convictions (see SG, para 122). The Guidance further states that if the sponsor or any other 'relevant person' (▶see 86) is issued with a civil penalty listed in Appendix C (apart from for employing illegal migrant workers) (▶see 87) within the last five years, UKBA will issue a 'B' rating. That will not apply if the penalty was withdrawn by UKBA or cancelled on appeal. A 'B' rating will also be given if the organisation already has a 'B' rated licence and is applying to renew it (SG, para 121).

'Action plans'

This is an agreed course of action between the sponsor and UKBA that is designed to enable the sponsor to improve so that it can be issued with an 'A' rating. Plans may involve, for example, improving record-keeping or communication between branches. The sponsor will also have to pay a fee to UKBA to cover the cost of the plan. Plans usually cover a period of three months but they can be extended up to a maximum of twelve months. If the action plan is not complied with, or if the sponsor does not improve sufficiently to be able to be uprated to an 'A', then UKBA will withdraw the sponsor licence (SG, paras 128–135).

Notification of decision

After a decision has been made, UKBA will write to the organisation that applied for the licence to tell them whether they have granted or refused the licence and whether the sponsor has been given an 'A' or 'B' rating. If the licence has been refused, or if the sponsor has been 'B' rated, reasons will be given (SG, para 111). When sponsors apply for a licence, they indicate how may certificates they wish to assign and, if the licence is approved, UKBA states the number of certificates that the sponsor has been allocated (SG, para 111, but ▶see below 106 on the 'cap' on certificates that may be issued in the Tier 2 (General) Migrant category).

Leaving aside the 'cap', among the factors that UKBA takes into account in deciding what the limit should be, are the sponsor's: estimate of how many it will need; previous record in dealing with UKBA; type and size of business; and the length of time it has been in business (SG, para 161). For Tier 4 applications, UKBA takes into account: the sponsor's previous record in dealing with UKBA, the type and size of the organisation, the total student capacity and the length of time that it has been operating (Student SG, para 181). At the end of a year, when the licence needs to be renewed, the sponsor indicates again how many certificates will be needed for the next year. Certificates that are unallocated over the 12 months may not be carried to the next year (SG, paras 165–166).

Successful applicants are issued with a sponsor licence number which should be cited on all future correspondence with UKBA (SG, paras 115–116).

Remedies for refusal

Decisions to refuse a licence are not 'immigration decisions' under the 2002 Act and so there is no appeal right. The proposed sponsor can apply again for a licence but should ensure that the reasons given for the previous refusal no longer apply. If the sponsor does re-apply, UKBA is likely to carry out a site visit in deciding the application (SG, paras 113–114). Organisations refused a licence who believe that the grounds for refusal are unlawful may challenge the decision by judicial review.

Renewing a licence

A sponsor licence runs for four years from the date it was issued. Before it expires, if the organisation wishes to continue to sponsor migrants, it will have to apply to renew the licence and it must do this even if it does not wish to sponsor any new migrants. Normally sponsors are not required to provide all of the documents that were produced at the time of the original application, but will generally need to show that the organisation is still operating lawfully in the UK (SG, paras 511–517). If a Highly Trusted Sponsor's licence expires without being renewed, or it withdrawn or surrendered, UKBA will reassess the sponsor and decide whether to grant it a standard Tier 4 licence. No new application is required for this (Student SG, para 15).

Surrendering a licence

Where an organisation does not have any further need to act as a sponsor for migrants, it may 'surrender' its licence using the sponsor change of circumstances form on the UKBA website and show that it no longer has responsibility for any migrants previously sponsored. An organisation that has surrendered its licence may apply again for a licence in the future (SG, paras 505–507).

OPERATING AS A SPONSOR AND COMPLYING WITH SPONSOR DUTIES

In order to operate their licence properly, sponsors should:

- properly manage the licence using the 'sponsor management system' (►immediately below);

- be aware of the procedures that apply in issuing certificates of sponsorship to those migrants it sponsors (►105);

- be aware of the guarantees it makes when issuing a certificate (►109);

- properly comply with the duties of a sponsor (►114);

- understand the procedures that apply and their duties if the sponsored migrant changes employment (►118); and

- be aware of their duties should there be a business reorganisation (►119).

Sponsor management system

After a licence has been approved, sponsors have access to the 'sponsor management system'. Level 1 and Level 2 users have access to different levels of use on the system. Using the sponsor management system, the sponsor:

- assigns certificates of sponsorship to migrants they wish to sponsor;

- asks to increase the limit placed on the number of certificates it may issue;

- may withdraw a certificate of sponsorship that has been assigned to a migrant but not yet used;

- makes changes to their key personnel (►see 95–98);

- reports changes about the sponsor organisation (name, address, etc) and reports changes about migrants (address, updates, etc) and or any failures of their sponsored migrants to attend or their suspicions about migrants – these reports are to be provided in accordance with the duties of a sponsor (►see 114 below).

Sponsors can gain access to the sponsor management system on the UKBA website at http://www.ukba.homeoffice.gov.uk/employers/points/sponsoringmigrants/sms/. Level 1 and 2 users must not disclose their passwords (sent by UKBA) to anyone else – if they do, the continuation of the licence could well be affected (SG, para 139).

Certificates of sponsorship: procedures

Migrants seeking to obtain entry clearance or leave to be admitted or remain in the UK under a category requiring sponsorship must be issued with a certificate of sponsorship by their sponsoring organisation. The certificate does not guarantee that entry clearance or leave will be granted because:

- the immigration authorities make the final decision on entry clearance and leave and they may 'cancel' a certificate if they find that the sponsor was not entitled to issue it; and

- even if a certificate is validly assigned, there may be outstanding requirements of the Immigration Rules, that are solely for the immigration authorities to make a decision under and which could be found not to be satisfied (SG, paras 11, 153, 168, 173–174).

If leave is not granted, the migrant may not enter/remain in the UK and may not work for or study with the sponsor. As a result, sponsors are advised by UKBA to ensure that the migrant will meet the requirements of the Rules relating to entry clearance, or leave to remain, before assigning a certificate to them (SG, para 173) and to check the terms of the leave granted to the migrant before allowing them to commence work or study (SG, para 365). A new certificate must be assigned if the sponsor and the migrant wish the migrant to extend their leave to remain in the UK in order to continue to work or study here with the sponsor (SG, para 367). For the periods of leave that are granted and the maximum periods allowed under the various categories and sub-categories, see the relevant chapter of this Guide dealing with the particular tier/category.

When a decision is made on the application for a licence to be a sponsor, the organisation will be told how many certificates of sponsorship it may issue (▶see above 103). There is, however, an overall 'cap' in place on the number of certificates that may be issued to sponsors in the Tier 2 (General) Migrant category (▶see box below 106; and for the permanent cap ▶see 208). The certificate itself is a virtual document that exists in the sponsor management system. When the sponsor assigns a certificate to a migrant it must record this in the sponsor management system and give the migrant the unique certificate reference number (SG, paras 141–142). In addition to completing the migrant and sponsorship screen, when it assigns a certificate, the sponsor is often required to input other details: salary, skill level or whether the job satisfies the resident labour market test (SG, para 150 ▶see below 109–114).

Under the Tier 5 (Creative and Sporting) category, a sponsor can assign a 'group certificate' to members of a group including the migrant's entourage or all members of a unit company eg a dance group (SG, paras 145–146).

Sponsor's role in guaranteeing maintenance

One of the means by which a Tier 2 migrant can show that they meet the maintenance requirements under the Immigration Rules is by their sponsor (provided the sponsor is 'A' rated) guaranteeing that they will support the migrant during the first month of employment. An 'A' rated Tier 5 sponsor can also indicate on the certificate of sponsorship of a Tier 5 (Temporary Worker) that it certifies the migrant's maintenance. Sponsors that do this must also tell the relevant migrants that they should not claim state benefits (SG, paras 352–359).

THE INTERIM CAP

Interim cap as introduced on 19 July 2010

The Government is committed to 'capping' non-EU employment and business migration to the UK. That policy goes beyond sponsored migrants. As far as it applies to sponsorship, on 19 July 2010, the Government introduced new Immigration Rules (HC 96) to limit the number of certificates of sponsorship available to be assigned to sponsors in any one period and to limit the number of certificates of sponsorship assigned to any specific sponsor in any one period. The intention was to apply these limits as an 'interim cap' until 31 March 2011. However, no actual limit was specified in the Rules, but the figures were, instead, left over to the PBS Guidance.

As a result of the failure to quantify the limits in the Immigration Rules so as to enable Parliament to consider them when the new Rules were laid, on 17 December 2010, the Divisional Court ruled that, following *Pankina* (►see 42–45), the interim cap was unlawful, see: *R (JCWI) v SSHD; R (English Community Care Association) v SSHD* (►see 49–50, 58–59).

New interim cap from 21 December 2010

In response to the *JCWI* case, the Government laid amending Rules with effect from 21 December 2010 (HC 698). Those Rules provide for a 'Tier 2 Interim Limit' on the number of certificates of sponsorship that can be assigned by the Home Office to sponsors in the Tier 2 (General) Migrant category between 21 December 2010 and 5 April 2011 (para 6 and App A paras 63B–K, HC 395 as amended). The Tier 2 interim limit, as stated in the Rules, is 10, 832 (App A, para 63B). That figure includes both the number of certificates of sponsorship that UKBA assigns to a particular sponsor *and* the number of certificates available to be assigned under an 'Exceptional Consideration Process' (App A, para 63D).

Operation of new interim cap from 21 December 2010

The interim cap introduced runs to 5 April 2011 after which the arrangements to cap the Tier 2 (General) Migrant category are likely to be rolled out with further amendments to the Rules. The operation of this interim cap is explained in an 'Addendum' to the version of the Tier 2 and 5 Sponsor Guidance Notes issued on 21 December 2010 (referred to below as 'SG Addendum').

Main features

The main features of the scheme as set out in the new Rules (▶above) and the SG Addendum are as follows:

- The interim cap only applies to certificates issued in the Tier 2 (General) category, including certificates used for extension applications.

- The interim cap does not include dependant applications.

- All certificates assigned by UKBA to a sponsor before 21 December 2010 and which have not been assigned by the sponsor to a migrant before 21 December 2010 were withdrawn (Rules, App A, para 63E).

- Sponsored migrants with an existing valid certificate and leave as at 21 December 2010 may continue to be sponsored and work while their certificate and leave remain valid (SG Addendum, para 8).

- It is for sponsors to decide how their interim allocation of certificates (determined in accordance with the Rules at App A, para 63D and 63F) that applies during the interim period is to be split between new sponsored migrants and existing sponsored migrants who require extensions (SG Addendum, para 10).

- The total number of certificates available to be assigned to sponsors as making up their interim allocation is 9,803 (App A, paras 63D(i) and 63G).

- However, in addition to that allocation, a sponsor may, on application, be assigned additional certificates under the 'Exceptional Consideration Process' (▶see below) (App A, paras 63D(ii), 63I).

- The remaining 1,029 certificates (making up the total of 10,832) are set aside for assignment under the 'Exceptional Consideration Process', (although that number will be added to if sponsors return any certificates that UKBA has assigned to them) (App A, paras 63J–63K).

- Existing sponsors who are downgraded to a 'B' rating will have their certificate allocation set at zero and will not be able to apply for exceptional consideration until they are 'A' rated once more. They can, however, continue to sponsor existing migrants who have continuing valid certificates and leave. New sponsors during the interim period who have a 'B' rating cannot apply for certificates until they have been awarded an 'A' rating (SG Addendum, paras 13–15, 21–23).

Exceptional Consideration Process

The 'Exceptional Consideration Process' (Rules, App A, paras 63D(ii), 63I) is appropriate where:

- an existing sponsor requires additional certificates during the period of the interim cap (SG Addendum, para 11);

- the sponsor is a new one, having been licensed during the period of the interim cap (SG Addendum, paras 16–18).

Applications under this process must be made using the 'Tier 2 (General) Request for Initial or Additional Allocation of Certificates of Sponsorship' form available on the UKBA website and will be considered by a 'panel' of UKBA managers.

To be admitted for consideration, the following requirements must be satisfied: the sponsor is 'A' rated on all their licences for all their tiers/categories; the number of certificates requested should take account of any available certificates remaining in the sponsor's allocation; and the sponsor must demonstrate that they have already undertaken a resident labour market test in respect of non-shortage occupations (SG Addendum, para 25).

The panel will proceed as follows (SG Addendum, paras 27, 32–37).

- It will meet to consider requests at the start of the calendar month and will consider all applications received by the 24th of the previous month.

- The available certificates each month is the limit for exceptional cases (above) divided evenly across the months of the interim limit.

- The panel will grant all applications for 'extensions' (provided they satisfy the requirements for consideration stated immediately above). In order to qualify as an 'extension' application for these purposes, the application must be: for a certificate for an existing migrant who is presently employed; the migrant must have leave as a work permit holder or under the Tier 2 (General) Migrant category; and the migrant's leave must be due to expire within the next 60 days.

- The remaining applications (ie those for 'new hires') are split into applications for shortage occupations and those not for shortage occupations and the certificates issued to each will be divided proportionally according to the number of applications for each.

- The applications are then ranked in order of salary bands (the highest band is at or above £40,000) to determine which cases will be granted first, up to the available limit.

If the limit is reached, some applications will not be granted. There is no right of appeal against a refusal, although sponsors can re-submit their request (SG Addendum, para 41). Note that UKBA states that it will monitor closely how a sponsor is using their certificates following a request for exceptional consideration (SG Addendum, paras 31, 42).

Applications for urgent Exceptional Consideration Process

Urgent requests for exceptional consideration should be made on the form: 'Tier 2 (General) – Request for Initial or Additional Allocation of Certificates of Sponsorship' marked 'urgent'. Decisions are made on such applications by the Deputy Director for Sponsorship or their deputy. UKBA states that there must be a "compelling reason for requesting urgent treatment" and gives the example of a sponsor with a new licence where the proposed sponsored migrant has leave that is due to expire before the next panel meeting (SG Addendum, paras 43–45).

For details of the development of the 'cap' generally ie including and beyond the sponsorship categories, ▶see Chapter 2 at 55–59 and for the permanent cap proposals from April 2011 ▶see 208–210.

Use of the certificate by the migrant

Using the unique sponsorship certificate reference number that they are given by the sponsor (▶above), the migrant can then apply for entry clearance (if seeking entry) or leave to remain in the UK (SG, paras 142, 151). Migrants with entry clearance giving rise to leave for more than six months, or who have been given leave to remain for more than six months, can enter, leave and return to the UK on multiple occasions during the period of their leave (SG, 155, 314; Leave to Enter and Remain Order). Where the migrant needs to do this as part of their employment, the sponsor should indicate this on the certificate of sponsorship.

However, if the migrant's leave is for six months or less and they wish to leave and re-enter, they will have to apply for a fresh leave with a new certificate even if they wish to re-enter within the period of the leave that was granted (SG, paras 314–315).

A migrant who is a non-visa national and who is assigned a certificate of sponsorship for a period of less than three months for a job in the Tier 5 (Temporary Worker) Creative or Sporting sub-category does not require entry clearance and special arrangements are in place at ports to enable them to enter (SG, paras 313, 316–319).

Getting the timing right

In order to sponsor a migrant to come to the UK, it is important to be careful with the timing of all the steps that need to be taken. Certificates of sponsorship are valid for three months from the date assigned and will become invalid if not used to obtain entry clearance or leave by the migrant during that time (SG, para 148). According to UKBA, those coming to the UK under Tiers 2 and 5 may not apply for leave more than three months before the date of the start of their employment as stated on their certificate of sponsorship (SG, para 362). So the certificate must be issued so as to enable the migrant to use it within three months and the date on which they do use it to apply for leave must be not more than three months before their employment starts. Note also that, if the position was advertised in order to satisfy the resident labour market test rules, the certificate must be assigned within six months of the first advertisement (SG, para 363).

Cancellation of certificate

UKBA may cancel a certificate if it finds that the sponsor was not entitled to assign it (SG, para 168). A migrant who does not want to make use of their certificate so as to be sponsored by their existing sponsor should contact the sponsor and ask them to withdraw it. The sponsor should do this within five working days. If the sponsor continues to fail to do this, the migrant should contact the UKBA Sponsor Licensing Unit directly, who will cancel it (SG, para 170).

Confirmations made by a sponsor when assigning a certificate to a migrant

As set out above, the final decision as to whether a migrant will be admitted to, or given leave for the UK is made by the immigration authorities, who may decide that a sponsor should not have been issued with a certificate of sponsorship in the first place (►see above 79–80, 105), or that certain other requirements of the Immigration Rules have not been followed. What follows immediately below must therefore be read together with the parts of this Guide which set out, in full, the requirements that need to be satisfied for a migrant to be admitted under the PBS. However, it is part of the sponsor's duty to (SG, para 398):

" ...only assign certificates of sponsorship to migrants who, to the best of the sponsor's knowledge and belief, will meet the requirements of the tier or category under which the certificate is assigned, and are likely to comply with the conditions of their leave."

This section flags up those conditions that sponsors are asked to confirm when they assign a certificate to a migrant in a particular category.

Tier 2 (General) Migrant

When assigning a certificate to a migrant under the Tier 2 (General) category, the sponsor confirms (SG, paras 177, 187, 400, 402–403):

- that it has carried out the resident labour market test and codes of practice (or that the job appears on the shortage occupations list – note that there is also an exception to carrying out a test of the resident labour market for post-graduate doctors/dentists who have started speciality training) and that the job will be paid at or above the rate at which it was advertised;
- that the migrant intends to and is able to do the specific skilled job which must be at or above S/NVQ skill level 3 (guidance about skill levels can be found in the codes of practice available on the UKBA website);
- that the migrant will be paid a salary and/or allowances (eg London weighting or accommodation where that would also be provided to a settled worker, but this does not include overtime, bonus or incentive pay or travel and subsistence) at or above the rate appropriate for that job in the UK; and
- that the job is a genuine one.

For full details about the requirements that must be satisfied for a migrant to enter in this category ►see 212, 222.

Tier 2 (Intra Company Transfer) Migrant

In assigning a certificate to a migrant under the Tier 2 (Intra Company Transfer) category, the sponsor confirms that (SG, paras 177–178, 401–404):

- if the migrant is being sponsored in the Established Staff sub-category, they intend and are able to do the specific skilled job which must be at or above S/NVQ skill level 3;
- if the migrant is being sponsored in the Graduate Trainee or Skills Transfer sub-categories, they intend and are able to do the specific job which must

be in a graduate occupation (guidance about such skill levels can be found in the codes of practice available on the UKBA website);

- the migrant has been working for the sponsoring organisation for the required period of time;
- the job is an intra company transfer;
- the migrant will be paid at or above the rate appropriate for that job in the UK (so that the resident labour market rate is not undercut), and
- the job is a genuine one.

For full details about the requirements that must satisfied for a migrant to enter in this category, ▶see 212, 222.

Tier 2 (Sportsperson) Migrant

In assigning a certificate to a migrant under the Tier 2 (Sportsperson) category, the sponsor (SG, paras 268–270 and 405):

- guarantees that the migrant intends to be based in the UK for the duration of his/her stay and that s/he will comply with the conditions of his/her leave and depart the UK at the expiry of their leave;
- must confirm that the migrant has been endorsed by the governing body for the sport, that s/he is internationally established at the highest level, will make a significant contribution to the development of his/her sport at the highest level in the UK and that it is appropriate to fill the post with a migrant who is not settled in the UK; and
- undertakes to accept the duties of sponsorship in respect of the particular migrant.

For full details about the requirements that must satisfied for a migrant to enter in this category ▶see 212, 237.

Tier 2 (Minister of Religion) Migrant

In assigning a certificate to a migrant under the Tier 2 (Ministers of Religion) category, the sponsor must (SG, paras 256, 406):

- guarantee that the migrant: is qualified to do the job in question; intends to be based in the UK for the duration of his/her leave to be here and will comply with his/her conditions of leave;
- give an undertaking that it accepts the sponsorship duties for the particular migrant;
- undertake to support the migrant; and
- confirms that it has undertaken a resident labour market test, or it must be the case that the relevant code of practice states that a resident labour market test is not required and the sponsor confirms that it is not filling a position that would otherwise be given to a settled worker.

For full details about the requirements that must satisfied for a migrant to enter in this category ▶see 212, 235.

Tier 5 (Temporary Workers) Creative and Sporting

In assigning a certificate to a migrant under the Tier 5 (Creative) sub-category for creative workers in dance, theatre, film and television, the sponsor confirms that it has followed the appropriate code of practice for the taking account of the needs of the resident labour market (SG, paras 297, 408). Where the migrant has a sole sponsor and there are no more than 14 calendar days between each event, the sponsor can issue one certificate of sponsorship for the whole period. Otherwise, separate certificates will be required (SG, para 299).

In assigning a certificate to a migrant under the Tier 5 (Sporting) sub-category, the sponsor confirms that it is satisfied by an endorsement from the governing body for the relevant sport that the migrant (player/coach) is internationally established at the highest level in their sport and/or that their employment will make a significant contribution to the development and operation of that particular sport in this country. Coaches must be suitably qualified (SG, paras 304, 309, 409).

In addition, where sponsors assign a certificate in the Tier 5 (Creative and Sporting) category, they are guaranteeing that the migrant (SG, paras 303, 312, 410):

• is coming to the UK to work or perform as stated in the relevant sector;

• is not intending to set themselves up in business in the UK;

• is not a threat to resident labour force; and

• will abide by their conditions of leave and will depart from the UK at the expiry of that leave.

For full details about the requirements that must satisfied for a migrant to enter in this category, ▶see 304, 310.

Tier 5 (Temporary Workers) Religious Workers

In assigning a certificate to a migrant under the Tier 2 Religious Worker sub-category, the sponsor (SG, paras 328, 412):

• vouches that the migrant is qualified for the job and will only take work in the UK as a religious worker;

• vouches that the migrant will only work in the locations specified (except where doing supplementary work, ▶309);

• undertakes to accept the responsibilities of sponsorship for the particular migrant;

• undertakes to support the migrant, through funds and/or accommodation, during the period of the certificate of sponsorship;

• guarantees that the migrant will not displace from or deny employment to a suitably qualified member of the resident labour force; and

• guarantees that the migrant will abide by their conditions of leave and will depart from the UK at the expiry of that leave.

For full details about the requirements that must satisfied for a migrant to enter in this category, ▶see 304, 314.

Tier 5 (Temporary Workers) Charity Workers

In assigning a certificate to a migrant under the Tier 2 Charity Worker sub-category, the sponsor guarantees that the migrant (SG, paras 323, 411):

- is intending to take voluntary fieldwork directly related to the purposes of the sponsoring charity;
- will not take up a permanent position;
- will abide by their conditions of leave and will depart from the UK at the expiry of that leave; and
- will not be paid (other than being provided with reasonable expenses).

For full details about the requirements that must satisfied for a migrant to enter in this category, ▶see 304, 313.

Tier 5 (Temporary Workers) Government Authorised Exchange

In assigning a certificate to a migrant under the Tier 2 Government Authorised Exchange sub-category, the overarching body that acts as sponsor is guaranteeing that the migrant (SG, paras 339, 413):

- is coming in order to work or train on a temporary basis through an approved exchange scheme;
- does not intend to set themselves up in business in the UK; and
- meets the requirements of the individual exchange scheme.

For full details about the requirements that must satisfied for a migrant to enter in this category, ▶see 304, 315.

Tier 5 (Temporary Workers) International Agreement

In assigning a certificate to a migrant under this sub-category, in order for him/her to be a servant in a private diplomatic household, the sponsor guarantees that the migrant (SG, paras 343, 414):

- is aged at least 18;
- will be employed as a private servant in the household either of a member of staff of a diplomatic or consular mission who has diplomatic privileges and immunity, or of an official employed by an international organisation who enjoys privileges and immunities under UK law;
- intends to work full-time in domestic employment;
- will not take up any other form of employment for that sponsor; and
- will depart the UK at the expiry of their leave.

In assigning a certificate to a migrant, under this sub-category, in order for him/her to be an employee of an overseas government or international organisation, the sponsor guarantees that the migrant will (SG, paras 345, 415):

- be under a contract of employment with the overseas government or international organisation;
- not take up employment for the sponsor other than that for which the certificate was assigned; and
- not, after entry, seek to switch to another form of worker under the 'international agreements' category.

To assign a certificate to a migrant, under this sub-category in order for him/her to be sponsored migrant under the GATS, or other international agreements, the sponsor guarantees that the migrant (SG, paras 348, 416):

- is employed by an employer or organisation, or is the national of a country, that: is a member of the World Trade Organisation, or has a bilateral agreement with the UK or the EU, or is a member of the EU;
- will be engaged in work that meets the terms of the relevant international agreement; and
- where relevant, works for the employer that was awarded the contract or will provide services to the UK client.

For full details about the requirements that must satisfied for a migrant to enter in this category, ▶see 304, 316.

Tier 4 (General) Student and Tier 4 (Child) Student

The role of the sponsor, the checks that it must have carried out and the guarantees that it makes when assigning a certificate (a 'confirmation of acceptance for studies') in these categories, is hard to summarise ▶see Chapter 8, particularly 251 onwards.

Sponsorship duties

Sponsors must comply with certain 'sponsor duties', the objectives of which are to: (SG, paras 12, 395):

- prevent abuse of the assessment procedures;
- catch early any patterns of migrant behaviour that cause concern;
- address possible weaknesses in the systems that may cause those patterns; and
- monitor compliance with the Immigration Rules.

A sponsor who fails to comply with its duties is at risk of having its licence withdrawn, suspended or downgraded, or having the number of certificates of sponsorship that it may issue reduced (SG, para 417 and ▶see 121–138 below). In *R (Leeds Unique Education) v SSHD* (14 May 2010), the Court put some emphasis to the need to focus on the actual duties that are placed on sponsors in the Guidance when it comes to decisions about withdrawal/suspension of licences, rather than more generally stated responsibilities (Judgment, para 19).

The duties set out below are applicable to all sponsors (for reference, see SG, para 398; SG, paras 419–424 and Appendix D on record keeping; Student SG, paras 296, 310–315).

Record keeping

Sponsors must keep:

- a photocopy or electronic copy of the sponsored migrant's passport, UK immigration status document showing evidence of his/her right to work or study in the UK (details of the responsibilities that apply here are further set out in UKBA's guidance on the prevention of illegal working – the link is available at para 398 of the SG);
- each sponsored migrant's up-to-date contact details;
- additional documents relating to the sponsored migrant that UKBA might require to see, for example documents dealing with the sponsor's recruitment practices so that (where required) UKBA can be sure that the migrant was recruited after a proper test of the resident labour market had been carried out, or documents dealing with the offer of a place on a course made to a student;
- where a student's course of study requires him/her to hold an Academic Technology Approval Scheme (ATAS) clearance certificate, that certificate should be kept;
- in the case of a child (aged under 18), a copy of a letter from their parents or legal guardian agreeing to the arrangements;
- an ID card if the sponsored migrant has one (from 2008, ID cards have been gradually introduced for foreign nationals – they are a new kind of immigration status document).

Reporting

Sponsors must report to UKBA:

- within 10 working days if a sponsored migrant does not attend for his/her first day at work;
- within 10 working days if the migrant does not enrol on his/her course;
- within 10 working days if the migrant is absent from work for more than 10 working days without permission;
- within 10 working days if a Tier 4 migrant misses 10 'expected contacts' and does not have the sponsor's reasonably granted permission for his/her absence;
- within 10 working days of a migrant ceasing his/her studies;
- within 10 working days of the migrant's contract of employment being terminated (the sponsor should provide the name and address of any new employer if the sponsor knows it);
- within 10 working days if the sponsor ceases to sponsor the migrant for any reason;

- within 10 working days of any significant changes in the migrant's circumstances, for example:
- promotion or change in job title/core duties (other than those that require a change of employment application);
- a change of salary (this does not include annual rises);
- if the location of the migrant's work or study changes;
- if there is any information that the migrant is breaching the conditions of his/her leave; or
- a change in the duration of the migrant's course of study (for the procedure where the migrant's employment changes, ▶see below at 118 and for the procedure if there are changes in a student's course or provider, ▶see 274–275);
- within 28 calendar days if there are any significant changes in the sponsor's circumstances, for example if the sponsor ceases trading, becomes insolvent, substantially changes the nature of its business, or is involved in a merger or takeover etc (▶see further below at 119);
- within 28 days, if a private, further or higher education institution appoints a new principal or changes owners; and
- the details of any third party or intermediary, in the UK or abroad, who has helped the sponsor with the recruitment of employees or students.

Sponsors should also report to the police any information that the sponsored migrant is engaging in terrorism or other criminal activity (SG, para 398; Student SG, para 296).

Changes to a sponsor's structure (▶see further below 119), address, key contact, Level 1 user, record of relevant criminal convictions and required number of certificates of sponsorship, should all be made on the sponsor management system (SG, para 520). The change of circumstances form (available on the website at http://www.bia.homeoffice.gov.uk/site content/applicationforms/pbs/sponsorcircumstancesform) should be used to report: a change of authorising officer; a replacement of the level 1 user or key contact where there is no other user who can do this using the sponsor management system; the appointment or change of a representative; the withdrawal of an application for a sponsor licence; or the surrender of a licence (SG, para 521) Some of the reporting requirements are relaxed for sponsors with HTS status and sponsors should refer to the Highly Trusted Sponsor Guidance (▶see Chapter 8 at 287).

Compliance

Sponsors are required to comply with the law by:

- making sure that the migrants that they are sponsoring to come to work in the UK are legally entitled to do the work that they are coming for and that they have the appropriate registration and/or professional accreditation where this is legally required – a copy of any relevant documents must be kept;

- not employing any migrant whose conditions of leave mean that s/he is not allowed to do the work in question and ceasing to employ any migrants who, for whatever reason, are no longer entitled to undertake the work; and
- only assigning certificates to migrants who, to the best of the sponsor's knowledge and belief, will meet the requirements of the tier or category under which the certificate is assigned and are likely to comply with their conditions of their leave.

Co-operating

In order to allow UKBA to manage the system effectively, sponsors are also required to:

- give UKBA officers access to any of the sponsor's premises when requested (with or without advance notice);
- comply with any action plan (▶see 102) set by UKBA; and
- minimise the risk of immigration abuse by complying with any good practice guidance issued by any sector body, or by UKBA.

Additional, tier-specific duties

The following duties are applicable to sponsors under certain tiers and are set out in general terms. In addition to those matters set out below, it is the sponsor's duty to be satisfied that the tier-specific conditions are met before it issues a certificate to a migrant, so that it can make the relevant confirmations and give the relevant guarantees (▶see above 109–114).

Tier 2 The sponsor must (SG, paras 400–403):

- ensure that the migrant intends and is able to do the specific skilled job in question;
- confirm when assigning the certificate that it has carried out the resident labour market test (where required) in accordance with the Sponsor Guidance and the relevant code of practice and that the migrant will be paid at or above the rate for which the position was advertised, or that the job is on the shortage occupation list, or that it is an intra company transfer; and
- indicate that the job will be paid at or above the rate appropriate for that position in the UK, that the job is a genuine vacancy and that it is at skill level S/NVQ 3 or above.

Tier 4 The sponsor must satisfy themselves that the student intends and is able to follow the course of study. The Student SG also deals with the responsibility of the sponsor to assess the student's ability and to check and verify the qualifications that the student holds (Student SG, paras 297–8).

Tier 5 Tier 5 sponsors must be sure to follow the applicable codes of practice for the sector that they operate in, respect the needs of the relevant resident labour market and confirm that their sponsored migrants will not set themselves up in business in the UK.

The above is a summary only of the tier-specific duties, for further details, see the Sponsor Guidance at paragraphs 400–416 and the Student Sponsor Guidance at paragraphs 297–315.

Duration of duties

A sponsor is responsible for the discharge of the above duties from the date the sponsor licence commences. A sponsor's duties cease when (SG, paras 397–8):

- the sponsor notifies UKBA that the migrant has ceased to be in their employment, or has ceased their course of study;
- the migrant leaves the UK and their entry clearance or leave to remain lapses;
- the migrant is granted further leave to remain with a different sponsor or in another immigration category not involving the present sponsor;
- the sponsor surrenders its licence; or
- UKBA withdraws the sponsor's licence.

Changes of employment

Not only must UKBA be informed, but a sponsored migrant under Tiers 2 or 5 must be issued with a new certificate of sponsorship and must make a new application for leave if the migrant (SG, paras 374–376):

- changes their employer unless s/he is moving to a new employer to do the same job as the result of a takeover, merger or de-merger (▶see 119) (SG, para 373); or
- changes their new job with the same employer unless the new job is within the same Standard Occupational Classification ('SOC') code with no drop in salary (other than relating to maternity leave etc, long-term sick leave or a reduction in hours as referred to below) and the change does not involve moving from a job that is on the list of shortage occupations to one that is not.

No new application needs to be made if the only change is that an employer reduces the working hours of a Tier 2 migrant as part of a company-wide policy to avoid redundancies provided the new arrangement will not last longer than one year. This applies provided that the reduction in pay must be proportionate to the reduction of hours, be reduced by no more than 30% and the sponsored migrant workers must be treated in the same way as settled workers (SG, para 379).

Tier 5 (Temporary Workers) may apply for a change of employment while in the UK but generally will only be given permission for up to the maximum time allowed under the particular sub-category. There are limited exceptions only to this which are set out in the Guidance (see SG, para 378).

Where a new certificate and application for leave is required, the migrant must not commence the new employment until UKBA has granted the application. Pending this, the migrant may continue to work for the existing sponsor provided their leave continues (SG, para 376).

Changes of course

For procedures where a student changes their course and/or sponsor, ▶see Chapter 8 on Tier 4 at 274–275.

Sponsor takeover and/or transfer of employment

Takeovers and mergers are covered in the Sponsor Guidance (SG, paras 523-539). A situation may arise where an existing sponsor (or a 'branch' of that sponsor) becomes a part of a separate entity and takes the sponsored migrants with it. If both the original and the new organisation have a sponsor licence, then both sponsors should update UKBA as to the change in the organisation (updating can be done through the sponsor management system or by emailing SCOC@ukba.gsi.gov.uk, SG para 528). This should be done within 28 days of the change occurring. It should be clear who is responsible for sponsoring the transferred migrants after the change in circumstances. The new sponsor may need to apply to increase its existing allocation of certificates in order to accommodate the transferred migrants. Note that it is advisable to notify UKBA of the change in the structure of the organisation even if the sponsored employees or students are not transferring.

If the new (receiving) organisation does not have a licence, then it will have to obtain one and in its application for a sponsor licence, it should include information about the entity from which it has taken on the migrants. This should again be done within 28 days of the takeover/ change in structure occurring. The previous sponsor should also tell UKBA of the changes that are taking place.

Further details are given in the Sponsor Guidance as to the position where a takeover is only partial, or there is only a partial split from an existing sponsor organisation and only some migrants will be transferred to the new organisation (SG, paras 532–539).

ENFORCEMENT: DOWNGRADING, SUSPENSION AND WITHDRAWAL OF LICENCES

The Sponsor Guidance states (SG, para 445):

"The vast majority of those who employ overseas workers are honest and willing to comply with their duties. Because sponsorship transfers a significant amount of responsibility for selecting migrants to sponsors, we have a duty to ensure that we deal appropriately with the minority who do not comply with their duties."

In order to ensure compliance with sponsor duties, UKBA monitors sponsors (►immediately below). If a sponsor is found not to be compliant whether through dishonesty or incompetence, UKBA is likely to take action including downgrading or removing their licences (►below at 121 onwards). If UKBA cannot be persuaded through representations not to take the threatened action, the only real remedies are to apply again or to make a claim for judicial review (►below at 128 onwards). When UKBA does suspend/withdraw the licence, the consequences for sponsors and migrants are serious (►see 135–138).

Monitoring of sponsors

After a licence has been issued, there are a number of ways in which UKBA monitors sponsors and their compliance with the scheme. When the sponsor signs the declaration on the licence application form and submits their application, they are taken to agree to this monitoring.

The main measures that are in place to monitor sponsors are as follows.

- UKBA monitors the information that it receives via the sponsor management system.

- When a sponsor has assigned all of the certificates that it has been allotted and requests a further allocation through the sponsor management system, UKBA may review the sponsor's performance.

- Periodically UKBA may require a Tier 4 sponsor to provide spreadsheets with information relating to its sponsored students. UKBA then reviews that information for compliance.

- In addition, a Tier 4 standard sponsor will be reviewed after six months of being issued with a certificate, or after their first intake of students (whichever is soonest).

- Tier 4 sponsors are reviewed if they apply for, but fail to be awarded, HTS status (►see above 101).

- If a sponsor is given only a 'B' rating and an action plan (►above at 102) is agreed, UKBA will review the sponsor's compliance in the course of determining whether or not the necessary changes have been made according to the plan.

- UKBA officials may carry out visits to the sponsor in order to check compliance (see SG, paras 428–441).

As to visits by UKBA officers, these may be made while a sponsorship application is being considered and also after a licence has been granted and is in force. Visits may be pre-arranged but UKBA officials may also arrive unannounced. At all times, officers should carry UKBA identification papers. When UKBA does visit an organisation to run checks, that does not necessarily mean that it has concerns about whether the sponsor is operating properly. UKBA states that it may make checks at random (SG, paras 425–426).

Downgrading, suspension and withdrawal of licence: general factors

If UKBA does find some failures in compliance, it will have to decide what to do about it. It may downgrade the licence from an 'A' rating or HTS status. It may suspend the licence with a view to considering whether the licence should be withdrawn. In deciding what, if any, action to take against a sponsor, UKBA states that it will generally take into account all the facts of the case and will, in particular, consider (SG, para 458):

- the seriousness of the sponsor's actions and the harm caused – UKBA will treat seriously anything that the sponsor has done or not done that has resulted in migrants going missing;

- whether the actions of the sponsor are part of a consistent record of non-compliance;

- any action that the sponsor has taken to mitigate and lessen the consequences of what it has done – for example if the sponsor has promptly informed UKBA that a sponsored migrant has stopped attending, or the sponsor has addressed the cause of any difficulties within its own organisation, that will obviously help; and

- whether the sponsor has been issued with any civil penalties.

According to the Sponsor Guidance, the particular facts are less important where withdrawal of the licence is referred to in that Guidance as being 'mandatory' ie as circumstances in which UKBA 'will' withdraw the licence (see below) (SG, para 458).

Downgrading a sponsor licence

UKBA *will* downgrade a licence from an 'A' to 'B' rating (for rating, ▶see 101–102), if the sponsor has certified that a Tier 2 or 5 migrant will not claim state benefits but s/he subsequently does claim benefits with the sponsor's knowledge (SG, para 454).

UKBA *may* downgrade a sponsor licence if (SG, paras 455-457; Student SG, para 356):

- the sponsor, authorising officer, key contact, level 1 user, an owner or director of the organisation, or anyone involved in its day-to-day running, is convicted of a serious offence connected to the running of the business and this leads UKBA to doubt the sponsor's suitability (convictions that are 'spent' under the Rehabilitation of Offenders Act 1974 are left out of account – see also SG, para 105, footnote 3);

- the sponsor assigns a certificate of sponsorship indicating that a vacancy was in a shortage occupation when it was not;

- any of the Level 1 or 2 users disclose their sponsorship management system password to someone else;

- the organisation sponsors more than five migrants in the Tier 2 (Intra Company Transfer – Graduate Trainee) category with start dates in the same financial year;
- the organisation continues to sponsor a student after s/he has twice failed a re-sit or a period of study (but ▶see the position for sponsors with HTS status, Chapter 8 at 287);
- the courses offered in the Tier 4 (General) Student category are below S/NVQ Level 3 or equivalent (or for English language courses, below CEFR level B2 – although there are some exceptions, ▶see 259);
- any work placement accounts for more than 50% of the total length of the course (unless there is a UK statutory requirement that requires it);
- the study element of any course is not undertaken on the premises of the sponsor;
- the sponsor has assigned certificates to students, who are not from majority English-speaking countries, in order to do English language courses or courses below degree level (excluding foundation degrees) without properly assessing the students' English language ability;
- the sponsor is 'A' rated and it has offered places to Tier 4 (General) students on courses at NQF level 3 (or equivalent);
- the sponsor is 'A' rated and it has offered places courses to Tier 4 (General) students below degree level (excluding foundation degrees) that include a work placement;
- the sponsor has offered places to Tier 4 (General) students where the main course of study does not lead to an UKBA approved qualification; or
- a Tier 4 sponsor ceases to meet the additional ratings criteria for an 'A' rated sponsor (▶see 101).

Procedure on downgrading a licence

If UKBA is considering downgrading a sponsor licence from 'A' to 'B', it will notify the sponsor of its proposed reasons, and give the sponsor 28 calendar days to make written representations in response, enclosing any relevant evidence. The 28-day period may be extended on request if there are exceptional circumstances. UKBA will then notify the sponsor of its decision whether to downgrade or not within 14 calendar days of receiving the sponsor's written responses. The decision will take effect from the date of the letter informing the sponsor of it (SG, paras 459–464). If the licence is downgraded, then the sponsor will be required to agree an 'action plan' (▶see 102) with UKBA which is intended to enable the sponsor to re-gain their 'A' rating. The sponsor will not be able to assign any more certificates to sponsored migrants until it has signed up to the measures set out in the action plan (SG, para 129).

Withdrawal and suspension of a sponsor licence

If a licence is suspended or withdrawn, that action will take effect in respect of *all* tiers, categories and subcategories in which the sponsor holds a licence (SG, paras 465, 477).

When UKBA *will* withdraw a sponsor licence

UKBA will withdraw a sponsor licence where (SG, paras 466 467; Student SG, para 365):

- the sponsor stops trading or operating;
- the sponsor ceases to be accredited or registered with a body that it needs accreditation/registration with in order to obtain a licence;
- the authorising officer, key contact, a level 1 user, owner or director of the organisation, or anyone involved in its day-to-day running, is issued with a civil penalty for employing one or more illegal workers under section 15 2006 Act and the fine that was imposed in respect of at least one of those workers is set at the maximum amount (presently £10,000) (this applies unless the penalty is withdrawn, reduced or cancelled by UKBA or on an appeal);
- any of the persons mentioned immediately above is issued with a civil penalty for a first offence where the fine is below the maximum amount but has failed to pay the fine within the 28-day time limit that is given;
- any of the persons mentioned immediately above has been issued with a civil penalty for a repeat offence within the period of the validity of their sponsor licence;
- the sponsor has been 'B' rated and not complied with an action plan for a period of 12 months or more;
- the sponsor has been 'B' rated and has assigned a certificate stating that a vacancy was in a shortage occupation, although that was not the case;
- the sponsor has been 'B' rated because it is a new further education provider with stage 2 accreditation and has failed to achieve full accreditation within 12 months (▶see above at 91);
- it is a private further, or higher education institution and has not reported a change in its ownership or the appointment of a new principal within 28 days of that change; or
- having been 'B' rated, the sponsor fails to pay the action plan fee within 14 calendar days.

When UKBA *will normally* withdraw a licence

The sponsor's licence will normally be withdrawn where (SG, para 468; Student SG, para 367):

- the sponsor, authorising officer, key contact, level 1 user, an owner or director of the organisation, or anyone involved in its day-to-day running, is: convicted (and the conviction is not spent under the Rehabilitation of

Offenders Act 1974) of an offence under the Acts of 1971, 1988, 1993, 1999, 2002, 2006 or 2007, or of an offence of trafficking for sexual exploitation, or of any other offence which indicates that the person is a risk to immigration control (including the offences listed in Appendix B to the Sponsor Guidance);

- any of the persons mentioned immediately above is dishonest in any of their dealings with UKBA (including by making a false statement, or failing to disclose essential information when applying for a sponsor licence or assigning a certificate);

- any of the persons mentioned immediately above becomes legally prohibited from acting as a company director;

- any of the persons mentioned immediately above becomes an undischarged bankrupt;

- the sponsor employs a migrant in a job that would not satisfy the appropriate skill level (for a Tier 2 (General) Migrant, that is S/NVQ level 3 or above);

- the sponsor fails to pay a migrant in the Tier 2 (skilled workers) category at least the salary (and/or allowances or benefits) specified on the certificate; or

- from 6 October 2010, or within six months of being granted a Tier 4 licence or receiving an intake of students (whichever is earlier), the sponsor fails to achieve the additional ratings criteria that applies to a 'B' rated sponsor (▶see 91); or

- the sponsor fails to comply with an action plan that has been drawn up by UKBA.

When UKBA *may* withdraw a licence

The sponsor's licence may be withdrawn where (SG, para 472; Student SG, para 371):

- the sponsor fails to comply with any of its duties (▶see 114–118);

- as a result of information UKBA's visiting officers have obtained, it is not satisfied that the sponsor is using the processes or procedures necessary to fully comply with its duties;

- the sponsor, authorising officer, key contact, level 1 user, an owner or director of the organisation, or anyone involved in its day to day running, is convicted of an offence that is considered by UKBA to be serious and the offence is not spent under the Rehabilitation of Offenders Act 1974;

- UKBA finds that migrants sponsored by the sponsor have not complied with the conditions of their leave in the UK and the sponsor has not been following good practice guidance set out by UKBA or a sector body;

- the sponsor or other organisation that the sponsor (or any of the persons referred to immediately above) have been involved with in a similar role, had its authorisation removed by the Office of the Immigration Services

Commissioner (OISC) (the OISC regulates those who provide immigration advice and services);

- the sponsor is 'B' rated and any of the sponsor's level 1 or level 2 users disclose their sponsor management system password to another person;

- the organisation sponsors more than five migrants in the Tier 2 (Intra Company Transfer – Graduate Trainee) category with start dates in the same financial year;

- the sponsor continues to sponsor a student after s/he has already twice failed to resit, or twice repeated a period of study (but ▶see Chapter 8 287 for the position in relation to sponsors with HTS status);

- the courses it is offering to sponsored students in the Tier 4 (General) category are below S/NVQ level 3 (or for English language courses, below CEFR level B2 – although there are exceptions, ▶see 259);

- any work placement accounts for more than 50% of the total length of a Tier 4 student's course (unless there is a UK statutory requirement that requires it);

- the study element of any course offered to a sponsored students is not undertaken on the premises of the sponsoring educational institution;

- the sponsor has assigned certificates to students, who are not from majority English-speaking countries, in order to do English language courses or courses below degree level (excluding foundation degrees) without first properly assessing the students' English language ability;

- the sponsor has offered places to General students on courses at NQF level 3 (or equivalent);

- it has offered places to General students for courses below degree level (excluding foundation degrees) that include a work placement; or

- it has offered places to General students where the main course of study does not lead to an UKBA approved qualification.

Withdrawal procedure: when UKBA 'will' withdraw the licence

In any of the circumstances listed above as situations in which UKBA 'will' withdraw the licence, UKBA states in its guidance that it will withdraw the licence with immediate effect (SG, para 467). If UKBA does this without giving the sponsor any chance to make representations, in our view it may be vulnerable to challenge. This is because, even in circumstances in which UKBA considers the withdrawal to be mandatory, the sponsor may have a case to make about whether the facts said to give rise to the withdrawal are actually established. A sponsor might, for example, wish to make representations on the question of whether it really has stopped trading, or whether one of its key personnel really has been given a civil penalty which they really have failed to pay within the required time (etc). It may also be that, even if the primary facts for the mandatory withdrawal of the licence are made out, there are some exceptional or mitigating circumstances that the sponsor wishes to put forward.

In addition, the Sponsor Guidance is not completely clear on whether no notice is to be given. Users will note that, although paragraph 467 refers to withdrawal with immediate effect, an earlier paragraph under the heading 'Downgrading to A B rating' states:

"453. When we believe a sponsor has not been complying with its duties, has been dishonest in dealing with us or poses a threat to immigration control, we may *withdraw* its licence or downgrade it to a B rating. *We will give the sponsor an opportunity to explain its case to us before taking any action*." (emphasis added)

This paragraph appears to suggest that UKBA will give advance notice of any decision to withdraw.

Suspension and withdrawal procedure: when UKBA 'may' or 'will normally' withdraw the licence

If the situation is one which is described by the above Sponsor Guidance as one in which UKBA 'may' or 'will normally' withdraw the licence, then the Guidance states that the following procedure applies. If UKBA considers that the available evidence shows that the sponsor is breaching its duties or posing a threat to immigration control such that withdrawal of the licence may need to be considered, then it will suspend the licence while a more detailed investigation is carried out (SG, paras 470, 473, 475, 480).

However, if UKBA does not believe that suspension is necessary, it is still likely to downgrade the licence to a 'B' rating (SG, paras 471, 474, 480). In fact, part of the Guidance states that in circumstances where UKBA 'will normally' or 'may' withdraw the licence, UKBA will first consider whether to downgrade the licence (SG, para 480; Student SG, para 379).

If UKBA does decide to suspend the licence, it states that it will then adopt one of the following two procedures.

- UKBA may write to the sponsor giving "detailed reasons" for the suspension and giving them 28 calendar days to make representations. The 28-day deadline is extendable in 'exceptional circumstances'. UKBA will then make a final decision within 14 calendar days of receiving the sponsor's response. If new relevant evidence comes to light during the 28-day period for the sponsor's response, UKBA may ask for a further response from the sponsor, giving them a further 28 days to provide it (SG, paras 482–488).

- Alternatively, UKBA may write to the sponsor giving its "initial reasons" for the suspension pending a full investigation. UKBA will then proceed to make its full investigation and when that has been concluded, if the suspension is to be maintained, UKBA will write again giving its detailed reasons for the suspension. The same procedure as immediately above then applies regarding a response from the sponsor (SG, paras 489–495).

At the conclusion of the process, UKBA may either decide to withdraw the licence, or lift the suspension and reinstate the sponsor. It could also still decide at that stage to downgrade the sponsor to a 'B' rating and draw up an action plan.

However, the above paragraphs of the Sponsor Guidance do not state that the sponsor will be given any advance notice of the suspension itself. That is important because suspension may have an extremely detrimental effect on a sponsor during the period that it is in force, even if it is later lifted after representations have been made. This question was addressed in *R (Manchester College of Higher Education and Media Techno-logy Ltd) v SSHD* (8 December 2010). In that case the Court had to consider whether, at least in the case of a Tier 4 sponsor, there was a duty to give some advance notice with an opportunity to make representations before even a suspension of the licence could come into effect. The Court looked at paragraph 16 of the Student Sponsor Guidance which suggested that in a suspension "we will give the sponsor an opportunity to explain its case to us before taking any such action" (the equivalent paragraph in the present general Sponsor Guidance is para 15, although that paragraph excludes the words "before taking any such action"). The Court in the *Manchester College* case held that, in the circumstances of that case, both the Student Sponsor Guidance and the general ('common') law rules of fairness required advance consultation with the sponsor before the suspension took place. For the Manchester case in more detail, ▶see 133–135 below and see also *R (Langcomp Ltd) v SSHD* (▶below at 131).

As to the duty on UKBA to provide reasons for a suspension so that the sponsor may make representations, it is clear that it will not be sufficient for UKBA just to go through the motions. The reasons that are given must be sufficient to enable the sponsor to know in what respect/s they are said to be in default so that the sponsor can make effective representations to UKBA to demonstrate otherwise. It will not do if, in the final decision, UKBA introduces new grounds for withdrawal which the sponsor has not had the opportunity to make representations about (▶see the example of the *London Reading College* case in the table below 136–137).

During the period of any suspension, sponsors (SG, para 476):

- will not be able to issue any further certificates to migrants they may wish to sponsor; and
- must continue to comply with the sponsorship duties (▶114).

Remedies for suspension and withdrawal of sponsor licence

There is no right of appeal against a decision to suspend, downgrade or withdraw a sponsor licence. Those affected may make representations including within the procedure described above. Organisations that have had their licence withdrawn may also re-apply to become a sponsor. If they re-apply, UKBA will look to see whether the grounds for the with-drawal have been rectified. On the re-application, the organisation will have to pay the appropriate fee and produce all the relevant documenta-tion once again (SG, paras 508–510). The only means of legal challenge to negative decisions is through judicial review (▶below).

Judicial review

Sponsors may resort to judicial review as appropriate but will need expert legal advice before doing so. As indicated, the *London Reading College* case (▶see the table below at 136–137) is a useful illustration of the duty on UKBA to adopt a procedure that is fair to the sponsor by clearly setting out all its concerns so that the sponsor has a chance to address them properly. It also indicates that a sponsor's licence is a "possession" within the meaning of Article 1 of the First Protocol to the ECHR (the human right to the peaceful enjoyment of possessions) (▶see further, on this point, Chapter 12 at 430–435).

If judicial review is appropriate, then the sponsor may also consider applying to the court to obtain 'interim relief' ie an 'injunction' to prevent a decision of UKBA from taking immediate effect. This has been a par-ticular concern in the case of the suspension or withdrawal of sponsor licences, particularly of educational institutions, because suspension during the period that it takes to get a full legal resolution of the issue may fatally undermine the sponsor's business and have serious consequences for the migrants it sponsors.

Some judicial review case examples follow below. Many of the examples are of permission/interim relief hearings only and we include them in order to give users an idea of the kind of issues that have arisen and some basic pointers as to how the Courts have been approaching them. Care with the authorities must also be taken because, sometimes, they can turn on the particular Guidance that was in force at the time.

R (Waqar Bhatti, The Middlesex College Ltd & others) v SSHD **(6 Nov-ember 2009)** In this case, the Divisional Court held that the suspension of the college's sponsor licence was justified by either or both: (a) a police investigation into the facilitation of illegal immigration by the college; and (b) the college's suspension from its accreditation with the Accreditation Service for International Colleges (ASIC) (Judgment, paras 24-25, 28–29, 31(1)).

R (Hamilton College Ltd) v SSHD **(5 March 2010 and 14 May 2010)** When this case originally came before the Court, Black J felt that it was not possible to deal with the question of permission to apply for judicial review of the suspension of the College's licence because there had, in recent days, been a very substantial flow of information relating to the case that had led to some confusion. The Court considered only the question of interim relief. Black J balanced the detriment to the College (financial loss, students opting to go elsewhere, students seeking recovery from the College of fees for their courses) against the interests of immigration control. The Judge also noted that, if the College were able to continue issuing certificates, new students might be done a disservice by being granted certificates for a College which might not in the end be able to allow them to finish their courses (March transcript, paras 12–13). On balance the Judge decided to refuse interim relief but instead indicated that the case should be expedited (paras 15–16).

By the time that the case came back before the Court in May 2010 (before Nicol J), a decision to withdraw the licence had been made and the case was listed and decided together with the similar case of *Leeds Unique Education* (for which, ▶see 132 below). The Court granted permission to apply for judicial review of the original suspension decision because the level of information/reasons provided at the time of the initial suspension and even up to the time that the claim for judicial review was brought, was extremely limited (May transcript, para 32). The Court also granted permission for judicial review in relation to the later withdrawal of the licence. In part this was because, although the withdrawal was based on the ground that the College was not properly assessing the intentions of its students before assigning a visa letter (ie a certificate), it appeared that only 6% of the total students to whom a visa letter had been issued did not enrol. It was also felt that it might be rash to assume that the eventual failure of a migrant to enrol automatically meant that the student was exercising deception, that was not picked up by the College, at the outset when the College assigned a certificate (May transcript, para 36(c)).

Interim relief was granted to the College pending the full hearing of the judicial review claim. In deciding the 'balance of convenience' (the test generally used to decide whether to give interim relief) in favour of the claimant, the Court took into account (May transcript, paras 38–40):

- the substantial loss that the College would suffer: if all of the presently sponsored students who had more than six months of their leave to run demanded a full refund of their fees, the College would face a bill of £2.5 million;
- in the particular case, the claimant's grounds for seeking judicial review against UKBA were strong not weak;
- the interim order could still allow the SSHD to take measures against the College if some new cause arose that showed a risk to immigration control; and
- the pressure on Court listings meant that a full hearing of the claim for judicial review in the immediate future was unlikely.

The Court noted (para 39):

"The SSHD is of course entitled and obliged to take proper measures to prevent breaches of immigration control, but that is not a good reason for refusing interim relief where the claimant has strong grounds for saying that the actions taken against it so far are not lawful."

Finally, it is to be noted that, possibly because of the view that Black J had earlier taken about the disservice to students waiting in the wings to whom the College might issue a certificate, the claimants offered to give an undertaking not to issue any certificates to new students during the period while any interim order was in place. The Judge indicated that he would not insist on such an undertaking before granting interim relief (para 40).

R (Guildhall College Ltd) v SSHD (5 March 2010) In this case, following a visit to the College, UKBA suspended its licence on 14 January 2010. On that date, UKBA wrote to the College stating that it had 28 days to make any representations including, if it wished, to submit evidence in response to the letter. The letter continued "…we will aim to decide what action, if any, to take within 14 days of receiving any representations" (para 9). The College indicated that it would make representations but it did not do so within the 28-day time period. UKBA then wrote again on 16 February 2010, this time stating that it had withdrawn the licence (para 12).

In its judicial review challenge, the College relied on the part of the then Sponsor Guidance which stated that, after a visiting officer had recommended withdrawal or downgrading of a sponsor licence, it would write to the sponsor to tell it "what action we propose to take and why". The Court decided that it was arguable that UKBA had failed to follow its own Guidance and approach in the letter, because it had only indicated in the January letter that it would be deciding what action it would take and there was no further letter stating that it had decided upon withdrawing the licence subject to any further representations. The departure from the Guidance was particularly material since UKBA knew that representations were on their way (paras 18–19). The Court also considered it arguable that the withdrawal was disproportionate given the options available to impose a lesser sanction in a case where the College had made efforts to improve its performance (para 22).

The Judge granted the College permission to apply for judicial review and interim relief that stayed the *withdrawal* of the licence but only restored the College to the position of having its licence *suspended* until the final outcome. The factors taken into consideration in making the decision on interim relief were:

a) the decision to withdraw the licence had been taken without the information required in order to properly reach that decision;

b) the evidence of any difficulties in the College was not of such significance to require that the licence be treated as withdrawn during the period of the court proceedings;

c) equally it would be undesirable for any new students to rely on visa letters/certificates issued by the sponsor for the time being – so the licence should stay suspended; and

d) the impact on the existing students of the suspension was relatively limited (paras 25–30).

R (Langcomp Ltd) v SSHD **(23 March 2010)** (Note: there are two transcripts of the hearing for the same day). In this case, the College sought permission to apply for judicial review of a decision to suspend a licence and also interim relief to stay the existing suspension and any future withdrawal/revocation of the licence pending the outcome of the judicial review proceedings. The Court granted these orders (see second transcript paras 1–5, 12–13). What is of particular interest is the fact that, although it was acknowledged that the Sponsor Guidance itself does not require UKBA to give advance notice of a decision to suspend a licence, the Court appeared to accept the claimant's submission that it may still be unfair to suspend a licence without advance notice to the sponsor with an opportunity to respond (▶see similarly the *Manchester College* case below at 133). To not give any notice in this particular case seemed to be especially unfair because UKBA had suddenly suspended the licence having very recently, and after a site visit, indicated that all was well (see first transcript, paras 11, 26, 36–44, 89–90, 117; second transcript para 30).

Collins J also agreed with the claimant College that it was "absurd" to suggest that, because 22 students of a total of 1,145 at the College had decided to drop out, that meant the College was not taking enough care to establish the intentions of its proposed sponsored students before assigning certificates to them. If the same logic were applied to Entry Clearance Officers or Immigration Judges, who grant entry clearance or allowing appeals in respect of a number of students, a small proportion of whom later failed to attend the College, a large number of ECOs and IJs would have to be sacked ! (see first transcript, paras 97–101, 117).

The Judge also indicated that, although there is no way of institutions recovering damages for financial losses caused by maladministration by UKBA, there might be a suggestion of misfeasance in some of UKBA's behaviour which might lead to claims for damages (second transcript, para 32).

London College of Excellence v SSHD **(7 May 2010)** In this case, the claimant College was refused permission to apply for judicial review of the revocation of its licence when the Court upheld UKBA's decision to the effect that:

a) sponsors were under a duty to check the UKBA website regularly for the up-to-date version of the Sponsor Guidance and to obtain the correct email address to use when reporting any changes to UKBA;

b) high levels of non-attendance at the College did show failures in the College's recruitment policies which are intended to ensure that those issued with a certificate have a genuine intention to study; and

c) the College had not been following the requirements of the Guidance regarding record keeping and attendance monitoring.

R (Leeds Unique Education) v SSHD **(14 May 2010)** This case raised similar questions to *R (Hamilton College Ltd) v SSHD* (▶above) and the permission/interim relief hearing on 14 May 2010 was heard together with that case. UKBA had withdrawn the College's sponsorship licence. Among the reasons for granting permission to apply for judicial review were that the decision that the College was not conscientiously carrying out its duties to assess whether students had the intention and ability to carry out their studies in advance of issuing a visa letter/certificate, was flawed (para 20):

"The chain of reasoning appears to have been as follows: attendance rates were low; those students who had such low attendance rates were not properly carrying out their studies; those same students did not intend to (or would not have had the ability to) carry out their studies at the time they were assessed and granted visa letters; the College (or its agents) had been deficient in their duties because they had failed to identify these matters. However, it is arguable, as the College contends, that these steps do not follow logically from each other. So, for instance, students who attend few lectures may still do well in their examinations or other assessments. Intervening events after the issuing of a visa letter may have changed their ability or intentions. A reasonable and proportionate assessment system will not always be able to identify applicants who lack the intention or ability to complete their studies."

Nicol J also granted Leeds interim relief having regard to the following factors:

a) the judicial review claim was strongly arguable;

b) the withdrawal of the licence was having a "devastating" impact on the business of the College – it had refunded £23,000 in fees already with a possibility of having to refund a further £0.5 million; it had reduced its staff from ten to four and also shed eight part-time staff;

c) the College continued to be accredited by its accrediting organisation, the British Accreditation Council and UKBA had not taken issue with the quality of teaching or other provision offered by the College – UKBA was not saying that the College was 'bogus';

d) the College's business plan was geared to students from South and South-East Asia, it would be difficult for them to switch to obtain a new complement of students from within the EU ie those who did not need to be assigned a certificate; and

e) as to the possibility of the College making a further application for a licence and that UKBA might make a lawful decision on that application, that was not of strong weight in deciding whether the College should have interim relief against the existing unlawful decision (paras 26–29).

In *R (New London College Ltd) v SSHD* (19 October 2010) In this case, the claimant College, after having obtained permission to apply for judicial review, applied for 'interim relief' to remove the suspension of its licence until the Court could make a final decision on the claim for judicial review. The College stated that it was suffering the following forms of substantial detriment after the suspension of the licence and pending the hearing of the claim: financial prejudice; staff redundancies/reduction in salaries; knock-on detriment to suppliers of printing and cleaning services; students unable to extend their leave to continue studying at the College; some students unable to sit their exams because certain examining bodies refused to register them while they were studying at a college whose licence had been suspended; and the possibility of the College being forced to close for business.

However, Cranston J agreed with UKBA that, despite action taken by the College since the suspension decision, a further visit by UKBA to the College had revealed that it remained non-compliant with its sponsor duties. In deciding where the 'balance of convenience' lay pending the final outcome of the judicial review claim, the Court gave very heavy weight to the public interest in immigration control and held that UKBA was entitled to maintain the suspension during that period. It concluded:

"12. There is no doubt that...there are very serious implications for the College of the continuation of the suspension. In my view the public interest in immigration control through colleges which are compliant with the licences outweighs that in the balance and I refuse interim relief."

R (Manchester College of Higher Education and Media Technology Ltd) v SSHD **(26 October 2010, permission and interim relief)** Having granted permission to apply for judicial review, the Court found that on the facts of the case, interim relief had to be granted. It was clear that there were a substantial number of non-EU students who would be affected. UKBA asserted that an entirely fresh application to UKBA for a licence could be made but the Judge, HHJ Waksman QC, was of the view that that could not cure the present problem because such an application would inevitably take time (paras 29–30).

R (Manchester College of Higher Education and Media Technology Ltd) v SSHD **(8 December 2010, full judicial review hearing)** The College had obtained a Tier 2 and Tier 4 sponsor licence in 2009 but only with a 'B' rating. It tried to upgrade its status to either trusted or HTS and to increase its allocation of certificates. After a site visit, the College was informed that a recommendation would be made to increase its allocation as requested. However, UKBA subsequently alleged that an email from the College, sent on 9 October 2010, had set out to deliberately mislead the decision-makers. On the basis of that, UKBA suspended the licence right at the start of the academic year (paras 7, 9).

The Judge considered the following paragraph of the Student SG (ie the present 10/10 version):

"Where we consider that a sponsor has not been complying with its duties, has been dishonest in its dealings with us or otherwise poses a threat to immigration control, we may withdraw, suspend or downgrade it to a B (Sponsor)-rating or reduce the number of confirmations of acceptance of studies it is allowed to assign. If we decide to suspend or downgrade the licence to a B (Sponsor)-rating, we will give the sponsor an opportunity to explain its case to us before taking any such action."

Later parts of the Student SG suggested that a licence would be suspended first and *then* there would be consultation with the sponsor with a chance to make representations (see Student SG, para 374). However, the Judge, HHJ Pelling QC, held that paragraph (para 374) dealt with cases where there was an allegation that the sponsor had breached his/her sponsor duties, or posed a threat to immigration and that was not the nature of allegation in this case. The allegation in the present case was that the sponsor had been *dishonest* which was a separate category of case and was referred to in paragraph 16 of the Sponsor Guidance (▶above). Accordingly, it was that paragraph of the Guidance that was relevant to this case. That meant that, on the Guidance alone, the sponsor was entitled to advance notice and a chance to make representations before the suspension (see Judgment, paras 13, 21, 24).

In addition and perhaps more importantly because the Guidance is always liable to change, the Judge also relied on the general, common law duty of fairness set out in cases such as *R v SSHD ex parte Doody*. The Judge referred to the importance of what was at stake for the College and its students and made reference to the high value that attaches to a sponsor licence as identified in the *London Reading College* case (see below). The Judge also referred to the delay in UKBA taking any action ie from the date of the offending email to the date of the suspension. This showed that this was not a case in which it appeared that immediate suspension was necessary. In those circumstances, the Judge held that the common law duty of fairness required that advance notice be given to the sponsor with an opportunity to make representations before the suspension came into effect (see Judgment paras 9, 14–15, 25):

"25. I am also entirely satisfied, to the extent that it is necessary for me to be so satisfied, that the common law rule of fairness required in the circumstances of this case that the claimant would be consulted before such a draconian step was taken. As I have said, there may be circumstances in which an immediate suspension will be called for. That is catered for in the subsequent provisions within the guidelines but this was not such a case."

The Judge went on to state that, although there had been a breach of the duty of common law fairness and the Guidance, that would not in itself be enough to justify quashing the decision, unless it could be shown that it was likely that a different outcome would have resulted if the relevant consultation process had taken place (see para 27). The Judge's conclusion was that it would indeed have made a difference and the suspension was therefore quashed (see para 44). However, although judicial review is a discretionary remedy, some may question whether the Court will always need to be satisfied that there may have been a different outcome if a fair procedure had been adopted, before the Court can intervene. In this context, we would draw attention to the following passage of the judgment of Lord Woolf MR from the well known case of *R v Home Secretary ex parte Fayed* (at pp777H–778B):

"It is true that until areas of concern are identified so that it can be ascertained whether the Fayeds would be in a position to make further representations it will not be possible to say whether an injustice has occurred. However justice must not only be done but be seen to be done and it has not been seen to be done in relation to the application of the Fayeds. They have not had the fairness to which they were entitled and the rule of law must be upheld. This being so the Secretary of State is not entitled to take advantage of his own error and contend that the Fayeds have failed to show they have been prejudiced. It follows that the Secretary of State's decisions must be quashed so they can be retaken in a manner which is fair. This is the concern of the courts, Parliament not having excluded the obligation to be fair. They are not concerned with the merits of the decision which should then be made. That is the concern of the Secretary of State."

See further the useful case of *London Reading College* ▶below 136–137.

Impact on migrants of suspension of licence

If the migrant has been issued with a certificate of sponsorship and leave to enter/remain in the UK *before* the suspension, it appears that the suspension of the licence will not have an immediate effect on them pending a final decision (▶see below for what happens if the licence is withdrawn).

Where a licence has been suspended and until a final decision has been made, UKBA will not make a decision on an application for entry clearance or leave to remain by any migrant who was issued with a certificate before the suspension, (SG, para 496). An application for entry clearance or leave by a migrant who was issued with a certificate *after* their sponsor's licence was suspended will be refused (SG, para 497).

Where entry clearance has been issued to a migrant before a suspension but the sponsor's licence is then suspended before they travel, UKBA will not prevent the migrant from coming to the UK and commencing work with the sponsor (SG, para 498). However, UKBA recommends that migrants in that position to do not travel (SG, para 498).

Impact on migrants of withdrawal of licence

When UKBA *withdraws* a licence, it treats any certificate issued by that sponsor as automatically invalid (SG, para 503). As to the existing migrants in the UK who were being sponsored by that licence holder, UKBA will (SG, para 500):

SUSPENSION AND WITHDRAWAL OF A LICENCE
THE LONDON READING COLLEGE CASE

Facts

In *R (The London Reading College Limited) v SSHD*, decided in October 2010, after conducting a visit to the College's premises, UKBA suspended LRC's licence on the basis of various deficiencies regarding the maintenance of student files, LRC's inability to provide sufficient records of its students or staff and an inability to determine from the records whether students were completing the required 15 hours per week of daytime study (Judgment, paras 17, 34).

The College made representations and there were improvements in its operation. A further visit by UKBA followed (paras 18–22). UKBA then wrote a further letter revoking the licence with immediate effect on the basis that not all issues had been resolved and that it had "serious concerns regarding the level of English language of some migrant students", that there was no evidence that LRC carried out English language skills testing of potential students and that this constituted a "breach of Tier 4 Sponsor obligations as per the published Guidance" (paras 24, 44). The effect was that LRC had to refund all its students with their fees for the academic year as it could no longer be their sponsor (para 24).

Findings of the court

The Judge allowed the claim for judicial review on the following grounds.

• The decision to revoke the licence was reached in breach of the rules of procedural fairness because the complaint about the lack of students' language skills was a "fresh allegation of which the College had no prior notice". Even if it was a complaint about record keeping, it was of a "wholly different" nature from the original record keeping matters that had been flagged up in the suspension decision which referred to the need to keep records of the identity and attendance of students, not their linguistic ability (paras 44, 48, 54). The point mattered because the LRC alleged that, had it been given the opportunity to make representations on the language issues, it had a satisfactory explanation. It stated that its policy was not to enrol students unless they had obtained either an IELTS score of 5.5, or they came from a Commonwealth country where education is provided in English (para 45). The Judge also referred to some further allegations of dishonesty that UKBA had made against the LRC that had not been properly and plainly put to the College for it to be able to respond (paras 47–48).

• The Court would grant relief to the LRC against UKBA's unlawful decision to withdraw the licence. It would not withhold that relief on the basis of UBKA's argument that the relevant bodies had withdrawn its accreditation. It would be wrong to do that since the LRC would not have got into difficulties with their accreditation in the first place had it not been for the withdrawal of the licence which had been unlawful (above). The Judge indicated that the accrediting bodies would doubtless now consider a fresh application for accreditation (para 53) (see, though, on this point, the different outcome in *R (Waqar Bhatti, The Middlesex College Ltd & others) v SSHD* at paras 30(2), 31(2), although that case concerned only the suspension of the licence).

- There had been a violation, by UKBA, of Article 1 of the First Protocol of the ECHR (the right to the peaceful enjoyment of possessions) (paras 64–68). UKBA accepted that a licence was capable of being a "possession" in certain circumstances. Any deprivation of a person's possessions had to be carried out in the public interest, subject to the "conditions provided for by law" and the principles of international law. Since the withdrawal of the licence was carried out in a way that was procedurally unfair (the first finding above), the revocation was not "subject to the conditions provided by law" which included the UK law requirement for procedural fairness (▶see further 430–435).

Note that the LRC also tried to challenge UKBA's decision on the grounds that the revocation of the licence was irrational and disproportionate. The Court's response in rejecting that ground ought to be borne in mind (paras 60–62). The Judge held (para 60):

"60. The capacity for damage to the national interest in the maintenance of proper immigration control is substantial if colleges are not assiduous in meeting their responsibilities. In these circumstances, it seems to me that [UKBA] are entitled to maintain a fairly high index of suspicion as they go about overseeing colleges and a light trigger in deciding when and with what level of firmness they should act..."

"62. ...In my judgment, it is not for the Court to weigh with a finely calibrated scale just what response was justified..."

It follows that the courts will apply a high threshold in deciding whether to intervene in a decision where the ground of challenge is irrationality.

A final important aspect of the Judgment is the importance and value that the Court attached to the possession of a sponsor licence (see para 9).

- immediately end the leave to enter/remain in the UK of any migrant who UKBA believes was "actively involved (complicit)" in any dishonesty by the sponsor – the leave of these migrants will be 'curtailed' so that there is no leave left;

- curtail to 60 remaining calendar days the leave to enter/remain in the UK of any other of that sponsor's migrants, ie those migrants who were not actively involved in any dishonesty – however if the migrant already has less than six months of his/her leave left remaining, UKBA will not curtail the leave at all.

Subject to any appeal, migrants in the first category above are required by UKBA to leave the UK immediately. The purpose of giving migrants in the second category ie the more deserving, a period 60 days is so that they have the opportunity of finding an alternative sponsor (SG, paras 500–502). In *JA (Revocation of registration – Secretary of State's policy) India*, the UT held that the policy of curtailment to 60 days did not give applicants who had no existing leave a legitimate expectation that they would be granted a 60-day grace period of leave to find another sponsor (see the decision at paras 12, 16–17, 19).

If a sponsor's licence has been withdrawn but an applicant who has been assigned a certificate by that sponsor has not yet come to the UK or applied for leave, then the consequences are (and see SG, para 503–504):

- any application for entry clearance and/or leave that were dependent on the licence will be refused;

- if the applicant has already been granted entry clearance but has not yet travelled to the UK, the entry clearance will be revoked by the entry clearance officer under paragraph 30A(ii) of the Rules on the grounds of a change of circumstance;

- if the applicant travels to the UK with an entry clearance, they will be refused entry to the UK under paragraph 321(ii) of the Rules (change of circumstances).

Criminal prosecution/civil penalties/other sanctions

In addition to taking action in relation to the sponsor licence (above), UKBA states that its visiting officers, who may carry out checks before a licence has been issued or once it is in force, are "fully trained in identifying and investigating illegal working and may issue civil penalties or refer cases for prosecution where appropriate" (SG, para 448, see also paras 16–17). Sponsors are recommended to be fully familiar with the UKBA guidance relating to preventing illegal working (see at http://www.ukba.homeoffice.gov.uk/employers/preventingillegalworking) and more information on the penalties that may be imposed is contained at http://www.ukba.homeoffice.gov.uk/sitecontent/documents/employersand sponsors/prepreventingillegalworking/currentguidanceandcodes/summary guidance 0208.pdf? view=Binay) (see SG, para 421 and 449).

Among the additional penalties that UKBA states sponsors may face, or be referred for by visiting officers in connection with illegal working, are the following (SG, para 450):

- written warnings for employing a worker who is not lawfully entitled to be employed in the UK;

- being served with an 'on the spot' civil penalty (fine) under section 15 of the 2006 Act (additional penalties may be imposed for each worker);

- prosecution for knowingly employing a worker with no lawful entitlement to be employed in the UK under section 21 of the 2006 Act;

- prosecution for possession (without reasonable excuse) of an identity document that is false or improperly obtained or which belongs to another under section 25 of the Identity Cards Act 2006;

- prosecution for facilitation or trafficking under s25 1971 Act (as amended); or

- being disbarred from serving as a company director or officer following a prosecution.

5 Tier 1: highly-skilled and high net-worth migrants and entrepreneurs

This chapter covers the following:

Tier 1 of the PBS replaced the following previous categories under the Immigration Rules;

- the Highly Skilled Migrants Programme (HSMP);
- businesspersons;
- Investors; and
- the International Graduates Scheme.

The purpose of Tier 1 is to allow the admission of highly-skilled migrants who are likely to contribute to the UK economy. Unlike other tiers of the PBS, Tier 1 does not require applicants to be sponsored by an employer or other institution in the UK.

As well as the Rules, this chapter makes detailed reference to the Policy Guidance made by UKBA. The Guidance referred to is abbreviated as follows (see the end of this Guide for further abbreviations).

T1 (General) PG   Tier 1 (General) of the Points-Based System – Policy Guidance, 14 December 2010

T1 (Ent) PG   Tier 1 (Entrepreneur) of the Points-Based System – Policy Guidance, 14 December 2010

T1 (Inv) PG   Tier 1 (Investor) of the Points-Based System – Policy Guidance, 14 December 2010

T1 (PSW) PG   Tier 1 (Post-Study Work) of the Points-Based System – Policy Guidance, 14 December 2010

PBS Dependant PG Points-Based System (Dependant) Policy Guidance, version 12/10, for applications made on or after 14 December 2010

References to 'App' A, B, C and E are to Appendices A, B, C and E of the present Immigration Rules.

THE FUTURE OF TIER 1

Tightening access to the UK under Tier 1 is central to the Government's plan to make significant reductions in the level of migration. In her speech to the Policy Exchange on 5 November 2010, the Secretary of State set out the Government's position as follows.

"Recent Home Office research showed that nearly a third of the Tier 1 migrants sampled – that is, people who are supposed to be highly-qualified and highly-skilled migrants – were not currently employed in highly-skilled jobs. They have come across examples of so called 'highly-skilled' migrants working doing jobs that most of us would not classify as highly-skilled. There is the individual who was issued with a Tier 1 visa and later became a duty manager at a well-known high street chain of fried chicken restaurants.

"At the same time, last year the UK only attracted 275 high-value investors and entrepreneurs.

"I want a new approach: one that is more selective; that brings in more of the genuinely skilled; and those who will make a real difference to our economy. Operating effectively, Tier 1 should only be used by investors, entrepreneurs and people of exceptional talent; in short, the genuinely highly-skilled. Not only that, we also want to actively encourage entrepreneurs to come ... we will reform the rules for entrepreneurs so that if you have a great business idea, and you receive serious investment from a leading investor, you are welcome to set up your business in our country."

On 23 November 2010, the Home Secretary made a statement to Parliament reiterating the Government's concern that 30 per cent of Tier 1 migrants end up in low-skilled occupations such as "stacking shelves, driving taxis or working as security guards", while some are unemployed. She set out the decision of the Government to:

- close the Tier 1 (General) route altogether (it had already been the subject of an interim cap (▶see below) on the basis that it is not, as planned, attracting the "brightest and best" to the UK;
- restrict Tier 1 to the following categories: investors; entrepreneurs and a "new route within Tier 1 for people of exceptionally talent – the scientists, academics and artists who have achieved international recognition, or are likely to do so";

- impose a cap on Tier 1 entrants of 1,000 for the first year (reducing the number by more than 13,000 over the previous year).

Changes will be introduced from April 2011. The cap of 1,000 persons is part of the Government's permanent cap on non-EU migration. The remainder of the cap will fall on Tier 2 (►see Chapter 6 208–210). For full details of the operation of the (unlawfully imposed) interim cap from 19 July 2010 and the re-imposed interim cap from 23 December 2010 to April 2010, ►see Chapter 2 55–59 and Chapter 4 106–108.

For the phasing out of Tier 1 (General) ►see immediately below. For transitional provisions ►see 211.

For further details of UKBA's proposals for change to the Tier 1 (Entrepreneur) category ►see below 164–165.

For further details of UKBA's proposals for change to the Tier 1 (Investor) category, ►see below 173.

For the proposals that have emerged from the general student (Tier 4) consultation for substantial change to the Tier 1 (PSW) category, ►see Chapter 8 292–295.

For further details of UKBA's newly-proposed 'Exceptional Talent' category, ►see below 203–204.

TIER 1 (GENERAL) MIGRANTS

The Tier 1 (General) category replaces and is almost identical to the HSMP Programme under the old Rules. It is aimed at "highly-skilled" individuals who the UK government believes are likely to contribute to the UK economy by obtaining employment, or becoming self-employed in the UK (Rules, para 245A) and to contribute to "growth and productivity" (Explanatory Memo to HC 321, para 7.2). Like the HSMP, Tier 1 (General) does not require applicants to have secured employment, or even have an offer of employment, before entry. The category was introduced in stages by amendments made to the Rules by HC 321 and HC 607 (the amending Rules also deleted the HSMP subject to transitional provisions – see Rules, para 245F). Applications for leave to remain under Tier 1 (General) could be made from 29 February 2008. Out-of-country applications commenced from India from 1 April 2008 (see HC 321); and from elsewhere from 30 June 2008 (see HC 607). Explained below are the requirements as they are stated in the Rules before April 2011. There have been various amendments since the introduction of the category and those amendments have included some transitional provisions.

The phasing out of Tier 1 (General)

On 19 July 2010, the Government imposed an 'interim cap' on the number of applications for entry clearance and leave to enter (but not leave to remain) within the Tier 1 (General) category (HC 59). UKBA began limiting the numbers of grants of entry to 600 per month (▶see Chapter 2 56–57). On 17 December 2010, the Divisional Court ruled that the means by which the Government implemented the cap were unlawful (▶49–50, 58–59). Following this, on 21 December 2010, the Government closed the category to new applicants from overseas (see the amendments to the Rules made by HC 698) (▶59). After that the route only remained open for:

- those who had already applied for entry clearance *before* 23 December 2010;
- those seeking to extend their leave in the UK, including by switching.

As indicated above, the Government has stated that it will close the route completely in April 2011. For the transitional provisions for those in the Tier 1 (General) category before 6 April 2011 ▶see 211. The Rules below will continue to apply for those in the Tier 1 (General) category who wish to extend their leave.

WHAT THE RULES SAY

Entering and remaining under Tier 1 (General)

The requirements to be met by those seeking to enter or remain in the UK in the Tier 1 (General) category are that the applicant must (paras 245C–D, HC 395):

- not fall for refusal under the general grounds for refusal (▶see Chapter 11);
- if seeking leave to remain, not be an illegal entrant;
- if applying for leave to remain and s/he has, or last had, leave as a Tier 1 (General) migrant, a Highly Skilled Migrant, as a Writer, Composer or Artist, or as a Self-employed Lawyer, score a minimum of 75 points for 'attributes' set out in paras 1–31 of Appendix A of the Rules;
- if the applicant is applying for leave to remain but does not have (or was last granted) leave in one of the categories referred to immediately above, score a minimum of 80 points for the 'attributes' set out in paras 1–31 of Appendix A;
- if the applicant is applying for entry clearance, score a minimum of 80 points for the 'attributes' set out in paras 1–31 of Appendix A;
- score 10 points for 'English language' as set out in paras 1–2 of Appendix B of the Rules;
- score 10 points for the 'maintenance' requirements as set out in paras 1–3 of Appendix C to the Rules;
- if seeking leave to remain, have or have last been granted entry clearance or leave under one of the following categories/tiers (ie it is possible to 'switch' in-country to the Tier 1 (General) from any of the following categories):

- Highly Skilled Migrant Programme;
- Tier 1 (General);
- Innovator;
- Fresh Talent: Working in Scotland Scheme;
- International Graduates Scheme (or its predecessor, the Science and Engineering Graduates Scheme);
- Postgraduate Doctor or Dentist;
- Student,
- Student nurse;
- Student Re-sitting an Examination;
- Student Writing-up a Thesis;
- Work Permit holder;
- Businessperson;
- Self-employed Lawyer;
- Tier 1 (Entrepreneur);
- Tier 1 (Investor);
- Tier 1 (Post-Study Work);
- Writer, Composer or Artist;
- Tier 2;
- Tier 4; or
- partner of a Tier 4 migrant; and
- if s/he is presently being sponsored by a government, or an international scholarship agency (or has been so sponsored although the sponsorship came to an end within the last 12 months) and s/he has, or was last granted, leave as a student, postgraduate doctor or dentist, student nurse, student re-sitting an examination, student writing-up a thesis or as a Tier 4 migrant, have the unconditional written consent to his/her application of the sponsoring government or agency (for the documents that specified by the Guidance for applicants to prove that they have this consent, see T1 (Gen) PG, paras 39–40).

Those who have sought to enter in this category, must have obtained a valid entry clearance enabling them to do so (Rules, para 245B).

For dependants of Tier 1 (General) migrants, ▶see 194.

WHAT THE RULES MEAN

Attributes

The points that are awarded for attributes are set out in Appendix A of the Rules (paras 1–31). In this category, points for attributes can be scored for:

- qualifications;
- previous earnings;
- UK experience; and
- age.

Applicants must score a minimum of either 75 or 80 points from any combination of the points awarded for attributes. However, applicants do not need to score points from each attribute category and can score the necessary 75 or 80 points from, for example, two of the four attributes categories.

The division into two thresholds (75 points and 80 points) was introduced by amending Rules from 19 July 2010 (Rules, paras 245(c); App A, paras 1, 1A and Table 2 as amended by HC 59). The threshold remained at 75 points for those already in the UK in the Tier 1 (General) category and those applying to switch into it from one of the predecessor categories for highly-skilled migrants (ie HSMP; Writer, Composer, Artist; Self-employed Lawyer). The purpose of increasing the threshold to 80 for everyone else, ie 'new' applicants, was to "ensure that only the brightest and most able migrants are granted entry to the United Kingdom" (Explanatory Memo to HC 59, para 7.14).

The maximum scores for the various attributes are: 50 points for qualifications; 80 points for previous earnings; 5 points for UK experience; and 20 points for age.

Automatic route for attributes: certain MBA graduates

There is one automatic route to scoring 80 points. This applies to those who have a Master of Business Administration (MBA) Degree from one of the institutions listed in paragraph 58A of Appendix A to the Rules and who (Rules, App A, para 1A):

- began the course of study that led to that degree on or before 29 June 2008;
- applied for entry clearance or leave to remain within 12 months of being awarded the qualification by the relevant institution; and
- provide the documents specified in the Policy Guidance to prove the above.

The automatic route is not available to those applying for leave to remain in the Tier 1 (General) category who already have, or were last granted, leave either as a Tier 1 (General) Migrant; under the HSMP; a Writer, Composer or Artist; or a Self-employed Lawyer (Rules, App A, para 1A). The route was added to the Rules from 27 November 2008 by HC 1113 in order to allow MBA graduates from the top business schools around the world to qualify. This was done so as to respect the expectations of those who had joined one of the relevant MBA courses on the understanding that, if successful, they would be permitted to come to the UK under the HSMP. Those expectations had existed since it was announced in the 2004 Budget that there would be a provision to allow graduates of some of the top business schools to work in the UK after completing their MBAs. The MBA provision was then launched on 12 April 2005 as part of the HSMP. The specified documents that applicants must produce to take advantage of this route are referred to in Annex C of the T1 (Gen) PG.

Qualifications

The points available for qualifications are set out in Appendix A of the Rules in Table 1 and paras 4–7. Applicants seeking to enter the UK, or applying for leave to remain under Tier 1 (General), will receive:

- 45 points if they have a PhD;
- 35 points for a Master's degree; and
- 30 points for a Bachelor's degree.

However, the above rule is modified where the applicant is applying for leave to remain in the following two situations:

- If the applicant has, or last had, leave under the HSMP, as a Writer, Composer or Artist, a Self-employed Lawyer, or as a Tier 1 (General) Migrant under the rules in place before 31 March 2009, s/he will be awarded: 50 points for a PhD; 35 points for a Master's degree and 30 points for a Bachelor's degree.
- If the applicant has, or last had, leave under Tier 1 (General) under the rules in place between 31 March 2009 and 5 April 2010, s/he will be awarded: 50 points for a PhD; 35 points for a Master's degree and no points for a Bachelor's degree.

Points can only be awarded for an academic qualification if it is deemed by the National Recognition Information Centre for the UK (UK NARIC) to meet or exceed the recognised standard of a Bachelor's or Master's degree or PhD in the UK. Points may be awarded for vocational and professional qualifications that are deemed by UK NARIC, or the appropriate UK professional body, to be equivalent to a Bachelor's or Master's degree or a PhD in the UK (Rules, App A, paras 5–6).

Applicants are advised by UKBA to check the level of their qualifications by using the 'points-based calculator' on the UKBA website. The calculator contains information from UK NARIC on the equivalence of overseas qualifications (T1 (Gen) PG, paras 85–7). UKBA also advises any applicants who are unable to find details of their qualification on the calculator to contact UK NARIC directly for an assessment of the level of their qualification (www.naric.org.uk). For professional/vocational qualifications that the applicant is unable to find on the calculator, applicants are advised to obtain written confirmation from the appropriate UK professional body who should be able to comment on the qualification's equivalence to UK academic levels (T1 (Gen) PG, paras 88–90).

Unless they were last granted leave under Tier 1 (General) or the HSMP categories and they previously scored points for the same qualification, applicants are required to produce specified documents as evidence of their qualification (App A, para 4). The documents specified in Guidance are (see T1 (Gen) PG, paras 92–95 for further details):

- original certificate of the award of the qualification;

- original academic reference from the institution that is awarding the degree together with an original academic transcript.

In cases where the applicant has not been able to find the details of his/her academic qualification on the calculator, s/he should, in addition to the above documents, submit an original letter/certificate from NARIC confirming the level of the qualification. Similarly, where the professional/vocational qualification cannot be located on the calculator, applicants should submit an original letter from the UK professional body confirming the relevant level (T1 (Gen) PG, paras 96–7).

Previous earnings

The points available for previous earnings are set out in tables 2–2A and paras 8–23 of Appendix A to the Rules. Applicants may claim points for their previous earnings whether in the UK or abroad. Income for any consecutive 12-month period during the 15-month period immediately before the date of application may be relied on and there are concessions for those who can show that they have been on maternity or adoption leave in the past 12 months (App A, paras 9–10). If an applicant fails to identify the period they rely on (or gives a period that does not comply with the above) then UKBA will assess them against the 12 months immediately before the date of the application (App A, para 12).

An applicant does not need to have actually worked for all of the 12-month period, because the necessary points are awarded not for the length of time that applicants work, but for the level of income earned in a maximum period of 12 months.

Earnings include (but are not limited to): salaries (including full-time or part-time employment, and bonuses); earnings from self-employment; earnings from business; statutory and contractual maternity or adoption pay; allowances forming part of a remuneration package (eg accommodation, schooling or car allowances); dividends from investments (provided the applicant is involved in the day to day running of the company, or where s/he has been paid a dividend as part of a remuneration package); property or rental income where this is part of the applicant's business and payments in lieu of (ie in place of) notice (App A, para 13).

Applicants are not limited to one employment or business. Their earnings may come from a number of sources, including different salaried or self-employed activities. The earnings may also come from different employers and the work done can be full-time, part-time, temporary and short-term (T1 (Gen) PG, para 119–121).

UKBA will not, however, count *unearned* sources of income such as interest on savings; inheritance; pension; state benefits; dividends where the applicant is not involved in the day-to-day running of the company and which are not received as part of a remuneration package; and property rental income where this does not form part of the applicant's business (further examples are also given at App A, para 16). Earnings are also not counted if they were made at a time when the applicant was in the UK in breach of the immigration laws (Rules, App A, para 17).

Salary, wages and business profits from self-employment, or other business activities, are all assessed on a gross basis, ie before tax (Rules, App A, paras 14–15).

The general rule is that the following points are awarded (Rules, App A, Table 2):

- 80 points for earnings of £150,000 or more;
- 45 points for earnings of £75,000–149,999;
- 40 points for earnings of £65,000–74,999;
- 35 points for earnings of £55,000–64,999;
- 30 points for earnings of £50,000–54,999;
- 25 points for earnings of £40,000–49,999;
- 20 points for earnings of £35,000–39,999;
- 15 points for earnings of £30,000–34,999;
- 5 points for earnings of £25,000–29,999.

However, separate and more generous points/earnings figures are given in Table 2 of Appendix A where the applicant is applying for leave to *remain* in the following circumstances:

- the applicant has, or last had, leave under the HSMP, as a Writer, Composer or Artist, a Self-employed Lawyer or as a Tier 1 (General) Migrant under the Rules in place before 31 March 2009;
- the applicant has (or last had) leave as a Tier 1 (General) Migrant under the rules in place between 31 March 2009 and 5 April 2010.

Applicants relying on earnings made overseas will need to convert the relevant amount into pounds sterling. Conversions should be carried out by using the currency converter on the Oanda website (www.oanda.com/convert/classic) selecting the date of conversion as the last day of the period for which the applicant is claiming earnings (App A, paras 18, 20).

After they have been converted, the overseas earnings should be multiplied according to the multiplier for the country in which the earnings were made as shown in Table 2A of Appendix A of the Rules (App A, para 21). This multiplier, as with the previous HSMP multiplier, takes account of the different average income levels throughout the world. For instance, income earned in Japan (or the UK) has a multiplier of 1 (ie there is no increase in the figure). Income earned in Sierra Leone has a multiplier of 11.4, so earnings made in that country should be converted into sterling and then multiplied by 11.4 to give the final figure. However, the multiplier is not applied to the overseas earnings of applicants who are applying for leave to remain and have presently, or have last been granted, leave under the Tier 1 (General) category, the HSMP, as a Writer, Composer or Artist, or as a Self-employed lawyer (App A, para 22).

The applicant must produce "specified" documents as evidence of previous earnings (App A, para 8). Applicants wishing to use concession for those who have been on maternity or adoption leave so as to be able to rely on a period of time before the 15 months immediately before the date of the application, are required to prove their absence from work on those grounds by producing the documents specified at paragraph 112 of the T1 (Gen) PG.

The same Guidance specifies that each source of earnings must be supported by two different forms of supporting evidence and that each form of supporting evidence must be from a different source. The example is given that while both P60s and payslips are acceptable as evidence, UKBA considers them to be from the same source, so another form of evidence would be required in addition (T1 (Gen) PG, para 137). The documents that are specified for this purpose are (and see T1 (Gen) PG, para 141 for the further details relating to each type of specified document):

- payslips (formal payslips or on company headed paper);
- personal bank statements showing payments made to the applicant – bank statements must be on official bank stationery and must show each of the payments that the applicant is claiming;
- letter from the applicant's previous and/or present employer;
- official tax documents produced by the tax authority or employer showing earnings on which tax has been paid or will be paid in a tax year;
- dividend vouchers;
- for self-employed applicants, letter from the applicant's accountant confirming that the applicant received the exact amount claimed, or the net profit to which s/he is entitled;
- invoice explanations or payment summaries from the applicant's accountant;
- company or business accounts that clearly show the net profit of the company or business;
- business bank statements showing the payments made to the applicant – again bank statements provided should be on official bank stationery and show each of the payments that the applicant is claiming;
- where an applicant is submitting a combination of bank statements and a letter/invoice summary from their accountant, they must also provide any invoices generated during the period for which earnings are being claimed.

Applicants are also asked to provide full contact details for each source of income so that UKBA can, if necessary, verify the evidence (T1 (Gen) PG, paras 144–5).

Evidence that is produced from an accountant or an accountancy firm must be from a fully-qualified chartered accountant, or a certified accountant who is the member of a registered body (T1 (Gen) PG, para 139 sets out the further details). Those relying on earnings while self-employed must also provide documents to show that they are registered as self-employed and that they were paying class 2 national insurance contributions during the periods of self-employment. The Guidance sets out the documents that are specified to show these contributions (T1 (Gen) PG, paras 140, 142–3).

UK experience

Points available for UK experience are set out in Table 3 and paras 24–30 of Appendix A. There are only two possible scores: 0 points, or 5 points. The *general* rule is that 5 points will be awarded for 'UK experience' if *either*:

- £25,000 or more of the previous earnings for which points were claimed were earned in the UK; or
- the applicant has a relevant qualification (▶see below) obtained in the UK.

However, the rules differ from the above in the following two circumstances, both where the applicant is applying for leave to *remain*.

- If the applicant has, or was last granted, leave under the HSMP, as a Writer, Composer or Artist, as Self-employed Lawyer or as a Tier 1 (General) Migrant under the Rules in place before 6 April 2010, then 5 points will be earned for UK experience if £16,000 or more of the previous earnings for which points were claimed, were earned in the UK. In these cases, there is no provision to score points in the alternative for a UK qualification (App A, Table 3 and para 24).
- If the applicant has, or last had, leave as a Tier 1 (General) Migrant under the Rules in place on or after 6 April 2010, 5 points will be earned for UK experience if £25,000 or more of the previous earnings for which points were claimed were earned in the UK. In these cases, also there is no provision to score points in the alternative for a UK qualification (App A, Table 3 and para 24).

Points cannot be claimed for both previous earnings and UK qualifications: the maximum score is always 5 points (App A, para 25). Previous earnings will not be taken into account for the purposes of UK experience if the applicant was in breach of the UK's immigration laws at the time when those earnings were made (App A, para 30).

Qualifications for the purposes of UK experience Points can only be awarded for UK experience for qualifications if all of the following conditions are met (App A, paras 26–28):

- the qualification is a Bachelor's or Master's degree or a PhD, and is deemed by UK NARIC to meet or exceed the recognised standards in the UK; *or* if it is a vocational or professional qualification, it is deemed by the relevant UK professional body to meet or exceed the recognised standard of a degree in the UK;

- the qualification was awarded (ie the applicant was first notified by the institution in writing that it had been awarded) no more than five years before the application was made;
- at least one academic year (or three consecutive terms) of the course must have involved full-time study in the UK; and
- the applicant must produces documents specified in the Policy Guidance as evidence of the qualification.

Note that the qualification does not have to be the same one for which the applicant claims points for attributes (App A, para 29). The Guidance states that qualifications will be assessed by the points-based calculator available on UKBA's website, which contains information provided by UK NARIC, and points will be scored accordingly. Applicants should therefore check the level of their qualification by using that calculator (T1 (Gen) PG, paras 161–4).

As to the evidence of the qualification that should be produced, the T1 (Gen) PG specifies an original letter from the UK institution/UK-based overseas institution at which the applicant studied (see para 170 for greater details). Where the applicant cannot find details of their qualification on the points-based calculator, they may still wish to claim points but they must then contact UK NARIC directly for an assessment of the level of their qualification and, as evidence, must also submit an original letter or certificate from UK NARIC confirming the equivalence of the level of the qualification (T1 (Gen) PG, paras 165, 172). Where professional or vocational qualifications are relied on but details cannot be found on the calculator, the applicant should provide an original letter from the appropriate UK professional body confirming the equivalence to UK academic levels (T1 (Gen) PG, paras 168, 173).

Where the applicant relies on the same qualification that has been provided in order to score points under the general head of 'qualifications' (ie aside from points for UK experience, ▶see above), then the original certificate of award, or an original letter from the institution of study, should already have been supplied for that purpose (T1 (Gen) PG, para 171).

Age

The points available for age are set out in Table 4 of Appendix A. The age of the applicant is taken as at the date of the application (T1 (General) PG, para 66). The applicant must produce the documents specified in the Policy Guidance as evidence of age (App A, para 31). The general rule is that applicants will receive:

- 20 points if they are under 30 years;
- 10 points if they are aged between 30 and 34 years; and

- 5 points if they are aged between 35 and 39 years.

  However, the above general rule for the allocation of points in respect of age is modified in the following circumstances where the applicant is applying for leave to *remain*.

- Where the applicant has, or last had, leave as a Tier 1 (General) Migrant under the Rules in place on or after 6 April 2010, s/he is awarded: 20 points (aged under 32); 10 points (aged 32–36); and 5 points (aged 37–41).

- Where an applicant has, or last had, leave as a Writer, Composer or Artist, Self-employed Lawyer or as a Tier 1 (General) Migrant under the Rules in place before 6 April 2010, s/he is awarded: 20 points (aged under 31); 10 points (aged 31–32); and 5 points (aged 33–34).

- Where an applicant has, or last had, leave under the HSMP, s/he is awarded: 20 points (aged under 30); 10 points (aged 30–31); and 5 points (aged 32–33).

  In order to demonstrate their age, the Guidance specifies the production of a current valid original passport or travel document. In the exceptional circumstances of those documents having been lost, stolen, expired and returned to the issuing Government, or submitted to another department or agency, UKBA may accept instead a valid national identity document, or a valid UK driving licence (Tier 1 (General) PG, para 75).

English language

Applicants must score 10 points for English language under paragraphs 1–2 of Appendix B to the Rules (Rules, para 245C(d)). Applicants will automatically receive 10 points for language if they have at any time previously been granted leave under the Tier 1 (General) or Tier 1 (Entrepreneur) categories (App B, para 2(d)). The same applies if the applicant has been granted leave under the HSMP under the Rules following the changes made on 5 December 2006 (App B, para 2(e)).

Otherwise, 10 points for language will only be awarded if the applicant meets any one of the following three conditions (App B, para 2(a)(b)(c)).

- The applicant has a knowledge of English that is equivalent to C1 of the Council of Europe's Common European Framework for Language Learning (CEFR) or above. The applicant must prove this by either:
- taking the secure English language test from a provider approved by the Secretary of State for these purposes and providing the original test certificate with the results showing s/he has attained level C1 (see 11 (Gen) PG, paras 190–1); or
- by providing specified evidence to show that s/he has obtained an academic qualification (not a professional or vocational qualification) which is deemed by UK NARIC to meet or exceed the recognised standard of a UK degree and which NARIC has confirmed was taught or researched in English to the C1 level.

Note that if an applicant's existing leave is about to run out and they must make their application before they have taken or received the results of their language test, they may submit their application without the test results as long as they give UKBA the date of the test within ten working days of submitting the application and also provide the results within five working days of receiving the certificate (see T1 (Gen) PG, paras 184-9).

- The applicant is a national of one of the following (majority English speaking) countries: Antigua and Barbuda; Australia; The Bahamas; Barbados; Belize; Canada; Dominica; Grenada; Guyana; Jamaica; New Zealand; St Kitts and Nevis; St Lucia; St Vincent and the Grenadines; Trinidad and Tobago; or the USA, *and* produces the specified documents to show it. The documents specified by the Guidance are: valid original passport or travel document or, exceptionally, current national identity document or original letter from the applicant's home government or embassy (see T1 (Gen) PG para 180).

- The applicant has obtained an academic qualification (not a professional or vocational qualification) which is deemed by UK NARIC to meet or exceed the recognised standard of a UK degree from an educational institution in one of the following countries: Antigua and Barbuda; Australia; The Bahamas; Barbados; Belize; Dominica; Grenada; Guyana; Ireland; Jamaica; New Zealand; St Kitts and Nevis; St Lucia; St Vincent and the Grenadines; Trinidad and Tobago; the UK; or the USA, *and* produces specified documents to show it. The documents that are specified by the Guidance are the original certificate of award *or* an academic reference from the institution awarding the degree together with an original academic transcript confirming the award (T1 (Gen) PG, para 200).

Maintenance

Applicants must score 10 points for maintenance under paragraphs 1–3 of Appendix C to the Rules (Rules, para 245C(e)). The maintenance rules for Tier 1 (General), Tier 1 (Entrepreneurs) and Tier 1 (Post-Study Work) applicants are the same. The necessary 10 points may be scored by showing a level of funds of (App C, para 2(a)(b):

- £2,800 in entry clearance cases; and
- £800 if the applicant is applying for leave to remain.

Originally, the requirement that applicants have the above level of funds for "at least three months prior to the date of application" was contained only in Policy Guidance and not in the Rules. The question of whether the Home Office could enforce the requirement in those circumstances was successfully challenged in *Pankina*. For full details of the *Pankina* case, ►see Chapter 2 41–45. The Home Office responded to *Pankina* by laying new Immigration Rules (HC 382), which came into force on 23 July 2010. The relevant wording of Appendix C is now that the applicant should have the funds at the date of the application (para 1A(a)) and, importantly (para 1A(b)):

"...if the applicant is applying for entry clearance, leave to enter or leave to remain as a Tier 1 Migrant (other than a Tier 1 (Investor) Migrant, a Tier 2 Migrant or a Tier 5 (Temporary Worker) Migrant, the applicant must have had the funds referred to [above] for a consecutive 90-day period of time, ending no earlier than one calendar month before the date of application."

So, it is now set out in the Rules themselves that applicants must show that they have the required funds over a three-month period. That period can end at any time in the last calendar month before the date that the applicant applies for entry clearance or leave to remain. As a result of *Pankina*, there is a transitional policy which disapplies the 'three-month' requirement for pre-23 July 2010 cases. For details of the policy, ▶see Chapter 2 46–47.

The Rules state that any funds that were obtained while the applicant was in the UK can only be relied on for maintenance purposes if they were obtained while the applicant had valid leave and was not acting in breach of any conditions of leave (App C, para 1A(d)).

The Rules also require that applicants must provide the documents that are specified in Policy Guidance in order to show that they meet the maintenance requirements (App C, para 1A(e) read with Rules, para 245AA) (▶below).

For the case-law generally interpreting the maintenance requirements under the PBS, ▶see 181–188 and for the additional maintenance requirements for the dependants of PBS migrants, ▶see below 196–200. For the relevance of human rights to cases where the strict requirements cannot be met, ▶see Chapter 12 414–420.

Maintenance: Policy Guidance

On the question of maintenance, the present Policy Guidance relating to the different categories of Tier 1 is *almost* the same. References below are given to the T1 (Gen) PG. The similar Guidance for the other relevant tiers can be found at T1 (Ent) PG, paras 154–164 and T1 (PSW) PG, paras 92–103.

It is important to bear in mind that, after *Pankina* (▶41–45) and the case law referred to below (▶181), advisers should take note that it may not be possible for UKBA to rely for their decisions on certain parts of the Guidance as a basis to refuse applications. It will not be possible for UKBA to do so where the particular part of the Guidance can be said to impose additional mandatory substantive requirements on applicants that are not contained in the Immigration Rules themselves. There will also be cases where the question of whether UKBA can rely on the particular relevant part of the Guidance is debateable.

For the content of the Guidance itself, ▶see the table below.

TIER 1 POLICY GUIDANCE: MAINTENANCE

The Guidance states that the evidence must be original and it must be issued by an authorised official of the relevant organisation (T1 (Gen) PG, para 210). The evidence must be of funds in cash such as in current or savings accounts. It is acceptable if notice is needed for withdrawal of funds from the account. Other accounts, or financial instruments like shares, bonds, pension funds, are not accepted (T1 (Gen) PG, para 211).

The Guidance further states that, if an applicant produces evidence from a single account, UKBA will always assess the available funds from the closing balance given on the document and that, where two or more pieces of evidence from a single account are given, it will assess the funds on the basis of the closing balance of the most recent document (T1 (Gen) PG, paras 213–215).

Where a joint account is produced, UKBA requires that the applicant is named on the account along with the other named person/s (T1 (Gen) PG, para 212) (Note that this particular paragraph is not repeated in the T1 (Ent) PG or T1 (PSW) PG).

The specified documents are as follows (T1 (Gen) PG, para 216):

• Personal bank or building society statements covering the relevant 90-day period. The most recent statement should be dated within one calendar month before the date of the application. The statements should be dated, show the applicant's name, account number, the financial institution's name and logo and show any transactions during the 90-day period. The statements should show a balance of £2,800 or £800 (as relevant) covering the 90-day period.

The T1 (Gen) PG and T1 (Ent) PG add that all statements should be on the bank's stationery unless the applicant is providing electronic statements. This Guidance further states that ad hoc statements on the bank's letterhead/ stationery are also acceptable (but that this does not include mini-statements from cash points). The T1 (Gen) and T1 (Ent) PG further states that electronic statements from online accounts can be provided, as long as they contain all of the above details and the applicant provides a supporting letter from his/her bank, on headed paper, confirming that the statements are authentic, or an electronic bank statement with the official stamp of the bank provided the stamp appears on every page. UKBA states it will not accept statements showing the balance on a particular day as such statements do not show that the applicant holds the funds over the full period required.

• Building society pass book covering the relevant 90-day period which ends no more than one calendar month before the date of the application. The pass book should show the applicant's name, account number, the financial institution's name and logo and any transactions during the 90-day period. The statements should show a balance of £2,800 or £800 (as relevant) covering the 90-day period.

• Letter from the applicant's bank or building society confirming that funds have been held for the relevant 90-day period ending no more than one calendar month before the date of the application. The letter should be dated no more than one calendar month before the date of the application and it should show the applicant's name, account number, the financial institution's name and logo, the funds held in the account and that the funds of £2,800 or £800 (as relevant) have been in the account for the 90-day period on and immediately before the date of the letter. The letter should be on the institution's letterhead/official stationery.

- letter from a financial institution regulated either by the Financial Services Authority or, in the case of overseas accounts, the home regulator (ie the official regulatory body for the country where the institution is and where the money is held), confirming the funds and that they have been held for the 90-day period ending no more than one calendar month before the date of the application. The letter should be dated no more than one calendar month before the date of the application and it should show the applicant's name, account number, the financial institution's name and logo, the funds held in the account and show that the funds of £2,800 or £800 (as relevant) have been in the account for the 90-day period on and immediately before the date of the letter. The letter should be on the institution's letterhead/official stationery.

Leave, conditions and extensions

The rules set out above cover both entering and applying to remain in the UK under the Tier 1 (General) category. The period of leave given to applicants and the conditions attached to the leave are set out in para 245D of the Rules. Before April 2010, leave was generally granted for three years with two years to follow on an extension application. From 6 April 2010, amending Rules (HC 439) changed the position so that, generally, applicants are first granted two years, to be followed by three years on the extension application. The purpose of this change was to "test that the migrant has become engaged in highly-skilled employment in the UK at an earlier stage" (Explanatory Memo to HC 439, para 7.3). However, even after the introduction of this change, if the applicant is applying to switch from any of the following predecessor categories of the Tier 1 (General) category, they will be treated in the same way as if they were applying for a second grant of Tier 1 (General) leave, ie given three years: HSMP; Innovator; Self-employed Lawyer; or Writer, Composer or Artist (Rules, para 245D(b)(ii)–(vi)).

During the period of their leave, Tier 1 (General) migrants have free access to the UK employment market and are able to work for any employer without prior permission from UKBA, as well as entering into self-employment.

The following conditions are attached to all grants of leave (Rules, para 245D(d)):

- Applicants must not have recourse to public funds.
- If required to do so by the Rules (see Rules, para 326), applicants must register with the police.

- Applicants must generally not engage in employment as a doctor or dentist in training *unless* the applicant *either*:
  - has obtained a degree in medicine or dentistry at Bachelor's level or above from a UK institution that is a UK-recognised or listed body (▶see below), or which holds a sponsor licence under Tier 4 of the PBS; *or*
  - is applying for leave to remain and has, or has last been granted, entry clearance or leave that did not have a condition restricting their employment and s/he has been employed during that leave as a doctor or dentist in training;
- Applicants must not enter employment as a professional sportsperson, including as a sports coach (this restriction was added from 6 April 2010 by HC 439 in order to prevent applicants from circumventing the requirement for governing body endorsement that is in place under Tiers 2 and 5).

Note that, for the purposes of the above rules, a 'UK-recognised body' is an institution that has been granted degree-awarding powers by either a Royal Charter, an Act of Parliament or the Privy Council. A 'UK-listed body' is an institution that is not a UK-recognised body but which provides full courses that lead to the award of a degree by a recognised body (Rules, para 6). The Policy Guidance sets out the procedure that should be followed and documents that should be produced in order to benefit from the potential exemption from the restriction on taking employment as a doctor or dentist in training (see Annex D to the T1 (Gen) PG). The Rules concerning work as doctors and dentists in training were amended to the present position in October 2009 (Cm 7701) and April 2010 (HC 439).

There is no requirement for Tier 1 (General) migrants to engage in employment once granted their visa but a low income in the twelve-month period prior to any extension application may have an adverse affect on the application.

Settlement

On completion of "a continuous period of five years lawfully in the UK" as a Tier 1 (General) migrant, applicants can apply for settlement (Rules, para 245E). Applicants whose last period of leave was under the Tier 1 (General) category can also apply for settlement if they have spent a total continuous period of five years lawfully in the UK in any combination of the following categories (Rules, para 245E(a)(b)):

- Tier 1 (General) Migrant;
- HSMP;
- Work Permit holder;
- Innovator;
- Self-employed Lawyer;
- Writer, Composer or Artist;

- Tier 2 (General) migrant, Tier 2 (Minister of Religion) migrant, Tier 2 (Sportsperson) migrant; or
- Tier 2 (Intra Company Transfer) migrant provided the continuous period of five years includes a period as a Tier 2 (ICT) migrant granted under the rules in place before 6 April 2010.

For the calculation of "a continuous period of five years lawfully in the UK" ▶see 1080 193.

Where the application is made under the terms of the HSMP ILR Judicial Review policy document, a continuous period of four years lawfully in the UK is required, of which the most recent must have been spent with leave as a Tier 1 (General) migrant. The applicant may have spent their time with leave in any combination of the following categories: Tier 1 (General); HSMP; Work Permit holder; or Innovator (Rules, para 245E(a)(b)).

In addition, Tier 1 (General) migrants seeking settlement must establish that they are economically active in the UK, either by being employed, or self-employed, or both (Rules, para 245E(c)). They must also not fall for refusal under the general grounds for refusal set out in the Rules, nor be an illegal entrant (Rules, para 245E(a)). As with most settlement applications, Tier 1 (General) migrants seeking to settle must also show sufficient knowledge of the English language and of life in the UK unless the applicant is aged under 18 or over 65 at the time of the application, or is applying under the HSMP ILR Judicial Review Policy Document (Rules, para 245E(d)).

TIER 1 (ENTREPRENEUR) MIGRANTS

The Tier 1 (Entrepreneur) category provides a route of entry to the UK for migrants who wish to establish, join or take over one or more businesses in the UK. A 'business' for these purposes means an enterprise as a company registered in the UK, a sole trader or a partnership (Rules, para 245H(a)(b)). This category replaced the previous "businessperson" category and was introduced from 30 June 2008 by HC 607.

For the present proposals to change the Tier 1 (Entrepreneur) category, ▶see the table below 164.

WHAT THE RULES SAY

Entering and remaining in the UK in the Tier 1 (Entrepreneur) category

The requirements to be met by those seeking to enter or remain in the UK in the Tier 1 (Entrepreneur) category are that the applicant must (paras 245J, 245K, HC 395):

- not fall for refusal under the general grounds for refusal (▶see Chapter 11);
- if seeking leave to remain, must not be an illegal entrant;

- score a minimum of 75 points for 'attributes' set out in paras 32–41 of Appendix A to the Rules;
- score 10 points for the English language requirements set out in paras 1–3 of Appendix B to the Rules;
- score 10 points for the 'maintenance' requirements set out in paras 1–2 of Appendix C to Rules;
- if seeking leave to *remain*, have or have last been granted entry clearance or leave to enter or remain as a Tier 1 (Entrepreneur) Migrant, or in one of the following categories (so applicants in any of the following categories can, in principle, switch to the Tier 1 (Entrepreneur) category):
  - HSMP;
  - Tier 1 (General) Migrant;
  - Tier 1 (Investor) Migrant;
  - Tier 1 (Post-Study Work) Migrant;
  - Businessperson;
  - Innovator;
  - Investor;
  - Fresh Talent: Working in Scotland Scheme;
  - International Graduates' Scheme (or its predecessor, the Science and Engineering Graduates' Scheme);
  - Postgraduate Doctor or Dentist;
  - Self-employed Lawyer;
  - Student;
  - Student Nurse;
  - Student Re-sitting an Examination;
  - Student Writing-up a Thesis;
  - Work Permit holder;
  - Writer, Composer or Artist;
  - Tier 2 Migrant; or
  - Tier 4 Migrant; and
- if seeking to enter the UK, or to "switch" into the Tier 1 (Entrepreneur) category, while having existing leave (or having last been granted leave) as a Student, Postgraduate Doctor or Dentist, Student Nurse, Student Re-sitting an Examination, Student Writing-up a Thesis or as a Tier 4 migrant *and* the applicant is sponsored by a government or international scholarship agency (or was so sponsored within the last 12 months), have the unconditional written consent of the sponsoring government or agency to the application and provide the specified documents to show it (for the specified documents, see T1 (Ent) PG, paras 39–41).

Those seeking to enter in this category must have a valid entry clearance enabling them to do so (Rules, para 245I).

For dependants of Tier 1 (Entrepreneur) migrants, ▶see 194–203.

WHAT THE RULES MEAN

Irrespective of whether applicants are seeking to enter the UK or remain in the UK as a Tier 1 (Entrepreneur) migrant, they must:

- score a minimum of 75 points for attributes;
- score 10 points for English language; and
- score 10 points for maintenance.

The rules for English language are the same as for the Tier 1 (General) category (▶above 151).

The Rules for maintenance are also the same as for the Tier 1 (General) category (▶above 153). For the relevant case law on maintenance, ▶see below 181.

Attributes

The attributes and their respective points are set out in the Rules at Appendix A, paras 32–41 and Tables 5–6.

Available points

For 'new' applicants ie entry clearance applicants and applicants for leave to remain who have not last been granted entry clearance, or leave as a Tier 1 (Entrepreneur) or under its predecessor categories (Business persons or Innovators), the following is they basis for the points to be scored for attributes (Annex A, para 33 and Table 5):

- the applicant has access to not less than £200,000 (25 points);
- the money is held in one or more regulated financial institutions (25 points);
- the money is disposable in the UK (25 points).

Provided the points are obtained for all of the above, the applicant will score the necessary 75 points.

Existing Tier 1 (Entrepreneurs) and those who have leave as Business-persons or Innovators who are applying to extend their leave, have a different and more burdensome task to score the required points for attributes. Such applicants must (App A, para 34 and Table 6):

- have invested (or had invested on their behalf) not less than £200,000 in cash directly into one or more businesses in the UK (20 points);
- have;
- registered with HM Revenue and Customs as self-employed, or
- registered a new business in which s/he is a director, or
- registered as a director of an existing business (20 points if one or more of these requirements is met);

(Note that in order to obtain points, an existing Tier 1 (Entrepreneur) applying to extend their leave must show that they met one of the above "registration" conditions *within three months* of their entry to the UK (if granted entry clearance under this category and there is evidence of entry), or within three months of the date of the grant of leave to remain.)

- be engaged in business activity at the time of his/her application for leave to remain (15 points);
- have:
- established a new business or businesses that has or have created the equivalent of at least two new full-time jobs for persons settled in the UK, or
- taken over or joined an existing business or businesses and his/her services or investment have resulted in a net increase in the employment provided by the business or businesses for persons settled in the UK by creating the equivalent of at least two new full-time jobs (20 points if either of these requirements is satisfied).

(Note that, where the applicant's last grant of entry clearance or leave was as a Tier 1 (Entrepreneur), the jobs must have existed for at least 12 months of the period for which that previous leave was granted)

Again, the necessary 75 points will be scored if all the above requirements are satisfied.

Below we look at some of the terms referred to in the above requirements and also at what evidence must be produced to show that the requirements are satisfied.

'Access to not less than £200,000'

Generally this is quite easy to prove. Applicants can rely upon funds in their own bank account, whether abroad or in the UK.

The funds do not have to be the applicant's savings and may be funds that have been made available by a third party. In such circumstances a declaration will be need to be obtained from the third party, stating that the money is available to the applicant (or the business that the applicant is running or seeking to run) and the declaration must be supported by evidence from a legal representative confirming that the declaration is valid (T1 (Ent) PG, para 58). Funds held by the partner of an applicant are also viewed as third party funds and will require a similar declaration (T1 (Ent) PG, para 59; for a template of the declaration see Annex C, Document 2 of the Guidance).

'Money held in regulated financial institutions'

This means that, if an applicant relies upon funds held in a bank account, the bank in question must be regulated by the relevant official regulatory body of the country in which the institution operates (App A, para 37). In the UK, the relevant regulatory body is the Financial Services Authority (FSA). If the funds are located abroad, the financial institution that holds them must be regulated by the 'home regulator' which is an official regulatory body in that country (T1 (Ent) PG, para 60).

'Disposable in the UK'

To receive points, applicants must show that they have £200,000 in funds that are "disposable in the UK". This means that the money must be held in a UK-based financial institution, or be freely transferable to UK and able to be converted into pounds sterling (App A, para 38). If the £200,000 is held in an overseas account in an institution that has a UK presence and is regulated by the FSA, UKBA will assume that the money can be transferred freely into the UK. If not, the applicant will have to prove that the money is transferrable with evidence from the financial institution (T1 (Ent) PG, paras 63–4).

'Investment of not less than £200,000 in cash directly into one or more businesses in the UK'

The investment cannot include the value of any residential accommodation, property development, or property management (App A, para 40). Similarly, if applicants have purchased properties which include residential accommodation, the value that can be relied upon for investment is only the amount of the business investment and not any part of the residential accommodation value. Investment can take the form of a director's loan provided it is unsecured and in favour of the business (App A, para 41). Applicants are not permitted to rely on any of the £200,000 investment as evidence of maintenance funds (T1 (Ent) PG, para 155).

'Engagement in business activity at the time of application for extension of leave'

In order to meet this requirement, applicants must either be self-employed, or the director of a company. The business activity relied on at the date of application does not need to be the same business activity that the applicant engaged in on the initial grant of leave as a Tier 1 (Entrepreneur), Businessperson or Innovator. If an applicant is engaged in both self-employed activity and is a director of a company, then only one such activity can be relied upon in order to score points.

'Creation of new full-time jobs for settled workers'

Employment will be accepted as 'full-time' if it consists of at least 30 hours work per week. However, UKBA looks at the hourly equivalent of two full-time jobs, and does not require two actual full-time employees. The number of employees can be one, two or more, provided the total number of hours amounts to the equivalent of two 'full-time' positions and provided the terms of the employment comply with the UK's regulations (eg the working time directive). So, two or more part-time jobs that add up to 30 hours per week will count as a full-time job (App A, para 41; T1 (Ent) PG, paras 93–4, 96). Where a single worker is employed for 24 months, points can be awarded (see T1 (Ent) PG, para 96). The jobs relied on must be as employees; self-employed contractors doing work for the business do not count (see T1 (Ent) PG, para 94).

The Policy Guidance sets out what UKBA considers to be a 'settled worker' as follows (see T1 (Ent) PG, Annex A, A27):

- UK nationals;
- EU nationals (although A8 and A2 nationals must be registered on the appropriate schemes unless they are exempt from worker authorisation);
- British overseas territories citizens other than those from the Sovereign Base Areas in Cyprus;
- Commonwealth nationals permitted to enter on the grounds of having a grandparent born in the UK;
- persons with settled status in the UK.

As to the requirement that, where the applicant's last grant of leave was in the Tier 1 (Entrepreneur) category, the jobs must have existed for at least 12 months of the period for which the previous leave was granted, there is no requirement that the 12 months period be consecutive and the jobs do not need to be in existence on the date of application (App A, para 41).

Evidence required

The Rules state that documentary evidence must be provided in all cases and that the documents specified in the Policy Guidance must be produced as evidence of investment (App A, para 36) and as evidence of business activity that took place during the period that the applicant had leave under the Tier 1 (Entrepreneur) category (App A, para 39, with reference to the Rules, para 245AA).

In order to provide evidence of funds, the Guidance states that applicants should provide a letter from each financial institution holding the applicant's funds to confirm the amount of money available. UKBA will use the *Oanda* database to convert any monies not held in the UK. The letter that is produced should meet the requirements set out in the Guidance and a template is given (see T1 (Ent) PG, para 65 and Annex C, Doc 1). Where the funds are those of a third party, applicants should produce a declaration from every third party that they have made the money available for the applicant to invest in the UK as well as a letter from a legal representative that confirms the validity of the signatures on each third party declaration that is provided (see T1 (Ent) PG, para 66).

When it comes to applying to extend leave, in order to show that the applicant has made the required investment into a business/es in the UK, the specified documents are: audited accounts; unaudited accounts and an accountant's certificate of confirmation; and, if the applicant has made the investment in the form of a director's loan, the legal agreement for the loan. Applicants are directed to produce as many of the specified documents as are necessary to show the full amount of the investment (for details see T1 (Ent) PG, para 71 and see Annex A to the Guidance at A19–20).

There are also documents that are specified to show that the business that has received the investment is indeed a *UK* business (see T1 (Ent) PG, para 72 and table; and see Annex A to the Guidance at A21) and to show that the above 'registration' conditions were met within the required three months (T1 (Ent) PG, paras 76–78).

The Guidance also specifies documents to be produced to show that the migrant is engaged in business activity at the point that s/he applies to extend (see T1 (Ent) PG, paras 84–90). Careful attention should also be given to the detailed evidence that is specified as required to show the creation of new employees (see T1 (Ent) PG, para 97–127).

Leave, conditions and curtailment

Applicants seeking to enter the UK under the Tier 1 (Entrepreneur) category, or those seeking to switch into the Tier 1 (Entrepreneur) category, will be granted leave for a period of three years (Rules, paras 245K and 245M(a)(ii) HC 395). Existing Tier 1 Entrepreneurs applying for extensions, may be granted a period of further leave of two years (para 245M(a)(i) HC 395). After five years, applicants become eligible for settlement (below).

The following conditions are attached to all leave granted in this category (paras 245K and 245M(b) HC 395):

* applicants must not have recourse to public funds;
* if required to do so under the Rules (see para 326), applicants must register with the police;
* applicants must not engage in employment other than working for the business that they have established, joined or taken over.

Curtailment

The general grounds for the curtailment (cutting short) of leave are dealt with in Chapter 11. However, the Tier 1 (Entrepreneur) Rules include an additional ground on which those in this category may have their leave curtailed. This ground was added to the Rules by HC 113 from 27 November 2008. Tier 1 (Entrepreneurs) may have their leave to enter or remain curtailed if, within three months of their entry to the UK (if granted entry clearance under this category and there is evidence of entry), or otherwise within three months of their grant of entry clearance or leave to remain, they have not either (Rules, para 245M(c)(d)):

* registered with HM Revenue and Customs as self-employed; or
* registered a new business in which s/he is a director; or
* registered as a director of an existing business.

However this additional curtailment provision does not apply to applicants who are already enjoying their second grant of leave under this category, or their first grant in this category if, immediately before it, they had leave in one of the predecessor categories of Businessperson or Innovator (Rules, para 245M(e)).

Settlement

On completion of a continuous period of five years lawfully in the UK as a Tier 1 (Entrepreneur) an applicant can apply for settlement (para 245N, HC 395). Applicants whose last period of leave was granted in the Tier 1 (Entrepreneur) category can also apply for settlement if they have spent the five year continuous period partly as a Businessperson or Innovator under the pre-PBS Rules and partly as a Tier 1 (Entrepreneur).

Applicants for settlement in the Tier 1 (Entrepreneur) category must be engaged in business activity at the time of their application and must provide specified evidence of this (►see above). Applicants must also show sufficient knowledge of the English language and life in the UK (unless the applicant is aged under 18 or over 65), must not fall for refusal under the general grounds of refusal and must not be an illegal entrant.

For the calculation of "a continuous period of five years lawfully in the UK" ►see 188–193.

Proposals for changes to the Tier 1 (Entrepreneur) category

The proposed overhaul of Tier 1 generally is set out above ►140–141. The proposals, for the Entrepreneur category in particular, which are *not* fixed, are set out in the table below.

PROPOSALS FOR CHANGES TO THE TIER 1 (ENTREPRENEUR) CATEGORY

The Government has indicated that it wishes to attract greater numbers in this category and that the revamped category will be exempt from a cap on numbers.

The essential proposals are:

- Allow applicants to be absent from the UK for up to 180 days in any twelve month period while still retaining eligibility for settlement (►see 188–193 below for details about the present position regarding continuity of presence in the UK and settlement).

- Allowing applications for settlement at an earlier stage (after three years) if the applicant's business has created at least ten full-time jobs which have been in place for six months, or where the business has generated more than £5m in turnover during the first three years (for start-up companies) or an additional £5m in turnover compared with the previous three-year average (for existing businesses).

- Allowing the entry of entrepreneurs who have less than the presently required £200,000 funding if, for example, the business has received investment of £50,000 or more from a restricted list of investors (eg a registered venture capitalist forum, or an investment body affiliated to the Government).

- Allowing the entry of support staff required to help set up the business outside

Tier 2. The Home Office suggests that up to four employees might be admitted depending on the level of investment in the business. It is proposed that for four migrants to be able to come with the applicant, an investment of £1m would be necessary. These additional support staff would have to have knowledge and experience that was essential to the successful establishment of the business and there would be a limit on their stay to 12 months after which they would have to qualify under Tier 2 to remain further.

- Give entrepreneurs a period of six months in which to register with Companies House.

- Provide alternative means of succeeding on an application for an extension, ie by allowing those who have created more than five new jobs to succeed even if they have not invested the full £200,000 in the business.

TIER 1 (INVESTOR) MIGRANTS

Tier 1 (Investor) category provides a route of entry for high net-worth individuals seeking to make a substantial financial investment in the UK (Rules, para 245O). It replaces the 'Investor' category and was introduced from 30 June 2008 by HC 607. The route enables millionaire applicants to come to the UK and eventually settle here provided that, within three months of their leave being granted, they invest £750,000 in UK bonds, share or loan capital in active UK registered companies. Applicants will also be permitted to take employment with only minor restrictions.

For the present proposals to change the Tier 1 (Investor) category, ▶see the table below 173.

WHAT THE RULES SAY

Entering and remaining in the UK in the Tier 1 (Investor) category

The requirements to be met by those seeking to enter or remain in the UK in the Tier 1 (Investor) category are that an applicant must (Rules, paras 245Q, 245S):

- not fall for refusal under the general grounds of refusal (▶see Chapter 11);

- if seeking leave to remain, not be an illegal entrant;

- score a minimum of 75 points for the attributes set out in paras 42–50 of Appendix A to the Rules;

- if seeking *leave to remain*, have or have last been granted entry clearance or leave to enter or remain either as a Tier 1 (Investor), or in one of the following categories (so applicants in any of the following categories can, in principle, switch to the Tier 1 (Investor) category):
- HSMP;
- Tier 1 (General) Migrant;

- Tier 1 (Entrepreneur) Migrant;
- Tier 1 (Investor) Migrant;
- Tier 1 (Post-Study Work) Migrant;
- Businessperson;
- Innovator;
- Investor;
- Student;
- Student Nurse;
- Student Re-sitting an Examination;
- Student Writing-up a Thesis;
- Work Permit holder;
- Writer, Composer or Artist;
- Tier 2 Migrant; or
- Tier 4 Migrant; and

• if seeking *entry* and the applicant has, or was last granted, leave as a Student, Postgraduate Doctor or Dentist, Student Nurse, Student Re-sitting an Examination, Student Writing-up a Thesis or as a Tier 4 Migrant, they must have the unconditional written consent to the application of the sponsoring Government or agency if they are presently being sponsored, or were sponsored within the last 12 months and must provide evidence of this;

• if seeking *leave to remain* and the applicant has, or was last granted, leave as a Student Nurse, Student Re-sitting an Examination, Student Writing-up a Thesis or as a Tier 4 Migrant, the applicant must have the unconditional written consent of the sponsoring Government or agency if they are presently being sponsored, or were sponsored within the last 12 months by a government or international scholarship agency (for the specified documents to be produced, see T1 (Inv) PG, paras 39–40).

Those seeking to enter in this category must have a valid entry clearance enabling them to do so (Rules, para 245P).

Applicants under the Tier 1 (Investor) category do not have to score points for Maintenance or English language (see App B, para 1; App C, paras 1A(b), 1). This is because in showing their net worth, they will already have demonstrated that they can support themselves and also because they should not need to work, although they are permitted to do so and so do not need to have English language skills for that purpose (T1 (Inv) PG, paras 52–3).

For dependants of Tier 1 (Investors), ▶see 194–203.

WHAT THE RULES MEAN

Attributes

Tier 1 (Investor) applicants must score 75 points for attributes (Rules, paras 245Q(b), 245S(b); App A, para 42). The points that may be scored are set out at paragraphs 42-50 and Tables 7-8 of Appendix A to the Rules.

For 'new' Investor applicants ie those seeking entry clearance or seeking to 'switch' into the Tier 1 (Investor) category, 75 points for attributes can be scored either of the two following ways (App A, para 43 and Table 7):

- An applicant can show that s/he "has money of his own under his control held in a regulated financial institution and disposable in the UK amounting to not less than £1 million".

- Alternatively, the applicant can show that s/he "owns personal assets which, taking into account any liabilities to which they are subject, have a value exceeding £2 million" and s/he "has money under his control held in a regulated financial institution and disposable in the UK amounting to not less than £1 million which has been loaned to him by a financial institution regulated by the Financial Services Authority".

Existing investors, ie those who have, or who were last granted entry clearance or leave either as a Tier 1 (Investor) or as an 'Investor' under the old Rules, who are applying for leave to remain, face more burdensome requirements. In order to score the required 75 points, they have to show that they (App A, paras 44, 50 and Table 8):

- have money of their own under their control in the UK amounting to not less than £1 million; or

- own personal assets which, taking into account liabilities to which they are subject, have a value of not less than £2 million *and* have money under their control and disposable in the UK amounting to not less than £1 million which has been loaned to them by a financial institution regulated by the Financial Services Authority

(30 points are scored if either of the above conditions are satisfied); *and*

- have invested not less than £750,000 of their capital in the UK by way of UK Government bonds, share capital or loan capital in active and trading UK registered companies ie one doing business (T1 (Inv) PG, Annex A, A21) other than companies mainly engaged in property investment (the investment may not be a deposit with a bank, building society, or any other enterprise whose normal course of business includes accepting such deposits (App A, para 50) (30 points); *and*

- made the above investment within three months of:
- the date of his/her entry to the UK if the applicant was granted entry clearance as a Tier 1 (Investor) Migrant and there is evidence to establish his/her date of arrival in the UK); or

- the date of the grant of entry clearance as a Tier 1 (Investor) Migrant (ie if there is no evidence of the date of arrival); or
- in any other case, of the date of the grant of leave to remain as a Tier 1 (Investor); and
- the investment must have been maintained for the whole of the remaining period of that leave (15 points).

(Note that those last granted entry clearance or leave as an Investor under the old pre-PBS Rules do not have to show compliance with this 'three month' rule but will still obtain the required 15 points. They must, however, have made the investment before applying to extend their leave, see T1 (Inv) PG, paras 84–85).

In order to convert foreign currency funds to sterling for the purposes of the above requirements, UKBA will use the spot exchange rate to be found on www.oanda.com as on the date of application (App A, para 48).

Below we explain further some of the terms used in the above requirements and also look at the evidence that applicants are required to produce in order to show that the requirements are met.

'Disposable in the UK'

Money is 'disposable in the UK' if all of the money is held in a UK-based financial institution or if the money is transferable to the UK and convertible to sterling (App A, para 48). This requirement has been put in place by UKBA to ensure that the currency control laws in an applicant's country of origin do not prohibit or interfere with the free transfer of the funds to the UK (T1 (Inv) PG, para 64).

'Money of his own', 'personal assets' and 'his capital'

As to these terms, applicants may rely on money that belongs to, or is owned jointly by, their partner as long as specified documents are produced to show that the funds are under the applicant's control so that the applicant is free to invest them (App A, para 49). The applicant should have the unrestricted right to transfer and dispose of the money held jointly or solely by their partner. The Guidance states (T1 (Inv) PG, para 61):

"Under this section, applicants may rely on money that they own jointly with their husband, wife, civil partner, unmarried or same-sex partner. They may also rely on money that is owned solely by their husband, wife, civil partner or unmarried or same-sex partner. The applicant must have an unrestricted right to transfer and dispose of the money held jointly and solely by their civil partner, unmarried or same-sex partner, and the applicant must have permission from his/her husband, wife, civil partner, unmarried or same-sex partner to have control of this money in the United Kingdom."

Relevant investments

Applicants are required to invest in the UK in Government bonds, or share or loan capital in UK companies. The Policy Guidance sets out examples of a number of investments that will *not* be accepted for these purposes (T1 (Inv) PG, Annex A, A24):

- investments through an offshore company or trust;
- investments in 'open ended' companies, investment trust companies or pooled investments ie because it is not certain that they will be in the UK;
- investments in companies mainly engaged in property investment, property management or property development;
- deposits with banks or building societies whose normal business is deposits;
- ISAs, premium bonds, savings certificates issued by the National Savings and Investment Agency (if the applicant was previously permitted to stay under the Tier 1 (Investor) category);
- 'leveraged' investment funds (unless the applicant was previously given leave under the 'Investor' category).

Maintaining the investment of £750,000

UKBA does not expect investors to keep the same actual investments but they must keep the necessary level of investments. If the investment is reduced below the required level as the result of fluctuations of prices on the stock market, then this will not mean that the applicant automatically fails in their application, but the investment should be swiftly corrected (T1 (Inv) PG, paras 85–86).

UK company

UKBA states that investments as loan or share capital must be in a business operating in the UK economy and subject to UK taxation. It will consider a UK company to be one that has its registered office in the UK and has a UK business or bank account. It will also accept multinational companies that are registered as UK companies with a registered or head office in the UK (T1 (Inv) PG, Annex A, A22).

'Owns personal assets which, taking into account any liabilities to which they are subject, have a value exceeding £2 million'

Assets held by the spouse, civil partner, unmarried or same-sex partner (whether held jointly or solely in the partner's own name) can be taken into account when assessing the applicant's net worth (T1 (Inv) PG, Annex A, A19).

Evidence required

The Rules state that the documents specified in the Policy Guidance must be provided as evidence of the investment (App A, para 46 read with

Rules, para 245AA).

In order to show that the applicant has the necessary funds disposable in the UK, applicants should provide one or more of the following documents (T1 (Inv) PG, para 62, note the Guidance is also specific as to what is required of each document):

- Portfolio report or breakdown of investments in a letter produced by an authorised financial institution ie one that is regulated by the FSA (a template letter is included at Annex C, document 1 of the T1 (Inv) PG).

- Where the applicant manages his/her own investments, or has a portfolio manager who does not operate in the UK and is not regulated by the FSA, s/he should provide documentary evidence of the holdings s/he is using to claim the funds. The evidence should cover the three consecutive months in the period directly before the date of the application. In these circumstances, applicants are required to produce one or more of the following: certified copies of bond documents; share documents; the latest audited annual accounts of the organisation where the investment has been made clearly showing the relevant investment; or a trust fund document.

- Personal bank statements from a bank regulated by the home regulator showing the money available.

- Letter from a bank regulated by the home regulator.

Whether the monies are held in the UK or overseas, if the funds have not been held in the bank account or portfolio for at least three months, the applicant must provide evidence of the source of those funds. The source may be gift; deeds of sale; evidence from a business; will; divorce settlement; or award/winnings. In each case the Guidance sets out in detail the documents that should be provided as evidence (T1 (Inv) PG, para 63).

In order to show that money not held in the UK is 'transferable' here, applicants should provide a letter from the bank or financial institution confirming that the monies can be transferred to the UK if the application succeeds (T1 (Inv) PG, paras 65–7).

Where the monies that the applicant is relying on are held jointly with, or solely by, their partner, applicants should provide all of the following (T1 (Inv) PG, paras 68–9, further details are given in the Guidance of the documents):

- the original marriage certificate or civil partnership certificate to confirm the relationship, or evidence of a two-year relationship similar to marriage or civil partnership;

- a declaration from the partner that s/he will allow all joint or personal money used to claim points to be under the applicant's control in the UK (a template for this declaration is shown in Annex C, document 3 of the T1 (Inv) PG); and

- a letter from a legal adviser confirming that the declaration is valid.

To show that an applicant owns personal assets with a value exceeding £2 million and that s/he has £1 million loaned by a financial institution regulated by the FSA, applicants must provide a letter of confirmation provided by an authorised financial institution in the UK confirming that the applicant has £1 million available to them to borrow and that the applicant's personal net worth is at least £2 million (see T1 (Inv) PG, para 74).

The Policy Guidance specifies the following documents as evidence of the funds actually invested in the UK economy (T1 (Inv) PG, paras 87, see the Guidance itself for more details of what is required of each document):

- A portfolio of investments certified as correct by an authorised financial institution regulated by the FSA.

- Where an applicant's original grant of leave was made under the previous 'Investor' category and the applicant cannot produce the evidence immediately above because s/he manages his/her own investments, or has a portfolio manager who works from outside the UK, the applicant must provide documentary evidence of his/her holdings used to claim points which may be in the form of certified copies of bond documents; share documents; or the latest audited accounts of the organisation in which the investment has been made.

Where an applicant has invested less than £1 million in bonds, share capital or loan capital in UK companies and relies on the evidence of the further funds (up to £250,000) to show the required overall £1 million, then the Guidance specifies one of the following as evidence of this (T1 (Inv) PG, para 90):

- documents confirming the purchase of assets (eg property) in the UK;

- statements of accounts;

- a letter from the financial institution that holds the cash on deposit.

Leave, extensions, conditions and curtailment of leave

Applicants either entering the UK or 'switching' into the Tier 1 (Investor) category will be granted leave for a period of three years (Rules, paras 245R, 245T(a)(ii)). Those extending their leave as an existing Tier 1 (Investor) will be granted leave for an additional period of two years (para 245T(a)(i) HC 395). After five years, investors are eligible for settlement (▶below).

All who are granted entry clearance, leave to enter or remain will have the following conditions attached to their leave (paras 245R and 245T(b) HC 395):

- applicants must not have recourse to public funds;

- if required to do so under the Rules (para 326), applicants must register with the police; and

- applicants must not engage in employment as a doctor or dentist in training *unless either*: (a) they have obtained a degree in medicine or dentistry at Bachelor level or above from a UK institution that is a UK-recognised or listed body (for which ▶see above 145), or which holds a sponsor licence under Tier 4 of the PBS; or (b) the applicant is being granted leave to *remain* and either has (or was last granted) entry clearance/leave that did not prevent him/her from working as a doctor or dentist in training and has, during that leave, been employed in either of those capacities (for details about obtaining this exemption from the employment condition, see T1 (Inv) PG, Annex D).

Curtailment

The general grounds on which leave may be curtailed (cut short) are set out in Chapter 11. The Rules relating to Investors were amended from 27 November 2008 by HC 1113 to contain an additional ground on which leave as a Tier 1 (Investor) may be curtailed. Where, after an applicant has been given their first entry clearance/grant of leave in the Tier 1 (Investor) category, they fail within three months, to invest £750,000 in UK bonds, or in share/loan capital in active and trading UK registered companies (as stated above), they may have their leave curtailed (para 245T(c)–(e), HC 395). The three-month period begins either:

- on the date of the applicant's entry to the UK (where the applicant was granted entry clearance as a Tier 1 (Investor) Migrant and there is evidence to establish the applicant's date of entry);
- on the date of the grant of entry clearance to the applicant (where the applicant was granted entry clearance as a Tier 1 (Investor) Migrant but there is no evidence to establish his/her date of entry to the UK); or
- in any other case, from the date of the grant of leave to remain in the UK.

This additional curtailment provision does not apply to applicants who are already enjoying their second grant of leave under this category, or their first grant in this category if, immediately before it, they had leave in the predecessor category of Investor (under the pre-PBS Rules) (Rules, para 245T(e)).

Settlement

On completion of a continuous period of five years lawfully in the UK as a Tier 1 (Investor), applicants can apply for settlement (para 245U HC 395). Applicants whose last period of leave is in the Tier 1 (Investor) category can also apply for settlement if they have spent the five-year continuous period partly as an Investor under the pre-PBS Rules and partly as a Tier 1 (Investor). With the exception of the first three months, applicants for settlement must have maintained their investment throughout the five-year period. Applicants must also show sufficient knowledge of English language and life in the UK (unless s/he is aged under 18 or over 65), must not fall for refusal under the general grounds of refusal and must not be an illegal entrant.

For the calculation of "a continuous period of five years lawfully in the UK" ▶see 188–193.

Proposals for changes to the Tier 1 (Investor) category

The proposed overhaul of Tier 1 generally is set out above ▶140–142. The particular proposals, for the high net-worth 'Investor' category, which are not fixed, are set out in the table below.

PROPOSALS FOR CHANGES TO THE TIER 1 (INVESTOR) CATEGORY

The essential proposals are:

- Introduce shorter periods of qualification for settlement in the UK depending on the size of the applicant's investment. The Home Office suggests:
- five years for an investment of £1m to £5m;
- three years for an investment of £5m to £10m;
- two years for an investment greater than £10m.

- Allow applicants to be absent from the UK for up to 180 days in any twelve-month period while still retaining eligibility for settlement (▶see 188–193 below for details about the present position regarding continuity of presence in the UK and settlement).

- Open the route up to wealth creators as well as those who are already personally wealthy.

- Increase the Tier 1 Investor entry clearance fee from £750 to £5,000.

TIER 1 (POST-STUDY WORK) MIGRANTS

The Tier 1 (Post-Study Work) category replaces the Science and Engineering Graduates Scheme (SEGS), the International Graduates Scheme (IGS) and the Fresh Talent: Working in Scotland Scheme (FT: WISS) and those previously granted leave under those schemes are automatically granted the required points for attributes under this category of the PBS (see below). As with the Tier 1 (Entrepreneur) and Tier 1 (Investor) categories, Tier 1 (PSW) was launched from 30 June 2008 by HC 607. The purpose was to "retain the most able international graduates who have studied in the UK" (Explanatory Memo to HC 321, para 7.2). The idea is to allow graduates from overseas who have taken their degrees in the UK, to remain in the UK and do skilled or highly-skilled work (Rules, para 245V). Leave is granted for a maximum of two years after which those in Tier 1 (PSW) will have to switch into another category if they wish to extend their leave and potentially eventually qualify for settlement. Tier 1 (PSW) migrants frequently switch into Tier 2 at the end of their two years, although in principle they can also switch into the other categories of Tier 1.

The Government considers that, as with Tier 1 (General), this category has not been fulfilling its role and that those admitted under it have often been found doing low-skilled work, or even not working at all. For the proposals that have emerged from the General Student (Tier 4) consultation for substantial change to the Tier 1 (PSW) category, ▶see Chapter 8 292–295.

WHAT THE RULES SAY

Entering or remaining in the UK under Tier 1 (Post-Study Work)

The requirements that must be met by people seeking to enter or remain in the UK under the Tier 1 (Post-Study Work) category are that they must (Rules, paras 245X, 245Z with reference also to para 245ZA(a)(i)):

- not fall for refusal under the general grounds of refusal (▶see Chapter 11);
- if applying for leave to remain, not be an illegal entrant;
- not previously have been granted entry clearance or leave to remain as a Tier 1 (Post-Study Work) migrant (ie no extensions to existing Tier 1 (PSW) leave are granted);
- if applying for entry clearance, not previously have been granted entry clearance or leave to remain under: FT: WISS, IGS or SEGS (the predecessor categories of Tier 1 (PSW));
- score a minimum of 75 points for attributes under paras 51–58 of Appendix C to the Rules;
- score 10 points for 'English language' under paras 1–3 of Appendix B to the Rules;
- score 10 points for 'maintenance' under paras 1–2 of Appendix C to the Rules;
- if seeking *leave to remain* have, or have last been granted, entry clearance, or leave to enter/ remain in one of the following categories (ie it is possible to switch from any of the following categories into the Tier 1 (PSW) category):
- a participant in the FT:WISS (provided the last leave granted under FT: WISS was for less than two years);
- a participant in the IGS (or its predecessor, the SEGS) (provided the last leave granted under the IGS or FT: WISS was for less than two years);
- a Student (who has not previously been granted leave under FT: WISS, IGS or SEGS);
- a Student Nurse (who has not previously been granted leave under FT: WISS, IGS or SEGS);
- a Student Re-sitting an Examination (who has not previously been granted leave under FT: WISS, IGS or SEGS);
- a Student Writing-up a Thesis (who has not previously been granted leave as a Tier 1 migrant or under FT: WISS, IGS or SEGS);
- a Tier 4 Migrant (who has not previously been granted leave as a Tier 1

(PSW) migrant or under FT: WISS, IGS or SEGS);

- as a Postgraduate Doctor or Dentist (who has not previously been granted leave under Tier 1 (PSW) or FT: WISS, IGS or SEGS);

• if seeking leave to remain having existing (or last been granted) leave under the FT:WISS, must be either a British National (Overseas) Citizen, a British Overseas Territories Citizen, a British Overseas Citizen, a British Protected Person, or a British Subject; and

• have the unconditional written consent of the sponsoring Government or agency to the application, if the studies which lead to the relevant Post-Study Work qualifications (ie those qualifications that the applicant relies on to score points for attributes) were sponsored by a Government or an international scholarship agency within the last 12 months (and the applicant must produce the documents specified in the Guidance to show this consent, for which see T1 (PSW) PG, paras 39–40).

The above rule that permits 'students' to switch to Tier 1 (PSW) refers to those granted leave as students under the old student rules (ie what were paras 57–62 of the Rules). It does not include, for example, switching from 'student visitors'. This is because 'student' is defined in paragraph 6 of the Rules. This is also the interpretation that was set out to ILPA in an UKBA letter dated 8 August 2008.

Those seeking to enter in this category must have a valid entry clearance enabling them to do so (Rules, para 245W).

For dependants of Tier 1 (PSW) migrants, ▶see 194–202.

WHAT THE RULES MEAN

Irrespective of whether applicants are seeking to enter the UK or remain in the UK as a Tier 1 (PSW) migrant, they must score a minimum of 75 points for 'attributes', 10 points for 'English language' and 10 points for 'maintenance'.

The Rules for maintenance are the same as for the Tier 1 (General) category (▶above 152–155). For details about the case law relating to the maintenance requirement, ▶see below 181–188.

Attributes

The attributes and the points that can be scored are set out in paragraphs 51–58 and Table 9 of Appendix A to the Rules. The sole attribute for which points are available is 'qualifications' and applicants must score 75 points.

Those applying for leave to remain who are switching from the Tier 1 (PSW) predecessor categories: IGS, SEGS or FT:WISS (ie who either have, or were last granted, leave in those categories) are automatically awarded the full 75 points. This is a transitional provision because, with time, this route will disappear as leave is no longer being granted under the IGS, SEGS or the FT: WISS.

All other applicants will have to score points, as described below, for: their degree (20 points); the institution where they studied for their degree (20 points); the immigration status they had during their study (20 points); and the time at which they make their Tier 1 (PSW) application (15 points).

Degree

Applicants will receive 20 points if they have been awarded either (App A, Table 9):

- a UK-recognised degree at Bachelor, Masters or PhD level;
- a UK postgraduate certificate in education (PGCE), or a professional graduate diploma of education; or
- a Higher National Diploma (HND) from a Scottish institution.

According to the Policy Guidance for the qualification to be accepted as a UK-recognised degree at the relevant level it must have been awarded by a UK 'recognised body', which is defined as an institution which has been granted degree-awarding powers by a Royal Charter, an Act of Parliament or the Privy Council. It includes all UK universities and some higher education colleges (T1 (PSW) PG, paras 54–5; Rules, para 6). To check that their institution is a recognised body, applicants should consult the website of the Department for Innovation, Universities and Skills (DIUS) at http://www.dcsf.gov.uk/recogniseddukdegrees. A HND from a Scottish Institution should be at level 8 on the Scottish Credit Qualifications Framework (App A, para 58; T1 (PSW) PG, para 58).

Note that the Rules when originally laid enabled applicants to score points for *any* postgraduate certificate or diploma, but were restricted from 31 March 2009 so as to permit only UK postgraduate certificates of education (HC 314) and were amended again from October so as to permit points to be also scored for a professional graduate diploma of education (Cm 7701).

The following qualifications will not attract any points (Tier 1 (PSW) PG, para 59):

- foundation degrees;
- honorary degrees;
- qualifications awarded in the UK by overseas awarding bodies;
- qualifications undertaken solely at an overseas campus of UK institutions;
- professional and vocational qualifications (unless they also fall within the definition of what does qualify – see above); and
- postgraduate certificates and diplomas (unless one of the certificates/ diplomas of education referred to above).

In *Kan (Post-Study Work – degree award required) India*, the applicant had not been 'awarded' the relevant qualification either at the date
of the decision or the hearing. The Tribunal held that the plain meaning of
the words in Appendix A was that an applicant could only score points if
s/he 'has been awarded' the relevant qualification and that this interpretation was supported by the Policy Guidance concerning the date when
the qualification is treated as having been awarded (paras 9, 11 and 14).
The Tribunal also held that the Policy Guidance (now contained in T1
(PSW) PG, para 62) allowing applicants without a certificate to provide a
letter from the institution to confirm that the certificate will be issued, did
not mean that the Rules could be satisfied if the award itself would occur
later. It reasoned that the ability to produce the *certificate of the award*
later did not mean that there did not have to be an *existing* award (para
13). In *NO (Post-Study Work – award needed by date of application)
Nigeria*, the Tribunal supplemented *Kan* in the context of the requirement to have made an application within 12 months of the award (▶see
below).

In a detailed case involving a number of Tier 1 (PSW) applicants who had
been studying at the Cambridge College of Learning, *NA & Others
(Cambridge College of Learning)*, the AIT held that, in a case where the
applicants had relied on certificates to show qualifications on a course
that the institution did not in fact legitimately run, the application could
be refused on the basis that producing the document amounted to a false
representation under para 322(1A) of the Rules. In *AA (Nigeria)* the
Court of Appeal made it clear that a false representation for these
purposes had to involve deception (a point acknowledged in the later
Tribunal case involving the same college, *TR (CCOL cases)* at para 14).

Institution where studied

A further 20 points will be awarded if the applicant (App A, Table 9):

- has studied for his/her award at a UK institution that is a "UK-recognised
  or listed body", or which holds a sponsor licence under Tier 4 of the PBS;
  or

- if s/he is claiming points for having been awarded an HND from a Scottish
  Institution, studied for that diploma at a Scottish publicly-funded institution of further or higher education, or a Scottish *bona fide* private
  education institution which maintains satisfactory records of enrolment
  and attendance.

A list of bodies that hold a sponsor licence under Tier 4 can be found on
UKBA's website at www.ukba.homeoffice.gov.uk/sitecontent/ documents/
employersandsponsors/pointsbasedsystem/registerofsponsorseducation.
A "UK-recognised body" is one that has been granted degree-awarding
powers by either Royal Charter, an Act of Parliament or the Privy Council.
A "UK listed body" is an institution that is not a UK-recognised body but
which provides full courses that lead to the award of a degree by a UK-

recognised body (Rules, para 6). Information on both UK-recognised and listed bodies can be found at www.dcsf.gov.uk/recognisedukdegrees. The Guidance states that the Scottish institution must be on the Register of Education and Training Providers list, see at www.ukba.homeoffice. gov.uk/sitecontent/documents/employersandsponsors/pointsbasedsystem/ diusregister.pdf (Tier 1 (PSW) PG, para 67).

Immigration status during study

A further 20 points will be awarded if the applicant's periods of UK study and/or research towards his/her qualification were undertaken while they had entry clearance, leave to enter or leave to remain in the UK that was not subject to a restriction preventing them from undertaking a course of study and/or research (App A, Table 9). In other words the qualifications being relied on must have been obtained at a time when the applicant had leave in the UK which permitted them to study. This requirement, as it now stands, was liberalised from October 2009 (see Cm 7701). Previously, only applicants who had studied while in the UK as a student, Tier 4 migrant or dependant could score the necessary points. It is not necessary, however, that applicants have remained in the UK throughout the entire period of their study. Periods of overseas studies or research do not disqualify an applicant (T1 (PSW) PG, para 71).

Timing of Tier 1 (PSW) application

The further final 15 points can be awarded if the application for entry clearance or leave to remain as a Tier 1 (PSW) migrant is made within 12 months of obtaining the relevant qualification, or within 12 months of completing a UK Foundation Programme Office affiliated foundation programme as a postgraduate doctor or dentist (App A, Table 9). The ability to make use of Tier 1 (PSW) after completing Foundation Programme training, which is undertaken under Tier 4, was added to the Rules from April 2010 (HC 439).

For the purposes of 'obtaining' the relevant qualification, the 12-month period starts from the date the applicant is first notified in writing by the awarding institution that the qualification has been awarded (App A, para 55). Guidance states that the notice may have been given directly to the applicant, or it may have been given by the institution publishing the details of the award, for example on a notice board or website (Tier 1 (PSW) PG, para 79). In *NO (Post-Study Work – award needed by date of application) Nigeria*, it appears that the applicant could prove that he had obtained his degree by the time of the hearing (para 6). However, the Tribunal, drawing on the ruling in *NA & Others (Tier 1 Post-Study Work-funds)*, held that the requirement to make the application within 12 months of obtaining the relevant qualification related to a historic timeline. It: "clearly requires an applicant to have obtained the relevant qualification by the date of the application, and not more than 12 months before" (*NO* paras 19, 23). In the instant case, the applicant had not completed the dissertation on which the award depended by the date of the application and so his appeal failed (*NO* para 25).

Evidence required

The Rules state that documents specified in Policy Guidance must be produced as evidence of the qualification that the applicant relies on to score points for attributes (or, where relevant, as evidence of the applicant completing a foundation programme as a postgraduate doctor or dentist) (Rules, App A, para 54 read with Rule, para 245AA).

The documents specified are (T1 (PSW) PG, paras 61–62):

- original certificate of award clearly showing the applicant's name, title of the qualification and the name of the awarding body; or
- if the certificate has not yet been issued, an original letter from the institution at which the applicant studied towards his/her eligible qualification on the letter head of the institution, issued by an authorised official confirming the applicant's name, title of the qualification, date of the award, the body awarding the qualification and explaining the reason why the applicant cannot produce the original certificate and confirming that a certificate will be issued.

In order to show the applicant's immigration status during their period of study/research in the UK, the Guidance specifies that applicants should produce original passports/travel documents or Biometric Residence Permits ('BRP') showing the relevant grants of leave, and an original letter from the institution at which they studied containing the start and end dates of the applicant's period of study or research for the qualification (T1 (PSW) PG, para 73). If the passport/travel document or BRP are not available through theft, expiry or because it is already with UKBA, officials will try to verify the applicant's status using electronic records (T1 (PSW) PG, para 75–6).

The evidence required in order to show that the application for entry clearance or leave to remain was made within 12 months of obtaining the relevant qualification should be in the form of an original document from the institution where the applicant studied (T1 (PSW) PG, para 82)

English language

Tier 1 (PSW) applicants must score 10 points for English language under Appendix B to the Rules (Rules, paras 245X(d), 245Z(d)). The only way in which Tier 1 (PSW) applicants can score the necessary 10 points for language is by scoring the required 75 points for the PSW attributes under Appendix A of the Rules (see above) (App B, para 3). Having done this, the applicant will have demonstrated that s/he has obtained an appropriate English qualification (Tier 1 (PSW) PG, para 90).

Leave, conditions, extension and settlement

Those granted entry will be given leave to enter for a period of two years (Rules, para 245Y). Those seeking to switch into the Tier 1 (PSW) category from any category other than the predecessor categories (IGS, SEGS, FT:WISS) will also be granted leave for two years (Rules, para 245Z(a)(ii)). But those who have, or were last granted, leave under the IGS, SEGS or FT:WISS, will be granted leave so as to bring their total leave up to two years when the last grant of IGS, SEGS or FT: WISS leave and the leave that is presently being applied for, are added together. This means that, if the previous leave under the IGS, SEGS or FT: WISS was for two years more, the present application will be refused (Rules, para 245Z(a)(i)).

During the period of their leave, Tier 1 (PSW) migrants have free access to the UK for the purposes of entering into employment and self-employment. All who are granted entry clearance, leave to enter or remain will have the following conditions attached to their leave (Rules, paras 245Y 245ZA(b)):

- they must not have recourse to public funds in the UK;
- if required to do so by the Rules (para 326), applicants must register with the police; and
- applicants must not enter into employment as a doctor or dentist in training *unless either*:
- they have obtained a degree in medicine or dentistry at Bachelor's level or above from a UK institution that is a recognised or listed UK body (for which, ►see above at 177) or which holds a sponsor licence under Tier 4;
- or the leave being granted is leave to remain and the applicant has, or has last been granted, entry clearance or leave that was not subject to any condition restricting employment and the applicant has been employed, during that leave, as a doctor or dentist in training (for details about obtaining this exemption from the employment condition, see T1 (PSW) PG, Annex B).

As with the Tier 1 (General) category, there is no requirement for the Tier 1 (PSW) migrant to engage in employment once granted leave, but not working may make it difficult or impossible to switch into the Tier 1 (General) or Tier 2 (General) category afterwards.

Entry clearance or leave granted in the Tier 1 (PSW) category is a 'one-off' grant. It cannot be extended in the same category and there is no route to settlement in this category alone. However, a Tier 1 (PSW) migrant can, in principle, switch into the other categories of Tier 1, or the Tier 2 (General) category which, in turn, may lead to settlement after five years.

MAINTENANCE REQUIREMENTS UNDER THE PBS: THE CASE-LAW

The Rules and relevant Policy Guidance relating to maintenance for the different Tiers and categories under the PBS vary. For the different Rules and Guidance, ▶see 152–155 (Tier 1); 220–222 (Tier 2); 263–270 and (Tier 4); 299–300, 307–308 (Tier 5) and 194–203 (dependants of PBS migrants).

The relevant case-law spans the different Tiers and categories and while the Rules and policy vary, some of the principles are common. For this reason, we set it out here in one place but users should use it with great care, bearing in mind the need to consider the applicability of each case to the particular category in which the applicant is applying and note that the Policy Guidance, in particular, is prone to and has changed over the years.

The landmark case is, of course, *Pankina* decided on 23 June 2010 and care should be taken with the cases pre-dating it. The immediate effect of *Pankina* was to prevent UKBA from relying on a requirement set out only in Guidance and not the Rules, that the applicant show that s/he had the required funds over a 90-day period before the application. The Home Office responded to the decision by placing the 90-day requirement in the Rules. However, *Pankina* has much wider implications for the inter-relationship between the Rules and Guidance under the PBS. For this reason *Pankina* and other cases dealing with that broad question are covered in Chapter 2 ▶41–45, 47–52. It is likely tht new Rules from 6 April 2011 will put more of the Guidance into the Rules.

We deal with the other maintenance cases below in chronological order (where the Tribunal decisions give a date of hearing rather than date of decision, we have used the date of hearing).

For the human rights issues that may arise when an applicant fails to meet the strict maintenance requirements under the Rules, ▶see 412–420. For maintenance issues about the evidence that can be taken into account on appeals, ▶see 441–442.

NA & Others (Tier 1 Post-Study Work-funds) (heard 24 April 2009)

NA was decided at a point when the requirement to have held funds for 90 consecutive days in Tier 1 cases was only contained in the Guidance and not in the Rules. It was also decided before *Pankina* (decided on 23 June 2010) which held that the Guidance could not be enforced to this effect. *Pankina* implicitly overruled the finding in *NA* to the effect the Guidance, read together with the Rules, meant that an applicant had, in a Tier 1 (PSW) case, to show that s/he held £800 for each and every day of the three-month period (see *NA*, paras 76–78, 86–89).

However, in *Pankina*, the court considered whether, in the alternative, if the monies did have to be held for three months (as the Rules have now been amended to confirm), it was enough if, by the time of any appeal hearing, the money could be shown to have been in the account for three months, even if it had not been there for three months before the date of the original application. The Court in *Pankina* held that the wording (albeit in the then Guidance) required that the funds had been held in the account for three months by the date of the application, ie not by the time of an appeal (*Pankina*, paras 38–9). In that finding, *Pankina* implicitly upheld the decision in *NA* which had been to similar effect (*NA*, paras 58–9).

In *NA*, the Tribunal did go on to find, however, that it was at least possible for applicants to rely on evidence first produced at appeal (ie even if that evidence had not been produced at the application stage) to show that the 'three-month' requirement had been met as at the date of the application itself (see *NA*, paras 66–67 and 74–75; this was later endorsed by the UT in *CS (Tier 1 – home regulator) USA*, para 13 and in *AM and SS* at para 5, ▶both below). This will be the case until s85A 2002 Act is brought into force which states that the Tribunal may only consider evidence in PBS cases if it was submitted at the time of the application, ▶see on appeals at 442–444).

NA also held:

- the relevant maintenance rules contained no discretion and did not make allowance for sickness or other mitigating circumstances (paras 54–56); and

- the relevant amount (of £800 in that case) could be shown in the form of a personal or joint account (paras 90–91) and could be shown in the form of personal savings held in overseas accounts (para 92).

SK (Tier 1 – Transitional provision – maintenance) Republic of Korea (decided 30 July 2009)

In *SK*, the Tribunal acknowledged a transitional arrangement in place for Tier 1 (PSW) applicants who applied on or before 31 October 2008, allowing them to show that they had a closing balance of £800 in their account at some point in the 30 days before their application (as opposed to complying with the new 90-day requirement). The Tribunal held:

- that this *only* applied to those who submitted their applications on or before 31 October 2008 and not if they applied later (paras 21–22, 30); and

- that the applicant had no legitimate expectation, based on information provided by the Home Office, that the transitional policy would be extended beyond this (paras 33, 35).

However, as a result of the decision in *Pankina*, applicants in SK's position, who applied before 23 June 2010, can seek the benefit of the policy introduced for such cases after the decision of the Court of Appeal (▶see Chapter 2 46–47).

SE & CJ v SSHD (approximately June/July 2009)

In this case the Home Office conceded a claim for judicial review and agreed to grant leave to a Tier 1 (General) applicant whose bank balance fell significantly below the required £1,333 (applicant plus dependant husband) for about 15 days of the required three-month period (the case arose in 2009 pre-*Pankina* when the three-month period was required under the Policy Guidance). No doubt important to the reason for conceding the claim were the general circumstances relating to the couple's finances: they held the required amount at the date of the application; had an established record in the UK as Work Permit holder and dependant, during which time they had been able to maintain themselves without recourse to public funds; they had deposited large amounts in their accounts in the seven months before the date of the application and they had large investments in US brokerage accounts. Significant also was the Home Office's explanation given in the response to the letter before claim why prescribed amounts were required to be shown. It was:

"[to ensure that applicants] have a sum of money available so that they can support themselves and any dependants if, for example, they experience periods of unemployment. This applies even if the migrant has a job offer when he or she arrives, because the migrant could lose, or resign from, that job without this affecting his or her immigration status. It is important that migrants who enter the UK are able to support themselves and their dependants. If they cannot, they face financial hardship, as they do not have access to most state benefits. Allowing the entry of those unable to support themselves will have negative social consequences."

PO (Points-based scheme: maintenance: loans) Nigeria (heard 28 August 2009)

This appeal concerned a Tier 1 (PSW) migrant and the Policy Guidance as then in force. The Tribunal held that the Guidance did not permit an applicant to show that s/he met the funds requirements by producing evidence of an agreement for a loan (in this case an overdraft facility). At the very least the Guidance required that the sum of money had actually been credited to the relevant account. The Tribunal went on (para 6):

"If the money is in the account, the respondent does not require an applicant to demonstrate that the money is his, rather than merely having been lent to him. Thus the evidence may be evidence of a loan that has been made. Nothing in any document we have seen shows that a person can meet the maintenance requirements by showing that there is an agreement for a loan, or in any other way that does not include showing the relevant sum as a credit balance in the account."

Note that it appears that the present Policy Guidance under Tier 1 (PSW) does not repeat the reference to 'loans' to which some of the Guidance referred to in both this case and *IK* (▶below) referred (see T1 (PSW) PG, para 98).

For loans under Tier 4, ▶see 268–269.

R (Ayokunnu Ebelechukwu Adeyemi-Doro) v SSHD (decided 23 September 2009)

This short application for permission for judicial review is notable only because it refers to the fact that there are examples of the Home Office conceding some claims for judicial review where certain failings (in relation, it appears, to maintenance) had come to light (para 10).

IK (Immigration Rules – construction – purpose) Pakistan (heard 4 November 2009)

IK is a good example, in our view, of how the inflexible PBS rules, compared to the pre-PBS rules relating to maintenance, can produce unfair results. The Immigration Judge had found in favour of the applicant, a Tier 1 (PSW) migrant, on the basis that, although he did not have the prescribed £800 in his bank account for the whole three-month period, he had the benefit of an overdraft facility of £2,000 in total (which he could at any time have drawn on, placed in his savings account and, presumably, by that means, shown that he had the required funds!). The applicant had also recently loaned £13,000 to his uncle (which he clearly proved) knowing that he was expecting a work bonus, which the applicant did receive but not till later than expected. The Immigration Judge said that, looking at the applicant's position overall, including his ability to loan such an amount to his uncle and his property worth £55,000 in Pakistan, it was clear he could show that he satisfied the Rules (see para 12).

On appeal, however, the Tribunal concluded that the Rules were plain (para 19), that having regard to the Oxford Dictionary definition of 'funds' contained in the Rules ('permanent stock of something ready to be drawn upon; or a stock of money especially one set apart for a purpose') that it was by no means plain that an overdraft facility, which concerned the bank's stock of money rather than that of an applicant, could be the 'funds' of the applicant (para 20). The Tribunal went on to find, including by reference to the Policy Guidance, that the applicant could not rely on his overdraft facility and that he did not meet the requirements of the Rules (paras 22-23). Insofar as the decision relied on the Policy Guidance, it may now be vulnerable following *Pankina*.

OK (paragraph 245Z(e) – transitional provisions – Maintenance (Funds)) Ukraine (heard 5 January 2010)

In essence, this decision looked again at the arguments relating to the 2008 transitional protection policy for those Tier 1 applicants who applied in the wake of the change in the Policy Guidance, requiring that applicants show that they held the relevant funds for 90 days. The

Tribunal upheld the position that such applicants had to apply by 31 October 2008 and rejected attempts to overturn the earlier similar decision of the Tribunal in *SK* (above).

CS (Tier 1 – home regulator) USA (heard 30 April 2010)

In this case before the UT a Tier 1 (PSW) migrant had relied on a letter from a Bank of America customer support officer in Florida confirming the information provided in bank statements that had also previously been provided (para 2). The Immigration Judge below had held that (then) para 96(iv) of the Policy Guidance applied. That Guidance referred to a "letter from a financial institution regulated by the [FSA] or, in the case of overseas accounts, the home regulator (official regulatory body for the country in which the institution operates and the funds are located) confirming funds...". The Immigration Judge held that the applicant could not satisfy the Rules because there was no letter from a regulator in the country of origin (see paras 4–5) (the present equivalent Policy Guidance is T1 (PSW) PG, para 103(iv)). The UT held:

- The applicant had produced evidence from a bank in the form of bank statements fulfilling the Guidance and that was sufficient to enable the appeal to be allowed. The reference in para 96(iv) to 'financial institutions' was to *other* financial institutions ie separate from those institutions earlier referred to in the Guidance ie banks and building societies. Therefore, there was no need, beyond the bank statements, for a separate letter at all. The Guidance provided a list of "separate specified alternative documents rather than a series of cumulative requirements". Accordingly, there was no need to produce the kind of evidence that is needed where reliance is placed on a separate type of financial institution other than a bank or building society (paras 10–14).

- Aside from this, the Immigration Judge had also interpreted the part of the Guidance that he thought was relevant, incorrectly. The relevant Guidance required, in the case of an overseas account held in an 'other' financial institution, a letter from that institution. It did *not* require a letter from the home regulator itself, simply that the institution be regulated by the home regulator. In deciding this, the UT corrected the decision in *MM (Tier 1 PSW; Art 9; 'private life') Zimbabwe* on the point (paras 15–17).

Note that, although this case was decided before *Pankina*, the UT made it clear that it was assuming, for the purposes of its decision, but without deciding, that the Guidance formed part of the Rules and could be a source of mandatory obligations on claimants as had been found in *NA* (*CS* at para 10).

AM and SS (PBS – Tier 1 – joint accounts) Pakistan (heard 11 May 2010)

In this case, concerning a Tier 1 (PSW) applicant, the UT held that a joint account bearing the name of the applicant meets the relevant evidential requirements of the Guidance and that further evidence of actual ownership of the funds in the account was not required. The relevant joint account was held in the name of one of the appellants and a friend of his (para 4). The Immigration Judge had rejected the joint account held with someone who did not have an important interest turning on the application because it was impossible to know at any given time whether the funds were personally available to the applicant. The Tribunal stated:

"10 Provided the money is in the account, it does not appear to matter who it belongs to. It may, for example, have been borrowed simply for the purpose of having bank statements meeting the requirements of the Guidance. The Immigration Judge's comments are obviously sensible. His mistake was to apply common sense to the interpretation of the points-based scheme. There is no perceptible rationale behind the conclusion that the possession of £800 (and not a penny less) for three months (and not a day less) is showing that [if] an application is granted, the applicant will be satisfactorily maintained for what may be a very long period in the future. The rules are simply hoops which have to be jumped through"

"11 Whoever it was that was properly to be regarded as the owner of the money in the joint account, that account clearly met the requirements in the Guidance..."

FA & AA (PBS: effect of Pankina) Nigeria (heard 23 July 2010)

FA was heard on the same date as two other Tier 1 (General) Student cases (below), all a month after the decision in *Pankina*. They were all heard by the same constitution of the UT (including the President and Vice-President). The Tribunal rejected attempts to use the Policy Guidance as a means of restricting the ability of applicants to show that they satisfied the maintenance requirements as contained in the Rules themselves.

In *FA* the UT had to consider whether a Tier 4 (General) student could rely on funds in a bank account that was in the sole name of her husband. The Tribunal held that once it is accepted that the Guidance does not have the status of Immigration Rules, there was no reason why the applicant could not show that she met the requirements of the Rules to have the required level of funds 'available' to her by a bank account in her husband's name (paras 18, 21). The Tribunal allowed the appeal having regard to the fact that it was clear that there was no reason to doubt the existence of the funds, or that the husband had made them available to his wife.

We comment that applicants must beware though. In *FA*, there was clear evidence that the husband would make the funds available to the applicant – the main reason he rather than she actually held them was cultural. An applicant must show, as a matter of fact, that the funds are 'available' to them and that may, of course, be more difficult if the monies relied on are held by others. The evidence that funds are in fact available may need to be more cogent if those funds are not held or owned by the applicant.

CDS (PBS: 'available': Article 8) Brazil (heard 23 July 2010)

In *CDS*, the UT allowed an appeal brought by another Tier 4 (General) student who relied on funds held by two sponsors who happened to be doctors and who were not the parents/legal guardian of the applicant. The Tribunal stated (para 13):

"In the absence of specific additional requirements of the Immigration Rules, it seems to us that funds are 'available' to a claimant at the material time if they belong to a third party but that party is shown to be willing to deploy them to support the claimant for the purpose contemplated."

HM & Others (PBS – legitimate expectation) Malawi (heard 23 July 2010)

The appellants had evidence of very substantial sums held in an account in their joint names in the National Bank of Malawi. The difficulty was that the prevailing Malawian currency exchange controls would only permit them to transfer a total of US$1,000 to the UK. The appellants proposed instead to obtain access to sterling in the UK from people who wished to remit funds to Malawi to whom they (the appellants) would transfer the equivalent funds from their Malawian bank account. The UT held that the fact that the appellants had the necessary funds under their control in an overseas bank account was sufficient to show that they were 'available' to them for the purposes of the Rules. The UT indicated that the appellants clearly had the ability to circumvent the exchange control regulations and it was unwilling to impose a limitation on the meaning of the Rules such that the funds would not be considered 'available' because they could not be immediately accessed due to the exchange controls (see paras 11, 13 and concluding part of para 14).

Further in *HM*, the UT noted that the relevant Policy Guidance set out that proof of availability of funds could be shown by bank statements of overseas accounts provided that the statements complied with certain requirements. On that basis, the Tribunal made the further alternative finding, also in favour of the appellants, that they had a legitimate expectation that the Secretary of State would deal with their application on the basis of the Guidance (see para 14). We comment that this is an example of how the Policy Guidance can actually help an applicant in a case in which s/he might not otherwise be successful under the Rules alone. It is worth noting exactly what the UT said in this alternative finding:

"14 Further or in the alternative, we do not consider that the appellants are precluded from relying upon the Guidance which, though as *Pankina* makes clear, cannot be employed adversely to an appellant, nevertheless in our view can give rise to a legitimate expectation that the Secretary of State will adhere to that Guidance when considering an appellant's claim…the Tier 4 Guidance states that proof of availability of funds can be shown by bank statements including overseas accounts so long as the specified information as set out in the Guidance is declared on the bank statement. The Guidance does not require that the funds have to be available in the sense of being immediately accessible or otherwise. Proof of liquid assets in bank accounts is, in effect, sufficient. Nor is there any requirement that the funds should be available for withdrawal or accessible within a specified time period. Bearing these matters in mind, we conclude that even if we are wrong in our view that the appellants are entitled to rely upon the wording of paragraph 11 of Appendix C, in the alternative they had a legitimate expectation that the Secretary of State would deal with their application in accordance with the wording of the Policy Guidance and as a consequence there would be a denial of that legitimate expectation if they were not allowed to so rely."

DN (student – course 'completed' – established presence) Kenya (decided 1 November 2010)

This was a Tier 4 case in which the applicant was trying to show that they had an 'established presence' studying in the UK with the effect that they would not have to show as high a level of available funds as would otherwise be the case. The UT held that, for the purpose of the definition of 'completed' a course that was relevant to showing an established presence, an applicant did not have to show that s/he had 'successfully completed' that course, ie by passing the relevant exams. For the full context, ▶see Chapter 8 at 263–264.

SETTLEMENT: COMMON REQUIREMENTS

Tier 1, Tier 2 and Tier 5 (international agreement sub-category, working as a private servant in a diplomatic household only) of the PBS provide routes to settlement if a number of requirements, that are individual to each Tier and category, are satisfied. There are also some common rules. The common requirements are that the applicant must:

- have spent a 'continuous period of five years lawfully in the UK' (with leave of a specified kinds which is different for each category);
- not fall for refusal under the general grounds for refusal (▶see Chapter 11);
- not be an illegal entrant; and
- have sufficient knowledge of the English language and sufficient knowledge about life in the UK (see also Rules, paras 33B–D), unless the applicant is aged under 18 or over 65.

The relevant settlement Rules are: para 245E (Tier 1 (General) ▶156; para

245N (Tier 1 (Entrepreneur) ▶164); para 245U (Tier 1 (Investor) ▶172); para 245ZH (Tier 2 migrants ▶242–243) and para 245ZS (Tier 5, private servant in diplomatic household). Note that the Tier 1 (PSW) category does not lead directly to settlement. Nor does the Tier 2 (ICT) category, unless a portion of the applicant's leave was granted under the Rules in place before 6 April 2010, or under the previous work permit scheme on the basis of an intra-company transfer.

Continuous period lawfully in the UK

The most recent Guidance issued by the Home Office about the calculation of the continuous lawful period is contained in the table below.

UKBA GUIDANCE ON 'CALCULATING CONTINUOUS PERIOD IN UK'

The Guidance set out below was issued by UKBA's 'Modernised Guidance team' on 26 January 2011 under the heading 'Indefinite leave to remain – calculating continuous period in UK – v1.0 ext'.

Calculating the continuous period in the UK

You can ignore short absences abroad if it is clear that the applicant has continued to be based in the UK. For example, an absence for:

- a holiday consistent with annual paid leave entitlements
- business trips consistent with maintaining employment or self-employment in the UK.

Tier 2 migrants

You can count the period between the migrant being granted entry clearance and the date they entered the UK towards the five-year period providing it is no longer than three months.

Discretion when continuous residence has been broken

Exceptionally, you may add periods spent in the UK to form unbroken continuous residence in cases where:

- there have been no absences abroad (apart from those described above) and authorised employment or business has not been broken by:
- any single interruption of more than three months or
- interruptions that total more than six months.

- there have been significant absences abroad but the reasons for these were:
- compelling ones of a compassionate nature or
- to do with the applicant's employment or business in the UK
- no single absence abroad should be for more than three months at a time and they must not total more than six months.

Decisions on discretion

The decision to apply discretion must be made by someone at the appropriate grade.

> An HEO or above must make the decision whether to allow discretion if breaks in residence come under the exceptional circumstances above.
>
> An SEO or grade 7 must make the decision whether to allow discretion if breaks in residence and/or employment or self-employment are longer than those above, or of a different type."

JCWI's view is that the UKBA approach set out in the table above is too restrictive as an interpretation of the Rules. Although the approach set out by UKBA makes concessions for holidays, business trips consistent with maintaining employment in the UK and compassionate reasons, the maximum amount of time that an applicant is apparently permitted to spend outside the UK is 'not more than six months' in total over the five-year period. That is to say the applicant must not, in order to qualify for settlement, spend more than 10% of their time outside the UK.

In what follows, we set out a chronological account of the development and interpretation of the rule.

Approach under HC 251 and HC 395

The 'continuous period' requirement was first introduced into the Rules by way of an amendment to HC 251 (the consolidated Statement of Immigration Rules that was in force until 1 October 1994, when the present HC 395 was introduced). HC 251 had a single settlement provision that was amended by HC 725 with effect from 26 July 1993 so that it entitled a relevant applicant to settle "if he has remained here in that capacity for a continuous period of four years". A similar provision was adopted in HC 395 which also, for many years, enabled settlement on the basis of four (rather than five) years' residence in the relevant capacity. The approach to the requirement that was taken is apparent from the following materials that span both the consolidated statements of the Rules, HC 251 and HC 395:

- A Home Office letter to a London solicitor dated 15 February 1994 concerning sole representatives and businessmen stated:
  "As you know, under the Immigration Rules, a person is eligible for settlement when they have remained here in the relevant capacity for four years. However, we have long recognised that a person engaged in business with overseas companies might find it difficult to achieve this. It was therefore felt that a realistic solution was to allow absences from the UK of up to 25% of the person's time over that four-year period."

- In *Khoury (1994)*, decided by an Immigration Adjudicator under HC 251, the main dispute concerned the method of calculating absences. However, the Adjudicator also accepted that 'continuous' "could not mean literally continuous, that is to say without any departure from the jurisdiction at all". The Adjudicator continued "this must be right: a sole representative is by definition doing business with overseas principals, and must inevitably need to return to base from time to time … So in my view 'continuous' does not mean literally unbroken by a single day". Having found that 'continuous' in this context does not have its literal meaning, the Adjudicator appeared to have found that it was capable of tolerating absences of up to 25%, in line with Home Office policy.

- In a further letter from the Home Office of 26 April 1996 to another London solicitor in response to a request for clarification of "policy regarding absences from the [UK] by persons here in the Investor category", the Secretary of State stated.

"I can confirm that the policy described at the ILPA [Immigration Law Practitioners' Association] conference remains unchanged. Whilst to qualify as an investor the relevant paragraph (224[i]) requires only that an applicant makes the United Kingdom his main home, to be eligible for indefinite leave to remain, an applicant must have spent at least 75% of the four-year period here (para 230[iii] states a continuous period of four years). Failure to achieve this will usually, if all other requirements have been met, result in a further grant of leave to remain."

- In the Immigration Appeal Tribunal case of *Shahbakhti* reference was made to the general practice of disregarding absences of three months in any one year, and, exceptionally longer periods (in that case 20 months' absence in four years was too long for a work permit holder) (*Shahbakhti* was mentioned briefly in *BD (work permit – 'continuous period') Nigeria* – ▶see below).

- In *Gurung (2002)*, a settlement application on behalf of a private servant in a diplomatic household, an Adjudicator had construed the settlement rule literally. Before Collins J (sitting as the President of the IAT), it was agreed by the Home Office that the rule was not to be construed in that way (at para 4):

"...the Home Office applies a rule of thumb in other cases which require a continuous period of four years to be spent in the United Kingdom before a particular leave can be granted. The Home Office has decided that absences for a period not exceeding three months in any one year should not prevent the period being continuous. That is to say, they have accepted that the word 'continuous' in the rule is not to be read literally and does not mean that there has to have been no day when the relevant individual has not been outside the United Kingdom. We are bound to say that if 'continuous' were to have the meaning that the Adjudicator says it does we cannot see that there are likely to be any private servants in a diplomatic household who would succeed."

Both in *Gurung* and *Khoury*, the statutory appeal bodies dealt with the matter with deference to Home Office policy which indicated that absences of up to 25% (ie three months a year) could be tolerated.

2005 undisclosed policy and judicial review challenge

In 2005, it came to light that the Home Office was operating on the basis of an undisclosed Immigration Directorate Instruction (IDI) ie one that was not posted on the website. The policy was very similar to UKBA's present approach set out in the table above and we reproduced the relevant extract from the 2005 policy in the 2006 Edition of the *JCWI Handbook* (see pp438). The policy prohibited settlement if the applicant had been absent for more than six months in total. Over a four (rather than a five) year qualifying period, this tolerated absences of anything up to 12.5% of an applicant's time (not more than six weeks per year) – a greater restriction than is required, for example, under the British Nationality Act 1981 for naturalisation purposes.

The policy was challenged on a number of grounds by an investor (under the pre-PBS Rules) in Judicial Review proceedings during the summer of 2005. The case did not need to be heard in court since, in the face of challenge, the Home Office conceded the immediate case. At the same time the Home Office accepted that its policy for Investors on the calculation of the four-year period for settlement purposes is that periods of absence of up to 25% in total would be tolerated (provided that none of the individual trips was for more than three months). As far as all of the other categories of the Rules were concerned, the Home Office stated that it would review how the four-year residence rule operated and would publish revised guidelines (see statement as reported in the *Financial Times*, 1 August 2005, p1 and letter circulated to ILPA dated 1 September 2005; for other articles referring to the matter, see: *The Economist*, 2 July 2005; *Sunday Times*, 10 July 2005).

It is not clear what became of the review but in Guidance issued after the concession of that case (see the IDI issued in December 2006 relating to the 'Calculation of the five-year period for settlement', IDI, Chapter 5, section 1, para 3; and in Guidance issued under the PBS), the Home Office has reverted to its long-stop prohibition of settlement if the applicant has spent a total period of more than six months outside the UK. That is the position that is repeated again, most recently, in the January 2011 UKBA Guidance (▶see table above). The inconsistency with the previous approach (▶above) is quite apparent. In addition, having been challenged on a 12.5% absence tolerance rate by an investor and having agreed that, at least in that category, absences of up to 25% should be tolerated, the Home Office has now reverted to a position where applicants in all categories (including Investors) must not be absent for more than 10% of their time. The Home Office has not attempted to justify its approach by attempting to distinguish between the wording of the PBS rules from the pre-PBS ones and it would be difficult to see the justification for doing so.

BD (work permit – 'continuous period') Nigeria

UKBA's position is also inconsistent with the most recent Tribunal case on the issue, heard in October 2010, *BD (work permit – 'continuous period') Nigeria* and decided under the pre-PBS work permit Rules requiring the applicant to have "spent a continuous period of five years lawfully in the UK" (then Rules, para 134). The appellant appealed against a decision dismissing his appeal by an Immigration Judge. The facts were that appellant had been recruited in the UK to a large British company and issued with a work permit. He continued in approved work permit employment for the next five years but *more than half* of his time was spent abroad, posted to branches of the British company overseas. All the appellant's earnings were paid into his bank account in England and he paid UK tax and national insurance. He had also enrolled onto the company's UK pension plan and indeed bought a house of his own in the UK. The Tribunal noted that, unlike the Rules on long residence (HC 395, para 276A), there was no definition dealing with breaks in continuity contained in the Rules themselves. It considered that (para 10):

"[the] reason for this, we apprehend, is that for categories which do not in themselves lead to settlement, the strength of connection to the United Kingdom which merits the grant of indefinite leave is established by actual residence in the United Kingdom for most of the ten years, with a cap being put on the amount of time spent abroad"

Dealing with the Rule and the case before it, the Tribunal continued (para 11):

"As a literal construction makes no sense, the rule has to be construed sensibly. It clearly imports a discretion – a discretion which can be exercised by us – as to how much absence can be disregarded in the calculation of a 'continuous period' of five years. Of relevance, in our view, will be the reason for the absence and the strength of the person's ties to the United Kingdom, as shown in other ways. In the instant case, the appellant's absences have been required of him by his employer, a British company, and he has at all times retained his base in the United Kingdom. He is domiciled here for tax purposes, and would seem to have established a domicile of choice for other purposes. He has clearly made this country his home. In those circumstances, we find that he does meet all the requirements of rule 134..."

Reform of settlement

It was clear from the Home Secretary's statement to Parliament made on 23 November 2010 that the Government intends to restrict access to permanent settlement and that changes would be introduced affecting settlement from and after April 2011. It also appears from the proposals referred to above for changes to the Tier 1 (Entrepreneur) category (►see above 164) and the Tier 1 (Investor) category (►see above 173), that the Home Office has been considering some relaxation of the rules relating to absences and settlement.

For the latest on settlement, taken from the February 2011 Statement of Intent ►see 212. There is likely to be a consultation on further changes to settlement in May/June 2011.

DEPENDANTS OF PBS MIGRANTS

The rules for the grant of entry clearance and leave for the dependants of migrants admitted under Tiers 1, 2, 4 and Tier 5 (Temporary Worker) are gathered together in paragraphs 319AA–319K of the Rules. There is no provision for the admission of dependants of those admitted under the Tier 5 (Youth Mobility Scheme). Applications are made on form PBS (Dependants). Where the main applicant holds a Biometric Residence Permit (BRP), any dependant making an in-country application must also make sure that they apply for such a document (PBS Dependant PG, para 24).

Strangely, the Rules appear also to apply to dependants of those admitted as 'Tier 4 Migrants' (para 319AA), which is defined as migrants under the Tier 4 (General) Student category and the Tier 4 (Child) Student category (para 6). This may have been an error since the PBS (Dependant) Policy Guidance makes it clear that "the dependant route is not available for a family member of a Tier 4 (Child) Student migrant" (para 78; see also Tier 4 PG, para 253). In addition, the Tier 4 (Child) Student rules make it clear that a child must have no minor children for whom they are responsible (Rules, para 245ZZA(e)).

Where we refer below to dependants of a 'PBS migrant', that is shorthand for main applicants admitted under Tiers 1, 2, 4 or 5. There are some variations in the Rules across the tiers and these are also pointed out below.

Entry clearance

All dependants who are seeking *entry* to the UK must have a valid entry clearance for this route otherwise entry clearance/leave to enter will be refused (Rules, para 319B(a), 319G(a)). The only exception is that a dependant of a Tier 5 (Temporary Worker) may be admitted without an entry clearance provided that all the other conditions are met and (Rules, paras 319B(b), 319G(b)).

- the applicant is not a visa national; and
- the applicant is accompanied by the Tier 5 (Temporary Worker) on whom they are dependent and that that person is, at the same time, being admitted under para 245ZN(b) of the Rules, namely as a non-visa national, entering under the creative and sporting sub-category of the Tier 5 (Temporary Worker) route with engagements in the UK for up to a maximum of three months.

Partners of PBS migrants seeking entry or leave to remain

The general Immigration Rules relating to the age of partners and polygamy also apply in PBS dependant cases (Rules, para 319A with reference to paras 277–280 and 295AA of the Rules). Note that in *DQ (Chile) & SB and another v SSHD* (December 2010), the Court of Appeal held that the amendments to the Rules introduced in November 2008 that prevented the grant of entry clearance/leave in circumstances where the applicant or sponsor are aged under 21, were a disproportionate inter-ference with fundamental common law and human rights. The Rule was not struck down, but the Court left it to the Home Office to either revise or drop the scheme. The Court of Appeal refused the Home Office permission to appeal to the Supreme Court but the Home Office has indicated that it will apply directly to the Supreme Court itself. As we go to press in this Guide, the situation is, therefore, not completely resolved. Formally the existing Court of Appeal ruling applies only to cases in which the sponsor is a British citizen but, arguably, the same reasoning applies where one party is settled as well.

WHAT THE RULES SAY

The requirements that have to be satisfied in order to qualify for entry clearance or leave to remain as the partner (ie spouse, civil partner, unmarried or same-sex partner) of a PBS migrant are (Rules, para 319C):

- the applicant must not fall for refusal under the general grounds of refusal (▶see Chapter 11);
- the applicant must be the spouse, civil partner, unmarried or same-sex partner of a person with valid leave as a PBS migrant or who is being granted entry clearance/leave as such;
- if the applicant is the unmarried or same sex partner of a PBS migrant then: any previous marriage, civil partnership or similar relationship of the applicant or the PBS migrant must have permanently broken down; the applicant and the PBS migrant must not be so closely related that they could not marry in the UK and the applicant and PBS migrant must have been living together in a relationship similar to marriage or civil partnership for at least two years;
- the relationship must be subsisting;
- the applicant and PBS migrant must intend to live with each other in their existing relationship throughout the applicant's stay in the UK;
- the applicant must not intend to stay in the UK beyond any period of leave granted to the PBS migrant;
- there must be a sufficient level of funds available to the applicant as set out in Appendix E to the Rules (▶see below 196) (but this require-ment does not apply if the PBS Migrant is a Tier 1 (Investor) Migrant);
- if the applicant is applying for leave to remain, ie while in the UK, she/must not be an illegal entrant;
- if the applicant is applying for leave to *remain*, the applicant must have, or must have last been granted leave: as the partner of a PBS migrant; or as the partner of the same person but under another category of the Rules where that person has since (or is now) being granted leave as a PBS migrant; or under any category of the Rules,

provided that the PBS migrant has or is being granted leave to remain as a Tier 5 (Temporary Worker) migrant in the creative and sporting sub-category on the basis of their being a sports visitor or entertainer visitor under para 245ZQ(b)(ii) of the Rules; and

- if the PBS migrant is a Tier 4 migrant, then s/he must be applying for or have entry clearance/leave for a course of studies that is for longer than six months.

Maintenance requirement

The Rules require that there must be a sufficient level of funds available to the applicant applying as a dependant as set out in Appendix E to the Rules (paras 319C(g), 319H(g)).

There is no maintenance requirement specified for the dependants of Tier 1 (Investor) Migrants. That is because, if the applicant can satisfy the substantial capital/investment requirements of that category, it is not necessary to subject their dependants to a further maintenance test.

In addition, if the applicant is applying as the dependant of a Tier 2 migrant, then, provided the following three conditions are all met, the maintenance requirements will be deemed to be met without the applicant having to fulfil the requirements set out below (Rules, App E, para (i)):

- the Tier 2 migrant either has, or is being granted, leave under Tier 2;
- the Tier 2 migrant's sponsor is 'A' rated; and
- that sponsor gives a written undertaking that, if it became necessary, the sponsor would maintain the dependants of the Tier 2 migrant to the end of the first month of the Tier 2 migrant's employment at least up to a limit of £533 per dependant.

The level of funds (▶see below) must be shown to be available for each dependant applicant (see PBS Dependant PG, para 40). Where the PBS migrant on whom the applicant is applying as dependant is applying for entry or leave at the same time, the amounts shown below are additional to the funds that must be shown for the PBS migrant themselves (Rules, App E, para (e)).

If the funds relied on were obtained while the applicant or PBS migrant was in the UK, then they must have been obtained at a time when they had leave and were not in breach of any conditions of that leave (Rules, App E, para (h)).

Amount of funds required

Tier 1 PBS migrant outside UK, or in UK for less than 12 months Where the PBS migrant is a Tier 1 migrant, there must be an amount of £1,600 if the PBS migrant (Rules, App E, para (a)):

- is outside the UK; or
- has been in the UK for a period of less than 12 months.

Tier 1 (other than above), Tier 2 and Tier 5 Where the PBS migrant is a Tier 1 migrant who is in the UK and has been here for 12 months, or the PBS migrant is a Tier 2 or Tier 5 migrant, then the amount required is £533 (Rules, App E, para (b)).

An example given in the PBS Dependant PG (para 42) is as follows. If a Tier 1 migrant has been in the UK for six months and is making an application at the same time for his/her spouse and two children, the amounts that must be shown as available for support are:

£800 (for the Tier 1 migrant him/herself, ie making an application for leave to remain); plus
£1,600 (for his/her spouse); plus
£1,600 (first child); plus
£1,600 (second child).
Total = £5,600

Tier 4 Where the PBS migrant is a Tier 4 migrant (Rules, App E, para (ba)):

- if the Tier 4 migrant is studying in inner London (for which, see below), there must be £533 in funds for each month for which the applicant, if successful, would be granted leave, up to a maximum of £4,797 (ie nine months);

- if the Tier 4 migrant is not studying in inner London, there must be £400 in funds for each month for which the applicant, if successful, would be granted leave, up to a maximum of £3,600 (ie nine months).

The Tier 4 migrant is treated as studying in inner London if the address where s/he is studying is in one of the following London Boroughs: Camden; City of London; Hackney; Hammersmith and Fulham; Haringey; Islington; Kensington and Chelsea; Lambeth; Lewisham; Newham; Southwark; Tower Hamlets; Wandsworth and Westminster (PBS Dependant PG, para 54). UKBA treats the site that the student attends for the majority of their time as the relevant one and will use the main site named by the sponsor on the CAS as that relevant one (PBS Dependant PG, paras 56–7).

According to the PBS Dependant PG, where the Tier 4 migrant has an "established presence studying in the UK", the dependant family member can qualify for reduced maintenance levels whether the dependant him or herself is applying from inside or outside the UK (see paras 51, 60, 62). Where the Tier 4 migrant has an "established presence" it is only necessary to show the necessary living costs (at the same rates for inner London and outside inner London as above) for a maximum of *two* rather than *nine* months (PBS Dependant PG, paras 64, 72–3, 75–6). According to the Guidance, the Tier 4 migrant has an established presence studying in the UK if they either (PBS Dependant PG, para 61):

- completed a course that was at least six months long within their last period of leave and that leave finished within the last four months; or

- are applying for continued study on a course where they have studied at least six months of that course and have been studying within the last four months; or

- are applying to continue in Tier 4 as a sabbatical officer, or as a post-graduate doctor or dentist and they have completed a course that was at least six months long within their last period of leave and this leave ended within the last four months.

Availability of funds

The funds must be shown to be 'available' to either the applicant or the PBS migrant (Rules, App E, para (c)(f)(i)(ii)). If the applicant is a child, they may be shown to be available to the applicant, the PBS migrant whom they are applying as a dependant of, or the child's other parent provided that that other parent is lawfully present in the UK, or being admitted/ granted leave at the same time as the applicant (Rules, App E, para (d)(f)(iii)).

Period over which funds must be shown to exist

For dependants of PBS Tier 1, 2 or 5 migrants, the funds must be shown for a consecutive period of 90 days. The 90-day period can end on any day within the calendar month immediately before the date of the application (Rules, App E, para (g)(i)).

For dependants of PBS Tier 4 migrants, the funds must be shown for a consecutive period of 28 days. The 28-day period can end on any day within the calendar month immediately before the date of the application (Rules, App E, para (g)(ii)),

Evidence requirements

The evidence required to demonstrate the required level of funds may be 'specified' in Policy Guidance (see Rules, para 319K; App E, para (j)). The PBS Dependant PG states that the evidence must be original, on the official letterheaded paper or stationery of the organisation and bearing its stamp and issued by an authorised official of that organisation (para 83). It is also stated that evidence must be in the form of cash funds and that evidence of shares, bonds, pension funds etc are not acceptable (para 84). If the evidence is in the form of a joint account, the main applicant as well as the applicant (or for children the other parent) must be named on the account with one or more other named person (para 85). The evidence is to be dated not more than a month before the application is submitted (para 86). Where the funds are not in sterling, UKBA will convert them on the basis of the exchange rate as at the date of application taken from www.oanda.com (para 87).

For dependant applications made where the PBS migrant is admitted under Tiers 1, 2 and 5, the 'specified' documents are (PBS Dependant PG, para 88):

- personal bank or building society statements covering the three-month period immediately before the application showing the name of the main applicant or applicant (or, where the applicant is a child, the other parent), the account number, the date, the financial institution's name and logo and the transactions over the three-month period;

- building society passbook showing the name of the main applicant or applicant (or, where the applicant is a child, the other parent), the account number, the financial institution's name and logo and the transactions over the three-month period;

- letter from bank confirming funds and that they have been in the bank for at least three months, showing the name of the main applicant or applicant (or, where the applicant is a child, the other parent), the account number, the date of the letter, the financial institution's name and logo, the funds held in the account and that they have been in the bank for at least three months without the balance falling below the required amount;

- letter from a financial institution regulated by either the FSA or, in the case of overseas accounts, the home regulator, confirming the funds and showing the name of the main applicant or applicant (or, where the applicant is a child, the other parent), the account number, the date of the letter, the financial institution's name and logo, the funds held in the account and that they have been in the institution for at least three months without the balance falling below the required amount.

Note also in relation to this evidence the Guidance states (PBS Dependant PG, para 88):

- it must show that there are sufficient funds in the account (either the required £1,600 or £533) over the *whole* three-month period in question and that the funds have not dipped below that amount for any time during that period;

- in the case of bank or building society statements, only the most recent statement must be dated within one month of the date of the application;

- *ad hoc* bank statements printed on the bank's letterhead are acceptable but should include the details normally required (above) for bank/building society statements (this excludes, however, mini-statements printed from cash points);

- if the applicant is submitting electronic bank statements from an online account, they must contain all the details listed above and, in addition, the applicant will need to provide either a supporting letter from the bank on headed paper confirming the authenticity of the statements, or to ensure that the electronic statement has the official stamp of the bank on every page.

Where a dependant of a Tier 2 migrant wishes to rely on the provision of the Rules that 'deems' the maintenance requirements to be met (Rules, App E, para (i), ▶see above 196), the evidence from the sponsor certifying maintenance must be a letter from the A-rated sponsor on official letter-headed paper or stationery, signed by a senior official of the sponsor and it must contain (PBS Dependant PG, para 89):

- the applicant's name;
- the sponsor's name and logo;
- confirmation that the sponsor has certified the maintenance; and
- details of any limit applied to the undertaking.

For dependant applications made where the PBS migrant is admitted under Tier 4, the requirements for evidence are the same as under Tiers 1, 2 and 5 above *except* that (PBS Dependant PG, para 94):

- the required period over which the funds must be held is 28 days rather than three months; and
- the amount of money that needs to be shown as available is different to that required under Tiers 1, 2 and 5 (▶see above 197).

For dependant applications made where the PBS migrant is admitted under Tier 4 but has official financial sponsorship and that sponsorship is intended to cover the costs of the dependants, then the applicant should provide a letter of confirmation from the Tier 4 migrant's sponsor. The official financial sponsor might be: the UK Government; the Tier 4 migrant's home government; the British Council; an international org-anisation; an international company or a university. The letter provided should (PBS Dependant PG, paras 96–7):

- be on official letterheaded paper or the stationery of the relevant org-anisation;
- have the official stamp of the organisation on it;
- give the Tier 4 migrant's name and the name of the applicant/s;
- be dated;
- give the length of the sponsorship; and
- state the amount of money that is being provided and that the organisa-tion will cover the applicant/s' maintenance.

If the official sponsor is covering only part of the applicant's maintenance, then the remaining funds must be shown separately as set out above. If the dependant is applying at the same time as the main applicant and the official sponsor is supporting both of them, the evidence must show sufficient support for the main applicant as well as for the dependant/s (PBS Dependant PG, paras 98).

Length of leave and conditions

If the above requirements are all satisfied, entry clearance/leave will be granted for a period of time in line with the PBS migrant and subject to the following conditions (Rules, para 319D):

- no recourse to public funds;
- registration with the police where such is required under para 326 of the Rules;

- no employment as a Doctor or Dentist in training unless the applicant has obtained a degree in medicine or dentistry at Bachelor's level or above from a UK institution that is a UK-recognised body, or which holds a sponsor licence under Tier 4 of the PBS; or the applicant is applying for leave to remain and has or has last been granted entry clearance, leave to enter or remain that was not subject to any condition restricting their employment and has been employed during that leave as a Doctor or Dentist in training (applicant's seeking to avoid a restriction on their employment as a doctor/dentist in training, on the basis that they have been working as such during their most recent period of leave, must provide with their application the documents set out in Annex A of the PBS Dependant PG);
- if the PBS migrant is a Tier 4 migrant who was granted leave for less than 12 months, the applicant will be prohibited from taking employment;
- if the PBS migrant is a Tier 4 migrant studying at below degree level study (excluding a foundation degree course), the applicant will be prohibited from taking employment.

Children of PBS migrants seeking entry or leave to remain

WHAT THE RULES SAY

The requirements that have to be satisfied in order to qualify for entry clearance or leave to remain as the child of a PBS migrant are the same as the Rules for partners set out above, except for the obvious differences and the following Rules that children must satisfy (Rules, para 319F, 319H):

- the applicant must be under 18 on the date of the application;
- if the applicant is over 18, s/he must be applying for leave to remain and must have existing leave, or last been granted leave, as the child of a PBS migrant, or as the child of the parent who had leave under another category of the Rules and has since been granted, or is at the same time being granted, leave to remain as a PBS migrant;
- the applicant must not be married or in a civil partnership, must not have formed an independent family unit and must not be leading an independent life; and
- both the applicant's parents must either be lawfully present in the UK, or being granted entry clearance or leave to remain at the same time as the applicant *unless* the relevant PBS migrant is the applicant's sole surviving parent, or has had sole responsibility for the applicant's upbringing, or there are serious or compelling family or other considerations which would make it desirable not to refuse the application and suitable arrangements have been made in the UK for the applicant's care.

UKBA states that it may consider a child to have formed an independent family unit where, for example, s/he is living with his/her partner, or has children of his/her own (PBS Dependant PG, para 103). It also states that it may consider an applicant to be living an independent life where s/he is living away from the family home (except where s/he is at a boarding school), where s/he is in full time employment or where s/he appears to be financially independent (PBS Dependant PG, para 104). Certain additional documentation that is to be submitted in support of applications that include dependent children is set out in the PBS Dependant PG at paras 105–8.

Length of leave and conditions

Entry clearance/leave will be granted for a period in line with the PBS migrant and subject to the following conditions (Rules, para 319I):

- no recourse to public funds;
- registration with the police where such is required under para 326 of the Rules;
- if the PBS migrant is a Tier 4 migrant who was granted leave for less than 12 months, the applicant will be prohibited from taking employment;
- if the PBS migrant is a Tier 4 migrant studying at below degree level study (excluding a foundation degree course), the applicant will be prohibited from taking employment.

Dependants of PBS migrants seeking indefinite leave to remain

Partners of PBS migrants will be eligible for indefinite leave provided (Rules, para 319E):

- s/he does not fall for refusal under the general grounds of refusal;
- s/he is not an illegal entrant;
- s/he is the partner of a PBS migrant who is, at the same time, being granted indefinite leave as a PBS migrant;
- s/he has, or was last granted, leave as the partner of a PBS migrant;
- s/he has been living together in the UK in their relationship with the PBS migrant for at least two years;
- the relationship is still subsisting;
- the applicant and the PBS migrant intend to live together permanently in their relationship; and
- the applicant has sufficient knowledge of the English language and about life in the UK (this does not apply if the applicant is aged 65 or over at the time the application is made).

Child dependants of PBS migrants will be eligible for indefinite leave provided (Rules, para 319J):

- s/he does not fall for refusal under the general grounds;
- s/he is not an illegal entrant;

- s/he is the child of a PBS migrant who is, at the same time, being granted indefinite leave as a PBS migrant;
- s/he has, or was last granted, leave as the child of a PBS migrant;
- s/he is not married or in a civil partnership, has not formed an independent family unit and is not leading an independent life;
- both of the applicant's parents are either lawfully present in the UK, or being granted entry clearance, limited leave to remain or indefinite leave at the same time as the applicant *unless* the PBS migrant is the applicant's sole surviving parent, or has had sole responsibility for the applicant's upbringing or there are serious or compelling family or other considerations which would make it desirable not to refuse the application and suitable arrangements have been made in the UK for the applicant's care; and
- the applicant has sufficient knowledge of the English language and about life in the UK (this does not apply if the applicant is aged under 18 at the time the application is made).

TIER 1 EXCEPTIONAL TALENT

As set out in the introduction above (▶140–141), the Government proposes to reform radically Tier 1 and to incorporate a new category of migrant under the heading of 'Exceptional Talent'. The proposals, which are *not* fixed, are set out in the table below.

HOME OFFICE PROPOSALS FOR TIER 1 EXCEPTIONAL TALENT

The Home Office explains that this route is intended as a 'niche' category for exceptional people in the fields of science, arts and humanities who wish to work and eventually settle in the UK. It is intended to apply in the following three situations:

- Migrants who hold a designated award – for example the Nobel Prize.
- Migrants who are internationally recognised in their field as a leading world talent and who are endorsed by a designated competent body.
- Young migrants who show exceptional promise and who are likely to become world leaders in their field and who are endorsed by a designated competent body.

The number of successful applicants will be subject to a cap (of 1,000 in the first year).

The Home Office is considering:

- what awards other than the Nobel Prize might be designated;
- whether all applicants would alternatively need to be endorsed by a designated body;
- whether an age limit should apply;

204 • Chapter 5: Tier 1

- who the designated bodies should be who are able to put people through to this route of entry – they are likely to be UK-based public bodies with a remit to promote excellence (among the examples given are the Royal Society, the Arts Council and the British Council);

- how such bodies would be designated;

- how the cap would apply.

  Applicants will have to be able to support themselves and the route is one that would lead to settlement after five years.

6 Tier 2: skilled workers

This chapter covers:

- the future of Tier 2 (►207–212);
- general requirements for entering and remaining under Tier 2 (►212–222);
- Tier 2 (General) and Tier 2 (Intra Company Transfer) (►222–235);
- Tier 2 (Minister of Religion) (►235–237);
- Tier 2 (Sportsperson) (►237–238);
- periods and conditions of leave granted under Tier 2 (►238–242);
- settlement under Tier 2 (►242–243).

This chapter refers, by paragraph, to two sets of Guidance issued by UKBA which we have abbreviated as follows:

T2 PG   Tier 2 of the Points-Based System – Policy Guidance, version 10/10, for use on or after 1 October 2010

SG   Tiers 2 and 5 of the Points-Based System – Sponsor Guidance, 21 December 2010 (version 12/10). *For UKBA's summary showing changes to the SG from 6 April 2011 ►see Appendix 2 at 458.*

Purpose

The purpose of Tier 2 is to allow employers to recruit non-EEA workers in order to fill particular vacancies in the UK that cannot readily be filled by British or EEA workers (Rules, para 245ZB(a)). The Tier was introduced by changes made to the Rules from November 2008 and it replaced the work permit system. It also replaced previous Rules for Ministers of Religion. From 27 November 2008, no further applications for work permits were accepted, although UKBA continued to accept applications for entry clearance and leave from those for whom UKBA had already issued a work permit.

Four categories

Tier 2 has four categories. They are described in the Explanatory Memorandum of the amending Rules (HC 1113) that introduced the Tier as follows (para 6.9):

- Tier 2 (General): for skilled workers coming to do jobs that cannot be filled from the resident labour market;
- Tier 2 (Intra-Company Transfer) ('Tier 2 (ICT)'): for skilled workers moving from an overseas branch of a company to a UK branch;
- Tier 2 (Ministers of Religion): for those coming to fill vacancies as religious workers with recognised religions, including preachers or pastoral workers;
- Tier 2 (Sportspersons): for elite sportspeople, or coaches, who are internationally established at the highest level and whose employment in the UK will make a significant contribution to the development of the sport at the highest level.

The Tier 2 (ICT) category is further broken down into the following three subcategories:

- Established Staff – for established employees of multinational companies who are being transferred because their job cannot be done by a new recruit from the resident workforce;
- Graduate Trainees – for recent graduates of multinational companies who are being transferred to the UK branch of the same organisation (this subcategory was added to the Rules from April 2010 by HC 439; the maximum period of stay in the UK is only 12 months);
- Skills Transfer – this allows overseas employees to come to the UK in order to learn skills or obtain knowledge that s/he will need in order to continue his/her job for the company overseas, or to are come to the UK in order to give the benefit of their own specialist knowledge to the UK workforce (this subcategory was added to the Rules from April 2010 by HC 439, with a maximum grant of leave of six months).

The need for a sponsor

To qualify under Tier 2, the applicant must have been assigned a certificate of sponsorship by their employer. In order to do this, the employer must have a valid sponsor licence. For details about employers qualifying for and obtaining a sponsor licence and operating the sponsorship system, ▶Chapter 4. Once a licensed sponsor has assigned a certificate to an applicant, UKBA makes only one decision in relation to the applicant: either to grant or refuse entry clearance or leave. There is no longer a two-stage process, as under the work permit system, where officials first made a decision as to whether to issue a work permit to the employer and then made a further decision as to whether to grant the applicant leave.

Even after leave is granted to a sponsored applicant, it may be curtailed if the sponsor ceases to be licensed, or if the migrant ceases work (▶see Chapter 11 on curtailment 399–400). For details about the suspension and withdrawal of sponsor licences and the consequences for sponsored migrants, ▶see Chapter 4 at 121.

This chapter

Some of the requirements for qualifying under Tier 2 are general across all of the categories, (or at least can be described in common terms even if there are some differences) and we look at those requirements at ▶212–222. After that we focus in on the categories and subcategories themselves (▶beginning at 222).

First we take a look at imminent developments for Tier 2 (immediately below).

THE FUTURE OF TIER 2

The Government has indicated that, from 6 April 2011, a number of significant changes will be made to Tier 2. Changes to Tier 1 are also planned (▶see Chapter 5 at 140–141, 164–165, 173, 203–204, 292–295 and see also below for planned transitional provisions relating to Tier 1); as are changes to Tier 4 (▶see Chapter 8 at 291–295).

As we go to press, the changes are not yet available either in amending Immigration Rules that will come into effect on 6 April 2011, or Policy Guidance. However, in February 2011, UKBA published *Tier 2 of the Points-Based System, Statement of Intent, Transitional Measures and Indefinite Leave to Remain* and we draw heavily on that document in this section. The Statement of Intent deals with changes to the Tier 2 (General) and Tier 2 (ICT) categories. It does not affect the Tier 2 (Minister or Religion) or Tier 2 (Sportsperson) categories. At Appendix B to the Statement of Intent, UKBA provides a table which usefully summarises Tier 2 as it will stand for those applying on or after 6 April 2010. Before the Rules themselves are laid and come into effect, it is impossible to be certain of the changes and their detail but we set out below what is presently known.

Skill level

The skill level under Tier 2 is being raised from NQF level 3 to occupations that are at graduate level. At Annex A to Statement of Intent is UKBA's 'Graduate Occupation' list as recommended by the Migration Advisory Committee (MAC). All the occupations listed are accompanied by a 'Standard Occupational Classification' (SOC) code (a number). According to the Statement of Intent, only jobs that are contained on that list, or the Shortage Occupation List, will be eligible under Tier 2 (General). That does not mean that applicants must hold a degree; it is the level of the *occupation* that is being targeted.

It is likely that the Shortage Occupation List will be amended in due course so that it is more closely aligned with the level of skills reflected in the Graduate Occupations List. This continues to be subject to review by the MAC.

Entry clearance applications

All Tier 2 applicants seeking entry clearance, or those switching employ-ers, will have a new test applied to them in order to obtain points for attributes. The 'qualifications' aspect of attributes will be dropped and instead applicants will need to score 30 points for a valid certificate of sponsorship and 20 points for an "appropriate salary for the immigration route and occupation" (the minimum salary necessary to score points will still be £20,000). Separate requirements will apply to Tier 2 (ICT) Migrants.

Limit on numbers: the interim and permanent 'cap'

From 19 July 2010, the Government imposed an 'interim' cap on the number of certificates of sponsorship that could be assigned to applicants in the Tier 2 (General) Migrant category (amending Rules, HC 96). The first interim cap was overturned by the JCWI case on 17 December 2010 as a result of the way it had been introduced.

In response, the Government laid new amending Rules (HC 698) effective from 21 December 2010 to impose a new (second) interim cap on the number of certificates that could be assigned by the Home Office to sponsors in the Tier 2 (General) Migrant category between 21 December 2010 and 5 April 2011 (see Rules, para 6 and App A paras 63B–K as amended). The Tier 2 (General) interim limit down to 5 April 2011 was set at 10,832. An 'exceptional consideration process' was introduced at the same time but the interim cap includes the certificates that may be issued under that exceptional process. For full details of the operation of the interim cap and exceptional consideration process, ▶see Chapter 4 dealing with sponsorship at 106–108 and see also Chapter 2 at 55–59.

It was always the Government's plan to introduce a permanent cap from April 2011. The Government has announced that, under the permanent cap, there will be a first year annual limit as follows:

* 20,700 on the numbers admitted under Tier 2 (General); and
* 1,000 under the new Tier 1 (Exceptional Talent) route (▶see 203–204).

The Government will review the cap on an annual basis both to see whether the numbers are right and also to determine whether the categ-ories it is applied to should be changed.

Which Tier 2 applicants will the permanent cap affect?

The permanent cap only applies to those applicants who require a 'restricted' (as opposed to an 'unrestricted') certificate of sponsorship. It appears that the cap will affect only applicants for entry clearance in the Tier 2 (General) category and that it will not affect Tier 2 (ICT), Tier 2 (Sportsperson) or Tier 2 (Ministers of Religion) applicants, whether they are applying for entry clearance or leave to remain.

The Statement of Intent lists the following circumstances as not affected by the permanent cap. In respect of these categories, sponsors may continue to issue 'unrestricted' certificates and they will be able to apply for additional certificates as they did previously:

- those applying under the Tier 2 (ICT) category (which itself is to be changed ▶see 211);
- those applying under the Tier 2 (Sportsperson) category;
- those applying under the Tier 2 (Ministers of Religion) category;
- Tier 2 migrants extending their leave with their original employers;
- Tier 2 migrants switching to a new employer;
- non-Tier 2 applicants switching into Tier 2 in-country;
- 'transitional arrangement' cases where those in the UK either under Tier 2, or as work permit holders, apply under Tier 2; and
- those applying under the Tier 2 (General) category whose salary will be £150,000 or more .

How will the cap be operated?

If a sponsor wishes to assign a 'restricted' certificate of sponsorship, then s/he will first have to apply to UKBA for permission to do so. UKBA will consider all such applications at a stated time once per month (a time-table will be published). There will be a monthly allocation of restricted certificates that are available to be issued so that the 20,700 available certificates are distributed throughout the year. UKBA has stated that, in the first month, it will make 4,200 certificates available and that, in each subsequent month, there will be 1,500 certificates up for allocation. Sponsors should not apply for a certificate more than three months before they plan to assign it because there is a requirement that the certificate is assigned to a migrant within three months of its issue.

If the monthly allocation is not full when all qualifying applications are counted up, then UKBA will issue a certificate to all applicants *provided* that they qualify. In order to qualify, the application must score a minimum of 32 points on the ranking system (▶see as set out in the table below). The unallocated certificates will be rolled forward and added to the next month's allocation.

If the monthly allocation is over-full, then UKBA will allocate certificates according to the same ranking system. Certificates will be allocated up to the monthly limit with those scoring the highest taking priority.

If the monthly limit bites at a point where there are a number of applicants who have scored exactly the *same* number of points, so that it is not possible to separate them, then the same-scoring applications will all be granted as long as that would not cause the monthly allocation to be exceeded by more than 100. The next month's allocation will be reduced by the amount of the excess in the immediate month's allocation. If the

RANKING APPLICANTS FOR 'RESTRICTED' CERTIFICATES OF SPONSORSHIP

	Points
Job on shortage occupation list:	75
PhD level posting and Resident Labour Market Test	50
Resident Labour Market Test	30
Salary	
£20,000–20,999	2
£21,000–21,999	3
£22,000–22,999	4
£23,000–23,999	5
£24,000–24,999	6
£25,000–25,999	7
£26,000–26,999	8
£27,000–27,999	9
£28,000–31,999	10
£32,000–45,999	15
£46,000–74,999	20
£75,000–99,999	25
£100,000–149,999	30

Note: a job with a PhD level posting does not mean that it is necessary to have a PhD in order to score the points for that job. The points are scored for the level of the job on the Standard Occupational Classification code that applies to it, not the specific qualifications of the applicant.

excess would be over 100, then all the 'bunched' applications that would otherwise lead the monthly limit to be exceeded will be refused and the 'spare' certificates will be carried over and added to the next month's allocation.

Where an employer is unsuccessful in their application, if they still wish the application to be considered, it will be necessary to apply again. Applications will not be automatically reconsidered in the following month's allocation.

Just because a 'restricted' certificate is issued, does not guarantee the applicant's entry to the UK. The same system will apply as previously ie the applicant must submit their application for entry clearance/leave and satisfy the requirements of the Rules in order to qualify.

English language

The Home Office will raise the English language requirements under Tier 2 (General) from basic to intermediate ie to level B1 on the Common European Framework of Reference for languages.

Changes to the Tier 2 (Intra Company Transfer) Migrants category

The essential changes for Tier 2 (ICT) Migrants are;

* the job that they do will have to be contained on the Graduate Occupation List;

* applicants paid between £24,000 and £40,000 will be granted leave up to a maximum of only 12 months, after which they will not be re-admitted under this category until at least 12 months have passed;

* applicants paid over £40,000 can be granted leave for up to three years and may extend that leave to bring it up to five years, after which they will not be eligible to apply again under the Tier 2 (ICT) category until at least 12 months have passed.

The 'Graduate Trainee' and 'Skills Transfer' subcategories of Tier 2 (ICT) are set to remain as part of the PBS.

Transitional provisions for Tier 1 and Tier 2

Applications made before 6 April 2010 will continue to be dealt with under the Rules in force before the 6 April changes. The new Rules will only be applied to applications made on or after 6 April 2010.

Although the Government announced in December 2010 that the Tier 1 (General) category would close, those with existing leave to enter or remain under the Tier 1 (General) category (or its predecessor categories: the HSMP; Writers, Composers and Artists; Self-employed Lawyers) will still be able to extend their leave under it. They will, however, have to score 100 points if they were required to score 100 points when they were first granted leave under Tier 1 (General).

Applicants who are not in already in the Tier 1 (General) or the above categories will not be able to switch into it from 6 April 2010. Those with leave under the Tier 1 (Post-Study Work) category (and its predecessor categories) and those in Tier 4 will be permitted to switch into Tier 2 (General) with an 'unrestricted' certificate of sponsorship, but not to switch into Tier 1 (General).

As for transitional measures and Tier 2, the new graduate level occupation requirement, the revised salary thresholds and the new English language requirements will not apply to those with leave either under Tier 2, or as a work permit holder, that was granted before 6 April 2010 and who are seeking to remain under Tier 2, or who are applying to remain as a Tier 2 migrant in order to change their employer. For Tier 2 Migrants affected by the permanent cap ►see 209.

6

In addition, the changes to the Tier 2 (ICT) category will not apply to applicants granted entry clearance before 6 April 2011. Those applicants will continue to be permitted to stay beyond five years. Those who are already transitionally protected from the earlier changes that were introduced from 6 April 2010 (ie the changes to restrict access to settlement for those in the Tier 2 (ICT) category), will continue to be protected and will retain their access to settlement.

Settlement

The changes to the eligibility for settlement for those in work and study routes will begin in April 2011. Further changes are expected to be rolled out later in the year. From April 2011, UKBA will make the following initial changes.

- There will be an income requirement for settlement applicants in the Tier 1 (General), Tier 2 (General) and Work Permit Holder categories. The purpose of this is to test, at the point of settlement, whether the applicant has, as expected, continued in skilled or highly skilled occupations. The intention is to apply the same income level requirement that is required when an applicant applies for further (limited) leave to remain.

- Applicants will only be able to satisfy the requirement to show knowledge of language and life in the UK by taking the Life in the UK Test, which is set at CEFR level B1.

- Applicants will need to be free of unspent convictions in order to obtain settlement. The Statement of Intent claims that this will "reform the criminality threshold for settlement to bring it more in line with that for citizenship (naturalisation) applicants". However, there is no absolute requirement to be free of unspent convictions under the British Nationality Act 1981, which imposes a test of 'good character'. In addition, the Guidance set out in Chapter 18 of the Nationality Instructions, makes it clear that the presence of an unspent conviction will not automatically mean that the applicant is not of good character. It will depend on the particular offence and other factors although in many cases an unspent conviction is stated to give rise to a presumption that the citizenship application will be refused. Under the present nationality framework at least there is always room for the exercise of judgment by the decision-maker.

It is understood that there is likely to be consultation on further changes to eligibility for settlement in May/June 2011.

GENERAL REQUIREMENTS FOR ENTERING AND REMAINING UNDER TIER 2

In this section we look at the general, common requirements for entering and remaining in the UK under the various categories of Tier 2. The additional requirements for the different categories under Tier 2 are looked at separately beginning ▶222.

Dependants

As with most other tiers of the PBS, it is possible for the partner and children of a Tier 2 Migrant to be granted entry clearance and leave as a dependant. For the requirements that need to be satisfied, ►see the section on dependants in Chapter 5 at 194–203.

WHAT THE RULES SAY

Applying for entry under Tier 2

In order to enter the UK under Tier 2 all applicants require an entry clearance granted for that purpose (Rules, para 245ZC).

In order to qualify for entry clearance and leave to enter the UK under Tier 2, the following requirements must be satisfied (Rules, para 245ZD):

- the applicant must not fall for refusal under the general grounds for refusal (►see Chapter 11);
- the applicant must be at least 16 years old;
- if the applicant is under 18 years of age, the application must have the support of his/her parents or legal guardian (or one parent if that parent has sole legal responsibility for the applicant);
- if the applicant is under 18 years old, his/her parents or legal guardian (or one parent if that parent has sole legal responsibility for the applicant), must confirm that they consent to the arrangements for the applicant's travel to and reception and care in the UK;
- if the applicant is applying under either the Tier 2 (General) Migrant, or Tier 2 (ICT) Migrant categories, s/he must score a minimum of 50 points for attributes under paras 59–84 of Appendix A to the Rules;
- if the applicant is applying as a Tier 2 (Minister of Religion) Migrant, s/he must score a minimum of 50 points for attributes under paras 85–92 of Appendix A to the Rules;
- if the applicant is applying as a Tier 2 (Sportsperson) Migrant, s/he must score a minimum of 50 points for attributes under paras 93–100 of Appendix A to the Rules;
- applicants must score a minimum of 10 points for English language under paragraphs 4–6 of Appendix B to the Rules (this requirement does not apply to applicants in the Tier 2 (ICT) category seeking entry clearance/leave to enter);
- applicants must score a minimum of 10 points for maintenance under paras 4–5 of Appendix C to the Rules;
- applicants who presently have, or who were last granted, leave as a student under the old rules, a Student Nurse, a Student Re-sitting an Examination, a Student Writing-up a Thesis, a Postgraduate Doctor or Dentist, or as a Tier 4 Migrant and who have been sponsored by a

government or international scholarship agency within the last 12 months, have to provide the unconditional written consent of their sponsoring Government or scholarship agency to their present application (and applicants are required, by the Rules, to produce 'specified documents' to show that this requirement has been met; see T2 PG, paras 179-180 requiring an original document on the official letter-headed paper or stationery of the relevant organisation); and

• if the sponsor is a limited company, the applicant must not own more than 10% of that company's shares (this requirement does not apply to the Tier 2 (ICT) category – the restriction was lifted from Tier 2 (ICT) from 1 October 2009 on the basis that it serves no useful purpose for this category and was a barrier to board members of multinational companies applying to work in the UK, see Explanatory Memo to Cm 7701, para 7.7).

WHAT THE RULES SAY

Applying for leave to remain under Tier 2

In order to succeed on an in-country application for leave to remain an applicant must (Rules, para 245ZF):

• meet the same requirements as set out for entry (above) relating to:
- general grounds of refusal;
- age;
- support and consent of the applicant's parents where the applicant is under 18;
- the points that must be scored for attributes;
- the points that must be scored for maintenance;
- the points that must be scored for English language (except that, in an application for leave to remain, Tier 2 (ICT) migrants are only excused the need to score points for English as long as the extension they seek would not lead to their leave being extended to a total period of more than three years in this capacity);
- the circumstances where the applicant has been sponsored through their studies by a government or scholarship agency;
- the circumstances where the applicant is sponsored by a limited company; and
- not be an illegal entrant.

In addition, the Rules set out in detail the existing leave that applicants must have (or have last been given) in order to allow them to apply to extend their leave under Tier 2. The Rules differ depending on which particular category and subcategory of Tier 2 the applicant is applying to remain in. This is explained immediately below.

Immigration status when applying for leave to remain in Tier 2

Those applying for leave to remain under Tier 2 must have, or have last been granted entry clearance, leave to enter or remain in a particular category.

Applying to remain as a Tier 2 (General) Migrant, a Tier 2 (Minister of Religion) Migrant or a Tier 2 (Sportsperson) Migrant

Those applying to remain in any of these three categories must have, or have last been granted, entry clearance or leave as (Rules, para 245ZF(e)):

- a Tier 1 Migrant;
- a Tier 2 (General) Migrant;
- a Tier 2 (Minister of Religion) Migrant;
- a Tier 2 (Sportsperson) Migrant;
- a Tier 2 (ICT) Migrant as long as the applicant has, or was last granted, entry clearance/leave in the 'Established Staff' subcategory of Tier 1 (ICT), or under the Rules in place before 6 April 2010 and the applicant's sponsor is not the same as the sponsor when s/he was last granted leave;
- a Highly Skilled Migrant;
- an Innovator;
- a Jewish Agency Employee;
- a Member of the Operational Ground Staff of an Overseas-owned Airline;
- a Minister of Religion, Missionary or Member of a Religious Order;
- an Overseas Qualified Nurse or Midwife;
- a participant in the Fresh Talent: Working in Scotland Scheme;
- a participant in the International Graduates' Scheme;
- a participant in the Science and Engineering Graduates' Scheme;
- a person Writing-up a Thesis;
- a Postgraduate Doctor or Dentist;
- a 'Qualifying Work Permit Holder' (ie a Work Permit Holder who was issued a work permit either under the business and commercial, or sports and entertainment parts of the previous work permit arrangements, see Rules, para 6);
- a Representative of an Overseas Business;
- a Representative of an Overseas Newspaper, News Agency or Broadcasting Organisation;
- a Student;
- a Student Re-sitting an Examination;
- a Student Nurse;
- a Student Union Sabbatical Officer;

6

- a Tier 4 Migrant;
- a Tier 5 (Temporary Worker) Migrant (but see immediately below for the further restrictions); or
- the partner of a Tier 4 Migrant.

If the applicant has, or was last granted leave as a Tier 5 (Temporary Worker) Migrant, it must have been granted under either the 'Government Authorised Exchange' or the 'Creative and Sporting' subcategories of that category (Rules, para 245ZF(g)). If it was granted under the Government Authorised Exchange subcategory, it must have been to enable work as an overseas qualified nurse or midwife and the applicant must have completed their registration with the Nursing and Midwifery Council (Rules, para 245ZF(h)). If it was granted under the Creative and Sporting subcategory, it must have been to enable work as a professional footballer (Rules, para 245ZF(i)).

Note that it is no longer possible to obtain leave in many of the above listed categories which have been replaced by the PBS. Paragraph 6 of the Rules (interpretation) still carries a definition of the abolished categories by referring to persons granted leave under the relevant paragraphs of the old Rules. For example 'Minister of Religion, Missionary or Member of a Religious Order' means "a migrant granted leave under paragraphs 178 to 185 of the Rules in force before 27 November 2008".

Applying to remain under the 'Established Staff' subcategory of the Tier 2 (ICT) category

Those applying to remain in the above subcategory of Tier 2 (ICT) must have, or have last been granted, entry clearance or leave as (Rules, para 245ZF(b)(i)):

- a Tier 2 (ICT) Migrant in the Established Staff subcategory;
- a Tier 2 (ICT) Migrant granted under the Rules in place before 6 April 2010;
- a Qualifying Work Permit Holder (ie a Work Permit Holder who was issued a work permit either under the business and commercial, or sports and entertainment, parts of the previous work permit arrangements; Rules, para 6) and the work permit must have been granted because the applicant was part of an intra company transfer; or
- the Representative of an Overseas Business.

In addition, the applicant must still be working for the same employer as s/he was working for at the time of the earlier grant of leave in the above categories (Rules, para 245ZF(b)(ii)).

Applying to remain under either the 'Graduate Trainee' or 'Skills Transfer' subcategories of the Tier 2 (ICT) category

Those applying to remain in the above subcategories of Tier 2 (ICT) must have, or have last been granted, entry clearance or leave in the *same* subcategories as they are now seeking leave to remain in ie only a Graduate Trainee can seek leave to remain as a Graduate Trainee and only a person in the Skills Transfer subcategory can seek leave to remain for that same purpose. In both cases the applicant must still be working for the same employer who s/he was working for at the time of the grant of the earlier leave (Rules, para 245ZF(c)(d)).

WHAT THE RULES MEAN

Applying to enter or remain under Tier 2

The requirements that must be satisfied in order to score points for attributes under Appendix A to the Rules are very particular to each of the different categories under Tier 2 and they are, therefore, set out when we look at the different categories (▶beginning 222 below).

English language requirements under Tier 2

Generally, Tier 2 applicants must score a minimum of 10 points for English language under paragraphs 4–6 of Appendix B to the Rules (Rules, paras 245ZD(e), 245ZF(m); App B, para 4). Not all Tier 2 applicants need to score points for English language. In either of the following two circumstances, the applicant does not need to satisfy any English language requirements (Rules, paras 245ZD(e), 245ZF(m); App B, para 4):

- the applicant is applying for entry clearance in the Tier 2 (ICT) category;
- the applicant is applying for leave to remain in the Tier 2 (ICT) category provided the applicant is not seeking a grant of leave that would mean that his/her total stay in the UK in the Tier 2 (ICT) category would be for more than three years.

Points for English language: Tier 2 (General), Tier 2 (ICT) and Tier 2 (Sportsperson)

If the applicant is applying in either the Tier 2 (General), Tier 2 (ICT) (and does not fall within the above exception) or Tier 2 (Sportsperson) categories, then they can score the necessary 10 points for English language if they meet *any* of the following conditions (see App B, para 5(a)–(e) and Table 1 with reference also to App B para 2(b)–(e)).

1) The applicant has competence in English to a basic user standard that includes the ability to understand and use familiar, everyday expressions, to introduce themselves and others and to ask/answer questions about basic personal details. In addition the applicant must either:

a) take an English language test with an UKBA-approved provider and provide the certificate showing that s/he has met the above standard of English language (UKBA may specify in Guidance the precise level that is to be met in order to show that the above standard is met); or

b) have obtained an academic (not a professional or vocational) qualification that is deemed by NARIC to meet the standard of a Bachelor's or Master's degree in the UK and it must be the case that NARIC has confirmed that the degree was taught/researched in English to the level of C1 of the Council of Europe's Common European Framework for Language Learning (CEFR), or the applicant can provide specified evidence to show that the qualification was taught or researched in English.

2) The applicant is a national of one of the following (majority English speaking) countries: Antigua and Barbuda; Australia; The Bahamas; Barbados; Belize; Canada; Dominica; Grenada; Guyana; Jamaica; New Zealand; St Kitts and Nevis; St Lucia; St Vincent and the Grenadines; Trinidad and Tobago; or the USA and produces the specified documents to show it. The documents specified by the Guidance are: valid original passport or travel document, or exceptionally, current national identity document or original letter from the applicant's home government or embassy (see T2 PG, paras 108–109).

3) The applicant has obtained an academic qualification (not a professional or vocational qualification) which is deemed by UK NARIC to meet or exceed the recognised standard of a UK degree from an educational institution in one of the following countries (note the list is slightly different to that in (2) above: Antigua and Barbuda; Australia; The Bahamas; Barbados; Belize; Dominica; Grenada; Guyana; Ireland; Jamaica; New Zealand; St Kitts and Nevis; St Lucia; St Vincent and the Grenadines; Trinidad and Tobago; the UK; or the USA and produces specified documents to show it. The documents that are specified by the Guidance are the original certificate of award or, if the applicant is awaiting graduation or no longer has the certificate and the institution is unable to provide another one, an academic reference (T2 PG, para 112 with reference to para 58).

4) The applicant has ever been granted leave under the Tier 1 (General) or Tier 1 (Entrepreneur) categories, or as a business person under the (old) Rules in force until 30 June 2008.

5) The applicant has been granted leave under the HSMP under the Rules following the changes made on 5 December 2006.

6) The applicant has been granted entry clearance or leave as a Minister of Religion under (old) Rules in force until 27 November 2008 provided that the leave was granted on or after 23 August 2004.

7) The applicant has ever been granted entry clearance or leave as a Tier 2 (General), Tier 2 (ICT) or Tier 2 (Sportsperson) Migrant, as long as when s/he was granted that leave, s/he scored points for English language under any of the routes in points (1)-(6) above.

8) The applicant has ever been granted entry clearance or leave as a Tier 2

(Minister of Religion) as long as when s/he was granted that leave, s/he scored points for English language under any of the routes in (1)-(6)(a) below relating to Tier 2 (Ministers of Religion). So, this route and route (7) above prevent these Tier 2 applicants from having to satisfy the language requirements again if they have already scored the necessary points for language on a previous application for the reasons given.

9) If the applicant is applying for leave to *remain* under the Tier 2 (General) or Tier 2 (ICT) categories, the applicant has obtained points from the transitional arrangements category in Table 11 and paragraph 83 of Appendix A to the Rules (▶see 224 below).

10) If the applicant is applying for leave to *remain* as a Tier 2 (Sportsperson) Migrant, the applicant has previously been granted entry clearance or leave as a Tier 2 (Sportsperson) or as a 'Qualifying Work Permit Holder' (ie one who was issued with a work permit in the business and commercial, or sports and entertainment, categories) provided that the relevant grant of entry clearance or leave was less than five years before his/her present grant of entry clearance or leave is due to expire and the applicant is working for the same employer for whom s/he was working, or intending to work, when last granted leave.

6

Points for English language: Tier 2 (Minister of Religion)

If the applicant is applying in the Tier 2 (Minister of Religion) category, then they can score the necessary 10 points for English language if they meet *any one* of the following conditions (App B, para 6(a)–(d) and Table 2, with reference to App B, para 2(b)–(e)).

1) The applicant has competence in English at least to level B2 (note the much higher level) of the CEFR for language learning. In addition the applicant must either:

a) take an English language test with an UKBA-approved provider and provide the certificate showing that s/he has met the above standard of English language (UKBA may specify in Guidance the precise level that is to be met in order to show that the above standard is met); or

b) have obtained an academic (not a professional or vocational) qualification that is deemed by NARIC to meet the standard of a Bachelor's or Master's degree in the UK, provides the specified evidence to show s/he has the qualification and UK NARIC must confirm that the degree was taught or researched in English to level C1 of the CEFR for language learning or above.

2) The applicant is a national of one of the following (majority English speaking) countries: Antigua and Barbuda; Australia; The Bahamas; Barbados; Belize; Canada; Dominica; Grenada; Guyana; Jamaica; New Zealand; St Kitts and Nevis; St Lucia; St Vincent and the Grenadines; Trinidad and Tobago; or the USA and produces the specified documents to show it. The documents specified are: valid original passport or travel document, or exceptionally, current national identity document or original letter from the applicant's home government or embassy.

3) The applicant has obtained an academic qualification (not a professional or vocational qualification) which is deemed by UK NARIC to meet or exceed the recognised standard of a UK degree from an educational institution in one of the following countries: Antigua and Barbuda; Australia; The Bahamas; Barbados; Belize; Dominica; Grenada; Guyana; Ireland; Jamaica; New Zealand; St Kitts and Nevis; St Lucia; St Vincent and the Grenadines; Trinidad and Tobago; the UK; or the USA and produces specified documents to show it. The documents that are specified by the Guidance are: the original certificate of award or an academic reference from the institution awarding the degree together with an original academic transcript confirming the award.

4) The applicant has ever been granted leave under the Tier 1 (General) or Tier 1 (Entrepreneur) categories, or as a business person under the (old) Rules in force until 30 June 2008.

5) The applicant has been granted leave under the HSMP under the Rules following the changes made on 5 December 2006.

6) The applicant presently has, or was last granted, entry clearance or leave either:

a) as a Minister of Religion under (old) Rules *provided* that the leave was granted on or after 19 April 2007; or

b) or as a Tier 2 (Minister of Religion) Migrant as long as, when granted that leave, s/he scored points for English language because s/he fell within any of (1)–(6)(a) immediately above.

7) If the applicant is applying for leave to *remain*, s/he has been granted continuous entry clearance or leave to enter or remain as a Tier 2 (Minister of Religion) Migrant, or as a Minister of Religion, Missionary or Member of a Religious Order under the old Rules over a period beginning less than five years before his/her present grant of entry clearance or leave is due to expire *and* the applicant continues to work for the same employer for whom s/he was working when last granted leave.

Maintenance requirements under Tier 2

Tier 2 applicants must score a minimum of 10 points for maintenance under paragraphs 4–5 of Appendix C to the Rules (Rules, paras 245ZD(f), 245ZF(n); App C, para 4).

'Automatic' routes to scoring points for maintenance under Tier 2

There are three 'automatic' routes to scoring the required 10 points for maintenance under Tier 2 as follows (App C, para 5(b)–(d)).

1) The applicant has existing entry clearance or leave as:

– a Tier 2 Migrant;

– a 'Jewish Agency Employee' (that is an applicant who was granted leave outside the Rules under the old concession relating to this category);

– a member of the Operational Ground Staff of an Overseas-owned Airline (under the old Rules);

- a Minister of Religion, Missionary or Member of a Religious Order (under the old Rules);
- a Representative of an Overseas Newspaper, News Agency or Broadcasting Organisation (under the old Rules); or
- a Work Permit Holder (under the old Rules).

2) The applicant is applying for leave to *remain* as a Tier 2 (General) Migrant and scores points under the Post-Study Work provisions in Table 10 to Appendix A of the Rules (►see below 220–229).

3) The applicant's sponsor is 'A' rated and gives a written undertaking that, if it were to become necessary, the sponsor will maintain and accommodate the applicant to the end of the first month of his/her employment. The sponsor may impose a limit on the undertaking but must give an undertaking to support the applicant to a minimum level of £800.

Scoring points for maintenance funds in all other cases under Tier 2

Where the applicant is newly applying under Tier 2, ie does not have entry clearance or leave under any of the Tier 2 categories and does not fit within any of the other automatic routes to scoring points for maintenance (►above), s/he will have to score points in the ordinary way. The maintenance test is the same for all Tier 2 applicants who do not automatically score points for maintenance. The necessary 10 points may be scored by showing a level of funds of £800 (App C, para 5).

Following the amendments to the Rules (by HC 382) after the Court of Appeal decision in *Pankina* (for the full details about the *Pankina* case, ►see Chapter 2 at 42–45), the relevant wording of Appendix C is now that the applicant should have the funds at the date of the application (para 1A(a)) and, importantly (para 1A(b)):

"…if the applicant is applying for entry clearance, leave to enter or leave to remain as a Tier 1 Migrant (other than a Tier 1 (Investor) Migrant), a Tier 2 Migrant or a Tier 5 (Temporary Worker) Migrant, the applicant must have had the funds referred to [above] for a consecutive 90-day period of time, ending no earlier than one calendar month before the date of application."

So, the Rules state that applicants must show that they have the required funds over a three-month period. That period can end at any time in the last calendar month before the date that the applicant applies for entry clearance or leave to remain. As a result of *Pankina*, there is a transitional policy which disapplies the 'three-month' requirement for pre-23 July 2010 cases. For details of the policy, ►see Chapter 2 at 46–47.

The Rules also state that any funds that were obtained while the applicant was in the UK can only be relied on for maintenance purposes if they were obtained while the applicant had valid leave and was not acting in breach of any conditions of leave (App C, para 1A(d)). The Rules also require that applicants must provide the documents that are specified in Policy Guidance in order to show that they meet the maintenance requirements (App C, para 1A(e) read with Rules, para 245AA) (▶below).

For the case-law generally interpreting the maintenance requirements under the PBS, ▶see 181–188 and for the maintenance requirements for the dependants of PBS migrants, ▶see 196–200. For the relevance of human rights to cases where the strict requirements cannot be met, ▶see Chapter 12 at 414–420.

Maintenance: Policy Guidance

The relevant part of the Policy Guidance dealing with maintenance is T2 SG, paras 133–148. The Guidance set out in those paragraphs is the same as that given in the Guidance for Tier 1 (General) Migrants and we set out the full details of that Guidance in a table in Chapter 5 ▶153–155. It is important to bear in mind that, after *Pankina*, it may not be possible for UKBA to rely for their decisions on certain parts of the Guidance as a basis to refuse applications. It will not be possible for UKBA to do so where the particular part of the Guidance can be said to impose additional mandatory substantive requirements on applicants that are not contained in the Immigration Rules themselves.

TIER 2 (GENERAL) AND TIER 2 (INTRA COMPANY TRANSFER) MIGRANTS: PARTICULAR REQUIREMENTS

The Tier 2 (General) category is for people coming to the UK with a skilled job offer to fill a gap in the workforce that cannot be filled by a settled worker. This is normally (but not always) demonstrated by showing that the Resident Labour Market Test (RLMT) (▶below) has been satisfied. Otherwise, the applicant may qualify on the basis that the position is included in the 'shortage occupation list' (▶below), or because s/he is switching into Tier 2 from Tier 1 (Post-Study Work). For details of the interim cap placed on the number of certificates of sponsorship that may be assigned under the Tier 1 (General) Migrant category, ▶see above at 208 and, in more detail, Chapter 4 at 106–108.

The Tier 2 (ICT) category is for overseas employees of multinational firms who have normally worked for the company overseas before the transfer, and are required to work for the UK entity. The branches (or entities) of the companies must show that they are linked by way of common ownership or control. The skills level for an ICT is the same as for a Tier 2 (General) applicant; however, due to the special nature of these transfers, there is no need to meet the RLMT.

The requirements for qualifying to be a *sponsor* are dealt with in Chapter 4. For the particular requirements that a body wishing to sponsor migrants under Tier 2 (ICT) must satisfy, ▶see 89.

In addition, when a sponsor assigns a certificate to a migrant, it confirms or even 'guarantees' certain matters. For the confirmations that a sponsor of a Tier 2 (General) Migrant makes when assigning a certificate and notifying the certificate to UKBA on the sponsor management system, ▶see Chapter 4 at 110. For the confirmations made by the sponsor of an Tier 2 (ICT) Migrant ▶see 110–111.

Applicants applying under the Tier 2 (General) or Tier 2 (ICT) Migrant categories must score a minimum of 50 points for attributes under paras 59–84 of Appendix A to the Rules (Rules, paras 245ZD(b), 245ZF(j); App A, para 59).

There are three attributes for which these points can be scored: sponsorship; qualifications; and prospective earnings.

There are two classes of applicant who score the entire 50 points for 'sponsorship' alone so that they do not need to show that they score points for 'qualifications' or 'prospective earnings'. They are:

- applicants whose jobs fall within the list of 'shortage occupations' (App A, Table 10) (▶below);
- applicants who fall within the 'transitional arrangements', ie the arrangements made in order to protect those who were work permit holders, or held a similar immigration status in November 2008 (and who may since have been granted leave under the Tier 2 (General) or Tier 2 (ICT) categories) (App A, para 61 and Table 11) (▶see below 224–228).

For all other cases (ie non-shortage occupation and non-transitional arrangements cases), applicants need to show that they can score the necessary points from a combination of (App A, paras 60 and Table 10) (for these cases, ▶see 228–235 below):

- sponsorship, for which points can be scored if:
- the job is an intra company transfer
- the job passes the RLMT or
- the applicant is switching to Tier 2 from Tier 1 (Post-Study Work);
- qualifications, for which points can be scored if the applicant has the equivalent of the following qualifications:
- GCE 'A'-level
- Bachelor's degree
- Master's degree or
- PhD;
- prospective earnings: applicants can score points for a gross annual salary of £20,000 and above.

Shortage occupations

The shortage occupations are those which appear on a list prepared by UKBA on the basis of advice received from the Migration Advisory Committee (MAC). It is updated regularly and can be found on the UKBA website. In these cases, the Home Office has already determined that there is a recognised shortage of suitably qualified and available resident workers to fill the positions in the work force. So, applicants being

6

sponsored to work in these occupations automatically score the necessary 50 points for attributes (App A, Table 10).

Transitional arrangements

The purpose of the transitional arrangements is set out in the Explanatory Memorandum that introduced the new Rules (para 6.13):

" ...minimise the impact [of the Tier 2 (General) and Tier 2 (ICT) Rules] on existing work permit holders. Provided they are working for the same employer, their job meets our skill level requirements and their employer has obtained a sponsor licence, these migrants will be able to extend their stay in the UK up to a total of five years without having to meet the specific Tier 2 criteria for qualifications, prospective earnings and English language."

The transitional arrangements are therefore available for certain applicants applying for leave to *remain*, ie to extend their leave in the UK. Applicants who benefit from the transitional arrangements automatically obtain 50 points for attributes by scoring 50 points for 'sponsorship' (App A, para 61 and Table 11). It is not possible for applicants who are being sponsored as Ministers of Religion or as Sportspersons under Tier 2, to score points for attributes under the transitional arrangements (App A, para 64). Those who do not benefit from the transitional arrangements, must score points as normal ▶see 228–235

Classes of applicant who can benefit from the transitional arrangements

Applicants who have at the moment, or who were last granted, entry clearance or leave under any of the categories listed below, fall within the transitional arrangements provided they satisfy the additional conditions set out below for each one (for all these Rules, see App A, paras 61 and 83).

1) **Tier 2 (General) or Tier 2 (ICT)** The present sponsor must also have sponsored the applicant when s/he was last granted leave, which must have been given under these 'transitional arrangements'. In addition the job that the applicant is presently being sponsored to do must be the same as that which s/he was being sponsored to do when s/he was last granted leave (acceptable changes to the details of employment under UKBA Guidance that are notified will not affect the applicant's ability to come within the transitional provisions). Applicants should not have had a period of five years or more with continuous entry clearance or leave in either of these Tier 2 categories, or those categories listed in points 2) or 3) below (the five-year period is calculated so that it includes the period left remaining on the applicant's present grant of leave).

2) **'Qualifying Work Permit Holder'** This is a work permit holder who was issued with a work permit in the business and commercial, or sports and

entertainment, work permit categories. The present sponsor must also have issued the applicant with a work permit for the applicant's last grant of leave. In addition, the job that the applicant is presently being sponsored to do must be the same as that in respect of which the work permit was issued when s/he was last granted leave (acceptable changes to the details of employment under UKBA Guidance and that are notified will not affect the applicant's ability to come within the transitional provisions). Applicants must not have had a period of five years or more with continuous entry clearance, or leave, in either this category, or those categories listed in points 1) above or 3) below (the five-year period is calculated so that it includes the period left remaining on the applicant's present grant of leave).

3) **Member of the Operational Ground Staff of an Overseas-owned Airline; Representative of an Overseas Newspaper, News Agency or Broadcasting Organisation; or a Jewish Agency Employee** The first two of these are categories of (old) Rules that were in force until 27 November 2008. Jewish Agency Employees are those granted leave outside the Rules under a concession that was previously in force (Rules, para 6). In addition, the present sponsor must be the same person for whom the applicant was working, or intending to work, when s/he was last granted leave. Further, the job that the applicant is being sponsored to do must also be the same as the one s/he was doing, or intending to do, when s/he was last granted leave. Applicants should not have had a period of five years or more with continuous entry clearance, or leave, in any of these categories, or those categories listed in points 1) and 2) above (the five-year period is calculated so that it includes the period left remaining on the applicant's present grant of leave).

4) **Senior Care Worker** This is an applicant who is being sponsored in a job that UKBA Guidance defines as being a Senior Care Worker role and whose last leave was granted in order to work as a senior care worker either under the category of:

– 'Qualifying Work Permit Holder' (▶see above for definition); or

– Tier 2 (General) or Tier 2 (ICT) under the 'transitional arrangements'.

These applicants should also have not spent a period of five years or more in the UK in the above categories (ie Qualifying Work Permit Holder, Tier 2 (General) or Tier 2 (ICT)), or any combination of them. The five-year period begins with the applicant's last grant of entry clearance (Rules, para 6). Senior Care Workers and Established Entertainers (▶below) are the two classes of applicant who do not need to show that they are going to work for the same employer (T2 PG, para 159).

5) **Established Entertainer** This is an applicant who is being sponsored in a job that UKBA's Guidance defines as being in the entertainment sector and who has, at some stage, had entry clearance or leave as a Work Permit Holder (under the old Rules) under the sports and entertainment arrangements in order to do the same work in which s/he is presently being sponsored. In addition, the applicant's last grant of leave must have been as either:

- a Work Permit Holder under the sports and entertainment arrangements either in order to do the same work in which s/he is presently being sponsored, or in another occupation defined in UKBA's transitional Guidance as being a job in the entertainment sector; or
- a Tier 2 (General) or Tier 2 (ICT) Migrant, as long as that leave was granted under the 'transitional arrangements' and that it was granted in order to do the same work in which s/he is presently being sponsored, or in another occupation defined in UKBA's Transitional Guidance as being a job in the entertainment sector.

In addition, the present sponsor must confirm that the applicant will be paid a salary for the job that is at or above the appropriate entertainments industry rate and that the sponsor consulted with those bodies that UKBA designates in the Transitional Guidance as being bodies to be consulted before the sponsor employs an applicant. These applicants should also have not spent a period of five years or more in the UK as a 'Qualifying Work Permit Holder' (▶see above for definition), or as a Tier 2 (General) or Tier 2 (ICT) Migrant, or any combination of them. The five-year period begins with the applicant's last grant of entry clearance (Rules, para 6).

Requirements of skill level and salary: transitional arrangements

Unless the applicant is a Senior Care Worker or an Established Entertainer, the job that the applicant will do must be skilled to National Vocational Qualification (NQF) level 3 or above and appear on the UKBA list of those skilled occupations (the UKBA website has a detailed list of skilled occupations in the document 'Occupation codes of practice for Tier 2'). Unless the applicant is an Established Entertainer, the sponsor must have confirmed when assigning the certificate that the applicant will be paid at or above the appropriate rate for the job (as set out in UKBA Guidance). The salary must be at the same level or above that which the applicant was paid when last granted leave as a Tier 2 Migrant (App A, para 82).

In *R (Hussain Zulfiqar Alvi) v SSHD*, the claimant attempted to argue that if a person fell within the classes of applicant who can benefit from the transitional arrangements, they did not need also to satisfy the skills threshold under paragraph 82 of Appendix A in order to score 50 points for attributes. The claimant also argued, along *Pankina* lines, that the list of skilled occupations, not being part of the Rules, could not be enforced against him. Both arguments failed. The Judge concluded (at para 31):

"In my judgment C's proposition – that it is unlawful for D to enforce a requirement that applicants for leave to remain for work purposes have certain skill levels, without every job and skill being listed in detail in the Immigration Rules themselves (requiring a Parliamentary process to change the list) – is unrealistic and certainly not a legal requirement. It was not the intention of Parliament that the skills list should be an intrinsic part of the Rules or subject to specific Parliamentary legislative approval. The existence of the Tier 2 Codes of Practice and Policy Guidance does not involve changing in a material and substantive way the effect of the Rules or material extrinsic Guidance. There is no breach of the principles set out in *Pankina* and in *R (English UK Ltd)*."

As to the level of earnings, UKBA is committed to ensuring that:

- migrant workers are not exploited by employers paying them less than the going rate; and that
- the resident labour market is not undercut by cheap labour from overseas. UKBA's 'Codes of Practice' aim to establish the minimum salary that it considers should be paid to an individual as the 'going rate'. If the actual salary paid does not meet this minimum requirement, then the application will be refused. Sponsors should keep an eye on these minimum salaries to ensure that the required salary is paid. If UKBA discovers that salary that is being paid no longer falls within the guidelines, the usual course of action is that UKBA requests that it be raised. If the sponsor is unable or unwilling to comply, this may lead to more drastic action by UKBA, including a review of the sponsor's rating or licence.

Particular additional requirements for those applying in the 'Graduate Trainee' and 'Skills Transfer' subcategories

If the applicant is applying under either the 'Graduate Trainee' or the 'Skills Transfer' subcategories of the Tier 2 (ICT) category, then the job must appear on UKBA's list of graduate occupations and (App A, para 81 with reference to App A, para 69(c)(d)):

- if the applicant is applying as a Graduate Trainee, the job must be part of a structured graduate training programme as defined in the UKBA Guidance;
- if the applicant is applying under the Skills Transfer subcategory, the job must be for the sole purpose of transferring skills to or from the sponsor's UK work environment and the applicant must be appointed as additional to other staffing requirements, ie the applicant's position must only exist because of the need for skills transfer.

In addition, if the applicant is applying in the Graduate Trainee subcategory, s/he must have been working for the sponsor outside the UK for a continuous period of three months immediately before the date of the application. Such applicants are also required to produce specified documents to demonstrate this (App A, para 72(c)).

Procedural requirements

There are also a number of procedural requirements that must be satisfied before an applicant can score the necessary points for sponsorship. They are as follows (App A, para 81 with reference to App A, paras 63–68).

- When making his/her application to UKBA, the applicant must provide his/her certificate of sponsorship reference number (which the sponsor should give to the applicant when assigning the certificate). The applicant must not have previously been granted entry clearance or leave on the basis of the same certificate number.

- The certificate of sponsorship number must be a 'valid' one. In order to be 'valid', the details that it produces when UKBA checks its own electronic database of certificate reference numbers must match the applicant in terms of the applicant's name and the Tier 2 category in which s/he is being sponsored and is applying. Also in order for the certificate to be valid, the remaining three conditions below must be satisfied.

- The applicant's application must be made within three months of the date on which the sponsor assigned the certificate (with the relevant certificate reference number) to the applicant.

- The applicant's employment, as set out in the certificate, must be due to start no more than three months after the certificate was assigned.

- The certificate must not have been cancelled by either the sponsor or UKBA since it was assigned.

Applicants who need to score points for sponsorship, qualifications, prospective earnings

Applicants applying under Tier 2 (General) or Tier 2 (ICT) for:

- entry clearance; or

- leave to remain but who, for any reason, do not fall within the 'transitional arrangements' described above (perhaps because they are switching from one of the categories listed at ▶215–217 above that do *not* attract the transitional arrangements);

do not automatically score 50 points for sponsorship. They must, instead, make up the 50 points that they need for attributes from a combination of their sponsorship, qualifications and prospective earnings. The points available for them to score are set out in the table below (App A, para 60 and Table 10).

If included in the points that the applicant scores are points for sponsorship as a result of their job being an intra company transfer, and if their application is successful overall, then the applicant's entry clearance or leave will be granted in the Tier 1 (ICT) Migrant category. If it is otherwise successful, then entry clearance or leave will be granted in the Tier 1 (General) Migrant category (Rules, paras 245ZE(f)(i)(ii), 245ZG(i)(i)(ii)).

Note that an applicant can only score one set of points for sponsorship eg it is not possible for an intra company transfer applicant to score additional points if a Resident Labour Market Test is also carried out – the applicant can score points for one or the other (App A, para 65). In addition, points can only be scored for one qualification (App A, para 78). Where the applicant is being sponsored under Tier 2 as a Minister of Religion, or as a Sportsperson, s/he cannot score points for attributes under the table below (App A, para 64).

SCORING POINTS FOR ATTRIBUTES UNDER TIER 2 (GENERAL) AND TIER 2 (ICT) WHERE NO TRANSITIONAL ARRANGEMENTS APPLY

Sponsorship	Points
Job on the shortage occupation list	50
Job passes the Resident Labour Market Test (RLMT)	30
Qualifies as an Intra Company Transfer (ICT)	25
Switching from Tier 1 (Post-Study Work)	30
Qualifications	
None or below GCE 'A' level	0
GCE A-level	5
Bachelors' degree	10
Masters' degree or PhD	15
Prospective earnings	
Under £20,000	0
£20,000 – £23,999	10
£24,000 – £27,999	15
£28,000 – £31,999	20
£32,000 +	25

Source: Immigration Rules, Appendix A, Table 10

Skill level and salary

The work that the applicant will do as notified on the certificate of sponsorship must be at level 3 of the NQF and appear on the UKBA list of occupations as skilled to that level. The applicant's salary, as also notified, must be paid at or above the appropriate rate for the job as stated in UKBA Guidance. UKBA's 'Occupation codes of practice for Tier 2' set out the appropriate salary rates. UKBA will include allowances that are specified as acceptable in the Guidance (▶see below 235) (App A, para 69(a)(b)).

Shortage occupation list

To score points for sponsorship on the basis that the applicant's job is contained on the shortage occupation list, the job must (App A, para 70):

- have been on that list as published by UKBA at the time that the certificate of sponsorship was issued;
- be contracted for a minimum of 30 hours per week; and
- if the job appears on the 'Scotland only' shortage occupation list, be for employment in Scotland.

As indicated above, the shortage occupations are those which appear on a list prepared by UKBA following advice received from the MAC and can be found on the UKBA website where it is regularly updated (http://www. ukba.homeoffice.gov.uk/employers/points/sponsoringmigrants/employing migrants/shortageoccupationlist). The list is to be reviewed by the MAC in the light of the decision by the Government to raise the Tier 2 skills threshold to graduate level occupations and the publication of the Graduate Occupation List which is contained as an Appendix to the Tier 2 Statement of Intent of February 2011.

Applicants are advised to confirm with their sponsor that the sponsor has stated on the certificate of sponsorship that the job is on the shortage occupation list and to check that the SOC code and job description on the certificate show that the job is listed on the shortage occupation list (T2 PG, para 81).

Resident Labour Market Test

For the applicant to score points for sponsorship on the basis that the job offer passes the Resident Labour Market Test (RLMT), the certificate of sponsorship must indicate that the sponsor has met the requirements of that test as defined in UKBA's Guidance for that particular job (App A, para 71).

The RLMT is required for Tier 2 (General) applications where the role and skills required are not included on the shortage occupation list. The sponsor must be able to show that there are no suitably qualified settled workers available to do the job. The details about how sponsors should approach this are dealt with in the Tier 2 and Tier 5 Sponsor Guidance (SG, paras 192–226) and, to a lesser extent, the Tier 2 Policy Guidance (T2 PG, paras 82–6).

The sponsor is required to advertise the position as required in the Sponsor Guidance and the code of practice as particular to the type of job. This includes advertising in JobCentre Plus (JobCentre Online in Northern Ireland) plus one other industry-related advertising method that is permitted by the code of practice concerned (for the codes of practice, see http://www.bia.homeoffice.gov.uk/employers/points/sponsoringmigrants /employingmigrants/codesofpractice/) (SG, paras 193, 197–8).

Other examples of recruitment given in the Sponsor Guidance are national newspapers or professional journals (SG, paras 211–212); 'milkrounds', ie annual recruitment programmes where sponsors visit universities to give presentations to and to interview students, often as part of a university's careers fair – a minimum of three universities must be used (SG, paras 214–216); rolling recruitment campaigns (SG, paras 217–218); using a recruitment agency (SG, para 219); using specified internet sites (SG, paras 220–221); and using 'head-hunters' (SG, para 222). Even if no code of practice exists, the sponsor must still advertise using the JobCentre (▶above).

All vacancies must be advertised to settled workers for 28 calendar days in one of two ways (SG, para 194):

- advertise the vacancy for a single continuous period, with a minimum closing date of 28 calendar days from the date the advertisement first appeared; or
- advertise the vacancy in two stages, where both stages added together total a minimum of 28 calendar days.

An example given by UKBA (SG, para 194) is that the advertisement can initially run for 14 calendar days. If a suitable settled worker is identified, they may be appointed straight away. However, if no suitable settled worker is identified, the advertisement relating to the vacancy must be run for a further 14 days, making 28 calendar days in total (even if a suitable migrant worker had emerged after the first round of advertising). If no suitable settled workers are identified during either the first or second stage, the RLMT has been completed and a Tier 2 migrant may be appointed.

The advertisement must include (SG, para 196):

- the job title;
- the main duties and responsibilities of the job (the job description);
- the location of the job;
- an indication of the salary package, or salary range, or terms on offer;
- the skills, qualifications and experience needed; and
- the closing date for applications, unless the job is part of the organisation's rolling recruitment programme (in which case the advertisement should state the period of the recruitment programme).

The only jobs that do not need to be advertised through the JobCentre are (SG, paras 199–200) (but in these cases the other RLMTs as set out in the particular code of practice must still be met):

- jobs for named researchers;
- jobs in the creative sector where the code of practice states that advertising is not required because the migrant will be making an additional contribution to the UK labour market (see the creative sector codes for further information);
- jobs in the role of director, chief executive or legal partner, where the salary package is at least £130,000, or where there will be stock exchange disclosure requirements;
- 'milk round' graduate recruitment exercises; and
- jobs which do not require a Resident Labour Market Test, ie:
- where the job is on the shortage occupation list;
- where the applicant has leave under the Tier 1 (Post-Study Work) category (or in its predecessor categories: the International Graduates' Scheme; the Science and Engineering Graduates' Scheme; or the Fresh Talent: Working

in Scotland Scheme) and the applicant is switching into Tier 2 (General) to continue the same job with the same employer where s/he has already been employed for at least six months;

– the migrant has present leave to be in the UK as a Postgraduate Doctor or Dentist in Specialty Training and needs to apply for further leave under Tier 2 (General) to complete that training.

After a recruitment exercise has been carried out, the sponsor should keep the documents listed at Appendix D of the Sponsor Guidance as proof of the RLMT having been carried out (SG, para 205).

If a settled worker applies for the job but does not have the necessary qualifications, experience or skills, an employer cannot refuse to employ him/her unless it had specifically requested these qualifications, experience or skills in the job advertisement (SG, para 203).

The certificate of sponsorship must be assigned no more than six months after the job was first advertised (SG, para 201). If the vacancy has been advertised in two stages, as described above, the certificate should be issued within six months of the date when the first of the two advertisements appeared. This is to make sure that the outcome of the advertising reflects the present availability of the skills required in a changing job market. The only exceptions to this six-month rule are (SG, para 202):

• where a migrant has been recruited through a 'milk round', in which case a certificate of sponsorship may be assigned up to 48 months after the milk round took place; and

• where a migrant is employed as a research fellow at a higher education institution, in which case the certificate may be assigned up to 12 months after the recruitment process started.

When the sponsor assigns a certificate of sponsorship, s/he has to confirm either that a RLMT has been carried out but no suitable settled worker could be found, or that such a test is not required (SG, para 206).

Particular requirements for those applying under Tier 2 (ICT)

To score points for sponsorship on the basis of an intra company transfer, the sponsor must have confirmed that the applicant will be coming to the UK to work for the sponsor as a Tier 2 (ICT) Migrant (App A, para 72).

In addition, if the applicant is applying under the 'Established Staff' sub-category of Tier 2 (ICT), then s/he must have been working for the sponsor for a particular period (►see below) either (App A, para 72(a)):

• outside the UK; and/or

• in the UK as long as s/he had leave to work for the sponsor either:

• under the Tier 2 (ICT) Established Staff subcategory, or under the Tier 2 (ICT) Rules in place before 6 April 2010;

• as a 'Qualifying Work Permit Holder' as long as the work permit was granted on the basis of an intra company transfer; and/or

- as a Representative of an Overseas Business.

The period of time for which these Established Staff applicants must have worked for the sponsor is (App A, para 72(b)):

- a continuous period of 12 months immediately before the date of the application
- if, during that 12-month period, the applicant has either been on maternity/paternity or adoption leave, or has been working for the sponsor in the Tier 2 (ICT) 'Graduate Trainee' or 'Skills Transfer' subcategories, then an aggregate period of 12 months within the period of 24 months immediately before the date of the application is permitted (see also T2 PG, para 30).

Applicants must produce the specified documents to show that they have been doing the above work for the period in question (App A, para 72(a)). The relevant parts of the Policy Guidance are T2 PG, paras 43–50 (payslips, personal bank or building society statements or building society pass book and detailed Guidance is given with regard to evidence of maternity/paternity and adoption leave).

Particular requirements for those applying in the 'Graduate Trainee' and 'Skills Transfer' subcategories of Tier 2 (ICT)

If the applicant is applying under either the 'Graduate Trainee' or the 'Skills Transfer' subcategories of the Tier 2 (ICT) category, then the job that s/he is being sponsored for must appear on UKBA's list of graduate occupations and (App A, para 69(c)(d)):

- if the applicant is applying as a Graduate Trainee, the job must be part of a structured graduate training programme as defined in the UKBA Guidance;
- if the applicant is applying under the Skills Transfer subcategory, the job must be for the sole purpose of transferring skills to or from the sponsor's UK work environment and the applicant must be appointed as additional to other staffing requirements ie the applicant's position must only exist because of the need for skills transfer and the certificate of sponsorship should confirm this (T2 PG, para 23).

In addition, if the applicant is applying in the Graduate Trainee subcategory, s/he must have been working for the sponsor outside the UK for a continuous period of three months immediately before the date of the application. Such applicants are also required to produce specified documents to demonstrate this (App A, para 72(c)).

Particular requirements for those applying to switch into Tier 2 (General) or Tier 2 (ICT) from the Tier 1 (Post-Study Work) category

The requirements to be met in order to score points for sponsorship in the above table on the basis of switching from the Tier 1 (Post-Study Work) category are as follows (App A, para 73). The applicant must be applying for leave to *remain*. The applicant must have existing entry clearance or leave: in the Tier 1 (Post-Study Work) category; or as a participant in the International Graduates' Scheme, the Science and Engineering Graduates' Scheme, or the Fresh Talent: Working in Scotland Scheme.

In addition, the applicant must have been working for the sponsor (and must produce the specified documents to show this; see T2 PG, para 89 for what is required):

- for a continuous period of six months immediately before the date of the application; or
- if, during that six-month period, the applicant has either been on maternity/paternity or adoption leave, for an aggregate period of six months within the period of 18 months immediately before the date of the application.

Finally, the job that the applicant is now being sponsored to do under the application, must be the same as the job s/he is doing at the time of the application.

Qualifications

For the purposes of the table above, applicants are required to produce documents specified in UKBA Guidance as evidence of their qualifications (App A, para 74). For the relevant Guidance setting out the evidence required, see T2 PG, paras 51–64. In addition, applicants will only score points for a degree if it is deemed by UK NARIC, or UKBA in its published Guidance, to meet or exceed the recognised standard in the UK for a Bachelor's or Master's degree or a PhD (App A, para 75(a)).

Where the qualification is below the degree standards set out above, in order to score points, the applicant must submit specified evidence to demonstrate that it is equivalent to, or higher than, one or more passes at GCE 'A' level (App A, para 75(b)).

Points can also be scored where the qualification is a vocational or professional one as long as (App A, para 76):

- the qualification is deemed by UK NARIC (or the appropriate professional body) to be the equivalent of a UK Bachelor's or Master's degree or a PhD; or
- if the qualification is below the degree standards set out above, the applicant provides the specified evidence to demonstrate that it is equivalent to, or higher than, 1 or more passes at GCE 'A' level.

Prospective earnings

For the purposes of the table above, prospective earnings are calculated on the basis of the applicant's gross annual salary and, for this, UKBA will use the information provided to it by the sponsor on the certificate of sponsorship.

UKBA will include allowances provided as part of the salary where those allowances are specified as acceptable in UKBA's Guidance (App A, para 79). The Policy Guidance states that UKBA will consider basic pay (excluding overtime) plus allowances such as London weighting, as long as they would also be paid to a settled employee who is in similar circumstances. The allowances must be a guaranteed part of the applicant's salary package. Benefits such as bonus, incentive pay, travel and subsistence, will not be taken into account (T2 PG, paras 75–6)

If the applicant is paid by the hour, UKBA will only take into account salary earned on the basis of a maximum of 48 hours worked per week (App A, para 80). For the further relevant Guidance setting out the evidence required, see T2 PG, paragraphs 65–76.

Procedural requirements

The procedural requirements relating to the certificate that is assigned to the applicant and which must be satisfied in order to score points for sponsorship, are the same as in the case of applicants covered by the transitional arrangements (App A, paras 63, 66–68) (▶see above at 224).

TIER 2 (MINISTER OF RELIGION) MIGRANTS: PARTICULAR REQUIREMENTS

Applicants in this category must be coming to the UK to work in a job as a religious worker within a genuine religious organisation for up to three years. Their work may encompass (SG, paras 250, 252):

- preaching or performing pastoral duties;
- work as a missionary; or
- work in a religious order within a community which involves a permanent commitment, like a monastery or convent.

Pastoral duties include (SG, para 250):

- leading worship regularly and on special occasions;
- giving religious education to children and adults by preaching and teaching;
- officiating at marriages, funerals and other special services;
- offering counselling and welfare support to members of the congregation;
- recruiting, training and co-ordinating the work of any local volunteers and lay preachers.

As a missionary, in addition to preaching and teaching, work may also include (SG, para 253):

- the organisation of missionary activity – short of administration and clerical work, unless it is a senior post;

- supervising staff;
- co-ordinating the organisation of missionary work;
- being in charge of a particular activity such as accounts/finance, personnel management or IT; or
- translating religious texts.

Anyone studying for a qualification on a formal full-time course of study, or training in an academic institution that is outside the order, should apply under Tier 4, not Tier 2 (SG, para 254). In addition, working full-time as a teacher in a school run by a Church or missionary organisation does not count as missionary work according to the Guidance (SG, para 253). Teachers would have to apply as a sponsored skilled worker under Tier 2.

Applicants under the Tier 2 (Minister of Religion) category should provide an official letter from their sponsor with their application. The letter should be signed by someone with authority in the organisation. The purpose of the letter is to set out the applicant's proposed duties (▶see above), their pay and how the RLMT has been met (T2 PG, paras 98–99).

The relatively high level of English language required of Tier 2 (Minister of Religion) applicants (▶see above 219) is explained by UKBA as the need to "speak to and for the religious communities [the applicant] will represent, and in particular to communicate effectively with the younger generation" (T2 PG, para 104).

Scoring points for attributes in the Tier 2 (Minister of Religion) category

An applicant applying as a Tier 2 (Minister of Religion) Migrant, must score 50 points for attributes under paragraphs 85–92 of Appendix A to the Rules (Rules, paras 245ZD(c), 245ZF(k); App A, para 85).

For the particular requirements that must be satisfied by a body that wishes to become a sponsor of migrants under the Tier 2 (Minister of Religion) category, ▶see Chapter 4 89; and for the confirmations that such a sponsor makes to UKBA when s/he assigns a certificate to a Tier 2 (Minister of Religion) Migrant, ▶see 111.

Applicants under this category will score all of the 50 required points for 'sponsorship' (the only criterion) provided that they have been issued with a valid certificate of sponsorship by their sponsor (App A, para 86 and Table 12). In order to satisfy this requirement (App A, paras 88–92):

- the details that are produced when UKBA checks its own electronic database of certificate reference numbers must match the applicant in terms of the applicant's name and confirm also that the sponsor is sponsoring him/her as a Tier 2 (Minister of Religion) Migrant;
- the applicant's application must be made within three months of the date on which the sponsor assigned the certificate (with the relevant certificate reference number) to the applicant;

- the certificate must not have been cancelled, either by the sponsor or UKBA, since it was assigned;
- the applicant must not previously have been granted entry clearance or leave on the basis of the same certificate (identifiable by its reference number); and
- the sponsor must have confirmed when assigning the certificate (and UKBA's database record must show that the sponsor has confirmed) that:
  - the Resident Labour Market Test has been complied with in respect of the job (unless the applicant has existing, or was last granted, entry clearance or leave as a Tier 2 (Minister of Religion), or as a Minister of Religion under the old Rules and the sponsor is the same as the sponsor whom the applicant was working for, or intending to work for, when last granted that leave);
  - the applicant is qualified to do the job in question;
  - the applicant intends to base him/herself in the UK;
  - the applicant will comply with the conditions of his/her leave; and
  - the sponsor will maintain or accommodate the migrant.

TIER 2 (SPORTSPERSON) MIGRANTS: PARTICULAR REQUIREMENTS

Those entering in this category are elite sportspeople and coaches, where:

- they are internationally established at the highest level; and
- their employment will make a significant contribution to the development of their sport at the highest level in the UK; and who intend to base themselves in the UK.

Before issuing a certificate, the sponsor will need to obtain an endorsement for the applicant from the appropriate governing body for the sport confirming the above and that the post could not be filled by a suitable settled worker (T2 PG, para 92; SG, para 270).

Scoring points for attributes in the Tier 2 (Sportsperson) category

An applicant applying as a Tier 2 (Sportsperson) Migrant, must score 50 points for attributes under paragraphs 93–100 of Appendix A to the Rules (Rules, paras 245ZD(d), 245ZF(l); App A, para 93).

For the particular considerations that apply where a body wishes to become licensed to sponsor migrants under the Tier 2 (Sportsperson) category, ▶see 89–90. For the confirmations that a sponsor of a Tier 2 (Sportsperson) Migrant makes to UKBA when s/he assigns a certificate to the applicant, ▶see 111.

Applicants under this category will score all 50 points for 'sponsorship' (the only criterion) provided that they have been issued with a valid certificate of sponsorship by their sponsor (App A, para 94 and Table 13). In order to satisfy this requirement (App A, paras 96-100):

- the details that are produced when UKBA checks its own electronic database of certificate reference numbers, match the applicant in terms of the applicant's name and confirms also that the sponsor is sponsoring him/her as a Tier 2 (Sportsperson) Migrant;
- the applicant's application must be made within three months of the date on which the sponsor assigned the certificate (with the relevant certificate reference number) to the applicant;
- the certificate must not have been cancelled either by the sponsor or UKBA since it was assigned;
- the applicant must not previously have been granted entry clearance or leave on the basis of the same certificate (identifiable by its reference number); and
- the sponsor must have confirmed when assigning the certificate (and UKBA's database record must show that the sponsor has confirmed) that:
  - the applicant is qualified to do the job in question;
  - that the applicant has been endorsed by the governing body for this sport;
  - the applicant intends to base him/herself in the UK; and
  - the applicant will comply with the conditions of his/her leave.

PERIOD AND CONDITIONS OF LEAVE GRANTED UNDER TIER 2

This section deals with the periods and conditions of leave granted under the various categories and subcategories of Tier 2. In most, but not all, cases applicants will be able to obtain a second grant of limited leave to bring them up to five years after which time they will be able to apply for settlement (▶below at 242).

Period of leave: on entry

Entry clearance/leave to enter will normally be granted for a period of three years and one month provided that the applicant's 'period of engagement' is of that length or longer. If the period of the applicant's period of engagement is shorter than three years, the applicant will be granted entry clearance/leave for that shorter period plus one month (Rules, para 245ZE(c)).

The 'period of engagement' is simply the period between the start and end dates of the employment as notified to UKBA on the certificate of sponsorship (Rules, para 245ZB(b)). The Rules suggest that the additional period of one month will be divided between 14 days before the employment start date and 14 days following the end of the employment (Rules, para 245ZE(d)).

However, much shorter periods are granted in the 'Graduate Trainee' and 'Skills Transfer' subcategories of the Tier 2 (ICT) category.

- Graduate Trainees are granted entry clearance/leave for a maximum of one year. They are granted less than a year if the period of their employment, as notified to UKBA, is less than a year, in which case they are given leave for the period of their engagement plus one month (Rules, para 245ZE(a)).

- Applicants in the Skills Transfer subcategory are granted entry clearance/leave for a maximum period of six months. However, they too will be granted less than that if the period of their employment, as notified to UKBA, is not as long as six months, in which case they are given leave for the period of their engagement plus one month (Rules, para 245ZE(b)).

Period of leave: grants of leave to remain

This section looks at the period of leave granted when applicants are applying in-country for leave to remain. Note that, in the case of the first three of the five situations considered below, in addition to the period of leave stated, UKBA will also grant leave for the period between the point at which the application is decided (positively) and any later date on which the applicant is due to start their period of employment as notified to UKBA on the certificate of employment (Rules, para 245ZG(g)).

Where applicant was previously granted leave under categories replaced by Tier 2

Where the applicant was last granted entry clearance or leave in any of the categories and in the circumstances listed below, on a successful extension application under Tier 2, s/he will be granted a period of leave to bring him/her them up to five years in total. The five years is calculated by adding the new grant of leave to all the leave granted in any combination of the categories listed below, starting with the first grant of leave of the continuous period in those categories (Rules, para 245ZG(a)(i)(b)).

If the applicant needs less than a grant of leave of two years to reach the five-year mark, s/he will still be granted two years' leave (Rules, 245ZG(a)(ii)).

However, if, in any case, the applicant's period of engagement (ie the length of employment as notified to UKBA when the sponsor issues the certificate) is less than the period of leave that the applicant would otherwise be granted in order to bring him/her up to five years' leave in total, then the applicant will only be granted leave for the length of their period of engagement (plus 14 days) up to a maximum of two years (Rules, para 245ZG(a)(ii)).

The relevant categories of leave/circumstances referred to above are as follows (Rules, para 245ZG(b)):

- Jewish Agency Employee (under the old concession), provided the applicant is still working for the same employer;

- Member of the Operational Ground Staff of an Overseas-owned Airline (under the old Rules), provided the applicant is still working for the same employer;
- Minister of Religion, Missionary or Member of a Religious Order (under the old Rules), provided the applicant is still working for the same employer;
- Qualifying Work Permit Holder (under the old Rules) (ie a Work Permit Holder whose employer was issued with a work permit for him/her in the business and commercial, or sports and entertainment, work permit categories) provided the applicant is still working for the same employer;
- Representative of an Overseas Newspaper, News Agency or Broadcasting Organisation (under the old Rules) provided the applicant is still working for the same employer;
- Tier 2 (Minister of Religion), provided that applicant meets all of the following conditions, namely s/he:
- previously had leave as a Minister of Religion, Missionary or as a Member of a Religious Order (under the old Rules) and received his/her last grant of entry clearance or leave to enter in that category;
- was granted leave to remain as a Tier 2 (Minister of Religion) Migrant at some point during the above period of leave; and
- is still working for the same employer as when last in the UK with the above leave;
- Tier 2 (Sportsperson) provided that the applicant meets all of the following conditions, namely s/he:
- previously had leave as Work Permit Holder (under the old Rules);
- was granted leave to remain as a Tier 2 (Sportsperson) Migrant at some point during the above period of leave; and
- is still working for the same employer as when last in the UK with the above leave; or
- Tier 2 (General) or Tier 2 (ICT) provided s/he meets both of the following conditions, namely:
- s/he scores points in the present application under the 'transitional arrangements' (▶see above 224–228); and
- his/her last grant of leave was in any of the following categories: Qualifying Work Permit Holder; Representative of an Overseas Newspaper, News Agency or Broadcasting Organisation; Minister of Religion, Missionary or Member of a Religious Order; Member of the Operational Ground Staff of an Overseas-owned Airline (all categories under the old Rules); Jewish Agency Employee (under the old concession); a Tier 2 (Minister of Religion) or a Tier 2 (Sportsperson).

'Graduate Trainee' subcategory of Tier 2 (ICT)

If the applicant is applying in the Graduate Trainee subcategory of Tier 2 (ICT), s/he may only be granted leave in order to bring his/her total time in the UK, since his/her last grant of entry clearance/leave to enter under Tier 2 (ICT), up to a maximum period of 12 months. If the applicant has already had 12 months, the application for leave will be refused. If the applicant's period of engagement is for less than the period needed to bring the total period up to 12 months, the applicant will only be granted leave for the length of the period of engagement plus 14 days (Rules, para 245ZG(c)).

'Skills Transfer' subcategory of Tier 2 (ICT)

If the applicant is applying in the Skills Transfer subcategory of Tier 2 (ICT), s/he may only be granted leave in order to bring his/her total time in the UK, since his/her last grant of entry clearance/leave to enter under Tier 2 (ICT), up to a maximum period of six months. If the applicant has already had six months, the application for leave will be refused. If the period of the applicant's engagement is for less than the period needed to bring the total period up to six months, the applicant will only be granted leave for the length of the period of engagement plus 14 days (Rules, para 245ZG(d)).

None of the above apply but the applicant was last granted leave in Tier 2, is in the same job and working for the same employer

Where none of the above circumstances apply, but the applicant:

- has, or was last granted, entry clearance or leave as a Tier 2 Migrant; and
- s/he is still working for the same employer and doing the same job as s/he was doing at the time that earlier grant of leave;

then leave to remain will be granted for two years, or if the applicant's period of engagement is less than that, for the period of engagement plus 14 days (Rules, para 245ZG(e)).

All other cases

In any case not covered by any of the circumstances above, leave to remain will be granted for a period of three years, or if the applicant's period of engagement is less than that, for the period of engagement plus 14 days (Rules, para 245ZG(f)).

Conditions of leave

Entry clearance/leave to enter and leave to remain under Tier 2 is granted subject to the following conditions (Rules, paras 245ZE(e), 245ZG(h)):

- no recourse to public funds;
- registration with the police, if this is required (see Rules, para 326);
- no employment *other than*:
- working for the sponsor in the employment that the applicant is being sponsored to do according to UKBA's records (this does not prevent permitted changes to the details of employment notified to UKBA and permitted by it);
- 'supplementary employment' (▶see below);
- 'voluntary work' (▶see below);

– if the applicant is granted leave as a Tier 2 (Sportsperson) Migrant, employment as a sportsperson for his/her national team while that team is in the UK.

'Supplementary employment' This work must be in the same occupation and at the same professional level as the work for which the applicant is sponsored. Applicants must undertake no more than 20 hours per week supplementary employment and the work must be carried on outside the applicant's normal working hours. In addition, for the work to be 'supplementary', the applicant must continue to work for his/her sponsor as notified to UKBA on the certificate of sponsorship. Provided these conditions are all met, the applicant does not have to notify UKBA of any supplementary employment that they choose to do (T2 PG, paras 191–192).

'Voluntary work' Applicants can take voluntary work in any sector but they must not be paid for the work that they do except that they may receive reasonable expenses as set out in section 44 of the National Minimum Wage Act (T2 PG, paras 193).

Changes of employment

Where the applicant changes employer, or there is a change to the applicant's job with the same employer that involves changes to his/her core duties, or the applicant's pay reduces (other than due to company-wide pay changes that are defined as acceptable in UKBA's Guidance), the applicant will have to make a 'change of employment' application. This is treated in the same way as an initial application – a new certificate of sponsorship is required and all the normal relevant requirements must be met and points scored.

A change of employment application will not be required if the change is simply a technical one, for example where a sponsoring employer restructures a department, or renames a position, but the role and fundamentals of the job remain the same. Similarly if the applicant changes jobs but remains within the same Standard Occupational Classification code, or if the applicant's pay increases. In such cases, it is possible to notify a change of employment to UKBA without having to obtain a new certificate of sponsorship and make a change of employment application (see T2 SG at paras 198–204).

SETTLEMENT UNDER TIER 2

Those whose most recent period of leave in the UK was spent under Tier 2 are eligible for settlement if they have spent a "continuous period of five years lawfully in the UK". For details about the calculation of that period and absences from the UK, ▶see Chapter 5 188–193.

Apart from the most recent period (which must have been under Tier 2), for Tier 2 applicants the rest of the five years may have been spent in any combination of the following categories of leave (some of which have now been replaced by the PBS) (Rules 245ZH(b)):

- Member of the Operational Ground Staff of Overseas-owned Airline;
- Minister of Religion, Missionary or Member of a Religious Order;
- 'Qualifying Work Permit Holder' (ie a Work Permit Holder who was issued a work permit either under the business and commercial, or sports and entertainment, parts of the previous work permit arrangements, see Rules, para 6);
- Representative of an Overseas Business;
- Representative of an Overseas Newspaper, News Agency or Broadcasting Organisation;
- Tier 1 Migrant (other than as a Tier 1 (Post-Study Work) Migrant);
- Highly Skilled Migrant;
- Innovator;
- Tier 2 (General) Migrant;
- Tier 2 (ICT) Migrant (▶but see below);
- Tier 2 (Minister of Religion) Migrant; or
- Tier 2 (Sportsperson) Migrant.

The Rules were amended from April 2010 by HC 439 to prevent Tier 2 (ICT) Migrants from being able to progress to settlement. However, transitional provisions were put in place to ensure that existing Tier 2 (ICT) Migrants could still eventually obtain settlement. How this works is as follows. If part of the period relied on to qualify for settlement is as a Tier 2 (ICT) Migrant, the five continuous years of leave must include a period as a Tier 2 (ICT) Migrant under the Rules in place before 6 April 2010, or as a 'Qualifying Work Permit Holder' who was granted leave because s/he was the subject of an intra company transfer (Rules, para 245ZH(b)(x)).

In all cases, in order to qualify for settlement the following conditions must also be satisfied (Rules, para 245ZH(a)(c)(e)):

- the applicant must not fall for refusal under the general grounds of refusal (see Chapter 11);
- the sponsor who issued the certificate that led to the applicant's last grant of leave must state in writing that s/he still needs the applicant for employment; and
- the applicant must have sufficient knowledge of English and life in the UK unless s/he is aged either under 18 or over 65.

7   Tier 3: low-skilled workers

This very short chapter concerns Tier 3 of the Points-Based System.

The purpose of Tier 3 is to create routes for the admission to the UK of low-skilled workers for short-term purposes not intended to lead to settlement. The original intention was that Tier 3 would replace the Seasonal Agricultural Workers' Scheme (SAWS) and the Sectors-Based Scheme (SBS). Both were due to be phased out in 2006 but remain operational, although now reserved exclusively for Romanian and Bulgarian nationals. Meanwhile, Tier 3 and all the schemes falling under it presently stand suspended. We have provided some basic details about SAWS and SBS (▶below), not because they actually constitute Tier 3 of the PBS, but because they do at least provide the basic model for Tier 3 should it ever be implemented.

There seems to be no imminent prospect of Tier 3 becoming operative. The Migration Advisory Committee had recommended establishing a scheme that would fit under Tier 3 and it seems that the Labour Government's original intention, when the PBS was conceived, was that Tier 3 would be operative. However, the prevailing view seems to be that demand for unskilled labour can be met from within the EEA workforce (hence the restriction of SAWS and SBS to Bulgarians and Romanians) and through the other tiers of the PBS, particularly Tier 5 and incidental work carried out by students admitted under Tier 4.

Features of Tier 3

As Tier 3 has never been made operational, there has been no Statement of Intent fully detailing the features of the scheme. However, the Labour Government's Command Paper, *A Points-Based System: Making Migration Work for Britain* provided a broad description of how Tier 3 might work. It makes clear that the schemes under Tier 3 would be established on a temporary basis only and it gives some further details of what the schemes might look like.

Effective returns policy Only nationals of those countries with which the UK has 'effective returns policies' would be permitted to participate in Tier 3 schemes. The requirement for an effective returns policy is already a pre-condition for eligibility for the Youth Mobility Scheme under Tier 5.

According to the Tier 5 Statement of Intent, 'effective returns arrangements' are those showing that there is an effective means for the enforced return for the sending country's nationals and that the governments of those states show that they cooperate in the process of such returns by:

- accepting EU letters for the purposes of return;
- re documenting their nationals swiftly; and
- receiving the return of their nationals in a timely and appropriate manner.

It is not clear whether precisely the same requirements would be imposed under Tier 3.

Quota-based Like the Sectors-Based Scheme and the Seasonal Agricultural Workers' Scheme and, more recently, the interim and proposed long-term 'cap', it is proposed that schemes under Tier 3 would be subject to a quota.

Operator-led All schemes under Tier 3 would be 'operator-led'. The operators would be responsible for recruiting the migrant workers, potentially moving them between employers and issuing the relevant documentation. Options such as compulsory remittances, requiring open return tickets, and biometric requirements (as is presently the case under the PBS) were also under consideration.

Switching/settlement Tier 3 is not intended to provide a route to settlement. The proposal was for entry to be limited to a maximum period of 12 months.

English language requirements The Command Paper noted that there are some low-skilled jobs for which English language is required. The intention appears to have been that operators/employers would be responsible for setting the relevant standard of English required and for ensuring that those requirements are met by potential participants.

Dependants It is not envisaged that the dependants of those admitted under Tier 3 would be eligible to join them in the UK

Seasonal Agricultural Workers Scheme

The SAWS category remains in the Immigration Rules (paras 104–109), although the only persons now able to benefit from it are Bulgarian and Romanian nationals who are full-time students. Participants must be aged over 18 and the holders of a valid Home Office work card issued by the 'operator' of a scheme that has been approved by the Home Office.

In order to obtain such a card, participants apply directly to one of the operators of the scheme for a placement in order to do the agricultural work (a list of the operators is available on the UKBA website). Participants must intend to work only as permitted on their work card and intend to leave the UK at the end of their period of leave under SAWS. They must also be able to maintain and accommodate themselves without recourse to public funds. Participants may be admitted for up to six months, but they can return to the UK again after a gap of at least three months. There is now a quota on the number of SAWS participants who will be admitted each year. There is no specific provision to enable participants to be accompanied by dependants.

Sectors-Based Scheme

Information on the operation of the SBS is available in detailed SBS Guidance posted on the UKBA website. The purpose of the SBS, as presently constituted, is to allow UK employers to recruit Bulgarian and Romanian nationals to fill specific posts in the food and manufacturing sectors. Employers may apply to UKBA for a 'letter of approval' to enable them to employ a particular participant in order to fill one of the specific posts referred to in the Guidance. The participant then submits the letter of approval to UKBA, together with an application for an 'accession worker card', on from BR3 (itself available on the UKBA website). The participant may not commence work until they have obtained an accession worker card. The criteria to obtain authorisation for the employment are as follows (SBS Guidance, 1 March 2010, para 3):

- there must be a UK-based employer;
- the participant is to be an employee of the UK employer;
- there is a genuine vacancy for the participant in the UK;
- the employer is responsible for the post;
- the gross pay and conditions of employment are equal or exceed those normally given to a resident worker doing similar work;
- the employment complies with UK legislation and any requirements for registration or licensing that are necessary for the employment;
- the skills, qualifications and experience needed to do the job meet specific requirements;
- the person is suitably qualified or experienced to do the job on offer;
- suitable arrangements have been made to provide accommodation for the participant;
- the participant is between the ages of 18 and 30 years;
- the post on offer is within a sector covered by the SBS arrangements;
- the post itself matches one of the posts covered by the SBS arrangements;
- the participant will be working full-time; and
- there are no suitably qualified or experienced 'resident' workers available.

Employers are also expected to provide appropriate levels of support by way of making sure that all relevant health and safety guidelines have been communicated to the participants in a language that they can fully understand before they commence work. There is no specific provision for participants to bring their dependants, although dependants can seek to qualify in their own right.

7

8   Tier 4: students

This chapter covers:

- Tier 4 (General) Students: qualifying for entry ▶250–273;
- period and conditions of leave under the Tier 4 (General) Student category ▶273–277;
- Tier 4 (General) Students: qualifying for leave to remain ▶277–279;
- Tier 4 (Child) Students ▶279–286;
- Highly Trusted Sponsor status ▶287–291;
- December 2010 proposals for change ▶291–295.

The transition to Tier 4 of the PBS

The great majority of those coming to the UK for studies now do so under the Tier 4 (General) Student category and the Tier 4 (Child) Student category, both part of the Points-Based System. These categories were introduced into the Rules from 31 March 2009. From that date, amending Rules (HC 314) deleted the following pre-existing student categories which had been contained in part 3 of the Rules which dealt with studies:

- Student;
- Student Nurse, *apart from* for applications for extensions of leave by those who already have leave to enter/remain as an overseas qualified nurse or midwife, (Rules, paras 69P–R);
- Student Re-sitting an Examination;
- Student Writing-up a Thesis;
- Postgraduate Doctor or Dentist; and
- Student Union Sabbatical Officer.

As a transitional provision, applications for those in the above categories made on or before 30 March 2009 continued to be determined under the old Rules (which are reproduced in Annex F of the Rules).

Also from 31 March 2009, the Home Office terminated the operation of published concessions outside the Rules relating to (see Explanatory Memo to HC 314, para 7.27):

- sandwich students;
- bar students;
- music students;
- pupil barristers;
- Wellbeck College students;
- Association of American Study Abroad Programmes; and
- the Pestalozzi Children's Trust.

Those who, as at 30 March 2009, had leave in any of the above deleted categories under the Rules or concessions could continue to enjoy the remainder of their leave. However, applications by them for leave on or after 31 March 2009 had to satisfy the new requirements of Tier 4. One of the most telling changes was the new requirement to have a confirmation of acceptance of studies (CAS) issued by an educational institution with a sponsor licence (when the scheme began, a 'visa letter' served the purpose of a CAS). For the requirements that must be satisfied by an educational institution in order to become a licensed sponsor and the requirements that must be satisfied, ▶see Chapter 4.

Study or academic routes outside Tier 4

There are, however, some relevant study or academic routes that remain outside the PBS. They are dealt with in other parts of this Guide and are as follows.

Business visitors coming as academic visitors (▶324–325), visiting professors (▶326) or to act as trainers in restricted circumstances (▶327).

Student visitors (▶336–338) must be adults and may come for a maximum of six months. There are no restrictions on the level of course that can be followed by those in this category, although there are restrictions on which educational institutions the applicant may study with. Work, inside and outside term time, is prohibited. From 10 January 2011; the Home Office has operated a further concession to this category allowing English language students to be admitted as student visitors for up to 11 months.

Child visitors (▶338–340) may also come for educational purposes. This may be either:

- to attend a course of study at an institution outside the maintained sector; or
- for an educational exchange or visit.

Prospective students may enter the UK outside the PBS as a form of 'special visitor'. But the purpose of admitting them is so that they can research courses, obtain a place and then switch into Tier 4, meeting all the relevant requirements (▶340–341).

Tier 5 (Youth Mobility Scheme) (▶Chapter 9) This enables nationals of certain participating countries, aged between 18 to 31 years, to come to the UK in order to experience life and work here. Those admitted may study on a privately-funded basis.

EEA nationals EU rights of free movement cover people moving within the European Economic Area for the purpose of study. These rights are not covered in this Guide.

TIER 4 (GENERAL): QUALIFYING FOR ENTRY

The Tier 4 (General) Student category is for those who wish to study in the UK who are aged 16 years or over (Rules, para 245ZT). A 16- or 17-year-old student who will be studying on a course at NQF level 3 (for example, A-levels) or above, may apply either under this category or under the Tier 4 (Child) Student category (▶below 279–286). If the course is below that level, then the same applicant will have to apply under Tier 4 (Child) category. A 16- or 17-year-old proposing to study on an English language course, unless it is a pre-sessional one, will have to apply under the Tier 4 (General) category.

All those seeking entry under the Tier 4 (General) category must have entry clearance (Rules, para 245ZU).

WHAT THE RULES SAY

In order to qualify for entry clearance to enter under the Tier 4 (General) category, the following requirements must be satisfied (Rules, para 245ZV):

- the applicant must be at least 16 years old (a student's age is considered to be that on the date of application, Tier 4 PG, para 250);
- *if* the applicant is under 18 years of age, s/he must show that the application is supported by his/her parents or legal guardian (or just one parent if that parent has sole legal responsibility for him/her);
- *if* the applicant is under 18 years of age, s/he must show that his/her parents or legal guardian (or just one parent if that parent has sole legal responsibility for him/her) have confirmed that they consent to the arrangements for the applicant's travel to, reception and care in the UK;
- the applicant must not fall for refusal under the general grounds (▶see Chapter 11);
- the applicant must score 30 points for attributes, which is achieved by being issued with a valid 'confirmation of acceptance of studies' (CAS) under paras 113–120 of Appendix A of the Rules – there are a range of requirements that must be met in order for the CAS to allow the applicant to score points (▶see below);
- *if* the course is below degree level, the entry clearance applied for must

not lead to the applicant spending more than three years in the UK as a Tier 4 Migrant, since the age of 18, studying courses that did not consist of degree level study;

- *if* the course is below degree level and contains a work placement, the sponsor must be a 'Highly Trusted Sponsor' (HTS), unless the course is a foundation degree;

- *if* the course is at level 3 on the National Qualifications Framework (NQF), or level 6 on the Scottish Credit and Qualifications Framework (SCQF), the Sponsor must be a HTS;

- the applicant must score ten points for maintenance under Appendix C of the Rules;

- *if* the applicant is presently being sponsored by a Government or international scholarship agency, or within the last 12 months has come to the end of such a period of sponsorship, s/he must provide the written consent of the sponsoring Government or agency to the application and must provide specified documents to show that this requirement has been met;

- *if* the applicant is applying to study certain science, maths, technology or engineering courses, s/he must hold a valid Academic Technology Approval Scheme (ATAS) clearance; and

- *if* the applicant wishes to be a post-graduate doctor or dentist on a recognised foundation programme, certain further specific requirements must be met.

Further details about these requirements are set out below.

8

WHAT THE RULES MEAN

Scoring 30 points for attributes: a valid CAS

Applicants must score 30 points for attributes. That can only be done by being issued with a valid CAS (Rules, para 245ZV(b); App A, paras 113–120). The CAS is a virtual, electronic document issued by the applicant's sponsor showing that it has accepted the applicant for a course of study. Each CAS has a unique reference number. It exists as a database record, rather than a piece of paper. The record made on the CAS contains details about the applicant (student) and their course. The particular course of study for which it has been issued is stated, as is the start and end date of the course. The CAS also has details confirming that the sponsor is happy that the applicant meets the requirements for the programme of study and about monies paid to the sponsor for course fees and/or living expenses.

When Tier 4 was launched on 31 March 2009, the document that educational sponsors issued was a 'visa letter'. This began to be phased out in favour of the CAS from 1 October 2009. From 22 February 2010, all Tier 4 applications are required to be supported by a CAS rather than a visa letter (see the amending Rules, Cm 7701 and HC 120).

When the applicant applies for entry clearance or leave, s/he must include on the application form the CAS reference number that s/he has been issued with (Tier 4 PG, para 96). A CAS may only be used to apply for leave once. If the application is refused and the applicant wants to apply again, a further CAS must be obtained.

However, in some cases one CAS will be sufficient for both a 'pre-sessional' course and a main course that follows it. A pre-sessional course may be an intensive English language course, or any other course, that the applicant takes to prepare him/her for a main course of study. In the following circumstances, a single CAS may be issued by the sponsor to cover both and UKBA will give leave for both courses at the same time (Tier 4 PG, paras 268–9, 272):

- the applicant has an *unconditional* offer of a place on his/her main course;
- the pre-sessional course is taken in order to prepare the applicant for study with either the same Tier 4 sponsor as the main course, or with a partner institution that is named on the Tier 4 sponsor's licence.

Where the offer of a place on the main course is conditional only, the applicant will need to apply for the pre-sessional course first and then obtain a new CAS and make a further application in order to study on the main course after the earlier one has been completed.

In order for the CAS to be accepted as valid and allowing the applicant to score points for attributes, a number of requirements must be met. These are set out below and relate to:

- procedural matters;
- the documents that were used to obtain a place on the course;
- the academic level of the course;
- work placements;
- English language proficiency;
- the academic level of English language courses;
- that the course leads to an 'approved' qualification;
- the site(s) where the applicant will be taught;
- the hours of the applicant's study; and
- the circumstances if the applicant is taking re-sits.

Procedural requirements

First, the following procedural requirements must be satisfied (Rules, App Λ, paras 116, 117):

- the application must be made within six months of the issue of the CAS – after six months the CAS expires;

- the application for entry clearance must be made within the three months before the start date of the course;
- the sponsor must not have withdrawn the offer of a place since the CAS was issued;
- the CAS must have been issued by an institution with a Tier 4 (General) licence;
- the sponsor educational institution must still hold the licence at the time that the application for entry clearance is determined;
- the CAS must contain "such information as is specified as mandatory" in Guidance published by UKBA;
- if the CAS was not issued for a course of studies, it must have been issued for a full-time, salaried, elected executive position as a student union sabbatical officer, to an applicant who is part-way through their studies, or who is being sponsored to fill the position in the academic year immediately after their graduation; and
- the CAS reference number that the applicant provides on their application matches a record that UKBA has, ie it matches a CAS Checking Service entry that names the applicant as the migrant and confirms that the stated sponsor is sponsoring him/her under Tier 4; and
- the CAS must not have been cancelled by the sponsor or UKBA since it was assigned.

Note that the 'CAS Checking Service' is defined in the Rules as (para 6):

"...a computerised interface with the [PBS] computer database which allows a [UKBA] caseworker or entry clearance officer assessing a migrant's application for entry clearance, leave to enter or leave to remain to access and review details of the migrant's [CAS], including details of the migrant's sponsor, together with details of the job and other details associated with the circumstances in which the [CAS] was issued."

For what happens to applicants and students where a sponsor's a licence is suspended or revoked, ▶see Chapter 4 135–138.

Requirement to produce documents used to obtain place on the course

As part of his/her application, the applicant must provide specified documents that s/he used to obtain the offer of a place on a course from the sponsor (Rules, App A, para 118(a)). The documents that are specified in the Guidance are (Tier 4 PG, para 97):

- the original certificate/s of qualification, clearly showing the applicant's name, the title of the award, the date of the award and the name of the awarding institution (original provisional certificates are not acceptable); or

- the original transcripts of results, clearly showing the applicant's name, the name of the academic institution, the course title and confirmation of the award.

It is important that the applicant knows what evidence was referred to in the CAS so that s/he can include it with his/her application (Tier 4 PG, para 98). In general terms, evidence produced in Tier 4 applications must be original documents and issued by an authorised official of the issuing organisation and on the official heading or stationery of the organisation. Documents not in English or Welsh must be accompanied by a certified translation that meets the requirements of the Guidance (for those requirements, see Tier 4 PG, paras 11–14).

If the course is at NQF level 3 or above and the applicant was assessed by the sponsor using means other than qualifications (eg references or a portfolio of work), it is not essential to produce those documents, although the sponsor should include details on the CAS of how they assessed the ability of the student. The same applies if the student has been offered a further course on the basis of progress made on existing studies (Tier 4 PG, paras 99–100).

English language courses Where the applicant is intending to study an English language course at level B2 of the Common European Framework of Reference for languages ('CEFR'), and the sponsor has assessed him/her by using references, then in addition to the above requirements, the sponsor must include details of those references on the CAS. For each such reference, the applicant must include with their application, the original reference which must be dated and contain: the applicant's name; the type/level of the course or previous experience; the date of the previous study/experience; and the referee's contact details. If the original reference is not available, a copy may be provided as long as a letter is also produced from the sponsor that confirms that the document is a true copy of the reference that they saw when assessing the applicant (Tier 4 PG, paras 107–111).

Postgraduate doctors/dentists taking a recognised foundation pro-gramme Included with the evidence of qualifications that these applicants send must be the original certificate and/or transcript of results of the UK-recognised degree in medicine or dentistry that s/he completed in the UK (Tier 4 PG, para 112).

General academic level of the course

On 12 November 2009, the then Prime Minister announced a review of Tier 4 based on concerns that it was being abused by economic migrants, particularly by those studying at below degree level and those studying on English language courses. On 10 February 2010, the Home Secretary made a statement announcing new measures to be taken intended to address issues raised during the review.

As far as the academic level of the courses that could be offered under Tier 4 were concerned, the Home Secretary announced that, from 6 April 2010, only Highly Trusted Sponsors (▶see below 287–291) would be permitted to offer courses at NQF Level 3 and its equivalents, eg level 6 of the SCQF. In addition, it was announced that courses that are below degree level (excluding foundation degrees) and which offer work placements could only be offered by those with HTS status (see immediately below for work placement courses). The idea was that all of these courses were attractive to economic migrants and should only be offered by sponsors with a strong record of student compliance. The introduction of the new category of HTS sponsors also went live from 6 April 2010. The changes were initially made by HC 439 from April 2010.

As a result, the present minimum academic requirements for those studying in England, Wales or Northern Ireland are (Rules, App A, para 120(a)(i)(ii) as inserted from 23 July 2010 by HC 382):

• the course must be at NQF Level 3 or above (in England, Wales and Northern Ireland) if the sponsor is:

– a HTS (below ▶287–291);

– an 'A' rated sponsor (▶see Chapter 4 101–102) *provided* CAS was assigned on or before 30 April 2010;

– an 'A' rated sponsor with an application for HTS status pending determination by UKBA *and* the CAS was assigned between 1 May 2010 and 30 June 2010; or

– a 'B' rated sponsor (▶see Chapter 4 101–102) *and* the CAS was assigned on or before 5 April 2010 (ie before the introduction of HTS status);

• if the sponsor does not have HTS status and none of the above transitional measures apply to the sponsor, then the course must be at the higher academic level of NQF level 4 or above.

The minimum academic requirements for those studying in Scotland are exactly the same as above, except that the required academic level where the sponsor is an HTS (or the above transitional measures apply) is that the course must be accredited at Level 6 or above in the SCQF by the Scottish Qualifications Authority. If not, then the course must be accredited at Level 7 or above in the SCQF (Rules, App A, para 120(a)(iii)(iv) as inserted by HC 382).

So, at present a sponsor without HTS status may still provide some courses at below degree level (degree level is NQF level 6/SCQF level 9) but those courses must be at NQF level 4 or above (SCQF level 7 or above). However, under the Government's latest proposals, made in December 2010, non-HTS providers will only be able to provide courses at degree level (for the proposals, ▶see 291–295). If these proposals are introduced, there is likely to be some transitional protection.

The above requirements do not apply if the course is a short-term study

8

abroad programme in the UK as a part of the applicant's qualification at an overseas higher education institution. That qualification must be confirmed as at the same as UK degree level by the National Recognition Centre for the UK ('NARIC') (see www.naric.org.uk). They also do not apply if the course is a recognised foundation programme for postgraduate doctors or dentists (App A, para 120(a)(v)(ix)).

Guidance indicates that an exception to the normal NQF level 3 threshold is that a Tier 4 (General) CAS may be issued to an applicant in order to attend a pre-sessional course at an independent school, which may include some academic study as well as English language, which the applicant undertakes in preparation for his/her full-time course of study at NQF level 3. The guidance states that such pre-sessional courses may be at any level (Student SG, para 193; Tier 4 PG, para 270). Other pre-sessional courses must meet the normal academic level (Student SG, para 229).

For the rules that apply to the academic level of English language courses ▶see below.

Requirements where the course offers a work placement

Where the course involves a work placement, the period spent on that placement must not be more than half of the total length of the course spent in the UK *unless* there is a UK statutory requirement that the placement must be more than half the length of the course. If the course is below degree level (excluding foundation courses) only sponsors with HTS status (or a sponsor to which one of the above transitional provisions relating to sponsorship applies ▶see under 'general academic level of course' at 254) may offer a course with a work placement (Rules, App A, para 120(e)). The placement should form an assessed part of the course (Tier 4 PG, para 263). Students who are enrolled on a higher education course at an overseas higher education institution who are coming to the UK to do part of their course can also spend some of their time in the UK on a work placement – again the work done must not be for a period of over 50% of the total course time (Tier 4 SG, para 238).

Under the present proposals (▶see below 293), the ratio between work placement and study would be changed so that applicants could only spend a third of their time on placements.

English language proficiency

Another of the Home Secretary's measures announced on 10 February 2010, applying to students studying on all courses, including English language courses, was to require applicants to take and provide the results of a secure test to show that their English language proficiency was at least at level B1 on the CEFR. According to the Home Secretary's statement, the Prime Minister's review found that students were coming to study at below degree level with a very low proficiency in English. The introduction of a test was seen as better than simply allowing sponsors to make their own assessment because, according to the Home Office, the test would (Explanatory Memo to HC 382, para 7.10):

" ... help ensure that sponsors are not duped by students offering false or fake documents to prove their English language ability."

The new secure test The requirement to take the new secure test was introduced into the Rules by HC 382 from 12 August 2010 subject to exceptions and transitional provisions partly depending on when the CAS was issued (►see below). The test certificate must be issued from an English language test provider approved for the purpose by the Secretary of State and which is "within its validity date" (Rules, App A, para 118(b)(vii)(3)). A list of the approved language tests, including the period for which they are valid, together with the scores that applicants must obtain is contained on the UKBA website at http://www.ukba.homeoffice. gov.uk/studyingintheuk/adult-students/evidence/visa-letter/ (Student SG, para 208). Where the requirement applies, the test certificate must be provided. Unless the applicant is exempt from sitting any component of the test through disability, the applicant must achieve or exceed level B1 in *all four* of the test components: reading, writing, speaking and listening (Rules, App A, para 118(b)(vii)(3)(ii)).

Exceptions There is no specific test or check on English language proficiency that applies in any of the following six circumstances (Rules, App A, para 118(b)(i)–(vi)):

- the CAS was assigned before 3 March 2010 (although note that any such CAS will now be out of date if it has not been used to make an application; App A, para 116(a));
- the course is at degree level of study;
- the course is a foundation degree course;
- the course is a pre-sessional course before a degree level course;
- the applicant is a Government-sponsored student and the course is an English language course; or
- the applicant is a national of one of the following (majority English speaking) countries: Antigua and Barbuda, Australia, the Bahamas, Barbados, Belize, Canada, Dominica, Grenada, Guyana, Jamaica, New Zealand, St Kitts and Nevis, St Lucia, St Vincent and the Grenadines, Trinidad and Tobago or the USA, and provides the "specified documents".

In the above, 'degree level study' means a course which leads to a recognised UK degree at bachelor's level or above, or an equivalent qualification that is at level 6 (or above) of the NQF, or level 9 (or above) of the SCQF (Rules, para 6). 'Foundation degree' means a programme of study leading to a qualification awarded by a higher education institution with degree-awarding powers and which is at a minimum of level 5 (or equivalent) on the NQF (Rules, para 6). In Scotland, level 8 SCQF is equivalent to foundation degree level.

8

Circumstances in which the sponsor must confirm the applicant's language proficiency If none of the above six exceptions apply but the case falls into any of the following three categories, the applicant does not have to take the secure test itself. However, when the sponsor comes to issue the CAS, it must confirm that the applicant is proficient in English to level B1 of the CEFR (Rules, App A, para 118(b)(vii)(1)(2)(4)):

- the course is an English language course, in which case the applicant must provide documents to support the sponsor's assessment of his/her knowledge of English (▶see also below under 'academic level of English language courses' imposing the B2 level for the course itself from 23 July 2010 only);

- the CAS was issued before 12 August 2010 (but after 3 March 2010), in which case the applicant must provide documents to support the sponsor's assessment of his/her knowledge of English;

- the applicant has successfully completed a course either as a Tier 4 (Child) Student, or as a 'student' under the old Rules in place before 31 March 2009, where s/he was given leave while under 18 and that leave was at least six months in length and ended within two years of the date that the sponsor assigned the CAS.

In the above cases, it is for sponsors to explain on the CAS how the student's English language ability has been assessed and to state the level which the applicant has reached (Student SG, paras 201, 204, 302). Examples given by UKBA of how it might be assessed are: conducting an interview with the student in English; verifying that the applicant's existing studies have been taught in English, or that the applicant holds a recognised English qualification (Student SG, para 300). If the assessment is based on a qualification or test result, the relevant certificate should be included with the applicant's application for leave (Student SG, para 302; Tier 4 PG, para 101).

Proposal for change Under the Government's December 2010 proposals, the level of English language proficiency would be raised from B1 to the upper intermediate level of B2. In addition, it is proposed that even those studying on courses at degree level or above would have to provide independent evidence of their competency by taking and passing the secure language test (▶below 292).

Academic level of English language courses

UKBA considers that a course is one of English language if the student is studying English as a foreign language. A course that contains English language with non-English language subjects as well is not considered to be an English language course, nor is a course that is assessed against the NQF framework eg an English language A-level (Tier 4 PG, paras 84–5; Student SG, paras 199–200).

On 10 February 2010, the Home Secretary announced that, from 3 March

2010, the Tier 4 Guidance would be changed to raise the minimum level of English language course that could be studied under Tier 4 from 'A2' to 'B2' of the CEFR (roughly GCSE standard). There would be exemptions for those sponsored by overseas Governments and for students on pre-sessional English language courses which prepare them for full degree courses. The relevant changes were made to the Guidance but with no accompanying changes to the Rules themselves.

However, on 9 July 2010, the Administrative Court decided the case of *R (English UK) v Secretary of State for the Home Department*. It held that, following *Pankina*, the raising of the academic level by Guidance alone was unlawful and could only be done by amending the Rules themselves (for full discussion of these cases, ▶see Chapter 2 42–45, 47–49). Shortly after the judgment, the Home Office responded by putting the relevant changes into the Rules themselves (see HC 382). As the Explanatory Memo to HC 382 makes clear, the amendment to the Tier 4 Rules "restores the position taken before…judgment was handed down" (see paras 7.11–7.13).

The academic requirements for English language courses, as set out in the Rules *from 23 July 2010*, are that the course must be an English language course at level B2 or above of the CEFR (Rules, App A, para 120(a)(vi) as amended by HC 382 from that date). There are three exceptions (App A, para 120(a)(vii)(viii); Student SG, para 193):

- if the applicant is a Government Sponsored student, the course may be an English language course at any level;
- if the course is a pre-sessional course before a degree course (▶see further below), the course may be an English language course at any level;
- if the CAS was assigned before 23 July 2010, the course may be an English language course at the much lower level of A2 or above of the CEFR (this last exception recognises, in line with the *English UK* case, that the requirement that the course be at level B2 was not lawful until it was introduced by the Rules themselves from 23 July 2010).

For the purpose of the above exceptions, UKBA interprets 'pre-sessional' course to mean (Tier 4 PG, para 270):

- a pre-sessional English language course which the student takes immediately before taking up an unconditional offer of a full-time course of study at NQF level 6 (degree level) or above, where both courses are covered by a single CAS (for such circumstances, ▶see above 252) issued by a higher education provider acting as the student's sponsor; or
- a pre-sessional English language course which will allow a student, if s/he successfully completes it, to progress to his/her full time course of study at NQF level 6 or above for which s/he already possesses a conditional offer from a higher education provider and where the same provider is to be the sponsor for both courses and has assigned a CAS for the first course.

8

Providers of English language courses do not have to obtain HTS (Student SG, para 194).

Alternative route: student visitor An alternative route for those wanting to come to the UK to study English language, or indeed any short course, is to come as a student visitor. Those using this route can study English language courses at any level. In addition, in a statement on 13 December 2010, the Minister, recognising that the stringent academic levels imposed under Tier 4 "do not meet the special needs of the English language sector", announced a concession outside the Rules for English language courses. Under the concession, student visitors on English language courses may be admitted to the UK for up to 11 months (the maximum period under the Rules is six months). The concession came into operation on 10 January 2011. For further details about the student visitor category, ▶see Chapter 10 336–338.

The Government's December 2010 proposals (▶see below 292) are for the minimum academic level for English language courses to be raised to C1 CEFR for which the applicant would have to show an existing level of B2.

Approved qualification

Except in the case of pre-sessional courses, the course must lead to an 'approved qualification' as defined in UKBA's Sponsor Guidance (Rules, App A, para 120(b); Student SG, para 229). An 'approved course' for UKBA purposes is one that is (Student SG at para 212):

- validated by Royal Charter;
- awarded by a recognised body on the 'recognised bodies' list operated by the Department for Innovation, Universities and Skills;
- recognised by one or more recognised bodies via a formal articulation agreement with the awarding body;
- in England, Wales and Northern Ireland, on the National Database of Accredited Qualifications at NQF level 3 or above;
- in Scotland, accredited at level 6 or above on the SCQF by the Scottish Qualifications Authority;
- an overseas qualification which is at a level equivalent to level 3 or above on the NQF (UK NARIC advises on the validity of such qualifications); or
- covered by a formal legal agreement between a UK-recognised body and another education provider or awarding body.

The Student Sponsor Guidance indicates that it is not necessary that pre-sessional courses lead to a recognised qualification (SG, para 212).

Place of study

All the study on the course must take place on the premises of the sponsoring educational institution, except when the applicant is on a work placement (Rules, App A, para 120(c)). The use of a temporary location authorised by the sponsor is acceptable. So, for example, there is nothing wrong with field trips. However, the time that an applicant spends at a work placement on different premises cannot contribute to the 15 hours per week of classroom study that is required below degree level courses (Sponsor SG, para 213).

Nature of course/hours of study

The course must be either (Rules, App A, para 120(d), Student SG, para 195):

- a 'full-time' course at degree level;
- an overseas course of degree level study that is recognised as being equivalent to a UK Higher Education course and is being provided by an overseas Higher Education Institution; or
- if not at degree level, a full-time course of study involving a minimum of 15 hours per week of organised daytime study. UKBA interprets 'organised' as meaning classroom and 'daytime' as meaning between 8.00 and 18.00, Monday to Friday.

Writing-up Where a postgraduate student is writing-up a thesis, UKBA states that a Tier 4 sponsor may still continue its sponsorship provided the sponsor requires the student's continued participation and provided the sponsor believes it can continue to discharge its sponsor duties relating to that student. If the student's participation is not required for 60 days or more, the sponsor must, at the very least, be confident that it can meet its sponsor duties in relation to the particular student (Student SG, para 277).

Re-sits

If the sponsor holds a standard ('A' or 'B') rated licence and the applicant is re-sitting the examination, or repeating a module of a course, s/he must be doing either his/her first or second re-sit of that exam or module. Further re-sits or repeats are not permitted. This restriction does not apply if the sponsor is an HTS. HTS providers can assign a CAS to allow more than two re-sits or repeats provided that the re-sit/repeat has been approved by the sponsor's own internal panels and boards who authorise re-sits or repeats in exceptional circumstances.

UBKA states that it retains the right to seek further information if "unusual patterns" are detected relating to re-sits (HTS SG, paras 11, 47–8; Student SG, paras 273). UKBA also states that where an applicant has to do a re-sit or a repeat, the sponsor should review the student's abilities in order to decide whether or not s/he is likely to be able to pass the course and, in the light of that, whether to continue sponsoring him/her (Student SG, paras 274).

8

Intention and ability to follow course

The Student Sponsor Guidance states that a CAS may only be assigned under Tier 4 if the sponsor is satisfied that the student is able and intends to follow the particular course of study. It also states that it is the sponsor's responsibility to consider the applicant's abilities and to state what evidence they have used to make their assessment. This may be done by confirming qualifications that the student already holds and by verifying them (Student SG, paras 297–8). The Sponsor Guidance states that a CAS does not guarantee admission partly because the immigration authorities themselves may 'cancel' the certificate if they find that the sponsor was not entitled to issue it (as well as if there are any outstanding requirements of the Rules that are not satisfied) (SG, paras 11, 153, 168, 173–4).

'Intention and ability' to follow a course does not form part of the Immigration Rules. Indeed an important part of the purpose of the PBS was to remove (as it has) 'subjective' criteria such as "intention" and "ability" to follow a course from the requirements of the Rules but to devolve any decision-making in those areas to sponsors. However, the Guidance referred to above seems to suggest that UKBA might refuse an application by second-guessing a sponsor's assessment of the student. The absence of a provision in the Rules to refuse on these grounds, as well as the lack of any statutory foundation for the sponsorship scheme itself, means that the legal basis on which this could be done is very shaky indeed.

The following extract of an email from UKBA International Group to the UK Council for International Student Affairs (UKCISA), dated 10 November 2010, explains how entry clearance managers in China have been approaching the issue:

"Paragraph 297 of the sponsor guidance says 'A confirmation of acceptance for studies may only be assigned under Tier 4 if the sponsor is satisfied that the student both *intends* and is able to follow the course of study concerned'.

"Institutions have an obligation to satisfy themselves both of an applicant's academic ability and intention to complete a course, how they do this is at their own discretion, but we are always happy to offer advice should it be requested. This summer we have processed and issued 1,000s of student visas and all Tier 4 applications go through a process of risk assessment. In the minority of cases where we identify concerns with an application, we will often call the applicant in for an interview.

"An Entry Clearance Officer has no grounds to refuse an application if the applicant presents a valid CAS, proof of funds and genuine supporting documents. However, on occasion the interview leads to a suspicion that the applicant may not be genuinely intending to complete their course or even enroll on it in the first place, irrespective of their ability to score 40 points. Of the 1,000s of applications that have been processed in China this summer, interviews with fraction [sic], around 100 applicants, have caused concern.

"Whenever concerns are raised with an applicant's intentions, we write to sponsors alerting them. It is not in the sponsor's or UKBA's interests to issue a Tier 4 visa to a non genuine student. It is entirely up to an institution to choose how they wish to progress, however it should be remembered that we only write where we have serious concerns. Before writing every application will have gone through a risk assessment process, been assessed by an Entry Clearance Officer, been interviewed by an Entry Clearance Officer and translator, and then the case will have been reviewed by an Entry Clearance Manager. The alert flags the concern to the sponsor giving them the opportunity to further investigate the applicant to satisfy themselves that the applicant is genuine. If the sponsor is unable to satisfy themselves that the applicant is genuine, we recommend they withdraw sponsorship. Of the 100 cases we have referred back to institutions this summer, around 75% have decided to withdraw sponsorship.

"If an institution chooses to maintain sponsorship then we will issue the visa. However if the applicant is later found in breach of the immigration rules, considering we have explicitly highlighted concerns around the case, further action may be taken".

Where the course is below degree level

The Rules state that, if the course is below degree level, the grant of entry clearance must not lead to the applicant having spent more than three years in the UK "as a Tier 4 Migrant", since the age of 18, studying courses that are not at degree level (Rules, para 245ZV(g)). Note that time spent studying at below degree level under the student rules in force before the introduction of Tier 4 (ie before 31 March 2009), will not count towards these three years (Student SG, para 245).

In addition, for courses at below degree level, the Rules repeat themselves by stating that only a HTS sponsor can offer: a work placement (unless the course is a foundation degree); or courses at level 3 on the NQF or level 6 on the SCQF (Rules, para 245ZV(g)(1)(2)). These conditions are also imposed under the Rules which state when a CAS is valid and capable of allowing the applicant to score points (▶see above 254–256).

Scoring points for maintenance

The applicant must score 10 points for maintenance under Appendix C of the Rules (Rules, para 245ZV(c); App C, para 10). In order to score those points, applicants have to show that they have a prescribed level of funds that is "available" to them (App C, para 11). The Rules also state that the applicant must have the prescribed level of funds as at the date of the application (Appendix C, para 1A(a)) but there are specific Rules about what funds must be shown over what period (▶see below).

Further details about maintenance and the relevant case law as it applies to all PBS cases is set out in Chapter 5 ▶see 181. For the relevance of human rights arguments where the strict maintenance requirements are not shown to be met, ▶see 414–420.

The requirements set out below that are specifically applicable to the Tier 4 (General) Student category, are contained in Appendix C at paragraphs 10–14 and in the table that accompanies those paragraphs. Where the applicant also has dependants applying to enter or remain with him/her, they must also meet certain maintenance requirements, for which, ▶see Chapter 5 413–420.

The prescribed level of funds that must be shown to be "available" to the applicant under the Tier 4 (General) Student category depends on three main factors:

- whether the applicant has an "established presence" studying in the UK;
- whether the applicant is studying in "inner London" or elsewhere in the UK; and
- the length of the course.

The Rules set a prescribed level of funds that must be shown for both the course fees and for personal living costs. Obviously, the precise amount required for the course fees will also depend on what those fees are as shown by the Tier 4 sponsor on the CAS.

Established presence studying in the UK An applicant has an "established presence" studying in the UK if *either* (Rules, App C, para 14):

- s/he has completed a course in the UK in the last four months and that course of was at least six months long and it was completed within their last period of leave either as a Tier 4 migrant, under the old student rules or as a postgraduate doctor or dentist; or
- the applicant is applying for continued study on a course that s/he has completed at least six months of and which s/he has been studying within the last four months.

In *DN (student – course 'completed' – established presence) Kenya*, the Upper Tribunal considered that the meaning of "completed" a course for the purposes of showing an 'established presence' did not mean "successfully completed". So, if the applicant is relying on a course that has concluded (the first bullet point above), s/he does not have to show that s/he has passed the relevant exams: it will be enough to show that s/he attended and studied on the course to its conclusion.

Studying in inner London An applicant will be considered to be studying in "inner London" if the institution, or branch of the institution at which the applicant is studying, is based in a London Borough specified in UKBA Guidance (App C, para 12). Under that Guidance, study is in inner London if it takes place in any of the following London boroughs: Camden, City of London, Hackney, Hammersmith and Fulham, Haringey, Islington, Kensington and Chelsea, Lambeth, Lewisham, Newham, Southwark, Tower Hamlets, Wandsworth or Westminster (Tier 4 PG, para 123). Where the applicant's studies take place partly in inner London and partly outside inner London, UKBA will treat the study as in inner London if the applicant's CAS states that the applicant will be spending the majority of their time studying at sites situated in inner London (App C, para 12; Tier 4 PG, para 123). In order to check whether their site is in inner London, applicants can enter the relevant postcode on the following website: www.aboutmyvote.co.uk.

Where the applicant does not have an established presence studying in the UK

If the applicant does *not* have an established studying presence (▶see above) in the UK and is studying in *inner London* (▶see above) (App C, paras 10–14 and table):

- if the length of the course is a year or more, the applicant must have the full course fees for the first academic year of the course;
- if the length of the course is less than a year, the applicant must have the full course fees for the entire course;

plus

- the applicant must have £800 for living costs for each month of the course but up to a maximum of nine months.

Note that when calculating living costs for each month, UKBA will round any part of a month up to the next whole month. So a student studying on a course for five months and two weeks, will have to show living costs for six months (Tier 4 PG, para 133).

If the applicant does *not* have an established studying presence in the UK and is studying in *outer London or elsewhere* (App C, paras 10–14 and table):

- if the length of the course is a year or more, the applicant must have the full course fees for the first academic year of the course;
- if the length of the course is less than a year, the applicant must have the full course fees for the entire course;

plus

- the applicant must have £600 for living costs for each month of the course but up to a maximum of nine months.

Where the applicant does have an established presence studying in the UK

If the applicant *does* have an established studying presence in the UK and is studying in *inner London* (App C, paras 10–14 and table):

- if the applicant is applying part-way through an academic year, s/he must have the full course fees required for the rest of the academic year;

8

- if the applicant will continue or begin a new course at the start of the next academic year, s/he must have the full course fees required for that next academic year;
- if the course is less than a year in length, s/he must have the full course fees required for the entire course;

plus

- the applicant must have £800 for living costs for each month of the course but up to a maximum of two months.

If the applicant *does* have an established studying presence in the UK and is studying in *outer London or elsewhere* (App C, paras 10–14 and table):

- if the applicant is applying part-way through an academic year, s/he must have the full course fees required for the rest of the academic year;
- if the applicant will continue or begin a new course at the start of the next academic year, s/he must have the full course fees required for that next academic year;
- if the course is less than a year in length, s/he must have the full course fees required for the entire course;

plus

- the applicant must have £600 for maintenance for living costs for each month of the course but up to a maximum of two months.

At what point in time must the applicant hold the required funds?

When the Rules were first laid, they did not state a period over which applicants had to hold the required level of funds. That was left to Policy Guidance instead. However, in *Pankina*, the Court of Appeal had to consider the requirement, contained in guidance applicable to Tier 1 (Post-Study Work) cases, that applicants must have held the required level of funds for 'three months'. The Court found that it was unlawful for such time periods to be contained in Policy Guidance alone: they had to be in the Rules (for further details about *Pankina*, ▶see Chapter 2 42–45). The Government responded by issuing new Rules (HC 382 inserting new para 1A into App C of the Rules from 23 July 2010). As far as Tier 4 is concerned, the relevant new wording is:

"1A...(c) If the applicant is applying for entry clearance or leave to remain as a Tier 4 Migrant, the applicant must have the [relevant funds] for a consecutive 28-day period of time, ending not earlier than one calendar month before the date of the application." (see also Tier 4 PG, para 150)

This means that the applicant:

- must show that s/he held the relevant funds over a continuous period of 28 days; and
- the last day of that 28-day period must be any day between the first day

of the calendar month before the date of the application and the date of the application itself.

For details of the transitional policy that applies in cases that pre-date 23 July 2010, when the '28-day' period was made part of the Rules, ▶see Chapter 2 46–47.

Evidence that must be produced

Applicants are required to produce the documents "specified" in Guidance in order to show that they have the required level of funds (Appendix C, para 1A(e)). As we indicate below, after *Pankina*, the extent to which compliance with each of the precise requirements of the Guidance can be rigidly insisted upon by the Home Office is likely to be the subject of ongoing debate and controversy. Immediately below, we summarise the relevant requirements of the Tier 4 Guidance, but this must now be read with reference to the developing case law following *Pankina* which also follows below.

According to the Guidance, the evidence must be of (Tier 4 PG, para 136):

• cash funds, including a current or savings account;

• a loan; or

• official financial or government sponsorship.

The Guidance states that it is not acceptable to produce other documents such as evidence of shares, bonds, overdraft facilities, credit cards and pension funds (Tier 4 PG, para 136).

The Rules state that UKBA Guidance may set out when funds will be "available" to the applicant, including the circumstances in which the money must be the applicant's own money and the extent to which a sponsorship arrangement will be sufficient (App C, para 13). The Guidance states that students can use money that is held by their parents or legal guardian but that they will have to provide evidence of their relation to the parent or legal guardian and also that the parent/legal guardian has given the applicant permission to use the funds (Tier 4 PG, para 135). According to the Guidance, in order to show the relationship with the parent/s or legal guardian, applicants should produce either (Tier 4 PG, para 158):

• their birth certificate showing the name/s of their parent/s;

• their adoption certificate also showing the names of their parent/s or guardian; or

• a court document (original or notarised copy) naming the legal guardian of the applicant.

In order to show that the parent/s or guardian have given their permission to the applicant to use the funds, the applicant should provide a letter from them confirming the relationship and their consent to the applicant using the funds to study in the UK (Tier 4 PG, para 158). The Guidance also states that if the student wants to produce a joint account as proof of his/her money, s/he must be named on the account along with the other person (Tier 4 PG, par 156).

Cash funds According to the Guidance, applicants can produce any of the following documents (Tier 4 PG, para 156):

- Personal bank or building society statements covering the relevant 28-day period and showing either the applicant's or their parent/s' or legal guardian's name, the account number, the date of the statement, the financial institution's name and logo and the amount of money available. Ad-hoc statements on the bank's letterhead are also acceptable (this does not include mini-statements from cash points). Electronic statements from online accounts can be provided, as long as they contain all of the above details and the student provides a supporting letter from his/her bank, on headed paper, confirming that the statements are authentic. In the alternative, an electronic bank statement with the official stamp of the bank will be accepted, provided the stamp appears on every page. UKBA states it will not accept statements showing the balance on a particular day as such statements do not show that the applicant holds the funds over the full period required.

- Building society pass book covering the relevant 28-day period and which shows the applicant's or their parent/s' or legal guardian's name, the account number, the financial institution's name and logo and the amount of money available.

- Letter from the applicant's bank or building society confirming that funds have been held for the relevant 28-day period and showing the applicant's or their parent/s' or legal guardian's name, the account number, the date of the letter, the financial institution's name and logo, the money in the student's account and that there is enough money in the account to cover the course fees and living costs.

- Letter from a financial institution regulated either by the Financial Services Authority or, in the case of overseas accounts, the home regulator (ie the official regulatory body for the country where the institution is and where the money is held), confirming that funds have been held for the relevant 28-day period and showing the applicant's or their parent/s' or legal guardian's name, the account number, the date of the letter, the financial institution's name and logo and the money in the student's account.

Loan According to the Guidance, applicants can produce a letter from a financial institution regulated by either the Financial Services Authority, or in the case of overseas accounts, the home regulator, which confirms the loan. The loan letter must show the applicant's name, the date of the letter, the financial institution's name and logo and the money available as a loan. Loans held in a parent/s or legal guardian's name cannot be used as evidence of money held by the student. Where students are travelling from overseas then, unless the loan is an academic or student loan from his/her country's national government and the loan will be released to the student by his/her national government on arrival, the funds must be available before the applicant travels to the UK. The loan should not be subject to any conditions other than that the student is granted leave under Tier 4 (Tier 4 PG, para 156).

Official financial sponsorship If the Tier 4 sponsor includes details of official financial sponsorship that they are giving to the student on the CAS, then no further documents are needed (Tier 4 PG, para 148). If those details are not included on the CAS, then the applicant will need to produce a letter of confirmation from his/her official financial sponsor on letter headed paper or stationery (with official stamp) with full details of the sponsorship as set out in the Guidance (Tier 4 PG, para 149). If the sponsor is only going to provide some of the funds, then the applicant will have to show that s/he has the rest of the required amounts available to him/her (Tier 4 PG, para 144).

Money that has already been paid to the sponsor for fees, or for university or college accommodation, will be deducted from the amount that needs to be shown, provided the applicant can demonstrate that it has been paid (Tier 4 PG, paras 140–141). If the applicant has provided funds to his/her sponsor for fees and/or living costs and the sponsor confirms the details of those monies as paid on the CAS, then no further documents are required (Tier 4 PG, para 146). If the Tier 4 sponsor has not included those details on the CAS, the student must include in their application an original paper receipt issued by the Tier 4 sponsor confirming what has been paid (Tier 4 PG, para 147).

Tier 4 (General) Student case-law following *Pankina*

The case-law following *Pankina* (for which, ▶see 47–52) has already undermined UKBA's right to rigidly rely on the Guidance as a source of additional mandatory requirements not otherwise contained in the Rules. The case-law on maintenance is looked at in greater depth in our section dealing with the maintenance requirements and the PBS categories generally (▶see Chapter 5 181). However of immediate note are the three Tier 4 (General) Student cases, all heard on 23 July 2010 by the same constitution of the Upper Tribunal (including the President and Vice-President). In all three cases, the Tribunal rejected attempts to use the Policy Guidance as a means of restricting the ability of applicants to show that they satisfied the maintenance requirements as contained in the Rules themselves.

In *FA & AA (PBS: effect of Pankina) Nigeria*, the UT had to consider whether a Tier 4 (General) Student could rely on funds in a bank account that was in the sole name of her husband. The Tribunal held that once it is accepted that the Guidance does not have the status of Immigration Rules, there was no reason why the applicant could not show that she met the requirements of the Rules to have the required level of funds "available" to her by a bank account in her husband's name (paras 18, 21). The

Tribunal allowed the appeal having regard to the fact that it was clear that there was no reason to doubt the existence of the funds, or that the husband had made them available to his wife.

Applicants must beware though. In *FA*, there was clear evidence that the husband would make the funds available to the applicant – the main reason he, rather than she, actually held them, was cultural. An applicant must show, as a matter of fact, that the funds are "available" to them and that may, of course, be more difficult if the monies relied on are held by others. The evidence that funds are in fact available may need to be more cogent if those funds are not held or owned by the applicant.

The UT reached a similar conclusion to that in *FA* in *CDS (PBS: 'available': Article 8) Brazil*. In that case, it allowed an appeal brought by another Tier 4 (General) Student who relied on funds held by two sponsors who happened to be doctors and who were not the parents/legal guardian of the applicant. The Tribunal stated (para 13):

"In the absence of specific additional requirements of the Immigration Rules, it seems to us that funds are 'available' to a claimant at the material time if they belong to a third party but that party is shown to be willing to deploy them to support the claimant for the purpose contemplated."

In *HM & Others (PBS – legitimate expectation) Malawi*, the appellants had evidence of very substantial sums held in an account in their joint names in the National Bank of Malawi. The difficulty was that the prevailing Malawian currency exchange controls would only permit them to transfer a total of US$1,000 to the UK. The appellants proposed instead to obtain access to sterling in the UK from people who wished to remit funds to Malawi to whom they (the appellants) would transfer the equivalent funds from their Malawian bank account. The UT held that the fact that the appellants had the necessary funds under their control in an overseas bank account was sufficient to show that they were "available" to them for the purposes of the Rules. The appellants clearly had the ability to circumvent the exchange control regulations and the UT was unwilling to impose a limitation on the meaning of the Rules such that the funds would not be considered "available" because they could not be immediately accessed due to the exchange controls (see paras 11, 13).

Further in *HM*, the UT noted that the relevant Policy Guidance set out that proof of availability of funds could be shown by bank statements of overseas accounts provided that the statements complied with certain requirements. On that basis, the Tribunal made the further alternative finding also in favour of the appellants that they had a legitimate expectation that the Secretary of State would deal with their application on the basis of the Guidance (see para 14).

Government or scholarship agency sponsored students

If the applicant is presently being sponsored by a Government or international scholarship agency, or within the last 12 months has come to the end of such a period of sponsorship, s/he must provide evidence of the written consent of the sponsoring Government or agency to the application. The Rules state that s/he must provide documents that are "specified" in the Guidance to show that this requirement has been met (Rules, para 245ZV(f)). The Tier 4 PG refers to these official sponsors as being the UK government, the student's home government, the British Council, any international organisation, international company, university or UK independent school (para 38). For these purposes "sponsored" means wholly supported in terms of both fees and living costs (Tier 4 PG, para 40).

As far as providing "specified documents" is concerned, the Guidance does not seem to go much further than the Rules. It states (Tier 4 PG, para 41):

"The student must provide us with his/her financial sponsor's unconditional consent in writing. This must confirm that the sponsor has no objection to the student continuing his/her studies in the [UK]."

Academic Technology Approval Scheme

An applicant who wishes to undertake any of the following studies must hold a valid Academic Technology Approval Scheme (ATAS) clearance (Rules, para 245ZV(d)):

- postgraduate studies leading to a doctorate or Master's degree by research in one of the subjects that are listed in paragraph 1 of Appendix 6 of the Rules;
- postgraduate studies leading to a taught Master's degree in one of the subjects listed in paragraph 2 of Appendix 6 of the Rules; or
- a period of study or research in excess of six months in one of the subjects listed in paragraphs 1 or 2 of Appendix 6 of the Rules at an institution of higher education where this forms part of an overseas postgraduate qualification.

The subjects listed in paragraph 1 of Appendix 6 are all related to: medicine; biological sciences; veterinary sciences, agriculture and related subjects; physical sciences; mathematical and computer sciences; and technologies. The subjects listed in paragraph 2 of Appendix 6 (taught Master's courses) are: materials science; physics (including nuclear physics); mechanical engineering; aerospace engineering; and materials technology/materials science. All of these subject are identified by their 'JAC' code references.

The aim of the Rule is to exclude the possibility of applicants making use of knowledge and experience gained through UK education for the purposes of the proliferation of weapons of mass destruction. In order to obtain an ATAS clearance, applicants must apply online on the Foreign and Commonwealth Office website (www.fco.go.uk/atas). When the applicant comes to apply for entry clearance/leave, s/he must include a print-out of the ATAS clearance certificate (Tier 4 PG, paras 103, 106).

Postgraduate Doctors or Dentists

If the applicant wishes to be a Postgraduate Doctor or Dentist on a recognised foundation programme, she must (Rules, para 2245ZV(e)):

- have successfully completed a recognised UK degree in medicine or dentistry from either an institution with a Tier 4 licence, a UK publicly-funded institution of further or higher education, or a UK *bona fide* private education institution which maintains satisfactory records of enrolment and attendance;

- previously have been granted leave either as a Tier 4 (General) Student, or under the previous 'student' category for the final academic year of the studies referred to immediately above and for at least one other academic year of those studies;

- if s/he has previously been granted leave as a Postgraduate Doctor or Dentist, not be seeking entry clearance, or leave to enter or remain, to a date beyond three years from the date on which s/he was first granted leave to enter or remain in that category; and

- if s/he has previously been granted leave as a Tier 4 (General) Student to take a course as a Postgraduate Doctor or Dentist, s/he must not be seeking entry clearance or leave to enter or remain to a date beyond three years from the date on which s/he was first granted leave to take such a course.

Those applying as Postgraduate Doctors or Dentists on a recognised foundation programmes must have a valid CAS from the 'Foundation Programme Office' which is the only sponsor that is licensed for these applicants (Sponsor SG, para 219).

Dependants

Partners and children of those given, or to be granted, leave in the Tier 4 (General) Student category may apply for leave as dependants. For full details about the requirements to be satisfied by PBS dependants, including Tier 4 dependants, ▶see Chapter 5 194–203.

Note that, from the outset of Tier 4 in March 2009, Tier 4 dependants have not been permitted to take employment in the UK if the Tier 4 (General) Student is granted leave for less than 12 months (Rules, paras 319D(b)(iv), 319I(b)(iii)). The following further restrictions were added from 3 March 2010 by HC 367.

- Partners and children of a Tier 4 (General) Student who is following a course of study of six months or less in duration can no longer be granted leave to enter/remain in the UK as dependants (Rules, paras 319C(i), 319H(i)).

- Partners and children admitted as the dependants of a Tier 4 (General) Student who is following a course of study that is below degree level (excepting foundation degree courses) are not permitted to take employment in the UK (Rules, paras 319D(b)(v), 319I(b)(iv)). If such dependants wish to work, they must qualify for a category of leave permitting them to work in their own right. To facilitate this for Tier 4 dependants who are already in the UK, the amending Rules made from 3 March 2010 made provision to allow them to 'switch' to remain in the UK in the following categories: Tier 1 (General); Tier 2 (General); Tier 2 (Minister of Religion); Tier 2 (Sportsperson) (Rules, paras 245C(f)(xx), 245ZF(e)(xxv)).

The above two changes do not affect applications made by Tier 4 dependants before 3 March 2010 (see the preamble to HC 367).

The Government's present proposals are to impose yet further restrictions on Tier 4 dependants (▶see below 293).

Dependants of those who still have leave granted under the old student rules that were in force before 31 March 2009 may still apply under the rules for dependants of those students (Rules, paras 76–81). They must show that they can be maintained and accommodated without recourse to public funds but the prescribed levels of funds set out under the PBS scheme do not apply and nor does the Policy Guidance. Leave granted under these rules allows access to employment provided the student has been granted leave for at least 12 months (Rules, paras 77, 80).

PERIOD AND CONDITIONS OF LEAVE FOR TIER 4 (GENERAL) STUDENTS

Entry clearance/leave to enter will be granted for the duration of the course *plus* a short period both before and after the course in accordance with the table ▶below (Rules, para 245ZW(a)(b)). The periods of leave and conditions that they are subject to are the same when UKBA grants leave to remain (Rules, para 245ZY).

Indefinite leave

There are no specific Rules allowing Tier 4 Migrants to obtain indefinite leave. In order to obtain indefinite leave, students will have to eventually qualify under Tiers 1 or 2. A popular route has been to switch into Tier 1 (Post-Study Work) and then Tier 2 (▶see further below 279).

Conditions of leave

The conditions that will be attached to the leave are (Rules, para 245ZW(c)):

- no recourse to public funds;

TIER 4 (GENERAL): PERIODS OF LEAVE TO ENTER GRANTED

Type of course	Period of entry clearance to be granted before the course starts	Period of entry clearance to be granted after the course ends
12 months or more	1 month	4 months
6 months or more but less than 12 months	1 month	2 months
Pre-sessional course of less than 6 months	1 month	1 month
Course of less than 6 months that is not a pre-sessional course	7 days	7 days
Postgraduate doctor or dentist	1 month	1 month

Source: Rules, para 245ZW; see also the table in the Student SG at para 243.

- registration with the police if such is required by the Rules (see Rules, para 326);
- no employment *except* as set out below (and the exceptions are significant);
- no study at any institution other than that of the applicant's official sponsor;
- no study prior to UKBA's decision on an application (or determination on an appeal from it) unless the application was supported with a CAS assigned by a HTS and was made while the applicant still had existing leave, in which case the study must be at the applicant's HTS's institution (see also HTS SG, para 49);
- no study other than the above unless it is "supplementary" study, in which case it does not need to be at the sponsor's institution.

Further details are given below about both employment and studying restrictions.

Conditions restricting study and applying to change sponsor

The power to attach a condition to leave that restricts the studies that an applicant may undertake in the UK was introduced from 21 July 2009 (s50 2009 Act amending s3(1)(c) 1971 Act). From 1 October 2009, the Rules were amended so that those in Tier 4 will have conditions restricting them to studying at their sponsoring institutions (Cm 7701).

Only the conditions actually imposed on the particular applicant count, but those who made applications for entry clearance or leave to remain from 5 October 2009 onwards, should find that the restriction is imposed on them (for the 5 October date, see the Explanatory Memo to HC 382, para 7.5 and Student SG, paras 243, 260). In such cases, any student who wishes to do anything more than "supplementary" study at a different institution, including where the planned progression of their studies necessitates changing to a new institution, will need to apply to vary their leave.

Applicants who need to vary their leave in order to study at a new institution cannot generally begin their further study until they have received a positive decision on the application. UKBA has recognised that the surge in study applications over the summer months may mean that, apart from for applicants who manage to get a 'same day' decision premium appointment at a PEO, the delay in processing posted applications may mean that many applications are not dealt with in time for the applicant to begin their new course. As a result, from 23 July 2010, the Home Office introduced the measure (set out above) allowing students to commence study at the new sponsor institution before receiving a decision on the application if the provider has HTS status (amendment made to Rules, para 245ZW(c)(iv) by HC 382).

UKBA also considers that even students who applied for leave before 5 October 2009 (and who presumably do not have conditions restricting their study) also need to obtain its permission in order to take up a course of study with a new sponsor. They can apply for that permission by emailing the details of the proposed change to MigrantReporting@ukba. gsi.gov.uk. UKBA states that it will give permission for the change of sponsors in such cases as long as:

- the new institution has a relevant Tier 4 licence;
- the new provider is happy to sponsor the applicant; and
- the new course meets the Tier 4 requirements.

Such applicants may begin the new course while they are waiting for a decision (Student SG, paras 260–65).

Those seeking to change course but remaining with their existing sponsor do not need specific permission, although the sponsor should notify the change (Student SG, paras 270–72). The new course should meet the Tier 4 requirements as they applied at the time that the applicant obtained his/her existing leave.

"Supplementary studies", for example evening classes, are permitted. These additional courses do not have to relate to the course of study for which leave has been granted and no specific permission is required. Nor does the applicant have to tell his/her sponsor about them." (Student SG, paras 278–9; Tier 4 PG, para 274).

Employment conditions

Tier 4 (General) Students are restricted in the employment that they can take as follows (Rules, para 245ZW(c)):

- employment of an unlimited number of hours may be taken during vacations;
- those studying at degree level, or on foundation degree courses, may take term-time employment of up to 20 hours per week;
- those studying at below degree level (excluding foundation degree courses) may take term-time employment of up to ten hours per week;
- employment may be taken where it is part of a course-related work placement which forms an assessed part of the course, provided that the time spent on the placement is not more than half of the total length of the course except where it is a UK statutory requirement that the placement should be for more than half the total length of the course (note that the employment that a student may take (▶see above) is in addition to any work placement, Student SG, para 287);
- employment may be taken as a Student Union sabbatical officer for up to two years provided that the applicant was elected to the post and that the post is at the same institution where the applicant is studying; and
- postgraduate doctors or dentists on recognised foundation programmes may be employed in that capacity.

Additionally, a Tier 4 (General) Student may not (Rules, para 245ZW(c)):

- be self-employed;
- be employed as a doctor or dentist in training (other than taking a vacancy on a recognised foundation programme);
- work as a professional sportsperson (including a sports coach);
- work as an entertainer; or
- fill a permanent full-time vacancy (▶see below), other than a vacancy on a recognised foundation programme or as a students' union sabbatical officer.

The restriction on those studying at below degree level to term-time employment of up to ten hours per week was introduced from 3 March 2010 by HC 367. Previously, below degree level students could work for up to 20 hours per week during term time. The change was made following the Prime Minister's review of Tier 4 that was announced on 12 November 2009 which was itself prompted by concerns about the rise in student applications since the introduction of Tier 4. The change was made in order to "reinforce the message that the student route is one for study rather than work" and to redress the previous balance which had allowed students to spend a minimum of 15 hours per week in organised daytime study but allowed them to work 20 hours per week in term time (Explanatory Memo to HC 367, para 7.3). At the same time, restrictions were also imposed on Tier 4 dependants (▶see 272 above).

Sponsors are encouraged to make sure that students are aware what their exact term and vacation dates are so as to ensure that students do not work in breach of the above conditions (Student SG, para 286).

Although Tier 4 students may not fill a "permanent full-time vacancy", that does not prevent them from filling a "full-time" non-permanent vacancy during vacations. The Rules were deliberately amended to this end from 1 October 2009 (Rules, para 245ZW(c)(iii) and 245ZZB(c) as amended by Cm 7701, paras 38 and 46).

The Government's present proposals are to impose greater employment restrictions on Tier 4 migrants (▶see below 293).

TIER 4 (GENERAL): QUALIFYING FOR LEAVE TO REMAIN

Students seeking to extend their leave in the UK are required to obtain a Biometric Residence Permit. In order to obtain this the student has to give his/her fingerprints and have their facial image taken. Further details about this process can be found at http://www.ukba.homeoffice.gov.uk/employers/preventingillegalworking/checking-id-cards.

WHAT THE RULES SAY

In order to be able to extend their stay ie obtain leave to remain in the UK under the Tier 4 (General) Student category, an applicant must satisfy the following requirements in common with the requirements for entry (Rules, para 245ZX):

- the applicant must be at least 16 years old;
- if the applicant is under 18 years of age, s/he must show that the application is supported by his/her parents or legal guardian (or just one parent if that parent has sole legal responsibility for him/her);
- if the applicant is under 18 years of age, s/he must show that his/her parents or legal guardian (or just one parent if that parent has sole legal responsibility for him/her) have confirmed that they consent to the arrangements for the applicant's care in the UK;
- the applicant must not fall for refusal under the general grounds (▶see Chapter 11);
- the applicant must score 30 points for attributes (that is achieved by being issued with a valid 'confirmation of acceptance of studies' (CAS) under paras 113–120 of Appendix A of the Rules – there are a range of requirements that must be met in order for the CAS to be treated as enabling the applicant to score these points, ▶see above 251–263);
- if the course is below degree level, the grant of leave to remain sought must not lead to the applicant having spent more than three years in the UK as a Tier 4 Migrant since the age of 18 studying courses that did not consist of degree level study, ▶see above 263;
- if the course is below degree level and contains a work placement, the sponsor must have HTS status, unless the course is a foundation degree;
- if the course is at level 3 of the NQF, or at level 6 of the SCQF, the sponsor must have HTS status;

8

- the applicant must score ten points for maintenance under Appendix C of the Rules (▶see above 263–271);
- if the applicant is presently being sponsored by a Government or international scholarship agency, or within the last 12 months has come to the end of such a period of sponsorship, s/he must provide the written consent of the sponsoring Government or agency to the application and must provide specified documents to show that this requirement has been met (▶see 270);
- if the applicant wishes to study specified certain science, maths, technology or engineering courses, s/he must hold a valid ATAS clearance (▶see above 271); and
- if the applicant wishes to be a postgraduate doctor or dentist on a recognised foundation programme, certain further specific requirements must be met ▶see 272.

The above requirements repeat those for entry clearance/leave to enter and reference should be made to the explanations given in the section dealing with entry above. However, applicants for leave to remain must *in addition* meet the following three requirements (Rules, para 245ZX(a)(b)(l)):

- the applicant must not be an illegal entrant;
- the applicant's proposed course must begin within a month of the expiry of the applicant's present leave; and
- the applicant must have, or have last been granted, entry clearance, or leave to enter or remain as a:
  - Tier 4 (General) Student;
  - Tier 4 (Child) Student;
  - Tier 1 (Post-Study Work) Migrant;
  - Tier 2 migrant;
  - participant in the International Graduates' Scheme (or its predecessor, the Science and Engineering Graduates' Scheme);
  - participant in the Fresh Talent: Working in Scotland Scheme;
  - Postgraduate Doctor or Dentist;
  - prospective Student;
  - Student;
  - Student Nurse;
  - Student Re-sitting an Examination;
  - Student Writing-up a Thesis;
  - Student Union Sabbatical Officer; or
  - Work Permit Holder.

It follows from the above that the Rules allow students who have existing leave, or who were last granted leave in the Tier 4 (General) Student category, to extend their leave in-country in the same category. The same goes for students and others granted leave in any of the above categories – they are permitted to 'switch' into the Tier 4 (General) category. The Rules do not expressly require the applicant to actually have leave at the point of the application (because they refer in the alternative to applicants who were 'last granted' leave in the particular category). So a person who overstays for a short time may still qualify although this is not to be recommended and may have future immigration consequences.

Also note that the Rules require that course for which the applicant is applying to stay must begin within a month of the expiry of their leave (Rules, para 245ZX(l)). Not surprisingly, that means that the course must be due to commence within a month of the expiry of the substantive period of limited leave as previously granted to the applicant by the immigration authorities. The automatic extension of leave under s3C 1971 Act that may be triggered when an applicant makes an in-time application to extend leave that is not decided before the expiry of the leave as granted, does not count for this purpose (see *QI (para 245ZX(l) considered) Pakistan* (IAC), para 10; confirmed in *HM & Others (PBS – legitimate expectation – paragraph 245ZX(l)) Malawi)* para 21).

Period and conditions of grant of leave

Leave to remain will be granted for the duration of the course plus a short period both before and after the course. The rules about the period and conditions of leave are the same as for entry clearance/leave to enter (▶above 273–277 including the table) (Rules, para 245ZY). The Tier 4 (General) category does not provide a direct route to indefinite leave, although many applicants 'switch' to other categories as permitted by the Rules. Often this has been to the Tier 1 (Post-Study work) category (see Rules, para 245Z(f)(vii)) and then later from that to another category leading to indefinite leave. Students have also been able to switch to the following categories: Tier 1 (General) Migrant (but note that this category will close from 6 April 2011), Tier 1 (Entrepreneur) Migrant, the Tier 1 (Investor) Migrant or the Tier 2 (Intra Company Transfer) Migrant categories (for these switching provisions, see the paras 245C(f)(xix), 245L(e)(xx), 245S (c)(xiv) and 245ZF(e)(xxiii) of the Rules).

TIER 4 (CHILD) STUDENTS

Children aged between four and 17 (inclusive) may apply to be educated in the UK under the Tier 4 (Child) Student category. The category allows children aged four and above to come to the UK to attend independent schools. Those aged 16 and above may study with any licensed provider.

Children aged 16 or 17 years who are studying at NQF level 3 or above (for example, A-levels), may choose to apply under the Tier 4 (General) category (above) or under this category. Unlike the Tier 4 (General) category, there is no minimum academic threshold of study in the Tier 4 (Child) category.

Tier 4 (Child) applicants are excluded from qualifying if they have minor children who are financially dependent on them or living with them. Any partner of a Tier 4 (Child) should also qualify to come to the UK in their own right rather than as a dependant. Parents of children under 12 attending fee-paying independent schools on a day basis may accompany them in a special visitor category (▶see Chapter 10 340).

The Home Office considers that the Tier 4 (Child) category has not generally been abused and it does not suggest, in its December 2010 proposals for change, that it will tighten the category further.

All those seeking entry under the Tier 4 (Child) Student category must have a valid entry clearance in this capacity (Rules, paras 245ZZ–ZZA).

WHAT THE RULES SAY

In order to qualify for entry clearance to enter under the Tier 4 (Child) Student category, an applicant must satisfy the following requirements (Rules, para 245ZZA):

- the applicant must be at least four years of age and under the age of 18;
- the applicant must show that the application is supported by his/her parents or legal guardian (or just one parent if that parent has sole legal responsibility for him/her);
- the applicant must show that his/her parents or legal guardian (or just one parent if that parent has sole legal responsibility for him/her) have confirmed that they consent to the arrangements for the applicant's travel to, reception and care in the UK (a written letter should be provided for these purposes);
- if a foster career or a relative (not a parent or guardian) of the applicant will be responsible for the care of the applicant, then the arrangements must meet the requirements laid down in Guidance published by UKBA, the applicant must provide details of those arrangements and specified documents to show that this requirement has been met;
- the applicant must have no children under the age of 18 who are either living with him/her, or for whom s/he is financially responsible;
- the applicant must not fall for refusal under the general grounds of refusal (▶see Chapter 11);
- the applicant must score 30 points for attributes (this is achieved by being issued with a valid 'confirmation of acceptance of studies' (CAS)

under paras 121–126 of Appendix A of the Rules – there is a range of requirements that must be met in order for the CAS to be treated as enabling the applicant to score these points ▶see below);

- the applicant must score ten points for maintenance under Appendix C of the Rules ▶see below; and

- if the applicant is presently being sponsored by a Government or international scholarship agency, or within the last 12 months has come to the end of such a period of sponsorship, s/he must provide the written consent of the sponsoring Government or agency to the application and must provide specified documents to show that this requirement has been met.

Consent and care arrangements

UKBA is required to have regard to the need to safeguard children and promote their welfare (BCIA 2009, s55) and it considers that all children studying in the UK must have suitable care arrangements in place for their travel, reception and living arrangements (Tier 4 PG, para 42).

A letter must be provided from the applicant's parent/s or legal guardian that confirms the relationship and their consent to the application and to the travel, reception and living arrangements for the child. If one parent is signing the letter, it must be confirmed that that parent has sole custody of the child, otherwise both parents must sign (Tier 4 PG, para 241). If the child is aged 16 or 17 and will be living independently, the letter should confirm the parent(s)' or legal guardian's agreement to them travelling to the UK and living independently there (Tier 4 PG, paras 242–3).

Guidance relating to private foster arrangements states that the parent and carer must notify their UK local authority of the arrangement. That authority will make sure that the foster carer is suitable and will provide that carer with any support and guidance that they need. Where the child is under 16, the application to UKBA must include the letter of notification to the local authority and the local authority's confirmation of receipt of that letter. However, if it is a 'close relative' who will look after the child, the arrangement does not have to be registered with the local authority. For these purposes, close relatives are: grandparents, siblings, step-parents, uncles or aunts, any of whom must be over 18 (Tier 4 PG, paras 45–7, 246–7).

Whether the child is living with a close relative or in a private foster care arrangement, the following evidence is specified as required to show that suitable arrangements have been made (Tier 4 PG, para 244):

- a written undertaking from the intended carer confirming the care arrangements (the undertaking must contain specified information: see para 244(i));

8

- the letter (above) from the parent(s) or legal guardian must confirm the care arrangement showing the nature of the relationship with the carer and the address in the UK where the child and the child's intended carer will live and that the parent(s) or legal guardian support and authorise the arrangement; and

- evidence that the intended carer is permitted to be in the UK (ie their passport or certificate of naturalisation – UKBA will generally accept notarised copies).

Information about the standards that are applied where children are at further education colleges, boarding schools and residential special schools can be found at the links provided in the Tier 4 Policy Guidance (Tier 4 PG, para 44).

Scoring points for attributes: a valid confirmation of acceptance of studies

The applicant must score 30 points for attributes which can only be done by producing a valid CAS (Rules, para 245ZZA(b); App A, paras 121–123 and Table 17). In order to score points from the CAS, a range of conditions must be met relating to:

- procedural matters;
- the documents that the applicant produced to the sponsor in order to obtain the place;
- the nature of the educational institution; and
- the nature of the course.

These are looked at in turn below.

Procedural requirements

As with the Tier 4 (General) category, there are a number of procedural requirements that must be satisfied in order for the CAS issued to a Tier 4 (Child) Student to allow him/her to score points (Rules, App A, paras 124–125):

- the entry clearance application must be made within six months of the issue of the CAS;
- the application for entry clearance must not be made more than three months before the start date of the course of study applied for;
- the sponsor must not have withdrawn the offer since the CAS was issued;
- the CAS must have been issued by an institution with a Tier 4 (Child) Student sponsor licence;
- the educational institution must still hold the licence at the time that the application for entry clearance is determined;
- the CAS must contain "such information as is specified as mandatory" in Guidance published by UKBA; and

- the CAS reference number that the applicant provides on their application for entry clearance/leave matches records held by UKBA (ie it matches a CAS Checking Service entry that names the applicant as the migrant and confirms that the stated sponsor is sponsoring him/her under Tier 4); and
- the CAS reference number has not been cancelled by the sponsor or UKBA since it was assigned.

Documents to be produced relating to child's educational ability

The Policy Guidance requires that the applicant provides his/her CAS reference number on the application form (Tier 4 PG, para 176). Children under the age of 16 do not need to produce further documents relating to their educational ability (Tier 4 PG, para 178). However, children who are 16 and above, whose sponsor has assessed them on the basis of their qualifications, should send those qualifications with the application. The same Guidance as for the Tier 4 (General) category is given about the nature of the documents that must be produced and the evidence to be produced if the applicant was assessed by the sponsor using other means (Tier 4 PG, paras 179–182).

Nature of institution

Where the applicant is aged under 16, s/he must be intending to study at an independent fee-paying school. The CAS will only be considered valid and capable of allowing the applicant to score points if it was issued by such a school (App A, para 124(a)). It is not possible for a child of any age to use this category to study at a publicly-funded school. Applicants aged 16 or above may, however, study at a publicly-funded further education college that is able to charge fees for international students (Tier 4 PG, para 164).

Nature of the course

The course must meet one of the following requirements (Rules, App A, para 126); it must be either:

- taught in accordance with the National Curriculum;
- taught in accordance with the NQF;
- accepted as being of equivalent academic status to either of the above by Ofsted (for England), the Education and Training Inspectorate (Northern Ireland), HM Inspectorate of Education (Scotland), or Estyn (Wales); or
- provided in accordance with the requirements of the existing independent school education inspection standards.

Guidance adds that the course may also be a pre-sessional one in order prepare the child for his/her main course of study where that main study meets the above conditions (para Student SG, para 221; Tier 4 PG, para 168). The course may also be one with a work placement, where the placement forms an assessed part of the course (Tier 4 PG, para 263).

The Student Sponsor Guidance adds that English as a foreign language is not a course meeting the above criteria (unless taken as a pre-sessional course) and that those wishing to study English language must generally use the Tier 4 (General) Student category or the student visitor category (if aged 18 or above), alternatively the child visitor category (Student SG, para 227).

Where the applicant is 16 or over and is studying at level NQF 3 (for example, A-levels) which is the minimum level for the Tier 4 (General) category, the child may apply for leave under either the Tier 4 (Child) or the Tier 4 (General) category. If, however, the applicant wishes to study at NQF level 2 (eg GCSEs), this can only be done under the Tier 4 (Child) category (Student SG, paras 216, 226).

A separate CAS should be assigned for each 'course' of study, so that a new CAS will be required when the student progresses from GCSE-level to A-level studies (Student SG, para 228).

Scoring points for maintenance

The requirements for scoring ten points for maintenance for this category that are set out below are all contained in Appendix C of the Rules at paragraphs 15–20 and the accompanying table. As with those in the General (Student) category, the requirement is that the Child (Student) can show that they have had the required funds for a consecutive 28-day period of time ending not later than a calendar month before the date of the application for entry clearance/leave (App C, para 1A(c)). However, UKBA assesses maintenance requirements *according to which of the particular circumstances as set out below*, the child student is in. The Policy Guidance on maintenance for the Tier 4 (Child) category (see Tier 4 PG at paras 183–240) is also tailored to the assessment of the maintenance under the different circumstances set out below that apply where a child is under 16 and not able to live independently. Where the requirements below are the same or similar to the requirements for maintenance for the Tier 4 (General) category, the Guidance is also similar (▶see above 267–269).

Child students boarding at residential independent schools

For a child studying and boarding at a residential independent school, UKBA will require evidence of sufficient funds to pay school fees for one academic year plus any additional accommodation fees required by the school (App C, para 16, table).

Child students attending independent schools but living at home in a private foster care arrangement

For a child studying at a non-residential independent school in a private foster care arrangement, or cared for by a close relative (grandparent, sibling, step-parent, uncle, or aunt), UKBA will require evidence of sufficient funds to pay school fees for one academic year plus an undertaking from the foster carer or relative to provide maintenance and accommodation for the child for the duration of the course. The foster carer or relative must also show that they have at least £500 per month for up to a maximum of nine months to support the child in the UK (App C, para 16, table).

Child students who are under 12, attending independent schools but living at home with their accompanying parent

UKBA continues to allow children studying at independent schools under the age of 12 to be accompanied to the UK by a parent who will be responsible for their care (for the rules relating to this ▶see Chapter 10 340). In this case, UKBA will require evidence of the funds required to pay school fees for one academic year plus £1,333 per month for each month up to a maximum of nine months. If more than one child is accompanying the applicant and the parent, then there should be an additional £533 per month available for each additional child, again up to a maximum of nine months (App C, para 16, table).

Child students aged 16 or 17 years of age living independently

Where the child student is aged 16 or 17 and will be living independently, the prescribed level of funds that is required depends on three main factors:

- whether the applicant has an "established presence" studying in the UK;
- whether the applicant is studying in "inner London", or elsewhere in the UK; and
- the length of the course.

The requirements are detailed and are the same as for those in the General (Student) category as explained above ▶263–270.

Period and conditions of leave

If successful and provided they request it, applicants will be granted leave for the length of their programme up to a maximum of six years (three years if the applicant is aged 16 or over) (Rules, para 245ZZB(a)(ii)(b)(ii)). The period of leave given will also include a period of approximately one month before the course starts, plus four months following the end date of the course (Rules, para 245ZZB(a)(i)(iii)(b)(i)(iii)). The maximum period of leave for students aged 16 or over was increased from two to three years in April 2010 by amending Rules (HC 439). The purpose of this was to allow students applying under the Tier 4 (Child) category to be offered programmes at NQF level 3, as well as any earlier preparatory courses.

If the child student becomes 18 or 19 while s/he still has leave granted under the Tier 4 (Child) category, s/he may continue with his/her course until that period of leave comes to an end. In general any application made to extend leave after the applicant turns 18 must be made under the Tier 4 (General) category (Student SG, table at p40). However, so that child students who were given leave before 6 April 2010 do not miss out on the opportunity of the now extended (from two to three years) period of leave, the Home Office has made an arrangement for 18-year-old students falling in that category to apply to extend their stay to bring it up to three years in total. In order to benefit from this the applicant must have been present in the UK studying as a Tier 4 (Child) Student, or as a student under the student rules in force, before 31 March 2009 and have been granted leave while under 18 (see Student SG, addendum; Tier 4 PG, Appendix A para 2).

Conditions

The conditions that will be attached to the leave in this category regarding recourse to public funds, registration with the police, employment and study, are the same as for those in the Tier 4 (General) category (►above 273) except that (Rules, para 245ZZB(c)):

- those aged under 16 may not take any employment at all;
- those aged 16 or over may take employment of no more than ten hours per week during term time (ie like Tier 4 (General) students studying at below degree level), so there is no provision in this category allowing for study of 20 hours per week during term time; and
- there is, naturally enough, no provision to take employment as a post-graduate doctor or dentist on a recognised foundation programme.

Qualifying to extend leave as a Tier 4 (Child) Student

The requirements for qualifying to extend leave, ie to obtain leave to remain as a Tier 4 (Child) Student, are the same those for entry except that an applicant seeking leave to remain must (Rules, para 245ZZC(a)(b)(j)):

- not be an illegal entrant;
- be applying to study on a course that begins within a month of the expiry of his/her present leave; and
- have, or have last been granted, entry clearance, or leave to enter or remain as:
- – a Tier 4 (Child) Student;
- – a student under the old student rules;
- – a prospective student (►see 340 341).

The periods of leave that will be granted and the conditions that will be attached to leave are the same as for Tier 4 (Child) Students entering the UK (above) (Rules, para 245ZZD).

HIGHLY TRUSTED SPONSORS

The requirements that need to be satisfied to obtain a sponsorship licence, as well as the duties that apply and the sanctions that can be imposed on sponsors, are dealt with in Chapter 4. That chapter deals with sponsors under Tiers 2, 4 and 5. That chapter also looks at the system for giving sponsors an 'A' or 'B' rating (▶101–102). Those features are common to all forms of sponsorship.

However, from 6 April 2010, Tier 4 sponsors only have the option of moving beyond a 'standard' (ie 'A' or 'B' rated) licence to obtain 'Highly Trusted Sponsor' (HTS) status. In order to obtain HTS status, a sponsor must first have held an 'A' rated sponsor licence for a minimum of six months. Separate Guidance is available for those seeking to obtain HTS status: 'Tier 4 of the Points-Based System – Highly Trusted Sponsor Guidance' (HTS SG). The present version is 07/10 dated 23 July 2010.

The purpose of the HTS scheme is (HTS SG, paras 8–9):

"...to identify those sponsors who are achieving the highest levels of compliance with their sponsor obligations and whose students are showing the greatest compliance with the terms of their visa or leave.

"By identifying those sponsors who are achieving high levels of compliance, [UKBA] can both target our resources elsewhere on areas of high risk, and can provide additional services and freedoms which recognise the good track record demonstrated thus far by those who qualify..."

Benefits of HTS status

The advantages of obtaining HTS status are set out below.

Wider range of courses Only HTS providers can offer courses at NQF level 3 and SCQF level 6. In addition, only HTS providers can offer courses at below degree level (excluding foundation degrees) which include work placements (▶above 256). Under the Government's presently proposed changes, it will be necessary to have HTS status in order to offer any courses to adults below degree level, ie at NQF 3, 4 and 5 and SCQF 6, 7 and 8 (▶see 292 below).

Re-sits Only HTS providers may assign a CAS to enable a third re-sit of an examination.

Commencing studies before positive decision The study restrictions that are imposed on students as conditions of their existing leave allow them to commence studies at a new institution before receiving a decision on their application to do so if the new provider is an HTS. This applies provided that: the HTS has issued a CAS for the particular applicant, the applicant has applied to UKBA for an extension of their leave using that CAS and the applicant has existing leave to study in the UK (Rules, para 245ZW(c)(iv); HTS SG, para 49).

Relaxation of reporting duties Some of the reporting duties relating to sponsors (▶see Chapter 4 115–116) are relaxed for HTS providers. HTS providers may replace the 'ten expected contacts' requirement, under which sponsors must report to UKBA within ten days of a tenth missed contact, with a system where the sponsor carries out two checkpoints during the reporting year and reports any withdrawals within ten days of those checkpoints. However, even if an HTS adopts the 'checkpoint' system, it is still expected to report, within ten days, any non-enrolments or students who formally withdraw from their studies (HTS SG, paras 50–52; Student SG, para 312).

Account manager HTS providers are allotted a specific UKBA account manager who is directly contactable by telephone and email. The specialised account manager is expected to have some expertise of the particular sector, to understand the sponsor's requirements and to build relationships with the sponsor's staff and be in a position to assist the sponsor with any queries (HTS SG, paras 42–3).

Requirements for qualifying for HTS status

Providers need to apply to UKBA in order to obtain HTS status. All publicly-funded sponsors with an 'A' rating who had been subject to a full institutional inspection were automatically entitled to the benefits of HTS status when the scheme commenced on 6 April 2010. However, in order to retain that deemed status, these providers were required to apply for an HTS licence by 30 June 2010. If they did not do so successfully, their status reverted to that of a standard licence.

There are nine 'values' by which applications for HTS status are judged (▶see table below). If a sponsor applicant fails to meet the standards expected by the criteria in one or two areas, that will not automatically result in refusal. UKBA looks at the picture of compliance overall to determine the outcome, but it also reserves the right to refuse if the sponsor is lacking in just one area (HTS SG, paras 20, 24).

Procedures for obtaining HTS status

In order to apply, sponsors must complete the application form 'Application for a Highly Trusted Sponsor licence under Tier 4 of the Points-Based System' which is available on the UKBA website and return it to 'UK Border Agency, Highly Trusted Sponsors, PO Box 589, Durham, DH99 1AB'. It must be signed by the present registered authorising officer and there is a fee of £400. In assessing the application, UKBA may ask for full details about the sponsor's existing students and it may request a spreadsheet showing student details and attendance. Officers may cross-check all information received against their own systems which record entry clearance and leave to enter/remain decisions and their records of movements in and out of the UK. UKBA may also make a site visit to the sponsor. Note that UKBA may make use of information provided in sup-

CRITERIA FOR QUALIFYING FOR HTS STATUS

The nine criteria or 'values' set out by UKBA are as follows (HTS SG, para 23):

- There must have been a minimum period of 6 consecutive months prior to the date of the application during which the sponsor held an 'A' (trusted) rating for Tier 4. The sponsor must also, at the time of the application, be 'A' rated for any other tiers in which it holds a licence.

- The sponsor must have recruitment practices in place that ensure, as far as possible, that only genuine students are accepted and issued with a CAS (UKBA expects sponsors to have followed the published Guidance and also its 'Tier 4 sponsor recruitment practices – Information sharing' document).

- The sponsor must not have been issued with a civil penalty in the last three years. Any civil penalty issued before that time must have been paid in full.

- The sponsor must have systems in place aimed at minimising the number of refusals of leave for migrants applying with a CAS that it has issued.

- The sponsor should carefully vet students before issuing them with a CAS so as to ensure that they intend to study. UKBA expects that no more than 2% of those issued with entry clearance or leave will not enrol within one month of the start of the course.

- Sponsors should take all reasonable steps to ensure that their sponsored students will attend and complete their course of study.

- UKBA expects that no more than 5% of the total number of sponsored students who have been granted leave under Tier 4 will have either failed to enrol or to complete their course.

- Sponsors must ensure that monitoring for attendance and progression is carried out in accordance with the sponsor duties.

- There must not have been any serious concerns raised following an UKBA inspection or review in the previous 12 months.

The HTS Sponsor Guidance also sets out circumstances in which an application will be refused. Among the reasons are (HTS SG, para 56):

- the sponsor no longer meets the standard Tier 4 criteria, or its Tier 4 licence is downgraded or withdrawn before the HTS application is determined;

- the submission of false documents or information with the application;

- there is either a failure to submit, or an incomplete submission of, a student evidence spreadsheet after it has been requested by UKBA within a given time period;

- unspent convictions by the sponsor or "another relevant person" (see below) for offences under certain immigration legislation, trafficking for sexual exploitation, or for any other offence which indicates to UKBA that the sponsor applicant poses a risk to immigration control;

- the sponsor or another relevant person is legally prohibited from becoming a company director (unless this is because s/he is an undischarged bankrupt);

8

- the sponsor or another relevant person has been dishonest in any previous dealings with UKBA (or the Immigration and Nationality Directorate before that);
- the sponsor or another relevant person has a previous record of non-compliance or poor compliance with sponsorship duties;
- the sponsor or another relevant person has failed, on request, to provide evidence to enable UKBA to decide whether the sponsor was complying with the sponsorship or work permit arrangements;
- the sponsor or another relevant person has previously had its HTS status withdrawn or refused by UKBA – in such cases the onus is on the sponsor to show that they have put their systems right in the area in which they were previously found to be lacking;
- the Office of the Immigration Services Commissioner (OISC) has removed the authorisation of the sponsor, or any organisation that the sponsor or another relevant person has been involved with in a similar role.

"Another Relevant person" for the above purposes means the sponsor's authorising officer, key contact or level 1 user (HTS SG, footnote 2 on p8). For an explanation of these personnel, ▶see Chapter 4 95–98.

port of an HTS application to review the existing standard licence and its rating.

Privately-funded institutions applying for HTS status on or after 1 May 2010 will not be able to issue a CAS to students for courses that only HTS providers can offer unless and until they have received a positive decision on the HTS application (HTS SG, paras 70–2). Those publicly-funded institutions which had deemed HTS status and which applied before 30 June 2010 to obtain formal HTS status could continue to issue a CAS for courses that only an HTS provider can offer unless and until the application for HTS status was refused (HTS SG, para 69).

If the application is successful, the name of the sponsor will be published on the UKBA Tier 4 register as having HTS status. An HTS licence is valid for 12 months only and the sponsor must apply, before its expiry, if it wishes to renew it (HTS SG, paras 83–7).

Unsuccessful applications, re-applying and challenging decisions

There is no right of appeal against a negative decision on the application and the sponsor applicant must wait at least six months before re-applying. This is in order to give the sponsor time to put right those areas in which they were found to be lacking (HTS SG, para 66). If the application is unsuccessful, the sponsor might also receive notice of an intention to review the existing standard licence (HTS SG, para 64). The same waiting period of six months applies before any further application can be made if an HTS licence is withdrawn. However, if a sponsor's standard licence is withdrawn, the sponsor may re-apply for that licence at any time (HTS SG, paras 81–2).

In the absence of a right of appeal, the only way to bring a legal challenge against negative decisions is by judicial review. Careful, specialist advice should be obtained before going down that route.

Duties of an HTS provider and loss of status

The duties of an HTS provider are the same as for holders of standard licences (▶see Chapter 4 114–118) (HTS SG, para 73). UKBA may carry out checks on the sponsor before and after a HTS licence is issued and the sponsor agrees to co-operate with these checks when it submits its application. Only those HTS providers who continue to meet the criteria set out in the table above are entitled to retain their HTS status. Failure to do so may result in the loss of their HTS licence.

UKBA states that it may carry out two reviews during the (12-month) life of the HTS licence. That is in addition to the assessment that is made in order to determine the application. If appropriate, UKBA may act to suspend or withdraw both the HTS licence and also possibly the original licence. UKBA will give the sponsor 28 days in which to make representations if it proposes to re-rate the sponsor (HTS SG, paras 78–80). For further details about suspension, downgrading and withdrawal of licences, ▶see Chapter 4 121–137.

If HTS status is removed and the sponsor reverts to their standard licence, then students who have already been granted leave are permitted to commence and complete their studies until the end of their leave. That is the case even if the course is one which, normally, only an HTS provider can offer. However, those applicants whose applications for leave in order to pursue a course that only an HTS provider can offer are still undecided, will be refused if the sponsor's HTS status is removed. If the CAS has been assigned but the applicant has not yet applied for leave in order to study on a course that only an HTS provider can offer, then the sponsor is required to cancel the CAS. No further CAS should be issued by the sponsor for such courses (HTS SG, paras 88–90)

DECEMBER 2010 PROPOSALS FOR CHANGE

On 7 December 2010, the Government announced a consultation on making yet further changes to Tier 4. The table below sets out the proposals made in the consultation paper. The clear purpose of the proposed changes is to attack the numbers of students coming to the UK and, for those that do, to impose a presumption that they will return abroad after their studies. This is part and parcel of the coalition Government's aim to make significant reductions to net migration. The aim is to bring the number of international students arriving broadly in line with the number of those leaving. According to Government figures, 273,000 visas were

THE STUDENT IMMIGRATION SYSTEM: A CONSULTATION

On 7 December 2010, the Government launched a consultation on its proposals to change the student immigration system.

In summary, the main proposals made in the consultation paper are as follows.

Raise the level of courses students can study

The Government proposes to restrict Tier 4 mainly to degree level courses and child students. Only providers with HTS status will be able to offer courses to adults at below degree level (ie NQF 3, 4 and 5; SCQF 6, 7 and 8). Those holding standard ('A' or 'B' rated) licences will only be able to offer courses at degree level ie NQF level 6 and SCQF level 9. The changes earlier in 2010 had restricted courses at NQF level 3 to HTS providers and this proposal would obviously go even further.

Introduce tougher English language proficiency criteria for students

The Government proposes to raise the Tier 4 English language proficiency requirement from the (existing) level of B1 of the CEFR to B2 (upper-intermediate level). This is proposed to apply to all Tier 4 applicants.

It is proposed also that the minimum level at which Tier 4 English language courses would be taught would also shift upwards, from B2 to C1 (with B2 as the necessary proficiency level for entry on to the course).

The Government also proposes that a wider group of students would actually have to take and pass the secure English language test in order to prove their competency, rather than being able to rely on their sponsor to assess their language abilities. So those studying at degree level or above would have to take the test. It is proposed that only the following categories would be exempt from the test:

- those from majority English-speaking countries;
- those who have recently studied in the UK as children;
- those who have been awarded a qualification equivalent to UK degree level or above that had been taught in a majority English-speaking country.

Ensure that students return abroad after their course

The Government proposes that students who want to remain in the UK after their initial course will have to have shown clear evidence, in the form of confirmation from their sponsor, of academic progression to a higher level. This might suggest a return to something like the requirement under the old rules of having to show "evidence of satisfactory progress in [his/her] course of study including the taking and passing of any relevant examinations" (and see the decision in *Goo* for how the Court of Appeal approached that requirement). It is also considering requiring such students to return overseas to apply again to re-enter as students. The aim is to promote the understanding that the presumption is that applicants return abroad after their studies, rather than assume that they will be permitted to stay on in the UK.

Closure or severe restriction of the Tier 1 (Post-Study Work) route

The Government's view is that many graduates who presently take advantage of the Tier 1 (Post-Study Work) route are not finding skilled work and it also points to a general high level of graduate unemployment in the UK. The Government also cites the large numbers of Tier 1 (Post-Study Work) migrants in the UK (in 2009, 38,000 applications were granted together with 8,000 dependants). As a result, the Government proposes either:

- closing the Tier 1 (Post-Study Work) route (with the possibility of transitional arrangements); or

- severely restricting the route, for example by limiting it to those with higher degrees such as PhD.

In a speech made at the conclusion of the consultation period at the end of January 2011, the Minister made a further alternative suggestion that the period of the Tier 1 (Post-Study Work) leave might be restricted from its present length of two years.

The Government's general reasoning in the consultation papers is that international graduates who want to work in the UK must qualify under Tier 2. To this end, the consultation paper states that the Government does not propose to end the present system of granting leave for an additional four months at the end of a course that is longer than 12 months in duration. This is intended to allow graduates time to obtain sponsorship from a UK employer. It is also stated that the Government intends to continue the practice of not requiring employers to carry out the Tier 2 Resident Labour Market Test when recruiting such graduates through the 'milk round'.

Limit the entitlement of students to work and sponsor dependants

The Government proposes that:

- students will only be permitted to work on campus during the week;

- students will only be permitted to work for external employers, off campus, at weekends and during the vacations;

- on courses offering work placements, the minimum work/study ratio will change from the existing 50:50 to allowing the student to attend a placement for only a third of their time (that is unless there is a UK statutory requirement that the placement should be longer than a third of the length of the course);

- only Tier 4 students who are studying for more than 12 months will be permitted to bring their dependants to the UK;

- no Tier 4 dependants will be permitted to work (unless the dependant separately qualifies independently under Tier 1 or Tier 2).

Introduce simpler procedures for checking low-risk applications

The Government proposes to change the requirements for evidence of maintenance and previous qualifications so that the requirements will be less onerous for some (low-risk applicants) as compared to others (high-risk applicants). It is proposed that the distinction will be made based either on nationality, or on whether the sponsor has a standard rating or is an HTS

8

provider. The Government is particularly concerned about the use of forged financial documents used to try to show that the maintenance requirements are met and about evidence that some applicants are using funds provided by agents which are then passed from applicant to applicant.

The proposal is to allow lower-risk applicants to self-declare that they have the required level of funds available to meet the maintenance requirements and that they have been awarded the educational qualifications necessary to obtain admission to their course. This would still remain subject to UKBA's right to ask for specific verification. All 'higher-risk' applicants would continue to be required to provide original documentation.

Introduce stricter accreditation procedures for education providers in the private sector

The Government proposes to tighten the accreditation regime in order to "ensure the quality of education provision within private institutions of further and higher education for Tier 4 purposes". Government figures show that, of the 56 Tier 4 sponsor licences that had been revoked by July 2010, nearly three-quarters of the holders were private institutions of further and higher education. The Government is concerned that the present system of accreditation and inspection of these institutions needs strengthening. It does not have the same concerns about independent schools. At present there are five UKBA approved accreditation bodies and the Government proposes to review their work and see how it can be improved.

Student visitor route

The Government proposes to retain the student visitor route (▶see Chapter 10 at 336–338) as offering an alternative means of entry for those wishing to attend short courses that are below the minimum academic requirements under Tier 4.

issued to students in 2009 (excluding student visitors) and approximately 30,000 dependant visas were issued.

The consultation closed on 31 January 2010. The Minister of State, Damian Green MP, issued a statement on the same day. Among his comments were the following:

"The Government has committed to making changes across the immigration system to achieve its overall aim of reducing net migration. The student route accounts for two thirds of migrants entering the UK each year which makes it a key focus for reform.

"...the Government wants to ensure that those who enter on a student visa genuinely come here to study. The Government is committed to minimising abuse of the student route by those whose primary motivation is not to study but to work and settle in the UK.

"By minimising abuse, we shall also take a further step towards our aim of reducing net migration to the UK to sustainable levels. The majority of non-EU migrants are students. They and their dependants accounted for around two thirds of visas issued last year under the Points-Based System. It is clear that the Government's aim to reduce net migration will not be achieved without careful consideration and action on the non-economic routes including students."

8

9 Tier 5: youth mobility and temporary workers

This chapter covers:

- the Youth Mobility Scheme (▶297–302); and
- Temporary Workers (▶302–318).

This chapter is about Tier 5 of the Points-Based System. The purpose of Tier 5 is to enable migrants to come to the UK on a temporary basis mainly for non-economic reasons, although enabling them to do some work while they are here.

All applicants under this Tier need a sponsor. For full details about qualifying and applying for a sponsor licence and operating as a sponsor, ▶see Chapter 4.

Tier 5 was introduced by changes to the Immigration Rules made by HC 1113 from 27 November 2008. The Youth Mobility Scheme and the Temporary Worker category are the two main categories in Tier 5, although the Temporary Worker category is broken down into a further five 'sub-categories'. The Youth Mobility Scheme replaces youth mobility routes that were contained both in the Immigration Rules and in concessions outside the Rules. The idea is that young nationals of those countries who are participating in the scheme will be able to come to the UK in order to experience life here for up to two years. During the time that they are here, they are able to do some work. The most well-known of the categories that it replaces was the 'Working Holidaymaker' scheme. The Temporary Worker category enables certain temporary workers to come to the UK for cultural, charitable, religious or international reasons.

The Immigration Rules dealing with Tier 5 are: paragraphs 245ZI–245ZS of the main Rules; Appendix A, paragraphs 101–112; and Appendix C, paragraphs 1A, 6–9. The Guidance issued by UKBA outside the Rules that is relevant to Tier 5, together with the abbreviations that we have used for it in this chapter, are as follows.

T5 (Youth) PG Tier 5 (Youth Mobility Scheme) of the Points-Based System – Policy Guidance, 31 July 2010

T5 (Temp) PG Tier 5 (Temporary Worker) of the Points-Based System – Policy Guidance, 14 December 2010

SG   Tiers 2 and 5 of the Points-Based System – Sponsor Guidance, 21 December 2010 (version 12/10). *For UKBA's summary of the changes to the SG from 6 April 2011 ►see Appendix 2 458.*

TIER 5 YOUTH MOBILITY SCHEME

The Youth Mobility Scheme allows a quota of young people of certain identified nationalities to come to the UK for up to two years to experience life here during which time they may work. Its formal title in the Rules is 'Tier 5 (Youth Mobility Scheme) Temporary Migrants'. The Scheme is also intended to promote the UK internationally, to enhance trade links and encourage tourism. The government of the applicant's country acts as their sponsor.

Applicants must obtain entry clearance in order to come to the UK under the Scheme (para 245ZJ HC 395). There is no provision in the Rules for applying for leave in-country or for extending leave under the Scheme. Those who obtain entry clearance under the Scheme are permitted to work in the UK and their employment is subject to a few restrictions only. Some self-employment is also permitted (►see below for the restrictions). Participants in the Scheme are also permitted to undertake voluntary work, study on a privately-funded basis and undertake au pair placements, although Guidance states that study should "not be the main purpose of the visit" (PG, para 285).

The following three types of non-British citizen British national may apply for entry under the Scheme (Rules, para 245ZK(b)(ii)):

- British Overseas Citizens;
- British Overseas Territories Citizens; and
- British Nationals (Overseas).

All three are defined in the British Nationality Act 1981 and they are described in the 2006 Edition of the *JCWI Handbook* (pp1406–12). As to foreign nationals, at present the Scheme applies only to nationals of the following five countries (Rules, para 245ZK(b)(i) and see Appendix G to the Rules; see also T5 (Youth) PG, Annex A):

- Australia;
- Canada;
- Japan;
- New Zealand; and
- Monaco

The above countries have made reciprocal agreements with the UK to allow at least 1,000 young UK nationals per year to visit their countries and work there for at least 12 months. The Home Office states that those countries also have "effective arrangements with the UK allowing us to return their nationals to them, and their nationals pose a low risk of abusing the UK's immigration controls". Nationals of the above countries will be deemed to be sponsored by their Governments if they have a national passport (Explanatory Memo to HC 1113 at para 6.18–6.19). Monaco was added to the list from April 2010 by HC 439 after accepting the UK Government's invitation to join the Scheme. If other countries are added, Appendix G to the Rules will be amended to show this.

Qualifying for entry

The requirements that must be satisfied in order to be granted entry clearance and be admitted to the UK under the Youth Mobility Scheme are as follows. Applicants must (Rules, para 245ZK):

- not fall to be refused under the general grounds of refusal (▶see Chapter 11);
- be a national of one of the countries listed above (ie in Appendix G to the Rules) or hold one of the forms of British nationality specified above;
- score a minimum of 40 points for 'attributes' under Appendix A to the Rules (▶see below);
- score a minimum of 10 points for maintenance under Appendix C to the Rules (▶see below);
- have no children under the age of 18 who are either living with them, or for whom they are financially responsible; and
- not have previously spent time in the UK either as a Working Holiday-maker or under the Youth Mobility Scheme.

But, even if all of the above requirements are satisfied, applicants will *still* be refused entry if the annual quota for the country of which they are a national has already been exceeded for the year in which they apply (Rules, para 245ZK and ▶see below).

Scoring points for attributes under the Youth Mobility Scheme

In order to be admitted, applicants must score 40 points for 'attributes'. They score those points by being a national of a particular country and by being of a particular age (para 245ZK(c) and paras 101–104, Table 14 of Appendix A, HC 395). The details are contained in the table below.

The date of application is taken to be the date the application fee is paid (T5 (Youth) PG, para 41). Points are only awarded where an applicant provides the specified evidence that s/he meets the above requirements (App A, para 104 read with Rules para 245AA).

Evidence of nationality An applicant is required to produce a valid passport confirming that s/he is a national of one of the five participating foreign countries, or that s/he is a British Overseas Citizen, a British Overseas Territories Citizen or a British National (Overseas) (T5 (Youth) PG, para 44).

Evidence of age The applicant's passport issued by the country participating in the Youth Mobility Scheme is generally used to determine whether points for age can be awarded (T5 (Youth) PG, para 46).

Criterion	Points awarded
Nationality	30
A citizen of a country in Appendix G to the Immigration Rules (Australia, Canada, Japan, New Zealand or Monaco); or	
A British Overseas Citizen, British Overseas Territories Citizen, or British Overseas National	
Age	10
Will be over the age of 18 when his/her entry clearance becomes valid for use; *and*	
Was/will be under the age of 31 on the date his/her application was made.	

Scoring points for maintenance under the Youth Mobility Scheme

Applicants must score 10 points for maintenance under paragraphs 6–7 of Appendix C, to the Rules (Rules, para 245ZK(d)). Appendix C requires applicants to have a level of funds of £1,600 in order to score the necessary 10 points (App C, para 7 and table). The applicant must have those funds at the date of the application and, if the funds were obtained while the applicant was in the UK, they must have been obtained while s/he had valid leave and was not in breach of any of the conditions of that leave (App C, para 1A(a)(d), T5 (Youth) PG, para 51). The level of existing funds shown above is the formal requirement for entry but applicants are also advised to take account of the cost of living in the UK. If they do not expect to receive any income from employment in the UK after the first month, they should ensure that they have enough money to support themselves (T5 (Youth) PG, para 52).

The Rules state that applicants must produce the documents that are specified in the Policy Guidance in order to score the necessary points (App C, paras 1A(e), 7 read with Rules para 245AA). For the affect on UKBA's ability to rely on the Policy Guidance since the decision of the Court of Appeal in *Pankina* and the associated case-law concerning maintenance, ▶see Chapter 2 42–45, 47–52 and Chapter 5 181. For the possible human rights arguments where the strict rules on maintenance cannot be met, ▶see Chapter 12 412–420.

As to the specified documents, the Policy Guidance states that they must be (T5 (Youth) PG, para 53):

- original;
- on the official letter-headed paper or stationery of the organisation;
- bear the official stamp of the organisation;

- be issued by an authorised official of the organisation; and
- be dated no more than one month before the application is submitted.

The specified documents themselves are as follows (T5 (Youth) PG, para 53):

- Building society/savings account pass book, which must clearly show the applicant's name, account number, the name and logo of the financial institution and that the balance is at least £1,600.
- Personal bank or building society statements, which must clearly show all of the same information as an account pass book (above), as well as showing the date of the statement. Statements printed on an ad hoc basis are acceptable as long as they are printed on the bank's letterhead. Mini-statements from cashpoints are not acceptable. Electronic statements from online accounts are acceptable as long as they contain all of the information listed above. If online statements are provided, the applicant will also need to produce a supporting letter from the bank on headed paper confirming the authenticity of the statements or the electronic statements must bear the official stamp of the bank on each page.
- Letter from a bank or building society confirming the funds. The letter must show the applicant's name, the account number, the date of the letter, the financial institution's name and logo and that there is at least £1,600 in the account.
- Letter from a financial institution regulated by the official regulator in the country in which the institution operates confirming the funds. The letter must show the applicant's name, the account number, the date of the letter, the name and logo of the institution and that at least £1,600 is held in the account.

No dependent children and previous time spent in the UK

The applicant is not required to produce documentary evidence to show that s/he meets the additional requirements of having no dependent children and not having previously spent time in the UK as a Working Holidaymaker or under the Youth Mobility Scheme. However, applicants are required to complete a declaration to confirm that these requirements are met (T5 (Youth) PG, para 55).

Annual quota

There is an annual allocation of places on the Youth Mobility Scheme for each of the foreign countries participating in the scheme that are listed in Appendix G to the Rules. Applications can only be accepted from nationals of those counties up to the point at which the annual allocation for the particular country has been filled. After that point, all applications will be refused, even if the applicant meets all the other requirements of the category (Rules, para 245ZK). However, there is no restriction on the number of applications that can be granted from British Overseas Citizens, British Overseas Territories Citizens or British Nationals (Overseas) (T5 (Youth) PG, para 57).

The Explanatory Memo to HC 1113 (the Rules that introduced the Scheme) states in relation to quotas:

"6.20 Each country listed in annex G has an annual allocation of places on the scheme, which will be notified to the authorities of the country concerned. Where we have established reciprocal youth mobility arrangements with a country, the allocation will be set at a figure equal to the number of UK nationals who went to that country in the previous year under the reciprocal scheme in question. However, the minimum allocation for all countries will be 1,000 places."

Terms and conditions

As stated, entry clearance is mandatory for admission under the Scheme and it is not possible to apply in-country. Switching from the Youth Mobility Scheme into other PBS work or study routes is not permitted and nor can participants extend their leave under the Youth Mobility Scheme, or apply for settlement. If the entry clearance application is accepted, applicants are admitted for a period of two years and may work for all of that period if they wish to do so, although subject to the following conditions (Rules, para 245ZL):

- no recourse to public funds;
- registration with the police, if required under paragraph 326 of the Rules;
- no employment as a professional sportsperson (including as a sports coach);
- no employment as a doctor or dentist in training unless the applicant has obtained a degree in medicine or dentistry at bachelor's level or above from a UK institution that is a recognised or listed body (for which, ▶see Chapter 5 177–178), or which holds a sponsor licence under Tier 4 of the PBS;
- self-employment is only allowed if:
- the applicant does not own permanent premises from which s/he does business (other than his/her home);
- the total value of equipment that s/he uses in the business does not exceed £5,000; and
- the applicant has no employees.

Applicants are prevented from 'owning' premises from which to carry out self-employed business, but that does not prevent them from *renting* the premises from which they work in a self-employed capacity. Applicants may also set up a company in order to do business and can hold shares (T5 (Youth) PG, para 35 and table).

9

Dependants

There is no provision in the Rules for the admission of dependants of those who are admitted under the Youth Mobility Scheme. However, the spouse or partner of an applicant may apply under the Scheme in their own right and, if they satisfy the criteria, they may then accompany their spouse/partner to the UK. Spouses or partners might also qualify for entry clearance in another capacity altogether. The Rules relating to the Youth Mobility Scheme exclude applicants who have children under the age of 18 either living with them, or for whom they are financially responsible (Rules, para 245ZK(e)).

The replaced categories and transitional provisions

The Youth Mobility Scheme replaces the following categories under the Rules and concessions:

* the Working Holidaymaker category (including children of Working Holidaymakers);
* the au pair category for non-EEA nationals;
* the British Universities' North America Club ('BUNAC') concession;
* the 'gap year'/working in UK schools concessions;
* the MPs' research assistants' concession; and
* the Japan Youth Exchange Scheme concession.

The Youth Mobility Scheme came into force on 27 November 2008 and since then no further grants of leave to enter have been permitted under the abolished categories unless the applicant had applied before that date. Those who had already been issued with entry clearance under one of the above abolished categories (as well as certain other categories/concessions that were also removed by HC 1113) could continue to use the leave that they had been granted (see preamble to HC 1113; Explanatory Memo to HC 1113, paras 6.43–6.48; T5 (Youth) PG, para 39). Leave under the abolished provisions may still be granted following a successful appeal where the initial application was made before 27 November 2008. It is not now possible to make an application for an extension of stay under one of the abolished categories.

TIER 5 TEMPORARY WORKERS

The purpose of this route is to enable "certain types of temporary worker whose entry helps to satisfy cultural, charitable, religious or international objectives" to come to the UK (Rules, para 245ZM). The main provisions dealing with Temporary Workers are contained in paragraphs 245ZM–245ZS of the Rules, paragraphs 105–112 of Appendix A and paragraphs 8–9 of Appendix C to the Rules.

There are five subcategories of Tier 5 (Temporary Worker). They are:

- **Creative and Sporting**. This is for people coming to the UK to work or perform as sports people, entertainers or creative artists.
- **Charity Workers**. This is for people coming to the UK to do voluntary work. It does not cover people coming to do paid work for charities.
- **Religious Workers**. This is for people coming to the UK to work as religious workers. The work could include preaching, pastoral and non-pastoral work.
- **Government Authorised Exchange**. This covers people coming to the UK under approved schemes that aim to share knowledge, experience and best practice.
- **International Agreement**. This is for people coming to the UK to provide a service that is covered under international law. It includes, for example, private servants in diplomatic households.

All of the above subcategories are looked at in more detail below. First we look at the common conditions for entry/stay under the Tier 5 (Temporary Worker) category.

Need to have a sponsor

All applicants under the Temporary Worker category must have a sponsor. The way that this works under the Rules is as follows. All applicants must score a total of 30 points for attributes under Appendix A of the Rules (Rules, paras 245ZO(b), 245ZQ(c); App A, para 105). The only way of scoring those points is by being issued with a Certificate of Sponsorship ('COS') by a sponsor (App A, para 106 and Table 15).

Need to have entry clearance

Most Tier 5 (Temporary Worker) applicants need entry clearance in order to enter the UK in this category (Rules, para 245ZN(a)). Applicants must also obtain their COS before applying for entry clearance. As a concession to the normal rule for the place where applications for (non-visit) entry clearances must be made, applicants in the Creative and Sporting subcategory may apply for entry clearance from a country that is not his/ her normal place of residence but is, instead, a country in which they are doing work similar to that which they wish to do in the UK (T5 (Temp) PG, para 112).

There is one exception to the requirement to obtain entry clearance. An applicant who is being sponsored (with a valid COS) in the Creative and Sporting subcategory, who meets all of the other requirements for entry, may be admitted without an entry clearance provided (Rules, para 245ZN(b)):

- s/he is not a visa national (ie a person who generally needs a visa for admission to the UK; the list of visa nationals is contained in Appendix 1 to the Rules);

9

- s/he has a valid COS according to a check that can be made on UKBA's electronic database which shows that s/he is being sponsored under the Creative and Sporting subcategory of Tier 5;
- that if the applicant has "consecutive engagements" (for which ▶see immediately below) in the UK, the total length of time of all his/her engagements (plus any gap between them) is three months or less; and
- that if the applicant does not have consecutive engagements, the total length of their engagement in the UK is three months or less.

"Consecutive engagements" An 'engagement' just means the particular employment that the applicant will be 'engaged' in as referred to on the COS which has been assigned to them. The COS should state the start and end date of the engagement. 'Consecutive' engagements refers to the situation where the applicant has been issued with more than one COS in order to meet their engagements in the UK and where there is a gap of no more than 14 days in between each engagement (Rules, para 245ZM(b)). So, where an applicant has been issued with more than one COS and has more than engagement in the UK, they can only be exempted from the need to have an entry clearance if they meet the above conditions *together with* the requirement that there are only 14 days between each engagement and that the total time that they need to spend in the UK comes to less than three months. All the engagements need to be sponsored under the Creative and Sporting subcategory.

Dependants

There is no prohibition on dependants joining the principal applicant under the Tier 5 (Temporary Worker) category as there is under the Youth Mobility Scheme. The requirements that must be met are largely the same as for those applying as dependants of the other categories of PBS migrants where the admission of dependants is permitted. They are described in Chapter 5 ▶194–203.

WHAT THE RULES SAY

Entering and remaining as a Tier 5 (Temporary Worker) Migrant

As stated above, most of those seeking entry require entry clearance (▶303). The further common requirements for obtaining entry clearance/ leave to enter and leave to remain in the UK under the Tier 5 (Temporary Worker) category are that (Rules, para 245ZO, 245ZQ):

- the applicant must not fall for refusal under the general grounds of refusal (▶see Chapter 11),
- if seeking leave to remain, the applicant must not be an illegal entrant;
- if the applicant is under 18 years of age, the application must be supported by his/her parents or legal guardian, or by one parent if that parent has sole legal responsibility for him/her;

- if the applicant is under 18 years of age, his/her parents or legal guardian, or just one parent if that parent has sole responsibility for him/her, must confirm that they consent to the arrangements for the applicant's travel to, reception and care in the UK (if the applicant is in the UK and the application is for leave to remain, it is obviously only the 'care' in the UK that consent is required for);
- the applicant must score a minimum of 30 points for attributes under paragraphs 105–112 of Appendix A to the Rules (▶see below); and
- the applicant must score a minimum of 10 points for maintenance under paragraphs 8–9 of Appendix C to the Rules (▶see below);
- if the applicant is seeking leave to remain, s/he must have last been granted entry clearance or leave to enter or remain as a Tier 5 (Temporary Worker) Migrant *unless* s/he falls within any of the exceptions set out below permitting switching from another category; and
- if the applicant is seeking leave to remain and was previously granted entry clearance or leave to remain as a Tier 5 (Temporary Worker) Migrant, s/he must be applying for and be sponsored under the same subcategory of the Tier 5 (Temporary Worker) category as the one s/he was last granted entry clearance or leave to remain in.

Switching

Switching both into the Tier 5 (Temporary Worker) category, and from that category to any other PBS route, is very restricted. The circumstances in which an applicant may 'switch' in-country in order to remain as a Tier 5 (Temporary Worker) migrant are as follows (see Rules, para 245ZQ(b)).

- The applicant was last granted entry clearance/leave as a Sports or Entertainer Visitor under the visit Rules (▶see Chapter 10 329–335) provided that, before the applicant entered the UK, s/he was issued with a valid COS in the Creative and Sporting subcategory of Tier 5. So, this allows an applicant to join together a period in the UK, first as a Sports/Entertainer Visitor and second under the creative/sporting subcategory of Tier 5 as long as they set up their Tier 5 sponsorship in advance.
- The applicant was last granted entry clearance/leave as an Overseas Government Employee (ie under paras 160–165 of the old Rules as deleted from 27 November 2008 by HC 1113), is now being sponsored and applying for leave in the International Agreement subcategory of Tier 5 and is continuing employment with the same overseas government or international organisation for which s/he was earlier given leave (this switching provision was added to the Rules from 22 February 2010 by HC 120).
- The applicant was last granted entry clearance/leave as a 'Qualifying Work Permit Holder' (ie one who was issued with a work permit under the old scheme in either the business and commercial, or the sports and entertainment categories; Rules, para 6), was previously issued with a work permit in order to be employed by an overseas government, is now being

sponsored and applying for leave in the International Agreement sub-category of the Tier 5 (Temporary Worker) category and is continuing employment with the same overseas government or international org-anisation for which s/he was earlier given leave.

- The applicant was last granted entry clearance/leave as a Qualifying Work Permit Holder (see immediately above for definition), was previously given a work permit for the purpose of employment as a sponsored researcher, is now being sponsored and applying for leave in the Government Authorised Exchange subcategory of the Tier 5 (Temporary Worker) category and is continuing employment with the same organisation for which s/he was most recently granted leave.

In the following circumstances, a Tier 5 (Temporary Worker) Migrant may switch into another category under the PBS.

- A footballer who is in the UK in the Tier 5 (Temporary Worker) category can switch into the Tier 2 (Sportsperson) category from within the UK. The applicant must meet all the requirements of the Tier 2 (Sportsperson category), including the English language requirement (Rules, para 245ZF(e)(xxiv)(g)(i)); T5 (Temp) PG in the table at pp 15)

- An overseas qualified nurse who is in the UK in the Government Author-ised Exchange subcategory of the Tier 5 (Temporary Worker) category, is able to switch to stay under Tier 2 in a job as an overseas qualified nurse or midwife on condition that the applicant has completed their registration with the nursing and Midwifery Council (Rules, para 245ZF(e)(xxiv)(g)(h); T5 (Temp) PG in the table at p15).

Scoring points for attributes under the Tier 5 (Temporary Worker) category

As stated above, all Tier 5 (Temporary Worker) applicants require 30 points for attributes which they can only score by being issued with a Certificate of Sponsorship (COS) (Rules paras 245ZO(b), 245ZQ(c); App A paras 105–6 and Table 15). The Rules do not describe the conditions for being sponsored or for the sponsor issuing a COS under the five different sub-categories. That is all dealt with in Guidance and we come to it below (▶beginning at 310). However, the Rules do set out a list of procedural requirements that must be met before the COS will allow the applicant to score the necessary points. They are (App A, paras 108–111);

- the COS must be valid, ie the reference number and the details of the COS that are given by the applicant in their application must match the details held by UKBA on its electronic database;

- the applicant must apply for entry clearance/leave to remain within three months of the issue of the COS (this does not apply where the applicant is applying for leave to *enter* and re-entering the UK using a COS which s/he has been granted leave to *enter* with before);

- the applicant will start the employment named on the COS within three months of the application for entry clearance/leave;

- the COS must not have been cancelled by either UKBA or the applicant's sponsor;
- the applicant must not have previously been granted entry clearance or leave to remain using the same COS; and
- where the COS is issued under the Creative and Sporting subcategory to allow the applicant to work as a sportsperson, the applicant must have been endorsed by the Governing Body of his/her sport and UKBA's records must show this (so UKBA should have received notice of this from the COS).

Finally, the Rules state that no points will be granted for a COS where it has been issued under the provisions of Mode 4 of the General Agreement on Trade in Services relating to intra-corporate transfers (App A, para 112).

Scoring points for maintenance under the Tier 5 (Temporary Worker) category

Applicants must score 10 points for maintenance under Appendix C to the Rules (Rules, paras 245ZO(c), 245ZQ(d); App C, para 8).

The maintenance requirement for those in the Temporary Worker category is different to that in the Youth Mobility Scheme. Whereas applicants under the Youth Mobility Scheme merely need to be able to demonstrate that they have a minimum of £1,600, those under the Temporary Worker category must either (App C, paras 1A(a)(b), 9 and Table):

- at the time of the application, show that they have at least £800 and that they have had those funds for a consecutive period of 90 days ending at any point in the calendar month before the date of the application; or
- have an 'A' rated sponsor (▶see Chapter 4 101–102) who has indicated on the COS that they certify that the applicant will not claim public funds during his/her period of leave under the Tier 5 (Temporary Worker) category (the guidance notes add that it is the duty of sponsors who provide this certificate to make the applicant aware that s/he should not claim state benefits during his/her period of leave, T5 (Temp) PG, para 135).

If the funds that the applicant relies on were obtained while s/he was in the UK, they must have been obtained at a time when s/he had valid leave and was not in breach of any of the conditions of that leave (App C, para 1A(d)).

Evidence of maintenance

The Rules state that applicants must provide the documents that are specified in the Policy Guidance in order to score points for maintenance (App C, paras 1A(e), 9 read with Rules para 245AA). For the effect on UKBA's ability to rely on the Policy Guidance of the decision of the Court of Appeal in *Pankina* and the associated case-law concerning mainten-ance, ▶see Chapter 2 42–45, 47–51 and Chapter 5 181. For the possible human rights arguments where the strict rules on maintenance cannot be met, ▶see Chapter 12 412–420.

The requirements as to the evidence and 'specified documents' are set out in the Policy Guidance (see T5 (Temp) PG, paras 142–149). Aside from the references to the particular the level of funds that are required under the Tier 5 (Temporary Worker) category (ie £800), the Guidance on mainten-ance is almost identical to that for Tier 1 (General) migrants which is contained in T1 (Gen) PG. For details of what this guidance contains, ▶see Chapter 5 154–155. There is, however, no reference in the T5 (Temp) PG to the acceptability of joint accounts as there is in the T1 (Gen) PG (at para 212). But this could simply be an oversight. Note the comments made by the Tribunal relating to this point, although they were made in a case concerning the Tier 1 (PSW) category and guidance relating to that category (*AM and SS (PBS – Tier 1 – joint accounts) Pakistan*):

"8. Mr Deller [the Senior Home Office Presenting Officer] told us that provisions relating to joint accounts had been accidentally omitted from the version of the Guidance applicable to the present application, but he agreed with our observation that, when provisions as to joint accounts had been included in the Guidance, they appeared to add nothing to the requirements for individual accounts."

Conditions of leave

The periods of leave that are granted under the Tier 5 (Temporary Worker) category are particular to each category and are dealt with below. The conditions that are normally attached to the leave can be set out together. The conditions are (Rules, paras 245ZP(e), 245ZR(g):

- no recourse to public funds;
- registration with the police where required (see Rules, para 326);
- applicants must only work for their sponsor in the employment for which they are being sponsored under their COS except that:
- applicants may take what is called "supplementary employment" (▶see below);
- those in the Government Authorised Exchange subcategory can also work for anyone whom the sponsor directs them to work for as long as the work is still the employment that the COS records that the applicant is sponsored to do; and
- those in the Creative and Sporting subcategory of Tier 5 can take employ-ment as a sportsperson for their national team while that team is in the UK.

"Supplementary employment"

The Policy Guidance sets out that applicants may undertake work that is 'supplementary' to the work for which the COS was issued. Supplementary work must meet the following three conditions; it must be (T5 (Temp) PG, paras 150–152):

- in the same sector and at the same level as the work for which the COS was issued.
- for no more than 20 hours per week; and
- outside the applicant's normal working hours for which the COS was issued.

For the work to be 'supplementary', applicants must also continue to work for their sponsor in the sponsored employment. Applicants are not required to tell UKBA about their supplementary work as long as it meets the above conditions (T5 (Temp) PG, paras 151–2). If they wish to do work that does not meet the above conditions, applicants must apply to UKBA in order to do so (T5 (Temp) PG, para 153).

Change of employment

Changes of employment, either with the same or a different sponsor, may be permitted under Tier 5 but applicants must apply to vary their leave in order to do it. A change will only be allowed if the new work is with a licensed sponsor and a new COS is required. Applicants will only be granted an extension of leave to stay to reach the maximum period permitted under the relevant subcategory of the scheme (▶below). Applicants cannot switch into another subcategory of Tier 5, or another category or tier of the PBS (T5 (Temp) PG, paras 154–157 and see Rules explained above).

Leaving and re-entering the UK

Those who have been granted entry clearance, or given leave for longer than six months, can re-enter on multiple occasions within the period of their leave (SG, paras 314–315; Immigration (Leave to Remain and Enter) Order 2000, Art 13). In the case of others, their leave will 'lapse' if they leave and they will have to apply for fresh leave, including applying for entry clearance again, unless they fall within the exception to those who need entry clearance (▶see 303). The Policy Guidance indicates also that it is possible to be issued with a multiple COS but that this is not necessary where the applicant wishes to go abroad for leisure, domestic or for business trips. The Guidance further states that where the applicant has been given entry clearance (or leave to remain for more than six months) and s/he is returning within that period of leave, s/he may can re-enter without obtaining a new COS (T5 (Temp) PG, paras 161–64).

Note that the Rules were amended from 1 October 2009 by Cm 7701 so as to enable migrants in the Creative and Sporting subcategory, who have entered without entry clearance, to use the same COS for multiple entries to the UK within a three-month period. Neither the Rules, nor the amendment to them appear to completely clearly drafted but the Explanatory Memo to the amending Rules states that the intention is to allow such persons to re-enter within the three-month period without obtaining a new COS (Rules as amended at App A, para 109A(a), 110); Explanatory Memo to Cm 7701 at para 7.9; T5 (Temp) PG, para 110; SG, para 318).

Sponsorship

An applicant under the Tier 5 (Temporary Worker) category is required to have a 'sponsor'. Generally, a sponsor is the UK-based organisation that the applicant wishes to work for. In order for an organisation to employ a particular applicant under the PBS they must be registered as a licensed sponsor. The sponsor must also have assigned a certificate of sponsorship (COS) for the applicant before s/he can submit his/her application for entry clearance/leave under the Tier 5 (Temporary Worker) category. In order to be able to assign a COS for a Tier 5 (Temporary Worker), the sponsor must have a licence which covers the sponsor for the particular subcategory in which the COS is to be issued.

The purpose of the COS is that it acts as an assurance that the applicant is able to undertake a particular job and intends to do so. The COS is not an actual document. It is a record with an individual reference number that contains the required information. The sponsor is responsible for providing the reference number to the applicant.

For full details about who may qualify to be a sponsor, applying to be a sponsor and how sponsorship operates, ▶see Chapter 4.

In the Tier 5 (Temporary Worker) category, the sponsor is not always the employer. The Tier 5 requirements can be met even if there is no direct employer/employee relationship. UKBA acknowledges that, in some sectors, particular arrangements may apply. For example, in the arts and entertainments sector, a migrant may be employed through a 'Special Purpose Vehicle'. In those cases, UKBA would still expect that the sponsor will be a producer or a general management company. In the Government Authorised Exchange subcategory, of course, an 'overarching' sponsor is used but is not the direct employer of any migrants. UKBA states that, in those cases where the sponsor is not directly employing the applicant, it will look very carefully at the arrangement in place to make sure that the applicant is being properly sponsored and that the sponsor duties (see also Chapter 4) are being met (PG, paras 288–90).

Creative and Sporting subcategory

This subcategory is intended for applicants who are coming to the UK in order to take up short-term contracts in the Creative and Sporting sectors (T5 (Temp) PG, para 98). It does *not* cater for those who entered or seek to enter the UK under the old permit-free concessions for entertainers including permit-free festivals and sportspeople. Those concessions are now contained in the specific Rules dealing with Entertainer and Sportsperson visitors (▶see Chapter 10 329–335; SG, para 295).

If an applicant has more than one sponsor because s/he is due to take up a number of different engagements in the UK, it is possible for each sponsor to issue a COS for each event. The periods of work specified in the COS must not overlap. If there is only one sponsor who is sponsoring the applicant for a number of different engagements, then the sponsor may issue only one COS as long as there is no more than 14 days between each engagement (T5 (Temp) PG, paras 114–5; SG, para 299). Note that the period of the engagement on the COS can include rehearsal periods. However, the COS must only cover the period of the engagement to include those rehearsals and if UKBA discover, perhaps through a visit, that that the COS has been issued to cover a longer period, it may take action against the sponsor (SG, para 301).

A 'group' COS may be issued for an applicant together with their entourage. The 'entourage' must be made up of people whose work is directly related to the employment of the applicant entertainer, artist or sportsperson and who have technical or other specialist skills (T5 (Temp) PG, para 113).

For the distinct requirements that must be met in order to apply for a licence to sponsor applicants under this subcategory ▶see Chapter 4 99–93.

Sportspeople

In order to issue a COS for a sportsperson, the sponsor must obtain an endorsement for the applicant from the governing body of the applicant's sport. The endorsement must confirm three things (T5 (Temp) PG, para 100; SG, paras 304, 309):

- that the player/coach is internationally established at the highest level (coaches must also be suitably qualified);
- that the applicant will make a significant contribution to the development of his/her sport at the highest level in the UK; and
- that the post could not be filled by a suitable settled worker.

Approved sporting governing bodies are listed on the UKBA website. When the sponsor assigns a COS, s/he must enter the governing body endorsement unique reference number into the electronic sponsor management system (SG, para 310).

Creative Workers

For creative workers operating in dance, theatre, film or television, the sponsor has to commit to following a specified 'code of practice' where that code takes account of the needs of the local resident labour market.

If the particular job does not have a code of practice that is associated with it, then in order to issue the COS, the sponsor needs to be able to show that the particular job could not have been done by a settled worker. The sponsor may show this by evidence of their own recruitment activity and attempts to recruit, or by written evidence from an industry representative body (T5 (Temp) PG, para 103; SG, para 297).

Guarantees given by issuing the COS

In issuing a COS under the Creative and Sporting subcategory, the sponsor guarantees that the applicant (T5 (Temp) PG, para 104; SG, paras 303, 312, 410):

- is seeking leave to enter the UK to work or perform in the relevant sector;
- is not intending to base themselves in business in the UK;
- does not pose a threat to the resident labour force; and
- will comply with the conditions of leave and depart from the UK when it expires.

Entry clearance/leave to be granted

If there are no more than 14 days between each of the engagements (ie the engagements are 'consecutive'), then entry clearance is granted to cover the whole period of the engagements *plus* a period of 14 days before the start of the first engagement *plus* a period of 14 days after the last engagement. If there is just one engagement, the same applies in that the applicant will be granted leave to enter for the period of the engagement plus 14 days either side. If there are more than 14 days between the engagements, the applicant is advised to leave the UK and apply again in order to re-enter to take up the next engagement. However, the *maximum* period of leave that can be granted is 12 months (Rules, para 245ZP(c); T5 (Temp) PG, paras 115–116; SG, paras 292, 300).

If the applicant is exempt from the need to obtain entry clearance (▶see 303 above) and arrives without such clearance, then the same rules as above apply for the period that is granted except that the maximum period of leave to enter that can be granted is only three months (Rules, para 245ZP(a)(b)).

If successful on an application to extend their leave, applicants will be granted a period of leave in line with their engagement/s, plus 14 days but up to a maximum of 12 months altogether (ie counting also the length of time spent in the UK under this category since his/her last entry). If the applicant has already spent 12 months here, the application will be refused (Rules, para 245ZR(a)(b)(c)). However, if the applicant is a *creative* worker and continues to sponsored *by the same sponsor as previously* also as a creative worker, then s/he may be given further leave for the length of his/her engagements plus 14 days, up to a maximum of two years altogether ie counting also the time spent in the UK under this category since his/her last entry (Rules, para 245ZR(e)(f); see also SG, para 292).

Creative and Sporting category applicants arriving without an entry clearance

As set out above (▶303), the Creative and Sporting subcategory is the only one under the Tier 5 (Temporary Worker) category in which it is possible for certain applicants to be admitted without entry clearance. Those arriving without such clearance are advised to expect a wait at the port while their status is checked. They should be ready to tell officers their COS reference number and have evidence with them to show that they satisfy the maintenance rules. They should also have with them contact details for their sponsor (T5 (Temp) PG, paras 107–109; SG, para 317).

Charity Workers

This subcategory is only for people wishing to undertake voluntary (and not paid) work in the UK. That work must be in line with the aims of the sponsor and the applicant must intend to carry out fieldwork directly related to the purpose of the sponsoring organisation (T5 (Temp) PG, paras 117–118; SG, para 320).

By issuing a COS, the sponsor guarantees that the applicant (T5 (Temp) PG, para 119; SG, paras 323, 411):

- intends to undertake voluntary fieldwork directly related to the purpose of the charity;
- will not be paid or receive other payment for their work;
- will not take up a permanent position; and
- will comply with the conditions of their leave and depart from the UK when it expires.

Although applicants cannot be paid, they are permitted to receive reimbursement of their reasonable expenses as outlined in section 44 of the National Minimum Wages Act.

Period of leave granted

Entry clearance/leave to enter is granted for the period of the engagement (or engagements provided there is no more than 14 days between them) plus 14 days either side of the engagement/s up to a maximum period of 12 months (Rules, para 245ZP(c)). The leave may be extended in-country but only up to a maximum period of 12 months including the original period of leave that was granted (Rules, para 245ZR(b)).

9

Religious Workers

Religious workers may be sponsored to come to the UK in order to take part in activities such as preaching and both pastoral and non-pastoral work (T5 (Temp) PG, para 120). This subcategory can also be used by those who are employed overseas in the same job as they wish to take up in the UK even if the exact nature of the responsibilities in the UK may differ to what they were doing abroad. The applicant's employment overseas should not cease as such, it should be continuing and their UK period of employment should be consistent with a career break. In addition, this subcategory may be used by members of religious orders, for example a community of monks or nuns, or a similar religious community that involves a permanent commitment to the order or community (SG, para 325).

For those applicants coming to the UK as members of religious orders, the work that they do must either be within the order itself, or it can be other work that is directed by the order. The Sponsor Guidance states that applicants in the following circumstances will not qualify under this subcategory (SG, para 329).

- Teachers working in schools that are not maintained by the order are not eligible. They must, instead, apply under Tier 2 (General).
- Those studying for a qualification on a full-time course in an academic institution that is not maintained by the order also cannot apply under this subcategory. They should apply under Tier 4 instead (although novices, whose training includes taking part in the daily community life of their order, can apply under this subcategory).
- Those who are working or studying within the order/community but who are not members of the religious order or community, are also not eligible to apply under this subcategory.

By issuing a Certificate of Sponsorship the sponsor guarantees that (T5 (Temp) PG, para 122; SG, paras 328, 412):

- the applicant is qualified to do the job in question;
- the applicant will not do work other than as a religious worker;
- the applicant will only work at the specified location except when doing 'supplementary' work;
- they accept the responsibilities of sponsorship for the applicant;
- they undertake to support the applicant through funds and/or accommodation which is sufficient to maintain the applicant throughout the period of the sponsorship;
- the applicant will not displace or deny an employment opportunity to a suitably qualified member of the resident labour force; and
- the applicant will comply with the conditions of their leave and will depart from the UK when it expires.

The Policy Guidance requires that, when they apply, applicants produce a letter from the sponsor outlining their duties, details of remuneration and an explanation of how what the applicant will do passes the Resident Labour Market Test. Further Guidance for sponsors in relation to the Resident Labour Market Test is set out in the Codes of Practice for sponsors (www.ukba.homeoffice.gov.uk/employers/points/sponsoringimmigrants/ employingimmigrants/codesofpractice (T1 (Temp) PG, para 123).

For the distinct requirements that must be met in order to apply for a licence to sponsor applicants under this subcategory, ▶see Chapter 4 89.

Period of leave granted

Entry clearance/leave to enter is granted for the period of the engagement plus 14 days either side of the engagement up to a maximum period of two years (Rules, para 245ZP(d)). It may be extended in-country but only up to a maximum period of two years including the original period of leave that was granted (Rules, para 245ZR(b)).

Government Authorised Exchange

The aim of this subcategory is to allow applicants to come to the UK through approved schemes, the purpose of which is to share knowledge, experience and best practice through work placements. The intention is also to allow applicants to experience the wider social and cultural environment of the UK. The subcategory is not for the purpose of filling job vacancies or bringing unskilled labour to the UK (T5 (Temp) PG, para 124).

Under this subcategory an 'overarching body' will normally manage the exchange scheme. and will act as the sponsor and be responsible for issuing a COS to each applicant who meets the requirements of the scheme and is participating in it. Both the particular exchange scheme and the sponsor must have the support of a UK government department (T5 (Temp) PG, para 126). A COS may only be assigned for skilled work ie equivalent to N/SVQ (National/Scottish Vocational Qualification) level 3 or above. The only applicants who are not required to undertake skilled work are those who come to the UK as part of the EU Lifelong Learning Programme (LLP) (T5 (Temp) PG, para 127). The LLP is a European funding programme which supports education and training across Europe. It provides funding for all stages of lifelong learning; for activities at school, at college, at university, in the workplace and in the community. Applicants who come to the UK under the LLP scheme can undertake vocational education and training at a lower level.

Individual employers and organisations are not permitted to sponsor migrants under the Government Authorised Exchange subcategory. The reason for this is to prevent potential abuse of the subcategory and also to prevent the formation of small individual schemes. The only exceptions to

9

this rule are that sponsored researchers may be recruited by Higher Education institutions under a scheme approved by the Department for Innovation, Universities and Skills and also where the sponsor is a government department or the executive agency of such a department (T5 (Temp) PG, para 125).

In assigning a COS, the overarching body that acts as sponsor guarantees that the applicant (T5 (Temp) PG, para 128; SG, paras 339, 413):

- is seeking entry to the UK to work or train temporarily through an approved exchange scheme;
- does not intend to establish a business in the UK; and
- meets the requirements of the individual exchange scheme.

For the distinct requirements that must be met in order to apply for a licence to sponsor applicants under this subcategory, ▶see Chapter 4 93–94.

Period of leave granted

Entry clearance/leave to enter is granted for the period of the engagement plus 14 days either side of the engagement up to a maximum period of two years (Rules, para 245ZP(d)). It may be extended in country but only up to a maximum period of two years including the original period of leave that was granted (Rules, para 245ZR(b)).

International Agreement

Applicants who wish to come to the UK under a contract to provide a service that is covered under international law may apply under the International Agreement subcategory. This includes:

- private servants in diplomatic households;
- services covered by other agreements between the UK and another country;
- services covered by the General Agreement on Trade in Services (GATS); and
- employees of overseas governments and international organisations.

Note that those who want to come to the UK under the intra-corporate transfer commitment of GATS are not eligible under this subcategory. They must apply under Tier 2 (ICT) of the PBS (see T5 (Temp) PG, para 129). Domestic workers in private households that are not diplomatic households are also not eligible under this subcategory (T5 (Temp) PG, para 130). They must qualify under the separate non-PBS Rules (▶see Chapter 10 94).

The guarantees given by sponsors in respect of applicants when they issue a COS under this subcategory differ depending on the type of applicant.

Servants in private diplomatic households

The guarantee that the sponsor gives when issuing a COS for a servant in a private diplomatic household is that the applicant (T5 (PG) para 130; SG, paras 343, 414):

- is aged 18 years or over;
- will be employed as a private servant in the household of:
- a member of staff of a diplomatic or consular mission who has diplomatic privileges and immunity as defined by the Vienna Convention on Diplomatic Relations; or
- an official employed by an international organisation with certain privileges and immunities under UK or international law;
- intends to work in full-time domestic employment;
- will not take up any other form of employment for the sponsor other than as a private servant in the specified household; and
- will leave the UK at the expiry of his/her leave.

Transitional arrangements for private servants in diplomatic households, who were working in the UK on or before 27 November 2008, were introduced at the time Tier 5 came into force. If UKBA approved their applications to extend their stay, they were given a one-off permission to stay for up to five years, which is the threshold for them to be able to apply for settlement (▶see below). UKBA continued to accept applications under these arrangements after that date until 26 May 2010 so as to ensure that everyone eligible to apply under the transitional arrangements had an opportunity to do so.

Employees of overseas governments and international organisations

The guarantee given in respect of employees of overseas governments and international organisations is that the applicant will (T5 (PG) para 131; SG, paras 345, 415):

- be under a contract of employment with the overseas government or international organisation;
- not take up any job for the sponsor other than that for which the COS was assigned; and
- not try to avoid immigration controls by switching to a different category of worker within the International Agreements subcategory after entering the UK.

GATS

The guarantee given in respect of applicants under GATS, or other international agreements, is that the applicant (T5 (Temp) PG, para 132; SG, paras 348, 416):

- works for an employer or organisation of a country that either:
- – is a member of the World Trade Organisation;
- – has a bilateral agreement with the UK or the European Union; or
- – is a member of the European Union;
- will be engaged in work that meets the terms and conditions of the relevant international agreement; and
- where relevant, works for the employer that was awarded the contract or will provide services to the UK client.

For the distinct requirements that must be met in order to apply for a licence to sponsor applicants under this subcategory, ▶see Chapter 4 94.

Periods of leave granted

Entry clearance/leave to enter is granted for the period of the engagement plus 14 days either side of the engagement up to a maximum period of two years (Rules, para 245ZP(d)). It may be extended in country but only up to a maximum period of 2 years, including the original period of leave that was granted (Rules, para 245ZR(b)).

However, those in the International Agreement subcategory who are being sponsored as overseas government employees or private servants in a diplomatic household may extend their limited leave up to a maximum of six years altogether (Rules, para 245ZR(d)). Private servants are even able to apply for settlement in the UK (▶immediately below).

Settlement for private servants in diplomatic households

The only direct route to settlement under Tier 5 is for those sponsored as private servants in diplomatic households under the International Agreement subcategory of the Tier 5 (Temporary Worker) category. The Rules were amended from 31 March 2009 to allow these applicants a route to settlement (see HC 314). In order to obtain indefinite leave (ie settlement), the applicant must (Rules, para 245ZS):

- have spent a continuous period of five years lawfully in the UK with leave in the above subcategory, working as a private servant in a diplomatic household (for further details about the calculation of this "continuous period", ▶see Chapter 5 189–193);
- not fall for refusal under the general grounds of refusal (▶see Chapter 11);
- not be an illegal entrant; and
- have sufficient knowledge of the English language and of life in the UK, unless s/he is aged under 18, or over 65 at the time of the application.

10 Non-PBS work/study routes and employer sanctions

This chapter covers:

- Visitors (▶320–341) including:
- – General Visitors;
- – Business Visitors;
- – Sports Visitors;
- – Entertainer Visitors;
- – Student Visitors;
- – Child Visitors coming for educational reasons;
- – parents of a child at school;
- – Prospective Students;

- employment under the Rules (▶341–353) including:
- – Postgraduate Doctors and Dentists including doctors undertaking the PLAB test, doctors undertaking clinical attachments and dentists undertaking clinical observer posts;
- – representatives of overseas businesses;
- – UK ancestry;
- – domestic workers;

- Employment outside the Rules (▶353–354):

- Exempt categories (▶354–355):
- – crew of ships, trains and aircraft;
- – offshore workers;
- – armed forces.

- Working without permission; consequences for employers and employees (▶355–374).

This chapter sets out those routes for work or study which remain outside the Points-Based System. It also addresses the consequences, for both employers and employees, of working without permission.

Some of these routes have long been in the Immigration Rules as permit-free employment routes which may lead to settlement, for example sole representatives and Commonwealth citizens with UK ancestry. Others have existed as concessions outside the Rules, such as offshore workers, film crews on location and sportspersons, which were temporary routes and did not lead to settlement. Others, such as aircrews and armed forces, are exempt from immigration control by virtue of section 8 of the 1971 Act and the Immigration (Exemption from Control) Order 1972 SI 1972/1613.

The underlying policy has been to incorporate as many as possible of all the various categories either into the PBS or the Immigration Rules and to move away from having routes dealt with by concessions (▶see the table in Chapter 2 showing routes of entry pre- and post- the PBS 38–40). Some routes do not easily fit within the structure of the PBS and so have been retained, some temporarily, others indefinitely, in the Rules.

It is important to appreciate that since these routes are outside the PBS, decisions on whether to grant entry clearance or leave remain subject to decisions based on the often subjective criteria under the Rules, such as an assessment of the 'intentions' of the applicant by the relevant official. It is not like the PBS where a person either achieves the specified points score or does not – if he does not, he will be refused; if he does, then, in the absence of a reason for refusal under the general grounds of refusal entry clearance or leave will be granted. On the other hand, these categories are not subject to the prescriptive documentation regime, or the maintenance or English language tests, under the PBS.

VISITORS

Business Visitors used to be admitted under the generic rule for 'Visitors', and the limits of their permitted economic activities were set out in the IDI, which also contained a number of concessions allowing permit-free employment outside the Rules for those wishing to visit in order to participate in sport or provide entertainment. Following a consultation process by the Government during 2008, the Rules were amended by Rules laid on 4 November 2008 (HC 1113) in order to create:

- the category of General Visitor, which replaces the old generic visitor category;
- a distinct category under the Rules for Business Visitors (which includes 'Academic Visitors' and 'Visiting Professors'); and
- separate and distinct categories under the Rules for Visiting Sportspeople and Entertainers, based on the previous concessions.

Below, we look at all of these categories. We take only a brief look at the General Visitor category (▶321) since this chapter concerns those coming for visits for *work or study* purposes. General Visitors must not be coming for such purposes, but we look at them because, in many instances, the requirements relating to the other categories of visitor refer back to the General Visitor requirements.

The Rules laid on 4 November 2008 defined a range of other categories of visitor as Special Visitors, namely those coming (para 6 HC 395 as amended by para 1 HC 113):

- for private medical treatment;
- for marriage;
- as Student Visitors;
- as Prospective Students;
- as Child Visitors;
- as parents of a child at school;
- as visitors in transit.

Of these 'special visitor' routes, we cover below those that relate to either work or study, namely: Student Visitors (▶336); Prospective Students (▶340); Child Visitors (where they are coming for educational reasons) (▶338); and parents of children at school (▶340). We do not cover medical visits, visits for marriage/civil partnership, or transit visitors (all similarly listed as forms of Special Visitor). We also do not cover visitors under the 'Approved Destinations Status' Agreement with China.

There remain a few categories which are not specified in the rules as Special Visitors but for whom there is provision/guidance in the IDI, which include carers (IDI, Ch 17, section 2), people coming to take part in archaeological excavations (IDI, Ch 2, paras 2.19) and child minders for relatives (IDI, Ch 2, paras 2.20).

Visitors and entry clearance

Visitors who are visa nationals (see the list of countries whose nationals are 'visa nationals' in Appendix 1 of the Immigration Rules) must obtain an entry clearance (often known as a 'visa') from a British embassy, high commission or consulate before travelling to the UK. Applicants for entry clearance must be outside the UK at the time they apply. Applications can be made to any post that is designated to accept visit entry clearance applications (Rules, para 28).

Visitors who are not visa nationals do not need to obtain entry clearance, though they may do so if they wish. Alternatively they may apply for leave to enter on arrival at a British port. There are always advantages (such as an in-country right of appeal against refusal of leave to enter) and disadvantages (such as the possibility of a refusal) in applying for entry clearance where it is optional. Often the best course depends on the particular circumstance of the case, but the formal requirements of the Rules remain the same.

General Visitors

The General Visitor category applies to those coming for visits for general purposes, for example for holidays or to see family or friends and other purposes not specifically dealt with in the other visit categories. It is beyond the scope of this chapter to give a full analysis of the General Visitor rule. A detailed discussion of the former generic visitor rule can be

10

found in Chapter 9 of the *JCWI Handbook* 2006 edition (on pp213–247). It is necessary, however, to set out the basic requirements because other categories of visitor refer to the need to comply with some of the General Visitor conditions as well as meet the specific requirements of the applicable rule for that type of visit.

Those seeking entry to the UK as General Visitors must show that they (Rules, paras 41–43):

- are genuinely coming for a limited period as stated by them not exceeding six months;
- intend to leave the UK at the end of their visit;
- do not intend to take employment;
- do not intend to produce goods or provide services within the UK, including the selling of goods or services direct to members of the public;
- do not intend to undertake a course of study;
- will maintain and accommodate themselves and any dependants out of resources available to them without recourse to public funds or taking employment, or will be so supported by relatives and friends;
- can meet the cost of their return or onward journey;
- are not a child under 18
- do not intend to do any of the activities provided for in the Rules relating to Business Visitors, Sports Visitors or Entertainer Visitors;
- do not intend to marry or form a civil partnership (*note*: there is a separate visitor category for this purpose);
- do not intend to receive private medical treatment during their visit (*note*: there is a separate visitor category for this purpose); and
- are not in transit to a country outside the common travel area (*note*: there is a separate visitor category for this purpose).

Duration of leave If they satisfy the above requirements, applicants are usually admitted for six months with a condition prohibiting employment. Leave to remain beyond the six-month maximum in the General Visitor category will only be granted outside the Rules in the most exceptional compassionate circumstances.

Frequency and duration of visits There is no formal restriction on the number of visits a person may make to the UK, nor any requirement that a specified time must elapse between successive visits. The fact that a person has made a series of visits with only brief intervals between them should not, in the absence of any other relevant factors, constitute suffi-cient ground for refusal. It is reasonable, however, for the immigration officer to consider the stated purpose of the visit in the light of the length of time that has elapsed since previous visits. The IDI state that a visitor should not, for example, normally spend more than six out of any 12 months in the UK. This is calculated on a rolling 12-month basis, which means that on arrival the immigration officer counts back 12 months from that date of arrival and calculates how much time the passenger has spent in the UK since then.

The IDI say that, occasionally, a Business Visitor may be required to stay for a period of weeks or even months (for example where machinery is being installed or faults being diagnosed and corrected). The immigration officer should be satisfied, however, that a person's presence here on business for more than six out of any 12 months does not mean that s/he is basing himself here and holding down a specific post which constitutes employment and would therefore require the individual to seek entry under the PBS.

Children coming for the purpose of a general visit

Children cannot qualify as General Visitors but there they can be admitted for the same essential purposes as a General Visitor under the separate category under the Rules, for 'Child Visitors' which applies to those who are under 18 (Rules, para 46A–46C). In addition to being required to satisfy most of the above requirements, Child Visitors must also show that: suitable arrangements have been made for them in the UK; they have a parent or guardian in their home country who is responsible for them; and, if a visa national, that they have an entry clearance either as an unaccompanied child, or one that is endorsed so as to identify the adult that they are travelling with. However, the requirement that applies to General Visitors that prevents them from undertaking a course of study (Rules, para 41(v)) does not apply to Child Visitors (see Rules, para 46A(ii)). Instead, the Child Visitor rules make specific provision for children to come for educational purposes (▶see below 338).

Business Visitors

The IDIs describe Business Visitors as persons who work abroad but who intend to visit the UK for short periods of time in order to transact business on their own or their overseas employer's behalf (IDI, Ch 2, para 2.2). They also state that, as well as meeting all the normal requirements for leave to enter as a General Visitor, applicants must show that they (IDI, Ch 2, para 2.2):

10

- are based abroad and have no intention of transferring their base to the UK, even temporarily;

- will not receive a salary from a UK source, although a Business Visitor is allowed to receive reasonable expenses to cover the cost of his/her travel and subsistence (some multinational companies will be administered from the UK, including the payment of worldwide salaries – in these circumstances, entry as a Business Visitor may still be appropriate, provided the person is based abroad and intends to continue to be so); and

- are not involved in selling goods or services direct to members of the public.

The Rules themselves state that a Business Visitor must (Rules, paras 46G–46I):

- be genuinely seeking entry as a Business Visitor for a limited period stated by him/her which must not exceed six months (or 12 months in the case of an Academic Visitor);
- meet all the applicable rules for General Visitors (▶above); and
- be coming to the UK for one of a number of specified purposes.

The list of specified purposes contains eight specified activities and introduces another generic activity called a "permissible activity". While the eight activities are listed in the Rules themselves and therefore can only be changed by means of a Rule change and the applicable Parliamentary procedure, "permissible activity" is defined in paragraph 6 of the Rules as a business activity "of a type listed in UKBA guidance specifying the activities that a business person may undertake during a short-term business visit to the UK". This means that the UKBA can add, remove or change any "permissible activity" by means of issuing amended Guidance, a simple administrative procedure. For the difficulties of a system where requirements for admission under the Rules are delegated to policy-making outside the Rules, ▶see Chapter 2 at 40–45.

Accordingly, in order to gain entry, the Business Visitor must intend to do one or more of the following during his/her visit (Rules, para 46G(iii)):

- carry out a "permissible activity" as defined (▶see box below 328);
- take part in a location shoot as a member of a film crew – this includes actors, producers, directors and technicians, provided they are employed or paid by an overseas company;
- represent overseas news media, including as a journalist, correspondent, producer or cameraman, provided s/he is employed or paid by an overseas company and is gathering information for an overseas publication or programme;
- act as an Academic Visitor but only if s/he has been working as an academic in an institution of higher education overseas, or in the field of his academic expertise immediately prior to seeking entry (▶see further below);
- act as a Visiting Professor (▶see further below);
- be a secondee to a UK company which is directly contracted with the visitor's overseas company, with which it has no corporate relationship, to provide goods or services, provided the secondee remains employed and paid by the overseas company throughout the secondee's visit (▶see further below);
- undertake some preaching or pastoral work as a religious worker (eg, to attend a conference), provided his/her base is abroad and he is not taking up an office, post or appointment;
- act as an adviser, consultant, trainer or trouble-shooter to the UK branch of

the same group of companies as the visitor's overseas company, provided the visitor remains employed and paid by the overseas company and does not undertake work, paid or unpaid with the UK company's clients (▶see further below);

- provide specific, one-off training on techniques and work practices used in the UK (the training could typically be classroom based and/or involve familiarisation or observation) where:
  - the training is to be delivered by the UK branch of the same group of companies to which the individual's employer belongs. (The IDI give the following example: where an overseas branch sends an employee to find out about the UK branch's marketing systems, IDI, Ch 2, para 2.2.3); or
  - the training is to be provided by a UK company contracted to provide goods or services to the overseas company (The IDI give the following example: training on how to use a piece of computer software that has been purchased, IDI, Ch 2, para 2.2.3); or
  - a UK company is contracted to provide training facilities only to an overseas company (the IDI give the following example: Provision of a classroom or piece of equipment, IDI, Ch 2, para 2.2.3).

Academic Visitor The IDI gives further details about Academic Visitors (IDI, Ch 2, paras 2.3.1–2.3.2). They state that Academic Visitors should be:

- persons on leave from an overseas academic institution who wish to come to the UK to make use of his/her leave to carry out his/her own private research or exchange information on research techniques – this may include some collaboration with staff at the host university or use of facilities;
- academics (including doctors) taking part in arranged exchanges, for example where a university in the UK is collaborating with an overseas university on research and exchanges personnel for some or all of the duration of the project – any salary should continue to be paid by the academic's own overseas institution; or
- eminent senior doctors and dentists (ie those considered to be top of their field of expertise) coming to take part in research, teaching or clinical practice.

The IDI go on to state that Academic Visitors must:

- not receive funding for their work from any UK source (payments of expenses, including travel or those to cover needs while in the UK can also be disregarded as can payments made on an exchange basis);
- not intend to take employment or engage in any work other than the academic activity for which they are being admitted;
- not be filling a normal post or genuine vacancy.

In addition, the IDI give examples of those unlikely to qualify as Academic Visitors:

- recent graduates, ie who are unlikely to have reached the necessary level of expertise;

- postgraduate researchers who are entering the UK in order to study for an accredited UK academic qualification – they should normally enter as Students;

- lecturers who want to come to the UK in order to give a series of lectures for which they will be paid – they will normally be required to obtain entry under Tier 2; however academics coming to participate in a single event which is not a commercial venture might enter as an ordinary Business Visitor;

- sponsored researchers – they should use the Tier 5 Government Authorised Exchange route.

Visiting Professor Students from overseas academic institutions who come to the UK on study abroad programmes may be accompanied by their professor/s who are overseeing their study. The professor may undertake teaching in the UK provided it is limited to the institution that is hosting the students and teaching should not be the visiting professor's main purpose in coming to the UK. The professor must be employed and paid by the overseas institution and they must not intend to base themselves in the UK (IDI, Ch 2, para 2.6).

Secondees The IDI state that this provision relates specifically and only to the situation where a UK company is to provide goods or services to an overseas company on a direct contractual basis, not vice versa; and where there is no corporate relationship between the two companies, ie, they are not part of the same group of companies. The individual will be seconded for the purpose of assisting the UK company to deliver the contract, for example to clarify his company's specifications. The secondee must remain employed and paid by the overseas company throughout his/her visit. Where a person is employed by an overseas company and is being seconded to a UK company which is related to the overseas employer, he must qualify to do so under the Intra Company Transfer (ICT) arrangements of Tier 2 of the PBS (▶see 222). Therefore, those who meet the ICT rules should not be granted leave under these arrangements for secondees. Persons coming to work in the UK in any other circumstances must qualify to do so under the relevant tier of the PBS. The IDI state that "Secondees should be granted leave to enter for a maximum of six months at any one time. In some cases such secondment arrangements can continue legitimately for longer than six months. Some are likely therefore to return to the UK for further periods. Provided the Immigration Officer is satisfied that they are returning for the same purpose for which they were originally granted leave to enter and that they meet General Visitor requirements, multiple entry should be permitted" (IDI, Ch 2, para 2.2.1).

Advisers/consultants etc The IDI state that those admitted for this purpose cannot intend to conduct work, paid or unpaid, for or on behalf of the UK branch, including, but not limited to, providing services for the UK branch to other companies, working in a supernumerary capacity (eg internship, project managing or by way of short-term temporary cover for the UK branch), or have direct involvement in producing goods for the UK company's clients. They must remain employed and paid by the overseas company throughout the visit and typically their visit would be of a one-off, short-term nature (IDI, Ch 2, para 2.2.2).

Specific, one-off training etc Although the Rules only refer to the three situations given above, the IDI state that this provision under the Rules also covers where the visitor is an employee from the same group of companies overseas as the UK company and is participating in a corporate training exercise provided to the UK company by an *outside* provider (IDI, Ch 2, para 2.2.3).

The IDI state that it is reasonable to expect those coming to the UK as Business Visitors (to attend meetings etc) to want to make use of their laptop/Blackberry whilst here. Provided this is solely to enable the Business Visitor to keep up to date with their own workload abroad, or to liaise with contacts in the UK, UKBA would not consider this as 'work' for the purposes of the Rules (IDI, Ch 2, para 2.2.4). A Business Visitor may also undertake tourist activities (ie visiting tourist attractions, friends, etc). They may also carry out activities permitted for Sports and Entertainer Visitors whilst in the UK (IDI, Ch 2, para 2.2.4).

Great care should be taken by international companies who have a PBS sponsor licence for their UK operations when deciding whether or not overseas employees can validly enter as Business Visitors. When there is any element of doubt whether the employee falls within the precise terms and scope of any of the above eight specified activities, or any of the permissible activities, the Business Visitor route should not be used in place of a validly issued Tier 2 certificate under the ICT category. Abuse of the Business Visitor route in these circumstances could lead to sanctions against the licensed sponsor (for further details ▶see Chapter 4).

10

Length of admission and dependants

Business Visitors may be admitted for a maximum of six months, with the taking of employment prohibited and they may not extend any one stay in the UK beyond that period. The only exception to that is Academic Visitors who may be admitted for up to 12 months provided they arrive with an entry clearance (Rules, paras 46H–46L). Dependants of Business Visitors should be treated as General Visitors (▶above) or, if under the age of 18, as Child Visitors and granted a maximum of six months (12 months in the case of dependants of Academic Visitors, Rules paras 42 and 46B) leave to enter with a prohibition on employment.

PERMISSIBLE ACTIVITIES

The following are listed in UKBA's Guidance (current at the date of writing) as permissible activities for Business Visitors for the purposes of paragraphs 6 and 46G(iii)(a) of the Rules (see IDI, Ch 2, para 2.24):

- attending meetings, including interviews that have been arranged before coming to the UK or conferences;

- attending trade fairs provided this is restricted to promotional work and does not involve selling direct;

- arranging deals, negotiating or signing trade agreements or contracts, undertaking fact-finding missions;

- conducting site visits;

- delivering goods and passengers from abroad such as lorry drivers and coach drivers provided they are genuinely working an international route;

- tour group couriers who are contracted to a firm outside the UK, who are seeking entry to accompany a tour group and who intend to leave with that tour group;

- speaking at a conference where this is not run as a commercial concern (organisers not making a profit) and the conference is a 'one-off';

- representing computer software companies coming to install, debug or enhance their products. Representatives of such companies may also be admitted as Business Visitors in order to be briefed as to the requirements of a UK customer but if they are to provide a service involving the use of their expertise to make a detailed assessment of a potential customer's requirements this should be regarded as consultancy work for which entry under the PBS would be required;

- representing foreign manufacturers by coming to service or repair their company's products within their initial period of guarantee;

- representing foreign machine manufacturers coming to erect and install machinery too heavy to be delivered in one piece, as part of the contract of purchase and supply;

- interpreting or translating for visiting businesspersons, provided the interpreter/translator is employed by the overseas company and is coming solely to provide this service for the visiting company member;

- monteurs (eg mechanics or serviceperson) coming for up to six months to erect, dismantle, install, service, repair or advise on the development of foreign-made machinery; and

- board-level directors attending board meetings in the UK provided they are not employed by a UK company, although they may be paid a fee for attending the meeting.

PLAB Test and clinical attachment/dental observation

It should be noted that doctors taking the Professional and Linguistic Assessment Board (PLAB) Test and those seeking entry for clinical attachment/dental observation are included within the definition of 'Business Visitors' in paragraph 6 of the Rules, although provision for these categories is actually dealt with in the part of the Rules covering studies (paras 75A–75F and 75G–75M, HC395) ▶see below 344–346 for further details of these two categories.

Sports Visitors

The 'creation' of the Sports Visitor and Entertainer Visitor categories (▶below) was, in reality, the transfer into the Rules of concessions that previously existed outside them. The distinguishing feature of these two new classes of visitor is that generally they should not be paid for the activities that they do in the UK.

Paragraphs 46M–46R of the Rules replace the previous concessions for: 'sportspersons coming for specific events'; 'persons coming for charity events' (exhibition matches etc); amateurs joining amateur teams; 'polo grooms'; personal coaches (etc). The intention is to enable sportspersons coming to the UK for one of these purposes to do so outside the PBS but within the Rules.

As will be seen from the chapters covering Tiers 2 and 5 of the PBS, sportspersons coming to base themselves in the UK to work, will need to qualify under either of those Tiers. Tier 2 (Sportspeople) is for elite sportspeople and coaches who are internationally established at the highest level, or whose employment will make a significant contribution to the development of their sport in the UK. Tier 5 is for individuals in the sporting sector who are coming to the UK temporarily for up to 12 months.

The requirements to be met by a person seeking leave to enter the UK as a Sports Visitor are that s/he (Rules, para 46M–46O):

10

* is genuinely seeking entry as a Sports Visitor for a limited period as stated by him, not exceeding six months;
* meets the requirements of the General Visitor rule (▶above); and
* intends to do one or more of the following during his/her visit:
– take part in a particular sporting event as defined in Guidance published by UKBA, tournament or series of events (▶see definition below)
– take part in a specific one-off charity sporting event, provided no payment is received other than for travelling and other expenses;
– join, as an amateur, a wholly or predominantly amateur team provided no payment is received other than for board and lodging and reasonable expenses;
– serve as a member of the technical or personal staff, or as an official, attending the same event as a Visiting Sportsperson coming for one or more of the above purposes.

Definitions

There are some helpful definitions in relation to the Sports Visitor category, as follows.

'Series of events' This is defined in the Rules as "two or more linked events, such as a tour, or rounds of a competition, which do not add up to a league or a season" (para 6). The IDI (Ch 2, para 2.8.2) expand on this, giving as an example football teams coming to the UK to participate in pre-season friendly matches against English clubs, in competitions. This would also include those coming for a series of events that, although not part of the same competition, are being held in the UK at the same time. For example the AEGON Tennis Championship is held immediately before Wimbledon and players are not expected to return home and seek fresh entry clearance.

'Amateur' In the Rules an "amateur" is defined, for the purpose of distinguishing him from a professional who is paid a salary for participation in sport (e.g. someone contracted to play for a sport or club), as "a person who engages in a sport...solely for personal enjoyment and who is not seeking to derive a living" from the sport (para 6). The IDI actually misquote this, adding the words "either wholly or in part" after the words "derive a living" (Ch 2, para 2.8.2). It should be remembered that the IDI do not have the force of law, nor are they an aid to the construction of the Rules. They are merely directions issued by the UKBA to its officials about the implementation of the rules (see *ZH (Bangladesh v Secretary of State for the Home Department)*. There is always the possibility that the AIT will not necessarily agree that they are correct or indeed lawful. So if a Sports Visitor seeking entry under this limb, is refused it because s/he derives a living partly from the sport, it may be challengeable. For practical purposes, though, both amateur and professional sportspeople may enter as Sports Visitors (▶see above).

Amateurs may not receive fees and sponsorship but may receive cash prizes as well as board, lodging and living expenses. The IDI say that sportspersons who are amateurs not paid for playing at home, will be able to join a club in the UK as a Sports Visitor provided that the team is made up of wholly, or predominately, amateur players and they are not being paid by the club, other than board, lodgings and living expenses. 'Predominantly amateur' would normally be considered to mean that the club has only one or two professional players. The club must be regarded within their sport as an amateur one (ie, one where the players are not normally paid or contracted to play for the club) and would not normally be in a league regarded as professional within the sport (IDI, Ch 2, para 2.8.2).

WHO MAY BE ADMITTED AS A SPORTS VISITOR?

The IDI state that Sports Visitors include (Ch 2, para 2.8):

- Amateurs and professionals coming to the UK to take part either as individuals or as a team in a specific event or tournament (eg, Wimbledon) or a series of events:

"Participation in an event not considered to be a sports competition

Those coming to take part in competitions that do not fall within the definition of 'sports' for the sports visitor provision, (for example Chess Tournaments) may be regarded as general visitors provided they meet the requirements of the Rules for general visitors. They should not receive any fee or sponsorship for their participation but may receive cash prizes, board, lodging and living expenses." (IDI, Ch 2, para 2.8.1)

- Members of the technical or support staff of amateurs or professionals, who are attending for the same event as the sportsperson. Examples of such staff include team managers, personal coaches, doctors, physiotherapists, dieticians, bodyguards and press officers.

- Polo grooms, providing they are not intending to base themselves at the stables for the season.

- Officials, including those coming on a voluntary basis, attending the same event as the sportsperson. Examples include linespersons and umpires.

- Amateurs and professionals coming as either an individual or a member of an overseas team, for a specific one-off charity sporting event or exhibition match, such as the London Marathon, provided the organisers are not making a profit and the sportsperson is not receiving a fee.

- Those seeking entry for personal appearances and promotions such as book signings, television interviews, negotiating contracts or to discuss sponsorship deals.

- Sportspeople seeking entry for 'trials' provided that the trial is not in front of an audience, either paying or non-paying.

- Those coming for training for short periods (whether as an individual or as part of a team) provided that they are not basing themselves in the UK, not being paid by a UK sporting body or joining a UK team; and any matches they are involved in are of the friendly/exhibition type.

10

Conditions

Six months, with a condition prohibiting employment, is the maximum permitted leave which may be granted to a Sports Visitor. Sports Visitors may undertake the 'permissible activities' of Business Visitors, ▶see above 328. They may also undertake Entertainer Visitor activities (▶below). It is not permissible under the Rules for a Sports Visitor to switch to a purpose covered in the PBS after entry to the UK. However, if a person was issued with a certificate of sponsorship under Tier 5 (Creative and Sporting) before they came to the UK, they may use this to apply for leave to remain to continue with the Tier 5 work without leaving the UK (see IDI, Ch 2, para 2.8.6).

Entertainer Visitors

Paragraphs 46S–46X of the Rules replace the previous concessions for entertainers, which allowed them to come to the UK for a short time, without a work permit, in order to take part in certain major arts festivals, music competitions and charity events. The present intention is to enable entertainers and their entourage to come to the UK for one of these purposes within the Rules but outside the PBS.

Entertainers coming to base themselves in the UK to work will need to qualify to do so under either Tiers 2 or 5. Tier 2 (General) is for entertainers who are coming for more than 12 months. Tier 5 (Creative and Sporting) is for people in those sectors coming to the UK temporarily for up to 12 months.

The requirements to be met by a person seeking leave to enter the UK as an Entertainer Visitor are that s/he (Rules, para 46S):

- is genuinely seeking entry as an Entertainer Visitor for a limited period as stated by him/her, not exceeding six months;
- meets the requirements of the General Visitor rule; and
- intends to do one or more of the following during his visit:
- take part as a professional entertainer in one or more music competitions;
- fulfil one or more specific engagements as either an individual amateur entertainer or as an amateur group;
- take part, as an amateur or professional entertainer, in a cultural event (or one or more of such events) that appears in the list of events to which this provision applies that is published in Guidance issued by the UKBA; and/or
- serve as a member of the technical or personal staff, or of the production team, of an entertainer coming for one or more of the above purposes.

A person seeking leave to enter to the UK as an Entertainer Visitor may be admitted for a period not exceeding six months, subject to a condition prohibiting employment, provided that officers are satisfied that each of the requirements of paragraph 46S is met (Rules, para 46T). Six months is the maximum permitted leave which may be granted to an Entertainer Visitor.

As with Sports Visitors (▶above), 'amateur' is defined as "a person who engages in a...creative activity solely for personal enjoyment and who is not intending to derive a living from the activity" (Rules, para 6).

The 'Permit Free Festival List'

The 'Permit Free Festival List' sets out those festivals which entertainers may be admitted to the UK as Entertainer Visitors to attend on one of the

WHO MAY BE ADMITTED AS AN ENTERTAINER VISITOR?

The IDI state that Entertainer Visitors include (Ch 2, para 2.9):

- professional entertainers coming to take part in music competitions;

- internationally famous people coming to the UK to take part in broadcasts or public appearances provided they are not performing and are not being paid;

- those undertaking an audition provided this is not performed in front of an audience (either paying or non-paying);

- amateur entertainers seeking entry as individual performers for a specific engagement;

- amateur entertainers seeking entry as part of a group, such as a choir or youth orchestra, coming for a specific engagement. This may include conductors, choreographers, stage managers and other non-performing staff supporting the group;

- professional entertainers taking part in a charity concert or show where the organisers are not making a profit and no fee is to be paid to the entertainer;

- amateur or professional entertainers taking part in a cultural event sponsored by a government or recognised international organisation or a major arts festival included in the 'Permit Free Festival List' (▶see table below 334–335);

- members of the technical or support staff of amateurs or professionals who are attending the same event as the Entertainer Visitor. Examples of such staff include make-up artists, personal bodyguards and press officers;

- officials attending the same event as the Entertainer Visitor. Examples include choreographers, and stage managers.

bases for admission set out in the table above. The Government has stated that it intends to review the arrangements and criteria for festivals and cultural events that do not require participants to qualify to come to the UK under the PBS. However, it has taken applications to be included on the list for the year 1 May 2011 to 30 April 2012. Applications were to have been submitted before 18 February 2011 to:

Permit free festivals,
Non-PBS Operational Policy Team
UK Border Agency
Level 2
Vulcan House – Steel
UK Border Agency
PO Box 3468
Sheffield
S3 8WA

10

The criteria for inclusion are:

- the event/festival must have been established for at least three years;
- it must have an expected audience of at least 15,000 over its course;
- at least 15 non-EEA performers must have performed at the event for each of the last three years.

The list for the year 1 May 2010 to 30 April 2011 is as set out in the table.

PERMIT-FREE FESTIVAL LIST

The Permit Free Festival List for 1 May 2010 to 30 April 2011 is as follows:

- Alnwick International Festival
- Barbican Festivals (Summer, Autumn 1, Autumn 2 & Only Connect)
- Bath International Music Festival
- BBC Proms
- Belfast Festival at Queen's
- Birmingham International Jazz Festival
- Breakin' Convention
- Brighton Festival
- Brouhaha International Festival
- Cambridge Folk Festival
- Celtic Connections Festival
- Cheltenham Festivals (Jazz/Science/Music/Literature)
- City of London Festival
- Cornwall International Choral Festival
- DaDa Festival
- Dance Umbrella
- Edinburgh Festival Fringe
- Edinburgh International Festival
- Edinburgh Military Tattoo
- Festival Republic's Music Festivals (Reading Festival, Leeds Festival, Latitude, The Big Chill)
- Glasgow International Jazz Festival
- Glastonbury Festival
- Glyndebourne
- Greenbelt Festival
- Harrogate International Festival
- Huddersfield Contemporary Music Festival
- Live Nation: Download, Wireless

- Llangollen International Musical Eisteddfod
- London African Music Festival (Joyful Noise)
- London International Festival of Theatre
- Norfolk and Norwich Festival
- Salisbury International Arts Festival
- Scottish International Storytelling Festival
- Southbank: Meltdown Festival
- T in the Park
- V Festivals Hylands Park & Weston Park
- WOMAD Festival
- Zee Carnival

The IDI state that Sikh religious entertainers (Kirtani players) are not covered by the Entertainer Visitor category, but need to seek entry to the UK under the Religious Worker subcategory of tier 5 of the PBS (Ch 2, para 2.9.2).

Conditions and Tier 5 (Creative and Sporting) options

Entertainer Visitors may be granted a maximum of six months leave with a condition prohibiting employment (Rules, paras 46T–46X). Entertainer Visitors may undertake the permissible activities of Business Visitors and Sports Visitor activities (▶see above).

Switching to a purpose covered in the PBS after entry to the UK as an Entertainer Visitor is not generally permissible. However, if a person has been issued with a certificate of sponsorship for Tier 5 (Creative and Sporting) by a licensed sponsor before they come to the UK, they may use this to apply for leave to remain to continue with the Tier 5 work without leaving the UK (IDI, Ch 2, para 2.9.6). There are several options for performers coming to the UK in these circumstances (IDI, Ch 2, para 2.9.7):

- If the Tier 5 sponsor for the employment covered by the CoS is willing to extend the CoS to cover the period(s) the performer will be appearing at Permit Free Festival(s), leave to enter under Tier 5 may be granted on entry to non-visa nationals who are coming for three months or less. If the performer is expecting to stay in the UK for longer than three months, s/he will need to obtain prior entry clearance regardless of whether he is a non-visa national or not. As now, all visa nationals would need prior entry clearance to cover the whole period, regardless of the duration of their stay.

- If the Tier 5 sponsor does not wish to extend the certificate and the Permit Free Festival(s) is before the performance(s) covered by the certificate, the performer may enter the UK as an Entertainer Visitor, undertake the Permit Free Festival appearance(s) and then apply to UKBA to switch into Tier 5 of PBS to perform at the covered events. To do this, the performer will need to submit an application to vary his/her leave, paying the appropriate fee, (using the certificate issued by his Tier 5 sponsor before the performer's arrival in the UK). Provided the performer meets the requirements of Tier 5, s/he will be granted leave to remain for the duration of the period specified by the sponsor when the certificate was issued, plus 14 days (up to a maximum of 12 months). If the performer intends to then do further Permit Free Festival appearances during the period for which he has been granted leave to remain under Tier 5, he may do these appearances as 'supplementary employment'.

- Alternatively, the performer can enter the UK under Tier 5, after obtaining entry clearance, if necessary. S/he will be granted leave to enter for 14 days before the beginning of his/her Tier 5 employment, and 14 days after the end of that period of engagement, up to a maximum of 12 months, and may undertake festival appearances as 'supplementary employment' during his/her period of Tier 5 leave.

- Switching is only allowed from the Visitor categories into Tier 5 in the circumstances described above. There is no other switching from Visitor categories to the PBS. If the Permit Free Festival appearances are to take place beyond the period for which the performer has been granted leave to enter or remain under Tier 5, the performer would need to leave the UK and seek entry as an Entertainer Visitor to return to undertake further festival work.

Student Visitors

General Visitors must not undertake courses of study in the UK (Rules, para 41(v)). However, it is possible for a visitor to undertake studies if the applicant enters in the capacity of Student Visitor. This category is only open to adults (for children, ▶see below at 338). In the December 2010 consultation paper that sets out the Government's proposals to restrict Tier 4 yet further, the Home Office points to the Student Visitor route as providing a means of access to the UK for those who cannot qualify to come to the UK to take their proposed course of studies under the PBS. The consultation document states (para 3.2):

"It is important to bear in mind that unlike competitor countries, the UK will retain its student visitor route which will continue to provide a route of entry for those wishing to study short courses under six months' duration, which may be below the minimum academic level permitted under Tier 4."

The requirements that must be satisfied by Student Visitors are that they (Rules, para 56K–M):

- must be genuinely seeking entry to the UK as a Student Visitor for a limited period stated by them and which must not exceed six months;

- have been accepted on to a course of study provided by an institution which:
  - is the holder of a Tier 4 sponsor licence (▶see Chapter 4); or
  - has valid accreditation from a UKBA-approved accreditation body; or
  - is inspected or audited by one of the bodies set out in Guidance published by UKBA; or
  - is an overseas Higher Education Institution offering only part of their programmes in the UK, holding its own national accreditation and offering programmes that are an equivalent level to a UK degree;
- intend to leave the UK at the end of their visit;
- do not intend to take employment in the UK;
- do not intend to engage in business, to produce goods or provide services in the UK;
- do not intend to study at a maintained school;
- will maintain and accommodate themselves and any dependants adequately out of resources available to them without recourse to public funds or taking employment, or will be so supported by relatives or friends;
- can meet the cost of return or onward journey;
- are not under 18;
- do not intend to do any of the activities provided for in the Rules relating to Business Visitors, Sports Visitors or Entertainer Visitors;
- do not intend to marry or form a civil partnership (*note*: there is a separate visitor category for this purpose);
- do not intend to receive private medical treatment during their visit (*note*: there is a separate visitor category for this purpose); and
- are not in transit to a country outside the Common Travel Area.

The inspection or auditing bodies set out in Guidance published by UKBA are:

- the Quality Assurance Agency for Higher Education (UK-wide);
- the Office for Standards in Education (Ofsted);
- the HM Inspectorate Education (Scotland);
- Estyn (Wales);
- the Education and Training Inspectorate (Northern Ireland); and
- the Independent Schools Inspectorate (IDI, Ch 2, para 2.14).

People who are studying overseas for UK qualifications who may need to visit the UK for classes or revision can apply under this category (IDI, Ch 2, para 2.14).

Conditions

Applicants may be admitted for a maximum period of six months subject to a condition prohibiting employment (Rules, para 56L). Student Visitors do not, therefore, benefit from the limited provision to work that applies to those entering under Tier 4.

Concession relating to Student Visitors studying English language courses

On 13 December 2010, the Minister of State, Damian Green MP, issued a statement recognising that the present academic requirement for English language courses, which requires prior knowledge at a minimum level of B1 on the Common European Framework of Reference for languages, and the proposed enhanced requirement, requiring prior knowledge at the B2 level, do not "meet the special needs of the language sector". He went on to say that, following representations received from the sector, he had agreed to put in place a "temporary measure that will allow English language students on a longer duration course to be given leave to enter as Student Visitors for a period not exceeding 11 months".

In order to benefit from this concession, unlike other visitors, applicants will need to obtain entry clearance whether they are visa nationals or not. They should also provide evidence of the duration of their course. The other requirements and conditions of leave remain the same as for other Student Visitors (▶above). The concession went live from 10 January 2011. As to how long the concession will operate for, the Minister stated:

"This concession is intended to create flexibility to allow legitimate English language colleges to continue to offer opportunities to genuine students. I shall monitor closely the practical impact to ensure that it does not become a loophole, and take a decision on making it permanent in due course".

UKBA has stated that it intends to carry out a review of the extended Student Visitor concession within 12 months of its launch.

Child Visitors coming as visitors for educational purposes

These visitors have to be divided into two categories:

- those coming for a course of study;
- those coming for exchange or educational visits.

Both are provided for by the 'child' visitor rules (▶above at 323) (Rules, para 46A–46D) and applicants must *in addition to the conditions described below* satisfy the other requirements of those Rules. Applicants may be admitted for up to six months in total (12 months if the child is accompanying a person admitted as an Academic Visitor, ▶above 325) subject to a condition prohibiting employment (Rules, paras 46B and 46D).

Those coming for a course of study

Unlike the General Visitor rules for adults, the Child Visitor rules do not contain the requirement that applicants must not intend to take a course of studies in the UK (compare Rules 41(v) and 46A(ii)). Therefore, this limb of the Child Visitor rule includes provision for children that is otherwise covered for adults by the above Student Visitor category. Child applicants who have been "accepted for a course of study" may be admitted if (Rules, para 46A(vii)):

- the course is to be provided by an institution that is outside the maintained sector;
- the provider is the holder of a sponsor licence for Tier 4 of the PBS; and
- the provider is inspected by one of the bodies set out in Guidance published by UKBA (▶see under Student Visitors above 336).

The relevant inspection bodies for the above purposes are (IDI, Ch 2, para 2.13.7):

- Office for Standards in Education (Ofsted);
- the HM Inspectorate Education (Scotland);
- Estyn (Wales);
- the Education and Training Inspectorate (Northern Ireland); and
- the Independent Schools Inspectorate.

However, the IDI go on to state that (Ch 2, para 2.13.7):

"…where a child visitor is undertaking an activity based programme within the duration of their leave, the organisation will not be required to obtain accreditation. Activity based programmes may include some tuition, eg English language. This tuition should clearly be an incidental part of the main, activity based programme. It must not form the larger part of the programme."

Exchange or educational visits

According to the IDI, exchange or educational visits are not viewed as being courses of study but rather they are "principally about enrichment, broadening horizons and deepening intercultural understanding" (Ch 2, para 2.13.8) and they continue:

"The precise nature of the visit is for the school to decide but short visits are likely to involve the young person attending some school lessons but he or she would probably not be expected to do any homework. There would normally be an extensive programme of cultural visits organised for the visitors (day trips, attending sporting event etc). The balance of activities is likely to change for longer visits with the young person expected to attend more/most lessons and do homework. The school's expectations of those on an exchange visit are not likely to be the same as for its own students. (For example those on exchange visits would not be expected to sit tests/exams or wear the school's uniform."

Children making use of this limb of the Child Visitor rules must attend:

- a school in the maintained sector; or
- a non-maintained special school; or
- an independent non fee-paying or an independent fee-paying school, as described in guidance published by the UK Border Agency.

There are extensive definitions of these schools provided in the IDI (Ch 2, para 2.13.9). This limb was added to the Rules from 1 January 2010 by HC120 and it replaces and supersedes the temporary concession that permitted such visits until 31 December 2009. The Explanatory Note accompanying the rule change commented that exchange visits "provide a valuable opportunity for UK children to improve their language skills and promote better understanding between different cultures" (para 7.3).

Parents of children at school

The purpose of this category is to enable parents of children at independent, fee paying day primary schools to stay with them in the UK (Rules, paras 56A–56C). The child must be under 12 years of age, meet the requirements of Student rules that enable them to study in the UK at such a school and must in fact be attending the school. In addition, the parent must:

- meet all the requirements for General Visitors set out above (▶321–323) other than the requirement to be seeking entry as a General Visitor for a period not exceeding six months;
- provide satisfactory evidence of adequate and reliable funds for maintaining a second home in the UK;
- not be seeking to make their main home in the UK; and
- not have been last admitted to the UK under the Approved Destination Status (ADS) Agreement with China.

Other than for those present in the ADS category, it is possible to switch to remain as the Parent of a Child at School. Leave is given for periods of up to 12 months and will be given with a condition prohibiting employment (Rules, para 56B). The IDI (Ch 2, para 2.12) give the impression that a parent may only stay for 12 months in total in this capacity, although our view is that the intention of the Rules is to restrict each grant of leave to a maximum of 12 months rather than to prevent further grants of leave.

Prospective Students

This category applies to those who wish to study in the UK but who have not yet actually enrolled on a course of study. It is intended to enable people to enter for up to six months, outside the PBS, in order to research and obtain a place of a course of study and then, later, to switch into Tier 4. The requirements are that the applicant (Rules, paras 82–84):

- can show a genuine and realistic intention of undertaking, within six months of the date of their entry, a course which meets the requirements of the Tier 4 (General) or Tier 4 (Child) Student category (▶see Chapter 8);
- intends to leave the UK on the completion of their studies, or on the expiry of his/her leave to enter if s/he is not able to meet the requirements for an extension as a student under the Tier 4 (General) or Tier 4 (Child) Student categories; and
- is able, without working or recourse to public funds, to meet the costs of his/her intended course and his/her accommodation and maintenance and that of any dependants.

Unlike other Visitors, Prospective Students must have an entry clearance for entry (Rules, para 82(iv)). They are later permitted to switch into Tier 4 (provided they meet all the relevant requirements, for which ▶see Chapter 8) (Rules, paras 245ZX(b)(viii) and 245ZZC(b)(iii)). While they remain Prospective Students prior to their switching to Tier 4, they will be prohibited from taking employment in the UK (Rules, paras 83 and 86).

EMPLOYMENT UNDER THE RULES

Most employment-based categories of entry, whether for short-term or long-term employment, have been incorporated into the PBS. However there remain a few residual categories of long-term employment (known as permit-free employment) which have been left under the rules and this section deals with such categories. First we will look at considerations which are common to these categories.

General common rules about entering and staying for long-term permit-free employment

In what follows, we set out the general common rules. There are some exceptions, which we address immediately below. In all cases, entry clearance is mandatory. In order to obtain entry clearance and leave to enter, the following general requirements need to be satisfied:

- applicants must intend to work in the particular capacity for which leave is granted, and not to take any other form of employment;
- applicants must be able to maintain and accommodate themselves and any dependants without claiming public funds (see pages 308–318 of the *JCWI Handbook* 2006 edition for full details about these requirements). Unlike under the PBS, there are no prescribed levels of funds to meet this requirement. We wait to see if entry clearance officers will continue to apply the long-established practices and principles to assess this requirement or whether they will use the prescribed PBS levels as a benchmark and whether this will be susceptible to challenge.

Applicants will need to obtain confirmation of their job offer, and then submit those details to the entry clearance officer in support of their

10

application for entry clearance. In some cases, the ECO may refer the application to the Home Office in the UK to confirm details of the job or other details before making a decision about granting entry clearance.

Entry clearance will be issued enabling leave to enter to be granted for the period specified under the relevant rule. Applicants must also continue to meet both the specific rules relating to their category and the common rules outlined above. The applicant for an extension must have been originally admitted in the category in which they seek the extension. Leave will be granted subject to conditions prohibiting access to public funds and restricting work to that for which leave was originally granted.

Settlement After five continuous years' leave in the relevant qualifying category, during which time the requirements of the rules have been met, and provided the applicant is still working and their employer confirms that they are still required, the worker can be granted settlement.

Family Spouses, civil partners, children and unmarried partners may be admitted to stay and obtain settlement in the UK as dependants of the principal worker, in the same way as for dependants of PBS migrants. Persons admitted as family members will generally be admitted without any working or business restrictions.

Postgraduate Doctors and Dentists

Prior to 3 April 2006, the category under the Rules for postgraduate doctors and dentists enabled non-EEA doctors and dentists to train in the UK at the following levels:

- foundation programmes;
- basic specialist training – this refers to Senior House Office (SHO) and equivalent grades; and
- higher specialist training – this refers to Specialist Registrar and equivalent grades. The General Practice Vocational Training Scheme (GPVTS) is also considered as higher specialist training.

Under rules in force since April 1985, since postgraduate doctors and dentists are strictly trainees, they were not considered to be in employment in the UK for immigration purposes and they were allowed to come for 'permit free training'. That enabling them to enter and remain and take up a training post without a work permit. After training was complete, or a four-year period had expired, they were required to return home and apply to come under a work permit. From April 2003, these classes of entrant could also benefit from the Highly Skilled Migrant Programme enabling them to both train in the UK and remain in employment in the UK after their period of training had ended and without having to return home.

By approximately 2005, the needs and the structure of the health service and medical training programmes had changed considerably since this category was introduced. In particular, the number of places in UK medical and dental schools had increased, meaning that there were more UK and EEA national medical graduates seeking relevant training posts. There was therefore no longer a need for a specific category in the Rules to enable doctors and dentists to train in the UK for many years and then obtain rights to work and settle here. The concern was expressed in a witness statement provided to the Court in the case of *R (BAPIO Action Ltd) v Home Secretary* as follows (see judgment at 1009D):

"There was a risk of IMGs [International Medical Graduates] displacing a significant number of United Kingdom doctors. Many IMGs in the [UK] are highly skilled and have several years' experience in their chosen field. Accordingly, they are highly attractive to NHS trusts seeking to provide services at junior doctor levels."

In order to confront this issue, the Rules relating to permit-free training were amended with effect from 3 April 2006 (HC 1016), limiting the provision so that:

- only those who had graduated from UK medical schools could qualify;
- they could only undertake the first period of postgraduate training (ie, the foundation programme); and
- for a period that was not extendable after three years.

Those in SHO or Specialist Registrar posts (or posts at the equivalent grades of either of these) were no longer eligible for a grant of leave as a Postgraduate Doctor or Dentist in permit-free training. These doctors and dentists could continue to come to the UK but only if they could qualify under the work permit scheme. In order to prevent those in the UK under the HSMP from being able to do this work, the Secretary of State for Health (after being unable to get the agreement of the Home Office for an Immigration Rule change dealing with HSMP) issued employment guidance to NHS Trusts to the effect that only IMGs whose leave to be in the UK extended beyond the post on offer should be offered jobs using the same procedure as for UK/EEA nationals. All others should only be offered posts if there were no other suitable candidates in the resident labour market. The failure to implement these changes to HSMP through the Immigration Rules led a ruling by the House of Lords in April 2008 that the Health Department's guidance was invalid (see *BAPIO* above).

The system now in place, including under the PBS, is as follows.

- Those migrants who have successfully completed a *recognised UK degree* in medicine or dentistry, can apply to take up a recognised Foundation Programme (ie, the first stage of training only) under the Tier 4 (General) student category. For this purpose, the UK Foundation Programme Office was formally approved as a Tier 4 Sponsor on 3 July 2009. This means that it will act as sponsor to the non-EEA graduates of UK medical schools.

- The restriction on access by foreign-trained doctors and dentists to training positions is carried through to Tier 1 of the PBS, where all four subcategories (Post-Study Work, the Highly Skilled, Investors and Entrepreneurs) are prohibited from working as Doctors in Training, defined under para 6 of the Rules as "employment in a medical post or programme offered by the NHS which has been approved by the Postgraduate Medical Examination and Training Board as a training programme or post".

- Other postgraduate doctors and dentists are treated like other skilled migrant workers and need to be issued with a certificate of sponsorship under Tier 2 from a licensed employer if they wish to take up work in the UK, which, except in the case of shortage occupations, will involve a resident labour market test.

- There remain, under the Rules, two categories for short-term admission, outside the PBS, under which overseas doctors can take exams in the UK and under which graduate doctors and dentists may undertake clinical attachment or dental observer posts (▶see immediately below) – both are similar to the visitor categories.

Note also that there remains some limited scope under the non-PBS Rules for overseas qualified nurses or midwives who have previously been given leave to enter or remain in that capacity in order to carry out training, supervised practice or an adaptation programme, to extend their existing leave for the same purpose (Rules, paras 69P–69R).

PLAB Tests

Overseas doctors may be admitted to take the Professional and Linguistic Assessment Board ('PLAB') test in the UK (Rules, paras 75A-75F). The purpose of the test is to examine both knowledge of English as well as medical ability. Part 2 of the test may only be taken in the UK. Doctors who are qualified overseas with qualifications that are not recognised by the UK have to pass the PLAB test in order to be able to register with the General Medical Council. Before coming to the UK in this capacity, applicants are required to pass a 'pre-assessment test in English language under the International English Language Testing System ('IELTS'). That is to ensure that they have a reasonable command of English sufficient in order to sit the PLAB test (IDI, Ch 2, para 2.4.1).

In order to be admitted, applicants must show that they:

- graduated from a medical school and intend to take the PLAB test in the UK;

- have documentary evidence of a confirmed test date and their eligibility to take the test;

- do not intend to take employment;

- do not intend to produce goods or provide services within the UK, including the selling of goods or services direct to members of the public;

- do not intend to undertake a course of study;

- will maintain and accommodate themselves and any dependants out of resources available to them without recourse to public funds or taking employment, or will be so supported by relatives and friends;
- can meet the cost of their return or onward journey; and
- intend to leave the UK at the end of the leave granted in order to take the test *unless* they are successful in the PLAB Test and are granted leave to undertake a clinical attachment (▶see below).

If the above requirements are satisfied, leave to enter may be granted for a period of up to six months. Extensions may be granted but only up to a maximum period of 18 months in the UK for the purposes of taking a PLAB test (Rules, para 75D(v)).

Doctors undertaking clinical attachments, dentists undertaking clinical observer posts

Rules also remain in place for those seeking entry or leave to remain for the purposes of undertaking a period of clinical attachment or a dental observer post (Rules, paras 75G–75M). The purpose of this Rule is to enable overseas doctors or dentists who wish to work in the UK to undertake periods of clinical attachments or dental observation posts in order to familiarise themselves with UK working practices. These clinical attachments and dental observation posts are *unpaid* and involve observation only and not treatment of patients.

Overseas doctors and dentists can apply for leave to enter to undertake clinical attachment or dental observation posts. Since these posts can be undertaken at any stage of the doctors' or dentists' careers, doctors who are already in the UK with leave to take the PLAB test, or on leave as postgraduate doctors, dentists and trainee general practitioners, can undertake clinical attachments or dental observation posts under their existing leave. They will only have to apply separately under the specific Rules on clinical attachments or dental observation posts where their period of existing leave (to take the PLAB Test or as a postgraduate doctor/dentist/trainee general practitioner) is due to expire before the end of the clinical attachment or dental observation post (see IDI, Ch 2, paras 2.4.9, 2.5, 2.5.7).

In order to qualify, applicants must (Rules, para 75G):

- be a graduate from a medical or dental school and intend to undertake a clinical attachment or a dental observer post in the UK;
- be able to provide documentary evidence of the clinical attachment or dental observer post which will be unpaid and involve only observation, not the treatment of patients;
- intend to leave the UK at the end of the leave granted to them for this purpose;
- not intend to take employment;

10

- not intend to produce goods or provide services within the UK, including the selling of goods or services direct to members of the public;
- not intend to undertake a course of study;
- be able to maintain and accommodate themselves and any dependants out of resources available to them without recourse to public funds or taking employment, or will be so supported by relatives and friends;
- be able to meet the cost of their return or onward journey; and
- not be seeking leave so as to mean that, when added to other periods of leave under this category, they would be in the UK for over six months altogether with leave for this purpose.

If the above requirements are met, the applicant is normally granted leave to enter for a six-week period at any one time up to a maximum limit of six months in total (Rules, para 75H). In addition to those in this category extending their existing leave, those present in the UK who were given leave either to take the PLAB test, as a postgraduate doctor, dentist or trainee GP, or as a work permit holder, can apply for leave to remain in order to undertake a clinical attachment or dentist clinical observer posts. Such applicants must satisfy the same requirements as above (Rules, para 75K).

Those in the UK on clinical attachment or dental observer post are not permitted to switch into any skilled employment route under the PBS.

Representatives of Overseas Businesses

This category now encapsulates two former categories, namely 'sole representatives' and 'representatives of overseas media organisations'.

UKBA originally intended to delete the sole representative rule and bring the category within Tier 2 of the PBS. However, it was persuaded that it was entirely inappropriate to require an overseas firm with no UK operations or representatives, nevertheless somehow to find a UK-based sponsor in order to send an employee to the UK to set up operations. So, for the time being, the route survives, but the UKBA has indicated that it is intended to delete it in due course as and when they have worked out how to fit it within the PBS.

In the case of overseas media representatives, this category was deleted from the Rules on 27 November 2008 and subsequently had to be brought back as a concession outside of the Rules, only to be reintroduced back into the Rules on 1 October 2009.

Because media representatives need not be the sole representative in the UK of the media organisation, the title of the overall category has been amended to remove the word 'sole'. A representative of an organisation that is not a media organisation is still required to be the sole representative of that organisation.

The two categories are set out in a single rule (Rules, paras 144–151). A 'sole representative' must, as previously, be seeking entry as a senior employee with full authority to take operational decisions on behalf of the overseas business for the purpose of representing it in the UK by establishing and operating a registered branch or wholly owned subsidiary of the overseas business. The applicant must also be the sole representative of the employer present in the UK. The rule as now set out introduces a new requirement that the branch or subsidiary must be concerned with same type of business activity as the overseas business.

A 'media representative' must be seeking entry as an employee of an overseas newspaper, news agency or broadcasting organisation being posted on a long-term assignment as a representative of their overseas employer. In the IDI of February 2009 relating to what was then the concession for overseas media representatives, UKBA stated that overseas media representatives must be directly involved in newsgathering for publication or broadcast abroad and that employees other than journalists may be considered, for example, producers, news cameramen and front of camera personnel. Secretaries and other administrative staff, however, must apply under Tier 2 of the PBS. There has been no suggestion that this will change now that the former concession has been brought back into the Rules.

A sole representative must intend to be employed full-time as a representative of that overseas business and must not be a majority shareholder in the overseas business. This latter requirement is to ensure that the application is not being made to get round the strict requirements of the businessperson rule, which has now been replaced by the Tier 1 (Entrepreneur) category under the PBS.

A requirement for English language skills at a basic user standard, in line with the language requirement for working in the UK under Tier 2 of the PBS, has also been introduced for both categories. Slightly confusingly the Explanatory Memorandum to the changes to the Rule explains that ability to speak English is now regarded as essential for a sole representative to make an effective economic contribution and will help to protect this category from abuse. However, although the language requirement applies to both, the Note makes no reference to the overseas media representatives in the explanation for the introduction of this additional requirement.

10

The additional common Rules for both categories are that:

- entry clearance is mandatory for applicants entering in this category;
- the overseas business must be based overseas – it must have its headquarters and principal place of business outside the UK;
- the representative must have been recruited or taken on as an employee outside the UK;
- applicants must not intend to take employment except within the terms

of this Rule; and

- applicants must be able to maintain and accommodate themselves in the UK without recourse to public funds.

The ECO will require documentary evidence confirming the legal, physical and trading existence of the overseas firm, and a detailed explanation of why the company requires a permanent presence in the UK, and why the proposed person is suited for that role.

Conditions and period of leave

The initial grant of leave will be subject to the following conditions (Rules, para 145):

- no recourse to public funds;
- registration with the police, if this is required (ie under para 326 of the Rules); and
- no employment other than working for the business which the applicant has been admitted to represent.

During the initial period of leave (two years was granted under the former rule, but the initial grant of leave under the present rule is three years in line with Tiers 1 and 2 of the PBS, see Rules para 145), the sole representative is expected to set up a registered branch or a wholly-owned subsidiary of the company in the UK, and to continue to run it. This does not have to be done within any particular time scale but it must have been done the end of the initial grant of leave to enter in order to obtain an extension (Rules, para 147(ii)(b); see *Trivedi*). The ECO will expect the sole representative to be intending to spend at least nine months of the year in the UK but, exceptionally, will be prepared to admit some applicants who will spend considerably less than this time in their first year. This discretion will typically be exercised in the case of full-time senior employees of the parent company who continue to work overseas, but who have been given responsibility for setting up a limited operation in the UK to test the market (IDI, Ch 5, s3, annex J, para 3). The sole representative can also hire local staff, or apply for a sponsorship licence in order to issue a certificate of sponsorship for prospective employees overseas to join them in the UK as employees of the company.

Extensions

The Rules specify that to qualify for an extension for the next three years (or two years for those admitted under the new Rule) the representative will have to show that (Rules, para 147):

- they entered the UK with valid entry clearance as a sole representative or a media representative
- in the case of a sole representative admitted under the present rules:
- the overseas firm still has its headquarters and principal place of business outside the UK;

- s/he is employed full-time as a representative of that overseas firm and has established and is in charge of its registered branch or wholly-owned subsidiary; and
- is still required for the employment in question as certified by his/her employer;
- in the case of a media representative admitted under the present rules:
- is still engaged in the same employment; and
- is still required for the employment in question as certified by his/her employer;

- they do not intend to take employment except as a sole representative or a media representative; and

- can maintain and accommodate him/herself and any dependants adequately without recourse to public funds.

The IDI (Ch 5, section 3, para 3.1) elaborate on the rules to the extent they stipulate that caseworkers must satisfy themselves that in the case of a sole representative s/he has generated business, principally with firms in the UK, on behalf of his employer since his/her entry to the UK or his last extension of stay here – and that s/he should be asked to provide evidence of this, which could be in the form of branch accounts, or copies of invoices, or contracts, or letters from firms with which the applicant has done business, giving an indication of the amounts of money involved in the transactions. This exceeds the requirements of the Rules under which there is no obligation to show that the representative has generated business, and this should be pointed out to UKBA if necessary.

An applicant who has served a continuous period of five years in the UK in these categories is eligible to apply for settlement (Rules, para 150).

Switching into the category

Applications for leave to remain as the Representative of an Overseas Business from an applicant who entered the UK in another capacity will be refused. Applicants who are already here in this capacity and apply to change employers will not be able to meet the requirement that they are working for the same organisation. Therefore such applications will also be refused.

Domestic Workers

For over 20 years, beginning in 1980, this category was operated as a concession outside the Rules. It was finally brought within the Rules on 18 September 2002 (paras 159A–159H, inserted by Cm 5597).

The UKBA originally wanted to delete the category altogether when the PBS was launched. According to Government ideology, it was low-skilled work which was covered by Tier 3 of the PBS, but that tier was going to remain suspended, at least for as long as restrictions on Bulgarian and Romanian access to the labour market continued to apply. So no provision was going to be made for this category, on the basis that there were sufficient low-skilled workers within the Europe-wide labour market to fill these positions. After extensive lobbying, however, the UKBA agreed to keep it in existence for the time being.

Unquestionably, it will remain under close scrutiny. In the UKBA response to the consultation on visitors in 2008, it recognised that overseas domestic workers may be the subject of abuse and exploitation and referred to research and analysis being carried out as a prelude to further consultation. UKBA stated:

"We are committed to ensuring that future arrangements concerning overseas domestic workers minimise any risk of abuse or exploitation. In addition, the current route will be preserved and then reviewed as appropriate after the first two years' operation of the reformed immigration system and when we will have properly road tested our anti-trafficking strategy. The results of the research and analysis will inform the development of any future arrangements and we will work closely with stakeholders to develop a package of reform."

To qualify under the Rules, domestic workers in private households must be aged between 18 and 65 years. For a period of at least a year before the entry clearance application is made, they must have been employed under the same roof as the employer, or in a household that the employer uses regularly. The purpose of this is to ensure that there is a genuine existing employer/employee relationship. Applicants must also have an entry clearance for entry in this capacity.

The work the domestic worker will do does not, as was once the case, need to be at any particular level. Typically, domestic workers will include cleaners, chauffeurs, gardeners, cooks and some nannies and carers. It must be intended that, in the UK, the domestic worker will be working full-time under the same roof as his/her employer, or in a household the employer regularly uses. Accordingly, the employer must normally be present in the UK. It is possible, however, for applications to be successful even if the employer spends a substantial amount of time abroad. UKBA gives the example of a housekeeper who is looking after property in the absence of her employers, and of a cook who works for the employer's family and who remains in the UK while the employer, him/herself, is abroad. In all cases, it will be necessary to show that the employer is in the UK for some of the time, and applicants should expect to explain their circumstances clearly if the employer's absences are for more than six months in a year (see IDI, Ch 5, s12, para 5.1).

Applicants coming initially must intend to travel to the UK in the company of their employer or the employer's spouse or child. Some flexibility is applied here so that domestic workers may be admitted if travelling alone, provided that the time-lapse is not excessive. In such cases, they should also carry a letter from their employer explaining why they are travelling alone (IDI, Ch 5, s12, para 2.5).

The ECO will normally require a written undertaking from the employer that they will provide adequate maintenance and accommodation (with a separate bedroom if the domestic worker is living in) for the applicant, and set out the main terms and conditions of employment in writing. The worker must be given a copy of this statement and must confirm that they agree with it. The British post should check the type and hours of work, and that the worker wants to come to the UK. The British post must interview the worker on their own, at least on the first application for entry clearance, to ensure that the worker understands the position. Again, they should also be provided with an information leaflet explaining their rights in the UK. Experience shows, however, that these procedures are frequently not implemented properly. All too often, workers ask for advice after having arrived in the UK, unaware of their immigration status and without their passport, which has been retained by abusive employers whom they have fled. The ECO who issued entry clearance may need to be contacted in these circumstances in order to establish when and on what terms the worker was admitted.

Length of leave

If the employer is being admitted to the UK as a visitor, the domestic worker will normally be granted leave for up to six months, in accordance with the period granted to the employer. If the employer is admitted in any other capacity, leave will normally be given to the domestic worker for up to 12 months at a time (IDI, Ch 5, s12, para 4.3) (Rules, paras 159B and 159E). Applicants can apply to extend their leave in this capacity, provided they entered the UK with an entry clearance as a domestic worker (Rules, para 159D(i)). Settlement can be applied for after five years continuous presence in the UK in this category if the applicant can demonstrate that they have been in employment as a domestic worker through that time (Rules, para 159G).

Changes of employment

The entry clearance should not generally state the name of the employer, and the domestic worker may obtain new employment, without obtaining approval, in other domestic work. They may obtain extensions of leave on the basis of their new employment (note that the rule relating to extensions of stay states simply that the applicant's employment must be certified by their 'current employer' – para 159D(iii) HC 395). Although the Home Office has been issuing endorsements to domestic workers which state that 'changes must be authorised by the Secretary of State', it has nevertheless confirmed that this relates to changes to do work other than domestic work, and not changes of employer (letter to Bates, Wells and Braithwaite Solicitors, 7 June 2004). Domestic workers are able to change their employer, regardless of the reason for leaving their original employment. Nevertheless, they should notify the Home Office by letter of changes of employment (IDI, Ch 5, s12, paras 1.1, 5.2). It is desirable for

10

domestic workers to do this, because they will need to prove that they have been in employment as a domestic worker under the Rules for the duration of their leave when they seek an extension of stay (Rules, para 159D(ii)). The fact that a domestic worker has changed employers will not 'stop the clock' for the purposes of calculating the five years after which they may apply for settlement. However, the domestic worker is likely to need letters from employers to show that they have spent five years in that type of employment.

Ancestry (Commonwealth nationals with British-born grandparents)

Commonwealth citizens aged 17 or over with a British-born grandparent (paternal or maternal) can come to the UK to take or seek work (paras 186–193, HC 395).

Applicants must be able to show that their grandparent was born in either the UK, Channel Islands, Isle of Man or – if born before 31 March 1922 – in what is now the Republic of Ireland. They need to prove their descent from the person born in the UK, usually by producing the grandparent's birth certificate or marriage certificate, the birth certificate of their parent descended from the grandparent, their parents' marriage certificate, and their own birth certificate. Documents are likely to be carefully scrutinised, as the immigration authorities are particularly concerned about false documentation in this area.

If the parents or grandparents were not married, any other evidence to show the relationship would be helpful, such as statements from people who knew them to confirm that they are the grandparents and parents of the applicant, or any evidence from school or medical records showing the family connections. An adoptive relationship with the grandparent, provided it is an adoption recognised by UK law, is accepted. A line of descent through the father is acceptable for an illegitimate child, as long as fatherhood is proved. Applicants must be able to show that they either have a job lined up or that they have realistic chances of obtaining work. Account will be taken of their age and state of health. There is no claim to UK ancestry through step-parents.

Applicants should also be able to work and be able to maintain and accommodate themselves without recourse to public funds. Entry clearance in the capacity of a person with UK ancestry is mandatory. Prior to 25 October 2004, it was possible for those who qualified to switch in-country into this category. So, for example, a Commonwealth national with close UK ancestry could, during a visit, decide to stay in the UK to work, rather than having to return home and make the application again. The Rules, however, were amended to prevent switching (Rules, para 189(ii)). It is extremely unclear why the Government would want to tighten its switching Rules to the extent of precluding straightforward applications in this category, where a person's entitlement is based on his/her nationality and heritage.

An applicant who qualifies for admission should be granted leave to enter for up to five years and may extend their limited leave after entry. After an applicant has spent five years the UK in this capacity, s/he should be eligible for settlement, provided s/he is able to work and intends to continue in employment or to seek further employment in the UK and is able to maintain and accommodate himself and any dependants adequately (Rules, paras 190 and 192).

Although the Rules require a person applying for settlement by virtue of UK ancestry to have resided here continuously in this capacity for five years, there is no requirement that any employment taken must be continuous. If an applicant is in employment all that is required is a letter from his current employer confirming that s/he will continue in their employ. If, however, the applicant is not employed at the time of application, UKBA will likely wish to see evidence of his/her employment record throughout the five years and evidence of any attempts he has made to find employment. Where it is clear that the applicant has not been in employment for any length of time over the five years s/he is likely to be asked to provide reasons as to why he has failed to obtain employment. Unless there is a very good reason for his failing to obtain employment the application is likely to be refused. The IDI also state that, in such cases, enquiries should also be made as to how the applicant has been supporting themselves without a regular income.

EMPLOYMENT OUTSIDE THE RULES

One of the intents behind the PBS was to incorporate all routes into the Rules, so there should not be any concessions outside the Rules still existing. In one category, however, the opposite occurred. This was for representatives of overseas media organisations on long-term assignment. As has been seen above (▶324), overseas news media staff coming for six months or less may do so as Business Visitors. This category is only for representatives who are being posted on a long-term assignment, ie, for more than six months.

The category was originally set out in paragraphs 136–143 of the Rules which provided for representatives of overseas newspapers, news agencies and broadcasting organisations who had been posted to the UK for long-term assignments to be admitted to the UK. Those coming for less than six months could apply as Business Visitors instead – there was specific provision for them in the former IDI.

On 27 November 2008, these paragraphs of the Rules were deleted, except in relation to eligibility for settlement for persons already here in this category. The intention was that such applicants would apply under Tier 2 of the new PBS. However this was not possible for those media organisations with no established presence in the UK as they had no one to act as a Tier 2 Sponsor. So, following extensive lobbying the category was reinstated *as a concession*.

10

It was subsequently incorporated (under Cm7701) back into the Rules with effect from 1 October 2009, but not as a separate stand-alone category. It has been incorporated within the rules as an alternative to entering as a 'sole representative'. Since these representatives need not be the sole representative of the overseas media organisation in the UK, the title of the category has been amended to remove the word 'sole' (▶see above 346–349).

EXEMPT CATEGORIES

Exemption from immigration control is dealt with under section 8 of the 1971 Act and the Immigration (Exemption from Control) Order 1972. Those exempt do not need 'leave' under the 1971 Act to come and go from the UK and may carry out their various activities without such leave or qualification under the PBS. This only applies to narrow groups of people some of whom are set out below. In addition to those set out, note that certain government representatives and other international officials are also exempt from control.

Crew of ships, trains and aircraft

The law relating to crew members varies slightly, depending on whether they belong to a ship, aircraft or train. In very general terms, a person who arrives in the UK as part of a crew aboard one of these vessels, and who also intends to leave within a short period of time as a crew member, will be exempt from control. This exemption does not apply to those who are subject to deportation orders, or who were refused leave to enter on their last arrival in the UK, or who the immigration officer decides to subject to examination. Crew members who 'jump ship', and do not return as crew members aboard their own or another vessel, can be detained and removed from the UK under the 1971 Act.

Off-shore workers

Those working on installations at sea are not covered by UK immigration legislation, and therefore overseas nationals may take up work on off-shore installations without permission. These workers usually spend their shore-leave in the UK, however, and wish to base their family here. For this purpose they and their dependants do need leave, and will usually be given entry for 12 months at a time. The immigration officer must be satisfied that the only work that the applicant intends to do is offshore. (See IDI, Ch 17, s4.)

Armed forces

Members of the UK armed forces, members of a Commonwealth force undergoing training in the UK with UK armed forces, and members of visiting armed forces coming to the UK at the invitation of the Government, are exempt from immigration control. These armed forces members are not, however, exempt from deportation. Their dependants are not exempt from immigration control, and must seek leave to enter and remain in the UK. Before 15 March 2005, dependants had to apply outside the Immigration Rules but, from that date, specific provision has been made within the Rules for them (paras 276AD–276AI, inserted by HC 346). Applicants must not intend to stay beyond the entitlement to remain in the UK of their principal and the maintenance and accommodation requirements must be met. In cases of children joining one parent only, the 'sole responsibility' or 'exclusion undesirable' Rules must be met unless the other parent is dead. Leave will be granted for up to four years at a time.

Diplomatic exemption

Generally, people who are the 'members of a diplomatic mission' are fully exempt from control. They are:

- the head of the mission;
- the diplomatic staff;
- the administrative and technical and service staff (such as chauffeurs, cooks, cleaners).

Not all employees of embassies will be exempt however – those paying local taxes may well not be exempt. Those who are not part of the diplomatic staff must have been recruited to work in the mission while living abroad. Diplomats family members, who form part of their household, are also exempt. Note that high-ranking officers of organisations such as the UN also have diplomatic exemption.

WORKING WITHOUT PERMISSION – CONSEQUENCES FOR EMPLOYERS AND EMPLOYEES

Consequences for employees

Where non-EEA nationals, in breach of the law, take employment, the consequences can be very severe. People who work unlawfully may:

- be administratively removed from the UK if they are in breach of their conditions of leave which either prohibit or restrict employment and business (1999 Act, s10);
- have any remaining leave curtailed on the grounds that they have breached their conditions of leave, or that they no longer satisfy the rules under which leave was given (Rules, para 323(i)(ii) read with para 322(3);
- if their leave is curtailed, be administratively removed from the UK as overstayers (1999 Act, s10);
- if they were admitted in a category for which they had to show that they did not intend to take work, be declared illegal entrants and removed

from the UK, if the immigration authorities can prove that they intended to work in the UK at the time that they were originally admitted (1971 Act, s33 and para 9 Sch 2);

- be refused leave to enter or remain in the future on the grounds that they have previously breached their conditions of leave (see paras 320(11) and 322(3), HC 395);

- be committing a criminal offence (Immigration Act 1971, s24).

The legal environment those breaching immigration law has changed radically since the introduction of new general grounds of refusal in the form of paragraph 320(7B) inserted by HC 321 on 1 April 2008 (▶see Chapter 11, 385). Overstaying by more than 28 days, working in breach of conditions (or otherwise breaching them by, for example, not complying with police reporting requirements) and the use of deception all lead to an automatic ban on re-entry. The length of the ban varies, namely for one year, if the migrant left voluntarily at his own expense; for five years, if the migrant left voluntarily, but at the direct or indirect expense of the Secretary of State; and for ten years where deception has been used or a person has been removed or deported. There were transitional provisions excluding any immigration offender who was in the UK illegally on or after 17 March 2008 and who left the UK voluntarily at their own expense before 1 October 2008.

Immigration offenders now find themselves 'between a rock and a hard place'. When making an application using a form which requires answers to questions such as whether the applicant has worked in breach of conditions, overstayed or used deception, s/he has to be advised to disclose the previous breach, which will inevitably lead to a mandatory ban for the appropriate period. If the applicant tries to conceal the offence and the attempt is discovered s/he will be at risk of a finding of deception which will bring about a mandatory ten-year ban. Any adviser who assists in any such concealment, or who knowingly submits an application which does not disclose the offence, could personally be liable to prosecution under section 25 of the 1971 Act for facilitation, which carries a penalty on conviction on indictment of an unlimited fine and imprisonment for up to 14 years.

These possible consequences apply equally to those who work while prohibited from work entirely, and also to those who are restricted from working other than in the capacity for which they were admitted, and who then do different work. This latter category includes, for example, a work permit holder (for most now, holder of certificate of sponsorship) who has been promoted but for whom no notification of a technical change or application for change of employment permission has been given to UKBA (formerly, Work Permits (UK)). Experience of UKBA practice at the time of writing reveals that this will be treated as a breach of conditions, giving rise to a mandatory re-entry ban, unless overturned on appeal, and a refusal to take into account, for the purpose of scoring points under the PBS, any earnings made from the 'unauthorised' employment. It is worth noting that, under recent changes to the Guidance to Sponsors, that promotions in a job will amount to a change of employment necessitating the issue of a fresh certificate of sponsorship which will usually require a further Resident Labour Market Test.

Biometric Immigration Documents, also known as Identity Cards for Foreign Nationals (ICFN)

It is relevant to mention Biometric Immigration Documents ('BIDs') at this point because of a little known, but potentially significant, requirement under the implementing regulations relating to BIDs.

The power to issue BIDs is contained in section 5 of the UK Borders Act 2007. The scheme was implemented by the Immigration (Biometric Registration) Regulations 2008/3048 (the 'BID Regulations') and has been rolled out by UKBA, category by category. For those categories of admission that fall under this regime, which at the time of writing are as set out in the Appendix (▶456–457), leave to remain is recorded on the BID, there being no stamps or stickers (vignettes) in the passport or other immigration status documents

Under regulation 18 of the BID Regulations, as permitted under the enabling powers of section 5 of the 2007 Act, the holder of a BID must notify the Secretary of State as soon as reasonably practicable if, among other things, s/he knows or suspects that:

- information provided in connection with the document was or has become false, misleading or incomplete; or
- owing to a change of his/her circumstances s/he would no longer qualify for leave under the immigration rule governing his/her current leave to enter or remain in the UK.

This imposes a positive duty of candour (a duty to volunteer relevant information) on migrants. Now migrants who have been issued with a BID, or are subject to the BID regime, have to report not only relevant facts, but also their own suspicions as to whether they may no longer be eligible for the leave that they currently possess.

Failure to so notify gives rise to the power of the Secretary of State (reg 23, BID Regulations) to:

- refuse to issue a BID;
- disregard or refuse the person's application for leave to remain; or
- cancel or vary leave to enter or remain.

Quite what "disregarding" means remains to be seen but its plain meaning would enable the Secretary of State to receive an application, possibly take any fee accompanying it and then just ignore it, which would in the majority of cases turn the applicant into an overstayer, which may in due course give rise to a mandatory re-entry ban (▶above).

10

A Code of Practice concerning the 'Sanctions for Non-Compliance with the Biometric Code Registration Regulations' was adopted in November 2008 and that Code uses the terminology 'reject' instead of 'disregard'. So it would appear that the Secretary of State will give notice of his decision, as rejection implies some form of action, but a rejection after an applicant's leave has expired will nevertheless make him/her an overstayer.

However it turns out in practice that there is now a legal obligation on migrants who have been issued with a BID (and the aim is ultimately to issue them to all non-EEA migrants) to volunteer to the Government that they may no longer be eligible to stay in the country. This will impact on a number of situations, by way of example only, a relationship breakdown situation in which the migrant's status is as the dependant partner of another person. We wait to see how strictly this power will be enforced and what the ramifications will be for day-to-day practice of immigration law.

The Secretary of State must also consider giving a penalty notice to any migrant who fails to comply with any obligation under the BID Regulations, imposing a fine of up to £1,000 and may give further successive notices in the case of continued failure (Reg 23, BID Regulations). There are powers to object to, or to appeal against, any such penalty. But there is no right of appeal against the refusal to issue a BID. On the other hand, where the Secretary of State decides to refuse an application for leave or to curtail or cancel leave to enter or remain in the UK for failing to comply with a requirement, the person may have a right of appeal under section 82 of the 2002 Act to the First Tier Tribunal. The position concerning appeal rights where the Secretary of State 'rejects' an application remains unclear.

Only applicants for leave to remain in the UK are presently affected by the BID regulations. Foreign nationals seeking indefinite leave to remain and the settled population remain unaffected by the changes, as do applicants in other immigration categories who continue to receive a vignette in their passport.

Consequences for employers: general

The compliance and regulatory regime for employers is now the harshest it has ever been.

There are specific offences of employing someone who does not have the right to take the employment in question, with penalties varying from fines to civil penalties and even imprisonment. These are referred to as employer sanctions (▶below 361).

In addition, all the other offences under immigration legislation, such as facilitating a breach of UK immigration law under section 25 of the 1971 Act, will continue to be applicable if the Crown Prosecution Service chooses to use them against an infringing employer.

Readers will note that in the Guidance issued to Sponsors, around 93 immigration-related offences are listed in Appendix B. If the sponsor, any key personnel or those responsible for the day-to-day running of the sponsor's organisation have a conviction for any of these offences it could prevent the organisation being granted a sponsorship licence, or lead to it being withdrawn (▶see Chapter 4, 86–88, 121–125).

UKBA's Enforcement Instructions and Guidance (Ch 18, para 18.3.3) states that even where an employer has carried out the required document checks and kept the appropriate records, this does not preclude an employer from being prosecuted for other criminal offences, including the offence of knowingly employing an illegal migrant worker (under section 21 of the 2006 Act, applicable in respect of employees whose employment began on or after 29 February 2008) or facilitating a breach of UK immigration law under section 25 of the 1971 Act. Action will be taken against the employer where there is sufficient evidence available and where prosecution is considered to be in the public interest.

UKBA repeats throughout its published material that it takes the issue of illegal employment of migrants very seriously and will impose a range of penalties on those who employ people unlawfully.

In the Sponsor Guidance it is stated that sponsors who are found to be employing someone illegally may face any of the following consequences (SG, para 450):

- written warning for employing an illegal worker, followed by close attention from UKBA's enforcement and compliance teams;

- downgrading to a 'B' rating on the sponsorship register;

- cancellation of sponsor licence and removal from the sponsorship register – so an employer is unable to bring any migrant worker to the UK or keep any existent migrant;

- an on-the-spot fine (known legally as a civil penalty) – a sliding scale allows heavier penalties for repeat offenders;

- prosecution for having in his/her possession or under his/her control without reasonable excuse an identity document that is false or improperly obtained or that belongs to someone else, which may result in an employer being imprisoned for up to two years and/or receiving an unlimited fine (under section 25 of the Identity Cards Act 2006);

- prosecution for knowingly employing an illegal migrant worker whose employment began on or after 29 February 2008 – employers can be imprisoned for up to two years and/or receive an unlimited fine (under section 21 of the 2006 Act);

- disbarment as a company director or officer as a result of prosecution – employers convicted of knowingly employing an illegal migrant worker could be disqualified from forming or managing a company (under section 2 of the Company Directors Disqualification Act 1986);

10

- prosecution for facilitation of trafficking – employers can be imprisoned for up to 14 years and/or receive an unlimited fine (under section 25 of the 1971 Act).

This list of consequences should not have come as a surprise. In March 2007 the Home Office issued a publication titled *Enforcing the rules. A strategy to ensure and enforce compliance with our immigration laws* in which it said that UKBA will:

- create immigration crime partnerships with local authorities, police, HM Revenue & Customs and local agencies to detect those here illegally and block benefits;

- develop regional partnerships with workplace enforcement teams from other departments including HM Revenue & Customs (HMRC) and the Department for Work and Pensions (DWP), to track down and punish unscrupulous bosses who exploit the system;

- work jointly with local authorities to use fines of up to £20,000 against private sector landlords to tackle overcrowding – building on new search powers in the 2007 Act;

- create a watch list of illegal migrants that can be provided to other Government departments and agencies to deny access to services and run a pilot in three NHS Trusts to test how its data can help ensure that overseas visitors not entitled to free health care pay for it;

- review how the driver licensing system can be used to identify and combat illegal immigration;

- pilot using its data to prevent fraud against the financial services industry by illegal migrants who are likely to disappear;

- use the Proceeds of Crime Act 2002 more often to seize cash and for the forfeiture/disposal of property; and

- use existing powers to apply to the courts to disbar company directors convicted of an offence in connection with the management of a company, such as knowingly employing illegal workers.

As an example of the above, the development of regional partnerships with workplace enforcement teams from HM Revenue & Customs means that the UKBA can, with the assistance of HMRC, check an employer's tax records to establish whether they have been employing someone who is not permitted to be employed, and will then use that information to take enforcement action, against either or both the employer and employee. UKBA gives on its website the following case (▶see box below) as an example of this type of "joined-up" working with HMRC

Threats to use the Proceeds of Crime Act 2002 are not empty. In the case of *R v David Kai Ku*: *R v Lu Xu,* two brothers who were convicted of facilitating a breach by employing illegal workers in their restaurant business were also given a confiscation order under the Proceeds of Crime Act 2002. This was assessed at the proportion of their *total turnover for*

UK BORDER AGENCY/HMRC PARTNERSHIP WORKING (OPERATION JUMBO)

Since September 2007, the UKBA team at Eaton House has been working with HMRC to share information about businesses in the Heathrow area which are suspected of flouting legal obligations relating to the use of migrant labour. In one case, HMRC compared the information provided by an employer in his end of year tax return to the information he had given to UKBA when he was prosecuted for employing illegal migrant workers. They discovered the employer had provided several workers with living accommodation above the business premises, which is a taxable benefit. HMRC estimated the potential PAYE and National Insurance loss for the year as approximately £32,000. They are considering recovering up to six years' loss, meaning that as much as £193,000 could be recovered.

---

the duration of the illegal employment that the illegal workers bore to the total staff headcount (in this case 25%!).

Employer sanctions

There are *four* different regimes governing specific sanctions on employers who employ persons aged 16 or above who are not permitted to work in the UK. The applicable regime depends on the start date of the employment:

- before 27 January 1997 there was no specific applicable provision;
- between 27 January 1997 and 30 April 2004, the applicable regime was section 8 of 1996 Act and the Immigration (Restrictions on Employment) Order 1996;
- between 1 May 2004 and 28 February 2008, the applicable regime was section 8 of 1996 Act as amended by the 2004 Act and the Immigration (Restrictions on Employment) Order 2004;
- on or after 29 February 2008, the applicable regime is sections 15 and 21 2006 Act and the Immigration (Restrictions on Employment) Order 2007.

It is essential, therefore, to ascertain the start date in order to identify the relevant regime and the respective obligations, penalties and defences. The sanctions were initially introduced by section 8 of the 1996 Act from 27 January 1997, amended in 2004 (still in force for employment beginning before 29 February 2008: see art 5, SI 2008 No 310) and have now been replaced, for employees taken on from 29 February 2008, by sections 15 and 21 of the 2006 Act. We look in detail at the defences that employers may raise if they have inspected and kept documents relating to the employee, under the different 'regimes', ▶below starting at 361.

Section 8 1996 Act and the amendments made by the 2004 Act

Section 8 of the 1996 Act created the summary strict liability criminal offence, punishable with only a fine, of employing someone who is not permitted to work in the job in question or at all. However, the employer could raise a statutory defence by checking and keeping copies of various documents relating to the employee. It is up to the employer to ensure that there are procedures in place to provide the statutory defence. It is important to note that section 8 only applies to an 'employee', ie someone who is employed under a contract of employment, which is defined as "a contract of service or apprenticeship, whether express or implied, and (if it is express) whether it is oral or in writing". No offence is committed by the 'employer' if the relationship is that of a self-employed contractor. So, if a householder hires a self-employed plumber to fix some frozen pipes, there is no offence under section 8 even if the plumber is not entitled to enter into business in the UK.

section 8, as originally enacted, was a summary only offence, which meant that an employer could only be tried in a magistrates' court and on conviction a fine of up to £5,000 per illegal worker employee could be imposed. There is no custodial penalty. The fact of the existence of the employer-employee relationship is enough to make the employer potentially liable. Where an offence is proved to have been committed with the consent or connivance of, or to be attributable to any neglect on the part of, any 'officer' of an employer which is a company, that officer can be made personally liable as well. An example of the use of these powers under section 8 is set out in the box below.

As stated above, an employer can raise a statutory defence, however, by

TEMPTATIONS CHINESE RESTAURANT IN COLCHESTER – HARWICH MAGISTRATES' COURT (MAY 2009): EXAMPLES OF USE OF SECTION 8 1996 ACT

As reported on UKBA's website, six illegal workers were employed at the restaurant. The company employing them was found guilty of six offences contrary to section 8 of the 1996 Act. What made the case unusual is that, in addition, two directors of the company were personally charged with the offence as co-defendants in addition to the company itself. Both additional co-defendants were found guilty.

Each of the three defendants was fined £5,000 per offence – the maximum permissible at a magistrates' court – making a total of £90,000, plus £6,000 costs and £15 victim surcharge. This represented triple punishment for the same offence and demonstrates the heightened risks for directors and other officers.

UKBA states that this type of case is one of many that will be appearing before magistrates' courts around the country as UKBA cracks down on employers of illegal workers. UKBA also publishes on its website details of employers on whom civil penalties have been imposed, including the name of the employer, the name of the business, the level of fine and the number of illegal workers discovered.

inspecting and keeping copies of various specified original documents. It is extremely important that this inspection took place before the employment began, otherwise it is of no effect and does not provide the defence. The documents that needed to be checked were initially set out in the Immigration (Restrictions on Employment) Order 1996. Subsequently the Immigration (Restrictions on Employment) Order 2004 strengthened this legislation by tightening the lists of documents that employers were advised to check, eliminating documents which had proved vulnerable to forgery and requiring specific combinations of document to be seen.

In order to obtain the defence to any charge under section 8 the employer must prove that, before the 'offence' was committed, all of the following applied:

- particular document/s relating to the employee were produced to the employer (▶see below for the document/s which must have been produced);

- the employer either took copies of, or scanned into a database using 'Write Once Read Many' technology, all the relevant documents (strictly, only certain parts of passports and travel documents must be copied or scanned, but it is safest to keep a record of the entire document);

- the employer was satisfied that the documents appeared to relate to the particular employee (for example, any photographs appeared to be of the employee and the date of birth given on the documents reflected the apparent age of the employee); and

- where it was necessary that two documents were produced (▶see below), discrepancies as to the names on the document were explained by another document which was produced to the employer, such as a marriage certificate.

It should be noted that, if the employer *knew* that it would be an offence to employ the person in question, the defence was not available.

If a *bona fide* check has taken place, it provides a defence under section 8 for all time, even if it subsequently comes to the knowledge of the employer that the employee does not, or no longer has, permission to do the work. The employer does not have to terminate the employment for fear of being liable for the section 8 offence – ▶see 371–374 for further discussion about this.

From 1 October 2004, section 6 of the Asylum and Immigration (Treatment of Claimants etc) Act 2004 made the summary offence under section 8 triable either way, which means that there is no upper limit to the level of fine that can be imposed on employers if convicted on indictment in the Crown Court under the 1996 Act. Therefore, if someone employed an illegal migrant worker from 1 October 2004 to 28 February 2008 and did not establish a statutory defence the employer could still be prosecuted and receive an unlimited fine in a Crown Court.

10

Since the offence became triable in either court, there is no longer a time limit for bringing criminal proceedings against an employer. Proceedings in the magistrates' court must normally be brought within six months, but the section 8 offence contained provisions enabling an extension to this time limit. The extension was abolished by the 2004 Act, but only because it was no longer needed.

The 2006 Act

section 15 of the 2006 Act replaced the section 8 regime, but only for those whose employment started on or after 29 February 2008.

Under section 15 of the 2006 Act, the definition of employment is slightly different to that in the 1996 Act. It now reads "employment under a contract of service or apprenticeship, whether express or implied and whether oral or written", but it is not considered that much will turn on this different definition.

The structure of the offence is essentially the same under the 2006 Act, but three new aspects were introduced:

* the checks for those people whose permission to be in the UK has a time limit need to be *repeated at yearly intervals*;
* if it comes to the knowledge of the employer that the employee does not have valid permission to do the job, the employer loses the benefit of the defence obtained by checking the documents in the first place and essentially has to dismiss the employee to avoid ongoing liability; and
* the breach has been 'downgraded' from a criminal offence to a civil matter, and the sanction is the issue of a civil penalty of up to £10,000 for each illegal employee.

In order to obtain the defence to any allegation under section 15 (it is known as a statutory 'excuse') the employer must prove that, before the 'contravention' was committed, all of the following applied in relation to documents produced to them:

* the employer took all reasonable steps to check the validity of the document;
* the copy or copies were retained securely by the employer throughout the employment and for a period of not less than two years after the employment came to an end;
* if a document contains a photograph, the employer satisfied him/herself that the photograph was of the prospective employee or employee;
* if a document contained a date of birth, the employer has satisfied him/herself that the date of birth was consistent with the appearance of the prospective employee or employee;
* the employer took all other reasonable steps to check that the prospective employee or employee was the rightful owner of the document;

- if the document is not a passport or other travel document the employer retained a copy of the whole of the document in a format which cannot be subsequently altered;
- if the document is a passport or other travel document, the following pages of that document were copied in a format which cannot be subsequently altered –
- the front cover;
- any page containing the holder's personal details including nationality;
- any page containing the holder's photograph;
- any page containing the holder's signature;
- any page containing the date of expiry; and
- any page containing information indicating the holder has an entitlement to enter or remain in the UK and undertake the work in question; and
- if the document is a travel document in the form of a card, the employer retains a copy of the whole of that document in a format which cannot subsequently be altered.

The above requirements and documents or combination of documents that need to be checked before the employment begins are now set out in the Immigration (Restrictions on Employment) Order 2007 No. 3290. These are set out in Tables 4 and 5 (▶below 369–370).

The civil penalty under the 2006 Act is targeted at employers who have been negligent in their recruitment practices.

Alongside the civil penalty, the 2006 Act introduced a criminal offence under section 21 of knowingly employing an illegal worker, for which the maximum penalty is imprisonment of up to two years and an unlimited fine. It is important to understand that section 21 only applies to employees whose employment began on or after 29 February 2008.

As with the offence under section 8 of the 1996 Act, any officers of the company who have consented to or connived in the offence can be personally liable. Unlike section 8 1996 Act there is no personal liability where the commission of the offence is attributable to any neglect on the part of an officer. This is because negligence in relation to illegal employment is intended to be dealt with under the civil penalty notice regime under section 15 (▶above).

Section 22(1) of the 2006 Act provides that an employer "shall be treated as knowing a fact about an employee if a person who has responsibility within the body for an aspect of the employment knows the fact." Employers therefore need to have in place procedures to capture relevant information about any migrant worker employees that may have been given to anyone who has responsibility for an aspect of the employment. So, if for example a migrant worker employee tells a payroll clerk that s/he is no longer legally entitled to work, it is possible that the employer will be deemed to have acquired knowledge that it is employing an illegal worker.

10

In order to assist readers, the four different regimes and the applicable checks are set out below.

REGIME 1 – those whose employment started before 27 January 1997

Employers' legal responsibilities in respect of preventing unlawful working by migrants relate only to staff employed on or after 27 January 1997. Employers who did not check the entitlement to work in the UK of staff employed before this date are not liable to specifically tailored sanctions if such individuals are found to be illegal migrant workers.

REGIME 2 – those whose employment started between 27 January 1997 and 30 April 2004

This regime is governed by section 8 of the 1996 Act as originally enacted and the Immigration (Restrictions on Employment) Order 1996. The penalty is a fine of up to £5,000 per illegal worker. The documents to be produced to avoid liability are set out in Part II of the Schedule to the 1996 Order. We do not reproduce them.

REGIME 3 – those whose employment started between 1 May 2004 and 28 February 2008

This regime is governed by section 8 of the 1996 Act as amended by the 2004 Act and the Immigration (Restrictions on Employment) Order 2004. Document checks are set out in Tables 1–3 below. The penalty on summary conviction is a fine of up to £5,000 per illegal worker and on indictment an unlimited fine. In order to avoid liability, the employer must have seen and copied *either* one document from Table 1, *or* two documents from Table 2, *or* two documents from Table 3.

TABLE 1

DOCUMENTS PRODUCED TO AN EMPLOYER – ONE DOCUMENT OPTION

The employer must have seen and copied or scanned any one of the following documents:

- a UK passport showing that the holder is a British citizen or a CUKC with the right of abode in the UK;

- a passport containing a certificate of entitlement issued by the UK authorities stating that the holder has the right of abode in the UK;

- a passport or national ID card showing that the holder is an EEA National;

- a UK residence permit issued to an EEA national or to a Swiss national;

- a passport, travel document or residence document issued by the Home Office which states that the holder has a current right of residence in the UK as the family member of a named EEA national or Swiss national who is resident in the UK;

- a passport or other travel document endorsed to show that the holder has indefinite leave to enter or remain in the UK, has no time limit on their stay, or is exempt from immigration control;

- a passport or other travel document endorsed to show that the holder has current leave to enter or remain in the UK and is permitted to do the type of work in question (provided it does not require a work permit);

- an ARC issued by the Home Office to an asylum-seeker stating that the holder is permitted to take employment in the UK.

TABLE 2

DOCUMENTS PRODUCED TO AN EMPLOYER – TWO DOCUMENT OPTION FIRST COMBINATION

The employer must have seen and copied or scanned one document which meets the description in (a) below *and* any one of the documents listed in (b) below.

a) a document issued by a previous employer, the Inland Revenue, Department for Work and Pensions, Jobcentre Plus, the Employment Service, the Training and Employment Agency (Northern Ireland) or the Northern Ireland Social Security Agency and which contains the person's name and national insurance number – eg, P45, P60, NI card; *and*

b) one of the following documents:

- a birth certificate issued in the UK which includes the names of the holder's parents;

- a birth certificate issued in the Channel Islands, the Isle of Man, or Ireland;

- a certificate of registration or naturalisation as a British citizen;

- a letter issued by the Home Office to the holder which indicates that the person named in it has been granted indefinite leave in the UK;

- an 'Immigration Status Document' issued by the Home Office to the holder with a UK residence permit indicating that the holder has been granted indefinite leave to enter, or remain, in the UK;

- a letter issued by the Home Office to the holder which indicates that the person named in it has current leave to be in the UK, and which allows them to do the type of work in question;

- an Immigration Status Document issued by the Home Office to the holder with a UK residence permit which indicates that the holder has been granted limited leave allowing them to do the type of work in question.

10

TABLE 3

DOCUMENTS PRODUCED TO AN EMPLOYER – TWO DOCUMENT OPTION SECOND COMBINATION

The employer must have seen and copied or scanned both of the following:

a) a work permit or other approval to take employment issued by Work Permits (UK) (ie, an IED); *and*

b) *either* a passport or other travel document endorsed to show that the holder has current leave to be in the UK and is permitted to take the work in question, *or* a letter issued by the Home Office to the holder which confirms the same details.

REGIME 4 – those whose employment started on or after 29 February 2008

This regime is governed by sections 15 and 21 of the 2006 Act and and the Immigration (Restrictions on Employment) Order 2007. The document checks that the employer should have carried out and kept copies in order to avoid liability are set out in Table 4 (for those with no time limit on their stay in the UK) ▶below and Table 5 (for those with time limited stay) ▶370 below. The penalty under section 15 is a civil penalty notice of up to £10,000 per illegal worker. The criminal penalty under section 21 is an unlimited fine and imprisonment for up to two years.

Under the Code of Practice relating to Civil Penalties (February 2008) there is a framework for the assessment of whether to issue a penalty notice and, if so, at what level. It provides a sliding scale with minimum and maximum penalties, but the actual amount will be decided by UKBA on a case-by-case basis. The level of penalty to be imposed per worker may be increased or reduced according to different criteria, which include:

• the nature of checks conducted;

• whether the employer has reported suspected illegal workers to UKBA;

• whether the employer has co-operated with UKBA; and

• the number of offences the employer has committed in the past.

As an example of the level of penalties, in August 2009 UKBA put a news item on its website stating how a sandwich factory in Hayes had, following a raid based on a tip-off, been found employing 11 illegal workers and had been issued with a Notice of Potential Liability, telling them they faced a possible fine of up to £110,000 unless they could prove the correct right-to-work checks were carried out on their employees.

TABLE 4

DOCUMENT OR COMBINATION OF DOCUMENTS FOR THOSE WITH NO TIME LIMITS

1 A passport or ID card (under the ID Cards Act 2009) showing that the holder, or a person named in the passport as the child of the holder, is a British citizen or a citizen of the UK and Colonies having the right of abode in the UK.

2 A passport or national identity card or ID card issued under the ID Cards Act 2009, showing that the holder, or a person named in the passport as the child of the holder, is a national of the EEA or Switzerland;

3 A residence permit, registration certificate or document certifying or indicating permanent residence issued by the Home Office or the Border and Immigration Agency to a national of a EEA country or Switzerland.

4 A permanent residence card issued by the Home Office or the Border and Immigration Agency to the family member of a national of a EEA country or Switzerland.

5 A BID issued by the Border and Immigration Agency to the holder which indicates that the person named in it is allowed to stay indefinitely in the UK, or has no time limit on their stay in the UK.

6 A passport or other travel document endorsed to show that the holder is exempt from immigration control, is allowed to stay indefinitely in the UK, has the right of abode in the UK, or has no time limit on their stay in the UK.

7 An Immigration Status Document issued by the Home Office or the Border and Immigration Agency to the holder with an endorsement indicating that the person named in it is allowed to stay indefinitely in the UK or has no time limit on their stay in the UK, when produced in combination with an official document giving the person's permanent National Insurance Number and their name issued by a government agency or a previous employer.

8 A full birth certificate issued in the UK which includes the name(s) of at least one of the holder's parents, when produced in combination with an official document giving the person's permanent National Insurance Number and their name issued by a Government agency or a previous employer.

9 A full adoption certificate issued in the UK which includes the name(s) of at least one of the holder's adoptive parents when produced in combination with an official document giving the person's permanent National Insurance Number and their name issued by a Government agency or a previous employer.

10 A birth certificate issued in the Channel Islands, the Isle of Man or Ireland, when produced in combination with an official document giving the person's permanent National Insurance Number and their name issued by a Government agency or a previous employer.

11 An adoption certificate issued in the Channel Islands, the Isle of Man or Ireland, when produced in combination with an official document giving the person's permanent National Insurance Number and their name issued by a Government agency or a previous employer.

10

12 A certificate of registration or naturalisation as a British citizen, when produced in combination with an official document giving the person's permanent National Insurance Number and their name issued by a Government agency or a previous employer.

13 A letter issued by the Home Office or the Border and Immigration Agency to the holder which indicates that the person named in it is allowed to stay indefinitely in the UK when produced in combination with an official document giving the person's permanent National Insurance Number and their name issued by a Government agency or a previous employer.

TABLE 5

DOCUMENT OR COMBINATION OF DOCUMENTS FOR THOSE WHOSE STAY IS SUBJECT TO A TIME LIMIT

1 A passport or travel document endorsed to show that the holder is allowed to stay in the UK and is allowed to do the type of work in question, provided that it does not require the issue of a work permit.

2 A BID issued by the Border and Immigration Agency to the holder which indicates that the person named in it can stay in the UK and is allowed to do the work in question.

3 A work permit or other approval to take employment issued by the Home Office or the Border and Immigration Agency when produced in combination with either a passport or another travel document endorsed to show the holder is allowed to stay in the UK and is allowed to do the work in question, or a letter issued by the Home Office or the Border and Immigration Agency to the holder or the employer or prospective employer confirming the same.

4 A certificate of application issued by the Home Office or the Border and Immigration Agency to or for a family member of a national of a EEA country or Switzerland stating that the holder is permitted to take employment which is less than six months old, when produced in combination with evidence of verification by the Border and Immigration Agency Employer Checking Service.

5 A residence card or document issued by the Home Office or the Border and Immigration Agency to a family member of a national of a EEA country or Switzerland.

6 An Application Registration Card issued by the Home Office or the Border and Immigration Agency stating that the holder is permitted to take employment, when produced in combination with evidence of verification by the Border and Immigration Agency Employer Checking Service.

7 An Immigration Status Document issued by the Home Office or the Border and Immigration Agency to the holder with an endorsement indicating that the person named in it can stay in the UK, and is allowed to do the type of work in question, when produced in combination with an official document giving the person's permanent National Insurance Number and their name issued by a government agency or a previous employer.

8 A letter issued by the Home Office or the Border and Immigration Agency to the holder or the employer or prospective employer, which indicates that the person named in it can stay in the UK and is allowed to do the work in question when produced in combination with an official document giving the person's permanent National Insurance Number and their name issued by a Government agency or a previous employer.

Sanctions in relation to A2 and A8 nationals

There are separate sanctions in relation to nationals of the A8 countries and the A2 countries. Under the Accession (Immigration and Worker Registration) Regulations 2004, an employer can be fined a maximum of £5,000 per illegal worker if they continue to employ an unregistered, non-exempt, A8 worker after one month and have not retained a copy of that employee's Worker Registration application or, if already granted, their certificate of registration. An employer can also be fined for continuing to employ an A8 worker if they have been notified by the Home Office that their registration application has been refused.

Under the Accession (Immigration and Worker Authorisation) Regulations 2006, an employer can be fined a maximum of £5,000 per illegal worker for employing a non-exempt A2 (Bulgarian or Romanian) worker who does not have permission to undertake the employment in question from 1 January 2007.

What happens if an employer becomes aware that an employee has ceased to be entitled to work?

The answer to this depends on whether the employment falls under section 8 of the 1996 Act regime or section 15 of the 2006 Act regime (▶see above).

It is important first of all to restate what UKBA's Enforcement Instructions (Ch 18, para 18.3.3) and Guidance states, namely that, even where an employer has carried out the required document checks and kept the appropriate records, this does not preclude an employer from being prosecuted for other criminal offences, including the offence of knowingly employing an illegal migrant worker (under section 21 of the 2006 Act – applicable in respect of employees whose employment began on or after 29 February 2008) or facilitating a breach of UK immigration law under section 25 of the 1971 Act. The latter involves a maximum penalty on conviction of an unlimited fine, or imprisonment of up to 14 years. UKBA will take action against the employer where there is sufficient evidence available and where prosecution is considered to be in the public interest.

10

The position under section 8 of the 1996 Act regime

UKBA admits in one of its own publications that carrying out the correct document checks under section 8 of the 1996 Act at the point of recruitment will confer a defence once and for all in respect of the contract of employment with that individual. Accordingly "after acquired" knowledge that the migrant has become illegal will not take away the benefit of the defence. UKBA has, however, referred to this as a 'loophole'.

It has been suggested that there may be implications for employers who are licensed sponsors under the PBS and who discover that an employee, for whom they have carried out the correct document checks under section 8 of the 1996 Act regime, has become illegal, eg, by becoming an overstayer. Such sponsors have been encouraged to dismiss an employee falling into this category. This is because, under the ongoing sponsorship duties, they are required not to employ "a migrant if the conditions on the migrant's leave (or the migrant's lack of leave) mean that he or she is not allowed to undertake the work in question, and to stop employing any migrant who ceases, for any reason, to be entitled to undertake the work" (Sponsor Guidance, para 398, p55 of 73). The difficulty appears to be that, even though the employer may have a defence to the section 8 offence for continuing to employ the migrant in question, this does not prevent there from having been an 'infringement' that can be taken into account under the sponsorship regime under the PBS. (For the action that can be taken under the sponsor regime ▶see Chapter 4.)

Of course, when the reason that the employee ceases to be entitled to undertake the work is because his/her leave has expired, ie s/he becomes an overstayer, s/he is not in breach of the conditions of leave *by working* because, when leave has run out, there is nothing for any such conditions (such as a prohibition or restriction on employment) to attach to (*Suthendran v Immigration Appeal Tribunal*). Thereafter a person may be contravening the immigration law by overstaying, but not contravening any restrictions attached to the leave that has expired. Thus it is arguable that a person who takes (or continues) employment after the expiry of leave is not committing any additional offence by doing so. There may possibly, therefore, be an argument about whether UKBA is entitled to assert that there will be a breach of a sponsor's duty in these circumstances if they continue to employ because there is some difficulty in describing the situation as the migrant 'ceasing' to be entitled to take the work. However there is a clear argument the other way; UKBA is likely to take a very strict line on this and we would strongly advise caution.

The position under section 15 of the 2008 regime

What UKBA refers to as the 'loophole' under section 8 of the 1996 Act (▶see above) has been closed by section 15 of the 2006 Act for employees whose employment commenced on or after 29 February 2008. This removes the benefit of the statutory defence if the employer becomes aware, at any time (ie not just at the moment of recruitment) that the employment is not lawful.

The section also defines the contravention differently in that, whereas under section 8 of the 1996 Act, the offence is committed by employing someone whose "…leave is not valid and subsisting", under section 15 2006 Act, the offence is a continuing one that includes the employment of someone "…whose leave to enter or remain in the United Kingdom … has ceased to have effect (whether by reason of curtailment, revocation, cancellation, passage of time or otherwise)". This change of wording suggests that the draftsman intended to take away the statutory excuse in cases of after-acquired knowledge that the employment either was, or subsequently became, unlawful.

So, under section 15 of the 2006 Act an employer will lose the benefit of the statutory "excuse" (at the very least) when s/he carries out the (required) repeat check on a migrant worker who has time limited leave and discovers that the employment is no longer lawful.

What to do if an employee's immigration status becomes questionable

Difficult questions arise when an employee's immigration status becomes questionable, as distinct from someone whose entitlement to work has ceased. Should the employer dismiss them? Matters of employment law are beyond the scope of this chapter, but it should be mentioned that the law governing illegality in contracts of employment is technical and complicated and expert advice on employment law should be sought. It is essential for employers not to be frightened and rush into hasty decisions. If they get it wrong, they could end up on the wrong end of a claim for unfair dismissal and possibly also for discrimination, for which there is no upper limit to the amount of award that can be made.

It is essential to carry out a detailed analysis of the facts and the law to determine if the employee still has permission to stay in the employment before moving to dismissal on grounds related to immigration status. Whilst section 8 of the 1996 Act defence will survive the after-acquired knowledge test, the section 15 of the 2006 Act defence will be lost. But those are only relevant if the continuing employment is actually unlawful under the terms of those sections.

It must be remembered that a person's leave, unless it expires, will continue in force unless and until UKBA initiates any enforcement action. This is particularly so where a person's entitlement to work derives from their status as a family member of another migrant. This can be illustrated in the following example. Say a work permit holder has changed jobs and started employment with a different employer without getting approval to the change of employment. Of course the new employer should terminate the employment as soon as possible as they face the risk of a fine under section 8 of the 1996 Act or a civil penalty and/or prosecution under sections 15 and 21 respectively of the 2006 Act, as appropriate.

But what about the employee's wife who is employed by a different company on the basis that she is the spouse of a Tier 2 migrant or work permit holder, and whose employer becomes aware of the change to her husband's immigration status? Her leave will have no restriction on employment. While her husband has breached his conditions and is therefore liable for enforcement action, as she is his family member, what is the status of her leave? There is no question but that it remains valid and subsisting unless and until action is taken against her by the immigration authorities. So, while her future as a permanent member of staff may be in doubt, her immigration status permits her to continue lawfully in the employment and does not form a basis for her dismissal. Nor does it make her continuing employment unlawful under section 8 of the 1996 Act, or section 15 of the 2006 Act. She also has not ceased to be entitled to undertake the work in question for the purposes of sponsorship duties.

Avoiding discrimination

While employers must take care not to commit an offence under section 8 of the 1996 Act or sections 15 and 21 of the 2006 Act by employing those not entitled to work in the UK, they must also ensure that the procedures they adopt do not discriminate against potential employees on racial grounds.

The Secretary of State has issued specific codes of practice that employers should follow in order to avoid race discrimination in their recruitment practices. The first one in relation to section 8, titled 'Code of Practice for all employers on the avoidance of race discrimination in recruitment practice while seeking to prevent illegal working', came into force in June 2001. The second, issued under section 23 of the 2006 Act, titled 'Guidance for employers on the avoidance of unlawful discrimination in employment practice while seeking to prevent illegal working', came into force in February 2008. In the case of *Osborne Clarke Services v Purohit*, a firm of solicitors was found culpable for indirect discrimination by refusing to consider applications for training contracts from persons whose immigration status required them to obtain permission to work.

The above documents can be found on the UKBA website at: www.ukba. homeoffice.gov.uk/sitecontent/documents/employersandsponsors/ preventingillegalworking/.

Note on money laundering regulations

In the light of the case of the two brothers referred to above, *R v David Kai Ku*: *R v Lu Xu*, where the turnover generated by illegal workers was held to be the proceeds of crime and was, accordingly, confiscated, practitioners should also carefully consider and take specialist advice where necessary, on their own position relating to payment of their professional fees by the employer and whether there may be reporting obligations under whistle-blowing legislation.

11 General grounds for refusal

This chapter covers:

- how the general grounds work (▶immediately below);
- grounds for refusal of entry clearance or leave to enter (▶379);
- grounds for refusal of leave to enter for those in possession of an entry clearance (▶395);
- grounds on which leave to enter or remain can be cancelled at port, or while the holder is outside the UK (▶396);
- grounds of refusal of leave to remain or variation of leave to enter or remain (▶398);
- grounds on which leave to enter or remain may be curtailed or be subject to an alteration in its duration (▶399).

HOW THE GENERAL GROUNDS WORK

Each category under the Immigration Rules sets out a list of requirements that an applicant needs to satisfy in order to be granted entry clearance or leave, under the Rules, in that particular category. Part 9 of the Rules, however, contains 'general grounds' on which entry clearance or leave can be refused. It includes a set of general grounds on which entry clearance or leave to enter can be refused (Rules, para 320), a set of grounds on which leave to enter can be refused even where a person is in possession of entry clearance (Rules, para 321) and a separate set of general grounds on which leave to remain, or a variation of leave, can be refused (Rules, para 322). It also includes grounds on which existing leave to enter or remain can be curtailed (Rules, para 323). All of these Rules are expressed to be "in addition" to the bases upon which leave may be refused under parts 1–8 of the Rules. Parts 1–8 of the Rules contain all the normal requirements for the individual categories of entry. Requirements for entry and leave under the PBS are contained in Part 6A of the Rules.

For many of the categories in parts 1–8, the general grounds are relevant because the relevant Rules state that the applicant "may" (ie, not necessarily 'will') be admitted to the UK if they satisfy the requirements of the particular category that are listed. That indicates that, even if all of the particular requirements for the category are satisfied, the general grounds

11

may still prevent an application from being granted. For the PBS categories, a repeated formulation is for the Rules relating to the individual category to state that leave 'will' be granted if the listed requirements relating to that category are met. *However*, one of the listed requirements is that the applicant "must not fall for refusal under the general grounds of refusal". So, in PBS categories, the general grounds for refusal are also directly relevant to any decisions made on applications for entry clearance or leave.

Deciding the facts: burden and standard of proof

The first question in deciding whether the general grounds are to be used against an applicant, is to determine whether the underlying facts that are required in order to make out any of the criteria for refusal under any particular general ground are satisfied. The precedent facts under the general grounds often concern the conduct (or misconduct) of the applicant, or a third person. This conduct ranges from seeking entry for a purpose not covered by the Rules to deception, or even criminal conduct. The burden of proving the existence of those particular precedent facts, where they are contested, is on the decision-maker, ie the immigration authorities. After the underlying facts are established by the officer, the burden of proof on other issues shifts back to the applicant as is normal (*JC China*, paras 10, 15).

As to the standard of proof, the Tribunal in *JC China*, citing pre-existing case law, stated as follows:

"13. So far as the standard of proof is concerned, we consider that what the Immigration Appeal Tribunal said in *Olufosoye* [1992] Imm AR 141 still holds good: 'insofar as the justification consists of deception or other criminal conduct the standard of proof will be at the higher end of the spectrum of the balance of probability' (see also *R v IAT ex parte Nadeem Tahir* [1989] Imm AR 98 CA). This approach reflects that of the House of Lords in *R v Secretary of State for the Home Department ex p Khawaja* [1984] AC 74 and is consistent with subsequent case law (see eg, *Bishop* [2002] UKIAT 05532). In *R (AN & Anor) v Secretary of State for the Home Department* [2005] EWCA Civ 1605, Richards LJ stated at [62]: 'Although there is a single civil standard of proof on the balance of probabilities, it is flexible in its application. In particular, the more serious the allegation or the more serious the consequences if the allegation is proven, the stronger must be the evidence before a court will find the allegation proved on the balance of probabilities'."

Mandatory and discretionary grounds

Some of the grounds for refusal of applications for entry clearance/leave to enter and for leave to remain are 'mandatory' under the Rules and some are discretionary under the Rules. Where the ground is found to apply and it is mandatory, that means that, as a matter of the Rules alone, officers *cannot* grant entry clearance or leave. Where refusal is discretionary, officers have a discretion *within* the Rules whether to grant entry clearance or leave. The mandatory Rules state that entry clearance/leave "is" to be refused if the relevant circumstances apply. The discretionary Rules state entry clearance/leave "should normally" be refused if the relevant ground is made out. It is a presumptive discretion ie the normal course is that the application will be refused. So, in the case of discretionary refusals of applications, officers will have be persuaded that there is a good reason not to take the normal course, which would be to refuse.

One of the significant aspects of a discretionary ground under the Rules, albeit a presumptive one, is that, if officers decide to reject the application and there is a right of appeal, the Tribunal has the power to review the exercise of the discretion on its merits. That means that the Tribunal may decide for itself whether the discretion was correctly exercised against the applicant (see s86(3)(b)(6) 2002 Act).

Relatively newly-added mandatory grounds relate to previous breaches of immigration laws, the so called 'travel bans' (▶see 385). There have also been important amendments to the general grounds concerning the making of false representations (▶see 383).

Can an application be granted *even if* a mandatory ground applies?

Even if the factual basis for a mandatory refusal ground is established, all is not always lost. This means that application cannot succeed *under the Rules* but the immigration authorities always have a discretion to depart from the Rules, in an appropriate case, and to grant entry clearance or leave outside them. Whether the source of this discretion is the Prerogative of the Crown exercised by Ministers, or the 1971 Act itself (section 4), has never been made absolutely clear, although there are a number of recent authorities which suggest it lies in the Prerogative (see *BAPIO* and *Pankina*, for example).

This discretion is live even if the immigration authorities refuse the application on the basis of the mandatory rule which states that an application "is" to be refused if it is made for a purpose not covered by the Rules. The aim of that Rule is to try to make sure that, in all cases, the person hearing the appeal does not have the power to reconsider, on its merits, the exercise of the discretion of the immigration authorities to refuse to grant leave outside the Rules. That is because the application will be treated as one to "depart from" an Immigration Rule (see s86(6) 2002 Act) namely to depart from that general ground of refusal.

Where a person is having to rely on the discretion to grant leave outside the Rules, the immigration authorities are only likely to grant the application if a very strong case can be made. The ECG refers to the need to show "exceptional, compelling circumstances" to justify such a course where a mandatory general ground for refusal would otherwise apply

(ECG, RFL3.3). If the application is refused, the Tribunal cannot be asked to review the exercise of the discretion not to depart from the Rules on its merits. However, even a decision that is in accordance with the Rules and in relation to which the Tribunal cannot 're-exercise' the discretion, the decision might still be challenged before the Tribunal if it can be shown to be 'not in accordance with the law' (ie s86(3)(a) 2002 Act), for example not in accordance with a published policy.

Other bases upon which an application may still be granted, even if a mandatory general ground applies (or indeed if a discretionary ground applies and officers are minded to exercise the discretion under the Rules against the migrant) are human rights, or asylum grounds. Asylum is beyond the scope of this Guide. Chapter 12 looks at human rights issues that particularly arise in PBS cases. The courts and tribunal have accepted that a person present in the UK even on a temporary basis can acquire a private life interest sufficient to engage human rights arguments, so this can offer a potential solution even to Points-Based System migrants. The ECG specifically directs officers considering general grounds, to also consider (RFL3.3):

"...if there are any human rights grounds (in particular the right to family life under Article 8)...which would justify the issue of an entry clearance."

The operation of the general grounds where no application has been made

The general grounds do not only operate where an application for entry clearance or leave has been made. As will be seen, they may also be invoked by officers in order to curtail (ie, cut off), cancel or reduce the length of existing leave if certain circumstances arise, or are discovered, without the applicant having made any approach to the immigration authorities. The general grounds also deal with the circumstances in which a person who arrives in the UK with an entry clearance, or with continuing leave (that has not lapsed since their last departure) may be denied entry.

As with the general grounds relating to applications for entry clearance or leave, even if an apparently mandatory ground under the Rules applies, that does not prevent the immigration authorities from refraining from taking action, either by using their discretion to depart from the Rules, or because human rights or related considerations prevent them from doing so.

GROUNDS FOR REFUSAL OF ENTRY CLEARANCE OR LEAVE TO ENTER

The general grounds for refusal of entry clearance or leave to enter are set out in Table 1 below. As the table shows, some of the grounds lead to a mandatory refusal under the Rules (where leave "is" to be refused), whereas others are discretionary ("should normally" be refused). Many of the grounds are self-explanatory and do not need further comment. For some, we give some additional details below.

TABLE 1

GENERAL GROUNDS FOR REFUSAL OF ENTRY CLEARANCE OR LEAVE TO ENTER

Mandatory grounds

Entry clearance or leave to enter the UK 'is' to be refused under the Rules if (Rules, para 320(1)-(7)(7A)(7B)(7C)):

- entry is being sought for a purpose not covered by the Rules;

- the applicant seeking entry is currently the subject of a deportation order;

- the applicant seeking entry fails to produce to the Immigration Officer a valid national passport or other document that satisfactorily establishes his/her identity and nationality;

- a passenger who arrives, or seeks entry, through the Channel Tunnel with the intention of entering any other part of the Common Travel Area, fails to satisfy the Immigration Officer, that he is acceptable to the immigration authorities in that other part of the common travel area;

- in the case of a visa national, s/he fails to produce to the Immigration Officer a passport or other identity document endorsed with a valid and current UK entry clearance issued for the purpose for which entry is sought;

- the Secretary of State has personally directed that the exclusion of the person from the UK is conducive to the public good;

- the Medical Inspector confirms that, for medical reasons, it is undesirable to admit an applicant seeking leave to enter the UK (note that this does not apply if the person is settled in the UK, nor where the Immigration Officer is satisfied that there are strong compassionate reasons justifying admission);

- false representations have been made or false documents or information have been submitted (whether or not material to the application, and whether or not to the applicant's knowledge), or material facts have not been disclosed, in relation to the application (▶see 383–385; or

- *unless* one of the exceptions (below) applies, the applicant has previously breached the UK's immigration laws by:
- overstaying (unless the applicant overstayed for 28 days or less *and* left the UK voluntarily *and* did not leave at the direct or indirect expense of the Secretary of State); or

11

- breaching a condition attached to his/her leave; or
- being an illegal entrant; or
- using deception in an application for entry clearance, leave to enter or remain (whether successful or not).

This last mandatory ground of refusal only applies for a set period of time (below). For further details about this important ground ▶see 385–392.

Exceptions to 'previous breaches' ground

An applicant does *not* fall to be refused under the final mandatory ground above (previous breaches of immigration laws) if one of the following exceptions, contained in the Rules, applies (further concessions outside the Rules are referred to below ▶388–391):

- they are applying as:
- a spouse, civil partner or unmarried or same-sex partner under paragraphs 281 or 295A of the Rules;
- a fiancé(e) or proposed civil partner under paragraph 290 of the Rules;
- a parent, grandparent or other dependent relative under paragraph 317 of the Rules;
- a person exercising rights of access to a child under paragraph 246 of the Rules; or
- a spouse, civil partner, unmarried or same-sex partner of a refugee or person with Humanitarian Protection under paragraphs 352A, 352AA, 352FA or 352FD of the Rules; or

- the person was under the age of 18 at the time of his/her most recent breach of the UK's immigration laws.

Length of time for which 'previous breaches' ground applies

The final mandatory ground above (previous breaches of immigration laws) blocks an application for entry clearance or leave to enter under the Rules for:

- 12 months, where the applicant left the UK voluntarily and not at the direct or indirect expense of the Secretary of State (time runs from the departure);

- five years, where the applicant left the UK voluntarily but at the direct or indirect expense of the Secretary of State (time runs from the departure);

- 10 years, where the applicant did not leave voluntarily but was removed or deported from the UK (time runs from the removal/deportation);

- 10 years, where the applicant used deception in an application for entry clearance (time runs from the use of deception in the entry clearance application).

For how these periods of time apply to the various different scenarios that may arise, ▶see Table 2 at 391–392. JCWI understands that Rules to come in from 6 April 2011 will introduce a new category of two-year ban for those who leave promptly and voluntarily but at public expense.

Where more than one breach of the immigration laws has occurred, it is the breach which leads to the *longest* period of absence which is treated as the relevant one for the above purposes (Rules, para 320 (7B)).

Discretionary grounds

Entry clearance or leave to enter the UK "should normally" be refused under the Rules if (Rules, para 320(8)–(20)):

- the applicant who arrives in the UK fails to furnish the Immigration Officer with such information as may be required for the purpose of deciding whether s/he requires leave to enter and, if so, whether and on what terms leave should be given;

- an applicant who is outside the UK fails to supply any information, documents, copy documents or medical report requested by an Immigration Officer;

- an applicant, who is seeking leave to enter as a returning resident, fails to satisfy the Immigration Officer that s/he meets the requirements of paragraph 18 of the Rules (dealing with returning residents), or that s/he seeks leave to enter for the same purpose as that for which his earlier leave was granted;

- the applicant for leave to enter the UK produces a national passport or travel document issued by a territorial entity or authority which is not recognised by HM Government as a state, or is not dealt with as a government by them, or which does not accept valid UK passports for the purpose of its own immigration control;

- the applicant for leave to enter the UK produces a passport or travel document which does not comply with international passport practice;

- the applicant has previously contrived in a significant way to frustrate the intentions of these Rules – the Rules state that Guidance will be published giving examples of circumstances in which an applicant who has previously overstayed, breached a condition attached to his/her leave, been an illegal entrant or used deception in an application for entry clearance, leave to enter or remain (whether successful or not) is likely to be considered as having contrived in a significant way to frustrate the intentions of the Rules (for more details, ▶see 392–395 below);

- the applicant fails to satisfy the Immigration Officer that s/he will be admitted to another country after a stay in the UK (this does not apply to a person who is eligible for admission to the UK for settlement, or to a spouse or civil partner eligible for admission under paragraph 282 of the Rules);

- if a sponsor of the person seeking leave to enter the UK is requested but refuses to give an undertaking in writing to be responsible for that person's maintenance and accommodation for the period of any leave granted;

- whether or not to the holder's knowledge, false representations have been made, or there has been a failure to disclose any material fact for the purpose of obtaining an immigration employment document;

- in the case of a child under the age of 18 years who is seeking leave to enter otherwise than in conjunction with an application made by his/her parent(s) or legal guardian, there is a failure to provide the Immigration Officer, if required to do so, with written consent to the application from his parent(s) or legal guardian (this does not apply in the case of a child asylum seeker);

11

- the applicant refuses to undergo a medical examination when required to do so by the Immigration Officer (this does not apply to those who are settled in the UK);

- the applicant has been convicted in any country, including the UK, of an offence which, if committed in the UK, is punishable with imprisonment for a term of 12 months or any greater punishment or, if committed outside the UK, would be so punishable if the conduct constituting the offence had occurred in the UK (this does not apply if the Immigration Officer is satisfied that the applicant's admission would be justified for strong compassionate reasons) (note that officers should not refuse on the basis of convictions that are 'spent' under the Rehabilitation of Offenders Act 1974, see ECG RFL10.1 and RFL10.5);

- from information available to the Immigration Officer, it seems right to refuse leave to enter on the ground that exclusion from the UK is conducive to the public good; if, for example, in the light of the character, conduct or associations of the person seeking leave to enter, it is undesirable to give it; or

- a person who seeks entry to the UK fails to comply with a requirement relating to the provision of physical data to which s/he is subject by regulations made under section 126 of the Nationality, Immigration and Asylum Act 2002.

Note

The introductory provisions to the Immigration Rules also provide (para 26):

"An application for entry clearance will be considered in accordance with the provisions in these Rules governing the grant or refusal of leave to enter. Where appropriate, the term 'Entry Clearance Officer' should be substituted for 'Immigration Officer'."

Entry for a purpose outside the Rules

This ground applies where entry is sought for a purpose that is not covered in the Rules at all (Rules, para 320(1)). It does not apply where there are simply problems with meeting the particular requirements for a given immigration category or Rule. Sometimes the distinction between not satisfying the Rules and applying for a purpose not covered by them can be a fine distinction. However, most applicants have done at least some research into potential immigration categories before making an application and the use of this Rule is not often required.

Valid passport or identity document

The full ground for refusal is "failure by the person seeking entry to the [UK] to produce to the Immigration Officer a valid national passport or other document satisfactorily establishing his identity and nationality" (Rules, para 320(3)). Nationals of countries where the governing authorities have met with limited international recognition, for example Somalia, have sometimes had problems establishing their identity under this rule.

If this ground is used as a basis of refusal, officers sometimes also assert that there is no right of appeal because of the provisions of section 88(2)(3) 2002 Act which, among other things, deal with ineligibility to appeal if the ground for refusal is that the applicant does not have a particular 'immigration document', including a passport. It is clear from the decision of the Tribunal in *AM (Section 88 (2): 'Immigration Document') Somalia* that the one does not directly lead to the other. Just because the officer has refused on para 320(3) grounds (an issue of fact that can be reviewed by the Tribunal), does not necessarily mean that there is no right of appeal at all, unless a ground for the decision is clearly that the applicant does not possess one of the documents referred to in s88(2)(3). In *AM* itself, the decision was not based on that ground.

Conducive to the public good

This appears in both the mandatory and discretionary grounds for refusal of entry clearance or leave to enter, although it is set somewhat differently in each. Where the Secretary of State personally directs that the exclusion of the applicant is conducive to the public good, the ground is mandatory (Rules, para 320(6)). However, where the Secretary of State has not issued such a direction, there remains a discretionary power for officers to refuse where it seems 'right' to do so on the basis that the person's exclusion from the UK is conducive to the public good (Rules, para 320(19)).

Submission of false representations, documents or information

This mandatory ground for refusal was added to the general grounds with effect from 29 February 2008 (Rules, para 320(7A) as added by HC 321, para 33). The Explanatory Memo to the amending Rules noted that the Rules for Highly Skilled Migrants had already stated that any application in which forged documents were submitted should be refused and that (para 7.22):

"[b]ecause of the importance of ensuring that immigration applicants tell the truth, we are extending this to all applications, and to all forms of deception (not just the submission of forged documents)."

From 27 November 2008, the Rule was amended further so that it referred not only to false documents and representations, but also to "false information" (HC 1113, para 97). The purpose, according to the accompanying Explanatory Memo to those amendments was (para 6.27):

"...to ensure that the provision of false information to a sponsor in order to get a Certificate of Sponsorship is a ground for refusal."

So, the full text of the Rule is now as follows:

"(7A) where false representations have been made or false documents or information have been submitted (whether or not material to the application, and whether or not to the applicant's knowledge), or material facts have not been disclosed, in relation to the application."

11

The same mandatory ground was inserted into the general Rules for:

- refusing leave to enter for a person with entry clearance;
- cancelling leave at port and refusing leave to remain (Rules, paras 321(i), 321A(2), 322(1A) as amended by HC 321, also from 29 February 2008).

The first and third of those further Rules were similarly amended from 27 November 2008 to add in "false information" (Rules, paras 321(i) and 322(1A) as amended by HC 1113).

Important points to note about this general ground, insofar as it is set out under the Rules, is that, in order for it to apply:

- the false representation, document or information need not have been material to the application; and
- the applicant him or herself may be without fault and even without knowledge of the false representation, document or information.

However, under this ground, false representations, documents or information are only relevant insofar as they are submitted "in relation to the application", ie the present application for entry clearance or leave. They are not relevant if they do not relate to the present application but only to some earlier one. One of the other mandatory grounds, Rule 320(7B), applies to previous use of deception (▶379–380, 385), as does one of the discretionary grounds, Rule 320(11) (previous attempts to frustrate the Rules) (▶see below 392). Despite this, some officers wrongly rely on 320(7A) to refuse applications on the basis of allegations of the previous use of deception.

In the case of *AA (Nigeria) v SSHD*, the Court of Appeal held that 'false' for the purposes of this rule (320(7A)) means more than simply 'incorrect', it means that there must have been some 'dishonesty' (Judgment at para 66 and following).

Internal Guidance on Rule 320(7A)

As to false representations, the ECG states (RFL4.3):

"...you must not refuse an applicant because you suspect that false representations have been made or because of minor inaccuracies in the application, for example an inaccurate address or mis-spelt name on a visa application form."

The ECG also state that false documents, for the purpose of this Rule, include (RFL4.4):

- a genuine document which has been altered or tampered with;
- a counterfeit document (one that is completely false);
- a genuine document that is being used by an impostor;
- a genuine document which has been fraudulently obtained or issued;
- a genuine document which contains a falsified or counterfeit visa/endorsement.

The ECG also underline that the purpose of the reference to 'false information' in the Rule is to allow an application to be refused if false representations were used, for example, to obtain a certificate of sponsorship under the PBS (RFL4.5).

As to non-disclosure of material facts, the ECG states (RFL4.6):

"You must refuse the application if material facts are not disclosed. You need to show that the withheld information would have been relevant to your decision. But you cannot refuse an applicant on these grounds if you have not indicated to the applicant the kind of information that is relevant to the application. The Court of Appeal (in the case of *Iracki*) has held that an applicant is not obliged to volunteer information unless he is given an indication of the kind of information which is material to the application."

The standard of proof that applies under 320(7A) is referred to in the ECG as follows (RFL4.2):

"The legal standard of proof is 'to a higher balance of probabilities', so it must be more likely than not that the falsehood has been used. It is for us to prove that an applicant has used falsehood. This means that it is not enough for us simply to doubt that the applicant is telling the truth. In order to refuse under this Rule, we need positive evidence that they have used deception or false representations, or that a document that they have submitted is false."

Previous breaches of immigration law ('travel bans')

Rule 320(7B) and the exceptions to it that are contained in the Rules are set out in Table 1 above at ▶379–380. Certain further exceptions, introduced by way of concessions outside the Rules, are referred to below.

Those who have previously breached immigration control in the way described in paragraph 320(7B), ie, by overstaying for longer than 28 days, breaching a condition attached to leave, being an illegal entrant or using deception in an application for entry clearance or leave (whether successful or not), are subject to a mandatory bar upon their re-entering the UK for a set period of time. Breaches of conditions must be just that ie breaches of the actual *conditions* that were attached to the leave. There is a notable distinction between such breaches on the one hand and not fulfilling the requirements of the Rules upon which leave was granted on the other. The latter may lead to curtailment of leave (▶below), or to officers not being satisfied that that the requirements are met on a future similar application. But they are not breaches of conditions unless, in any particular case, the requirement for leave that was breached overlapped directly with a condition on the leave (and see *R (Zhou) v SSHD*).

This Rule is also sometimes referred to as imposing a 'travel ban'. It was introduced from 1 April 2008 by the HC 321 (para 47). The Explanatory Memo accompanying the new Rule stated (para 7.24):

11

"The previous Immigration Rules on this subject did not cover all the above breaches. They also gave a great deal of discretion to case-workers, with the potential for inconsistent decision-making. The new rules replace this by setting out a clear period during which a previous immigration offender will have any future applications to come here refused."

There was no consultation on HC 321 and it came as a shock and surprise to migrants and advisers. The change led to a great deal of lobbying, as a result of which a number of important concessions were introduced both within and outside the Rules.

Standard of proof

The ECG states (RFL5.2):

"The legal standard of proof is 'to a higher balance of probabilities', so it must be more likely than not that the applicant has previously breached UK immigration law and we must have good evidence, eg, our records showed the applicant overstayed."

See also the decision in *JC China* (▶above 376).

Lack of awareness of previous deception

In contrast to the position under paragraph 320(7A) (false representations etc in the present application, ▶above at 383), where the breach is alleged to have involved false documents or false representations in a previous entry clearance, leave to enter or leave to remain application and the applicant was "not aware that the documents or representations were false", the authorities appear to accept that an application is not to be refused under para 320(7B) (ECG, RFL5.4). However, the ECG imposes a burden on the applicant to prove their lack of awareness (RFL5.8). Arguably, this wrongly reverses the burden of proof. The Guidance continues:

"Where the documents relate directly to the applicant (for example, employment references, qualifications or financial details), such a claim would be likely to fail unless the applicant has clear evidence that an error has been made (eg, written confirmation from a financial institution that they had previously supplied us with incorrect information)."

Application to working holidaymakers

The ECG clarifies that refusal under 320(7B) for breach of employment conditions by a working holidaymaker will be appropriate if they are found to have worked for more than 12 months regardless of how long they stayed in the UK. The Guidance continues (RFL5.12):

"You cannot refuse a working holidaymaker under 320(7B) if they have worked in the UK for 12 months or less, even if you are satisfied that their work was not incidental to their holiday...So for example, a working holidaymaker who stays in the UK for 13 months and works 10 months has not breached this condition of their leave."

Working holidaymakers have been deleted as a category from the Rules, but the above Guidance is of relevance as it relates to the possibility of present refusal under para 320(7B) on the basis of a historical breach by a person who spent time in the UK in this category.

'Removal' for the purposes of para 320(7B)

The question of whether a person was previously 'removed' or 'deported', rather than having left 'voluntarily', is important under para 320(7B) because it helps determine *how long* the bar on their entry will be imposed for (▶see Table 1 above 380 and the Table 2 below 391). It is also important in deciding whether a bar can be applied at all in the case of a person who only overstayed for 28 days or less (▶see above 379 and Rules, para 320(7B)(i)).

The ECG states (RFL5.9):

"Remember that making a decision to remove a person (Form IS 141 A part 2 or IS 151B), or issuing a notice identifying him as an immigration offender (IS 151A) do not in themselves mean that the applicant has been removed from the country. It is perfectly possible for someone to leave the country voluntarily after a decision has been taken to remove him, in which case future applications should only be refused for one or five years, not ten."

Assisted voluntary returns through, for example, the Voluntary Assisted Returns and Re-integration Programme, is one that is voluntary but yet at public expense.

On the specific point of removal directions given at airports when an applicant is in the process of leaving voluntarily, in a letter to ILPA dated 29 February 2008, the Minister, Liam Byrne MP, stated:

"You then raise a practical question as to how we will treat migrants who are served with removal directions (Form IS151) at airports when leaving the UK of their own accord. I hope I can reassure you on this. Provided they leave voluntarily at their own expense, they will only have applications refused for one year. It is only those who are actually removed or deported by the Border and Immigration Agency who will be subject to the ten-year provisions."

The one-year, rather than the five- or ten-year ban, applies in respect of those who leave voluntarily and not at the expense of the Secretary of State.

11

Cases where the applicant is removed having been refused leave to enter at port

In his letter of 4 April 2008, the Minister, Liam Byrne MP, also gave a reassurance in relation to port cases:

"I am happy to give the assurance you seek on people refused at port. Paragraph 320 (7B) only applies to people who have broken UK immigration law. A passenger who seeks leave to enter at port and is proven to have used deception will therefore be subject to a re-entry ban, but someone who is refused entry and removed for some other reason (eg, for not having the correct visa) will not."

This appears to be a correct interpretation of the Rules. If there is no deception in an application for leave to enter made at port and no other basis upon which it is said that the person has previously breached the immigration law in the terms of para 320(7B), then there is no basis for a refusal under that paragraph. This is because there is no stand-alone ban for those who have been removed having sought, but been refused, leave to enter at port.

Exceptions to paragraph 320(7B) under the Rules

Paragraph 320(7B) does not apply to all applications. This is made clear on the face of rule 320(7B) itself which explicitly states that it is subject to rule 320(7C) which then makes exceptions from the general bans for a variety of family life type applications. In addition, the bans do not apply 'where the individual was under the age of 18 at the time of his most recent breach of the UK's immigration laws'. These exceptions are set out in Table 1 ▶380. The family life exception in the Rules is a recognition that a blanket ban on entry clearance or leave to enter in family cases, where there had been a previous breach, would not be compatible with the ECHR (article 8). The exceptions given in the Rules are not, though, exhaustive of all the cases in which the operation of para 320(7B) may violate an individual applicant's human rights and advisers should be astute to make such representations in appropriate cases.

These exceptions were introduced by amendments to the Rules introduced from 30 June 2008 (HC 607), although they first came into effect as concessions to the Rules from the date that they were announced by the Minister in the House of Commons, namely on 13 May 2008. A number of other concessions to paragraph 320(7B) have remained outside the Rules (immediately below). Note the new two-year ban category likely to be introduced from April 2011 (▶380)

Concession: voluntary departures by 1 October 2008

The new rules were implemented without any transitional provisions. However, by way of a concession announced by Lord Bassam in the House of Lords on 17 March 2008 (*Hansard* columns 96–100) and confirmed in a letter from the Minister, Liam Byrne MP, to ILPA, dated 4 April 2008, para

320(7B) will not be applied to anyone who was unlawfully in the UK on 17 March 2008 and who went home voluntarily before 1 October 2008.

The ECG states (RFL5.4 and 5.6):

"5.4...As concessions outside the Rules, you should not refuse an applicant under 320(7B) if:
[...]
the applicant was in the UK illegally on or after 17 March 2008 and left the UK voluntarily before 1 October 2008...

5.6...The concession only applies to voluntary departures whether or not at public expense. It does not apply where the immigration offender was removed or deported from the UK.

Remember that making a decision to remove a person (Form IS 151B), or issuing a notice identifying him as an immigration offender (IS 151A part 2) does not in itself mean that the applicant has been removed from the country. It is perfectly possible for someone to leave the country voluntarily after a decision has been taken to remove him. You therefore need to be satisfied on the balance of probabilities that the applicant was actually removed before deciding that the concession does not apply to him."

Now deleted parts of the ECG gave more details about this concession as follows:

"An applicant must have left the UK by 1 October 2008 to benefit from this concession unless their departure has been delayed through no fault of their own eg delays in UKBA obtaining their document or flight delays."

"Ministers have announced a concession to paragraph 320(7B), with the aim of encouraging people who are in the UK illegally to leave and apply to return under the Immigration Rules. In order to qualify under the concession, the applicant must meet the following conditions:

They must have left the UK voluntarily between 17 March 2008 (this is the date the concession was announced) and 1 October 2008 inclusive.

They must also not have contrived in a significant way to frustrate the immigration rules (eg by conducting a bogus marriage). This means that if a person's breach of our immigration laws was so serious that they would have been refused under the old paragraph 320(11) of the Immigration Rules (or would have been refused under those provisions had they overstayed or breached their conditions), then the concession should not be applied to them."

It will be for the individual to prove to an ECO when making a future application for entry clearance that s/he was in the UK on 17 March 2008 and left voluntarily before 1 October 2008. Advisers will need to consider how those facts can be proved and advise accordingly.

Note that migrants who left the UK *before* 17 March 2008 will not have the benefit of the concession (see Minister's letter to ILPA of 4 April 2008). For them, para 320(7B) will therefore have a retrospective impact in respect of their previous breaches of UK immigration laws.

The justification for not including this concession in the Rules is that it is time limited (Explanatory Memo to HC 607, para 7.43).

Concession: victims of trafficking

The ECG states (RFL5.4 and 5.7):

"5.4...As concessions outside the Rules, you should not refuse an applicant under 320(7B) if:
the applicant has been accepted by UKBA as a victim of trafficking...

5.7...Posts are unlikely to see very many cases where victims of trafficking apply for entry clearance. They will largely be dealt with by caseworkers in the UK. If an applicant states that UKBA has accepted them as a victim of trafficking, ECOs need to contact Evidence and Enquiry (using HO Referrals) to check the information."

This concession was first set out in a letter from Liam Byrne MP to Chris Huhne MP, dated 14 May 2008. The justification for not including the trafficking concession in the Rules is that it was temporary as an interim measure pending the UK's ratification of the Council of Europe Convention on Action against Trafficking in Human Beings (Explanatory Memo to HC 607, para 7.43; the Convention was later ratified by the UK in December 2008).

Concession: subsequently granted leave

The Minister's letter to ILPA, dated 4 April 2008, confirmed that the Government:

"...will not use paragraph 320(7B) to refuse someone for a past breach of our immigration laws if, subsequent to that breach, we granted them leave to enter or remain."

The ECG also confirms that an application should not be refused under para 320(7B) if (RFL5.4):

"...following their breach of UK immigration laws, UKBA issued a visa or leave to enter or remain in the knowledge of that breach eg a student who has overstayed but was granted LTE following an out-of-time application."

This should dispose of the concern that individuals who, for example, entered the UK illegally and were then granted discretionary leave (such as an unaccompanied minor asylum seeker) would be prevented from later returning to the UK with an entry clearance, say as a spouse.

Concession: certain students

A further apparent concession, exempting applicants from para 320(7B) and contained in the ECG, applies to students who were refused leave to remain after 1 September 2007, if they were refused solely on the basis that they had made an out-of-time application. Such students should not be refused under para 320(7B) on grounds of previous overstaying (RFL5.11).

Periods of exclusion

The periods of time over which para 320(7B) operates to cause the refusal of re-entry in the different classes of case is set out in Table 2 below. It should be read together with the notes and exceptions set out above.

TABLE 2
PERIODS OF BAN UNDER PARAGRAPH 320(7B) OF THE RULES

Grounds	Period of mandatory ban
Overstay for 28 days or fewer + left voluntarily not at expense of SSHD	No ban
Overstay of over 28 days or more + left voluntarily not at expense of SSHD	1 year
Breach of conditions + left voluntarily not at expense of SSHD	1 year
Illegal entrant + left voluntarily not at expense of SSHD	1 year
Deception used in an application *other than* for entry clearance + left voluntarily not at expense of SSHD	1 year
Overstay (any length) + left voluntarily at the expense of SSHD	5 years
Breach of conditions + left voluntarily at the expense of SSHD	5 years
Illegal Entrant + left voluntarily at the expense of SSHD	5 years
Deception used in an application *other than* for entry clearance + left voluntarily at expense of SSHD	5 years
Overstay, breach of conditions, illegal entry, deception used in an application + removed or deported	10 years
Deception in a previous application for entry clearance	10 years

Note:

1) Time runs from the date of the relevant departure (voluntary departure, removal or deportation); or in the case of deception being used in an entry

11

clearance application, from the date that the deception was used. This is apparent from the wording of the Rules and is confirmed by the ECG (RFL5.3).

2) Where more than one breach of the immigration laws has occurred, it is the breach which leads to the *longest* period of absence which is treated as the relevant one for the above purposes (Rules, para 320 (7B)).

JCWI understands that new Rules from 6 April 2011 will introduce a new category of a two-year ban for those who leave promptly and voluntarily but at public expense.

Previously contrived to frustrate the Rules

The present version of the relevant Rule states (Rules, para 320(11)):

"(11) where the applicant has previously contrived in a significant way to frustrate the intentions of these Rules. Guidance will be published giving examples of circumstances in which an applicant who has previously overstayed, breached a condition attached to his leave, been an Illegal Entrant or used Deception in an application for entry clearance, leave to enter or remain (whether successful or not) is likely to be considered as having contrived in a significant way to frustrate the intentions of these Rules."

This Rule was introduced from 30 June 2008 by HC 607. The purpose was to ensure that there was still a means of refusing an applicant whose previous breach was a particularly severe one but who is exempt from automatic refusal under paragraph 320(7B) (for which, ▶see above), because of the exceptions introduced to that rule (see Explanatory Memo to HC 607, para 7.41). Notably, there is no time limit in the Rule that attaches to when the previous breach occurred. In principle (although this does not seem to have been the purpose) it might also, therefore, be used to refuse a person whose previous breach was particularly severe and who would otherwise be caught by 320(7B) but for the fact that the relevant period of time since the breach had expired. Note, however, that in contrast with para 320(7B), para 320(11) is at least a discretionary ground for refusal.

It is plain from the wording of the Rule that only serious previous conduct will be sufficient to justify refusal on this ground. Overstaying, breaching a condition of leave, or using deception, will not, alone, be enough, otherwise the Rule could simply have been based on any of those features. The Rule refers to published Guidance as to the circumstances in which this Rule is likely to be applicable (▶below).

Guidance on para 320(11) – ECG

The ECG states (see also UKBA's 'Modernised Guidance' under 'General Reasons for Refusing', available on the UKBA website and to almost identical effect):

"RFL7.1 When can I refuse under 320(11)?
This is a discretionary refusal where an applicant has:

been an immigration offender or in breach of UK immigration or other law; and/or

received services or support to which they were not entitled;

and where there are aggravating circumstances.

It is not sufficient to have been in breach of immigration law or to be an immigration offender. There must be aggravating circumstances as well.

RFL7.2 What are the services or support to which they were not entitled? The following is not an exhaustive list, and are provided as examples only:

obtaining asylum benefits

state benefits

housing and housing benefits

tax credits

employment

goods or services

NHS care using an assumed identity or multiple identities or to which not entitled

RFL7.3 What are aggravating circumstances?
Please note that the list below is not an exhaustive list. Aggravating circumstances can include actions such as:

absconding;

not complying with temporary admission/temporary reporting conditions/bail conditions;

not complying with reporting restrictions;

failing to comply with removal directions (RDs) after port refusal of leave to enter (RLE);

failing to comply with RDs after illegal entry;

previous working in breach of visitor conditions within short time of arriving in the UK (ie pre-meditated intention to work);

previous recourse to NHS treatment when not entitled;

previous receipt of benefits (income, housing, child, incapacity or otherwise) or NASS benefits when not entitled;

using an assumed identity or multiple identities;

previous use of a different identity or multiple identities for deceptive reasons;

vexatious attempts to prevent removal from the UK eg feigning illness;

active attempt to frustrate arrest or detention by UK Border Agency or police;

a sham marriage/marriage of convenience/polygamous marriage in the UK;

harbouring an immigration offender;

facilitation/people smuggling;

escaping from UK Border Agency detention;

switching of nationality;

vexatious or frivolous applications;

not complying with re-documentation process.

All cases must be considered on their merits, the activities considered in the round to see whether they meet the threshold under paragraph 320(11), taking into account family life in the UK and, in the case of children, the responsibility for the breach.

Where an applicant falls to be refused under 320(7A) or 320(7B), the ECO must consider whether it is also appropriate to refuse the applicant under paragraph 320(11). Where 320(7C) applies which makes an applicant exempt from 320(7B), an ECO must consider whether a refusal under paragraph 320(11) is appropriate.

RFL7.4 Aggravating circumstances and appeal determinations
Full consideration must be given to an applicant's UK immigration history, including any appeal determinations, since it is aggravating circumstances which have occurred after the appeal determination which should be considered."

It should be noted that the UKBA definition of 'aggravating circumstances' is remarkably broad and in fact seems to include any conceivable breach of immigration law. It can be very strongly argued that allegedly aggravating circumstances such as overstaying, not complying with removal directions and not complying with the terms of temporary admission are relatively commonplace, do not represent a high level of breach of immigration law and do not amount to 'significantly contriving' to frustrate the intentions of the Rules. The paragraph appears designed to catch more serious behaviour such as sham marriages or false claims to nationality.

Concessions to paragraph 320(11)

The following concessions that apply to previous breaches under para 320(7B) of the Rules, also apply to paragraph 320(11) (see as confirmed in the Explanatory Memo to HC 607 at para 7.43):

- the concession relating to people who were in the UK on 17 March 2008 who returned home voluntarily by 1 October 2008 (▶see 388);

- the concession covering those who UKBA has accepted were trafficked to the UK (▶see 390).

GROUNDS FOR REFUSAL OF LEAVE TO ENTER FOR THOSE IN POSSESSION OF AN ENTRY CLEARANCE

An entry clearance is taken to be evidence of a person's eligibility for entry to the UK (s33(1) 1971 Act; Rules para 25). The purpose of the entry clearance system is so that it can be determined, in advance and before a person travels, whether they are admissible to the UK. As a result, a person who arrives with an entry clearance that was duly issued to him/her and which is still current can *only* be refused leave to enter on narrow grounds. They cannot be refused leave to enter on the basis of the general grounds for refusal of leave to enter unless those grounds also satisfy the specific grounds for refusal for a person in possession of an entry clearance.

The grounds for refusal of leave to enter for those in possession of an entry clearance are set out in Table 3 below.

Revocation of entry clearance

Note also that, even before a person travels to the UK, the Entry Clearance Officer has the power to revoke an entry clearance that has been issued to the person if satisfied that (Rules, para 30A):

- whether or not to the holder's knowledge, false representations were made or material facts were not disclosed, either in writing or orally, for the purpose of obtaining entry clearance;
- there has been a change in circumstances since the entry clearance was issued that has removed the basis of the holder's claim to be admitted to the UK; or
- the holder's exclusion from the UK would be conducive to the public good.

Overlap with cancellation of leave for those arriving with leave

The Immigration Rules treat separately:

1) refusal of leave to enter to a person with entry clearance; and
2) the cancellation of leave of a person who arrives with leave given to him/her before his/her arrival (for which, ▶see below),

However arguably there is an overlap since persons who arrive in the UK with an entry clearance that operates as leave to enter are to be treated, under the Immigration Acts, on their arrival, as persons who have been granted leave to enter before their arrival (article 4(2)(2B)(3)(3A), Leave to Enter and Remain Order 2000; and see as specifically indicated in the 1971 Act at Sch 2, para 2A(2A)). So, it is possible that, for those arriving with entry clearance that operates as leave to enter, it is necessary, in

11

TABLE 3

**GROUNDS OF REFUSAL OF LEAVE TO ENTER FOR
THOSE IN POSSESSION OF AN ENTRY CLEARANCE**

According to the Rules, a person seeking leave to enter the UK who holds an entry clearance that was duly issued to him/her and which is still current may only be refused leave to enter if the Immigration Officer is satisfied that (Rules, para 321):

- false representations were made or false documents or information were submitted (whether or not material to the application and whether or not to the holder's knowledge), or material facts were not disclosed in relation to the application for entry clearance (▶see further above 383);

- a change of circumstances since the entry clearance was issued has removed the basis of the applicant's claim to be admitted (this does not apply if the only change of circumstance is that a person has become over age for entry in one of the categories under paras 296–316 of the Rules, ie, relating to applications by children); or

- refusal is justified on the grounds of restricted returnability; medical grounds; grounds of criminal record; because the person seeking leave to enter is the subject of a deportation order or because exclusion would be conducive to the public good.

---

addition, to consider the criteria for cancellation of leave of a person who arrives with leave (▶see below).

GROUNDS ON WHICH LEAVE TO ENTER OR REMAIN CAN BE CANCELLED AT PORT OR WHILE THE HOLDER IS OUTSIDE THE UK

The grounds on which leave to enter or remain can be cancelled at port, or while the holder is outside the UK, are set out in Table 4 below.

A person may arrive in the UK with leave to enter or remain that is in force as the result of having left the UK with leave that did not lapse because it was granted for a period exceeding six months (see art 13(1)–(4) Leave to Enter Order 2000). In addition, on their arrival in the UK, the holder of an entry clearance which operates as leave to enter is generally treated as a person who has been granted leave to enter before their arrival (art 4(2)(2B)(3)(3A), Leave to Enter Order 2000). A final category of passenger who may arrive with existing leave are those granted leave by an Immigration Officer before their departure or *en route* to the UK (art 7, Leave to Enter Order 2000). These powers are used to grant leave to enter to groups the Home Office believes are at low risk of abusing controls, for example school groups and recognised tour groups.

The 1971 Act sets out that such people may be examined on their arrival and that their leave may be 'suspended' until the examination is completed (1971 Act, Sch 2, para 2, 2A, 2A(7)). On completion of the examination, the leave may be cancelled (Sch 2, para 2A(8); see also Rules, paras 10A–10B). If that does occur to a person who has entered with leave (whether or not with an entry clearance), the passenger is to be treated for appeal purposes as if s/he had been refused leave to enter at a time when s/he had entry clearance (Sch 2, para 2A(9)). The effect of that is to give an applicant an in-country right of appeal to the Tribunal, unless the ground of refusal was that the applicant's purpose in entering the UK was different to that stated in the entry clearance (see ss89, 92(1)(3)(3A)(3B) 2002 Act) (those who have made asylum or human rights claims are subject to a different regime – they will generally enjoy in-country appeals rights in any event, unless their appeal is certified as 'clearly unfounded', ss92(1)(4)(a), 94(2) 2002 Act).

The power to cancel leave which is in force on arrival is not to be exercised by an Immigration Officer acting alone, officers must always obtain the approval of a Chief Immigration Officer or an Immigration Inspector (Rules, para 10).

TABLE 4

GROUNDS ON WHICH LEAVE TO ENTER OR REMAIN CAN BE CANCELLED AT PORT, OR WHILE THE HOLDER IS OUTSIDE THE UK

Under the Immigration Rules, the immigration authorities have the power to cancel a person's leave to enter or remain that is in force: (a) on their arrival in the UK; or (b) while they are outside the UK, if (Rules, para 321A):

- there has been such a change in the circumstances of their case since the leave was given, that it should be cancelled;

- false representations were made or false documents were submitted (whether or not material to the application and whether or not to the holder's knowledge), or material facts were not disclosed in relation to the application for leave (►see further above 383);

- it is apparent that, for medical reasons, it is undesirable to admit that person to the UK (this does not apply if the person is settled in the UK, nor where the Immigration Officer or the Secretary of State are satisfied that there are strong compassionate reasons justifying admission);

- the Secretary of State has personally directed that the exclusion of that person from the UK is conducive to the public good;

- from information available to the Immigration Officer or the Secretary of State, it seems right to cancel leave on the ground that exclusion from the UK is conducive to the public good; if, for example, in the light of the character, conduct or associations of the person, it is undesirable for him/her to have leave to enter the UK; or

11

- where the person is outside the UK, they fail to supply any information, documents, copy documents or medical report requested by an Immigration Officer or the Secretary of State.

Note 1: The heading given to these grounds in the Rules is expressed in mandatory terms ie "grounds on which leave to enter or remain...is to be cancelled..." (emphasis added). While that heading suggests that the grounds are mandatory, the text of the Rule itself does not make the position clear.

Note 2: The first five grounds above are also contained (although, it should be noted, with some modification) in statutory provisions in the 1971 Act in respect of persons arriving with leave to enter or remain which is in force and granted prior to their arrival (1971 Act, Sch 2, paras 2A(1)(2)(2A)(3)(4)(8) read with article 13(5) Leave to Enter Order 2000). Where there is a difference, it is the grounds as stated in the statute that must take precedence. Those statutory provisions also contain an additional ground for examination and cancellation, namely that the passenger's purpose in arriving in the UK is different from that stated in the entry clearance (1971 Act, Sch 2, para 2A(2A)).

Note 3: The final ground above, relating to cancellation of the leave of a person outside the UK, is also referred to in article 13(7)(9) Leave to Enter Order 2000. That Order also gives the immigration authorities powers to 'vary' the leave of a person outside the UK. In determining whether to either vary or cancel leave using those powers, the provisions under Sch 2 1971 Act to seek information and the production of documents from an applicant who is being examined on entry to the UK, also apply (see art 13(6)(8), Leave to Enter Order 2000).

GROUNDS FOR REFUSAL OF LEAVE TO REMAIN OR VARIATION OF LEAVE TO ENTER OR REMAIN

The grounds on which the Secretary of State may refuse to grant an application for leave to remain, or to 'vary' their leave ('variation' is a term that applies to persons whose leave is altered when they already have it) are set out in Table 5 below.

TABLE 5

GROUNDS FOR REFUSAL OF LEAVE TO REMAIN OR VARIATION OF LEAVE TO ENTER OR REMAIN

Mandatory grounds

Applications for leave to *remain* or to *vary* leave to enter or remain in the UK "are" to be refused under the Rules if (Rules, para 322(1)(1A)):

- the variation is being sought for a purpose not covered by the Rules; or
- false representations have been made or false documents or information have been submitted (whether or not material to the application, and whether or not to the applicant's knowledge), or material facts have not been disclosed, in relation to the application (▶see further above 383).

Discretionary grounds

Applications for leave to *remain* or to *vary* leave to enter or remain in the UK "should normally" be refused under the Rules if (Rules, para 322(2)–(11)):

- false representations have been made or there has been a failure to disclose any material fact for the purpose of obtaining leave to enter or a previous variation of leave;
- the applicant has failed to comply with any conditions of leave;
- the applicant has failed to maintain or accommodate him/herself or any dependants without recourse to public funds;
- it is undesirable to permit the applicant to remain in the UK in the light of his/her character, conduct or associations or the fact that s/he represents a threat to national security;
- the applicant's sponsor refuses, if requested, to give an undertaking in writing to be responsible for the applicant's maintenance and accommodation in the UK or fails to honour such an undertaking once given;
- the applicant fails to honour any declaration or undertaking given orally or in writing as to the intended duration and/or purpose of his stay;
- the applicant fails to satisfy the Immigration Officer that s/he will be returnable to another country if allowed to remain in the UK for a further period (this does not apply to a person who qualifies for settlement in the UK or to spouse or civil partner of a person settled in the UK);
- failure by an applicant to produce within a reasonable time, information, documents or other evidence required by the Secretary of State to establish his claim to remain under the Rules;
- failure, without providing a reasonable explanation, to comply with a request made on behalf of the Secretary of State to attend for an interview; or
- in the case of a child under the age of 18 years who is seeking to vary his/her leave to enter or remain otherwise than in conjunction with an application made by his/her parent(s) or legal guardian, there is a failure to provide the Secretary of State, if required to do so, with written consent to the application from his/her parent(s) or legal guardian (this does not apply in the case of a child asylum seeker).

GROUNDS ON WHICH LEAVE TO ENTER OR REMAIN MAY BE CURTAILED OR SUBJECT TO AN ALTERATION IN ITS DURATION

The grounds on which leave to enter or remain may be curtailed, or subject to an alteration in its duration are set out in Table 6 below.

From 27 November 2008, specific amendments were made to the Rules by HC 1113 to enable a migrant's leave granted under Tier 2, Tier 4 or under the Tier 5 (Temporary Worker) category, to be curtailed or shortened if the sponsor ceases to hold a licence, or if the migrant ceases (or never starts) working or studying with the sponsor (Rules, para 323A – set out in Table 6). The present Rules presently in force reflect certain further modifications to these Rules after HC 1113.

The powers of curtailment are operated on the basis of a *discretion* within the Rules. So much is clear from the wording of the Rules (see also IDI, 'Curtailment' instruction, v.2.3, August 2009, para 2.8).

TABLE 6

GROUNDS ON WHICH LEAVE TO ENTER OR REMAIN MAY BE CURTAILED OR BE SUBJECT TO AN ALTERATION IN ITS DURATION

A person's leave to enter or remain may be curtailed if (Rules, para 323):

- false representations have been made, or there has been a failure to disclose any material fact for the purpose of obtaining leave to enter or a previous variation of leave;
- the person has failed to comply with any conditions of leave;
- the person has failed to maintain or accommodate him/herself or any dependants without recourse to public funds;
- it is undesirable to permit the person to remain in the UK in the light of his/her character, conduct or associations, or the fact that s/he represents a threat to national security;
- the person ceases to meet the requirements of the Rules under which his leave to enter or remain was granted;
- the person is the dependant, or is seeking to remain as the dependant, of an asylum applicant whose claim has been refused and whose leave has been curtailed under section 7 of the 1993 Act, and he does not qualify for leave to remain in his/her own right;
- the person's grant of asylum is being revoked for any of the reasons given in para 339A(i)–(vi) of the Rules; or
- the person's grant of humanitarian protection is being revoked for any of the reasons given in para 339G(i)–(vi) of the Rules.

A person who has leave to enter or remain under Tier 2, Tier 4 or as a Tier 5 (Temporary Worker) Migrant, may be curtailed or have its duration altered, *if* (Rules, para 323A):

- any of the grounds set out above for the curtailment of leave apply;
- the migrant's sponsor ceases to have a sponsor licence (for whatever reason);
- the migrant's sponsor transfers the business for which the migrant works or at which the migrant is studying to another person who does not have a sponsor licence *and* that (other) person:
- fails to apply for a licence within 28 days of the transfer;
- applies for a sponsor licence but is refused; or
- applies for a sponsor licence and is granted one but not in the category that would allow it to issue a certificate of sponsorship to the migrant;
- the migrant fails to commence, or ceases, working for the sponsor; or

- in the case of a Tier 4 Migrant:
- the migrant fails to commence studying with the sponsor;
- the migrant studies at an institution other than that which issued the visa letter on the basis of which the migrant's present entry clearance, leave to enter or leave to remain was granted, unless the sponsor is a Highly Trusted Sponsor or the UKBA has given its written consent for the migrant to transfer to another sponsor; or
- the migrant ceases studying with the sponsor.

12 Human rights and the Points-Based System

This chapter covers:

RESPECT FOR PRIVATE LIFE

Article 8 of the European Convention on Human Rights (ECHR) provides as follows:

"1 Everyone has the right to respect for his private and family life, his home and his correspondence.
2 There shall be no interference by a public authority with the exercise of this right except such as is in accordance with the law and is necessary in a democratic society in the interests of national security, public safety or the economic well-being of the country, for the prevention of disorder or crime, for the protection of health or morals, or for the protection of the rights and freedoms of others."

Article 8 protects four broad interests: private life, family life, home and correspondence (article 8(1)). The impact of the right to respect for 'family life' on immigration decisions that cause the separation of family members is very well known in immigration law (see as covered in the JCWI *Handbook* 2006 Edition, pp820–851, although there has been a good deal of further case law since that time).

There may, of course, be PBS cases where family life is relevant ie because the immigration decision prevents the PBS (or other work/study) applicant from being in the UK together with family members. We do not cover 'family life' cases here because our focus is on the particular human rights implications in PBS work and study cases. Advisers should nevertheless be alive to the need to check whether there are any relevant family life considerations in any case.

'Adding together' the interests under article 8

Advisers should bear in mind also that it is possible to add together elements of family life and private life connections and to argue that, when taken together, a negative immigration decision would be an unjustified interference with the article 8 interests. In *Nhundhu & Chiwera*, the Tribunal explained this point in the following way:

"In the context of immigration and asylum cases, the court has come to view the right to respect for private and family life as a composite right. This approach requires the decision-maker to avoid restricting himself to looking at the circumstances of 'family life' and to take into account also significant elements of the much wider sphere of 'private' life...One consequence of this approach is that a person may be able to establish a protected right under Article 8 either by reference to significant elements of family life or significant elements of private life or a mixture of both."

As will be come clear as we look at the different aspects of private life (▶below), it may therefore be that an applicant can build an article 8 case based on:

- family life; and/or
- relationships developed through work, study or business in the UK (private life ▶see below 405–407, 410–421); and/or
- residence in the UK and other social ties (falling short of family life) with those here (private life ▶see below, 408–421).

Structure of article 8 and proportionality

It will be clear from the terms of article 8 (▶above) that, in order to show a violation, a number of hurdles have to be jumped. An immigration decision will violate article 8 if:

1) the interest affected falls within the scope of those protected by the right (ie 'family' life, 'private' life etc); and

2) the decision 'interferes' with the 'right to respect' for that interest; and

3) the decision is either:
- not 'in accordance with the law'; or
- not made in order to further one of the legitimate interests of the state/community referred to (national security, public safety, economic

12

well-being of the country, prevention of disorder and crime, protection of health, protection of the rights and freedoms of others); or

– not 'proportionate' ie the extent of the interference with the protected interest/s cannot be justified as 'necessary in the interests of a democratic society' in order to fulfil the legitimate interest.

The burden of showing 1) and 2) above is on the applicant. If that is done, then the burden of showing that none of the aspects of 3) above apply is on the state.

In *Razgar*, the House of Lords established five questions for decision-makers to ask themselves (para 17) (and see as applied by the Tribunal to a PBS private life case in *MM Zimbabwe*, para 20):

- Will the proposed removal be an interference by a public authority with the exercise of the applicant's right to respect for private life or (as the case may be) family life?

- If so, will such interference have consequences of sufficient gravity as potentially to engage the operation of article 8?

- If so, is such interference in accordance with the law?

- If so, is such interference necessary in a democratic society in the interests of national security, public safety or the economic well-being of the country, for the prevention of disorder or crime, for the protection of health or morals, or for the protection of the rights and freedoms of others?

- If so, is such interference proportionate to the legitimate public end sought to be achieved?

In order to show an interference with the right to respect for the relevant interest, there is a threshold of a 'minimum level' of severity that must be crossed (see Lord Bingham in *Razgar*, para 18). In *AG (Eritrea)*, Sedley LJ, giving the judgment of the Court and after referring to Lord Bingham's analysis, stated (at para 28) (applied also in *MM Zimbabwe* at para 52):

"It follows, in our judgment, that while an interference with private or family life must be real if it is to engage art 8(1), the threshold of engagement (the 'minimum level') is not a specially high one. Once the article is engaged, the focus moves, as Lord Bingham's remaining questions [in Razgar] indicate, to the process of justification under art. 8(2). It is this which, in all cases which engage article 8(1), will determine whether there has been a breach of the article."

The 'in accordance with the law' requirement under article 8 is there in order to prevent an interference with a fundamental right from being arbitrary. Any interference must be sanctioned according to clear, accessible and predictable legal rules – we return to this below when looking at a similar requirement under article 1 of the First Protocol (deprivation of possessions) (▶430).

Decisions taken on the basis that a provision of immigration control set out in the immigration legislation or Rules, will almost always satisfy the requirement or having been made for the purpose of one of the legitimate interests of the state or community.

The element of 3) above that is most argued about in article 8 cases is 'proportionality' (►immediately below).

'Proportionality'

In *Huang v SSHD*, citing both *de Freitas* and *R (Razgar) v SSHD*, the House of Lords identified the following as the questions to be asked in order to determine whether a decision is 'proportionate':

- Is the objective "sufficiently important" to justify limiting a fundamental right?
- Is the decision/measure taken to meet the above objective "rationally connected" to it?
- Is the decision/measure taken which causes the interference "no more than is necessary to accomplish the objective"?
- Has a "fair balance" been struck between the interests of society and the interest of the individual/group of persons whose interests are being interfered with?

In relation to the last question, in *Razgar* the House of Lords had stated that the judgment on proportionality (at para 20):

"…must always involve the striking of a fair balance between the rights of the individual and the interests of the community which is inherent in the whole of the Convention. The severity and consequences of the interference will call for careful assessment at this stage."

Development of concept of 'private life' covering work/study

The general concept of 'private life' is a very broad one. In April 2002, the European Court of Human Rights ('ECtHR') decided the case of *Pretty v United Kingdom*. This was about whether a woman who was suffering from an incurable, degenerative disease should be able to control how and when she died, including if that meant obtaining assistance to die from others. The ECtHR reviewed the case law and the breadth of the right and said this (at para 61):

"As the court has had previous occasion to remark, the concept of 'private life' is a broad term not susceptible to exhaustive definition. It covers the physical and psychological integrity of a person…It can sometimes embrace aspects of an individual's physical and social identity…Elements such as, for example, gender identification, name and sexual orientation and sexual life fall within the personal sphere protected by art 8…Article 8 also protects a right to personal development, and the right to establish and develop relationships with other human beings and the outside world. Though no previous case has established as such any right to self-determination as being contained in

12

art 8 of the convention, the court considers that the notion of personal autonomy is an important principle underlying the interpretation of its guarantees."

The Court found that the applicant's choices about how she wished her life to come to a close were within the scope of 'private life' (para 67), although it concluded also that the ban on assisted suicides in the UK was not disproportionate and there was, therefore, no violation of article 8 taken as a whole.

Pretty pushed at the boundaries of private life by recognising that the right to self-determination could fall within the scope of article 8 in the circumstances that presented themselves. The consequences of the pursuit of a vocation in terms of work, occupation or study and the relationships and social interaction that they give rise to, comes within 'private life', as an element of the right to 'personal development' and pursuing relationships with others and the world outside (see also the extract from *Pretty*).

That private life covers personal development and outside relationships had been a feature of the case law long before *Pretty*. A decade before that case, in December 1992, in *Niemietz v Germany*, a case involving a police search of a lawyer's offices, the ECtHR had stated (at paras 29–31; see also *Amman v Switzerland* at para 65):

"29. The court does not consider it possible or necessary to attempt an exhaustive definition of the notion of 'private life'. However, it would be too restrictive to limit the notion to an 'inner circle' in which the individual may live his own personal life as he chooses and to exclude therefrom entirely the outside world not encompassed within that circle. Respect for private life must also comprise to a certain degree the right to establish and develop relationships with other human beings.

"There appears, furthermore, to be no reason of principle why this understanding of the notion of 'private life' should be taken to exclude activities of a professional or business nature since it is, after all, in the course of their working lives that the majority of people have a significant, if not the greatest, opportunity of developing relationships with the outside world...it is not always possible to distinguish clearly which of an individual's activities form part of his professional or business life and which do not. Thus, especially in the case of a person exercising a liberal profession, his work in that context may form part and parcel of his life to such a degree that it becomes impossible to know in what capacity he is acting at a given time...

" ...31. More generally, to interpret the words 'private life' and 'home' as including certain professional or business activities or premises would be consonant with the essential object and purpose of Article 8, namely to protect the individual against arbitrary interference by the public authorities..."

The above suggests that the more intertwined a person's work or business is with 'who they are' and how they relate to the world and the more they relate to the 'inner circle' of their life, the greater will be the impact upon their 'private life' of a measure that interferes with that work or business. The highly skilled and specialised nature of many of the occupations that are generally covered under Tiers 1 and 2 and the importance of the individual applicants that fall within these categories to the business (be it their own or another's), makes it more likely that their work will be closely associated with their sense of identity, personal development and social interaction.

In *Sidabras v Lithuania* (July 2004), the applicants were former Lithuanian KGB agents who, following Lithuanian independence, had been disbarred from both public and some forms of private employment. The Court considered the case under article 8 (private life) taken together with article 14 (discrimination on the grounds of their previous employment). The ECtHR held that the measures impacted on the applicants' private life as there was "no watertight division separating the sphere of social and economic rights from the field covered by the convention". The prohibition on their taking up private sector employment affected their ability to develop relationships with the outside world, pursue various professional activities to a significant degree and created serious difficulties for them as regarded the possibility of earning a living. That was found to have repercussions for their private life (paras 47–8, 50).

It is perhaps important to note that *Sidabras* concerned only the question of whether the circumstances fell within the 'ambit' of article 8 because the Court found a breach of article 8 taken together with article 14 (discrimination). In the *Countryside Alliance* case, Lord Bingham considered that *Sidabras* was an extreme case on its facts because the statutory consequence of the applicants' employment as KGB officers was to disbar them from employment in very many public and private employments. Effectively they were deprived of access to work and their ability to function as social beings was blighted as a result (para 15).

In a judgment given in August 1996, *C v Belgium*, the Strasbourg Court acknowledged that an applicant's 'social ties' involving his schooling and vocational training amounted to private life within the Convention (para 26).

One leading textbook explains (*Human Rights Law & Practice*, Lester and Pannick, 3rd edn, para 4.8.13):

"It is clear that the ECtHR considers that art 8 extends to individuals' involvement or potential for involvement in professional or business activity, or to public social activity, precisely because such is essential for normal people to achieve fulfilment, a personal identity and a sense of self. The ECtHR's approach...consistently shows that because an individual's private life may coalesce with or merge into professional or business activities..."

12

Long residence, social ties and private life

In March 1992, Judge Martens gave a concurring judgment in the case of *Beljoudi v France* in which he said the following (at pp 841–2 of the report):

"'Family life' already enlarges the circle but there are relatives with whom one has no family life *stricto sensu*. Yet the relationship with such persons, for instance one's parents, undoubtedly falls within the sphere which has to be respected under Article 8. The same may be said with regard to one's relationships with lovers and friends. I therefore share the view of the Commission, which has repeatedly held that 'respect for private life' comprises also to a certain degree the right to establish and develop relationships with other human beings, especially in the emotional field of the development and fulfilment of one's own personality."

In his dissenting judgment in *Boughanemi v France*, in April 1996, in which a young Tunisian, who had lived in France from the age of eight years, was being deported following serious criminal offences, Judge Martens picked up the same theme. He argued that the expulsion of an integrated alien could be unlawful even if it did not involve an interference with family ties and that it was time to acknowledge that the interference of long residing foreign nationals could raise issues concerned with their private life which were sufficient to prevent removal. Martens' judgments were later picked up in standard practitioner books in the UK.

In October 2003, in *Slivenko v Latvia*, the Grand Chamber of the ECtHR found that the expulsion of two long-term residents of Latvia to Russia amounted to an interference with private life. The applicants were a mother and daughter and were ethnically Russian, the mother having lived in Latvia since the age of just one month and her daughter was born in Latvia. Following the fall of the Soviet Union, the applicants' husband/father, a Soviet army officer, returned to Russia where the family had been provided with a flat. The applicants did not wish to leave to live in Russia and resisted doing so. There was no rupture in family ties, but the Court held that the requirement for the applicants to leave Latvia constituted an unlawful interference with their private life having regard to their inevitable degree of social integration in that country.

In June 2004, the case of *R (Razgar) v SSHD* was decided in the House of Lords. That concerned the separate question of the applicant's assertion that his removal to Germany would violate his private life interests on the grounds of the unavailability for him there of the necessary psychiatric treatment needed to address his condition. The Secretary of State asserted in his submissions to the Court that the "same principle" as with regard to an immigration decision causing a rupture of established family life applies (at pp 372F–G):

" ...where a disproportionate rupture to a person's private life occurs because removal takes place after long periods of residence in the removing state: see *Slivenko v Latvia* [▶above]...and *Nasri v France* (1995) 21 EHRR 458. In such cases the threat to private life is based on the links with the removing state which engage that state's responsibility."

In her review of the Strasbourg case-law in *Razgar*, Baroness Hale referred to Judge Martens' approach (▶above). In the context of her appreciation of the different circumstances in which an immigration decision may violate article 8, she also referred to the above decision in *Slivenko* (*Razgar* at paras 47, 49).

In October 2006, the Grand Chamber decided the important case of *Uner v Netherlands* in which the court reviewed the 'guidelines' that had been given in the earlier case of *Boultif v Switzerland* concerning the factors that are to be taken into consideration in the expulsion of non-nationals following criminal convictions. The Court in *Uner* expressly considered whether the criteria laid down in *Boultif* were comprehensive enough. It noted that not all migrants will necessarily have established a 'family' life in the host country and that, citing *Pretty* (▶above), article 8 protects also the right to establish and develop relationships with other human beings and the outside world. The ECtHR went on to accept that the "totality of social ties" between settled migrants and the community in which they are living constitutes part of the concept of 'private life' within the meaning of article 8. The Court stated (para 56, see also para 59 on the facts of the case):

"Regardless of the existence or otherwise of a 'family life', therefore, the Court considers that the expulsion of a settled migrant constitutes interference with his or her right to respect for private life. It will depend on the circumstances of the particular case whether it is appropriate for the Court to focus on the 'family life' rather than the 'private life' aspect."

Uner has since been cited and applied many times by the Strasbourg Court; see for example only *Hizir Kilic v Denmark* and *Maslov v Austria* (at para 63).

In *Maslov*, the applicant was a Bulgarian national who was admitted to Austria lawfully at the age of six years, together with his family and was granted settled status when aged 15. From approximately the same time, the applicant fell into crime and was arrested and convicted on 22 counts, including offences of attempted and aggravated gang burglary and gang extortion. Not long afterwards, the applicant was again convicted of a further 18 counts of aggravated burglary. The Court considered that the case involved aspects of both 'family' (the applicant's relationship with his parents and other family members although he had not yet formed a 'family' of his own) and private life (the totality of social ties formed by a settled migrant) (paras 62–3). Ultimately, the Court was of the view that

12

the offences were in the nature of juvenile delinquency and that removal was not proportionate (paras 80–81).

Most recently, the Supreme Court decided *ZH (Tanzania)* (February 2011). That case largely concerned the importance to be attached to the British citizenship of a child whose mother was to be removed and also the question of the child's 'best interests'. Although the case involved 'family life', the Supreme Court also appeared to endorse the significance of social ties arising as an element of private life. Giving the leading judgment, Baroness Hale referred to *Uner*, stating "[s]ignificantly for us . . . the Grand Chamber in *Uner* went on . . . 'to make explicit two criteria that may already be implicit'". One of these was the "solidity of social, cultural and family ties with the host country and with the country of destination" (para 17 and see also the references to the degree of the child's "integration" and "social links" at paras 29 and 31). In addition, at para 32, Baroness Hale adopted an extract from a text to the following effect: "In short, the fact of belonging to a country fundamentally affects the manner of exercise of a child's family and *private* life, during childhood and well beyond" (emphasis added).

Private life in action: coverage of work/study/residence in UK cases

That an applicant's connections to the UK comprised by social/emotional ties not amounting to 'family' life, and also ties underpinned by work, occupation and study, may fall within private life, is now well established in the UK case law (and ▶see also the cases at 412–421).

- In *Nhundu and Chiwera v SSHD*, one of the earliest detailed Tribunal decisions after the incorporation of the IAT, the proposition that study and/or work could give rise to elements of private life appeared to have been accepted (paras 26, 36).

- In the successful judicial review application in *Mthokozisi v SSHD*, the relevant interests were private, rather than family life and were founded on the applicant's relations with his foster family (see at paras 13 and 19).

- The close relationships with a particular family and other connections to the UK were regarded as amounting to private life in *N v SSHD*, although the facts were not strong enough to establish a breach of article 8 in that case (para 11); and see further *MT (Zimbabwe) v SSHD* (at paras 10, 12–13, 29)

- In *AG (Eritrea) v SSHD*, the Court of Appeal held (at para 40):
  "The private life established in this country by a lone 14-year old whose asylum claim is not processed for four years, who has no known family in Eritrea and cannot speak the language, and who has acquired an education, psychological support and a social circle here, not only brings him very plainly within art 8(1) but raises an obvious question about the necessity and proportionality of removing him notwithstanding the legality and proper objects of immigration control."

- In *JN (Uganda) v SSHD*, the relevant article 8 interest on the basis of which the Court proceeded, was the development of a 'social and private life' in the UK which included work for the local authority, voluntary work at a women's prison, involvement in a Church and with the Runnymede Christian Fellowship (see at paras 4–5, 10, 16). Having referred to paragraph 20 of the decision in *Huang*, Maurice Kay LJ commented:
  "Although expressed by reference to family life, that reasoning plainly applies equally to private life cases."

- In *OA (Nigeria) v SSHD*, the Court of Appeal upheld a careful decision of an Immigration Judge finding a violation of article 8 (private life) involving interference with an applicant's studies should she be returned. The applicant had been studying accountancy courses in the UK since the age of 16, from the stage of NVQ level to the expectation of obtaining a degree in accounting from Oxford Brookes University. In the course of her applications, she had been let down and cheated by an unscrupulous adviser who had wrongly advised her that she was entitled to apply for indefinite leave and who procured a non-genuine stamp in her passport. When this turn of events was discovered, the applicant did all she could to rectify the situation and assist the Home Office in their investigation of the adviser. The applicant showed satisfactory attendance and progress with her studies. Her latest application had been refused after significant delay on the basis that there was no evidence that she had re-enrolled, although the applicant had in fact re-enrolled in the meantime and no further enquiries had been made by the Home Office. The IJ found that the interruption with the applicant's studies amounted to an interference with her private life of sufficient gravity to engage article 8 and was disproportionate. He pointed out that the applicant: would be unable to complete her studies in the UK; had lost time spent on the course here while getting used to the curriculum and teaching; would experience delay before being able to enrol on a new course; had invested money, time and effort in her studies here; would bear the consequences for her dishonest representative's conduct; and had acted with due expedition after it came to light that her representative had conducted the matter fraudulently (Court of Appeal, para 21). The Court of Appeal considered that there was evidence of a serious impact on the applicant's studies of her being required, in the middle of an academic year, to leave the country and that the detriment was obvious. It upheld the IJ (paras 24–25, 29). The Court also pointed out that, but for the involvement of the corrupt representative, the applicant would have made the necessary applications and would almost certainly have succeeded under the student Rules (para 28).

Note, that, in *SSHD v QY (China)* the Court of Appeal drew attention to the strength of the facts in *OA*. In the different circumstances of *QY*, the applicant sought to rely on studies that she had arranged for herself after a lawful decision to remove had been taken but had been delayed through legal proceedings – the appellant was unsuccessful (see *QY*, paras 21, 23-5). *OA* was also distinguished in the case of *SZ (Zimbabwe) v SSHD* (see at para 31).

12

- In *SSHD v HK (Turkey)*, the Court of Appeal upheld a decision of the Tribunal to allow the applicant to remain in the UK notwithstanding serious criminal offending. The decision was based on ties established in the UK amounting to elements of family and a "well-developed and strong" private life, one aspect of which was the applicant's relations with his parents and siblings (paras 14, 18–19, 30-33).

- In both *JO (Uganda) v SSHD* (at paras 20–21) and *HM (Iraq) v SSHD* (paras 29–30), the Court of Appeal directed itself in accordance with the ECtHR decisions in *Uner* and *Maslov* (▶above) as to the need to consider carefully and balance the private life established in the UK of a relatively young applicant facing deportation for criminal offences, even though the individual had not yet founded a family life of his own.

- Users may also find the following Court of Appeal decisions of some interest: *MA (Afghanistan)* (paras 5, 15, 21–23, 25, 28); *RU (Sri Lanka)* (paras 31, 39, 40, 43); and *DM (Zambia)* (paras 17, 19–20).

Private and family life in action: points-based system cases

Since the PBS came into operation, applicants and their advisers (and, it is understood, some decision-makers) have been continually frustrated by refusals of applications that seem, in their eyes, to be based on technical and bureaucratic grounds. The stipulation in the Rules (para 245AA and elsewhere) to the effect that the requirements will not be found to be met unless the applicant submits the "specified documents" has often led to a situation where, although on any ordinary application of the evidence to the qualification criteria, an applicant would succeed, the application nevertheless fails.

Another frustration is that, because the PBS has been drawn so as to eradicate discretion, uncertainty and areas for dispute on appeal, it also removes judgment and common sense from the system. An applicant who may well be perfectly able to maintain and accommodate themselves and their dependants without recourse to public funds (and would previously have been found to be so able), may now be refused, not because they cannot, but because they have not ticked the required boxes (although the ability of the Home Office to require boxes to be ticked can no longer solely be set out in Policy Guidance where the requirement amounts to the introduction of a substantial criterion that should be contained in the Rules, ▶see *Pankina* dealt with in full in Chapter 2 42–45, 47–52).

The comments of the Vice-President of the Upper Tribunal in *AM and SS (PBS – Tier 1 – joint accounts) Pakistan* help to illustrate this problem (para 10):

"The Immigration Judge's comments are obviously sensible. His mistake was to apply common sense to the interpretation of the points-based scheme. There is no perceptible rationale behind the conclusion that the possession of £800 (and not a penny less) for three months (and not a day less) is showing that [if] an application is granted, the applicant will be satisfactorily maintained for what may be a very long period in the future. The rules are simply hoops which have to be jumped through."

Human rights are concerned with substance rather than form. If an applicant cannot meet the strict requirements of the Rules (read with Policy), not because they fall foul of any legitimate measure, or requirement of immigration control, but rather because they have not jumped through all the required "hoops", an interference with a qualified right (such as article 8 ECHR) caused by the decision, may be difficult to justify in terms of proportionality. As a result, if an applicant can bring their case within the scope of article 8 – and in many PBS or other work and study cases they will be able to do so, see the ambit of 'private' life set out extensively above – they may have a case that to refuse them would violate the Convention.

Taking another example, in *R (Pengiliang Fu) v SSHD*, a Tier 4 (General) Migrant got into trouble because he had failed to submit an application in the proper form. The learned Judge noted (para 33):

"I would not however wish to leave this case, which has not succeeded, without this observation. This claimant has plainly satisfied the requirements of the Immigration Rules throughout his stay up until the moment that he made a mistake when submitting his application on 29 May 2009. The error which he made was a simple mistake. I do not know how it occurred or why it occurred, but the Secretary of State might, when reconsidering or considering any application made by him in the future, take into account that but for the mistake, and nothing more than that, the claimant would unquestionably have been entitled to have been granted, and would have been granted, leave to remain to pursue his course of studies."

That is another type of case where, if article 8 can be engaged, it would be very difficult, on the basis of the circumstances, to justify a negative decision.

Even where the 'falling short' from the Rules does raise some legitimate concerns for the integrity of immigration control, depending on the importance of the default and the strength of the private/family life ties and the proposed interference with them, applicants may also have a Convention based claim.

12

In all article 8 cases, the applicant will have to demonstrate that the negative decision causes sufficient detriment to pass the minimum threshold identified in *AG (Eritrea)* (►above at 404) so as to show an interference with the right to respect for private/family life. In many cases an applicant may have invested heavily in their migration to the UK and may have spent many years saving or studying in order to plan their life around it. If an interference is shown, the question of whether it is justified, or whether a violation of the article taken as whole is made out, is decided in accordance with the principles of proportionality (▶above at 405).

A good explanation of the potential role of article 8 in PBS cases, concerning in particular, failures to satisfy the maintenance rules was given in *Pankina* itself (▶see table below).

PANKINA: THE HUMAN RIGHTS ANGLE

For the main findings in *Pankina*, ▶see Chapter 2 42–45.

One of the applicants in *Pankina* (Ms Malekia) was found not to qualify under the PBS relating to post-study work even on the basis that the three-month requirement in UKBA's Policy was found to be invalid. That was because she had not, at any time, had the requisite level of funds (£800) in her account.

For that reason and in case it was wrong on the main question, the Court went on to consider the application of article 8 ECHR within this limb of the PBS. The Court's findings on article 8 are all the more important given that the Home Office subsequently implemented the 'three-month' funds requirement through Immigration Rules (HC 382), having been told by the Court that it could not do so through Policy Guidance alone. On the human rights question, the Court of Appeal decided as follows.

1) The Court rejected the Home Office arguments that article 8 was "off limits", that the Rules were the "sole test of eligibility" and that "article 8 cannot be said to modify them". It affirmed that, in this context, section 6 HRA 1998 made it unlawful for a public authority to act in a way that was incompatible with ECHR rights. The Home Office could not rely on the Immigration Rules as a defence to an ECHR-based claim, ie under s6(2) HRA, because the Rules are neither primary legislation, nor (on the Court's findings) are they made "under" primary legislation. There is therefore "no obstacle in principle to the contention that in applying the Rules the Home Secretary must respect Convention rights whether or not the Rules explicitly introduce them" (paras 41–4).

2) In an important passage for PBS applicants, the Court went on to hold that: (para 45):

   "...in exercising her powers, whether within or outside the rules of practice [ie the Immigration Rules]...the Home Secretary...must have regard and give effect to applicants' Convention rights. This will mean in most cases evaluating the extent and quality of their family and private life in the United Kingdom and the implications, both for them and for the United Kingdom of truncating their careers here."

3) If an interference with article 8 is established, then in dealing with questions of proportionality, consideration must be given to the importance of the requirement/s of the Rule that the applicant cannot satisfy. The Court drew attention to the fact that if an applicant cannot satisfy an academic or language requirement under the Rules, then a "miss is likely to be as good as a mile", meaning that it may be very difficult to demonstrate that the article 8 interference is disproportionate. But, the Court indicated the opposite will be the case where, for example, an applicant falls "marginally or momentarily

short of a financial criterion which in itself has no meaning" because "its significance is as a rough and ready" measure of the person's ability to support themselves (para 46):

"Having £800 in the bank, whether for three continuous months or simply at the date of application, is in no doubt some indication of this; but people who are able to meet the test may fall on hard times after obtaining indefinite leave to remain, and others who fail it would, if allowed to remain, never become a charge on public funds. The Home Office has to exercise some common sense about this if it is not to make decisions which disproportionately deny respect to the private and family life of graduates who by definition have been settled here for some years and are otherwise eligible for Tier 1 entry."

4) In Ms Malekia's own case, she had qualified as a nurse in the UK, but she lived here alone with no relative closer than a cousin. The Court of Appeal indicated that one would expect in a case such as that a finding that the private (although not the family) life limb of article 8 was engaged but "not to an extent sufficient to outweigh the requirements of immigration control" (paras 52–3).

We now turn to look at some of the illustrative cases.

MM (Tier 1 PSW; Art 8 'private life') Zimbabwe (heard 17 July 2009)

This case was decided in the context of an application to remain in the UK by a Tier 1 (Post-Study Work) Migrant. The Tribunal conducted a review of the private life authorities, both domestic and those handed down in Strasbourg, many of which are referred to above. The Tribunal came to the following conclusions:

- Respect for private life does not include a right to work or study per se, but the social ties and relationships (depending on their duration and richness) formed during periods of study or work are capable of constituting 'private life' under article 8 (head note point 1 and see paras 28, 30, 34, 38–41, 47)

- The character of an individual's 'private life' is ordinarily by its very nature of a type which can be formed elsewhere, albeit through different social ties, after the individual is removed from the UK. In that respect 'private life' claims are likely to advance a less cogent basis for outweighing the public interest in proper and effective immigration control than are claims based on 'family life' where relationships are more likely to be unique and cannot be replicated once the individual leaves the UK. Each case must nevertheless be judged on its own facts and, applying *WB (Pakistan) v SSHD* at para 16, it is essential that a judicial decision is reached applying an "even-handed application of the proportionality tests". There can be no presumption about the outcome (head note point 3 and see paras 65–66).

The facts of *MM* involved a mother and daughter who had been in the UK

12

for some years. The applicant herself had taken a number of courses culminating in a BA (Hons) degree and had been employed as a cCommunity health worker. Her daughter had been at school in the UK between the ages of eight and 13. The applicant wished to be able to gain post-study work experience under Tier 1 and it was argued that the effect on the applicant's daughter of ending her schooling in the UK also engaged the right to respect for private life.

The Tribunal assessed that:

- an alternative private life, including school for the applicant's daughter, would be established in the country of origin – there was no reason to think otherwise;
- the applicant had always been in the UK on a temporary basis;
- although a private life had been developed through social ties and school, there was never any expectation of the applicant being permitted to remain in the UK unless she was able to comply with the Rules;
- the applicant could not satisfy the maintenance Rules by some margin when her dependent child was factored in; and
- both applicant and daughter could reasonably be expected to continue their lives in Zimbabwe.

The interference was held to be proportionate (see paras 67–69, with reference to para 14 on the true extent of the failure to comply with the maintenance Rules).

Notably the Tribunal in *MM* also cited with approval the following passage from an earlier Tribunal decision, *NA & Others (Tier 1 Post-Study work-funds)*, as to the difficulty that applicants switching into the Tier 1 (Post-Study Work) category face when invoking article 8 (*MM*, paras 63-65):

"105…whilst it is possible for a student in the course of his or her studies (and part-time working, if applicable) to have developed over time ties with the community that amount to significant elements of a private life within the meaning of Article 8 (a student may also have maintained or developed incidental family life ties here), they are persons who have come to the UK for a limited purpose and with no expectation of being able to stay except by meeting the requirements of the Immigration Rules. They do not thereby acquire a right to remain in the UK despite the Immigration Rules. A refusal under the Tier 1 (Post-Study) scheme may mean they fail to make their immigration prospects better; it does not mean they have been made worse."

MB (Article 8 – near miss) Pakistan (heard 16 July 2010)

In this case, shortly following *Pankina*, Sedley LJ, sitting in the UT, indicated that article 8 may assist an applicant in a case where s/he nearly misses the requirements of the Rules. He stated (para 5):

" ...we do no more than note that it is at least respectably arguable that if an Article 8 case is properly before a fact finding Tribunal or Tribunal of law in this field, one of the matters which may go to proportionality is what is described...as a near miss argument. That is to say, if one is considering on the one hand the demands of a firm and fair immigration control policy and on the other the situation of somebody whose family or private life is going to be disrupted in a material way by removal for non-compliance with the Rules. It may well matter what the nature and degree of non-compliance was."

CDS (PBS: 'available': Article 8) Brazil (heard 23 July 2010)

Here the UT allowed an appeal brought by a Tier 4 (General) student who relied on funds held by two sponsors who happened to be doctors, even though the sponsors were not the parents or legal guardian of the applicant as required in the Policy Guidance (see at para 13).

However, in case the UT was wrong in its construction of the Rules, it went on to consider the case under article 8. The Tribunal indicated that the Convention does not give a general discretion to IJs to disapply the Rules because the way they impact may appear to be unduly harsh and stated that it would be difficult to imagine how the private life of someone with no prior connection to the UK would require them to be admitted outside the Rules for the purpose of study (para 17). But the UT then went on:

"18. However, the appellant has been admitted to the UK for the purpose of higher education and has made progress enabling an extension of stay in that capacity since her admission in 2007. We acknowledge that that gives no right or expectation of extension of stay irrespective of the provisions of the...Rules...

"19. Nevertheless people who have been admitted on a course of study at a recognised UK institution for higher education, are likely to build up a relevant connection with the course, the institution, and educational sequence for the ultimate professional qualification sought, as well as social ties during the period of study. Cumulatively this may amount to private life that deserves respect because the person has been admitted for this purpose, the purpose remains unfulfilled, and discretionary factors such as mis-representation or criminal conduct have not provided grounds for refusal of extension or curtailment of stay."

The Tribunal noted that a change in the sponsorship Rules during the course of the period of study had had a serious effect on the applicant's ability to conclude her course. It noted also that, in some cases, the Rules may be of such importance that "a miss is as good as a mile" but then indicated that procedural/evidential rules relating to maintenance did not fall into that category:

"21. The points-based system aims to provide objective criteria for what

12

funds are needed to be demonstrated before an extension of stay is granted. If we are wrong on our first conclusion, we shall here assume that it may also set strict criteria as to how the availability of such funds is to be demonstrated and in whose accounts the funds may be. But where the appellant establishes by evidence that she has funds available to support her if needed, the strength of the public interest in refusing her an extension based on somewhat arbitrary provisions of guidance attached to an appendix to the rules, is in our judgment somewhat less than the failure to meet a central requirement of the Rules.

"22. But even central requirements are not determinative if the countervailing claim is of sufficient weight...

"23. Here the same sponsors who ensured that the appellant had sufficient funds at the beginning of her course were available with ample financial support to ensure that she met the substantive require- ments of Appendix C in order to continue with her studies. If minds had been applied to the problem the necessary funds could have been transferred to her account so both the letter and the purpose of the Policy Guidance was met.

"24. In our judgment, the application to this appellant of the Policy Guidance that prevented her from obtaining the extension at the time and in the circumstances set out above, was a disproportionate inter- ference with private life that deserved respect as long as she continued to meet the other requirements of the Rules and make appropriate progress in her course of studies here."

FA & AA (PBS: effect of Pankina) Nigeria (heard 23 July 2010)

This case was heard by the same Panel of the UT as that which heard *FA & AA* above. The UT held, by reference to *Pankina*, that regardless of what was contained in the Policy Guidance, under the Rules a Tier 4 (General) student could rely on funds in a bank account that was in the sole name of her spouse. The appeal was allowed on that basis since there was no reason to doubt the existence of the funds, or that the husband had made them available to his wife, the appellant.

Importantly for present purposes, the UT went on to say that, if it was wrong in its main finding, then it would be "quite likely that article 8 would prevent this appellant's course of studies in the United Kingdom being terminated for the reasons that it was" (para 27). That observation made in the alternative seems to underline that, if an applicant can clearly demonstrate, evidentially, to the satisfaction of the Tribunal that s/he will be properly supported in the UK, then even if the particular evidence pro- duced to show this is not that which the Rules and Guidance stipulates, it will be hard to justify a refusal of leave if the case engages article 8.

There are a number of UT authorities, however, that point up the limits of the extent to which article 8 may assist where the Rules cannot be satisfied. We now turn to these. Note that the first two cases below pre-date the decision in *Pankina* and the UT decisions in July 2010 cited above that shortly followed it.

SK (Tier 1 – Transitional provision – maintenance) Republic of Korea (heard 17 July 2009)

Aside from dealing with article 8, this case involved an argument about legitimate expectation and the transitional provisions that were implemented relating to the 'three-month' requirement relating to mainten-ance (for that argument, ►see 182).

As to article 8, the applicant had lived in the UK for almost six years, always in accordance with the Rules, had obtained a Bachelor of Arts degree in Fashion Photography and had, since graduation, been working as a professional photographer for various magazines. She had established very good contacts in the industry and recently co-founded a new magazine in the UK employing others. She had always maintained herself in the UK without recourse to public funds and she had only failed to meet the maintenance requirements by failing to keep a constant balance of £800 in her account. The cause of that was that she genuinely believed that she did not have to do so and that she could benefit from the transitional arrangements in respect of the 'three-month' require-ment. If she returned overseas, the applicant would not be able to re-apply under the Tier 1 (Post-Study Work) category because more than 12 months had elapsed since her graduation and she would therefore lose what she had established in the UK (see paras 38–39).

The Tribunal accepted that the applicant may have made a genuine mistake about qualifying under the transitional arrangements "probably because she did not properly address her mind to the issue or make proper enquiries. That however is her responsibility" (para 42). It found that the applicant had established a private life in the UK that would be interfered with if she were required to leave (para 45) and despite the fact that the applicant may have been able to satisfy the Rules but for a genuine misunderstanding on her part (para 46), the interference was propor-tionate. The applicant would lose the fruits of her opportunities and contacts in the UK but she would be able to build a new career in South Korea and would be "an asset in whatever society she settled" (paras 46–8). Many will view this assessment as decidedly harsh.

BN (Article 8 – Post-Study Work) Kenya (heard 2 February 2010)

The applicant could not satisfy the requirement (then in Guidance) to have the necessary level of funds in her account for three months pre-dating the application. The UT accepted that the applicant's five-year residence in the UK while pursuing studies that had led to two Masters' level degrees and her established social relationships and work at the university as an

12

international operations manager, gave rise to a private life "with some elements of significance". The UT also accepted that the negative immigration decision caused an interference with that private life. The applicant's history to date also indicated that she has been supported without recourse to public funds (para 30).

However and distinguishing *OA (Nigeria)* (▶above at 411), the UT pointed out that the applicant was not being prevented from completing a course of studies that she had previously been admitted to undertake. Rather she was being prevented from switching into employment (under the Tier 1 (Post Study Work) category). Although it was not a case of wilful flouting of the Rules (the applicant was merely unaware of the 'three-month' rule), it has held that she could have been expected to check the detailed, up-to-date evidential requirements of the new category under which she was applying. She could only have had an expectation to remain in the UK in the new capacity in order to work if she met the requirements of those Rules. Accordingly, the interference with the applicant's article 8 interests was held not to be disproportionate (paras 31–34).

MM & SA (Pankina: near miss) Pakistan (heard 17 November 2010)

In this case, the applicant had applied for a variation of leave as a Tier 4 (General) Student. However, while the application was outstanding, the sponsor licence of the educational institution that had issued the applicant's confirmation of acceptance of studies had been suspended. The applicant subsequently (shortly after the date of the decision) sent an email to the Home Office asking for permission to obtain a confirmation of acceptance of studies from a new Tier 4 sponsor. That was followed up by the submission of a letter from the new sponsor educational institution offering the applicant a place on a new course which the applicant subsequently commenced (see para 13).

The Tribunal found that the applicant could not meet the Rules because the email correspondence that she had sent did not amount to a Tier 4 application and the applicant could not, by reason of the letter that had been written by the new college, comply with the requirement in the Rules (116(a) of Appendix A) that only permits points to be scored for a confirmation of acceptance of studies if it was issued "no more than six months before the application is made". The Tribunal held that inherent within this was that the letter must have been issued "before" the application is made (paras 20–21).

Again, the UT considered that the decision constituted an interference with the applicant's private life under article 8 and the question that arose was the proportionality of that interference (para 25). Citing *CDS*, *MB* (both above) and *Huang*, the UT held that it was important to emphasise the point made in *CDS* that "Article 8 is not to be viewed as a means whereby the Immigration Rules can be ignored or in effect re-written, because a judicial fact-finder regards a person as having only narrowly failed to comply with the relevant rules" (para 27). The UT went on to distinguish the circumstances in *Pankina* relating to the evidential requirements of maintenance, which may more readily lend themselves to 'near miss' arguments, from circumstances such as the present. In the present case, the Rules relating to the issue of a confirmation of studies by a licensed sponsor prior to the application were clearly not met. The UT stated (para 28 and see also paras 30, 33):

"...judicial decision makers should be careful to identify and reject arguments based on an alleged near miss, which, on proper analysis, are an attempt to import extraneous qualifications into a provision of the Rules, such as that an applicant had no control over the failings of or other difficulties faced by an educational provider. Such factors might have a legitimate part to play in the proportionality exercise, as weighing in favour of an applicant who has an independently strong private or family life case; but they should not be used to diminish the weight to be given to the considerations described in paragraph 16 of Huang [ie the general administrative desirability of applying known rules if a system of immigration control is to be workable, predictable, consistent and fair as between one applicant and another and the damage to good administration and effective control if a system is perceived to be porous, unpredictable or perfunctory]."

The UT noted also that the case was not one in which the applicant was facing the premature termination of studies for which she had been admitted. Rather, when she had received notice of the suspension of the licence held by her original college, she had switched, without explanation, to an entirely different course of study (para 31). There was no evidence that the applicant could not undertake her new course of study in her country of origin, or of any other significant elements of private life. In all the circumstances, the Tribunal therefore found the interference to be proportionate (paras 31–32, 34).

SAB & Others (students – serious breach of conditions – article 8) Ghana (heard 23 November 2010)

In this case the UT upheld a decision to reject a private life claim where the IJ had found that the applicant, a Tier 1 (General) Student, had breached the conditions of his leave by working "hugely in excess" of the 20 hours per week permitted and where it had been found that the applicant's desire to remain in the UK was driven by the intention to obtain remunerative employment. The IJ was also sceptical of the assertion that the applicant needed to be in the UK during the remaining period of time while he wrote up his thesis (see the UT at paras 19–20). The UT held that the present case was "far removed from some minor technical infringement of the Rules" but that in a case such as this "the public interest was considerable, not least because this Appellant has committed a serious and long-term breach" (paras 41–2).

12

Limbo immigration status constituting an interference with private life

It has been established that there may be circumstances where persons who are residing in an ECHR-contracting state may be subject to an interference with their private life by reasons of the denial to them of access to employment and services so as to enable them to lead a relatively normal life. This is unlikely to happen in many cases based on the PBS, or where the applicant is claiming entitlement to work or study routes. If such applications are refused, then in most cases, the applicant will be required to leave and denial of access to work, study or other services while they resist removal will not generally amount to an infringement with human rights. This aspect of private life is only likely to be engaged where the applicant has an accepted basis for remaining, but yet is being denied the right to function as a normal member of the community otherwise than in accordance with the immigration law.

The situation in which such circumstances may arise are those of delays or administrative difficulties in affording an applicant a status to which s/he is entitled and which would enable access to work, study etc. Such might, if sufficiently prolonged or severe in its impact, have implications under article 8.

The following examples help to illustrate the point:

- In *Smirnova v Russia*, the ECtHR upheld a complaint under Article 8 in respect of an applicant who had been denied access to her internal passport over a prolonged period which had ramifications for her everyday life (exchanging currency, buying train tickets) as well as more crucial needs such as finding employment and medical care (see at paras 96–100).

- In *Aristimuno Mendizabal v France*, decided in January 2006, the applicant was a Spanish national who had been lawfully resident in France since 1975. From 1979 to 1989, she had been issued with temporary residence permits valid for one year each and after that she was issued with temporary 'receipts' of her applications (which counted as valid leave but only for three months at a time). She was finally issued with a ten-year residence permit in December 2003. The claimant argued that the denial of a long-term permit over a period of 14 years amounted to an interference with her private life. The ECtHR acknowledged that measures not related to 'removal' or 'expulsion' but with the maintaining of an individual in a situation of 'precariousness' and 'uncertainty' in their immigration status, may amount to an interference with the right to respect for private and family life under article 8. In the instant case, the impact on the applicant had given rise to an interference in her private life since she had only obtained casual and unskilled jobs, he had had social and financial difficulties and had not been able to rent premises and "carry on the professional activity for which she had undertaken training" (paras 70–72).

- In *Sisojeva & Others v Latvia* (2006, 2007), the ECtHR initially allowed the claim of the applicant Russian nationals, who had been resident in

Latvia over a considerable period but had apparently been refused any formal immigration status. The court noted that no formal order for the applicants' deportation had been made. However, it was not enough for the host state to refrain from deportation, the state was required to give those concerned, if necessary by taking positive measures, the possibility of exercising their rights without interference. However, when the case reached the Grand Chamber, the case was struck out on the basis of new evidence and facts which showed that, in fact, any insecurity or uncertainty in status had been caused by the applicants' own actions – they had obtained both Latvian and Russian passports and, contrary to Latvian law, registered themselves in both countries without telling the authorities. They had also not suffered difficulties in obtaining education and employment. The Latvian authorities were found to have done enough to respect the article 8 private life rights of the applicants while residing in the territory and, beyond that, it was not the Court's role to order that any particular immigration status, rather than another, be granted (see at para 91 and following).

• *R (S & Others) v SSHD)*, the Home Office conceded before the Court that the maintaining of the applicants, who could not be removed to Afghanistan as they were protected by article 3 ECHR, on a regime of temporary admission amounted to an interference with their private lives under article 8 ECHR. The applicants had drawn attention to the fact that they could not work, study (except in a very restricted way), access normal benefits and services and were required to report (see at para 108 of the decision of the Administrative Court, the point did not need to be further considered when the case went to the Court of Appeal).

• In *R (Dawit Tekle) v SSHD*, Blake J held in the Administrative Court that the blanket policy of refusing asylum seekers permission to work, take self-employment or establish a business during the period of lengthy delays in determining fresh applications for asylum, amounted in principle to an interference with private life. In doing so, he cited the earlier decision of the House of Lords in *EB (Kosovo) v SSHD*, in which that Court had noted that it was unreasonable to expect asylum seekers facing substantial delays in determining their claims to "put their lives on hold" and that such delays strengthened an article 8 case for non-removal on the grounds that such applicants could be expected to develop closer ties and establish deeper roots with the community (see at paras 31–32, 35–6, 51, 53–54). When the case went to the Court of Appeal and to the Supreme Court (*R (ZO (Somalia)) v SSHD*), it was dealt with on the basis of the applicants' rights under article 11 of Council Directive 2003/9/EC (reception conditions/permission to work). Both of those courts made clear that they did not feel the need to address the article 8 point (see Court of Appeal, paras 28–29 – although that Court indicated it considered the Home Office's grounds of appeal on the point arguable; Supreme Court, para 10).

12

RIGHT TO FREEDOM OF EXPRESSION

Article 10 of the ECHR provides:

"1. Everyone has the right to freedom of expression. This right shall include freedom to hold opinions and to receive and impart information and ideas without interference by public authority and regardless of frontiers. This article shall not prevent states from requiring the licensing of broadcasting, television or cinema enterprises.

"2. The exercise of these freedoms, since it carries with it duties and responsibilities, may be subject to such formalities, conditions, restrictions or penalties as are prescribed by law and are necessary in a democratic society, in the interests of national security, territorial integrity or public safety, for the prevention of disorder or crime, for the protection of health, morals, for the protection of the rights of others, for preventing the disclosure of information received in confidence, or for maintaining the authority and impartiality of the judiciary."

The structure of article 10 is very similar to article 8 ECHR (▶see as described above). They are both 'qualified rights'. It is similar too to the structure of article 9 (freedom of thought, conscience and religion) and article 11 (right to freedom of peaceful assembly and association) which also have potential relevance to the considerations covered below, although (with the exception of *Nolan* ▶below) most of the cases have been decided under article 10. The most important aspects of these various rights for present purposes are:

- the right to "receive and impart information and ideas" (article 10);
- the right to manifest religion or belief, in worship, teaching, practice and observance (article 9);
- the right to "freedom of association" (article 11).

In *R (Farrakhan) v SSHD*, Louis Farrakhan, the spiritual leader of the Nation of Islam, based in Chicago, USA, had been excluded from the UK. He wished to travel to the UK in order to address the organisation's followers here and they, in turn, had long been keen to receive a visit from him. The Secretary of State's concerns related to community relations, particularly those between Jews and Muslims, and the ramifications for public order. In addressing the applicability of article 10 ECHR, the Master of the Rolls stated that the Court drew the following conclusions based on the Strasbourg jurisprudence (see paras 52–6):

"53...Where entry is refused or an alien is expelled for reasons which are wholly independent of the exercise by the alien of Convention rights, the fact that this carries the consequence that he cannot exercise those rights in the territory from which he is excluded will not constitute a violation of the Convention...

...55 Where the authorities of a state refuse entry or expel an alien from its territory solely for the purpose of preventing the alien from exercising a Convention right within the territory, or by way of sanction for the exercise of a Convention right, the Convention will be directly engaged. This proposition is implicit in the observations of the Commission in *Agee v United Kingdom* 7 DR 164 and *Omkarananda and Divine Light Zentrum v Switzerland* 25 DR 105 and is expressly supported by the decision of the Court in *Piermont v France* 20 EHRR 301 and by the reasoning of the Commission in *Adams and Benn v United Kingdom* 88–A DR 137...

56 Thus, where the authorities of a state refuse entry to an alien solely to prevent his expressing his opinions within its territory, article 10 will be engaged. In such a situation the application of the provisions of article 10(2) will determine whether or not the interference with the alien's freedom of expression is justified."

The Court acknowledged that denial of entry did not just affect Mr Farrakhan but that it also prevented those members of the British public who wished to, from seeing and hearing from him. The receiving, as well as imparting, of views and information, falls within article 10 (see the terms of article 10 above and *Farrakhan*, para 77).

It is of note, however, that, in *Farrakhan*, the Court did not consider that the "reason why the Secretary of State excluded him was simply, or even predominantly, in order to prevent him exercising the right of freedom of expression in this country" (para 58). The reason for Farrakhan's exclusion was that his presence might prove a "catalyst for disorder" (paras 19, 58, 61, 78; there was also some recent evidence of his followers in the UK having engaged in criminal disorder, paras 18, 24). It was therefore to this (secondary) extent, ie that the Government did not wish Farrakhan to address meetings because they might prove the occasion for disorder, that one object of the exclusion could be said to have been to prevent free expression and which led to article 10 coming into play (para 62). The Court found that the merits of the case were "finely balanced" (para 79) but ultimately found for the Government.

The decision in *Farrakhan* was cited in *Huang* and in *GW (EEA reg 21: 'fundamental interests') Netherlands* (see at paras 42-4, 47), the Tribunal assumed, following *Farrakhan*, that article 10 was applicable in the similar circumstances of that case (although *GW* also engaged separate rights of free movement under EU law).

12

However, in the case of *Moon v ECO, Seoul*, Ouseley J, sitting in the Tribunal, decided: (1) that the decision in *Farrakhan* that article 10 could apply to a migrant seeking entry to the UK from outside the territory was 'obiter' (ie not strictly binding because the Court of Appeal had proceeded on the basis of a concession from the Home Office, rather than deciding the point in the face of argument); and (2) *Farrakhan* was wrong on the point: article 10 could not apply to these circumstances.

In *R (Naik) v SSHD* (November 2010), Cranston J, in the Administrative Court, followed *Moon* on the above points (see at paras 72–79). He held that all of the Strasbourg article 10 cases referred to in *Farrakhan* were cases where the applicants were claiming freedom of expression rights while in (and not outside) the jurisdiction (para 78). As with *Farrakhan* and *Moon*, Dr Naik, a Muslim orator of Indian nationality who had a multiple-entry visitor visa, and who planned to give public presentations at major events at Wembley Arena, the Sheffield Arena and Birmingham NEC, was presently outside the jurisdiction. Accordingly, the Secretary of State's decision to exclude him from entry could not be challenged on Article 10 grounds by reference to Dr Naik's interests alone.

However, Cranston J went on to find that article 10 was applicable in principle, on the basis of the approach taken to article 8 ECHR by the House of Lords in *Beoku-Betts* (para 79):

"In my view the territorial principle...means that Dr Naik is unable directly to assert article 10 rights, even in respect of rights to be exercised within the jurisdiction. However, article 10 contains an express right for others to receive the information. The imparting and receipt of information are two sides of the same coin. In my view the rights to impart and receive in this context must be viewed in the same integral way in which the court must approach article 8 rights: *R (Beoku-Betts) v Secretary of State for the Home Department* [2008] UKHL 390, [2009] 1 AC 115. That is especially so in this case where it is apparent that Dr Naik's question and answer sessions are significant to his public lectures. It is the ability to see, hear and interact that is a feature of Dr Naik's attraction...it seems to me that I should treat Dr Naik as asserting their rights, and for that reason, article 10 is engaged since they are clearly within the jurisdiction".

There is a potential danger in putting form over substance in the approach which treats an applicant as unable to invoke the article 10 rights if not actually on the territory. Take the example of *Piermont v France* that was relied on by the Court in *Farrakhan*. In that case a German MEP visited French Polynesia and New Caledonia in order to take part in and support pro-independence and anti-nuclear testing demonstrations. Her visit raised lots of local tensions and came at a time of local elections. As regards Polynesia, the exclusion order was made towards the end of her visit and was actually served on the MEP as she was on an aircraft *about to leave*. The order was one expelling her and prohibiting her re-entry. The purpose was obviously to prevent her from re-entering Polynesia, since she was already departing. The ECtHR found that the measure violated article 10. It might seem odd that, had the plane actually taken off before she was served, she would not be allowed to challenge the decision (see paras 12, 52, 77).

In any event, however, the wider Strasbourg case-law seems to demonstrates that applicants outside the territorial jurisdiction of the host state can raise article 10 objections to the denial of their admission.

- In *Cox v Turkey* (August 2010) a ban on re-entry was imposed on a US woman who had previously been in Turkey and expressed views on Kurdish assimilation and the expulsion and massacre of Armenians from Turkey that were controversial. She had also protested against the film *The Last Temptation of Christ*. She was prevented from returning to Turkey and applied to the Court. The ECtHR upheld her claim finding that, although her views might offend some, the immigration measure that prevented her coming to Turkey to express them engaged article 10 and violated the Convention (see paras 27, 30–31, 43–44). The court drew attention to the fact that article 10 rights are enshrined "regardless of frontiers" (para 21).

- In *Women on Waves & Others v Portugal* (3 February 2009), a Dutch women's foundation based in Amsterdam and others chartered a ship, the *Borndiep*, which they sailed intending to dock in Portugal. The plan was to have meetings on the ship promoting family planning, the decriminalisation of abortion and measures preventing sexually transmitted diseases. The Portuguese sent out a warship to block the entry of the boat into Portuguese territorial waters. The Court examined the case under article 10 and found there to have been a violation (para 30).

- A similar conclusion was reached in *Nolan and K v Russia* (July 2009) in a case involving the banning of the applicant from Russia which was found to violate *article 9* of the ECHR (right to freedom of religion) as it was designed to repress the exercise of the applicant's freedom of religion and stifle the spreading of the teaching of the Unification Church (see paras 62–66, 75).

There is an obligation in the UK system to follow the "clear and constant" jurisprudence of the Strasbourg Court in the absence of some special circumstances or strong reason not to: the intention is that the UK 'keeps pace' with Strasbourg (*R (Alconbury Developments Ltd) v Secretary of State for the Environment, Transport and Regions*, para 26; *R (Ullah) v SSHD*, para 2).

Relevance to PBS and work/study routes

The cases of *Farrakhan*, *Moon* and *Naik* all concerned the question of whether the particular applicants could be admitted to the UK in order to carry out a visit for the purpose of addressing their followers, or the interested public at large. One can see how such rights may also be in play, however, where an applicant is seeking leave for the somewhat longer term purposes under Tier 2 (Minister of Religion) Migrant or the Tier 5 (Temporary Worker) 'Religious Worker' categories. The Tier 2 (Minister of Religion) category covers applicants coming to the UK in order to undertake preaching and pastoral work including (Sponsor Guidance, para 250):

- leading worship regularly and on special occasions;
- providing religious education for children and adults by preaching or teaching;

12

- officiating at marriages, funerals and other special services;
- offering counselling and welfare support to members of the congregation;
- recruiting, training and co-ordinating the work of any volunteers and lay preachers.

They may also be applying for leave to carry out functions as missionaries, or as members of religious orders to live in a community here.

It is possible that there will also be elements of 'expression' inherent, for example, in those applying under the Tier 5 (Temporary Worker) subcategory for 'creative' workers including for the purposes of dance, theatre, film and television and even those coming for similar purposes under elements of the non-PBS visitor routes such as entertainer visitors (▶see Chapter 10 332–335). It may also be that the 'receiving and imparting information' aspect of article 10 is relevant to those applying for just such activities, for example the 'skills transfer' or 'graduate trainee' subcategories of the Tier 2 (Intra Company Transfer) category.

One important question, however, will be the extent to which the courts are prepared to entertain such claims when the applicant has little established nexus with the UK. It may be that it becomes relatively easy to justify any interferences where the primary connection is slight. The UT has, for example, indicated the difficulty inherent in raising a private life article 8 claim when a person, with no existing connection, is applying to come to the UK for studies (see, for example, *CDS* at para 17). It is however the case that in *Farrakhan* and *Naik*, article 10 was engaged by applicants seeking entry from outside.

Another important and fundamental question is whether the law will develop so that a decision that is taken to deny immigration rights *for reasons that are independent* of the rights of free expression, or manifestation of religious belief, can still be challenged on the basis of those Convention rights. So, will a decision taken to refuse a religious worker on the grounds, for example, that s/he does not have sufficient maintenance to meet the Rules, be challengeable on the basis considered here? In *Farrakhan*, *Moon* and *Naik*, the grounds for the exclusion decisions were connected to the exercise of the rights in question. As the above citation from *Farrakhan* sets out, the Strasbourg jurisprudence sets out that the Convention is engaged when the decision was made for the sole purpose of preventing the alien from exercising a Convention right within the territory (although, as is also pointed out above, in *Farrakhan*, the Court of Appeal did note that the reason for the exclusion in that case was not predominantly to prevent him from exercising the right of freedom of expression (para 58), but rather to preserve public order).

The decision of Sedley LJ in *Murungaru* concerning article 1 of the First Protocol was also based on whether it could be said that the *purpose* of the authorities' decision was to interfere with the peaceful enjoyment of possessions (the Convention right in question), or rather had to be viewed as an unrelated immigration measure (▶see below 435).

Perhaps importantly, the 'outside jurisdiction' Strasbourg cases that we have cited above do appear to draw some express inspiration from the decision in *Abdulaziz*, the landmark article 8 case requiring immigration controls to be exercised consistently with Convention obligations (see *Cox* at para 27 and note that *Farrakhan* itself also harked back to the article 8 case-law). In an article 8 case, one does not ask the question whether the expulsion or non admission decision has been taken *in order* to prevent the exercise of the (private or family) right in question. The immigration decision will normally have been taken because the applicant does not meet the requirements of the Rules, or because they are an overstayer, or have committed criminal offences (etc), not because of some objection or concern of the Home Office about the way in which the applicant is leading their private or family life. So, by analogy with the article 8 cases and if the foundation for the article 10 cases really does sprout from the same source, there may be room for some debate about whether the immigration measure really does have to have been taken for the purpose of denying the exercise of the (eg article 10) right in order for that right to be in play. The case-law will have to take another step, however, before decisons taken for unrelated immigration reasons could engage the Convention in this context.

The proportionality of any interferences in cases such as this will depend on factors such as the importance of the ability to access the UK to the applicant's own pursuit of their religion or self expression, the length of association between the applicant and the community/beneficiaries in the UK and the importance of the particular individual applicant to that community and the value of the particular role that they will play. It will also depend on the particular reasons given under the PBS for refusal. In the cases mentioned above, exclusion decisions had been made by the Secretary of State on the basis that the individuals' presence in the UK would not be conducive to the public good because of public order concerns or the applicant's potential to cause division within the British community, or because the applicant fell foul of the Secretary of State's policy concerning 'unacceptable behaviours' (glorifying terrorism and the like). They are very serious concerns and may weigh very heavily against any interference. However, as advisers are aware, many refusals under the PBS are often for fairly insubstantial failures relating to the inability to meet technical requirements. Such will obviously not weigh as heavily when measured against an infringement of fundamental rights.

In cases involving removal, it is to be noted that, in *Ullah*, the House of Lords rejected the suggestion that the Convention could not have 'extra-territorial' effect in the sense that it could never be used to prevent removal where an applicant would suffer harm in the foreign country that would be contrary to articles of the Convention beyond article 3. That meant that it is may be possible to rely on articles such as articles 9 and 10 (etc) to prevent removal if the applicant would suffer treatment contrary to those articles in the receiving state. However, *Ullah* decided that, outside of article 3, in such cases it would be necessary not only to show a breach of the relevant article of the Convention but that the violation would amount to a 'flagrant denial' of the right in question (also described as a 'gross violation', 'flagrant violation of the essence of the very essence of the right', 'flagrant, gross or fundamental breach', 'gross invasion of the person's fundamental human rights'). But that deals with the situation in what was described in *Ullah* and *Razgar* as 'foreign' cases ie where the harm would occur only in the receiving state.

In the other type of case ('domestic') cases, where the harm occurs within the host state, it is not necessary to show a gross violation. Included in 'domestic' cases are removal decisions that separate persons from family members established here in the UK (that is why the article 8 family life cases do not require a 'flagrant' breach to be shown before there is a violation of the Convention). It is possible, therefore, that a Tier 2 (Minister of Religion) Migrant or a Tier 5 (Temporary Worker) under the Religious Worker category who falls foul of the PBS requirements for some not particularly significant reason, might seek the benefit of articles 9–11. They might do so on the basis that the case is a 'domestic' one concerning their separation from members of their community for whom they play a very important role. But again this is new territory.

It is clear from *Beoku-Betts* above, as applied in *R (Naik) v SSHD*, that the rights and interests of the members of the religious community who benefit from the particular applicant's work must be considered as part of determining whether there has been an infringement of the right. Once the right is in principle engaged, ie the subject matter of the decision is found to fall within the scope of the right, the question whether the negative decision will be justified in any case will depend on the particular facts and the application of the principles of proportionality (for which, ▶see above 405). There is, however, no developed case law on this and applicants would be well advised to ensure that any such arguments are brought also under the head of article 8 (private life) which may, in any event, cover the essence of such cases.

For a fuller review of *Ullah*, *Razgar* and the question of territoriality and the distinction between 'foreign' and 'domestic' cases, see the *JCWI Handbook* 2006 Edition at pp787–792.

PEACEFUL ENJOYMENT OF POSSESSIONS

Article 1 of the First Protocol to the ECHR ('A1P1') provides:

> "Every natural or legal person is entitled to the peaceful enjoyment of his possessions. No one shall be deprived of his possessions except in the public interest and subject to the conditions provided for by law and by the general principles of international law.

"The preceding provisions shall not, however, in any way impair the right of a State to enforce such laws as it deems necessary to control the use of property in accordance with the general interest or to secure the payment of taxes or other contributions or penalties."

A1P1 has three parts, or as they have been called by the Strasbourg Court, three "distinct rules" (see *Sporrong & Lonroth v Sweden*, para 61). Although these rules do have a connection, the ECtHR has also sometimes decided a case with reference to just one rule. The first rule is that a person is entitled to enjoy their own possessions 'peacefully' (first sentence of the first paragraph). An interference with that enjoyment, even if it does not amount to actually taking the possessions away, is enough to engage the right. The second rule (first paragraph, second sentence) concerns interferences with property that amount to a "deprivation" of possessions ie the actual taking away or 'expropriation' of the possessions by the state. The third rule deals with another form of interference where the state operates a system to control the possessions.

In *R (The London Reading College Limited) v SSHD* (decided in October 2010), the College challenged a decision made by UKBA to withdraw its sponsor licence. The full circumstances of the case are described in Chapter 4 (▶see 136–137). Although no very detailed submissions were made before the Court on the point, in addition to its case based on fairness, the College also succeeded in its argument that the withdrawal of the licence was an unlawful violation of A1P1. UKBA accepted that a sponsor licence is capable of being a 'possession' for the purposes of A1P1.

UKBA argued that, although the licence was a possession, it is possible to deprive a person of their possessions in the 'public interest' as A1P1 states and that it was in the public interest to deprive the College of the licence in that case. However, the Judge held that, because the deprivation had been carried out in a way that was unlawful procedurally ie because the College had not been given proper notice of UKBA's concerns so as to be able to make effective representations, the deprivation had not been carried out "subject to the conditions provided by law" as required by A1P1 (see Judgment, paras 63–68).

"Conditions provided by law" is similar to other phrases that appear in the ECHR such as "prescribed by law" in articles 5 and 10(2) and "in accordance with the law" in article 8(2). They require that the decision taken to interfere with the right must have a 'lawful' basis, ie it must be set out in some clear and predictable part of the contracting state's laws, whether the law is formally written in a statute or it is unwritten, like British 'common' law derived from decided cases (see *R (Gillan) v CMP*, para 31; *Sunday Times v UK*, at para 47).

In the *London Reading College* case, the decision had not been taken fairly under ordinary British law and, therefore, the deprivation of the

12

College's possessions was not carried out in accordance with 'conditions provided by law' and there was a violation.

Because the decision to withdraw the licence was quashed in that case anyway (because of the lack of fairness), the only thing that the ECHR finding added was a right to claim damages against the College in accordance with the principles of 'just satisfaction' under the ECHR and section 8 HRA. Under these provisions, no award of damages is made for a breach of the ECHR unless the court is satisfied, taking account of all the circumstances, that an award is necessary in order to afford 'just satisfaction' to the person/s whose rights have been violated. Sometimes, a declaration of violation alone will be enough to provide the victim with 'just satisfaction' because the main purpose of the Convention is to protect human rights, rather than provide compensation for damage that is suffered (see *R v SSHD ex parte Greenfield*). In *Anufrijeva*, the Court of Appeal gave guidelines about damages in HRA cases indicating that awards would only be modest. *Anufrijeva* was, though, a case dealing with damages arising out of breaches of article 8 caused by maladministration, rather than quantifiable business losses such as can be foreseen with some precision when a sponsor licence is withdrawn.

Although in the *London Reading College* case, the withdrawal was found to be unlawful regardless of the human rights angle, there may be some cases where the Convention would make a difference. Although it is not expressly stated in A1P1 as far as all three 'rules' are concerned (particularly the first rule), in all cases, interferences with possessions must be justified as being in the public interest and proportionate; see *Sporrong & Lonroth v Sweden* (see at paras 69 and 73):

"**69. For the purposes [of the first sentence of the first paragraph ie the entitlement to the peaceful enjoyment of possessions] the Court must determine whether a fair balance was struck between the demands of the general interest of the community and the requirements of the protection of the individual's fundamental rights. The search for this balance is inherent in the whole of the Convention and is also reflected in the structure of Article 1."**

It may well be that, even if the sponsor is responsible for certain defaults in that s/he has failed in respect of certain of the 'sponsor' duties, the real question may be whether the removal of the licence can be said to be proportionate when regard is had to the principles of proportionality set out above (►see 405), in particular whether:

- withdrawal of a licence is "no more than is necessary" to achieve the immigration control objective; and

- a "fair balance" has been struck between the interests of society and the interest of the individual/group of persons whose interests are being interfered with.

No doubt the Courts will give significant weight to the public interest in immigration control when weighing any default by a sponsor in carrying out its duties and responsibilities under the sponsor system and the Court, in certain cases concerning sponsorship, has so held (▶see Chapter 4 at 128–135).

However, it will also be necessary to have regard to the importance and value to be attached to the licence which UKBA is trying to take away. In the *Reading* case (cited with approval on this point in *R (Manchester College of Higher Education) v SSHD*), although not here directly addressing the human rights context, the Judge made the following observation:

"It should be understood that establishing a college and achieving both accreditation and licensing is a substantial undertaking for an establishment. Having achieved this status and opened for business teaching students, the college will inevitably have made substantial financial commitments. The loss of a licence would have the most serious professional and financial consequence for the college and its proprietors. It would also have a serious impact upon both its students and its prospective students because, without a visa letter or a "Confirmation of Acceptance for Studies" document from a licensed college, the students' immigration status is undermined. It follows that a licence is a very valuable thing."

So, there may be room for arguing in some cases, that having regard to A1P1 and the extent or nature or seriousness of the particular breach of the Sponsor Guidance (for which ▶see Chapter 4), the decision taken by UKBA to suspend or withdraw the licence was not a proportionate one. Regard will be had, on the particular facts of the case, to the effect that it would have on the college and its, possibly very many, students. It may be that the college will have to close if the withdrawal stands and its owners may face financial ruin, for example by students demanding the return of fees paid for courses/exams that they are no longer able to take. The same may be the situation in the case of a business in which proprietors have invested and which cannot properly function without the staff that have been taken on from overseas. Thought and weight will also need to be given to the fact that the effect on the relevant sponsored students or employees may be as innocent parties caught up in the sponsor's mistakes.

It may be that in some cases, strong arguments could be made that it would be proportionate to adopt lesser measures than the revocation of a licence in order to deal with the perceived problem, for example downgrading the licence and requiring that an 'action plan' be implemented and adhered to (which is the case for all 'B' rated licences).

Some caution should also be adopted, though, in reliance on A1P1 because the Court in the *Reading* case did not consider the question of A1P1 in relation to licences in any depth and it is possible that the area may become the subject of further argument. A related question is

12

whether a negative decision concerning an individual's permission/leave to be in the UK in order to carry out an economic activity might constitute the interference with possessions within A1P1.

The Strasbourg court seems to have regarded the 'goodwill' and connected 'value' of a business or profession as a possession when it comes to decisions about whether the proprietor will be licensed to continue to carry out the business. So, in *Tre Traktorer Aktiebolga v Sweden*, when the applicant company had its licence to sell alcoholic beverages revoked, the Court held that the "economic interests connected with the running" of the business were 'possessions' within A1P1 and that its "withdrawal had adverse effects on the goodwill and value of the restaurant" (para 53). In *Murungaru v SSHD* (▶below), the view of the Court of Appeal was that, in *Tre Traktorer Aktiebolga*, it was not the licence itself but the "economic interests connected with the running of the restaurant, including its goodwill" that constituted the possessions (para 51).

Similarly, in *Van Marle & Others v The Netherlands*, where individual applicants had practised as accountants for some years and a new piece of legislation required them to seek registration in order to continue in practice (which they were refused), the ECtHR had regard to the "value of their clientele" in concluding that the case fell within the scope of A1P1 (at paras 41–42):

"41. The Court agrees…that the right relied on by the applicants may be likened to the right of property embodied in Article 1: by dint of their own work, the applicants had built up a clientele; this had in many respects the nature of a private right and constituted an asset and, hence, a possession within the meaning of the first sentence of Article 1."

These authorities suggest that, in the case of an existing, running business, it is the *economic value* connected to the client base and the *goodwill* that it has built up, that may constitute the 'possession', rather than the licence itself (although see also *Capital Bank AD v Bulgaria* at paras 130–131 in which the licence appears to have been acknowledged as the relevant possession).

In *R (Nicholds) v Security Industry Authority*, the UK Court had to consider whether the denial of a licence to work as a door supervisor under a new regulatory framework interfered with the A1P1 rights of a group of people who had, for many years, worked as door supervisors but who could not qualify under the new arrangements as a result of their criminal convictions. In deciding the case, Kenneth Parker QC was of the view that it was only licences or permissions that are "assets", in the sense that they had a monetary value and could be marketed either through sale, leasing or sub-licensing that could be treated as protected by A1P1. Other licences, such as the ones in question in the case, which were of value only to the holder because s/he could not carry on the economic activity without it, were not (see in particular paras 74–79).

Kenneth Parker QC's analysis was approved by Lord Bingham in the Supreme Court in *R (Countryside Alliance & Others) v Attorney General*, although he expressed the view that the connected case-law was not clear (para 21) (and see also now *Security Industry Authority v Stewart* at paras 45–6).

In the end, in the *Nicholds* case, the Judge, recognising the complexity of the matter (para 76), decided to approach it on the basis that the licences did amount to A1P1 possessions, despite his reservations (para 83 onwards).

Contractual rights and those seeking entry

A final case on A1P1 worth considering is *Murungaru v SSHD* (December 2008). The claimant in judicial review proceedings was a deposed Kenyan government minister whose visa for entry to the UK was revoked by the immigration authorities on the grounds that it would be contrary to the public good to allow him to re-enter.

One of the bases on which the applicant sought to challenge the decision was that he wished to enter to access private medical treatment and that he had a contract with his doctors in the UK for that purpose. He asserted that the contract amounted to a possession under A1P1. Accordingly, the applicant's case was that to deny him re-entry was to interfere unlawfully with his rights under the Convention.

The evidence relating to the existence of the contract was very thin (only a one-line assertion in a witness statement from his solicitor) but the Court of Appeal approached the case on the basis of the finding of Keith J in the Administrative Court that the applicant was indeed a party to a continuing contract for medical services to be provided at his election (paras 28–9).

Assuming that the measure could amount to an interference with possessions, Sedley LJ held that, on the facts, the decision under challenge was, in reality, to the withdrawal of a visa and that the disruption to the medical treatment was an unintended side-effect only (para 34). Lewison J analysed the nature of the contract itself and found that it was *not* sufficient to amount to a possession. This was because the contractual rights were: intangible, non-assignable, not transmissible (on this Lewison J cited Kenneth Parker QC in *Nicholds* above), not realisable and with no present economic value. He held that, therefore, they could not realistically be described as an 'asset' falling within A1P1 (see paras 45, 56–58).

12

RIGHT TO EDUCATION

The right not to be denied an education under article 2 of the First Protocol to the ECHR has been little used. In a number of cases, the Strasbourg Court and Commission have declared inadmissible claims that expulsion, which would result in inferior education for young children, breached Article 2 (see *Jaramillo*, *Sorabjee* and *Ajayi*).

In *R (Holub) v SSHD*, the Court of Appeal considered the case of a Polish girl who claimed that she had missed too much of the syllabus while in the UK. She claimed, in particular, that the Polish educational system was so inflexible and rigid as to the factual knowledge which is required to progress through the system, that she would be unable to catch up and would not be able to advance into higher education if she were to be returned to it. In essence, therefore, it was the dislocation in her education which was claimed would be detrimental to her were she required to leave education in the UK and try to re-integrate into the Polish system. The Court decided that, given her abilities and the fact that she had kept up her Polish, she would be able to manage and the extent of any educational prejudice which she faced was, therefore, not severe enough to breach the Convention. The Court of Appeal also stated their view that the right not to be denied an education could not have 'extra-territorial' effect.

This latter view, about extra-territoriality, was later stated by the Tribunal in *Kacaj* not to be 'authoritative' and the Tribunal refused to follow it in principle. Later, in *Ullah*, the House of Lords also decided that, in principle, it might be possible to bring ECHR claims against removal relying on articles of the Convention other than articles 3 and 8 (►see above). However, in a 'foreign' case, it would be necessary to show a 'flagrant' violation in the foreign state.

It seems unlikely that reliance on this right will take applicants under Tier 4 very far (and see also the comments made in *MM Zimbabwe*, paras 27 and 42). The only real possibility where progress might be made may be a case, very strong on its facts, where (as was attempted in *Holub*), there are very significant 'domestic' (see *Ullah* above for the meaning of this ►429–430) aspects to the alleged violation ie where the removal from a very particular education in the UK, perhaps because that education simply could not be replicated elsewhere, is what is at the root of the alleged infringement of the right. On the existing authorities, such cases might just as well be argued under article 8.

13 Challenging decisions

This chapter covers:

- rights of appeal to the First-Tier Tribunal (Asylum and Immigration Chamber) (▶below);
- administrative review (▶444–449);
- other remedies (▶449–455):
- judicial review (▶449–450);
- complaints / ombudsman / compensation (▶450–454);
- discrimination impact assessments (▶454–455).

Challenges may also be brought to decisions relating to sponsor licences under the PBS, for example the suspension or withdrawal of a licence to sponsor employees or students. Details regarding this and the (judicial review) case law that has built up are provided in Chapter 4 at ▶127–137.

RIGHTS OF APPEAL

This section deals with the rights of appeal that exist to the First-tier Tribunal (Immigration and Asylum Chamber), in particular the rights of appeal that exist in Points-Based System cases.

For details about the substantive requirements that apply in order to qualify under the various tiers, ▶see the relevant chapter of the Guide.

For details of the case-law including the Court of Appeal decision in *Pankina* about the limits to what can legitimately be provided for in Policy Guidance that is not otherwise contained in the Immigration Rules ▶see Chapter 2 at 42–45.

For the general case law concerning the maintenance requirements in PBS cases, ▶see Chapter 5 at 181–188.

For the impact of human rights under the PBS, ▶see generally Chapter 12 and for the particular human rights case law as relevant to PBS cases, ▶see Chapter 12 at 412–423.

Immigration decisions subject to appeal

Where an 'immigration decision' is made in respect of an applicant s/he may appeal to the First-tier Tribunal. An 'immigration decision' is one of the following (s82 2002 Act):

- refusal of leave to enter the UK;
- refusal of entry clearance;
- refusal of a certificate of entitlement under section 10 of the 2002 Act;
- refusal to vary a person's leave to enter or remain in the UK if the result of the refusal is that the person has no leave to enter or remain;
- variation of a person's leave to enter or remain in the UK if, when the variation takes effect, the person has no leave to enter or remain;
- revocation under section 76 of the 2002 Act of indefinite leave to enter or remain in the UK;
- a decision that a person is to be removed from the UK by way of directions under section 10(1)(a), (b), (ba) or (c) of the 1999 Act (removal of persons unlawfully in the UK);
- a decision that an illegal entrant is to be removed from the UK by way of directions under paragraphs 8 to 10 of Schedule 2 to the 1971 Act (control of entry: removal);
- a decision that a person is to be removed from the UK by way of directions under section 47 of the 2006 Act (removal: persons with statutorily extended leave);
- a decision that a person is to be removed from the UK by way of directions given by virtue of paragraph 10A of Schedule 2 to the 1971 Act (family);
- a decision that a person is to be removed from the UK by way of directions under paragraph 12(2) of Schedule 2 to the 1971 Act (seamen and air-crews);
- a decision to make an order under section 2A of the 1971 Act (deprivation of right of abode);
- a decision to make a deportation order under section 5(1) of that Act, and
- refusal to revoke a deportation order under section 5(2) of that Act.

There also exist certain rights of appeal based on the denial or removal of refugee status (sections 83-83A 2002 Act).

Specific restrictions on the rights of appeal in PBS cases

The 2002 Act provides for various restrictions and limitations on rights of appeal (section 88 2002 Act and following). We are concerned here only with the specific limitations that are particular to PBS cases (although other general limitations could arise in a PBS case).

Section 4 of the Immigration and Asylum and Nationality Act 2006 came into force on 1 April 2008 (see Immigration Asylum and Nationality Act

2006 (Commencement No 8) Order 2008 SI 310, art 3). This section cuts down the right of appeals to the Tribunal in respect of entry clearance decisions by inserting a new version of s88A 2002 Act. However, article 4 of the No 8 Commencement Order made savings in relation to the operation of section 4(1)(2) of the 2006 Act. The effect is to make the restrictions on the right of appeal against entry clearance have effect only insofar as the application that gave rise to the refusal was of a kind identified in Immigration Rules as required to be considered under the Points-Based System. So, pursuant to these amendments as presently in force, refusals of entry clearance applications for the PBS routes will not generally attract a right of appeal to the Tribunal. The replacement remedy for these cases is 'administrative review' (▶see below 444).

However, an applicant affected by these restrictions may still appeal to the Tribunal on the grounds referred to in section 84(1)(b) and (c) of the 2002 Act (see s88A(3)(a) 2002 Act as amended by the 2006 Act and brought into in effect in relation to PBS cases). These are that the decision is unlawful discrimination, and/or that the decision is unlawful under section 6 of the Human Rights Act 1998 (public authority not to act contrary to the Human Rights Convention) as being incompatible with the appellant's Convention rights.

For the impact of the ECHR in points-based cases, ▶see Chapter 12 and for PBS human rights cases, ▶see Chapter 12 at 412–423.

Evidence to be taken into account by the Tribunal and date of assessment

The Tribunal has a wide jurisdiction to review findings of fact made by the decision-makers, to correct factual errors and to consider evidence and facts that were not before the decision-maker (see, for example, *R v IAT ex parte Hassanin*).

Section 85(4) of the 2002 Act allows the Tribunal to consider any evidence that is relevant to the "substance" of the decision "including evidence which concerns a matter arising after the date of the decision". This does not, however, apply to an appeal against the refusal of an entry clearance or a certificate of entitlement (see s85(5) 2002 Act). In entry clearance/ certificate of entitlement cases, the Tribunal may only consider evidence of the circumstances as they existed as at the time of the decision to refuse. That is the case even if the entry clearance/certificate of entitlement decision is challenged on human rights grounds (see *AS (Somalia) v SSHD*; *SA (Pakistan)*, paras 17–19). The Tribunal may, however, in these cases, consider evidence about matters that post-date the decision but which cast light on the circumstances existing as at the date of the decision (see *DR (Morocco)*, paras 16, 22–25).

13

Section 85(4)(5) governs the situation at present but the Government has made provision for very substantially restricting the evidence that the Tribunal may take into account in PBS cases (see s85A 2002 Act as inserted by the 2007 Act). Section 85A is not yet in force. The position when it does come into force is described below (▶442).

Tribunal as primary decision maker: AS (Afghanistan) & NV (Sri Lanka)

The width of the powers of the Tribunal were made clear in *AS (Afghanistan) & NV (Sri Lanka) v Secretary of State for the Home Department* (Court of Appeal, 20 October 2009). In those cases, the appellants had applied for leave to remain, one as a person intending to establish herself in business and the other on the basis of long residence. Both applications were refused and the appellants appealed. In the course of their appeals, they raised, including by way of responses to a notice to state additional grounds, the assertions that they were entitled to remain, respectively, under the International Graduates' Scheme and the Rules relating to students. The latter grounds were not related to those on which they had been refused leave to remain in the decisions under appeal. Rather, they raised entirely separate categories under the Rules. In each case, the Tribunal refused to consider these new grounds on the basis of a want of jurisdiction.

The Court of Appeal, by a majority, allowed the appellants' appeals. It held that section 85(2) of the 2002 Act (Tribunal to consider any matter raised in a 'one-stop' statement which constitutes a ground of appeal under section 84), considered together with the interlocking provisions of sections 84, 96 and 120 2002 Act, required the Tribunal to consider the grounds raised. The Tribunal was not restricted to considering grounds that related to the reasons for the original decision, or the original grounds of appeal. The matters that the Tribunal was required to consider included grounds capable of supporting a fresh application. The Court was relaxed about the Tribunal acting as primary decision taker. It took the view that the legislation enabled an appellant to challenge the substance of the decision made against him or her as that decision affected his/her immigration status. Appellants were not restricted simply to attacking the grounds on which the decision was made – the 'decision' referred to in section 85(2) of the 2002 Act was an 'immigration decision' of the kind referred to in s82(2) 2002 Act (see at para 113). The decisions of the Tribunal in *SZ (Applicable Immigration Rules) Bangladesh* and *EA (Section 85(4) explained) Nigeria*, in which the Tribunal had suggested a more restrictive approach, were held by the Court of Appeal not to have considered how section 85(2) should work in harmony with the one-stop provisions (see para 114 and see also at paras 82–3).

Rules setting historic requirements: the limits to the effect of section 85(4) 2002 Act and AS *(Afghanistan)*

However, the broad approach in *AS (Afghanistan)* and indeed the breadth of section 85(4) of the 2002 Act (above), enabling the Tribunal to act as primary decision-taker in principle, will in certain cases be constrained by the requirements contained in the Immigration Rules themselves, upon which the Tribunal is required to adjudicate. There are provisions of certain Rules which fix a historic timeframe as to when certain conditions are required to have been met. In other words, an appeal cannot be allowed on the basis that the decision is 'not in accordance with the Immigration Rules' if the particular Rules at issue lay down a condition to be met at a specific point in time and that condition was not met at that point, although it was met later. .

This point was made in *Pankina*. In that case, the Court was, of course considering the 'three-month' maintenance requirement as set down in the Policy Guidance. But the reasoning applies equally now that that requirement has been added into Appendix C of the Rules. Paragraphs 1A(a) and (b) of Appendix C now require, in respect of the tiers/categories there referred to, that the applicant must have the relevant funds at the date of the application and that they must have had the relevant funds for a "consecutive 90-day period of time, ending no earlier than one calendar month before the date of application". That requirement could not be met by showing that, by the date of hearing but not by the date of the application, the applicant had had the relevant funds for a 90-day period (although there may well be a human rights case to be made if the requirement is satisfied by the stage of the hearing in an in-country case and ▶see generally 412–423).

In *Pankina*, Sedley LJ stated:

"38. If, contrary to my clear view, the material policy guidance forms part of the Appendix C criteria [the question is] at what date compliance is to be judged. In the present case, this means the date of application or the date of appeal. The £800 in the bank accounts of some of the applicants had not been there continuously for the three months preceding the applications but had been there for three continuous months by the time their appeals came up.

"39. Although argument has been directed to large issues of principle arising out of the phraseology of the legislation, the answer has in my judgment to be found in the provisions themselves. The rule as framed makes it clear that it is to the Home Office that the necessary proof must be submitted. The argument that a fresh opportunity arises on appeal is based on s.85(4) of the 2002 Act, which provides that on such an appeal the tribunal 'may consider evidence about any matter which it thinks relevant to the substance of the decision, including evidence which concerns a matter arising after the date of the decision'. There are many

13

instances of rule-based issues which need to be appraised as they stand at the moment of the appeal hearing, but the question whether at the date of the application the specified funds had been in the applicant's bank account for three continuous months cannot intelligibly be answered by evidence that they had not, albeit they now have been."

In so deciding, the Court of Appeal implicitly approved *NA & Others (Tier 1 Post-Study Work-funds)* on this narrow point. As was confirmed in that case, however, section 85(4) would operate to enable, for example, further evidence to be adduced after the application and at the stage of the Tribunal hearing, to show that the relevant funds had been held in the account at the relevant historic point in time as specified in the Rules (see para 67).

Further examples of the PBS Rules laying down a historic time-frame by which certain requirements must be met and which will not be satisfied by evidence that the requirements were met at a later point in time are as follows.

- In *NO (Post-Study Work – award needed by date of application) Nigeria*, the Tribunal held that Table 9 of Appendix A to the Rules clearly required that the Post-Study Work Migrant had obtained the relevant qualification by the date of the application and not more than 12 months before it. This disentitled the applicant from relying on a qualification that s/he hoped to obtain in the future (see paras 19, 23–25).

- In *MM and SA (Pankina: near-miss) Pakistan*, the UT arrived at similar conclusions in relation to the requirement contained in Appendix A to the Rules to the effect that a confirmation of acceptance of studies had to be issued not more than six months before the application for leave was made (see paras 10–12, 21). The Tribunal noted (para 21):
  "The true position is that, if a Rule specifically requires a particular state of affairs to pertain at a particular point in time, then that is what needs to be shown by evidence, albeit that that might include 'evidence which concerns matters arising since the date of decision'."

Further restriction on the evidence that can be taken into account in PBS cases: section 85A 2002 Act

Section 19(2) of the Borders Act 2007 inserts new section 85A into the 2002 Act. At the time of writing, the Government has yet to bring this new provision into force. If and when it is brought into force it will very severely limit the evidence that the IJ can consider when considering PBS appeals. The effect of the provision is to make new exceptions to the general rule contained in s85(4) 2002 Act which allows the Tribunal to:

"... consider evidence about any matter which [it] thinks relevant to the substance of the decision, including evidence which concerns a matter arising after the date of the decision."

The 'first exception' in section 85A simply repeats the existing exception (contained in section 85(5) 2002 Act, which will be repealed when section 85A comes into force) to the effect that s85(4) does not apply in appeals against refusals of entry clearance, or refusals of certificates of entitlement to the right of abode (s85A(2) 2002 Act).

However, the 'second exception' introduced by section 85A is new. It applies if all three of the following conditions are met (s85A(3)):

- the appeal is against a refusal of leave to enter, or a refusal of a decision to vary a person's leave to enter or remain (note that PBS appeals have largely been removed in relation to entry clearance appeals – above); and
- the immigration decision concerns an application identified in the Immigration Rules as one to be considered under a 'Points-Based System' (ie part 6A of the Rules); and
- the grounds of appeal include any of the following: that the decision is not in accordance with the Immigration Rules, that the decision is not otherwise in accordance with the law, or that a discretion conferred by the Rules should be exercised differently.

In the above circumstances, the IJ is restricted to considering the following evidence only (s85A(4) 2002 Act).

- The IJ may consider any evidence that was submitted in support of and at the time of the application to the immigration authorities (the Tribunal Procedure Rules may specifically define the circumstances in which evidence will be treated as submitted, or not submitted, in support of and at the time of the application, s85A(5)).
- The IJ may consider evidence that is adduced in support of any grounds other than that the decision was not in accordance with the Rules or the law, or that a discretion conferred by the Rules should be exercised differently.
- The IJ may consider evidence that is provided in order to prove that a document is genuine or valid.
- The IJ may consider any evidence that is provided in order to deal with a Home Office ground of refusal that is not related to the awarding of 'points' under the PBS but is adduced in instead to deal with a refusal based on any other requirement of the Rules, or an exercise of discretion under the Rules.

So, in sum, once section 85A comes into force, an IJ hearing a PBS case will generally only be able to consider evidence that was provided to the original decision-maker. Evidence that is provided after the date of the application, either to the decision-maker or to the Tribunal, cannot be considered, even if it is adduced to show facts existing at the date of the application, or the date of the decision.

The exceptions are that an applicant may still rely on later-submitted evidence in order:

13

- to support a ground of appeal (even in a PBS case) based on race relations, the ECHR, EU free movement rights, or the Refuge Convention;
- to prove the validity, or genuiness, of a document; or
- to deal with a ground of refusal that is not connected to the actual scoring of points, for example where the decision-maker, albeit in a PBS case, has relied on one of the general grounds of refusal, or the requirements relating to parental consent for an application from a child, or (in many cases) the requirements about the status that an applicant must have in order to switch into the relevant PBS category.

ADMINISTRATIVE REVIEW

Before the introduction of the PBS, most people applying for entry in a work-related category would have had a right of appeal to the statutory Tribunal (now the First-Tier Tribunal) under the 2002 Act against the refusal of entry clearance. Under the PBS, the right of appeal is largely replaced by 'administrative review'. The difference between the two is that appeals are to a wholly independent Immigration Judge, whose decisions may be appealed, on points of law, to the next rung (the Upper Tribunal) and, from there, to the Court of Appeal. Administrative review is a system of internal review under which the decision is looked at again but by a more senior civil servant, an Entry Clearance Manager ('ECM'). It seems that the formal procedure is that, where the 'administrative reviewer' (the ECM) thinks that a different decision should be made, s/he 'recommends' to the ECO that the decision be changed. The ECO then issues the further decision. There is no further right of appeal in administrative review, but like all decisions taken by public authorities, in principle negative decisions can be challenged by judicial review (▶see further below).

Applicants who are already in the UK cannot apply for an administrative review. The facility is only available to those who are overseas.

The system for administrative review is not contained in any legislation. It is set out in Home Office guidance only with the details contained in similar form in the annexes to each of the Policy Guidance documents for the tiers of the PBS.

What grounds can be considered on an administrative review?

The Guidance states that administrative review is a mechanism for reviewing entry clearance decisions where the applicant believes "an error" has been made in the decision. It also states that applicants who believe that an "incorrect decision" has been made can apply for a review.

Subject to the exceptions mentioned below, applicants are not permitted to submit new evidence for the purposes of an administrative review. The intention is that the administrative reviewer will consider the case on the basis of the documents submitted to the original ECO of which copies should have been kept at the post. So, for instance, if the applicant only submitted a copy document and the ECO decides that s/he can only be satisfied that the information contained in the document is accurate if they see the original version, then the applicant cannot remedy the situation by providing the original on an administrative review.

The same is true if the ECO is not satisfied for other reasons that the evidence that has been provided is sufficient to satisfy them that a requirement of the Rules is met. In order to succeed by submitting further evidence, the applicant would have to make a further application for entry clearance, pay another fee and re-submit all the evidence that was provided with the first application as well.

The PBS relies heavily on applicants providing documentary evidence to meet the relevant requirements; for example bank statements, educational qualifications and certificates and salary slips. It may be that an applicant fails to provide the necessary documents because s/he did not know that they were required. It may be that it is only when the applicant is refused entry clearance on the ground of non-production of a particular piece of evidence that it becomes clear that the document should have been provided in the first place and that a new application will have to be made to put the situation right. This all puts a premium on taking care with the original application and making sure that all the necessary evidence is provided from the outset.

The exceptions to the rule that applicants cannot produce new evidence for an administrative review are:

- where the applicant was refused under the general grounds contained in paragraph 320(7A) or 320(7B) of the Rules (▶see below); or
- when the ECM requests new evidence.

The Policy Guidance states that the decision may be changed on an administrative review if any of the following conditions are found to apply, namely the ECO:

- failed properly to consider evidence submitted with the original application;
- failed to apply the Immigration Rules correctly;
- made a mistake in processing the application; or
- failed to give adequate reasons for refusing entry clearance.

The Guidance further states that the decision will not be changed "simply because the applicant claims that there is a fault with [UKBA's] underlying processes or policies".

13

In reviewing the evidence, the ECM will check that documents have been correctly assessed and that any necessary verification checks have been properly carried out. Checking that the Rules have been properly applied will include making sure that points have been correctly awarded.

The administrative reviewer may decide that the result of the original application was correct (ie it should indeed have been refused) and that the only change that should be made to the decision is in relation to the reasons given for refusing it. There is no particular limitation on the administrative reviewer in terms of the requirements that they may review. The ECM may look at matters in the application that are separate from the grounds on which the review is requested. It is also, therefore, possible that the ECM may decide that the ECO was wrong not to raise a different or additional ground of refusal to those on which the original decision was based. In any such case the refusal notice will be replaced by another refusal which gives the different reasons.

Considering the general grounds of refusal on an administrative review

Naturally given that on an administrative review, the ECM can look at whether the Rules have been applied correctly, s/he may look at the general grounds for refusal. The Policy Guidance states that, if an applicant is refused under either of the following paragraphs of the Rules, s/he will be able to submit further "information" (for which we interpret also 'evidence') for the administrative review:

- paragraph 320(7A) ie where false representations have been made or false documents or information have been submitted (whether or not material to the application, and whether or not to the applicant's knowledge) or material facts have not been disclosed in relation to the application;

- paragraph 320(7B) ie refusals based on the applicant having previously breached the UK's immigration laws by:

- overstaying;

- breaching a condition of leave;

- being an illegal entrant; or

- "using deception" in an entry clearance or leave application.

Paragraphs 320(7A) and 320(7B) are covered in Chapter 11 (▶see 383–392). Paragraph 320(7A) relates to falsehoods used in the present application, but paragraph 320(7B) may be used to raise previous breaches against an applicant in any entry clearance decisions for years to come (ten years in the case of deception).

The Policy Guidance notes, in particular, that an applicant may, on an administrative review of a refusal based on paragraph 320(7A), want to establish that, even if a document was produced or a representation was made that was false, the applicant was not aware of the fact and therefore did not use deception. If the applicant can show that to the ECM's satisfaction then, although the existing refusal may have to stand because of the false document/representation/information, future applications would not be refused under paragraph 320(7B). The way that the

Guidance explains this is as follows:

"If an application has been refused because a false document was used or a false representation was made, the applicant may claim that they were unaware of the false documents or false representations. The refusal will still stand but the applicant would have to prove that they did not know that false documents or false representations were used, if they are not to have any future applications automatically refused for 10 years. Where the documents related directly to the applicant (for example, employment references, qualifications of financial details), such a claim would be likely to fail unless the applicant has clear evidence that an error has been made (for example, written confirmation from an employer, financial institution or educational establishment that they had supplied us with incorrect information at the time we verified the original documentation).

"If the administrative reviewer does accept that the applicant did not knowingly use false documents or false representations, the refusal will still stand, but the applicant will not automatically have any future applications refused under the rules (paragraph 320(7B)) where false documents or false representations were used."

Administrative review procedure

A PBS applicant refused entry clearance will be given an 'Administrative Review Request Notice' at the same time as receiving the refusal decision. If the applicant wishes to apply for an administrative review, they must fill out the notice in full and send it to the address stated on the notice.

Applicants should set out the reasons given for refusal of the application and explain fully why s/he thinks a mistake was made.

Applicants are not to send any other documents with their request. They should not, for example, send in any supporting evidence or their passport (if the refusal is later reversed, applicants will be asked separately for their passport). The exception to this is if the application was refused under the general grounds of refusal contained in paragraphs 320(7A) or 320(7B) (▶see above).

Time limit

Any request for administrative review must be made and received back by the entry clearance officers within 28 days of receipt of the refusal notice by the applicant. If the request is received outside that time limit, then in addition to setting out his/her grounds for review, the applicant should set out and explain the circumstances which have led to the request being made out of time. Officers will consider a request submitted outside the deadline only if there are "exceptional circumstances".

If the request is submitted out of time and the administrative reviewer

13

decides not to consider the review, the notice will be returned to the applicant with an explanation as to why it is not being considered.

How many requests for administrative review may be made?

Only one request for an administrative review of any one entry clearance refusal is permitted.

However, if the outcome of the administrative review is to uphold the decision but on different grounds, then the applicant may request a second administrative review and challenge the new grounds for refusal.

Who carries out the review?

The 'administrative reviewer' will be an ECM. ECMs are senior to ECOs. The ECM who carries out the review must not have been connected with the initial decision. For that reason, the reviewer may be situated at a different entry clearance post to that where the original entry clearance application was dealt with.

Time-frame for decision

The ECM will aim to issue a decision within 28 days of receipt of the request for the review. If, in exceptional circumstances, the ECM is unable to complete the review within that time, s/he will notify the applicant in writing and state when the applicant can expect the decision.

Outcome of the administrative review

On a review, the ECM can do one of three things:

- overturn the decision and decide to issue entry clearance;
- uphold the decision with the same reasons for refusal; or
- uphold the decision with revised reasons for refusal and recommend to the ECO that a new refusal notice is issued explaining the revised reasons.

The applicant will be notified of the outcome of the review by letter.

Where the decision is overturned and the ECM has decided to issue entry clearance, the applicant will be requested to provide his/her passport for it to be endorsed with an entry clearance.

In cases where the decision is upheld and the reasons for refusal remain the same, the applicant will not be entitled a further administrative review. If the applicant wishes to pursue their application, the only options are:

- submit a fresh application if it is the case that the existing grounds for refusal can be overcome by, for example, new evidence;
- challenge the decision by judicial review (▶see generally below) if the applicant believes that the decision of the ECM is unlawful.

In cases where the decision is upheld but with new reasons for refusal and the applicant is, as a result, issued with a new notice of refusal of entry clearance (GV51), the applicant will be entitled to ask for an administrative review of that refusal challenging the new reasons.

OTHER REMEDIES

This section looks at certain other remedies that may be available: judicial review; making a complaint, including to the ombudsman and discrimination impact assessments

Judicial review

Where a PBS decision cannot be challenged by an appeal, or by administrative review in the circumstances described above, then the only avenue of challenge left open will be judicial review in the Administrative Court (part of the High Court).

For the use of judicial review in order to challenge UKBA decisions about sponsor licences (eg suspending or withdrawing a licence), ▶see Chapter 4 at 127–137.

Judicial review will be the route of challenge in circumstances where:

- an applicant for entry clearance has exhausted the procedure for administrative review ie the ECM upholds the decision of the ECO on the same grounds; or
- an in-country applicant, for whatever reason, does not have, or has been denied, the right to appeal against the decision.

Great care should be taken. Judicial review is a procedure for challenging the lawfulness of a decision on narrow grounds. The court will not generally assess the facts for itself, or allow a claim for judicial review because a favourable decision might reasonably have been reached by another decision-taker. The court will only intervene on legal grounds. Judicial review can also be very costly. Applicants should take detailed legal advice before commencing judicial review proceedings. A general description of judicial review is provided in Chapter 38 of the 2006 Edition of the *JCWI Handbook*.

As to procedure, before a judicial review claim can be begun, the applicant, or his representative, must first provide a judicial review pre-action protocol 'letter before claim' notifying the decision-taker of the grounds on which it is alleged that the decision is unlawful and allowing (normally) 14 days for a response.

A claim for judicial review must be brought in accordance with Civil Procedure Rules ('CPR') 54. Such a claim must be brought:

1) promptly; and

2) in any event not later than three months after the grounds to make the claim first arose ie within three months of the decision in question.

13

The court may extend time but a full and proper explanation has to be given for the delay before the court is likely to consider this.

An applicant will not, in the absence of exceptional circumstances, succeed in bringing a claim for judicial review against the original ECO's decision in a PBS case, without seeking an administrative review from the ECM. This is because the court expects claimants to exhaust his or her remedies and to use judicial review only as a last resort.

It will not be appropriate to use judicial review in a situation where the application has been refused because of absence of a particular document or piece of evidence and the applicant now wishes to submit that evidence but cannot do so through the administrative review process. As with most cases of administrative review, in judicial review the court looks at the decision in the light of the evidence that was before the decision-taker at the time that the decision was made. Most 'new evidence' cases will have to proceed by way of a fresh application. For example where the ECM (administrative reviewer) has refused to revise the ECO's decision because the applicant has not been able to satisfy the ECM about his/her employment history on the basis of some error provided in the employer's reference about the applicant's employment experience, but no evidence to explain the error was presented to the ECO/ECM, then the court will not interfere with the ECM's decision.

The judicial review court may be expected to look with close scrutiny at an ECM decision on administrative review taken under paragraph 320(7A) of the Rules, where the outcome is a finding by the ECM that the applicant has used deception in knowingly providing false documents, or making false representations in support of the entry clearance application. Such a decision is of particular gravity because, not only does it deny the applicant entry on the present application, it also stands as a bar to the applicant succeeding on an application for entry clearance for the next ten years (see Rules, para 320(7B)). The burden is on the ECM to justify a refusal on this basis and to show, with clear evidence, that the applicant has used deception. Again, expert advice should be taken before attempting a judicial review.

Complaints/Ombudsman/compensation

In the 2006 Edition of the *JCWI Handbook*, we provided an outline dealing with complaints to the Home Office and to the Ombudsman (pp1223–1234). Complaints using these procedures arise where the applicant is unhappy with how their matter has been handled by the immigration authorities ie if the administration has been lacking, or if the applicant is unhappy about how officials have conducted themselves. They are not to be used in order to challenge the outcome of the decision for which the remedies above are relevant.

Internal complaints system

First it is important to follow the steps required by UKBA when making a complaint. The complainant should first notify the person responsible for the maladministration of their concerns and, if this does not prove successful, the next step is to refer the matter to their supervisor.

A formal complaint can be made by completing the 'complaints registration form' available on the UKBA website. For complaints about the handling of an in-country PBS application, if the applicant does not have a letter containing a contact address or phone number of where to send the complaints registration form, then it should be sent to the North East Yorkshire and the Humber Customer Service Unit which will forward the complaint to the relevant team. The contact details for this unit are: NEYHCustomers@ukba.gsi.gov.uk and the address is North East Yorkshire and the Humber Region CSU, PO Box 3468.

If the complaint is about an entry clearance application, the complaints registration form should be sent to the Visa Services Directorate Customer Service Unit at: Visa Customer Services, Visa Services Directorate – UKBA International Group, c/o Lunar House, 40 Wellesley Road, Croydon CR9 2BY.

UKBA aims to give a full response to formal complaints within 20 working days but indicates that dealing with some complaints may need careful investigation and take longer.

If the applicant is unhappy with how the complaint has been dealt with, it is possible to request a further review of the matter. After that has been done, applicants may decide to take up the matter with the Parliamentary Ombudsman (▶see below).

When filling out the complaints registration form, applicants should set out in detail the circumstances giving rise to their complaint and enclose any supporting evidence and correspondence. As explained in the *JCWI Handbook* (▶see above reference), if the applicant has suffered direct financial loss as the result of the error, it may be possible to claim a reimbursement. This will only be provided if the applicant's costs were reasonable and were lost as the unavoidable and direct consequence of the immigration authorities' actions. Evidence, for example receipts, of any such losses should be provided.

In exceptional circumstances not involving financial loss, consideration will be given to making a consolatory payment. Consolatory compensation, both under UKBA's internal scheme and in awards made by the Ombudsman (▶see below), are very low.

Parliamentary Ombudsman

A further complaint may be made to the Parliamentary Commissioner for Administration (the 'Parliamentary Ombudsman') who has a duty to

13

investigate complaints thoroughly and promptly. Complaints to the Ombudsman should be made after going through the UKBA complaints procedure and must be made through a Member of Parliament. UKBA has indicated its view that only exceptionally will it be appropriate to complain to the Ombudsman without first having complained internally.

Rarely will a case involving maladministration end up as judicial review, but even if it does, unless exceptional circumstances apply, it will be essential to have pursued all remedies by way of internal complaint and the Ombudsman first. In a case concerning a claim for compensation made under policy relating to maladministration in the child support system, *R (Humphries) v SSWPD*, the court ruled that the claimant should have first proceeded to make a further complaint to the independent case examiner relevant in those cases ('ICE') before seeking judicial review. The ICE was a body set up on the recommendation of the Ombudsman for complaints relating to child support, after the Ombudsman began receiving a large number of complaints concerning child support. The court stated in relation to such complaints/claims:

"The ICE has an expertise in dealing with them. They frequently involve detailed consideration of facts (as in part does the claimant). The ICE is well able to apply the policy of the Guide as he is required to. He is well able to consider its application in an individual case. If he errs legally or the Agency fails to follow his recommendation, judicial review will lie. It is not shut out by first going to the ICE. In the claimant's case, it would, for example, have been a straightforward exercise for the ICE and the Agency between them to agree a likely figure for a plasterer's earnings."

In addition, note that in *Anufrijeva v Southwark LBC*, a judicial review case concerning damages for maladministration under article 8 ECHR, the Court of Appeal held that applicants should generally seek other routes, such as the Ombudsman or alternative dispute resolution, rather than bringing costly public law proceedings.

It should also be noted that the Ombudsman can call for information and documents required in order to resolve the complaint/claim and is likely to be successful in getting the immigration authorities to produce the relevant material.

Common law claims

There is a thread of cases in which attempts have been made to bring claims in negligence against the immigration authorities based on the principle of assumption of responsibility, which results in loss and damage. It is beyond the scope of this Guide to set out the complexity of the law in detail but a brief summary of the main points follows.

A claim by an applicant that the ECO/ECM has acted negligently in assessing his application under the PBS may fail on grounds of public policy: *Denise Rowley v DWP* (Court of Appeal). There are, however, circumstances in which a claim for damages has proved possible. In *Kanidagli v SSHD* (Administrative Court), the claimant's loss did not arise as a result of pure omission; the immigration officers acted imperfectly; the relationship between the immigration officer and the immigrant was a close one and, accordingly, the court found in favour of the claimant. The Secretary of State owed a duty to the claimants to take care in the administrative implementation of the immigration decisions which had been made in their cases. To be precise, s/he owed a duty of care to ensure that an inappropriate condition on the applicant's entry clearance/leave was not endorsed on her passport so as to result in the applicant being prohibited from claiming public funds.

If there is good evidence that the ECO/ECM assumed responsibility towards the applicant and made representations to them that their application would be treated in a particular way and it later turns out not to have been, then depending on the facts of the case, the applicant may have a cause of action. As a general rule a sufficient relationship of proximity will exist to establish a duty of care when someone possessed of special skill (such as an ECO/ECM) undertakes to apply that skill for the assistance of the other person who relies upon such skill. There would also have to be direct and substantial reliance by the applicant on the ECO/ECM's skill.

In *Henderson v Merret Syndicates*, the House of Lords cited with approval a passage from *Hedley Byrne*:

"...reliance upon the assumption of responsibility by the other party will be necessary to establish a cause of action because otherwise the negligence will have no causative effect..."

The precise limits of the concept of assumption of responsibility are still in a state of development. There is no comprehensive list of guiding principles to help the courts determine when an assumption of responsibility can be said to arise. The courts look at all relevant circumstances to see whether they are closely analogous to and consistent with the situations in which liability has been imposed in a previous case. Some further pointers are as follows.

- An objective test will be applied when asking the question whether, in a particular case, responsibility should be held to have been assumed by the defendant.

- The fact that a provider of information does not think that s/he is assuming a duty of care is not determinative and in assessing the importance of what was contained in exchanges between the parties, the court would apply not the dictionary meaning of the words used, but the meaning which the parties might reasonably be supposed to have given to those words in that context (*Precise (521) plc v William M Mercer Ltd*, Court of Appeal).

- The fact that the defendant is providing a service pursuant to a statutory

13

duty does not absolve him/her (*Her Majesty's Customs and Excise Commissioners v Barclays Bank plc* at para 38; *Carty v Croydon LBC* at para 43).

- Once it is determined that the extended principle of *Hedley Byrne* (assumption of responsibility) applies, then there is no need to embark on any further enquiry of whether it is fair, just and reasonable to impose liability for economic loss (*Barclays Bank*, para 4).

Note that the assumption of responsibility principle was not relied on in *W v Home Office* (though it was accepted that it could give rise to damages, pp 311). In that case, the Court of Appeal held that there was no duty of care in the particular case in circumstances in which a questionnaire relating to a separate person had mistakenly been placed on the applicant's file causing him to be detained.

Discrimination impact assessments

Race relations legislation (s71 Race Relations Act 1976 and the Order made under it) and now the Equality Act 2010 (in force from 1 October 2010), make provision for the carrying out of discrimination 'impact assessments' to help ensure that proposed changes of Government policy are audited for possible discriminatory effect. The areas of potential discrimination are race, sex, pregnancy and maternity, gender reassignment, disability, age, sexual orientation and religion or belief.

The development of immigration policy, through the Immigration Rules in particular, are affected by the need to comply with duties under the equality legislation. As the Explanatory Memoranda to statements of changes in the Rules make clear, impact assessments relating to the changes are generally published on the UKBA website.

There is a developing body of case law showing how these duties are enforceable by judicial review as is illustrated by the following citations.

- In *R (Elias) v Defence Secretary*, Arden LJ stated (see at paras 273–4):

"It is the clear purpose of section 71 [of the Race Relations Act 1976] to require public bodies to whom that provision applies to give advance consideration to issues of race discrimination before making any policy decision that may be affected by them. This is a salutary requirement, and this provision must be seen as an integral and important part of the mechanisms for ensuring the fulfillment of the aims of anti-discrimination legislation."

This view was affirmed in the Administrative Court and the Court of Appeal in *BAPIO* (Administrative Court, paras 64–69; Court of Appeal, paras 1-4).

- It is good practice for explicit reference to be given to impact assessments so as to show that due regard has been had to them (*Baker & Ors, R (on the application of) v Secretary of State for Communities & Local Government & Ors*, Court of Appeal, para 37). If due regard is not had to these duties then the policy may well be unlawful (*R (Watkins – Singh) v Governing Body of Aberdare Girls' High School*, para 114).

- An incomplete or erroneous appreciation of the duties will mean that "due regard" has not been given to them; see the remarks of Moses LJ in *R (Kaur and Shah) v London Borough of Ealing* at para 45.

- The "due regard" duty must be fulfilled before and at the time that a particular policy that will affect the identified group is being considered by the public authority in question. It involves a conscious approach and state of mind (*R (Elias) v Secretary of State for Defence*, para 274; *R (C) v Secretary of State for Justice*, para 49).

- The duty must be exercised in substance, with rigour and with an open mind. It is not simply a question of "ticking boxes" (*R (Kaur and Shah) v London Borough of Ealing*, paras 24–25). Provided the duty has been conducted in substance and relevant factors were take into account, then the courts will not quash the Policy or Rule in issue (*Domb and Ors*, para 75; *R (Harris) v Haringey LBC*; *Margaret O'Brien & 5 Ors v South Cambridgeshire DC*).

- Breach of the s71 duty was not simply a technical matter. It was found to be a defect in following a procedure that is of very great substantial, and not merely technical, importance (*R (C) v Secretary of State for Justice*, para 54).

- The s71 duty was found to be a non–delegable duty; it always remained with the public authority charged with it (Brown, para 92).

13

Leave recorded on Biometric Registration Documents

This is the list of categories as referred to in Chapter 10 in relation to which an applicant's leave will be recorded on a Biometric Registration Document ('BID'), rather than in a stamp or sticker (vignette) in the applicant's passport, or other immigration status document/s (see Immigration Biometric Registration Regulations 2008, SI 2008 No. 3048, Reg 4).

The relevant categories under the Immigration Rules are:

- Tier 4 (General) Student;
- Tier 4 (Child) Student;
- Postgraduate Doctor or Dentist;
- Academic Visitor granted leave in the UK for a period exceeding six months;
- Spouse or civil partner of a person present and settled in the UK;
- Unmarried or same-sex partner of a person present and settled in the UK;
- Visitor for private medical treatment;
- Domestic Worker in a private household;
- United Kingdom ancestry;
- Retired person of independent means;
- Spouse or civil partner of a person with limited leave to enter or remain in the UK as a retired person of independent means;
- Child of a person with limited leave to enter or remain in the UK as a retired person of independent means;
- Representative of an Overseas Business;
- Tier 2 Migrant making an application under that category for leave to remain for a period which, together with any preceding period of leave, exceeds a cumulative total of six months leave in the UK as a Tier 2 Migrant;
- Tier 1 (General) Migrant;
- Tier 1 (Entrepreneur) Migrant;
- Tier 1 (Investor) Migrant;

- Tier 1 (Post-Study Work) Migrant;
- Tier 5 (Temporary Worker) Migrant;
- those applying for limited leave to remain as a dependant of a person who is applying, or has applied on or after 25 November 2008, for limited leave to remain under one of the above categories; and
- those applying in the UK to replace their passport or other document in which their limited leave had been endorsed.

Changes to the Tier 2 and 5 Guidance for Sponsors

Effective from 6 April 2011

Tier/ Category	Change	Paragraph(s)
T2 (ICT)	The established Staff sub-category has been replaced with 2 new sub-categories – Long Term Staff and Short Term Staff	4 285-296
All	Appendix A has been amended to include Planning permission/Local Planning Authority consent in List B but this will only have to be produced if we specifically ask for it.	30
All	Detailed explanation of how copies of original documents must be certified.	33 footnote
All	Explanation of what is (not) acceptable when applying to add a new Tier/category to an existing sponsor licence.	40
All	Explanation of what is meant by 'office holder' and a weblink giving more information	86 footnote
All	New policy – if you have had a sponsor licence before, but we revoked it, you are not eligible to apply for a licence again for a period of 6 months from the date we revoked your previous licence.	110 117 529
All	Now Policy – 'B' rated sponsors cannot sponsor any new migrants. The only CoS a 'B' rated sponsor is allowed to assign are for existing employees who need to extend their leave to continue working in the same job.	130
All	Further clarification on the policy which states that a CoS can only be used once to support an application for leave to enter, or remain in the UK. This applies where the application is refused or granted, but it does not apply where the migrant withdraws their application, or	148

Tier/ Category	Change	Paragraph(s)
	where their application is rejected. (The current exception under Tier 5 for migrants who are non-visa nationals and are employed in the creative sector still applies.)	
All	An explanation of how 'CoS years' work and the specific change that under these two tiers, the CoS year will always mirror the financial year. Also, clarification that sponsors cannot have annual allocation of 'restricted CoS'.	162-174
Tier 2 (General) Tier 2 (ICT)	New policy – all migrants sponsored under these Tiers must be paid into their own bank account. Sponsors must not pay migrants in these two tiers, in cash. This applies to all existing sponsored migrants and all new sponsored migrants.	183-185
All	New sanction – with regard to sponsoring under the age of 18. The existing policy is that all sponsors must ensure that they have suitable care arrangements in place for their travel, their reception on arrival in the UK and for their living arrangements while in the UK, as well as parental consent to these arrangements. Failure to comply with this will result in the sponsor's licence being revoked.	186 360
Tier 2 (General) Tier 2 (ICT)	Revised Policy – from 6 April 2011, all jobs under these two Tiers must be at graduate level. (Includes arrangements for existing migrants with leave under Tier 2 (General) granted under the rules in place before 6 April 2011, or as a Work Permit holder, who are eligible to extend their existing leave or make a change of employment application.)	187-189
Tier 2 (General) Tier 2 (ICT)	Revised explanation of what the 'appropriate rate' of pay is for migrants under these two tiers from 6 April 2011 when a change to the Immigration rules will require specific minimum salary levels under Tier 2 (General) and all sub-categories of Tier 2 (ICT)	190
All	Re-emphasis of existing policy on how to complete a CoS when you will be paying any allowances to a migrant.	192 326 337 359

Tier/Category	Change	Paragraph(s)
Tier 2 (General)	Introduction of the annual limit under this Tier for 2011–12 and 'restricted'/'unrestricted' CoS.	202-204
Tier 2 (General)	Full details on the limit for 2011–12 including how to apply for a restricted CoS and the rules on assigning a restricted CoS.	208-239
Tier 2 (General)	Information on the revised shortage occupation list which is for graduate occupations only.	240-243
Tier 2 (General)	Resident Labour Market Test. Removal of the exception from advertising jobs in Jobcentre Plus where the salary is £130,000 per annum or more. New, full exemption from the Resident Labour Market Test for any job paying £150,000 per annum or more.	254
Tier 2 (General)	Removal of the ability for a headhunter to recruit on behalf of a sponsor without having to advertise nationally. Headhunters will still be able to recruit where instructed by a sponsor but they must conduct a full Resident Labour Market Test as set out in this guidance, where one is required.	270-271 and Codes of Practice
Tier 2 (ICT)	Introduction and full details of two new sub-categories Long term Staff and Short Term Staff, which replace the 'Established Staff' route from 6 April 2011.	285-298
All	Change of employment rules updated to include circumstances where migrants are involved in a transfer of employment due to a merger, de-merger or takeover.	439-444
All	New sponsor duty – you must hold the appropriate planning permission or Local Planning Authority consent to operate your type/class of business at your trading address (where this is a Local Authority requirement)	463 f)
All	Revised list of circumstances in which we will downgrade a sponsor's licence to a 'B' rating.	517
All	Revised list of circumstances in which we will revoke a sponsor's licence.	528
All	Revised list of circumstances in which we may revoke a sponsor's licence.	530

Tier/ Category	Change	Paragraph(s)
All	Further clarification and revised instructions on what you must do if you are involved in a merger, de-merger or takeover.	586-602

ADDENDUM

1 This addendum provides information on the transitional arrangements for certificates of sponsorship (CoS) issued to sponsors and/or assigned to migrants under Tier 2 (General) and Tier 2 (Intra Company Transfer) on or before 5 April 2011. It also contains an important reminder for all sponsors assigning CoS under Tier 2 (ICT).

Changes to Tier 2 (General) and Tier 2 (ICT) – Established Staff

2 This edition of the sponsor guidance sets out how the limit on Tier 2 (General) will operate during the period 6 April 2011 to 5 April 2012. The Immigration Rules have also been amended to include this limit. It also sets out key changes to the minimum skill level allowed under Tier 2 (General).

3 In addition, it sets out how the Tier 2 (ICT) Established Staff sub-category will be replaced from 6 April 2011. In its place we are introducing two new sub-categories – one for Short Term Staff and one for Long Term Staff. It also sets out the minimum skill level for these new sub-categories.

4 If you are an existing Tier 2 (General) and/or Tier 2 (ICT) sponsor you will have already been notified that your CoS allocation for Tier 2 (General) and/or Tier 2 (ICT) will be reduced to zero from 6 April 2011 and you will most likely have already applied for a new annual allocation to start from that same date. However, it is important that you understand what will happen in respect of any CoS you *assign* up to and including 5 April 2011.

REMINDER – All Tier 2 (General) and Tier 2 (ICT) CoS currently allocated to your SMS account will be cancelled overnight on 5 April 2011 if you have not assigned them by that date. You will already have received a letter inviting you to apply for a further allocation to start from 6 April 2011.

Tier 2 (General) and Tier 2 (ICT) – Established Staff CoS assigned on or before 5 April 2011

5 As we have set out in this guidance and other communications to you during February and March 2011, there will be some significant changes to the requirements under Tier 2 (General) and Tier 2 (ICT) from 6 April

2011. We have also published a revised list of shortage occupations that will come into effect from 6 April 2011.

6 The following table explains what will happen where you have assigned a Tier 2 (General) or Tier 2 (ICT) – Established Staff CoS to a new migrant on or before 5 April 2011, when the migrant applies for leave to enter or remain in the UK.

	Application for leave is made overseas	Application for leave is made in the UK
Date of application for leave is on or before 5 April 2011	The migrant's application will be processed in accordance with the rules in place before 6 April 2011.	The migrant's application will be processed in accordance with the rules in place before 6 April 2011.
Date of application for leave is on or after 6 April 2011	The migrant's application will be processed in accordance with the rules in place from 6 April 2011.	The migrant's application will be processed in accordance with the rules in place from 6 April 2011

Example 1

7 You assign a Tier 2 (General) CoS to a migrant on 21 March 2011. The migrant is a 'new hire' who will apply from overseas for leave to enter the UK to start work for you in a job with a skill level of S/NVQ 3 on 25 April 2011.

- If the migrant makes their application for leave on or before 5 April 2011, it will be assessed according to the Immigration Rules in place on that day. This means that the skill level of S/NVQ 3 is acceptable and the application for leave *will not fail on that point*.

- If the migrant makes their application for leave on or after 6 April 2011, it will be assessed under the new Immigration Rules that come into force on that date. This means that *the application will fail* because the job is not at graduate level or above.

Example 2

8 You assign a Tier 2 (ICT) – Established Staff CoS to a migrant on 21 March 2011. The migrant will be transferred on 25 April 2011 to spend six months working in the UK and they will apply under the new Tier 2 (ICT) Short Term Staff sub-category. Their salary and allowances whilst in the UK will be £22,000 and this meets the requirements set out in the relevant code of practice.

- If the migrant makes their application for leave on or before 5 April 2011 under the Established Staff sub-category, it will be assessed according to the Immigration Rules in place on the day. This means that the salary of £22,000 is acceptable and the application for leave *will not fail on that point*.

- If the migrant makes their application for leave on or after 6 April 2011 under the Short Term Staff sub-category, it will be assessed under the new Immigration Rules that come into force on that date. This means that *the application will fail* because the salary is less than the required minimum of £24,000.

Important note about assigning Tier 2 (ICT) CoS

9   Any CoS that you assign to a migrant who wants to apply under the Long Term Staff or Short Term Staff route, must be assigned using the 'Established Staff' sub-category within SMS. However, you must add a note in the 'sponsor notes' box to confirm which route you are sponsoring the migrant under.

10 This also applies to any CoS you have already assigned but which will not be used by a migrant to apply for leave until on or after 6 April 2011. Again, you must add a sponsor note to the CoS to confirm which route you are sponsoring the migrant under.

11 We will shortly be making changes to the SMS to rectify this.

Abbreviations

2002 Act	Nationality, Immigration and Asylum Act 2002
2009 Act	Borders, Citizenship and Immigration Act 2009
A1P1	Article 1 of the First Protocol of the ECHR
App A	Appendix A of the Immigration Rules (attributes)
App B	Appendix B of the Immigration Rules (English language)
App C	Appendix C of the Immigration Rules (Maintenance – funds)
App D	Appendix D of the Immigration Rules (HSMP Rules, 31 March 2008)
App E	Appendix E of the Immigration Rules (Maintenance – funds – family)
App F	Appendix F of the Immigration Rules (Rules relating to HSMP, IGS, Fresh Talent: Working in Scotland, Businesspersons, Innovators, Investors and Writers/composers/artists as at 29 June 2008)
App G	Appendix G of the Immigration Rules (Tier 5 countries)
ATAS	Academic Technology Approval Scheme
BCIA 2009	Borders, Citizenship and Immigration Act 2009
BID	Biometric Immigration Documents
BRP	Biometric Residence Permit
CAS	Confirmation of Acceptance of Studies
CAS	Confirmation of Acceptance of Studies
CEFR	Common European Framework of Reference for languages
CEFR	Common European Framework of Reference for Languages
certificates or certificates of sponsorship	In Chapter 4 this generally refers to of certificates of sponsorship, confirmations of acceptance for studies and visa letters
COS	Certificate of Sponsorship
CPR	Civil Procedure Rules
ECG	Entry Clearance Guidance
ECHR	European Convention on Human Rights and Fundamental Freedom
ECM	Entry Clearance Manager
ECO	Entry Clearance Officer
ECtHR	European Court of Human Rights
EEA	European Economic Area
EU	European Union
FSA	Financial Services Authority
FT: WSS	Fresh Talent: Working Scotland Scheme

GATS	General Agreement on Trade in Services
HND	Higher National Diploma
HRA 1998 or HRA	Human Rights Act 1998
HSMP	Highly Skilled Migrants Programme
HTS	Highly Trusted Sponsor
HTS SG	Tier 4 of the Points Based System – Highly Trusted Sponsor Guidance, version 07/10, 23 July 2010
IAT	Immigration Appeal Tribunal
IDI	Immigration Directorate's Instructions
IELTS	International English Language Teaching System
IGS	International Graduates' Scheme
Leave to Enter and Remain Order 2000	Immigration (Leave to Enter and Remain) Order 2000
Leave to Enter Order 2000	Immigration (Leave to Enter and Remain) Order 2000
LLP	Lifelong Learning Programme
MAC	Migration Advisory Committee
MBA	Master of Business Administration
NARIC	National Recognition Centre for the UK
NQF	National Qualifications Framework
OISC	Office of the Immigration Services Commissioner
PBS	Points-Based System
PBS Dependant PG	Points-Based System (Dependant) Policy Guidance, version 12/10, for applications made on or after 14 December 2010
PEO	Public Enquiry Office
PG	Policy Guidance issued by the Home Office relating to the PBS
PLAB	Professional and Linguistic Assessment Board
RFL	'Refusal of Leave' part of Entry Clearance Guidance
RLMT	Resident Labour Market Test
Rules	Consolidated statement of Immigration Rules, HC 395, in effect from 1 October 1994
S/NVQ	Scottish/National Vocational Qualification
SAWS	Seasonal Agricultural Workers Scheme
SBS	Sectors-Based Scheme
SCQF	Scottish Credit and Qualifications Framework
SEGS	Science and Engineering Graduates' Scheme
SG	Tiers 2 and 5 of the Points Based System – Sponsor Guidance, 21 December 2010 (version 12/10)
SMS	Sponsor Management System
SOC	Standard Occupational Classification
SSHD	Secretary of State for the Home Department
Student SG	Tier 4 of the Points-Based System – Sponsor Guidance, October 2010 (version 1010)
T1 (Ent) PG	Tier 1 (Entrepreneur) of the Points-Based System – Policy Guidance, 14 December 2010

T1 (Entr)	Tier 1 (Entrepreneur)
T1 (Gen)	Tier 1 (General)
T1 (General) PG	Tier 1 (General) of the Points-Based System – Policy Guidance, 14 December 2010
T1 (Inv) PG	Tier 1 (Investor) of the Points-Based System – Policy Guidance, 14 December 2010
T1 (Inv)	Tier 1 (Investor)
Tier 1 (PSW)	Tier 1 (Post-Study Work) category
T1 (PSW) PG	Tier 1 (Post-Study Work) of the Points Based System – Policy Guidance, 14 December 2010
T1 (PSW)	Tier 1 (Post-Study Work)
T1	Tier 1
T2	Tier 2
T2 PG	Tier 2 of the Points Based System – Policy Guidance, version 10/10, for use on or after 1 October 2010
T3	Tier 3
T4	Tier 4
T5	Tier 5
T5 (Temp) PG	Tier 5 (Temporary Worker) of the Points-Based System – Policy Guidance, 14 December 2010
T5 (Youth) PG	Tier 5 (Youth Mobility Scheme) of the Points-Based System – Policy Guidance, 31 July 2010
The 'Rules'	The present consolidated statement of Immigration Rules laid before Parliament as required by the Immigration Act 1971, s1(4), 3(2). The official name for the present consolidated statement is HC ('House of Commons Paper') 395
The 'BID Regulations'	Immigration (Biometric Registration) Regulations 2008/3048
Tier 2 (ICT)	Tier 2 (Intra Company Transfer) Migrant
Tier 4 PG	Tier 4 of the Points-Based System – Policy Guidance, version 07/10, 23 July 2010
UK NARIC	National Recognition Information Centre for the UK. The national agency responsible for providing information advice and expert opinion on vocational, academic and professional skills and qualifications from over 180 countries world-wide
UKBA	United Kingdom Border Agency
UT	Upper Tribunal (Immigration and Asylum Chamber)

List of cases

References to law reports

AC – *Appeal Cases*

All ER – *All England Law Reports*

DR – *Decisions and Reports series of European human rights cases*

ECR – *European Case Reports*

EHRR – *European Human Rights Reports*

EWCA – *England and Wales Court of Appeal*

EWHC – *England and Wales High Court*

Imm AR – *Immigration Appeal Reports (the 'Green Books')*

INLP – *Immigration and Nationality Law & Practice*

INLR – *Immigration and Nationality Law Reports*

IRLR   *Industrial Relations Law Reports*

UKAIT – *UK Asylum and Immigration Tribunal*

UKHL – *UK House of Lords*

UKUT – *UK Upper Tribunal*

WLR – *Weekly Law Reports*

Tables and information boxes

Index

For cases referred to in the text please see alphabetical list of cases, pages 465–470

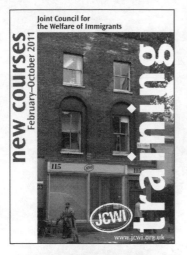